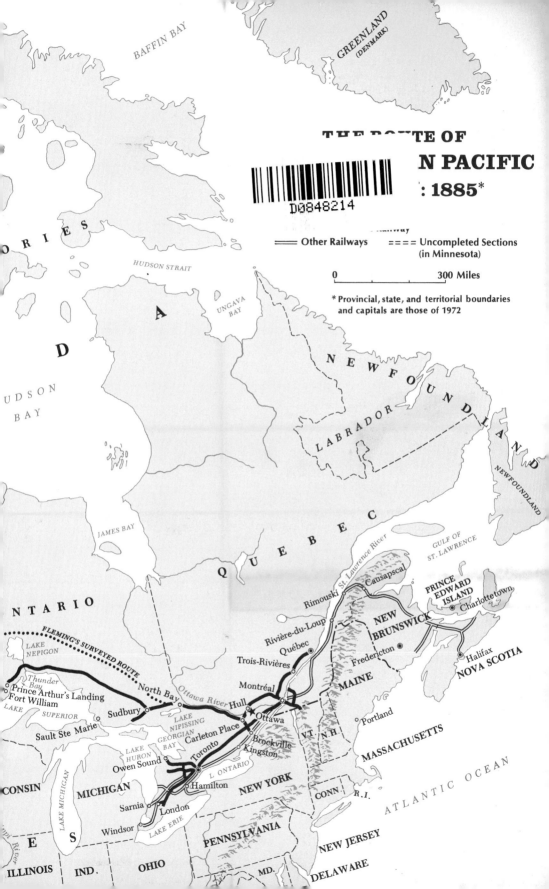

THE ROUTE OF
[CANADIA]N PACIFIC
[RAILWAY]: 1885*

═══ Other Railways   ════ Uncompleted Sections
(in Minnesota)

0 ——————————— 300 Miles

* Provincial, state, and territorial boundaries
and capitals are those of 1972

BAFFIN BAY

GREENLAND
(DENMARK)

...RIES

HUDSON STRAIT

A

D

UNGAVA
BAY

UDSON

BAY

NEWFOUNDLAND

LABRADOR

NEWFOUNDLAND

JAMES BAY

Q U E B E C

GULF OF
ST. LAWRENCE

St. Lawrence River

Causapscal

PRINCE
EDWARD
ISLAND

Charlottetown

Rimouski

NTARIO

FLEMING'S SURVEYED ROUTE

LAKE
NEPIGON

Rivière-du-Loup

Québec

NEW
BRUNSWICK

Fredericton

Halifax

NOVA SCOTIA

Trois-Rivières

Thunder
Bay
Prince Arthur's Landing
Fort William

North Bay

Ottawa River

Montréal

MAINE

LAKE
SUPERIOR

Sudbury

LAKE
NIPISSING

Hull

Ottawa

VT.

N.H.

Portland

Sault Ste Marie

GEORGIAN
BAY

Carleton Place

Brockville

MASSACHUSETTS

LAKE
HURON

Owen Sound

Toronto

Kingston

CONSIN

L. ONTARIO

MICHIGAN

Hamilton

NEW YORK

CONN.

R.I.

ATLANTIC OCEAN

LAKE MICHIGAN

Sarnia

London

Windsor

LAKE ERIE

E

S

River

PENNSYLVANIA

NEW JERSEY

ILLINOIS

IND.

OHIO

MD.

DELAWARE

MONTGOMERY COUNTY COMMUNITY COLLEGE

3 0473 00032715 8

46776

HE
2810   Berton, Pierre
C2   Impossible railway.
B44
1972

DATE DUE			
APR 6			

LEARNING RESOURCES CENTER
MONTGOMERY COUNTY COMMUNITY COLLEGE
BLUE BELL, PENNSYLVANIA

Books by PIERRE BERTON

The Royal Family (1954)
The Mysterious North (1956)
The Klondike Fever (1958)
The Big Sell (1963)
The Comfortable Pew (1965)
My War with the Twentieth Century (1965)
The Smug Minority (1969)
Voices from the Sixties (1967)
The Impossible Railway (1972)

For Younger Readers:

Stampede for Gold (1955)
The Secret World of Og (1962)

THE
IMPOSSIBLE
RAILWAY

Pierre Berton

THE IMPOSSIBLE RAILWAY

The Building of the Canadian Pacific

ALFRED · A · KNOPF / NEW YORK

1972

Copyright © 1970, 1971, 1972 by Pierre Berton Enterprises, Ltd.
All rights reserved under International and Pan-American Copyright
Conventions. Published in the United States by Alfred A. Knopf, Inc.,
New York. Distributed by Random House, Inc., New York.

Originally published in Canada in two volumes, as
The National Dream (1970) and
The Last Spike (1971), by McClelland & Stewart, Ltd., Toronto, Canada.

Library of Congress Cataloging in Publication Data:

Berton, Pierre, 1920–   The impossible railway.
First published in 2 v. under titles: The national dream (1970)
    and The last spike (1971)   Bibliography: p.
    1. Canadian Pacific Railway.   2. Railroads and state—Canada.
    3. Canada—History—1867–1914.   I. Title.
HE2810.C2B44   1972   385'.0971   72–2236
ISBN 0–394–46569–5

Manufactured in the United States of America

First American Edition

46776

Size is not grandeur, and territory
does not make a nation.

     —THOMAS HENRY HUXLEY

Until this great work is completed,
our Dominion is little more than a
"geographical expression."

     —SIR JOHN A. MACDONALD

All I can say is that the work has
been done well in every way.

     —W. C. VAN HORNE,
      at Craigellachie

Strand B.A. 7.50 1973/74.

Contents

Illustrations

Maps

Cast of Major Characters

THE POLITICIANS

Liberal-Conservatives (Tories)

SIR JOHN A. MACDONALD, Prime Minister of Canada, 1867–73, 1878–91.

SIR GEORGE ÉTIENNE CARTIER, Minister of Militia and Defence, 1867–73. Macdonald's Quebec lieutenant.

SIR CHARLES TUPPER, M.P. for Cumberland, Nova Scotia; President of the Privy Council, 1870–72; Minister of Inland Revenue, 1872–73; Minister of Customs, 1873; Minister of Public Works, 1878–79; Minister of Railways and Canals, 1879–84; Prime Minister of Canada, 1896; High Commissioner to London, 1884–96.

SIR FRANCIS HINCKS, Premier of United Canada, 1851–54; Minister of Finance, 1869–73.

HECTOR LOUIS LANGEVIN, Minister of Public Works, 1869–73; Postmaster General, 1878–79; Minister of Public Works, 1879–91. Cartier's successor as Macdonald's Quebec lieutenant.

J. J. C. ABBOTT, M.P. for Argenteuil, Quebec. Legal counsel for first railway syndicate leader Sir Hugh Allan in 1873; legal counsel for the CPR Syndicate, 1880.

JOHN HENRY POPE, Minister of Agriculture, 1878–85; Minister of Railways and Canals, 1885–89. Tupper's deputy during his absence.

SENATOR FRANK SMITH, Minister Without Portfolio, 1882–91. Wholesale grocer and railway executive.

EDGAR DEWDNEY, Indian Commissioner, Manitoba and North West Territories, 1879–88; Lieutenant-Governor of the North West Territories, 1881–88.

Liberals (Clear Grits and Reformers)

ALEXANDER MACKENZIE, Prime Minister of Canada and Minister of Public Works, 1873–78.

EDWARD BLAKE, M.P. for Durham West, Ontario; Premier of Ontario, 1871–72; Minister Without Portfolio, 1873–74; Minister of Justice, 1875–77; President of the Privy Council, 1877–78. Succeeded Alexander Mackenzie as Liberal leader, 1880.

LUCIUS SETH HUNTINGTON, Solicitor General for Lower Canada, 1863–64; M.P. for Shefford, Quebec, 1867–78; President of the Privy Council, 1874–75; Postmaster General, 1875–78. His speech in 1873 touched off the Pacific Scandal.

THE PATHFINDERS

SANDFORD FLEMING, chief engineer of the government-owned Intercolonial Railway; Engineer-in-Chief of the CPR, 1871–80; succeeded by Collingwood Schreiber. Devised a workable system of standard time.

MARCUS SMITH, in charge of surveys in British Columbia, 1872–76; Fleming's deputy in Ottawa, 1876–78. Strong proponent of Bute Inlet as CPR terminus. Government inspecting engineer on the Onderdonk contract between Port Moody and Emory in British Columbia.

WALTER MOBERLY, assistant surveyor general of British Columbia, 1865–66; in charge of mountain surveys for CPR, 1871–72. Discovered Eagle Pass.

HENRY J. CAMBIE, in charge of British Columbia surveys after 1876, replacing Marcus Smith. Engineer for Andrew Onderdonk on Contract 60 in the Fraser Canyon area and later for the CPR between Kamloops and Eagle Pass.

CHARLES HORETZKY, photographer and explorer. Conducted exploratory surveys in the Pine Pass and Kitlope River regions.

GENERAL THOMAS LAFAYETTE ROSSER, chief engineer of the CPR, 1881–82; former chief engineer for the Northern Pacific Railroad.

MAJOR A. B. ROGERS, engineer in charge of the mountain division of the CPR. Formerly locating engineer for the Chicago, Milwaukee and St. Paul Railroad.

THE ENTREPRENEURS

SIR HUGH ALLAN, Montreal shipowner and financier whose syndicate was awarded the CPR contract in 1872. His heavy subscriptions to the Conservative Party implicated him in the Pacific Scandal.

JAY COOKE, Philadelphia banker who financed the Northern Pacific Railroad and hoped to control the CPR.

GEORGE W. McMULLEN, Canadian-born promoter from Chicago who produced American backers for Sir Hugh Allan's railway company.

SENATOR DAVID L. MACPHERSON, Toronto railway builder and rival of Sir Hugh Allan. He made a fortune in Grand Trunk Railway construction contracts and headed the Interoceanic Company, which bid unsuccessfully for the CPR contract in 1872.

THE CPR SYNDICATE

GEORGE STEPHEN, president of the CPR, 1881–88. Former president of the Bank of Montreal. He helped Donald Smith and James J. Hill organize the St. Paul, Minneapolis and Manitoba Railway in the late 1870's.

DUNCAN McINTYRE, vice-president of the CPR, 1881–84. President of the Canada Central Railway.

JAMES J. HILL, Canadian-born fuel and transportation merchant in St. Paul, Minnesota. Member of the executive committee of the CPR, 1881–83. Organized the Great Northern Railroad in the United States.

NORMAN KITTSON, early Minnesota fur trader; Hill's partner in Red River Transportation Company and subsequent ventures. Member of the CPR Syndicate, 1880.

RICHARD BLADWORTH ANGUS, member of the executive committee of the CPR. Elected vice-president in 1883. Former general manager of the Bank of Montreal.

DONALD A. SMITH, George Stephen's cousin, M.P. for Selkirk, Manitoba, 1871–78; Labrador fur trader who rose to become resident governor and Chief Commissioner of the Hudson's Bay Company in Canada. A partner of Hill and Kittson in Red River Transportation Company and subsequent railroad ventures. Member of the CPR Syndicate, 1880. A major CPR stockholder and a director after 1883.

JOHN S. KENNEDY, New York banker allied with Hill, Stephen, and Smith in the St. Paul railway venture.

THE BUILDERS

JOSEPH WHITEHEAD, Liberal M.P., awarded contracts on the Pembina Branch of the CPR and on Section Fifteen between Cross Lake and Rat Portage, west of Lake Superior.

ADAM OLIVER, Liberal M.P.P. (Member of Provincial Parliament), awarded telegraph contracts west of Fort William, Ontario. Implicated in Neebing Hotel scandal.

J. W. SIFTON, awarded construction contract west of Fort William (with his brother Henry) and telegraph contract west of Winnipeg (with David Glass, M.P.). Father of Sir Clifford Sifton, founder of Sifton newspapers.

MICHAEL J. HANEY, construction boss who took over and completed Section Fifteen for the government after Joseph Whitehead suffered financial reverses. Superintendent of the CPR's Pembina Branch and Rat Portage divisions, 1882. General manager of the Onderdonk section, 1883–85.

ALPHEUS B. STICKNEY, general superintendent of the CPR's western division, 1881; formerly superintendent of construction on the St. Paul, Minneapolis and Manitoba Railway.

WILLIAM CORNELIUS VAN HORNE, general manager of the CPR, 1882; vice-president and general manager, 1884; president, 1888–99; chairman of the board, 1899–1910. Formerly general superintendent, Chicago, Milwaukee and St. Paul Railroad.

JOHN EGAN, superintendent of the CPR's western division after 1882. Formerly divisional superintendent, Chicago, Milwaukee and St. Paul Railroad.

THOMAS SHAUGHNESSY, general purchasing agent of the CPR, 1882–85; assistant general manager, 1885; vice-president and general manager, 1888; president, 1899–1917. Formerly general storekeeper, Chicago, Milwaukee and St. Paul Railroad.

HARRY ABBOTT, in charge of the eastern section of the CPR's Lake Superior construction.

JOHN ROSS, in charge of the western section of the CPR's Lake Superior construction.

JAMES ROSS, in charge of construction for the CPR's mountain division. Built the Credit Valley Railway, 1878–79.

ANDREW ONDERDONK, contractor in charge of government construction between Port Moody and Savona's Ferry on Kamloops Lake, 1881–85. Also built section of CPR line between Savona's Ferry and Craigellachie in Eagle Pass.

THE NATIVE PEOPLES

LOUIS RIEL, head of the métis (half-breed) provisional government in Manitoba, 1869–70, and leader of the Red River uprising. In exile, Member of Parliament for Provencher, 1873–74. Leader of the Saskatchewan Rebellion of 1885.

GABRIEL DUMONT, Riel's adjutant general, "the Prince of the Plains," formed métis government at St. Laurent, near Batoche on the South Saskatchewan, in 1873. Long-time chief of the Red River buffalo hunts.

CROWFOOT, head chief of the Blackfoot tribes, a noted warrior, veteran of nineteen battles, wounded six times. Refused to join in the rebellion of 1885.

POUNDMAKER, a Cree chief, Crowfoot's adopted son, one of the leaders agitating for concessions from the government for Indians along the North Saskatchewan between 1881 and 1885. Captured and imprisoned for his role in the Saskatchewan Rebellion.

BIG BEAR, chief of the Plains Crees, organizer of first Indian council, 1884. His followers precipitated the massacre at Frog Lake during the Saskatchewan Rebellion. His capture on July 2, 1885, signaled the rebellion's end.

THE BYSTANDERS

FREDERICK TEMPLE BLACKWOOD, Earl of Dufferin, Governor General of Canada, 1872–78. Succeeded by the MARQUIS OF LORNE.

GEORGE BROWN, former leader of the Reform Party; publisher and editor of the *Globe*, Toronto. Alexander Mackenzie's mentor. Murdered in May, 1880.

GEORGE MONRO GRANT, minister of St. Matthew's Church, Halifax,

1863–77; secretary to Sandford Fleming on the chief engineer's transcontinental trip, 1872. His book *Ocean to Ocean* describes that journey.

JOHN MACOUN, self-educated botanist; companion of Fleming and Grant on their trip from ocean to ocean. Examined the fertility of the North West for the government.

FATHER ALBERT LACOMBE, oblate missionary whose parish was the Far West. Pastor to railway workers east of Winnipeg, 1880–82.

JESSE FARLEY, receiver for the bankrupt St. Paul and Pacific Railroad. He later sued James J. Hill and Norman Kittson, claiming that the reorganization of the railroad was his idea. The suit failed.

SIR HENRY WHATLEY TYLER, president of the Grand Trunk Railway, 1876–95; British Member of Parliament and engineer. Formerly inspector of railways in Great Britain.

JOSEPH HICKSON, general manager of the Grand Trunk Railway, 1874–91.

ARTHUR WELLINGTON ROSS, Winnipeg real-estate agent and adviser on real-estate matters to the CPR. Member of the Manitoba legislature, 1879–82; Member of Parliament for Lisgar, Manitoba, 1882–96. A Conservative.

SAMUEL BENFIELD STEELE, in command of North West Mounted Police detachments along the line of CPR construction. Member of the original detachment of the NWMP. Acting adjutant of the Fort Qu'Appelle district.

THE
IMPOSSIBLE
RAILWAY

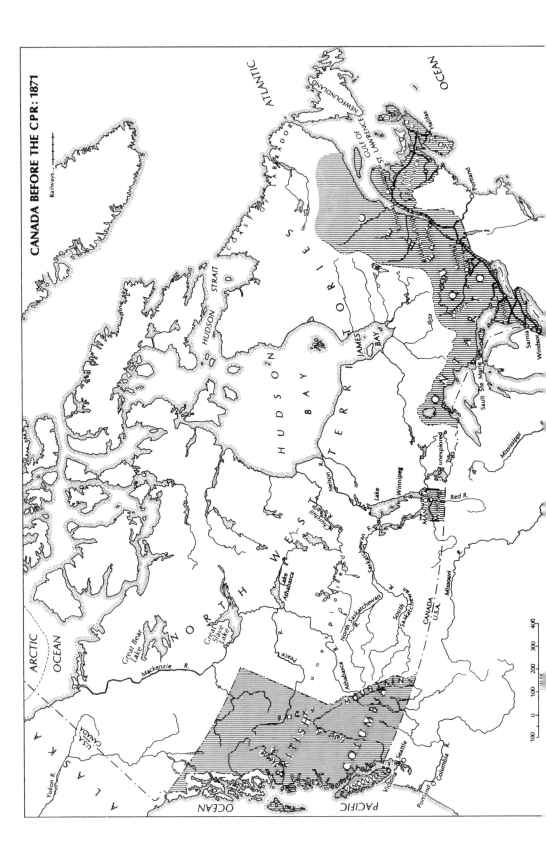

CANADA BEFORE THE CPR: 1871

Railways

From Sea to Sea

IT IS NEW YEAR'S DAY, 1871, *the year in which Canada will become a transcontinental nation, and in most of British North America it is bitter cold. In Ottawa, where it is eighteen below, the snow, gritty as sand, squeaks eerily beneath the felted feet of morning church-goers. A cutting wind, blowing off Lake Ontario, is heaping great drifts against the square logs of the Upper Canadian barns, smothering the snake fences and frustrating the Grand Trunk's Montreal–Toronto passenger schedule. On the St. Lawrence, in front of Quebec City, that annual phenomenon, the ice bridge, is taking form. In the harbor of Saint John, the rime hangs thickly upon the rigging, turning schooners and barkentines into ghost ships.*

Only at the colonial extremities is New Year's Day a green one. In the English gardens of Victoria, British Columbia, the occasional yellow wallflower still blooms shyly, and in the verdant colony of Prince Edward Island the fields are free of frost. The editorial comments are as salubrious as the climate. The potato farmers of Souris and Summerside read their Saturday Islander *with approval: "In our cosy little Island we have scarcely experienced anything but the blessings of Providence," it says. "It is probable that never at any previous period of our existence were we as rich a community as we are at the moment." There is cause for rejoicing: the Island colony is eagerly awaiting new proposals from Canada calculated to entice it into Confederation; the rumors say that these will be far more liberal than the ones that have been rejected. And why not? After all, British Columbia has been promised a railway!*

Three thousand miles to the west, the steam presses of the British Colonist *are pumping out a New Year's salutation for the morrow. For British Columbia, the editor writes, the outlook has never been brighter: "Clad in bridal attire, she is about to unite her destinies with a country which is prepared to do much for her." The paper carries a reprint from a Tory journal back east, praising the government for the nuptial present it is about to bestow.*

The world is in its customary turmoil—the Germans at the gates of Paris, the insurrectionists bedeviling Cuba—but in Canada there is nothing but good humor. Even George Brown, the caustic editor of the Globe, *is in a mellow mood. One can almost surmise a half-smile lighting up those long Scottish features as he scribbles an unusually benign editorial in his Toronto office. "Peace and plenty prevail," he writes, "and there is nothing for us but hope and encouragement as we welcome the advent of another year."*

It is the Lord's Day and all across settled Canada the curtains are drawn and the church bells are sounding. Only an eccentric would resist their summons. Because of the Sabbath, all the elegant and sometimes lusty New Year's rituals of the Canadian upper classes have been postponed for a day. The brass and rosewood, the sterling and cut glass, have all been polished to a high gloss by an army of servants, making ready for Monday's "calling." Then will the gentlemen of the towns, frock-coated and convivial, trudge unsteadily from threshold to threshold, to be greeted by well-bustled matrons with puckered lips and full decanters. The temperance movement is crying out against such debauchery. In Montreal, it is reported, some of the ladies have been persuaded to serve coffee. That city, a correspondent notes, has already given the New Year "a sober and orderly welcome."

Far off beyond the somber desert of the Canadian Shield, at Fort Garry in the new province of Manitoba, the welcome is not so orderly. Fiddles screech, pipes skirl, and the settlers caper like souls possessed to an endless succession of Red River reels, while nearby tables groan with smoking joints of venison and buffalo. The great Scottish feast of Hogmanay—New Year's Eve—is far more important than Christmas.

For one Scotsman, there is a special reason to celebrate. Donald A. Smith, late of Labrador, has just won a federal seat in his adopted province's first election. It is a significant victory. The events set in motion by the decisions of 1871 will change the current of Smith's life and enshrine his likeness in the history books of a later century, linking him forever with a symbolic railway spike in a distant mountain pass.

That pass is one thousand miles to the west of the Red River, and for all that thousand miles scarcely a light flickers or a soul moves. Awesome in its vastness and its isolation, the newly acquired North West—the heart of the new Canada—sleeps beneath its blanket of snow. Walled off from the Pacific by the vertebrae of the Cordilleras and from the settled East by a granite Pre-Cambrian wasteland, the great central plain is like an unconquered island.

The North West! The name is beginning to take on overtones of romance. In the winter, when the blizzard strikes and the heavens are blotted out, it can be a white hell; in the summer, by all accounts, it is an enchanted realm. One can travel for days, they say, along the ruts of the Carlton Trail between Fort Garry and Fort Edmonton without encountering humankind—only ridge after ridge of untrammeled parkland rolling on toward the high arch of the sky. Out there, they say, the eye can feast upon acres and acres of tiger lilies and bluebells, stretching to the horizon "as if a vast Oriental carpet had been thrown across the plains." The prairie chickens, they say, are so numerous that they mask the sun, while the passenger pigeons roost so thickly on the oaks that the very branches snap beneath their weight. And there are exquisite lakes, speckled with geese and swans, broad meadows where the whooping cranes stalk about in pairs, and everywhere the ultimate spectacle of the buffalo, moving in dark rivers through a tawny ocean of waist-high grass. Only a privileged few have gazed upon these marvels; the events of 1871 will ensure that they will soon be just a memory.

How many white men inhabit this empty realm? Perhaps twenty-five hundred. Nobody knows for certain because there has never been an accurate census. The North West is a scattered archipelago of human islets, each isolated from the others by vast distances and contrasting life styles—Scottish farmers, métis buffalo hunters, Yankee whiskey traders, French missionaries, British and Canadian fur merchants. In the lonely prairie between these human enclaves the nomadic and warlike Indian bands roam freely.

For all of the decade, this wild, misunderstood domain will be the subject of endless speculation, curiosity, political maneuver and debate. There are few Canadians yet who care greatly about it; most provincial politicians, indeed, are "either indifferent or hostile to its acquisition." Yet by the fact of its acquisition, the young Dominion has set itself upon a new course. The Conservative Prime Minister, Sir John A. Macdonald, has just promised British Columbia a great railway across the North West to Pacific tidewater. Once that decision is confirmed, as it must be in this pivotal year of 1871, nothing can ever again be the same.

1 · An "act of insane recklessness"

ITS POLITICAL OPPONENTS PRETENDED TO believe that the Macdonald Government had gone mad. "Insane" was the word the Liberal leader, Alexander Mackenzie, used, time and again for most of the decade of the seventies, to describe the pledge to build a railway to the Pacific. It was, he said in the House that spring of 1871, an "act of insane recklessness," and there were a good many Canadians, including some of John A. Macdonald's own supporters, who thought he was right.

Here was a country of only three and a half million people, not yet four years old, pledged to construct the greatest of all railways. It would be longer than any line yet built—almost one thousand miles longer than the first American road to the Pacific, which the United States, with a population of almost forty million, had only just managed to complete.

The Americans had more money, shorter mileage, and far fewer obstacles than the Canadians. For one thing, they knew where they were going: there were established and sophisticated cities on their Pacific coastline. But neither John A. Macdonald nor his surveyors had any idea where they were headed. The only settlement of account on the Canadian Pacific Coast was on an island; the indentations in the mainland were uncharted, the valleys were unexplored, the passes were unsurveyed.

For another thing, the United States was not faced with any barrier as implacable as that of the Pre-Cambrian Shield, that great desert of billion-year-old rock, whose southern tongue intruded between the settled valley of the St. Lawrence and the farmlands of the Red River basin. If the railway followed an all-Canadian route, its builders would have to blast their way across seven hundred miles of this granite wasteland, pocked by gun-metal lakes and overlaid with a patchy coverlet of stunted trees. There were ridges there that would consume three tons of dynamite a day for months on end; and, where the ridges ended, there was another three hundred miles of muskeg bogs, which could (and would) swallow a locomotive at a single gulp. This was land incapable of cultivation. There were many who held with Alexander Mackenzie that to build a railway across it was "one of the most foolish things that could be imagined."

After the Shield was breached, the road was to lead across the North West—a tenantless empire of waving grass (which many thought to be unproductive desert) bordered by the thinly forested valley of the North Saskatchewan River. Every sliver of timber—railroad ties, bridge supports, construction materials—would have to be hauled, league after league, across this desolate land where, it seemed, the wind never ceased.

At the far limits of the plains the way was blocked by a notched wall of naked rock, eight thousand feet high. Beyond that wall lay a second wall and beyond that wall a third. Here were gloomy trenches to be bridged, cataracts to be thwarted, and alpine buttresses to be dynamited. At the end of that sea of plumed mountains lay the unknown coastline, tattered like a coat beyond repair. George Étienne Cartier, acting for his ailing leader, had promised British Columbia that the railway would reach that coastline, ready to operate, within ten years. It was, cried Edward Blake, the intellectual giant of the opposing Liberal (or Reform) Party, "a preposterous proposition."

Some of Macdonald's parliamentary followers tended to agree with Blake. The Prime Minister was absent in Washington during the debate over the railway in April, but Alexander Morris, his Minister of Internal Revenue, reported to him that it was the hardest fight since Confederation four years before. Some twenty Government supporters, enough to cause the administration's defeat, were "weak kneed and alarmed." Morris rallied them with a tough speech, telling the caucus it was no time to stab an absent leader in the back; but the decision to build the great railway was a near thing.

The Government had promised the railway to British Columbia in order to lure that colony into the new Confederation of Ontario, Quebec, New Brunswick, Nova Scotia, and Manitoba. Macdonald's vision of Canada did not stop at the Great Lakes; his dream was of a transcontinental British nation in North America—a workable alternative to the United States. To achieve this dream, the railway was a necessity, or so the Prime Minister insisted: it would stitch the scattered provinces and empty territories of the West together, as the government-owned Intercolonial was intended to do in the East; it would be the means of colonizing the prairies; it would forestall American expansion; it would be the spine of empire, an Imperial highway linking the British Isles with the Orient and avoiding the appalling voyage around the Horn.

There were, almost certainly, more pragmatic reasons. Macdonald needed the diversion of the railway to maintain himself in office. The project was clearly a gamble, but the stakes were high. If he succeeded in fulfilling his pledge, the Conservative Party could probably look forward to a generation of power. No other *fait accompli*, even that of Confederation, could compete with such a triumph.

If the skeptics had considerable logic on their side, Macdonald had emotion. Could a country of three and a half million people afford an expenditure of one hundred million dollars at a time when a laborer's wage was a dollar a day? Perhaps not; but Macdonald meant to persuade the country that it could not do without a railway if it wanted to be a nation in the true sense of the word. Also, the Government insisted, the railway would not bring any rise in taxes: it could be paid for with land from the North West.

Why the fixed term of ten years? As Macdonald's opponent Mackenzie said, most of the railway would run through an uninhabitable wilderness: "It wouldn't be necessary to construct the greater portion of the line for another thirty years." That was also perfectly true; but Macdonald's attitude was that there might be no nation in thirty years without a railway. The cornerstone of his transcontinental policy was the settlement of the North West, and he and his Ministers pressed the view that without a railway the land would remain empty until the Americans moved in to fill the vacuum. Besides, they had the assurance of the chief British Columbia delegate, Joseph Trutch, that the ten-year clause was not a "cast iron contract" but more a figure of speech; the province would not hold the Canadian government to the letter of the wording.

It was the apparent insistence on an all-Canadian line that brought the harshest criticism. Few Canadians really believed that any railway builder would be foolhardy enough to hurdle the wilderness of rock between Lake Nipissing and the Red River. No white man had ever crossed all of it on foot and few reliable maps of the region existed.

Macdonald's opponents were all for diverting the line south of Lake Superior, through United States territory, and then leading northwest into Manitoba from Duluth. If North America were one nation, that would be the sensible way to go. But Macdonald did not believe that Canada could call herself a nation if she did not have geographical control of her own rail line. What if Canada were at war? Could troops of a belligerent nation be moved over foreign soil? The half-breed uprising of 1869 was still green in the Prime Minister's memory. Unable to use the colonists' route through St. Paul, the troops sent to the Red River had taken ninety-six days to negotiate the forty-seven portages across the Canadian Shield. A railway could rush several regiments to the North West in less than a week. Macdonald did not rule out another rebellion or even a border dispute with the Americans.

The Prime Minister, as he was to say so vehemently on more than one occasion, was born a British subject and meant to die one. His nationalism had two sides. On the positive side he was pro-Canadian, which in those days was much the same as being pro-British. On the negative side he was almost paranoiac in his anti-Americanism. The Americans, to Macdonald, were "Yankees," and he put into that term all the disdain that was then implied by its use: the Yankees were upstarts, money-grasping, uncouth, anti-British; and they wanted to grab Canada for themselves, throw off the monarchy, and turn solid Canadians into shrill, greedy tinsel copies of themselves.

Macdonald's opponents might feel that the price of holding the newly acquired North West was too high to pay, but he himself was well aware that some Americans, especially those in Minnesota, saw it as a ripe plum ready to fall into their hands. He believed, in fact, that the United States government "are resolved to do all they can, short of war, to get possession of the western territory." That being so, he wrote in January, 1870, "we must take immediate and vigorous steps to counteract them. One of the first things to be done is to show un-mistakeably our resolve to build the Pacific Railway."

There was reason for Macdonald's suspicions. In 1867, the very year of Confederation, William H. Seward, the United States Secretary of State, flushed with his purchase of Alaska, had told a Boston audience that the whole continent "shall be, sooner or later, within the magic circle of the American union." His successor, Hamilton Fish, was an expansionist, as was President Grant himself; though they were not prepared to fight for a piece of Canada, they were delighted to countenance, if not to encourage, a powerful group of Minnesota businessmen and politicians who saw their burgeoning territory extending north of the 49th parallel.

As Macdonald well knew, there were powerful influences working in the United States to frustrate the building of any all-Canadian railroad. In 1869, a United States Senate committee report declared that "the opening by us first of a Northern Pacific railroad seals the destiny of the British possessions west of the ninety-first meridian. They will become so Americanized in interests and feelings that they will be in effect severed from the new Dominion, and the question of their annexation will be but a question of time." A similar kind of peaceful penetration had led eventually to the annexation of Oregon.

It was the railwaymen who coveted the North West. "I have an awful swaller for land," the Northern Pacific's General George Washington Cass told the Grand Trunk's Edward Watkin. In 1869 the Governor of Vermont, John Gregory Smith, who also happened to be president of the Northern Pacific, determined to build that line so close to the Canadian border that it would forestall any plans for an all-Canadian railway.

By the following year, Jay Cooke, the banker who was the real power behind the Northern Pacific, was so sure of capturing the same territory as a monopoly for his railroad that he was using the idea to peddle the company's bonds. A Northern Pacific pamphlet decried the whole idea of a railway north of Lake Superior: the Americans, it said, would send any branches needed into British territory to serve their neighbors.

On one side of the mountains, the railway would siphon off the products of the rich farmlands; on the other side, it would drain the British Columbia mining settlements. "Drain" was the operative verb; it was the one the Senate committee used. As for the Minnesotans, they saw their state devouring the entire Red River Valley. Their destiny lay north of the 49th parallel, so the St. Paul *Pioneer Press* editorialized. That was "the irresistible doctrine of nature."

But it was Macdonald's intention to defy nature and fashion a nation in the process. His tool, to this end, would be the Canadian Pacific. It would be a rare example of a nation created through the construction of a railway.

In the Canada of 1871, "nationalism" was a strange, new word. Patriotism was derivative, racial cleavage was deep, culture was regional, provincial animosities savage, and the idea of unity ephemeral. Thousands of Canadians had already been lured south by the availability of land and the greater diversity of enterprise, which contrasted with the lack of opportunity at home. The country looked like a giant on the map, second only in size to China. But for most practical purposes, it stopped at the Great Lakes.

The six scattered provinces (British Columbia had just acceded) had yet to unite in a great national endeavor or to glimpse anything remotely resembling a Canadian dream; but both were taking shape. The endeavor would be the building of the Pacific railway; the dream would be the filling up of the empty spaces and the dawn of a new nation.

2 · *The dreamers*

FOR ALMOST FORTY YEARS BEFORE MAC-donald made his bargain with British Columbia, there had been talk about a railway to the Pacific. Most of it was nothing more than rhetoric. For most colonial Canadians at mid-century, the prospect of a line of steel stretching off two thousand miles into the Pacific mists was totally unreal.

Thomas Dalton, editor of the Toronto *Patriot*, has been credited with the first vision. He talked vaguely, in 1834, of an all-steam route by river, rail, and canal from Toronto to the Pacific and thence to the Orient. His friends dismissed him as a mere enthusiast, by which they probably meant he was slightly demented.

In 1851, when Allan Macdonell, a Toronto promoter, applied for a charter to build a railway to the Pacific, his scheme was turned down "as an hallucination to amuse for a moment and then to vanish." At that time Canada had built only about two hundred miles of railway. The United States, by comparison, had built ten thousand miles.

Then, two years later, the climate suddenly changed and the country entered into an orgy of railroad building. In this euphoric period was launched the partnership between railways, promoters, politicians, and government that became the classic Canadian pattern for so many public works.

Profits and politics tended to become inseparable, especially among Conservatives. Most Conservative politicians were business or professional men who welcomed the idea of a partnership between big business and government to build the country. By 1871, when Macdonald launched his Pacific railway scheme, there were forty Members of the House and twelve Senators—promoters, directors, contractors, or company presidents—with vested interests in railroads. The great majority were Conservatives.

The Liberals' opposition to Macdonald's railway policy stemmed in part from the excesses of the railway boom of the fifties. They had reason to be outraged. Between 1854 and 1857 an estimated hundred million dollars in foreign capital was pumped into Canada for the purpose of building railways. Much of it found its way into the pockets of promoters and contractors. The usual scheme was to form a company, keep control of it, float as much stock as possible, and then award lush construction contracts to men on the inside. Thomas Keefer, a respected engineer, was later to write of Cabinet Ministers accepting fees from promoters, contractors, and railway officials and making such men "their most intimate companions, their hosts and guests, their patrons and protégés." One American contractor, he said, virtually ran the Upper Canadian (Canada West) government in the fifties.

By 1858, it had, however, become fashionable to talk of a Pacific railway. Both the British and the Canadian governments began to take an active interest in examining the North West with an eye to possible railway routes, and a series of expeditions was launched at the end of the 1850's to explore all the country between Lake Superior and the Rockies—land still under the control of the Hudson's Bay Company.

Then, in 1862, Sandford Fleming, a railway engineer of stature, entered the picture and placed before the government the first carefully worked-out plan for building a railroad to the Pacific. When Fleming wrote his "Observations and Practical Suggestions on the Subject of a Railway through British North America," he was only thirty-five and most of his awesome accomplishments (including the conception of standard time) lay ahead of him. Typically, his outline for a "highway to the Pacific" was carefully thought out, measured, and detailed. It was to be built in gradual stages, it would cost about one hundred million dollars, and it would take at least twenty-five years to build.

It was the cautious and meticulous plan of a cautious and meticulous Scot, for Fleming, in spite of his inventive record (he had designed the first Canadian postage stamp in 1851 and founded the Canadian Institute), was nothing if not deliberate. He worked out every detail down to the last horse, crosstie and telegraph pole, and, of course, to the last dollar. His gradualness, he conceded, would not "satisfy the precipitate or impatient," but he included in his memorandum a reminder of Aesop's hare and tortoise, pointing out that the line of the railway extended over forty-five degrees of longitude, which was "equal to one-eighth of a circle of latitude passing entirely around the globe." After all, wrote Fleming, "half a continent has to be redeemed and parted at least from a wild state of nature."

It was an impressive memorandum and it undoubtedly did a great deal to advance Fleming's considerable ambitions. Eight years later, when Canada's pledge to British Columbia passed the Commons, the Prime Minister appointed Fleming Engineer-in-Chief of the Canadian

Pacific Railway in addition to his previous appointment to the same capacity with the government-owned Intercolonial then being built to link the Maritime Provinces with central Canada. Being a politician, though a Scot, Macdonald *was* both "precipitate and impatient" by Fleming's standards. George Étienne Cartier, on Macdonald's behalf, had promised British Columbia that the railway would be commenced within two years and finished in ten. Certainly ten years had a more attractive ring than twenty-five; and the Prime Minister would reassure himself that he had Joseph Trutch's promise that the Pacific province would not hold him too firmly to that reckless schedule.

3 · *"Canada is dead"*

IN THE PIONEER CANADA OF 1871, THE Canadian Shield was uninhabitable, the North West virtually unreachable. The real frontier was the American frontier, the real West the American West. As the decade opened, a quarter of all Canadians in North America were living south of the border.

Some went for adventure. These included the father of Buffalo Bill Cody, who had once kept a tavern in Toronto Township, and, significantly, two Minnesota steamboatmen from Rockwood, Ontario, and Sorel, Quebec—James J. Hill and Norman W. Kittson—who would, a few years later, help launch the Canadian Pacific Railway. Some went for greater opportunity. These would soon include the frustrated composer of the national anthem, *O Canada*, Calixte Lavallée. But most went for land. The good land ran out in Upper Canada in the 1850's, and over the next generation the country began to feel a sense of limitation as farmers' sons trekked off to Iowa and Minnesota never to return. The nation's lifeblood was being drained away.

A moving frontier is essential to the vitality of a burgeoning nation. It tends to draw to it the boldest and most independent spirits in the country; and they in turn, stimulated and tempered by its challenge, become a regenerating force. Canada, by its geography, was being denied this kind of transfusion.

The call of the land was far stronger than the call of country. "The young Canadian leaving his native country to seek his fortune in the United States feels no greater wrench than a young Englishman would feel in leaving his country to seek his fortune in London," the novelist Anthony Trollope noted during a voyage to North America. Nationalism, in the seventies, was a sickly plant.

Indeed, the very utterance of the phrase "Canadian nation" was denounced in some quarters. "Canada," said the *Globe*, "except by a mere play on words, is not a nation." The whole idea of a national spirit, or "national sentiment," to use the phrase of the day, was under suspicion as being slightly treasonous.

If far-off fields looked greener to many Canadians, it was because life at home often seemed drab and unrewarding. Trollope confessed that in passing from the United States into Canada one moved "from a richer country into one that is poorer, from a greater country into one that is less." An Irishman who had spent a brief period in Canada before succumbing to the lure of the United States set down, in 1870, his feelings about the land he had left behind: "There is no galvanizing a corpse! Canada is dead—dead church, dead commerce, dead people. A poor, priest-ridden, politician-ridden, doctor-ridden, lawyer-ridden land. No energy, no enterprise, no snap."

It was a harsh indictment, but there was some truth in it. The country was controlled by the landowning classes—the merchants, the professional people, and the farm owners. In the United States, manhood suffrage was universal; in Canada, the propertyless had no vote.

The new Dominion was not yet a cohesive nation but rather a bundle of isolated village communities connected by tenuous threads. Three-quarters of the population lived in comparative isolation on farms, where most activity ceased at dusk and where, at certain times of the year, the condition of the back roads made extended travel nearly impossible. There was scarcely a city worthy of the name "metropolis." Montreal, with a population of one hundred thousand, was really two cities—one French-speaking, one English. Toronto, with half that population, was still largely an oversized village dominated by men of narrow views—Methodists, Tories, and Orangemen; it reeked, as most cities did, of fresh manure, discarded garbage, and the stench of ten thousand outdoor toilets. Ottawa was beyond the pale. For a newly elected Member of Parliament, it was, in the words of George Rose, a British humorist, "simple banishment." Rose, who passed briefly through the new Dominion after touring the United States, thought of Canada as "at best the Siberia of Great Britain."

For the industrial worker, life was harsh and colorless: he toiled for longer hours and for lower pay than his counterpart across the border. (In Quebec the *annual* wage in industry was $185.) But there was not much industry; in all of Canada it employed fewer than two hundred thousand people. Thus there was little opportunity for those who wanted to escape the drudgery of the farms.

In those days of dawn-to-dusk labor, there were three major spare-time activities: for the landholders, there was politics; for the women, there was religion; for the laborers on farms and in factories, there was strong drink. It is small wonder, then, that under these conditions many a Canadian looked with longing eyes across the border, where the work opportunities were more varied, where social conditions were better, where every man had the vote, and where the way to the frontier farmland was not barred by a thousand miles of granite and swamp.

The country had a strangely intense love-hate relationship with the United States. Publicly the Americans were vilified; secretly they were admired. The very newspapers which attacked the hated Yankees published syrupy American serial stories on their front pages instead of solid Canadian news. The very people who scoffed at the ingenious Yankee labor-saving gadgets, such as the eggbeater, were the ones who bought them. Canadians sang Yankee songs, attended Yankee plays, minstrel shows, and circuses, read Yankee authors, and were beginning to accept Yankee customs—the boardinghouse rather than the British lodgings, for example. And almost everybody wanted the return of free trade with the United States. It could open up a tremendous and attractive market for Canadian products.

The Yankees were thought of as hustlers, and, though this propensity was publicly sneered at, many a Canadian felt his own country's business leaders lacked something of the Americans' commercial zeal. The attitude was well expressed by a British travel writer who reported that "in Canada everyone skates well. The Yankee rarely snatches time from his business for such recreation."

If the Yankees were envied, they were also feared. The Fenian raids of 1866 and 1870 by British-hating Irish Americans were still fresh in everyone's mind; the suspicion lingered that the Americans had secretly encouraged them. Canadians were still moving to the United States in disturbing numbers, but in spite of this—or perhaps because of it—any newspaper could be sure of a hearing if it launched a violent anti-American attack and any politician could secure a following by damning the Yankees. Making fun of the Americans was almost a national pastime and had some of the overtones of latter-day anti-Semitism. The cartoonist's stereotype, Brother (or Cousin) Jonathan, later superseded by Uncle Sam, was pictured in unflattering terms in the pages of such short-lived *Punch*-style humor magazines as *Diogenes* and *Grinchuckle*. He was a sharp storekeeper with hard, cold eyes, whittling on a piece of wood. He was a lecherous roué, or an unshaven suitor, rejected by an innocent Miss Canada. He was a red-nosed toper, kicked in the pants by a vigorous Young Canada, the precursor of Jack Canuck. Yankee speech was lampooned in painfully laborious dialect stories.

Americanisms such as "to velocipede" or "specimentary" came under attack from grammatical pedants, while such Yankee habits as serving ice water with meals or the chewing of tobacco—habits also indulged in by large numbers of Canadians—were sneered at in print.

All these attacks on the Yankees underlined the undeniable truth that they were different from the British. Aside from Quebec, Canada was still very much a British nation, with British habits, attitudes, speech, mannerisms, and loyalties. Almost all immigrants came from the British Isles, continued to think of the motherland as home, and often returned to it. The habit of giving three cheers for Queen and Country (the country being Great Britain), and for anyone else who was royal, at dinners, military parades, and political gatherings, was universal—among French-speaking Quebeckers as well as British-born Canadians. Royal and viceregal visits produced paroxysms of excitement. The Dominion was, indeed, more British than Canadian. Class was important; church and family traditions were often placed above money in the social scale, and the "best" families flaunted coats of arms. Titles were coveted by politician and merchant prince alike. That was the great thing about Canada in their eyes: its British background provided the climate for a merchant nobility that served as a bulwark against the creeping republicanism from south of the border, which the newspapers decried so vehemently.

The newspapers, which mixed advertising with news and opinion with fact in the most ambiguous fashion, led the attack on the Americans. They published dire warnings to those who would emigrate south of the border. American commerce was declining, they declared; prices in the States were excessively high; the rates of taxation were crushing. Most of all they harped on the dangers of "republicanism"; again and again they sought to demonstrate that it inevitably led to crime and corruption.

It is doubtful if these attacks prevented many young men from quitting the narrow back roads of Canada for the broader highways to the south. The railways were running west and prosperity followed them. In those halcyon days the building of a railway was automatically believed to spell good times: anyone who turned his eyes south and west could see that.

But railways meant something more. Out beyond that sprawl of billion-year-old rock lay an immense frontier, of which Canadians were dimly becoming aware. It was now their land, wrested in 1869 from the great fur-trading monopoly of the Hudson's Bay Company after two centuries of isolation; but they did not have the means of exploiting it. A railway could give them access to that empty empire. Canada in

1871 was a country whose population was trapped in the prison of the St. Lawrence lowlands and the Atlantic littoral. A railway would be the means by which the captive finally broke out of its cage.

4 · *The struggle for the North West*

THE NORTH WEST WAS, IN 1871, AN almost totally unknown realm. Until the sixties, it had been generally considered worthless to anyone but fur traders—a Canadian Gobi, barren, ice-locked, forbidding, and totally unfit for settlement. In 1855 the Montreal *Transcript* wrote that it would not even produce potatoes, let alone grain. This attitude was fostered and encouraged by the Hudson's Bay Company. The last thing the great fur-trading empire wanted was settlers pouring in. Even bridges were taboo: they might encourage colonists. When Father Lacombe, the saintly voyageur priest, finally had one built at the St. Albert oblate mission near Fort Edmonton, the Governor himself tried to have it destroyed. At that time it was the only bridge in all of Rupert's Land.

James Young, the Galt, Ontario, M.P., recalled that "even the most eminent Canadians were deceived by these representations. For example, up to the time of Confederation, Sir George Cartier strongly opposed its acquisition by this country. The Prime Minister himself, at that time, had no idea of the value of the North West from an agricultural, commercial or manufacturing point of view." As late as 1865, Macdonald had declared that "the country is of no present value to Canada."

Historically, Montreal had dominated the North West through control of the fur trade; but in the mid-fifties Toronto moved to seize the initiative from its metropolitan rival. The leading Toronto expansionist was George Brown, editor and publisher of the *Globe*, and head of the Liberal or Reform Party until 1867. In the summer of 1856, at the height of the railway-building spree, Brown launched a campaign designed to educate his readers to the potential of the North West and to make the Hudson's Bay Company the villain of the piece. This agitation led to the government-sponsored exploration of the North West in 1857 and the appointment the same year by the British House of Commons of a Select Committee to examine the whole question of the Hudson's Bay territories in North America. Twelve years later the company ceded all of it to Canada.

Macdonald's indifference to the North West continued until 1869, when the Red River uprising inflamed the nation and launched the tragic odyssey of Louis Riel. No other figure in Canada's frontier past has so fascinated historians and writers, not to mention playwrights and even librettists. Villain or hero, martyr or madman—perhaps all four combined—Riel dominates the story of the opening of the prairies.

When he set up his independent state in the heart of North America he was just twenty-five years old, a swarthy figure with a drooping mustache and a shock of curly hair. Some scores of literary scalpels have since attempted the dissection of that perplexing personality. All agree that he was a solitary man with few confidants except his priest and his mother. All agree that his Roman Catholic religion—the narrow ultramontane version absorbed during his college years in Montreal and at his mother's knee (she saw visions and heard the voice of God) — was a dominant force in shaping him; at the end of his life it was interwoven into his madness. The evidence shows that he was a passionate man with a quick temper and a love of popular adulation who liked to get his own way and who could be violent when crossed; it also shows that he preferred nonviolence and on more than one occasion practiced it to his own detriment. He could be as compassionate as he was pious, but he was hanged for a crime that some called murder and others termed execution. He was, by turns, politically pragmatic—the murder-execution was more pragmatic than vengeful—and mystically idealistic. A champion who was prepared to sacrifice himself for his people, he was also capable of taking a bribe (to quit the country) in 1871 and of asking for another (to abandon his people and his cause) in 1885. It is small wonder that it took a century before a monument was raised to him in the province he helped to found.

Riel was born a Westerner and a métis, which means he was a French-speaking Roman Catholic of mixed race. In his case his veins were tinctured with the merest dash of Cree blood. His father, who was to have been a priest, became an eloquent tribune of his people, and Louis, the eldest of eleven, inherited the mantle of political agitator. His schooling in Montreal, his brief period in the law office of a leading radical, and his own prairie heritage had shaped this clever, intense, and apparently humorless youth into a racial patriot ready to champion the half-breed cause at Red River.

The métis were in a state of turmoil when Riel arrived back at St. Boniface in 1868 because their status was threatened by the yeasty combination of events arising out of Confederation and the imminent sale of the Hudson's Bay lands to Canada. The settlement of the West, they knew, meant an end to their own unique society, the loss of the lands on which many of them had squatted, usually without title, and the eventual dispersion of their race.

Métis society was built on the law of the buffalo hunt, a twice-yearly event, which was run with a military precision that produced general-ship of a high order and led to the first stirrings of political organization among an essentially nomadic people. The statistics of such hunts are remarkable. The greatest employed four hundred mounted hunters, twelve hundred carts, and sixteen hundred souls, including women and children. This itinerant city crawled across the plains, stretching for miles, on its way to a border rendezvous with the métis of Dakota; there, near Pembina, it formed itself into a gigantic circle, one thousand feet in diameter, ringed with oxcarts placed hub to hub and a triple row of tepees. Then, after four days of painstaking organization, which saw the election of captains, soldiers, and guides, it rolled off once more —every cart in its exact place—toward the final encounter with the great herd. The climactic scene was awesome: the ground shaking as if from an earthquake, the sky blacked out by the immense clouds of dust, the phalanx of mounted hunters, with muskets raised, galloping toward the stampeding beasts, the prairie running red with the blood of the animals. Such a spectacle would be unthinkable in a land of roads and railways, fences and furrows. By 1869, with the Hudson's Bay Company about to yield up its lands to Canada, surveyors from the East, without a by-your-leave, were already setting up their transits on métis river lots.

The métis were not Canadians and did not think of themselves as such. Neither did the white Selkirk settlers of the Red River nor the Protestant half-breed farmers. Within the community there was a small "Canadian Party" whose orientation was white, Protestant, Orange, and Upper Canadian. It helped precipitate the métis uprising which Riel did not begin but which he did organize and shape with consummate skill.

By the end of 1869, without a single act of violence, Riel and the métis had raised their own flag over the Red River settlement and were preparing to treat on equal diplomatic terms with Donald A. Smith, the Hudson's Bay man from Montreal and Labrador, whom the government had hastily dispatched. Since the great fur company had formally relinquished its territory and Canada had yet to take it over (the métis prevented the erstwhile Lieutenant-Governor from crossing the border), Riel was in an interesting bargaining position. Soon he had the entire community behind him except for the incendiary members of the Canadian Party whom he had imprisoned. Had matters rested there, Louis Riel would undoubtedly have brought the community peacefully into Confederation on métis terms and taken his place as a great

Canadian statesman, his name enshrined on countless hospitals, ball parks, schools, and expressways.

This was not to be. Some of the prisoners escaped and mounted a countermovement. The métis quickly put it down, but one of the Canadians, a sinewy Orangeman named Thomas Scott, could not be put down. When he tried to murder Riel, he was summarily court-martialed and sentenced to be shot. In this single act of violence was laid the basis for a century of bitterness and controversy.

Of all the pivotal figures in Canadian history, Thomas Scott is one of the least engaging. His breed was not uncommon in Ontario—a bigoted Protestant Irishman, totally unyielding, always inflammatory, who was nourished by his own hatreds. Scott would have driven a less mercurial man than Riel into a fury: he attacked his guards, urged his companions to follow suit, taunted the métis, and vowed to escape and kill their leader. Riel made his death a deliberate act of policy: Canada must learn to respect the métis. One can pity Scott as he is dragged before the firing squad, faced for the first time with the realization that the popish half-breeds actually mean what they say (his shocked cry, "This is cold-blooded murder!", was to echo for decades through the back roads of Ontario); but one can never like him. He makes his brief appearance on the stage of history and is gone, writhing on the ground, not quite dead from the firing squad's volley, waiting for the *coup de grâce*. But his memory remains and his tragedy, mythologized out of recognition (as Riel's was to be), will kindle an unquenchable conflagration in Orange Ontario.

The massive demand for revenge forced the government to mount, in 1870, a largely unnecessary military expedition across the portages of the Shield to relieve a fort which Riel was preparing to hand over peacefully. The expedition did have one other purpose: Macdonald, now thoroughly alive to the perils of further indifference, was not unhappy about a show of military strength in the valley of the Red River, which the Minnesota expansionists clearly coveted. By January, 1870, the Prime Minister had determined that speedy construction of a railway across the new territory to the Pacific was a necessity. He was certain that Washington would try to use the Riel troubles to frustrate Canada's acquisition to the North West.

Riel's own story almost exactly parallels that of the railway. Unwittingly, he helped to launch it; unwittingly again, fifteen years later, he helped to save it; he was hanged within a few days of the driving of the last spike. Forced into hiding and finally into exile in the United States, Riel was twice elected to Parliament from the riding of Provencher in the new province of Manitoba, of which he was the undisputed founder. He could not take his seat—the Ontario government had put a price of five thousand dollars on his head—but before he vanished over the border, he indulged in one last dramatic piece of stagecraft.

The scene is Ottawa in 1874—a snowy afternoon in January. Two muffled figures appear at a side door of the Parliament Buildings. One tells the clerk on duty that a new Member has come to sign the roll. The bored clerk hands the stranger a pen: he scratches his name and slips away. Idly, the clerk glances at it and utters a startled cry. There are the words "Louis Riel" burning themselves into the paper. The clerk looks up, but the outlaw waves sardonically and vanishes. He will not return until 1885 to play his unknowing role at the most critical moment of all in the history of the Canadian Pacific Railway.

5 · *The land beyond the lakes*

BY 1871, WITH THE EVENTS IN MANITOBA still making headlines week after week, Canadians began to look upon their new North West with a mixture of wonder, guilt, and apprehension. *It must be wonderful to see it! Oh, if only one* COULD *see it, but it was so remote, so hard to reach! Something ought to be done about developing it; they said parts of it were very rich. But would you want to* LIVE *there—so far away from everything, in that dreadful climate? One day, of course millions would live there—that was certain. One day . . .*

If the attitudes toward the North West were vague, confused, and uncertain, part of the reason lay in the conflicting reports about it. Some said it was little more than a desert; others saw it as a verdant paradise. Even the two official government explorations of the territory launched in 1857—one by the British, one by the Canadians—differed in their assessments.

The better remembered of these expeditions was that of the British, mounted by a dashing Irish bachelor named John Palliser, who left his name on a triangle of supposed desert in what is now southern Alberta and Saskatchewan. Palliser and his companions were two years in the field, and their accomplishments, though obscured at the time, were monumental. They explored, by a variety of routes, all the country between Lake Superior and the Pacific Coast. One of Palliser's associates, James Hector, discovered the Kicking Horse Pass and was almost buried alive as a result. His horse, stumbling in the frothing waters, dealt him a hoof blow that rendered him insensible. The Indians, believing him dead, popped him into a freshly dug grave and were about to shovel in the earth when the supposed corpse, conscious but unable to utter a word, managed, by a single prodigious wink of one eye, to shock the would-be burial party into less precipitate action. With Hector in great pain and his companions close to starvation, the party plunged on through the newly named pass, following the turbulent river along the line of the future CPR.

But the idea of a railway in the shadows of those rumpled peaks was far from Palliser's mind. His knowledge of the country would never lead him to advocate a railway "exclusively through British territory." Across the prairies, certainly; but that armored barrier north of Lake Superior "is *the* obstacle of the country and one, I fear, almost beyond the remedies of art." The sensible method was to go through American territory south of the lake and cut up to Manitoba through Pembina on the border, if and when the Americans built their own lines to that point.

Meanwhile the government of the united Canadas had mounted, in 1857 and 1858, a series of similar expeditions. The Canadian explorers were far more optimistic about an all-Canadian railway than were the British. One, George Gladman, did not feel the difficulties to be "insuperable to Canadian energy and enterprise." Another, Henry Youle Hind, thought Palliser too sweeping in his condemnation of the route across the Shield, which was "of vast importance to Canada." Hind agreed with Palliser that the Great American Desert had its apex in the Far West, but along the wooded valley of the North Saskatchewan and some of its tributaries there was "a broad strip of fertile country." Hind wrote in his report that "it is a physical reality of the highest importance to the interest of British North America that this continuous belt can be settled and cultivated from a few miles west of the Lake of the Woods to the passes of the Rocky Mountains." He was impressed enough by that statement to render it in capitals. In Hind's view this was the route that any railway must take to span the great central plain. He borrowed the magic name of "Fertile Belt," which Palliser had first used, and the name stuck. To the south was an "Arid Belt"— Palliser's Triangle it came to be called—which Hind, too, felt was unfit for human habitation. Hind's enthusiasm for the Fertile Belt was to have a profound effect on the railway planners; from that point on, few gave serious consideration to taking the CPR farther to the south. Hind also helped promote the North West as a land of promise. "A great future lies before the valley of the Saskatchewan," he declared. "It will become the granary of British Columbia, the vast pasture field by which the mining industry of the Rocky Mountains will be fed."

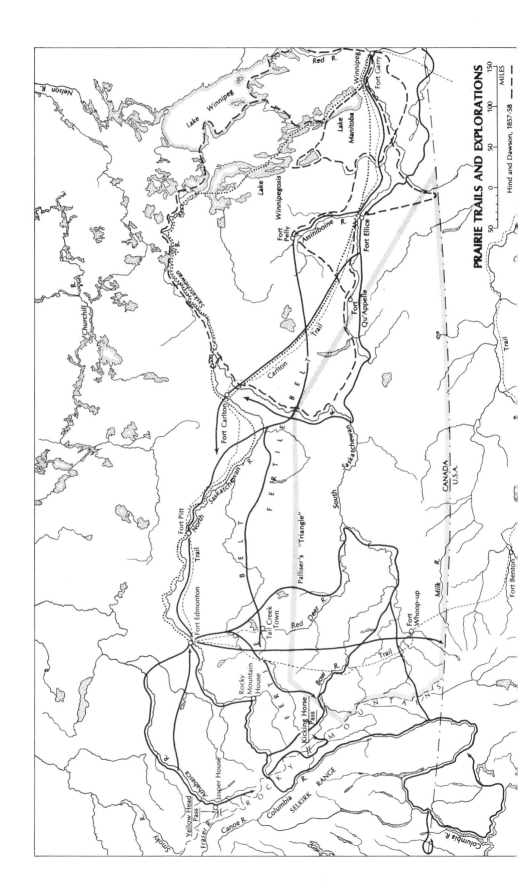

PRAIRIE TRAILS AND EXPLORATIONS

Hind and Dawson, 1857-58

MILES

0   50   100   150

Red R.

Nelson R.

Lake Winnipeg

Lake Winnipegosis

Lake Manitoba

Churchill R.

Fort Garry

Winnipeg

Fort Pelly

Assiniboine R.

Fort Ellice

Fort Qu'Appelle

Saskatchewan R.

Carlton Trail

Fort Carlton

Fort Pitt

North Saskatchewan R.

South Saskatchewan

Palliser's "Triangle"

FERTILE   BELT

Fort Edmonton Trail

Fort Edmonton

Rocky Mountain House

Fort Creek Town

Red Deer R.

Kicking Horse Pass

Bow R.

Fort Whoop-up

Milk R.

CANADA
U.S.A.

Fort Benton

Trail

ROCKY   MOUNTAINS

SELKIRK RANGE

Columbia R.

Canoe R.

Yellow Head Pass

Jasper House

Athabasca R.

Fraser R.

Smoky R.

Columbia R.

In 1871, a decade after Hind wrote those words, his vision still belonged to the future. The land beyond the lakes had not changed greatly since he and Palliser had explored it. To the men of the North West, Canada remained a foreign country: their world ran north and south. In the Far West, the mail bore United States postage, for it went out to civilization by way of Fort Benton, Montana. The Red River settlers' nearest neighbors lived in Minnesota, and the most traveled of the prairie trails was the one that ran from Fort Garry on the present site of Winnipeg to the railhead at St. Cloud, where the settlers did their shopping.

To cross the North West, in the days before the railway, was a considerable feat attempted by only a hardy few. The chief form of transportation was by Red River cart. These carts, pulled by oxen, were adapted from Scottish vehicles—two light boxes, each perched on a single axle with wheels six feet high. There was one difference: they contained not a single nail nor, indeed, a scrap of iron. Instead, tough strands of buffalo hide—the all-purpose shaganappi—were used. The axles could not be greased because the thick prairie dust would quickly immobilize the carts; as a result the wheels emitted an infernal screeching, "the North West fiddle," as some pioneers dubbed it.

With the clouds of yellow prairie dust that were raised in their wake, the brigades of carts were made visible and audible for miles. (A French visitor wrote that "a den of wild beasts cannot be compared with its hideousness.") They generally traveled in brigades, some of which were as long as railway trains. The most memorable, and surely the loudest, was the one organized in 1855 by Norman Kittson, the St. Paul trader. It contained five hundred carts and took a month to reach the Minnesota capital from Fort Garry.

The carts left deep ruts in the soft prairie turf, so deep that the wagons tended to spread out, the right wheel of one cart traveling in the wake of the left wheel of the cart ahead; thus, the prairie trails could be as much as twenty carts wide, a phenomenon that helps explain the broad streets of some of the pioneer towns.

These trails furrowed the plains like the creases on a human palm. The most famous was the Carlton Trail, winding for 1,160 miles from Fort Garry to the Yellow Head Pass in the Rockies. For half a century this was the broad highway used by every explorer, settler, trader, or adventurer who set his sights for the West. When the railway was planned, almost everybody expected it to follow the general course of the Carlton Trail. This was not to be, but a later railway did just that: it forms part of the Canadian National system today.

The trails crossed the domain of the buffalo, whose numbers in the early seventies were still legion. The open prairie was covered with their dried dung, which provided the only fuel for hundreds of miles; often, too, it was white with their bones—so many that, from a distance, it seemed as if a blizzard had covered the grass. As late as 1874, when the newly formed North West Mounted Police made their initial trek across the plains, their colonel estimated, within the range of his own vision, one million head stretching off to the horizon. And the sound of them! To the Earl of Southesk, "the deep, rolling voice of the mighty multitude came grandly on the air like the booming of a distant ocean." This was a domain which few men ever saw; it could not exist for men. The railway would mark its finish.

For the few who had come, nature might be idyllic but life was harsh. They huddled in drafty cabins, ill lit by candles made of grease or buffalo chips and heated by a single box stove. They slept on mattresses stuffed with prairie grasses, spread out on bunks fashioned from green lumber whipsawed by hand. The price of groceries was so astronomical that they were often obliged to do without. In the words of Mrs. David McDougall, who bore the first white child along the Saskatchewan in 1872, it was "meat, morning, noon and night until I could have cried for joy to have seen some fresh fruit."

The savage blizzards of winter could fell the hardiest; in summer the clouds of mosquitoes could drive oxen mad. Then there were the great fires that could leave the land a blackened ruin and the grasshoppers that, in plague years, could eat everything, including the curtains on the windows, leaving no green or living sprout behind.

In the East such phenomena were not understood. By 1872, the trickle of settlers westward was reaching the thousands. The soldiers who had struggled over the portages at the time of the métis uprising returned with tales of the rich humus in the Red River Valley. Their colonel, Garnet Wolseley, had himself written in *Blackwood's Magazine* that "as far as the eye can see, there is stretched out before you an ocean of grass, whose vast immensity grows upon you more and more the longer you gaze upon it." It brought, he said, "a feeling of indescribably buoyant freedom [that] seems to tingle through every nerve, making the old feel young again. . . . Upon the boundless prairies, with no traces of man in sight, nature looks so fresh and smiling that youth alone is in consonance with it."

These were heady words, but headier were to come. Another dashing and romantic Irishman was back from the North West, and very shortly the country would be agog with his descriptions of the region he called "The Great Lone Land."

6 · *Ocean to Ocean*

WILLIAM FRANCIS BUTLER HAS BEEN called hot-blooded and impulsive. He does not look it in his photographs; but one must remember that the photographs of that era had to support their subject on metal posing stands and hold their heads steady with neck clamps. Butler, circa 1870, is a solemn, dome-headed young subaltern, the long oval of his face exaggerated by his close-cropped Suvorov-style side whiskers and mustache. Only the eyes are alive.

But he *was* impulsive. He was stationed in England when he learned that the Canadian government was mounting an expedition against Riel. The news could not have come at a more propitious moment. A remarkably intelligent officer, who had seen twelve years' service in India, Burma, and Canada, he ought to have been promoted long before. But in those days commissions were purchased, not earned, and Butler did not have the fifteen hundred pounds it would cost him to accept the proffered command of a company.

He was faced with an unhappy choice: he could serve on as a junior officer or he could quit the service and face an equally cheerless existence as the governor of a penitentiary or the secretary of a London club. He was positively thirsting for adventure "no matter in what climate, or under what circumstances." The Red River uprising saved him. The news of the expeditionary force had scarcely reached England before Butler was off to the nearest telegraph office, dashing off the cheapest possible cable, consistent with politeness, to the expedition's commander, Colonel Wolseley: *"Please remember me."* Then, without waiting for an answer, he caught the first ship for North America.

When Butler reached Canada, he found to his chagrin that there was no job for him. Butler suggested one: that of an intelligence officer who, by traveling through the United States, might possibly enter Riel's stronghold from the south. Wolseley liked the idea and Butler leaped into his assignment with enthusiasm. He slipped past Riel and his men at the Red River, returned to the rebels' headquarters, where he interviewed Riel himself, and then, following the old voyageur route, paddled his way east to the Lake of the Woods, where he made his report to Wolseley.

When the troops entered Fort Garry, Butler was with them; but he found the subsequent anticlimactic weeks irksome. One night during a dinner at the home of Donald A. Smith, he suddenly announced that he was returning to Europe to resign his commission.

Smith had a better idea. Out along the North Saskatchewan there had been continuing disorders, which the local Hudson's Bay Company factors had been powerless to prevent. The Indians were being ravaged by smallpox and cheap whiskey, to what extent no one knew. Something in the way of troops might be needed. Why not send Butler to make a thorough report?

Shortly thereafter, the Lieutenant-Governor sent for Butler, outlined Smith's plan, and suggested that he think it over.

"There is no necessity, sir, to consider the matter," responded the impetuous officer. "I have already made up my mind and, if necessary, will start in half an hour."

It was typical of Butler that he made his mind up on the instant, regardless of the circumstances. He would not wait for the summer, when the trails were dry, the grouse plentiful, the shadberries plump and juicy, and the plains perfumed with briar rose. It was October 10 "and winter was already sending his breath over the yellowed grass of the prairies." With a single métis guide, Butler set off on a cold and moonless night, the sky shafted by a brilliant aurora, prepared to travel by foot, horseback, and dogsled across four thousand miles of uninhabited wilderness.

"Behind me lay friends and news of friends, civilization, tidings of a terrible war, firesides, and houses; before me lay unknown savage tribes, long days of saddle-travel, long nights of chilling bivouac, silence, separation and space!" Butler loved every minute of it.

He acquitted himself handsomely. It was his recommendation to the government, following his return, that led to the formation of the North West Mounted Police. But it was his subsequent book, *The Great Lone Land*, with its haunting descriptions of "that great, boundless, solitary waste of verdure," that caught the public's imagination. The title went into the language of the day. For the next fifteen years no description, no reference, no journalistic report about the North West seemed complete without some mention of Butler's poetic title. It was as well that the CPR was built when it was; long before the phrase was rendered obsolete, it had become a cliché.

But Butler's description of what he saw and felt on that chill, solitary journey across the white face of the new Canada will never be hackneyed: "The great ocean itself does not present more infinite variety than does this prairie ocean of which we speak. In winter, a dazzling surface of purest snow; in early summer, a vast expanse of grass and pale pink roses; in autumn, too often a wild sea of raging fire. No ocean of water in the world can vie with its gorgeous sunsets; no solitude can equal the loneliness of a night-shadowed prairie: one feels the stillness and hears the silence, the wail of the prowling wolf makes the voice of solitude audible, the stars look down through infinite silence upon a silence almost as intense. This ocean has no past—time has been nought to it; and men have come and gone, leaving behind them no track, no vestige, of their presence."

Butler went back to England to pursue a distinguished military career. Wealthy or not, his caliber was such that they had to make him a general. When the great British river flotilla went up the Nile in its vain attempt to save General Charles ("Chinese") Gordon from the Mahdi, Butler was in charge of it. He gathered many trophies and not a few decorations, but his book was his monument and his closing words rang down the corridor of the decade like a trumpet call: "Midst the smoke and hum of cities, midst the prayer of churches, in street or salon, it needs but little cause to recall again to the wanderer the image of the immense meadows where, far away at the portals of the setting sun, lies the Great Lone Land."

Butler's book was published in 1872. The following year another work on the North West made its appearance. It was so popular that it went into several editions and was serialized in the newspapers. Its title, *Ocean to Ocean*, also became part of the phraseology of the day. It was the saga of two bearded Scots who, in one continuous passage by almost every conveyance available, traveled entirely through British territory to the Pacific Coast—a feat which again captured the imagination of a country starved for frontier adventure.

The author of *Ocean to Ocean* was a remarkable Presbyterian minister named George Monro Grant, who was to become one of the most distinguished educators and literary figures of his time. He was already an outstanding preacher whose sermons, at St. Matthew's, Halifax, were so eloquent that sinners of the deepest dye were seen to emerge from their pews actually beaming after suffering the scourge of his tongue.

Grant was Sandford Fleming's choice for the post of secretary to the transcontinental expedition that the Engineer-in-Chief organized in 1872 to follow the proposed route of the new railway. The surveyor had determined to see the country for himself and discuss the progress of the field work at every point with the men on the ground.

Fleming was an impressive man, physically as well as intellectually, with a vast beard, a rugged physique and a questioning mind. He was forty-five years old at the time and he still had half of his life ahead of him in which to complete the Intercolonial and plan the Canadian Pacific, devise a workable system of standard time, plan and promote the Pacific cable, act as an ambassador to Hawaii, publish a book of "short daily prayers for busy households," become Chancellor of Queen's University, girdle the globe, and cross Canada by foot, snowshoe, dog team, horseback, raft, dugout canoe, and finally by rail.

In Grant, Fleming had a trail mate who was leather-tough and untroubled by adversity, a good man in the best sense, from whose bald brow there always seemed to shine the light of Christian good humor, in spite of an invalid wife and one retarded son. Grant himself had come through the fire, having been thrice at death's door in the very first decade of life: scalded half to death, almost drowned and given up for dead, and mangled by a hay cutter that cost him his right hand.

Grant was, in a London journalist's phrase, "the realized ideal of Kingsley's muscular Christian." When he joined Fleming's expedition, he was in the prime of life—a lithe thirty-seven, with a savant's high dome, flat straight nose, intense Scottish eyes, and the inevitable beard. He stood, at that moment, at the threshold of a career which would lead him to the principal's chair at Queen's. The notes for *Ocean to Ocean* were transcribed late at night, at the end of a hard day's travel, by the light of a flickering campfire, but the book itself, a polished and readable polemic for the new Canada, bore no sign of haste or hardship. In the words of Grant's son, "It revealed to Canada the glories of her northern and western territories, and did not a little to steel the hearts of many through the dark days that were to come."

The expedition set out across the Great Lakes by steamer into the stony wasteland of the Shield, where Fleming's surveyors were already inching their way—and sometimes meeting their deaths—in a land untouched by white men's moccasins. The party included Fleming's son and a Halifax doctor friend of Grant's, Arthur Moren. Soon another remarkable figure was to be enlisted.

Not long after embarkation, Fleming's attention was attracted by the enthusiasms of an agile and energetic man with a brown beard and twinkling eyes. This creature invariably leaped from the steamer the instant it touched the shoreline and began scrambling over rocks and diving into thickets, stuffing all manner of mosses, ferns, lichens, sedges, grasses, and flowers into a covered case.

It was only because the steamer whistled obligingly for him that he did not miss the boat. Sometimes, indeed, he was forced to scramble up the side after the ship had cast loose from the pier. The sailors called him "the Haypicker" and treated him with an amused tolerance, but his enthusiasm was so infectious that he soon had a flock of passengers in his wake, scraping their shins on the Pre-Cambrian granite as he plucked new specimens from between the rocks.

This was John Macoun, a botanist on the staff of Albert College in Belleville, Ontario, enjoying a busman's holiday in the wilds. Fleming asked him casually if he would care to come along to the Pacific, and Macoun, just as casually, accepted. Timetables in the seventies were elastic, and though the prospect of a twenty-five-hundred-mile journey across uncharted prairie, forest, mountain peak, and canyon might have deterred a lesser man, it only stimulated Macoun, in the garden of whose lively mind the images of hundreds of unknown species were already blooming.

Macoun was a natural botanist, almost entirely self-taught. At thirteen he had quit school and departed his native Ireland to seek his future in Canada. He began his new life as a farmhand but he could not resist the lure of plants. He determined to become a teacher in order that he might devote his spare hours to a study of botany. Partly by trial and error, partly by osmosis, and partly by sheer hard slogging, he slowly made himself a naturalist of standing in both Europe and America.

In 1869, he was offered the chair of natural history at an Ontario college. That summer he began the series of Great Lakes vacation studies that brought him, three years later, into the ken of Sandford Fleming.

By the time they left the steamer and headed out across the rock and muskeg toward the prairie, Macoun, Grant, and Fleming had become a close triumvirate. It makes a fascinating picture, this spectacle of the three bearded savants, all in their prime, each at the top of his field, setting off together to breast a continent: the comradeship was warm, the prayers earnest, the talk stimulating, and the way challenging.

The prairie, which all had read about in Butler's book, lured the three companions on like a magnet. One night, after supper, realizing that it was only thirty-three miles away, they decided they must see it and pushed on through the night, in spite of a driving rain so heavy that it blotted out all signs of a trail. The three men climbed down from their wagon and, hand in hand—the giant Fleming in the center, the one-handed Grant on the right, and the wiry Macoun on the left— trudged blindly forward through the downpour, leading the horse, mile after muddy mile, until a faint light appeared far off in the murk. When at last they burst through the woods and onto the unbroken prairie, they were too weary to gaze upon it. They tumbled, dripping wet, into a half-finished Hudson's Bay store and slept. The following morning the party awoke to find the irrepressible Macoun already up and about, his arms full of flowers.

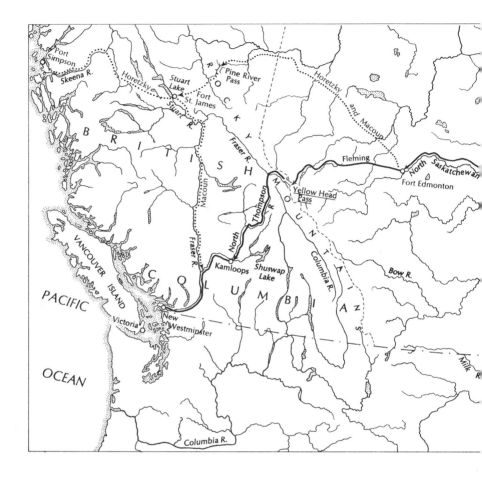

"Thirty-two new species already!" he cried. "It is a perfect floral garden."

"We looked out," wrote Grant, "and saw a sea of green, sprinkled with yellow, red, lilac and white. None of us had ever seen the prairie before and behold, the half had not been told us. As you cannot know what the ocean is without having seen it, neither in imagination can you picture the prairie."

In Winnipeg the party picked up a new companion, a strapping giant named Charles Horetzky, with brooding eyes and a vast black beard. This former Hudson's Bay Company man was to be the official photographer for the party. Though everything went smoothly at the time, Horetzky was to be a thorn in Fleming's side for all of the decade. Eight years later, the generally charitable Grant referred to him as "a rascal and . . . a consummate fool combined."

The party, a small brigade of six Red River carts and two buckboards, set out along the Carlton Trail. The meticulous Fleming had figured that they must make forty miles a day for a full month and,

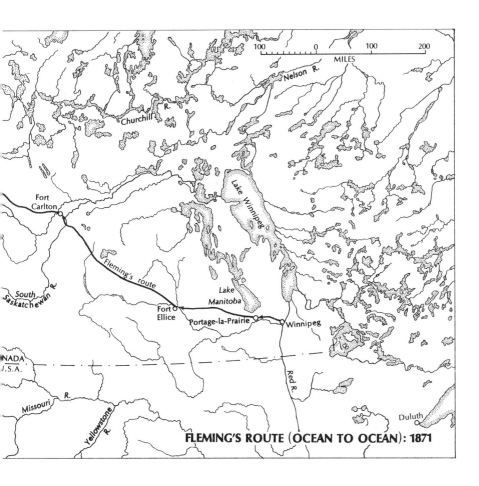

MILES

100   0   100   200

Nelson R.

Churchill R.

Lake Winnipeg

Fort
Carlton

Fleming's route

South
Saskatchewan R.

Lake
Manitoba

Fort
Ellice

Portage-la-Prairie

Winnipeg

NADA
U.S.A.

Red R.

Missouri R.

Yellowstone R.

Duluth

FLEMING'S ROUTE (OCEAN TO OCEAN): 1871

leaving nothing to guesswork, attached an odometer to one of the carts. They rose at sunrise and traveled until dark in three spells a day. There were surprises all along the line of route, some of them pleasant, some terrifying. At one point they happened upon a flat plain, twelve miles wide, which was an unbroken mass of sunflowers, asters, goldenrod, and daisies—an Elysian field shining like a multicolored beacon out of the dun expanse of the prairie. At another they were struck by a hailstorm so strong that the very horses were flung to the ground and the carts broken. In this chill Hades, the stones pelting from the sky were so large that a single blow from one of them could stun a man.

All along the way, the travelers read and reread Butler's book and, in addition, a pamphlet about the Peace River country by Malcolm Macleod, whose father had been the first Hudson's Bay Company man to cross the Rockies and who established in the heart of British Columbia the fort which bears his name.

At Fort Edmonton the party split up. Fleming, fascinated by Macleod's pamphlet on the agricultural resources of the Peace, suggested that Horetzky and Macoun go north and try to get through the mountains by way of that great river and then head for Fort St. James and thence for the coast. He and Grant would go through the Yellow Head Pass to meet one of Fleming's survey parties.

For Macoun it became a bizarre journey. The hardy botanist was no stranger to punishment. As a schoolboy in Ireland he had been whipped unmercifully almost daily. But in the Peace River country, Macoun was subjected to a more subtle chastisement. It became increasingly clear, as the days wore on, that the swarthy Horetzky felt that the botanist was a drag on the expedition and had resolved to get rid of him by fair means or foul—or at least that is what Macoun believed.

It soon developed that Horetzky had determined upon a different course from the one Fleming had proposed for the Peace River exploration. He had decided to go through the mountains by another pass, following the Pine River, a tributary of the Peace, and he did not want Macoun in the way. He tried to get the botanist to turn back, but Macoun told him that he would rather leave his bones in the mountains than fail.

He almost did. According to Macoun's later account, Horetzky planned to lure him into the mountains, then leave him with the encumbering baggage to die or make his own way out while he, Horetzky, pressed on, lightly equipped, to new and dazzling discoveries. Horetzky was now giving orders to the Indians in French, a language Macoun did not understand. But the botanist was no fool; he clung to his companion like glue. The two made a hazardous 150-mile journey through the mountains at twenty-six below zero, carrying their own bedding and provisions and struggling with great difficulty over half-frozen rivers and lakes. They finally reached Fort St. James, the exact center of British Columbia, on November 14.

It must have been a trying journey in other ways. The Hudson's Bay factor at the fort quietly let Macoun know that Horetzky, who was only a joint director of the expedition, appeared to have taken full charge, ordering all sorts of luxuries for himself but only minimal provender for the botanist.

"I told him I did not care what I got," Macoun later recalled, "as long as I got away from Horetzky with my life."

Horetzky was already planning to push on westward through virtually unknown country to the mouth of the Skeena, but Macoun had no intention of accompanying him. Macoun was penniless by now, totally dependent on the charity of the Hudson's Bay Company. Accompanied by two Indian guides, he fled south, wearing snowshoes seven feet long. He had never worn snowshoes in his life and soon abandoned them, content to flounder through drifts which reached above his knees. Eventually, on December 12, he reached Victoria, where he learned that his wife had been delivered of a fifth child. What she thought of her husband's extended summer vacation is not recorded.

Grant's journey with Fleming through the Yellow Head and down the Fraser lacked the cloak-and-dagger aspects of Macoun's struggle, but it was certainly arduous. There were long swamps "covered with an underbrush of scrub birch, and tough willows . . . that slapped our faces, and defiled our clothing with foul-smelling marsh mud." At times, in the Albreda area, the nine-year-old trail was buried by "masses of timber, torrents, landslides or debris." The horses' hooves sank eighteen inches into a mixture of bog and clay, but "by slipping over rocks, jumping fallen trees, breasting precipitous ascents with a rush, and recklessly dashing down hills," the crossing of the Thompson River was reached. To the one-handed clergyman, the comfortable parish of St. Matthew's must have seemed to have been on the far side of the moon.

By any standard, Grant and his companions had made an impressive journey. In 103 days of hard travel they had come 5,300 miles by railway, steamer, coach, wagon, canoe, rowboat, dugout, pack and saddle horse, and their own sturdy legs. They had made sixty-two camps on prairie, riverbank, rock, brush, swamp, and mountainside; and they were convinced that the future railway would follow their route across the Shield, up along the Fertile Belt, and through the Yellow Head Pass, which was Fleming's choice from the moment he first saw it. This physical accomplishment was magnificent, but its subtle concomitant was far more significant: in the most graphic and dramatic fashion, the clergyman and the surveyor had given the Canadian public a vision of a nation stretching from sea to sea.

7 · The ordeal of the Dawson route

IT WAS ONE THING TO HAVE AN ITCH TO go west. It was quite another to get there. At the start of the 1870's, the would-be homesteader had a choice of two routes, both of them awkward and frustrating. He could take the train to St. Paul and thence to the railhead and proceed by stagecoach, cart, and steamboat to Winnipeg; or he could take the all-Canadian route by way of the lakehead and the notorious Dawson route.

The rail route was undoubtedly the more comfortable, though "comfortable" in those days was a comparative word. The Miller coupling and the air brake had not yet been invented, so that passengers were jolted fearfully in their Pullmans. Having reached St. Paul by a series of fits and starts—for there were many changes and few through lines —the weary traveler could figure on at least another week before arriving at Winnipeg. The service on the St. Paul and Pacific Railroad was, to put it charitably, erratic. The faltering line, plagued by bankruptcies and plundering, ran to nowhere in particular, the exact location of the railhead being at all times uncertain and the condition of the rolling stock bordering on a state of collapse. "Two streaks of rust and a right of way," they called it. Who would have believed that this comic-opera line would one day become the forerunner of the two greatest railways to the Pacific—the Great Northern and the Canadian Pacific?

Once at the end of track, the passengers hoisted all their worldly belongings onto a four-horse stage and bumped along through clouds of acrid dust and flocks of whirring prairie chickens toward the steamboat landing at Twenty-Five Mile Point. During the summer the Hudson's Bay Company's steamboat *International* plied the Red River at uncertain intervals. Butler described it with his usual sharp eye: "Her engines were a perfect marvel of patchwork—pieces of rope seemed twisted around the crank and shaft—mud was laid thickly on boiler and pipes, little spurts of steam had a disagreeable way of coming out from places not supposed to be capable of such outpourings." The creaky vessel, 130 feet long, had difficulty negotiating the hairpin turns. In winter, of course, she could not operate; and when the water in the Red fell below two feet, she ran aground and the passengers had to take the Burbank stagecoach out across the bumpy, uninhabited prairie, laying over during the night at the atrocious stopping places where, in a single undivided attic, men, women, and children all slept together in beds jammed side by side.

This ordeal was idyllic compared to that suffered by those who chose the all-Canadian route (generally because it was cheaper). The route out of Prince Arthur's Landing at the head of lake transportation consisted of a corduroy road, interspersed with water stretches, and then a wagon road cut directly from the prairie turf. It was named for Simon J. Dawson, a sharp-featured surveyor from Trois-Rivières, who had explored it for the government in the late fifties. Dawson, who was later to become a Member of Parliament, was known as "Smooth Bore Dawson" because of his even temper and his quiet way of speaking. He needed to husband his reserves. The calumnies subsequently heaped upon him might have driven a more excitable man to dangerous excesses.

As the result of the report he made following his explorations of the Lake Superior country, Dawson was commissioned in 1868 to supervise the building of a series of corduroy links from Prince Arthur's Landing to connect the long chain of ragged lakes which lies between Superior and the Lake of the Woods. From that point the Fort Garry Road would lead on to the prairie and thence to Winnipeg. Between 1872 and 1873, a thousand settlers paid their ten dollars to use the Dawson route between the lakehead and Winnipeg.

It was a formidable route. A tug or steamboat was required on every lake and a different team of horses, together with harnesses and wagons, at each of the ten portages. Throughout its brief existence, there was never a time when some section of the Dawson road was not in need of repair.

In 1874 the Government decided to contract out the freight and passenger service to a private company. The contractors agreed to move passengers from the lakehead to Winnipeg in ten or twelve days and freight in fifteen to twenty. But because they were subsidized by the Government to carry passengers at low fares, it was in their interests to carry as few as possible and put most of the $75,000 subsidy in their pockets.

The story is told of one luckless settler arriving in a pitiable state of exhaustion and dilapidation at the office of Donald A. Smith, M.P., in Winnipeg and proclaiming: "Well, look at me, ain't I a healthy sight? I've come by the Government water route from Thunder Bay and it's taken me twenty-five days to do it. During that time I've been half starved on victuals I wouldn't give a swampy Indian. The water used to pour into my bunk of nights, and the boat was so leaky that every bit of baggage I've got is water-logged and ruined. But that ain't all. I've broke my arm and sprained my ankle helping to carry half a dozen trunks over a dozen portages, and when I refused to take a paddle in one of the boats, an Ottawa Irishman told me to go to h——l and said that if I gave him any more of my d————d chat he'd let me get off and walk to Winnipeg."

In June and July of 1874, the pioneer newspaper of Manitoba, the *Nor'wester*, began to carry the immigrants' complaints. They considered the stationmaster at Fifteen Mile shanty "a brute," and the men at the Height of Land "mean and surly." At Baril Lake, the baggage was flung helter-skelter into the hold of a barge where it rested in eight inches of water. On one passage across Rainy Lake, where, true to

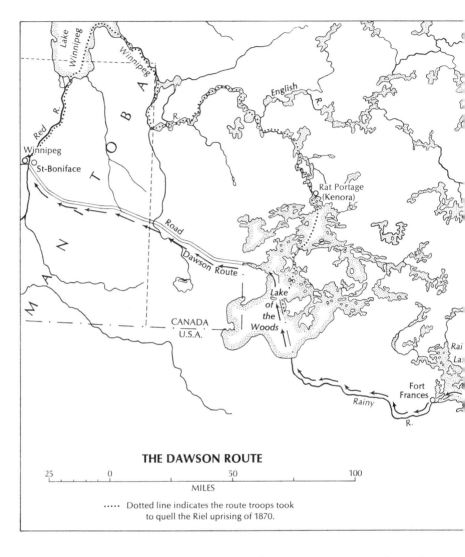

THE DAWSON ROUTE

25   0   50   100

MILES

····· Dotted line indicates the route troops took
to quell the Riel uprising of 1870.

nomenclature, a cloudburst descended, male passengers compassionately
took the tarpaulin off a woodpile and placed it over the heads of the
women and children. This so enraged the engineer that he seized an
ax and threatened to chop away at the customers unless the covering
was replaced instantly. It wasn't, whereupon the engineer "out of sheer
spite" held up the boat for five hours.

James Trow, an Ontario Member of Parliament who took a lively
interest in the North West, reported that paid American agents of the
Northern Pacific were on hand at Prince Arthur's Landing to try to
seduce immigrants away from the Dawson route, saying that "if we
persisted we might possibly get though before Christmas or New
Year's but in all probability our bones would be left to bleach on some
portage or sunk beneath the waves." The Americans urged the travelers

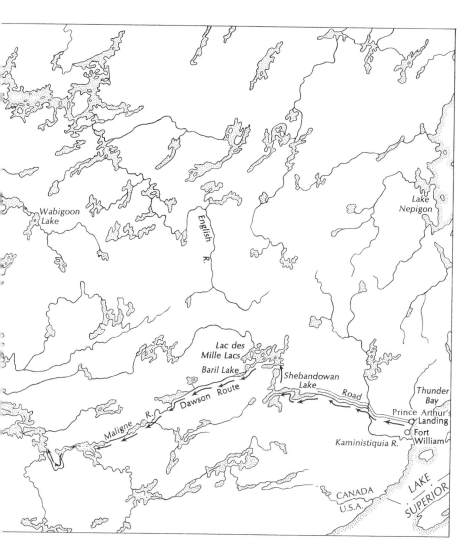

to give up any fancy of settling on the Canadian prairie and choose instead the more hospitable soil of Minnesota or Dakota.

Many a passenger was on the edge of revolt as a result of conditions on the trail. Scores arrived in Winnipeg in a state of semistarvation, obliged to subsist on fish they caught themselves, their effects destroyed by leaky boats. They were forced to work their own passage, sleep in dirty, neglected shanties, and walk when no wagons were available—all the time subjected to a volley of insults and threats by the employees of the contractors.

Complaints began to pour into Ottawa. In July, 1874, an alarmed government sent Simon Dawson himself out to investigate. When the surveyor arrived at the North West Angle of the Lake of the Woods, he was nearly mobbed by a crowd of infuriated and starving passengers who were vainly awaiting transportation to Winnipeg. Dawson scrambled about and found some half-breeds with Red River carts who arranged to handle the job, but his smooth-bore temperament must have been sorely tried. That year he quit in disgust and disappointment as superintendent of the route and advised the government that no further work should be done on it.

The road continued to operate in a desultory way. The Countess of Dufferin, the Governor General's lady, went over it in 1877 and was knocked about so much on the corduroy that she chose to get out and walk. Another traveler, Mary Fitzgibbon, wrote that she would never forget her own trip. The road by this time consisted of "round logs, loosely bound together, and thrown down upon a marsh, no two consecutive logs being the same size." Originally there had been some foundation, and there were still deep drains on each side, but "the logs had given way at different ends in some parts and altogether in others. It was bump, bump, bang and squash and squash, bang and bump; now up now down, now all on one side, now all on the other. Cushions, rugs, everything that could slide, slid off the seats . . . and one longed to cry out and beg to be stopped if only for a moment."

Finally the road was abandoned, along with a half-completed set of locks at Fort Frances, on which the Government had expended three years and $289,000. The days of canals and corduroy roads were over. The railroad was on its way.

1 · Poor Waddington

THE DEBATE ON THE TERMS OF ADMIS-
sion of British Columbia was not yet over when the first of the entrepreneurs arrived in Ottawa. This was Alfred Waddington of Victoria,
seventy-five years old and a fanatic on the subject of a Pacific railway.
His scheme was premature and ill-considered and he himself was suspect in the eyes of the Canadian decisionmakers; nonetheless his meeting in July, 1871, with Sir John A. Macdonald and his finance minister,
Sir Francis Hincks, touched off the complicated chain of events that
led to the nation's first great political crisis.

Old Waddy, as he was called, was a bland-looking man whose moon-
face was framed in ear-length locks and a little fringe of chin whiskers.
Only the hard, resolute line of his mouth hinted at an inner stubbornness. He was obsessed, almost to the point of irrationality, by the idea
of building the railway through the Yellow Head Pass to Bute Inlet,
a precipitous indentation in the British Columbia coastline on whose
beaches he had already been granted a townsite.

Waddington had been a trial to the Victoria political establishment
ever since he had arrived in British Columbia from San Francisco, with
the first wave of adventurers, after gold was discovered on the Fraser
in 1858. The well-educated son of an English squire, originally lured
across the Atlantic by the California gold rush, he came to the colony
a wealthy man, free to plunge with zest into politics and pamphleteer-
ing. As a member of the colonial legislature he became a constant and
pugnacious critic of the administration. For years Old Waddy battered

away at the unyielding ramparts of the tight little in-group that controlled the colony until, one autumn day in 1860, he suddenly abandoned it all and turned his attention to the promotion of what eventually became a transcontinental railway scheme.

The railway took over his life. Its terminus was to be at Waddington Harbour, a paper community he had created at the head of Bute Inlet, the narrow fiord that springs out of the mouth of the Homathco River, some 150 air miles north of Vancouver. The inlet and the river seduced Waddington as they were to seduce later surveyors. At an age when most men seek retirement, he spent five years struggling through the Homathco's gloomy canyons, beggaring himself on trailmaking and surveys.

The venture was marred by the Chilcoten Massacre of 1864. Nineteen of Waddington's men were slaughtered by Indians whose women had been molested and whose fears had been aroused by pranksters who had pretended to bottle enough smallpox to destroy the entire tribe.

But nothing seemed to deter Waddington, neither Indian ferocity nor the seventy-nine hairpin turns on the sheer cliffs of the mountain named after him. He was an incurable optimist. Where realists would have reckoned the odds insurmountable and retreated, the quixotic Waddington galloped forward towards disaster. By 1868 he had squandered sixty thousand dollars on his scheme, but his projected road was little more than a series of blazed trees and surveyors' markers while his envisioned metropolis, in which some Victoria merchants had recklessly speculated, remained a pretty map.

Undeterred, he joined forces with William Kersteman, another promoter of unbuilt railroads and, in March, 1871, descended on Ottawa. Both men were wildly overconfident and unrealistic. There was never any possibility of either or both successfully promoting the great railway to the Pacific. Historically, they were merely the means by which the sinister figure of George W. McMullen was introduced to the Pacific railway scheme.

McMullen was just twenty-seven years old, a stubby man with a pudgy face, luminous brown eyes, and short cropped beard. He came from a prominent Conservative family in Picton, Ontario, where his mother's relatives owned the local Tory paper. His father, Daniel, who had retired early from the Wesleyan Methodist ministry because, he said, his energetic revivalism had overtaxed his strength, was "greatly esteemed for his piety." The phrase scarcely applied to the son. Young McMullen had left for the United States several years before, a move which earned him the appellation of George Washington McMullen (the "W" actually stood for William). By 1871 he was a hard-nosed Chicago businessman, the proprietor, among other things, of a newspaper, the *Evening Post*, one of a host of short-lived journals that sprang up and died like weeds in that city during the period.

McMullen was interested in railways and canals. Indeed, he was interested in anything that might make him a dollar. He had an agile, inquisitive mind which, for all of his long life, intrigued him into the most curious ventures—the growing of aphrodisiacs, for example, and the development of a long-range cannon. He had come to Ottawa in the spring of 1871 as part of a Chicago delegation seeking the enlargement of the Chicago and Huron Shipping Canal. Waddington and Kersteman were both ardent Yankeephiles. Armed with surveys, maps, pamphlets, and copies of speeches, the two enthusiasts approached McMullen, who was intrigued enough to seek further support in the United States.

By July, McMullen had brought a covey of American businessmen into the scheme. Charles Mather Smith, a Chicago banker, became his joint promoter. Smith brought in W. B. Ogden, an original incorporator of the Northern Pacific. Ogden brought in General George W. Cass, heir presumptive to the presidency of the Northern Pacific, and, more important, Jay Cooke, the Philadelphia banker who controlled the railroad's purse strings and who had his clear, boyish eyes focused on the Canadian North West, which he hoped would become a tributary of his railroad.

Cooke's first hope was for out-and-out annexation, which would give the Northern Pacific a total monopoly of the land west of the lakes. Failing that, Cooke and his agents intended to work for a Canadian line which would be dependent on the U.S. road for an outlet. In his dreams, Cooke visualized an international railway, running from Montreal through American territory south of Lake Superior and then cutting back into Canada by way of the Red River to proceed westward across the prairies. The railroad, and eventually the territory itself, would be totally under American control. When Ogden wrote to Cooke in June, 1871, urging him to take preliminary steps to "control this project," it was exactly the opportunity that Cooke had been seeking. Thus the first people to call on the Canadian Government to offer to build the Canadian Pacific were the representatives of the very men whom the Canadian Pacific was intended to thwart.

The Americans arrived in Ottawa in mid-July, about a week before the contract was signed (on July 20) with British Columbia. They came armed with a set of documents stating the terms on which they would undertake to build the railway. They had brought some extra political muscle along in the person of a Tory lawyer from Toronto. But, in spite of his presence, the atmosphere in Sir Francis Hincks's office on July 13 was decidedly chilly, and it began to dawn on the Americans that Kersteman and Waddington had overrepresented their political influence. The following day the Prime Minister made it quite clear that any railway scheme was too premature for serious discussion. To Macdonald, who dismissed Waddington as a "respectable old fool," the only value this patently Yankee delegation had was as a kind of lever to force Canadian capitalists to take the matter of the railway seriously.

The Americans did not give up. Through their lawyer, they indicated that they would welcome some prominent Canadians on the board of their railway company. There was free stock to be distributed and a hint of ultimate profits for insiders. The questionable morality of all this seemed to escape Sir Francis Hincks, who merely replied: "I fear that you are going altogether too fast." The ambiguity of that statement was to return to haunt Hincks when the correspondence was made public two years later.

At this point, the Americans unceremoniously dumped both Waddington and Kersteman, though they apprised neither of their fate. Kersteman journeyed to England and came back, late in 1872, full of enthusiastic but vague promises of financial assistance. Macdonald palmed him off on Hincks. The promoter arrived on the Finance Minister's doorstep in Montreal on Christmas Day, where he found himself subjected to some unseasonable abuse. Events had passed him by; the Americans by this time had become a decided liability and the wretched Kersteman was dismissed as a troublemaker. It began to dawn on him, after four years of unremitting labor and twenty-five hundred dollars spent out of his own pocket, that nobody at any time, Canadian or American, had ever had the slightest intention of cutting him in on the Pacific railway company.

As for Alfred Waddington, he died on February 26, 1872, a victim of smallpox, the same disease that had indirectly caused the massacre of his survey party eight years before. The reports of his death and funeral were meager; the briefest of paragraphs mentioned his promotion of the railway. Back in Victoria, where he had so long made news, the *British Colonist* gave him a cursory eulogy. "Poor Waddington," it called him. The reference was not unkind and certainly not inaccurate.

2 · *Sir Hugh Allan's shopping spree*

As Waddington and Kersteman fade into the wings, the formidable figure of Sir Hugh Allan strides out to stage center. This vain, haughty, and politically naïve shipping magnate was the richest man and the most powerful financier in Canada.

In his Notman photograph, Allan looks like the prototype of the nineteenth-century robber baron. He is seen taking a pace forward as if to lunge upon the hapless photographer, and the fierceness of his terrier face is enhanced by a shaggy mane of hair and whiskers, snow white, which encircles his features like the frame of a picture. Allan's annual income was estimated at more than half a million dollars a year, a sum so immense that it is hard to grasp today. A dollar in 1871 was worth four or five in 1970; since there was no income tax, Allan's net income amounted to far more than two millions annually in modern terms. It allowed him to build and maintain his baronial mansion in Montreal, on which he bestowed the Gothic title of Ravenscrag. Here he had entertained Prince Arthur, the younger brother of the Prince of Wales, a piece of hospitality which undoubtedly contributed to his knighthood in 1871.

Like so many Canadian financiers of the period, Allan was a Scot and a self-educated as well as a self-made man. His father had been a shipmaster engaged in trade between the Clyde and Montreal, and young Allan was raised in the company of sailors. In 1825, he left school at the age of thirteen, emigrated to Montreal shortly after and went to work for a firm of commission merchants and shipbuilders. Within a dozen years, Allan had risen to senior partner, a driving, hard-working man who studied furiously in his spare hours to make up for his lack of schooling. Unlike most English-speaking Canadians of that time, he made a point of learning French; it was to his advantage to become fluent in the language.

Eventually, the penniless, half-educated Scottish boy became head of the Allan Line, one of the principal fleets of the world. If he was proud, egotistical, and single-minded, he had reason to be. Starting with nothing, he had amassed the greatest fortune in Canada. He was president of the Merchants' Bank, which he had founded, and of fifteen other corporations; he was vice-president of half a dozen more. His interests encompassed telegraphs and railways, coal and iron, tobacco and cotton, cattle, paper, rolling mills, and elevators.

It was the heyday of the uncritical journalistic eulogy, when merchant princes were revered and not reviled; and Allan was hailed as the very prince of merchant princes. Basking in the adulation of press and peer group, praised for his business acumen, his public philanthropies, and his regular church attendance, Allan could scarcely be blamed if he felt himself to be above other men. He *was* a good businessman—his habits so strict that he never acted on a question which involved the spending of money without first having the transaction reduced to writing; he *was* a good churchman—he often read the lesson or delivered a lecture from the pulpit. He was also imperious and uncommunicative. He had a healthy disdain for the public, the press, and the politicians. The first could be ignored, the latter two purchased. He was accustomed to making handsome loans, with vague terms, to newspapers: the Montreal *Gazette* and the influential French-language journal *La Minerve* were two which enjoyed his largesse. His only real politics, as one acidulous commentator remarked, were the politics of steamboats and railways. Allan undoubtedly felt himself above politics, more powerful than any politician and certainly more astute. He was a man long accustomed to getting his own way and it certainly never occurred to him, in the summer of 1871, that this very bullheaded self-confidence would frustrate his ambitions and besmirch his name.

It was to Sir Hugh Allan that Sir Francis Hincks dropped the news, early that August, that some Americans were interested in building the Pacific railway. It was too bad, Hincks added casually, that a work of such importance should be entrusted to foreigners. Allan was immediately interested. As the country's leading shipowner he could benefit, perhaps more than anyone else, from a railway link to the Pacific. It would place him at the head of a transportation colossus and probably bring him other laurels. Allan had just received a knighthood; the successful construction of the Pacific railway would surely lead to a baronetcy, and the Laird of Ravenscrag, as the press had dubbed him, wanted a genuine title perhaps more than anything else.

Allan lost little time in getting in touch with the Americans, whose names Hincks had obligingly supplied. In September he met McMullen and Smith in Montreal and proceeded to form a company which, though ostensibly Canadian, would be almost entirely controlled and financed by the Northern Pacific; it was planned, in fact, that it would be part of the Northern Pacific complex. Allan's reward was to be a large block of stock, and a secret fund of forty thousand dollars—later raised to fifty thousand—to distribute, in McMullen's phrase, "among persons whose accession would be desirable."

A serious obstacle existed, however, in the person of Sir George Étienne Cartier, Macdonald's dynamic but ailing Quebec lieutenant, who had done so much to launch the railway idea in the first place.

Cartier was unalterably opposed to any U.S. participation. "As long as I live," he had declared, ". . . never will a damned American company have control of the Pacific." He was prepared to resign rather than consent to it.

The Americans pressed on. They signed a formal agreement with Allan on December 23, 1871. The details were kept secret for good reason: Jay Cooke explained to his partner that "the American agreement has to be kept dark for the present on account of the political jealousies in the Dominion, and there is no hint of the Northern Pacific connection, but the plan is to cross the Sault Ste Marie through northern Michigan and Wisconsin to Duluth, then build from Pembina up to Fort Garry and by and by through the Saskatchewan into British Columbia."

At the same time a pretense would be made that an all-Canadian route was being constructed north of Lake Superior: "The act will provide for building a north shore road to Fort Garry merely to calm public opinion." Its actual construction, however, was to be delayed for years while the Montreal–Duluth link through the United States was put into operation, financed by Canadian Pacific bonds sold in London to investors who believed they were promoting an Imperial project.

Jay Cooke was then at the peak of his meteoric career—a big, apple-cheeked financier, boyish-looking in spite of his flowing beard, dreaming dreams of a railway empire that would devour half of Canada for America's manifest destiny. He was known throughout the financial world as The Tycoon, a name that had yet to be vulgarized by American journalism. "As rich as Jay Cooke" was a common expression of the day, and well it might be, for Cooke, the empire builder, lived like a prince of old, surrounded by three hundred costly paintings, in a million-dollar fifty-two-room Philadelphia palace, popularly known as "Cooke's castle." Here prayers were a morning ritual and religious service an evening duty, for Cooke was nothing if not pious. On the Lord's Day he engaged in a round of church and Sunday-school services; on weekdays he worked hard at manipulating newspapers, politicians, and governments, all of whom praised him to the skies.

"Manipulate" was a word that came easily to Cooke. The year before, he had written to a colleague to invite his aid "in manipulating the annexation of British North America north of Duluth to our country." It could be done, he suggested, without any violation of treaties but "as a result of the quiet emigration over the border of trustworthy men and their families." Cooke was secure in the belief that "the country belongs to us naturally and should be brought over without violence or bloodshed." In this scheme, he planned to use the new Canadian Pacific

Railway in which he and his associates would have a 55 per cent interest. Among other things, Cooke believed that a union between the two railroads (for that is what he ultimately envisaged) would strengthen the Northern Pacific's chances for a loan in London.

If it ever occurred to Allan that he was engaged in a secret plot with American businessmen to deliver the Canadian North West into the hands of the United States, he was able to rationalize it magnificently. Business, after all, was business, and American investment in Canada was not only desirable but also necessary. At one point he even wrote to General George W. Cass, who was about to become the new president of the American railroad, that "the plans I propose are in themselves the best for the interests of the Dominion, and in urging them on the public I am really doing a most patriotic action." What was good for Sir Hugh was, in his eyes, good for the country.

By the time this letter was written (with unconscious irony on July 1—Dominion Day—1872), Allan had for almost six months been engaging in a lavish shopping spree, using the Americans' money in an attempt to buy up politicians, newspapermen, and business opponents. On the question of who should be bought, and for how much, Allan differed from McMullen. The Chicago promoter was doing his best to suborn minor Members of Parliament. Allan thought this "a waste of powder and shot." He preferred to concentrate on bigger game such as Cartier and Senator David Macpherson, who was putting together a rival company to compete with Allan for the contract. Macpherson's Interoceanic Company had a directorate of prominent Toronto and Ontario capitalists. His stated object was to defeat Allan's scheme, which the Liberal press was denouncing almost daily as a front for the Northern Pacific.

It was not difficult for Macpherson or Allan to find partners for their ventures; they were clamoring to be let in. All directors of the successful company stood to make substantial profits with minimal risk, for the plan was that each director would get a proportionate share of the stock without paying for it.

Allan did his best to buy Macpherson off—or so he told his American backers on February 24. He claimed that Macpherson had insisted on a quarter million dollars' worth of stock and threatened opposition if he did not get it. A few days later Allan was back again with a list of a dozen other prominent Canadians he said would have to be paid off with fifty thousand to one hundred thousand dollars in stock apiece.

There is no evidence that Allan saw all or any of these men or offered them anything. Macpherson's subsequent account of their meeting was quite different. Allan, he said, had called upon him to join in forming the Canadian Pacific Railway Company with the understanding that he, Allan, would head it. There would be eleven directors—six Canadians, including Allan and Macpherson, and five Americans, all of them directors of the Northern Pacific. Macpherson objected strenuously to the Americans' involvement; all they needed to control the company was one vote, Allan's, and if they controlled the purse strings they certainly controlled that. The naïve idea that the Americans would own the company and yet allow the Canadians to run it was too much for Macpherson. He washed his hands of Allan and set about getting a charter for his all-Canadian company.

3 · *The downfall of Cartier*

SIR GEORGE ÉTIENNE CARTIER WAS ONE of the leading architects of Canadian Confederation and, next to Macdonald, the most important politician in Canada. His opposition to Allan's railway scheme could not be brooked; before Allan could succeed he must have Cartier with him. To achieve that end he was prepared to use brutal methods.

Cartier controlled the parliamentary action of forty-five Quebec Members who voted in a solid phalanx. The Government needed this Quebec vote since its majority was considerably less than forty-five. The defection of half could, on a tightly fought issue, put it out of office. If Allan could win over a slice of Cartier's following, he would then control the means to manipulate their leader. The lever, he shrewdly decided, would be the Quebeckers' hunger for a railroad along the north shore of the St. Lawrence from Quebec City, through Montreal to Ottawa. He himself headed the Northern Colonization Railway, which planned to build the Montreal–Ottawa link of the coveted line. Cartier, who had connections with the rival Grand Trunk Railway, could be presumed to oppose it. Allan began at once to spend the money provided by his American backers to stir up the French Canadians along the proposed route against Cartier.

He proudly reported to General Cass of the Northern Pacific the particulars of his successful campaign. He had, he said, paid several French-Canadian lawyers to write up the matter in the press. He had bought controlling stock in newspapers and subsidized others as well as their editors and proprietors. He had stumped the country through which his proposed railway would go, calling on the people, visiting

the priests, making friends, sending paid agents among the more prominent citizens, and making speech after speech himself, in French, to
show the habitants "where their true interests lay."

The scheme worked: Allan won over twenty-seven of Cartier's
forty-five followers. He now believed he could control the Government.
An election was in the offing for the late summer of 1872, and Cartier,
to his astonishment and dismay, woke up to the truth that he had lost
much of his political power. His surrender was total. On June 12,
Allan wrote to McMullen that it would not be necessary for either of
them to talk to the government in Ottawa: "I believe I have got the
whole thing arranged through my French friends, by means you are
aware of, and we now have the pledge of Sir G. that we will have a
majority, and other things satisfactory."

Meanwhile, Senator David Lewis Macpherson and his rival Interoceanic Company were proving an embarrassment to Macdonald. Macpherson was an Inverness Highlander of heroic stature "in whose
presence," Macdonald's astute secretary Joseph Pope recalled, "an
ordinary mortal felt very small indeed." He had a massive head, a huge
brow, pouched Oriental eyes, and a fantastic tangle of side whiskers,
which, with his immense soup-strainer mustache, effectively concealed
a receding chin. Somewhat pompous in manner, overdeliberate in
method, but generally sound in judgment, he could not be pushed an
inch. He remained utterly convinced, in spite of all disclaimers, that
Allan was prepared to deliver the railway into the hands of Yankee
freebooters.

Macpherson's stubbornness posed a real dilemma for the Prime
Minister, who was anxious to resolve the railway problem before the
election; there was no doubt it would strengthen his hand politically
in a tight contest. The Highlander was an old friend and a staunch
Conservative who had, the previous winter, raised a testimonial fund
of sixty thousand dollars to help free Macdonald from a crushing burden of political debt. Moreover, in the summer of 1871, Macdonald had
actually pressed his friend to take up the question of the railroad in
order to prevent the Americans from coming in. Now the Prime Minister was faced with an impossible choice: he could choose the Toronto
group and alienate French Canada, or he could choose the Allan group
and alienate Ontario. Clearly an amalgamation was indicated, but here
Macdonald came up against the stone wall of Macpherson's intractabil-
ity. Macdonald genuinely believed that Allan was the only possible
choice to head the venture. Only a man of his established wealth and
apparent business acumen could command the confidence of the international financial community. But Macpherson continued to insist

stubbornly that Allan was a tool of the American railway; and not even his own associates, who were moved to throw in with the Montreal group, could shake this belief. He would welcome amalgamation, but not with Allan as president.

As it turned out, Macpherson was right. It ought to have been clear to Allan by this time that the Government had no intention of allowing American control of the railway; and yet, while pretending publicly that his was an all-Canadian company, the imperious ship-builder retained his secret ties with New York and Chicago. On August 7, he told General Cass that the Government was obliged to stipulate that no foreigner could appear as a shareholder in the company: "The shares taken by you and our other American friends, will therefore have to stand in my name for some time." To McMullen he sent a reassuring letter: the Americans were to be excluded, but "I fancy we can get over that some way or other."

In vain Macdonald tried to effect a rapprochement between Mac-pherson and Allan. In July, with the election campaign under way, Macpherson suggested that the new directors—seven from his company and six from Allan's—elect their own president; but to this Allan would not consent. The Conservative Party desperately wanted to place the *fait accompli* of a strong railway company before the electors; but the principals remained deadlocked.

By this time Allan was hard at work trying to restore the political fortunes of the badly battered Cartier, who had been transformed from enemy into ally by his machinations of the previous spring. It was Allan's first and only entry into politics; indeed, he had rarely bothered to vote. But by August 9 he was so deeply involved in the campaign that he even appeared on the platform with Cartier at St. James Square. It was not a prepossessing beginning: both men had to duck a volley of stones and rotten eggs, and the taunts were so great that Cartier had difficulty being heard. Allan, it appeared, had done his work only too well.

It was this tortured alliance with Allan that was to becloud Cartier's reputation. He remains, save for this one fall from grace, an attractive figure: a totally dedicated Canadian patriot with all the vivacity of his race. In the familiar portrait of the Fathers of Confederation he occupies the front row center, next to Macdonald—a robust, almost dapper man with a mane of white hair. His black, darting eyes were a sign of his inner vitality: he was quite capable of working fifteen hours a day. His value to Macdonald was inestimable—together they forged and main-tained the uneasy alliance between the French and English nations in British North America. But in the election of 1872, Cartier was robust no longer: the telltale symptoms of Bright's disease—the swollen feet, the impaired judgment—had already appeared. George Étienne Cartier had less than a year to live.

If Allan threw himself, heart, soul, and pocketbook, into the election, it was because he believed he had a pledge from the Government to give him the charter for the railway. The events of July 29 and 30, when promises were made by Cartier and Macdonald, and election funds were pledged by Allan, can only be understood against the background of the political morality and practice of the time.

Elections in post-Confederation Canada were fought with money, and often enough it was the candidate who spent the most who cornered the votes. Dollars spoke louder than ideas, and out-and-out bribery was not uncommon. Indeed, during the seventies so many elections were controverted because of bribery that a kind of gentlemen's agreement existed between the parties to keep them to a manageable number. As late as 1874, there were official charges of bribery before the courts in no less than twenty-nine constituencies in Ontario and Manitoba. Charles Clarke, who was clerk of the legislature of Ontario, recalled that "for many years before Confederation, and after its creation, electoral corruption, gross intimidation, bludgeon arguments, and brutal force had been employed at various elections to the detriment and loss of electoral strength by one or other of the opposing candidates." Of the early seventies, Clarke wrote that "nearly every active politician who had experience in Canadian Parliamentary elections was aware of the existence of bribery and intimidation. So common was this experience that, although never seeing money actually exchanged for a vote, its use was as well known to me as was the existence, say, of the Queen of England, or the fact that she occupied the throne."

The entire country was almost totally partisan, which meant that, in the absence of any really burning issue, it was difficult to change a man's mind unless, in the euphemism of the period, you "treated" him —to a drink, a bottle, a dinner, or a five-dollar bill. Treating was against the law, as was the practice of driving or dragging reluctant voters to the polls, but these expensive customs, as Macdonald himself admitted, were common to both parties.

There was still no secret ballot in the 1872 election; it did not make its appearance until 1874. This meant that bribery was extraordinarily effective, since the party agents could check on the loyalty of their paid supporters.

The election was particularly hard fought, especially in Ontario, where the Liberals were on the rise: Macdonald thought that financially the Opposition had the better of it. He himself was hard pressed for funds and was scraping up every dollar he could wrest from reluctant friends.

Cartier was equally desperate, and this desperation was increased by the knowledge that he faced an uphill battle in his own constituency. For him the moment of truth came at the close of July. Allan had conferred with him on several occasions, urging him to procure the amalgamation of the two companies "upon such terms as I considered would be just to myself"—in short, the presidency for Allan. On the thirtieth, some six weeks after Allan had told McMullen that Cartier had been brought to heel, he and his lawyer, John J. C. Abbott, visited Cartier for a meeting that was to become memorable. Cartier had a telegram scribbled by Macdonald who, in the midst of fighting his own election battle in Kingston, had managed to crowd in another interview with Macpherson. Again Macpherson had insisted that the question of the presidency be left to a board of directors. Macdonald made his decision.

"Under these circumstances," he wired on July 26, "I authorize you to assure Allan that the influence of the Government will be exercised to secure him the position of President. The other terms to be as agreed on between Macpherson and Abbott. The whole matter to be kept quiet until after the elections."

Four days later Cartier showed the wire to Allan. It was not quite enough for the shipping magnate. What if Macpherson continued to be stubborn? What would the Government do then? The ailing Cartier was forced to concede that if a new amalgamated company could not be formed, then Allan's Canada Pacific Company would be given the charter. But Allan wanted that promise nailed down in writing.

Cartier suggested that Abbott draw up the necessary document and return with it that afternoon. Allan and Abbott rose to leave, and as he saw them to the door, Cartier asked in his abrupt way: "Are you not going to help us in our elections?" Allan asked how much Cartier wanted. Cartier replied that it might come to one hundred thousand dollars. Allan, the model businessman, suggested he put that in writing, too.

That afternoon—the date was July 30, 1872, the day on which Fleming, Grant, and Macoun first reached the open prairie—Allan and Abbott were back again with two letters. One, to be signed by Cartier, promised Allan the charter; the other, also to be signed by Cartier, asked for financial help in the elections. Cartier was not satisfied with either of the letters and both were rewritten. One was to become notorious:

"The friends of the Government will expect to be assisted with funds in the pending elections, and any amount which you or your Company advance for that purpose shall be recouped by you. A memorandum of immediate requirements is below.

NOW WANTED

Sir John A. Macdonald	$25,000
Hon. Mr. Langevin	15,000
Sir G. E. C.	20,000
Sir J. A. (add.)	10,000
Hon. Mr. Langevin	10,000
Sir G. E. C.	30,000"

In spite of promises to recoup, Allan did not really expect to see his money again.

Meanwhile, in Kingston, Macdonald was impatiently awaiting a reply to his telegram of July 26. When it finally arrived he was appalled. His immediate instinct was to go to Montreal at once and straighten out the mess into which Cartier had blundered; but the poll was about to begin and Macdonald could not afford to take time off from last-minute electioneering. Instead he wired Cartier, repudiating the letter: his original telegram of July 26 must be "the basis of the agreement." *Agreement!* The ambiguity of that word would return to haunt Macdonald.

Cartier broke the news to Allan, who gracefully withdrew the letter; but he did not withdraw his financial support. He increased it. The additional fifty thousand dollars in Cartier's original NOW WANTED memo was swiftly paid over—ten thousand to Sir Hector Louis Langevin, Macdonald's portly Minister of Public Works and Cartier's successor as the leader of the Quebec wing of the party, another ten thousand to the Prime Minister, and thirty thousand to Cartier's central election committee. That was not the end of it. Allan left for Newfoundland at the height of the campaign but was pursued by a telegram from Abbott asking another twenty thousand dollars for the committee and ten thousand more for Macdonald. When Allan returned he learned that these sums had actually been exceeded. All together he had distributed more than $350,000.

And for what? The Conservative Government barely squeaked into power. In Ontario it was badly battered and in Quebec, where most of the Allan funds had been spent, it managed to capture only a bare majority. Without the West and the Maritimes, Macdonald would have been ruined politically. As for Cartier, he suffered a stunning personal defeat, which had its own ironies. By some mysterious process, a large slice of Allan's money had been appropriated by the other side. On the day of the election, the open balloting revealed that man after man who had been paid in good hard cash to work for George Étienne had actually been in the secret service of the enemy all the while.

4 · *George McMullen's blackmail*

ALL THAT AUTUMN, AS SIR JOHN A. Macdonald, freed at last from the campaign, struggled to effect a compromise between the two rival companies, he was haunted by his secret promise to Allan. There was no way out of it. Senator David Macpherson remained utterly immovable and the Prime Minister had no means of budging him. He sent emissaries and long conciliatory letters to Macpherson, and at last he himself made a pilgrimage to the rambling and turreted Queen's Hotel in Toronto, where the two Scots downed a formidable succession of brandies and soda. The mission failed. Macdonald's personal charm was legendary, but in this case every conversation foundered on the rock of Allan's presidency.

If Allan were made president, Macpherson argued time and again, the Canadian public would be "seized with apprehension that the R^y. would be handed over to the Americans"; that feeling alone would affect stock sales. Everybody, Macpherson pointed out, believed the Americans were behind Allan: "You yourself must believe it."

Macdonald realized that he would have to form a new company without Macpherson. Like it or not, he had to keep his promise to the man who had been the biggest contributor to the Conservative coffers. At this juncture he ought to have entertained some doubts about Allan. On October 7, he was shocked to discover that the Montrealer, in spite of all his pious proclamations, had not actually broken off relations with McMullen and the others. Allan's alibi to Macdonald was that he was trying to let the Americans down gradually, but he was later to testify under oath that he believed the proposition to exclude foreigners was impolitic and unnecessary and that the Government would not insist upon it. Macdonald did insist, and Allan finally promised to obey. Was this the man who ought to be heading up the greatest national venture?

There was nothing the Prime Minister could do. He had made a promise through Cartier—Allan kept using that awkward word "agreement"—and he would have to stick by it. Macdonald uneasily began to wonder just what the agreement consisted of; the memory of that ambiguous telegram, dispatched at the height of a fatiguing campaign, when whiskey and wine were flowing freely, began to nag at him. What actually *had* Cartier promised Allan? Macdonald realized that he himself did not know the exact details. But already there were rumors floating around Montreal about Allan's gifts to the Cartier campaign.

Macdonald now learned from Allan the full extent of Cartier's financial dependence upon him. The Prime Minister was horrified. Was it possible that the once astute Cartier could have been so foolish? He could not believe it and sought reassurance from his old friend, who had sailed for England to seek medical aid for his disease. Cartier's reply confirmed Macdonald's worst fears.

In Chicago, George McMullen was also experiencing twinges of uneasiness as he studied Allan's reports of his lavish spending. On September 16, 1872 (Grant and Fleming reached the summit of the Yellow Head Pass that day), Allan informed him that he had paid out the staggering sum of $343,000 in gold for election expenses and other disbursements connected with the railway contract and still had $13,500 to pay.

Startled by the magnitude of these figures, McMullen lost no time in getting to Montreal to confront Allan, who managed to mollify him. Then, on October 24, Allan, under Macdonald's goading, finally broke the news to his American associates that he would have to dump them. McMullen was shocked and furious. There were angry letters, evasive replies, and finally, on Christmas Eve, a face-to-face meeting between the two men in Montreal. Here, at last, Allan made it bluntly clear to McMullen that it was all over: he was closing off all arrangements with the Americans and repudiating any obligations they might feel he was under to them. McMullen was in a state of rage. He had squandered more than a year of his time and tens of thousands of his and his associates' dollars, and now it appeared that he, like the frustrated Kersteman, had had no hope of success from the outset. Allan had deceived everybody. He had deceived the Government; he had deceived his friends; he had deceived his backers, and, above all, he had deceived himself—led on to greater and greater foolishness by what Lord Dufferin, the Governor General, was to call "the purse proud and ostentatious notion of domineering over everybody and overcoming all obstacles by the brute force of money."

The apoplectic McMullen suggested that if Allan had a scrap of honor left he would either stick to the original agreement or step right out of the picture. This Allan refused to do, whereupon McMullen threatened to tell the entire story to the Prime Minister; after all, he had in his possession all of Allan's indiscreet correspondence. McMullen had for some time considered these damaging letters to be his ace in the hole.

Allan, apparently sure of his ground because of his deal with Cartier, remained obdurate. Perhaps he did not believe that McMullen would carry out his threat. But McMullen was not a man to shilly-shally. He wanted compensation and, if he did not get that, he wanted revenge. Off he went to Ottawa with no less a purpose than to blackmail the Prime Minister of Canada.

The encounter, which Macdonald had been half expecting and certainly dreading for all of that autumn, took place on New Year's Eve, 1872. The politicians and businessmen of the seventies seem to have had a certain insensitivity to festive occasions. Allan and McMullen had battled it out on Christmas Eve. Hincks had given Kersteman a dressing down on the Yule. Now McMullen was waiting to see the Prime Minister while the rest of the nation was preparing jubilantly to usher in the new year of 1873—the blackest in all of Macdonald's long political career.

It makes a striking picture, this pivotal meeting in the Prime Minister's office. The youthful McMullen, his round eyes coldly furious, faced a man thirty years his senior, whose languorous attitude gave no hint of his inner emotions. Physical opposites, the two antagonists had certain common qualities. Both were possessed of lively imaginations, which allowed them to glimpse future benefits in schemes others thought harebrained. Both, as a result, enjoyed the steady nerves of committed gamblers. For Macdonald, the railway project had been an immense political risk; for McMullen, a considerable financial one. Oddly, McMullen, the apparently hardheaded businessman, was far more quixotic than the pragmatic politician who faced him across the desk. Macdonald's gambles—or visions or dreams (all three nouns apply)—had a habit of turning out far more successfully than McMullen's astonishing series of ventures, several of which were indeed harebrained.

The interview took up two hours. McMullen came armed with Allan's letters to him; he proceeded to read the Prime Minister some compromising extracts. He produced the correspondence with General Cass. He unfolded the secret contracts made the previous year with the Americans. He talked mysteriously about strange stories that Allan had told him about paying off Members of Parliament. He said he could name names in that connection—names of persons "who are very near to you." Macdonald was inwardly aghast, but at moments like this he knew enough to maintain a poker face. He denied that

Allan had bribed the Government. In that case, McMullen replied smoothly, Allan must be a swindler—he had taken almost four hundred thousand dollars from the Americans on just that pretext. He urged Macdonald either to stick to the original agreement or leave Allan out of the new company. Macdonald replied that he could do neither; if McMullen thought he was badly used, that was his problem. The Americans, said the Prime Minister, had been out of the company for some time.

Not so, replied McMullen, and he produced Allan's own correspondence in evidence. Again Macdonald was appalled, but he did not turn a hair.

"He [Allan] ought to have been more frank with you," Macdonald said. "He could not if he had tried obtained what he wanted to get. He must have ascertained that last session. He could not by any possibility have effected the purpose you wished him to effect of getting your associates, the American capitalists, interested in the company. He could not do so, the public feeling was so great."

McMullen grew more threatening. He began to talk about what would happen politically if the public knew all the facts, "as they certainly would, if Allan was put in and allowed to break his sacred obligations with his associates." Macdonald made no comment but asked for time to consult with Allan and Allan's lawyer, J. J. C. Abbott. On that note the encounter ended.

McMullen was back in Ottawa three weeks later. This time he brought along the Chicago banker Charles Mather Smith and another colleague, who had been privy to the early negotiations. Smith brought *his* correspondence with Allan and the three men indulged in a kind of Greek chorus of woe, bewailing their relationship with the perfidious Montrealer and crying out that they had advanced huge sums of money for the railway in good faith. Macdonald was properly sympathetic. He agreed that they had been badly used by Allan, who should certainly be made to refund the money. McMullen began to talk wildly about seizing Allan's ships in American ports and suing him in the courts.

"I think you are quite right," said Macdonald. "If I were in your place I would proceed against him."

With this the atmosphere grew almost genial. McMullen and Smith denied that they were trying to blackmail the Government and asked, wistfully, if there was any chance they could be given an interest in the railway. That, Macdonald told them, would not be possible.

McMullen offered to let Macdonald have copies of all the damaging correspondence, including some new documents nailing down Allan's dishonesty regarding the extent of the American interest in his company. These showed that on October 12, at the very time when Allan and Abbott had assured Parliament that negotiations with the Americans had been terminated, Allan was paying over American money to incorporate the railway company.

Although none of the men involved knew it at the time, this was not the full extent of Allan's duplicity. The day before he finally dumped McMullen, Allan had a long talk with Lycurgus Edgerton, Jay Cooke's itinerant commissioner in Canada, about the new company Macdonald was forming. Allan assured the Northern Pacific man that there was nothing in the charter to affect Cooke's plans. "Certain, unreasoning public opinion had to be conciliated by an apparent concession . . ." but this was "more in form than in substance." Edgerton was able to report to Cooke that there would be no all-Canadian route via the north shore of Lake Superior, if Allan remained in control. It was a "useless expenditure . . . dictated by a sentimental patriotism, and a narrow minded jealousy and prejudice." For the next five or ten years "if not for *all time*, the Canada Pacific must be subservient and tributary to the interests of the Northern Pacific."

Even without this knowledge it must have been clear by now to the Prime Minister that Allan was an unfortunate choice to head the new company. For almost a year Macdonald had been telling his colleagues, his friends, his political enemies, and the country at large (as well as himself) that Allan was the only possible choice for the job —a man of business acumen, probity, sagacity, and experience who commanded the total respect of the financial community. Now he stood revealed as a blunderer, a conniver, a liar, a double-dealer, and, perhaps worst of all, a Yankee-lover—a man whose imprudence, in Macdonald's own words, "has almost mounted to insanity." And this was the man who would shortly be setting off for London on a mission of the greatest delicacy to secure the underwriting of the world's largest railway project. Clearly, if the financial community or the public at large knew what Macdonald knew, the railway scheme would collapse like a soap bubble.

Would they find out? Worry gnawed at Macdonald as he prepared for the session of 1873. The Americans would have to be bought off, if indeed blackmailers could ever be bought off. He wrote to Hincks in Montreal and Hincks sought out Abbott, the lawyer who, more and more, was assuming the role of fixer in the various chapters of the continuing unpleasantness. Some bargaining then took place between Abbott and the Americans. McMullen had wanted more than two hundred thousand dollars. Abbott pared the sum down to $37,500 U.S. He paid him twenty thousand down and placed Allan's check for the rest in an envelope which he gave to Henry Starnes of Allan's Merchants' Bank. McMullen then placed the offending correspondence in another envelope and gave that to Starnes. The banker's instructions were to wait until ten days after the end of the coming session and then deliver the envelope with the money to McMullen and the envelope with the correspondence to Allan. This was the best arrangement that Abbott could make to keep the story from becoming public before Allan completed his negotiations in England and while Parliament was in session. The arrangement was not concluded until the very eve of Allan's departure.

But blackmailers are notoriously unreliable. George McMullen did not bother to collect the second envelope from Henry Starnes, the banker. He had already received a higher bid from Macdonald's political enemies.

3

1 · Lucius Huntington's moment in history

THE FIRST SESSION OF THE SECOND
Parliament of Canada opened on March 6, 1873, with no hint of the
storm that was gathering. The air was bracing and frosty and, though
the snow was piled in soiled mountains along the sidewalks, the sky
was blue and the sun bright. To the Earl of Dufferin, the dapper new
Governor General, setting off for Parliament Hill in his glittering four-
horse state carriage, the weather was "quite divine."

He was deposited promptly at three o'clock before the main arch-
way, to the accompaniment of clanking swords, jangling spurs, brass
band, and royal salute. As he entered the blood-red door of the Senate,
he found himself proceeding through what one observer aptly called
a "double file of living millinery." The crimson chamber had been
cleared of desks and the senatorial chairs were now occupied by the
wives and daughters of the parliamentarians and leading citizens, all
caparisoned in gowns from Paris, London, or New York.

It was Lord Dufferin's first Parliament and it was perhaps as well
that he could not foresee the trials that lay before him. He had served
as a diplomat at St. Petersburg, Rome, and Paris, but nothing in his
past had prepared him for the political hurly-burly of the Canadian
scene. As he marched easily toward the canopied chair known as the
Throne, Dufferin, who was more than a little snobbish, looked about
him with satisfaction. It was true that the Canadian Senators were not
draped in the robes of British peers, but "they looked a very dignified

body in their sober court dress." Indeed, he was "rather surprised to see what a high bred and good looking company they formed."

The Governor General took his seat and looked out across an ocean of fluttering Parisian fans, glistening pearls and diamonds, and silks in pale pastels framed against the darker velvets; it reminded him of a bed of flowers. Now, at the call of the Gentleman Usher of the Black Rod, the Members "swarmed in like a bunch of schoolboys" (there were four future Prime Ministers in that swarm). The Governor General read the speech from the Throne, feeling a little silly at having to repeat it in French.

One of the key paragraphs in the speech dealt with the railway: "I have caused a charter to be granted to a body of Canadian capitalists for the construction of the Pacific Railway. The company now formed has given assurance that this great work will be vigorously prosecuted, and the favourable state of the money market in England affords every hope that satisfactory arrangements may be made for the required capital."

Macdonald was not the only Member present who must have felt the hollowness of those words. By this time, the Opposition was in on the secret and, as the session progressed, rumors began to flit around Ottawa about a coming political earthquake. The *Globe*, which called the railway scheme "financially the maddest, and politically the most unpatriotic, that could be proposed," hammered away daily, in editorial after editorial, its two points: first, that Allan was backed by Yankee dollars, and second, that the Government never had any intention, at any time, of dealing with anybody else.

Then, on March 31, the Opposition's intentions were revealed when, at the opening of the day's proceedings, Lucius Seth Huntington of Shefford, Quebec, rose to give notice that before the House went into Committee of Ways and Means, he would move that a committee be appointed to inquire into matters generally affecting the Canadian Pacific Railway. Huntington sat down amid Opposition cries of "Hear! Hear!" and a tingle of excitement rippled through the House.

Thus when Huntington prepared to make his motion on the evening of April 2, the corridors of the House were filled to suffocation, the galleries were crowded, the Treasury benches were full, and every Opposition seat was occupied. The Commons was silent and expectant. Seldom had any Member faced such an attentive audience.

Huntington rose. At forty-six, he was a man of commanding presence, big-chested and handsome, with a classic head that a sculptor might covet—aquiline nose, poetic eyes, thick shock of light, wavy hair. He was a lawyer and politician of long experience. One day, with his parliamentary career behind him, the eloquent Huntington would retire to New York and publish a political novel.

Huntington began to read from a paper in his hand. He was a polished speaker, resonant and melodious, but now there was a tremor in his voice and he spoke so softly that the backbenchers had to lean forward to catch his words. He had every reason to be nervous, for he was putting his career on the line. If he could not prove his charges, he would certainly be forced to resign his seat; but if he *could* prove them, his name would go down in history.

His speech was astonishingly brief; it ran to no more than seven short paragraphs and was supported by no documentary evidence. As he spoke, he paused occasionally and glanced uneasily about him as if to weigh the effect of his words: the reaction from the Government benches was one of stolid indifference. Huntington charged that the Allan company was secretly financed by American capital and that the Government was aware of that fact, that Allan had advanced large sums of money, some of it paid by the Americans, to aid the Government in the elections, and that he had been offered the railway contract in return for his support. Lord Dufferin, who was a great-grandson of Richard Brinsley Sheridan and had some of the eloquence of that great playwright and parliamentarian, put the case more forcefully in his report to the Colonial Secretary. Huntington, he said, had charged that the Government had "trafficked with foreigners in Canada's most precious interests in order to debauch the constituencies of the Dominion with the gold obtained at the price of their treachery."

Dufferin did not believe a word of this. In spite of his official pose of strict impartiality, he had been seduced by the Prime Minister's considerable charm. He thought the scene in the House, which he could not witness, "a very absurd one" and Huntington himself "a man of no great political capacity."

But it was not absurd, as events were to prove. Huntington called for a parliamentary committee of seven members to inquire into every circumstance connected with the railway negotiations with power to subpoena papers, records, and witnesses. Then he sat down, "full of suppressed emotion," as a historian of the day recorded.

An oppressive silence hung over the House—a silence so deathly that some who were present recalled years later the solemn ticks of the parliamentary clock falling like hammer blows. Every eye had turned to the lean, sprawled figure of Macdonald. The Prime Minister, one hand toying with a pencil, remained "inscrutable as stone." There were those who said he was stunned by the charges, but this is scarcely credible; he had been expecting them ever since Huntington gave his notice. More likely he was bothered by their lack of substance. Why was Huntington holding back? Why hadn't he read the evidence into the record? What was the Opposition plotting?

The silence was broken at last by the Speaker, asking in a calm, impersonal voice for the question. The voting proceeded. The motion was lost by a majority of thirty-one—one of the largest the Government had enjoyed that session—and the House moved on to other business. Huntington's motion, unsubstantiated by any evidence, had produced no result. The *Globe*, the following day, referred to the Pacific Railway Scandal (the title was eventually shortened to Pacific Scandal), and, as might be expected, laced into the Prime Minister for his silence in the face of Huntington's charges; but it confessed itself surprised "at the equally silent policy of Mr. Huntington." Macdonald himself thought Huntington had blundered by allowing the Government to shut off debate so subtly and treat the whole matter as a vote of non-confidence. The Government press took the view that the motion was nothing more than a device to needle the ministry.

As far as the public was concerned, the cry of barefaced corruption had lost its potency from overuse by the newspapers. There was no such thing as an objective daily newspaper in the Canada of the seventies. The major papers were party organs, owned or subsidized by the Liberals or the Conservatives. The "news" stories emanating from Ottawa were no more impartial than the editorials and were not expected to be. Most people probably agreed with the Governor General, who saw in the vote over the Huntington motion a great victory for the Government.

Macdonald, however, was having second thoughts. He had faced a rebellion from his own followers between sittings. Many felt that the Government had given the appearance of riding roughshod over its opponents and that its silence in the face of charges so serious could be taken as an admission of guilt. Accordingly, the Prime Minister rose a week later to announce the appointment of a select committee of five to investigate the Huntington charges.

Now Macdonald proceeded to set in motion a series of tactics of the kind that would eventually earn him the sobriquet—an affectionate one—of "Old Tomorrow." His was to be a policy of delay. When Alexander Mackenzie, the Opposition leader, urged that the evidence before the committee be taken under oath, Macdonald obligingly agreed. It sounded like a concession to the Opposition, since Huntington's motion had not gone that far.

But before the witnesses could be sworn, a bill had to be introduced into the House providing for evidence to be taken under oath.

That could occupy almost a month. Macdonald was reasonably confident that such a bill would be *ultra vires* and that Mother England, if prompted, would disallow it. Such a disallowance would pave the way for a royal commission, which could, of course, examine witnesses under oath. From Macdonald's point of view, a royal commission composed of aging jurists of his own choosing was far preferable to a parliamentary committee with men of Edward Blake's caliber ready to tear into the Allans, the Abbotts, and the Langevins.

It was May 3 before the Oaths Bill received the Governor General's signature. On May 5, the committee met for the first time—but not for long. Again, with the help of the Tory appointees, Macdonald engineered delay. The hearings were postponed until July 2.

Delay was dangerous to the Liberal cause. Telegrams could be destroyed in the interval; originals of documents and letters could disappear, as indeed they did. The Liberal leadership belatedly realized that it had made a tactical error in not placing some of the evidence on the record when Huntington first made his charges in early April. It is clear that he had seen copies of the Allan-McMullen correspondence and knew where the originals were stored. The evidence was to show that the Liberal Party had purchased Allan's indiscreet correspondence from McMullen for twenty-five thousand dollars.

Outwardly, then, the Prime Minister was totally in command. Inwardly, he was sick at heart with grief, disappointment, and foreboding. In May he suffered two terrible blows whose force was not lessened by the fact he was braced to expect them.

By the middle of the month it was clear that Allan's negotiations with the English banking houses had met with total failure, destroyed by the whispers of scandal from across the water; and so Macdonald's railway policy lay in tatters. The settlement of the North West, the knitting together of the disunited provinces, the building of a workable transcontinental nation—all these remained an elusive dream. Two years had already slipped by since the pact with British Columbia, and there was now no chance in the foreseeable future of mounting the enterprise.

And the partnership of Macdonald and Cartier was no more. Macdonald's friend, confidant, bulwark, political comrade-in-arms, and strong right hand was dead in England of the kidney disease that had ravaged him for two years. At the nadir of his career, Macdonald had no one to turn to. Politically he stood alone, weary, overworked, tormented, dispirited. He wanted to resign, but his party could not let him; there was no one to replace him. When he suggested retiring to the backbenches, the Conservative hierarchy pointed out that his withdrawal could easily lead to a general exodus. And so, "very much harassed and out of health," he stayed.

He was, in fact, a Canadian fixture, and it was unthinkable that he should go. In those days, before the newspaper half-tone engraving was invented, politicians were not always instantly recognizable; but everyone knew Macdonald, whom his own sister Louisa referred to as "one of the ugliest men in Canada." The long, rangy figure, the homely face, the absurd nose, the tight curls around the ears made him a caricaturist's delight. J. W. Bengough, the country's leading political cartoonist, portrayed him week after week in *Grip* as a kind of likable rogue with matchstick legs and giant proboscis.

Likable he was, though often enough a rogue in the political sense. In those days of partisan hatreds, when one's political adversary really *was* the enemy, Macdonald's opponents found it hard to hate him. One Liberal, Joseph Lister, who attacked Macdonald viciously in Parliament, confessed he was so attracted to the man's personality that he dared not trust himself in his company.

This singular absence of bile is remarkable when set against the tragedies and travails of Macdonald's private life. His personal vicissitudes would have broken a lesser man. His first wife had been a hopeless invalid, bedridden for most of the fourteen years of their married life. His second baby boy had died of convulsions. His daughter Mary, the only issue of his second marriage, was mentally retarded and physically deformed. After Confederation, Macdonald's life savings were wiped out and he found himself plunged into heavy debt, partly because he had been forced by his political career to neglect his law practice, partly because of an unexpected bank failure. Never robust, always apparently on the edge of physical breakdown, he had been felled for six months in 1870 by a nightmarish attack of gallstones, which brought him to the brink of death (his obituary set in type and ready for release) and weakened him for life.

Now, in the late spring of 1873, piled on top of all these adversities, Macdonald was burdened by the loss of his closest associate, the collapse of his national dream, and the possible political destruction of himself and his party.

He turned, as he so often did in moments of stress, to the bottle; and for the next several weeks all who encountered him, from Governor General to hack reporter, were treated to the spectacle of the Prime Minister of Canada reeling drunk. "Indisposed" was the euphemism usually employed by the newspapers, but the public knew exactly what *that* meant. After all, the stories about his drinking were legion: how he had once mounted a train platform so drunk and shaken that he had been seen to vomit while his opponent was speaking but had saved the day by opening his speech with the words: "Mr. Chairman and Gentlemen, I don't know how it is, but every time I hear Mr. Jones speak it turns my stomach." How he had told a public gathering during his campaigns against the former Liberal leader and *Globe* editor: "I know enough of the feeling of this meeting to know that you would rather have John A. drunk than George Brown sober." How, when his colleagues urged him to speak to that other great toper, D'Arcy McGee, about his alcohol problem, he had said: "Look here, McGee, this Government can't afford two drunkards and you've got to stop."

Macdonald's affinity for alcohol—he was a nonsmoker—went back to his childhood when the Macdonald home dispensed what was then the universal form of hospitality: raw whiskey, obtainable at twenty-five cents a gallon and usually as easily available as water, being kept on tap or in a pail with a cup beside it. Macdonald's father, "Little Hugh," was addicted to it and his life was shortened by it. Macdonald's own drinking bouts—he would sometimes go to bed and consume bottle after bottle of port—were to become an endearing Canadian legend; but at the time they were a source of concern to his friends and colleagues and a perplexing embarrassment to his statuesque and highly moral wife, for whom, in the first glow of courtship, he had given up the bottle. To the sympathetic Dufferin, who was more than once publicly disconcerted by the presence of his tipsy Prime Minister, Macdonald suffered from an "infirmity." The prim and granite-faced leader of the Opposition, Alexander Mackenzie, was not so tolerant. To him, Macdonald was, quite simply, a "drunken debauchee."

Yet his powers of recuperation were marvelous. He had the ability to pull himself together, even after days of drinking, when there was necessary business to attend to. And at the end of June, Macdonald needed his faculties: the Oaths Bill was officially disallowed just five days before the investigating committee was due to meet. Macdonald was now prepared to renew his offer of a royal commission.

The Dominion Day holiday, the sixth since Confederation, intervened—a day of picnics and street dancing, quoits and croquet, train excursions and lacrosse games. Year by year, such national celebrations were giving the country a slight sense of community. The following morning, in the Montreal Court of Appeals, the select committee convened. Macdonald sent it a letter renewing his offer of a royal commission. A furious debate followed. The Government Members wanted to pack up the committee until Parliament briefly reconvened on August 13. The Opposition wanted to dispense with the oath and examine unsworn witnesses. The three Government supporters inevitably prevailed. Once again the Opposition had been frustrated in its attempts to get the evidence before the public. It was more than three months since Huntington had aired the issue and the country was in no sense aroused. There was only one course left open: the press.

2 · Scandal!

ON THE MORNING OF JULY 4, READERS OF the Toronto *Globe* and the Montreal *Herald* opened their slim papers to the scoop of the decade. PACIFIC RAILWAY INTRIGUES, the *Globe* headline read, and there, for column after column, was laid bare the correspondence of Sir Hugh Allan with his secret American backers. It was all in print for the country to ponder: Allan's remarks regarding Macpherson . . . Allan's list of prominent Canadians who, he said, were to be given free stock . . . Allan's detailed account of his victory over Cartier . . . Allan's long report to General Cass (whose name was withheld from the press) reporting on his coercion of the Quebec press and public . . . Allan's disbursements of $343,000 . . . Allan's double game with his American associates.

There were seventeen letters in total, and they all but ended Sir Hugh Allan's public career. One associate declared in Montreal that he would not be seen walking the streets with Sir Hugh. The board of the new railway company met hurriedly that afternoon while, not far away, a public meeting expressed its dissatisfaction with the investigation. For the first time the public had something it could get its teeth into, and the Pacific Scandal, as it was now universally called, became the major topic of the day.

The letters, the *Globe* insisted, showed that the Government was "hopelessly involved in an infamous and corrupt conspiracy." They scarcely showed that. Macdonald's name was mentioned only three times and always innocuously. There was only one suspicious paragraph in the letter of August 7 to General Cass, in which Allan wrote that "we yesterday signed an agreement by which, on certain monetary conditions, they agreed to form the company, of which I am to be President, to suit my views, to give me and my friends a majority of the stock, and . . . the contract for building the road." The letter was ambiguous enough to be capable of innocent explanation.

Meanwhile, a much-chastened Allan, at Macdonald's urgent behest and with Abbott's legal skill, was preparing a sworn affidavit to be published on July 6 in major Government newspapers. This lengthy document, which was seized on with relief by the Government's supporters, was designed to get the administration off the hook. It largely succeeded. Allan's sworn denials were explicit and positive. Though he certainly subscribed money to aid in the election of his friends, he had done so without any understanding or condition being placed upon such funds. None of this money, he swore, had come from the Americans. It was true that he had left the door ajar for his American friends until told specifically by the Government that they must be excluded; he felt honor bound to do so. As for McMullen, he had made such financial demands on Allan that "I declined altogether to entertain them." He was, of course, prepared to return all the money the Americans had expended, but he was not prepared to pay McMullen an exorbitant fee for his time.

The statement, which bears the imprint of Abbott's sensitive legal mind, was a masterpiece of tightrope walking. "He [Abbott] has made the old gentleman acknowledge on oath that his letters were untrue," Macdonald wrote gleefully to Dufferin. "This was a bitter pill for him to swallow, but Abbott has gilded it over for him very nicely." It was not easy for Allan to wriggle out of correspondence written in his own hand, but he did his best in a painfully contorted way: the letters, he said, were "written in the confidence of private intercourse in the midst of many matters engrossing my attention, and probably with less care and circumspection than might have been bestowed upon them had they been intended for publication. At the same time, while in some respects these letters are not strictly accurate, I can see that the circumstances, to a great extent, justified or excused the language used in them."

Allan, then, was the villain of the piece, and the ministerial press cast him in that role. The Government's position was also bolstered immeasurably by the fact, easily substantiated, that the *Globe* and *Herald* had deliberately suppressed two other letters which showed that Allan had finally broken off negotiations with the Americans. McMullen, too, was reviled as a scoundrel and a blackmailer. His own relatives on the Picton, Ontario, *Gazette* attacked him, carefully refraining from any reference to his local family connections.

Though the *Globe* regurgitated the correspondence daily, it was clear that Macdonald's ministry, though bruised, was by no means broken. The weary Prime Minister now felt that he could afford a short holiday at Rivière du Loup. It was while he was there, in his small cottage near the riverside, that the world crashed in on him.

On July 17, just as the public was growing weary of the newspapers' incessant harping on the scandal, the blow fell. It was devastating. The *Globe* ran a great bank of type on the right-hand column of its front page: THE PACIFIC SCANDAL: ASTOUNDING REVELATIONS. The revelations appeared identically and simultaneously in the *Globe*, the *Herald*, and *L'Événement* of Quebec, and they *were* astounding.

The story, which ran to several columns, took the form of a historical narrative by George McMullen, whose dubious presence had hung over the affair from the outset. McMullen, goaded by "the vilest slanders," laid about him with a scythe as he gave his version, often highly colored and inaccurate, of his role in the drama. He claimed that Allan had lent Macdonald and Hincks $4,000 and $4,500 respectively "with very good knowledge that it was never to be repaid." He identified the newspaper that Allan told him he had paid. He said that Allan had made an additional indefinite loan of ten thousand dollars to Hincks and had promised Langevin twenty-five thousand for election purposes, "on condition of his friendly assistance."

This was strong meat, though not of itself conclusive since McMullen, branded in the public mind as a blackmailer, was himself suspect. But unlike most newspaper stories, the sting of this one was in its tail. Appended to McMullen's narrative, deep inside the newspaper, was a series of letters and telegrams which contained political dynamite. They had been buried at the end by design in an attempt to divert suspicion from the source from which they had been obtained. They had been rifled from Abbott's safe in the dark of the night during the lawyer's absence in England, copied by his confidential secretary, George Norris, Jr., and an assistant, and sold for hard cash to the Liberal Party.

> *Cartier to Abbott, Montreal, August 24, 1872:*
> "In the absence of Sir Hugh Allan, I shall be obliged by your supplying the Central Committee with a further sum of twenty thousand dollars upon the same conditions as the amount written by me at the foot of my letter to Sir Hugh Allan on the 30th ult.
>
> GEORGE E. CARTIER
>
> "P.S. Please also send Sir John A. Macdonald ten thousand dollars more on the same terms."

"Terms"? "Conditions"? What price Allan's sworn denials now?

> *Memorandum signed by three members of the Central Committee, J. L. Beaudry, Henry Starnes, and P. S. Murphy:*
> "Received from Sir Hugh Allan by the hands of J. J. C. Abbott twenty thousand dollars for General Election purposes, to be arranged hereafter according to the terms of the letter of Sir George

E. Cartier, of the date of 30th of July, and in accordance with the request contained in his letter of the 24th instant."

Montreal, 26th Aug., 1872.

Again, that damning word: *terms*. It was well for the Government that poor Cartier was dead.

Telegram: Macdonald to Abbott at St. Anne's, Aug. 26, 1872, Toronto:
"I must have another ten thousand; will be the last time of calling; do not fail me; answer today."

And:

Reply: Abbott to Macdonald from Montreal, Aug. 26, 1872:
"Draw on me for ten thousand dollars."

"Three more extraordinary documents than these . . . never saw the light of day," Lord Dufferin wrote to the Colonial Secretary. The effect on the public was incalculable. Dufferin was later to refer, in his dramatic fashion, to "the terror and shame manifested by the people at large when the possibility first dawned upon them of their most trusted statesman having been guilty of such conduct." The Pacific Scandal became the sole topic of conversation in those late July days and continued so into the fall. The carnage among the party faithful was devastating. Even schoolboys found themselves embroiled. Sir John Willison, who was to become editor of the *Globe*, was a youth at the time and remembered how his village school at Greenwood, Ontario, broke into factions. Those who clung to the Tory leader were denounced by their classmates as "Charter Sellers"; and Willison admitted, even though he had been reared in a Tory household and still clung desperately to the faith of his fathers, "I fear that I wavered as I found lifelong Conservatives falling away from the standard." Many a loyal Tory was transformed, during that tempestuous summer, into a working Liberal.

In all his long career, nothing hit Macdonald so hard as the McMullen revelations. The news, which reached him at Rivière du Loup in a hurriedly scribbled letter from Langevin, "fairly staggered" him. It was, he later told Dufferin, "one of those overwhelming misfortunes that they say every man must meet once in his life." He had expected trouble but nothing so cataclysmic as this. He had certainly sent the telegrams, but he had never expected to be found out.

Alexander Campbell, Macdonald's old law partner and Senate

leader, was in touch with his chief immediately with a call for a hurried conference with Langevin in Quebec City. The strategy was clear: a royal commission was now an absolute necessity, preferably one that included "safe" judges. The indispensable Abbott was hurriedly called upon to assist in the negotiations. He reported a Montreal rumor that fresh revelations were due to appear at any moment. He had written "very guardedly" to Charles Dewey Day, a retired Superior Court judge, who was Chancellor of McGill University. Abbott had every confidence "in his acting judiciously." A sympathetic letter to Macdonald from the judge himself, two days later, made clear just what the cautious Abbott meant. Judge Day was squarely on Macdonald's side, disturbed by the fact that the correspondence as published in the press was "in a shape which tells against you." The judge wrote that "no time should be lost in endeavouring to change the current public opinion. If you think I can be of service in helping to place the matter upon a true and just footing I willingly accept the duty." Obviously, from Macdonald's point of view, Charles Dewey Day was the proper choice to head the royal commission.

With the crisis swirling around him, Macdonald took to the bottle and vanished from sight. No member of his Cabinet could reach him or learn of his plans or purpose. The press reported that he had disappeared from Rivière du Loup. His wife had no idea where he was. The frantic Governor General, in the midst of a state tour of the Maritimes, could get no answer to an urgent and confidential letter. He followed it with an equally urgent telegram; silence. On August 5, the Montreal *Daily Witness* published in its two o'clock edition a rumor that Macdonald had committed suicide by throwing himself into the St. Lawrence. The story, concocted by his political enemies, vanished from the next edition but was widely believed at the time; it seemed to confirm the Government's guilt. Suicide or no, the fact was that for several days, in a moment of grave political crisis, the Prime Minister of Canada could not be found by anyone. Dufferin finally unraveled the mystery and put it delicately in a private letter to the Colonial Secretary: "He had stolen away, as I subsequently found, from his seaside villa and was lying perdu with a friend in the neighbourhood of Quebec."

3 · *The least satisfactory royal commission*

THE THREE ROYAL COMMISSIONERS APpointed under the great seal of Canada on August 14 began to take evidence at noon, on September 4, in the same railway committee room that three weeks before had echoed with the angry cries of the Opposition.

In his choice of commissioners, Macdonald was not able to escape the shrill charge of collusion. Oddly, Judge Day, the chairman, who had at the time of his appointment come down so firmly on Macdonald's side, was not attacked by the press. The aging jurist with the big, luminous eyes and domed head was generally felt to be above politics, perhaps by virtue of his position as Chancellor of McGill. The other two choices were greeted with more skepticism. The *Globe* dismissed Judge Antoine Polette, another ex-politician and retired Superior Court judge, as "a bitter, prejudiced French Conservative and . . . a very dull man." It reserved its heaviest ammunition, however, for the Honourable James Robert Gowan, a cadaverous county court judge from Simcoe, Ontario, known to have been Macdonald's close friend for twenty-five years, whom the newspaper saw as a hack political appointee and party follower.

The commission was unsatisfactory on several counts. There was no commission counsel to cross-examine witnesses (Huntington was boycotting the entire proceedings on principle) and the commissioners did not seem to know what to ask them. Apart from the three elderly judges no one, except the Government in the person of Macdonald, was allowed the right of cross-examination. Several of the principals declined to appear. Of the thirty-six witnesses called, fifteen contributed nothing whatsoever to the proceedings, nor were they pressed to contribute more. They only knew, as the saying goes, what they had read in the papers.

It was obvious from the beginning why Macdonald had preferred a royal commission to a parliamentary inquiry. As Dufferin summed it up: ". . . elderly judges have hardly the disembowelling powers which are rife in a young cross-examining counsel."

Day after day, for all of September, the public was treated to the spectacle of powerful business figures and important politicians, by nature and training supposedly men of precision, fumbling about on the stand, delivering fuzzy or evasive answers, testifying to receipts that were "lost" or missing, prefacing their remarks with such phrases as "I cannot remember," or "It is not very likely."

The first witness was Henry Starnes, the president of Allan's Merchants' Bank and chairman of Cartier's election fund. Starnes was shrewd of feature, with hooded lizard's eyes and beaked nose, but he was a mountain of uncertainty when asked about contributions to the Cartier campaign: "I cannot say how all the money came but it was deposited with me, and by what means I do not exactly know."

This was the city's leading banker talking: Starnes, a lieutenant colonel in the militia and a former mayor of Montreal, came empty-handed to the witness stand; he had no financial statement for the fund, no record of receipts or disbursements, and apparently no memory of them. He could not name the exact amount the committee had received, or how much of that money Allan had supplied, nor was he asked by the commission to file any account.

Sir Francis Hincks was the second witness. He had arrived from Montreal, according to the *Globe*, "much put out by things as they are and consequently in a very bad humour." Small wonder: he was approaching the twilight of a long career in business and politics, and once again there was a cloud over his name. In 1854 he had been accused of corruption for accepting one thousand shares of Grand Trunk stock while actively pushing for that railway. For fifteen years after that Hincks exiled himself to the Caribbean, where he served as Governor, first of Barbados and then of British Guiana.

Now this shriveled old man with the sharp features and the stooped shoulders once again saw his name connected with shady political maneuvering. Because of his fierceness in debate he was known as "The Hyena," but now he was positively calflike on the witness stand. He professed ignorance that Allan had been "a liberal contributor to the election funds." Yet he must have known the money was coming from somewhere; he had got some himself.

When the managers of the Ottawa and Montreal telegraph agencies took the stand, it developed that copies of the telegrams of the previous year had been destroyed under new rules which had "nothing to do with the elections" but which provided that originals could be kept for only six months. Thus all copies of telegrams for the period under investigation were gone. The reasons given were lack of storage space and to prevent "our operators being dragged up to Court." The ubiquitous Allan, it turned out, was also president of the telegraph company.

Hector Louis Langevin, a bulky man with pouchy eyes, a pageboy hair style, and a tiny *mouche* beneath his lower lip, claimed he destroyed most of his mail. Macdonald's Minister of Public Works testified: "I don't keep any of these letters, nor any letters that are mere formal letters. It has always been a rule with me as soon as I have finished with a letter to destroy it, unless it is an official letter to be filed in the Department. But my own letters I destroy, and I think, from what I have seen since, that I was perfectly right in this."

Langevin admitted getting election funds from Allan, but "as far as I can recollect" there were no conditions attached to them. Yet he also admitted he had been given $32,600—an enormous sum to receive from a single source; in modern terms it would be equivalent to some two hundred thousand dollars.

The tendency of the commissioners to take statements at their face value without searching inquiry did not go unremarked. In the *Globe*, George Brown and his editorial writers pounded that point home daily. Brown had just returned from England, where he had been sent for reasons of health immediately following his publication of the McMullen revelations. The Scandal had worn *him* down, too. Once across the water, Macdonald's old adversary dined with one of *The Times*'s chief editorial writers, supplied him with documents dealing with the Scandal, and then went after the lesser dailies and periodicals. "Putting the press men right," he called it. The result was that when Macdonald testified before the commission, the major British papers were ready to pounce.

It was Macdonald's testimony that the country was waiting for. The Prime Minister, who had attended every session of the commission, delivered himself of a long narrative, starting with his first meeting with Alfred Waddington and taking the story down past the election of 1872. He denied or qualified many of the statements in the McMullen account, and he denied that Allan's election contribution had influenced the Government in any way. He also made it clear that the Government had never had any intention of allowing the Americans to control the railway. But there were two damning accusations that he could not and did not deny: he had asked Allan for election funds and he had promised Allan the presidency of the company.

Macdonald swore that he had not used one cent of Allan's money for his own election, but he was forced to make one other damaging admission: Allan's money had been spent in a manner "contrary to statute," in bringing voters to the polls and in "dinners and things of that kind." The Prime Minister's euphemisms and deliberate vagueness could not prevent the public mind from making the obvious deduction that the money had been used to bribe the voters. In his second capacity of Minister of Justice, he had knowingly broken the law.

The British press came down very hard on the Prime Minister. *The Times* declared that his testimony had confirmed the McMullen revelations. The *Pall Mall Gazette* cried that "the scandal of his conduct is without precedent." George Brown's spadework had paid off for the Liberal Party.

Two days later, Allan took the stand—a chastened and forgetful witness. He even forgot that he had signed a supplementary contract with his American backers on March 28, 1872, in which he was authorized to accept, if necessary, a smaller land grant for the railway than that originally proposed.

"I had no recollection of this contract until the last few days," the Laird of Ravenscrag declared. "And if I had been asked would have said I had never seen it." But there was no question that the contract existed and that the most astute business leader in Canada, who insisted that everything be in writing, had put his signature to it.

As for the notorious correspondence with McMullen, Smith, and Cass, they were "private letters for private information and not for publication at all." In Allan's view, that seemed to take care of that. He admitted that some of the statements in the letters "may appear to conflict" with his own evidence and then repeated his previously published explanation that they had been written carelessly.

In his testimony, Allan showed himself a master of double-talk. McMullen had charged that a secret agreement had been made between Cartier and Allan, with Macdonald's blessing, between July 30 and August 6, 1872, by which, for certain monetary considerations, Allan was to get the charter. And there, staring at him, was Allan's own letter to Cass of August 7.

He had also used the word "agreement" in an August 6 letter to McMullen. But in Allan's curious interpretation "yesterday" no longer meant "yesterday," "signed" didn't really mean "signed," and an "agreement" was actually, on second thought, not an agreement at all.

The word "yesterday," Allan insisted, was used inadvertently for "recently" or "some time ago." It was "merely a slip of the pen." "Signed an agreement" was an expression "used in the hurry of the moment." And though Allan was faced with a letter in which he had written that the contract decision was ultimately in the hands of one man—Cartier—he now denied that he ever thought that an agreement with Cartier was equivalent to an agreement with the Government. Then he added that until Macdonald sent the wire refusing to accede to it, he really *had* looked on it "as a kind of agreement."

Again the commissioners dealt lightly with the witness. What happened, exactly, to the money he paid to three Cabinet Ministers? Why, if it was a free gift freely given, did he make so much fuss about getting receipts? Was the nominally paid-up capital of the Canada Pacific all in cash or was some of it bogus? Was he normally in the habit of spending almost four hundred thousand dollars at election time? The Liberal press asked these questions rhetorically. The commissioners did not bother.

John Joseph Caldwell Abbott, M.P., took the stand following Allan's testimony. Even though the correspondence, telegrams, and testimony showed that he had been handing out cash on behalf of Allan by the tens of thousands, he denied that he was Allan's confidential agent with respect to money.

"No, I don't think I was. Sir Hugh asked me to assist him in this affair." With these carefully chosen words Abbott subtly moved to dissociate himself from the discredited knight. He was the most powerful corporation lawyer in Canada—his clients included the Hudson's Bay Company and the Bank of Montreal as well as the Allan Line—and he knew how to hedge. His testimony was peppered with "not likelys."

A remarkable man, Abbott sprang from a remarkable lineage. His father was a pioneering missionary, a distinguished scholar, a well-known writer, and first librarian and Vice-Principal of McGill. His mother was the daughter of another minister, a former midshipman with Captain James Cook. He was the kind of man who likes to be in charge of things, and obviously he had the ability to take charge.

He claimed to be unhappy in politics. Yet he could not avoid it: a corporation lawyer in those days was automatically immersed in politics. His dislike of politics seems to have been genuine—he was a man who automatically did his best (without notable success) to stay out of the public eye; but he remained in politics all of his life. For, above all else, Abbott was a survivor. The Pacific Scandal failed to sink him, even though his own role was among the least admirable. In all of the shady background maneuvering, from the time of Allan's dealings with Cartier to the final denouement of the royal commission, Abbott's guiding hand is to be seen. When secret agreements are drawn up, Abbott composes them. When election funds are promised, Abbott hands over the checks. When damaging letters are purchased, Abbott negotiates. When indiscreet papers must be destroyed, Abbott presides. When dissident clerks defect, Abbott dangles the bribe. When friendly commissioners are needed, Abbott comes up with the names. Seven years later, Abbott the fixer would still be around to draw up a new railway charter; "the most perfect organ of its kind" it would be called. By 1887 he would become mayor of Montreal, and in 1891–92 he would officiate for sixteen not too glorious months as the first native-born Prime Minister of Canada, in spite of his late leader's declared belief that he had not a single qualification for the office. But then, Macdonald never warmed to Abbott. He was an extraordinarily ugly man with a face like a homelier John Bull—a big pudgy nose and hard metallic eyes —but as Macdonald's secretary, Joseph Pope, remarked, his nature was agreeable and his smile was sweet. Macdonald slew Abbott with a single phrase: "Yes," he said, "a sweet smile. All from the teeth outward."

By the time Abbott took the stand, interest in the royal commission was fading fast. Very little had emerged from the tangle of evasion, hedging, and double-talk that the public did not already know. The newspapers were still publishing verbatim accounts of the proceedings, but the people were bored. When Abbott returned on September 27 to read and correct his deposition—a task that occupied two hours—one of the commissioners went into a calm sleep from which, at intervals, he would rouse himself to take snuff. Another paced the floor at the rear of the bench, pausing to help himself from the snuffbox of his slumbering comrade. Only Judge Day, the chairman, managed to stay alert.

Abbott's fine tenor voice, the pride of Christ Church Cathedral, droned on and on. The messengers nodded. The secretary of the commission read listlessly from the *Canada Monthly*. One of the three or four newspapermen present laid himself out on one of the cushioned seats that the public had abandoned, and he too slept.

Thus did the proceedings of the royal commission grind slowly towards their close. The commissioners made no report but simply published the evidence without comment. It was left to Lord Dufferin to write its epitaph as he sent his account of the affair off to the Colonial Secretary: "A greater amount of lying and baseness could not well be crammed into a smaller compass."

4 · Battle stations

THE FINAL ACT WAS PLAYED OUT ON Parliament Hill from October 23 to November 5 in what the parliamentarian-historian James Young called "one of the most remarkable and profoundly exciting debates of that period." There would be only one subject discussed in this new session of Parliament: the evidence taken before the royal commission.

Parliament opened on Thursday, October 23, a raw, wet day with an omen of snow already in the air. Millards, on Sparks Street, was advertising "thick-soled, water-defying, slush-repelling, damp-excluding, snow-dispelling, cold-defying, heat-contracting boots." The roads and sidewalks were in their usual terrible condition, pocked by cavities and riven by cracks, which caused one lady, that day, to sprain an ankle. But nothing deterred the crowds who congregated all along the principal streets early that morning. Tantalizing rumors were about. It was said that George McMullen was in town. It was said that Louis Riel, the

Member for Provencher, was in town to take his seat. It was said that the two brothers of Thomas Scott, Riel's victim, were in town to exact revenge. It was said that Macdonald was despondent over the criticisms of the British press. It was said that Macdonald was confident of a majority. It was said that Macdonald would retire into private life. In the cavernous stairwells of the Russell House, the famous hostelry which every visitor and parliamentarian of note made his headquarters, the whispers echoed as human eddies formed and parted and circulated and formed again to exchange gossip about the Scandal.

By noon a river of people was flowing toward Parliament Hill. By two, the galleries and corridors of the House were so tightly packed that it was difficult to breathe. Never before had there been such a crush within those Gothic walls. Outside, a damp wind was cutting through the thickest overcoats; inside, the temperature had become oppressive.

Once again Lord Dufferin found himself within the crimson chamber reading another man's speech in two languages—a speech that announced, among other things, that the report of the royal commission would be placed before the House and that the royal charter for the Canadian Pacific Railway would be surrendered for lack of financial backing. The House adjourned. The preliminaries were over. After the weekend, the real contest would begin.

At three that Monday afternoon the members of the Government and Opposition were in their places. Macdonald lounged at his desk to the Speaker's immediate right, presenting to the world a picture of jaunty indifference. Nearby, in Cartier's old place, squatted the rotund figure of Langevin, his new Quebec lieutenant, a shrewd and affable man, gentler than Cartier but embattled now by virtue of his role in the Scandal. It was a powerful front bench: Hincks, the aging Hyena, making his last appearance in Parliament; Leonard Tilley, a handsome New Brunswicker, untainted by any scandal; and Sir Charles Tupper, the doughty "Cumberland War Horse," perhaps the best tactician in the House, poised for the attack. Young George Ross of Middlesex, Ontario, sitting in the Opposition backbenches and looking over the political heavyweights with a tyro's eyes, thought that Tupper even in repose looked "as if he had a blizzard secreted somewhere about his person."

Directly across from Macdonald sat Alexander Mackenzie, Leader of the Opposition, perhaps the bleakest-looking man in the House, whose features might have been carved out of the same granite he himself had fashioned in his days as a stonemason. His desk was piled high with references for the speech that he had been working on all weekend.

The Liberal Party had a formidable offensive team of its own: Mackenzie himself, caustic and dry, an expert at invective; Edward Blake, the strongest man in the party, a master of satire whose every word carried conviction, his scorn so withering that he could crush an opponent with a phrase; Richard Cartwright, know as "the Rupert of Debate," his speeches models of classic purity and polished diction, a coiner of pungent, cutting phrases; the one-armed E. B. Wood, known as "Big Thunder" because of his roaring speeches, which came freely garnished with scriptural references and resounding passages from the great orators and poets; and, of course, the eloquent, sonorous Huntington. They stared across the no-man's land of the Commons at their enemies, hungry for the kill.

Both sides were confident of success. Though the Opposition had the public on its side, the Government still had the votes. At this stage of political development, party lines were not yet tightly drawn and whips could not exert the kind of discipline that was eventually to prevail. The Opposition itself was a loose amalgam of mildly radical Reformers and Ontario agrarian-based Clear Grits, working under the umbrella of the Liberal Party. Many of those who supported Macdonald called themselves Independents. In addition there were six Members from the new province of Prince Edward Island, who had never sat in the House before. Nobody had a clear idea of how they would vote.

At the close of the royal commission hearings, Macdonald counted his supporters and estimated a majority of twenty-five. He held to this estimate through most of October. Part of the parliamentary struggle, therefore, took place not on the floor of the House but behind the scenes, as one side struggled to hold its supporters and the other strove to capture them. Doubtful Members found themselves besieged day and night with promises, cajolery, threats, and even bribes. The Prince Edward Islanders were hotly pursued: Mackenzie had made a special trip to the island before the session with Tupper right behind him, both intent on swaying these new unknown quantities. Amor de Cosmos, the mercurial Victoria Member (he had been born plain William Smith), was besieged by representatives of both sides as soon as he entered Ontario; the Lover of the World stepped off the train at London into the arms of Edward Blake and J. D. Edgar, the Liberal Party whip, and when he left Toronto for Ottawa, Senator Alexander Campbell, Macdonald's old law partner, was practically in his berth. In Ottawa the whiskey flowed as freely as the waters of the Rideau and to such an extent that certain Government supporters known for their conviviality were kept under lock and key lest, in the phrase of the day, they be "spirited away" and persuaded to vote contrary to their expressed intentions.

By Monday, October 27, Macdonald could no longer be sure of his majority of twenty-five. The number had dropped to eighteen and then to sixteen; some thought it as low as thirteen. "There is no country in the world, I imagine, where the rats leave the sinking ship so fast," Dufferin remarked acidly. But if Macdonald could hold the debate down to three or four days and make one of his powerful speeches early in the game, he could probably win the vote.

But a short debate was not possible. Everyone wanted to speak (forty managed to do so); and everyone was on hand. Such a crowded House had not been seen in the short political history of the Dominion. Every seat seemed occupied except one: the elusive Louis Riel would not be heard from.

The battle was joined shortly after three, once the routine business was dispensed with. As the cheers of the Opposition echoed from the vaulted walls, a grim Mackenzie rose to his feet. He spoke for almost three hours, to the continual accompaniment of applause and cries of encouragement from his followers. It was a wickedly effective speech, in which Mackenzie told the House that it was being asked to vote that black was white—that Sir Hugh Allan had simply given his money as a good member of the Conservative Party, though the country had been told "very plainly by that gentleman that he had no party views at all." Mackenzie wound up with a motion of censure.

When Tupper rose to reply after the dinner recess, the galleries were jammed. The entire first row of the Speaker's Gallery was occupied by Lady Dufferin and her entourage. It was whispered that the Governor General himself was disguised in the audience—a scandalous suggestion, since no representative of the British Crown could appear in the Commons without invitation. Actually, the eager Dufferin had pleaded with Macdonald "to arrange some little closet for me in the House . . . a 'Dionysius ear' no matter how dark or inconvenient." Macdonald was too wise to allow such a breach. The idea that a *Globe* reporter, or some sharp-eyed Member, might uncover the person of the Queen's representative trespassing, like a secret agent, on such hallowed ground at this moment of crisis must have sent shivers down his spine.

Tupper was a master of the bludgeon. The robust Nova Scotia surgeon with the hard, unblinking eyes and the creased, pugnacious face believed in one tactic in debate: attack with every weapon available; admit nothing; pound, hammer, swipe, thrust; if an opponent dare utter a word, batter him down.

He leaped to his feet, rejoicing that "the time has come when I and my colleagues are in a position to discuss this question in the presence of an independent Parliament." After that barefaced opening, he never let up: The country's prosperity was being affected. Canada's fair name was being tarnished. The real plan was to frustrate the building of the railway, nothing more. The sum Allan had contributed was "of an insignificant character." Public feeling was strongly with the Government. The charges were false and scandalous. All loyal people would regard the Opposition with suspicion. No intelligent person could fail to perceive that they had entirely abandoned their case.

This show of bravado put the House in a spirited mood and the Cumberland War Horse had to trample his way through a thicket of catcalls, derisive cheers, and whoops of laughter. Totally undeterred, he galloped on for more than three hours and then gave way to the hero of the Opposition, Lucius Seth Huntington.

With the clock past eleven, Huntington plunged into a spirited defense of his own position and a sardonic attack upon his adversaries, among whom Charles Tupper led all the rest.

At one point, Huntington had the House roaring with laughter as he pounced on Allan's statement to General Cass that he had suborned twenty-seven of Cartier's phalanx of forty-five Parliamentary supporters: "As a mere matter of curiosity, I should like to know who are the twenty-seven." (*Cheers and laughter.*) "We have in this House a Sir Hugh Allan brigade consisting of twenty-seven members. We have it upon Sir Hugh Allan's authority that they were sent here to vote for the Government, and if any of the twenty-seven desire to stand up, I will sit down" (*loud laughter*).

Huntington continued, in the same vein, to twit the Prime Minister for being on the bench, in the dock, and acting as prosecutor all at the same time. He wound up, at 1:30, with a glance at the wavering Government supporters, by declaring that "the time comes when they have to choose between fidelity to party and fidelity to country."

Thus, day after day, the debate seesawed. On Wednesday night, a storm broke over Ottawa and the citizens awoke to find their city shrouded in the first snow of winter. But a more important question than the weather hung on every lip: What on earth was wrong with Macdonald? Why had he remained silent? His boasted majority was drifting away "like leaves in the Valley of Vallombrosa" (Dufferin's literary style again); and yet he had not joined in the debate. His friends were full of angry entreaties. He *must* speak; only he could stem the tide. Stubbornly, the Prime Minister refused.

He had started to drink again. By Friday, when he had an interview with the Governor General, he was clearly not himself. Haggard in appearance, he was weak with fatigue and ill with strain. Many assumed that he did not feel himself fit to take up the cudgels in his party's defense.

But this was not the case. Macdonald was waiting for Blake to speak because he was tolerably certain that the Opposition was holding some damning piece of evidence, some document of "a fatally compromising character," that Cartier had written. Or perhaps he himself had dispatched some damaging letter during the election; the appalling thing was that the Prime Minister could not be sure whether he had or not, for he had been in his cups for so much of that period. He *must* have the last word. He could not afford to make his move and then have Blake follow him with such a *coup de grâce*.

It was only at the end of the week that the truth began to dawn upon him that, for once, he had been shamelessly outmaneuvered. Blake was holding back on purpose, calculating that Macdonald's physical condition would deteriorate to the point where he could not speak at all. There would be no fresh revelations; the Liberals were waging a war of attrition.

It was dangerously late. J. D. Edgar, the Liberal whip, sat in his place in the House and tried to figure how a division would go. Without the new Members from Prince Edward Island, he thought he could count on ninety-nine votes. He expected four more from the new province. That would give the Opposition 103 votes out of 206—exactly 50 per cent. Three others were wavering; if they thought the Government would be defeated they would change sides. Edgar had been working mightily, buttonholing Members, talking, cajoling, and promising. His most recent trophy was David Glass, a black-bearded Irish criminal lawyer, who defected with a ringing speech which cut deep. Later Glass would be rewarded for his defection.

Macdonald resolved to enter the arena on Monday night. The preliminaries were not propitious. That very afternoon, Lord Dufferin noted that he was tipsy. And Robert Cunningham, the Manitoba journalist who represented Marquette, rose on a question of order to declare that an Ottawa alderman had offered him a government job in the North West and a bribe of up to five thousand pounds if he would cast his vote for the Government. At this point the Prime Minister had to be dragged to his feet before he could reply. Yet in just three hours he would have to make the speech of a lifetime.

5 · *Macdonald versus Blake*

NINE O'CLOCK MONDAY EVENING, November 3, 1873. On Parliament Hill the corridors are choked, for the report has been abroad since early afternoon that Macdonald will speak at last. Scores have forgone their dinners in order to hold their places in the packed galleries. Even the sacrosanct backbenches have been invaded by strangers. Hundreds more, holding useless tickets, stand outside, straining for a whisper of the proceedings within. People have poured into the capital anticipating the coming verbal duel between John A. Macdonald and his dour adversary, Edward Blake.

In the parliamentary restaurant, a few stragglers are finishing their coffee. Suddenly the word comes: "Sir John is up!" The cups scatter as the stragglers race to the floor.

Now every Member is in his seat, except the exiled Louis Riel. The buzz of conversation has been cut off as cleanly as if a muffler were placed over the House. Macdonald has risen slowly to his feet, pale, nervous, and haggard, "looking as if a feather would knock him down." Then, for the next five hours, he proceeds to electrify the House.

Those who were there would never forget it. Many felt it was the greatest speech Macdonald had ever made; some said it was the greatest they had ever heard. Even the vituperative *Globe* called it "extraordinary." Sick, dispirited, and weary he might be; but somewhere within himself this homely, errant, and strangely attractive political animal had tapped a hidden well of energy. Some said it was the straight gin, which his colleague Peter Mitchell insisted that alternate page boys poured at regular intervals into the water glasses at his elbow (each thought the other was pouring water); but Macdonald was driven by another, more powerful stimulation. He was fighting, with his back to the wall, for his career; only he could salvage it.

He began very slowly and in a low voice, but, bit by bit, he warmed to his audience. Gradually, tone and manner changed, the voice became louder, more strident: Macdonald began to fight. He struck savagely at Huntington: the object of his resolution, he said, was "to kill the charter in England and to destroy it." (*Cheers and catcalls.*) He kept on. Huntington's course, cried Macdonald, was governed from behind the scenes by a "foreign and alien power." The Yankee-lover sat in the House "not only by alien money but by alien railway influence." Here, all of Macdonald's inbred distrust of the Americans was coming to the fore—the same dark apprehensions that would one day force a railway across seven hundred miles of rocky desert rather than see it diverted through a foreign land.

As the clock ticked its way past midnight, Macdonald continued to goad the Opposition: "They have spies and thieves and men of espionage who would pick your lock and steal your notebook." Why, Huntington had paid McMullen seventeen thousand dollars for the famous documents! Huntington was on his feet in an instant with a denial, amid cheers from the Opposition and calls of "Order!" from the Government benches.

"I challenge the Honourable gentleman to combat!" cried Huntington. "I dare him, Sir, on his responsibility to take a committee . . . I challenge him to stand up and take a committee!"

(*More cheering, more cries of "Order."*)

"I dare him to do it!" Huntington kept shouting.

"It is very evident," said Macdonald, "I hit a sore spot."

Yes, he said; he would call a committee to investigate the whole matter of election expenses. He knew of one gentleman opposite who had spent twenty-six thousand dollars getting elected. Another had spent thirty thousand dollars. Others had spent from five to ten thousand dollars.

"Hear! Hear!" called a puckish voice from the opposite side of the House. It belonged to David Blain, a Scottish-born lawyer from West York who had married the sister of a wealthy and prominent Toronto hardware merchant.

Macdonald picked up the cry and turned it against his taunter. He would, he said, prove the payment of money to an elector to vote for Blain.

"Not a cent went out of my pocket!" cried the outraged Blain.

"Well, you know, if a man has not a pocket, his wife has," retorted Macdonald wickedly.

By now he had the Opposition benches in an uproar.

"How dare you make such a statement?" the aggrieved Blain was shouting above the cries of "Shame!" and "Order!" Macdonald's supporters were cheering him on. Blain was crying, "You ought to be ashamed of yourself!" The Speaker stepped in and the Prime Minister moved on to other subjects, reiterating, again and again, that there was no bargain, no contract, between his Government and Allan—and that Allan's contribution was merely an election subscription.

It was past 1:30. Not a soul had left the House. From her seat in the Speaker's Gallery, Lady Dufferin gazed down with admiration. What a tale she would have to tell at Rideau Hall!

Macdonald, roused now to a kind of fever pitch, intoxicated as much by the crowds and the cheers as by the glass in his hand, was reaching the climax of his address. No illegal expenditure had yet been proved before any legal tribunal against any Member of Parliament, he declared. He challenged the House, he challenged the country, he challenged the world to read the charter—to read it line by line and word by word to see if there was in it anything that derogated from the rights of Canada (*loud cheers*) or if there was in it "any preponderance of any one man of these thirteen [directors] over another" (*more cheers*).

"Sir, I commit myself, the Government commits itself, to the hands of this House, and far beyond this House, it commits itself to the country at large." (*Loud cheers.*) "We have faithfully done our duty. We have fought the battle of Union. We have had Party strife setting Province against Province, and more than all, we have had in the greatest Province, the preponderating Province of the Dominion, every prejudice and sectional feeling that could be arrayed against us.

"I have been the victim of that conduct to a great extent; but I have fought the battle of Confederation, the battle of Union, the battle of the Dominion of Canada. I throw myself upon this House; I throw myself upon this country; I throw myself upon posterity and I believe that I know that, notwithstanding the many failings in my life, I shall have the voice of this country, and this House rallying round me." (*Cheers.*) "And, Sir, if I am mistaken in that, I can confidently appeal to a higher Court, the court of my own conscience, and to the court of posterity" (*cheers*).

"I leave it with this House with every confidence. I am equal to either fortune. I can see past the decision of this House either for or against me, but whether it be against me or for me, I know, and it is no vain boast to say so, for even my enemies will admit that I am no boaster, that there does not exist in Canada a man who has given more of his time, more of his heart, more of his wealth, or more of his intellect and power, such as it may be, for the good of this Dominion of Canada."

It was over. He sat down, utterly exhausted, while his supporters, and even some of the Opposition, cheered him to the roof. Lady Dufferin, who had brought along Lord Rosebery, a future Prime Minister of England, as her guest, was already scurrying off to Rideau Hall. There, until five that morning, she would regale her husband with a spirited account of the speech. Maudlin it might have been, but it was, by all odds, a personal triumph for the Prime Minister, producing at Rideau Hall, as Dufferin reported to him, "a continuous chorus of admiration from all my English friends." More important, the speech had solidified Macdonald's hold upon his own party, a hold which had become increasingly weak and aimless. Without it he could scarcely have continued as leader.

In spite of the late hour, the House continued to sit. Now Edward Blake hoisted his big frame from his chair and stood, erect and commanding, peering somberly through his small silver-rimmed spectacles at his enemies across the floor. To this tousled and scholarly-looking lawyer with the powerful build and the strange pallor the Liberal Party had entrusted its final volley. Blake was a nemesis to many, a friend to few, and an enigma to all, a kind of political Hamlet who, seething inwardly with personal ambition, showed a strange distaste for those laurels that were dangled before him. Generally considered by his colleagues as the man most likely to succeed, he never quite succeeded. He had been Premier of Ontario for scarcely a year when he quit to enter the federal arena. He could have led the Liberal Party, instead of Mackenzie (who had once served under him in Ontario), but he declined the opportunity. All his life he would dally over similar honors.

The key to this diffidence lay in Blake's extraordinary sensitivity; an imagined slight could cause him to burst into tears in public. He once astonished the Governor General by crying in his presence over a remark Macdonald had made about him. As a brilliant lawyer— perhaps the most brilliant of the century—he had been used to the deference of his judges and his peers. He could not accustom himself to the coarse invective and bitter imputations of personal motive that were a feature of the politics of his day. And this was singular because Blake himself, when in full voice, was perfectly capable of reducing an opponent to jelly.

The Liberal Party, seeking to cap the debate with climactic oratory, had chosen well. The speech Blake was about to give was exactly the kind the situation called for and exactly the kind at which he excelled. It was Blake's strength that he built his speeches, brick by brick, on solid fact and hard evidence—and his weakness that he generally gave his listeners too much of both. He kept on talking until there was absolutely nothing left to be said, a quality that did not endear him to his associates; after all, they had speeches of their own to make. Blake took nothing for granted. He verified every statement by reference to the original documents and, long after he had proved his case conclusively, he kept piling it on and on, until, as a colleague remarked ruefully, "everyone became dizzy scaling the heights to which he was being lifted." No wonder Blake constantly appeared pale, nervous, and exhausted. While others were relaxing in the smoking room, the Hamlet of the House was grubbing away in the parliamentary library.

The two speeches, Macdonald's and Blake's, laid side by side, are mirrors of the two totally disparate men who made them. Where Macdonald had been hotly emotional, Blake was icily dispassionate. Where Macdonald had been witty, Blake was earnest. Where Macdonald had been personal and subjective, Blake was aloofly analytical.

He stood now, as the cheering died, left hand sunk characteristically deep into his side pocket, totally immobile—Blake the Avenger. He had neither the time nor the inclination for humor. Instead he cut right to the bone, scooping up Macdonald's closing plea and turning it against him: "It was not to these high and elevating sentiments that the right honourable gentleman appealed during the election, it was not upon the intelligent judgment of the people he relied, but upon Sir Hugh Allan's money!" This blunt beginning, James Young recalled, electrified the House. Blake kept on until 2:30 that morning, in his soft, resonant voice, and then for another four hours the following afternoon and evening, building his case, fact piled upon fact, every sentence deftly turned, the phrases all arranged in ringing parallels.

The ladies of the Dufferin household, who had slipped out immediately after Macdonald took his seat the previous evening and returned the following afternoon to watch Blake worrying the evidence like a terrier, thought it all a bore. "Dull and uninteresting and not nearly so amusing and lively as Sir John's," was Dufferin's verdict on the speech. Then he added: "But it reads well." It read very well indeed in its pitiless logic—far better than Macdonald's impassioned and lachrymose remarks. And, to the faltering members, Blake's very lack of histrionics —no arm waving, no rising inflections—added weight to his words.

"I believe that this night or to-morrow night will be the end of twenty years of corruption." (*Cheers.*) "This night or to-morrow night will see the dawn of a brighter and better day in the administration of public affairs in this country" (*continued cheering*).

When Blake took his seat, even some Government Members rendered him the accolade of their applause as some Liberals had for Macdonald. Macdonald was not present. He lay upon a couch in a committee room, half conscious, ill with fatigue.

The vote was still in doubt. How effective had Blake been? Had he managed to cancel out the morale-building effects of Macdonald's passionate appeal? The Liberals had still not been able to force a vote; every man was in his place, waiting hour after hour for the division that would not come.

After Blake was finished all eyes turned to the proud Scots face of David Laird, the leader of the new group of Prince Edward Islanders. It was the first time he had addressed such a gathering. "Was there ever a maiden speech so fraught with doom?" George Ross asked. Laird did not keep his listeners waiting long. In a calm voice he declared his opposition to the Government, and again the Liberal benches rang with cheers.

Now it was the turn of another independent Member, Donald A. Smith of Selkirk Riding, Manitoba, the tough former fur trader, who was becoming a power in the Hudson's Bay Company and the Bank of Montreal. Smith normally supported the Government; moreover, he had been a member of Allan's board of directors, but it was by no means certain how he would vote. Macdonald's supporters were hesitant about approaching this frosty and imperious man who managed, throughout his career, to remain constantly in the limelight without ever appearing to seek it. Finally the Prime Minister was himself persuaded to talk to Smith. The meeting was not a success; when the Member was taken to Macdonald's office he found him drunk and belligerent. Smith was received with more curses than flattery. Nonetheless the feeling in the Government ranks was that Smith was on their side.

It was one o'clock in the morning when Smith rose to an expectant chamber. The future Lord Strathcona was not unaware of the drama. His speech was brief but he managed to squeeze from it every possible ounce of suspense. His tone was bland, his manner inoffensive: he did not consider that the First Minister took Allan's money with any corrupt motive. In fact he knew personally that Allan at one time had thought of giving up the charter. In every instance he knew the provisions were made more and more stringent against Sir Hugh.

The Government benches began to cheer. W. T. R. Preston, a longtime Liberal organizer, later claimed that some twenty Tories rushed to the parliamentary restaurant, popped open bottles of champagne, prepared to drink Smith's health, and sang "Rule, Britannia!"

But Smith was not finished. He felt that the leader of the Government was incapable of taking money from Allan for corrupt purposes. He would be most willing to vote for the Government—the cheers from the ministerial benches were now gleeful—*could he do so conscientiously.*

Consternation on the Conservative side! Cheers and laughter from the Opposition.

It was with great regret, Smith said, that he could not do so: there was no corruption but "a very grave impropriety."

In the parliamentary restaurant the champagne was left untasted. The Members skulked back to their seats as Smith sat down and the Speaker, with only the slightest tremor in his voice, adjourned the House. As the Commons broke up, there was a storm around Smith. The Members rushed toward him, cheering, handshaking, reviling, threatening. Smith remained, as always, totally imperturbable. He had been Macdonald's choice to deal with the ticklish problem of Riel during the Red River uprising; the Prime Minister had always admired him. Now Macdonald felt betrayed, for he had always held to the concept that party must come before principle. For most of the decade the name of Donald A. Smith was anathema to the Conservatives.

It was, of course, all over. In the lobbies and the downstairs restaurant there was a buzz of activity. Suddenly the atmosphere had changed; the vanquished took their defeat in good part, the conquerors refrained from being overjubilant.

Macdonald did not wait for the ignominy of a vote. He resigned the following day and went, remarkably cheerfully, into Opposition and the country simmered down. "As is the case with this somewhat volatile people, the excitement . . . has disappeared," Lord Dufferin reported to England. It was painful to lose his First Minister. "It cut me to the heart," he wrote, "that a career so creditable to himself, and so serviceable to his country . . . should have ended in such humiliation."

Macdonald was not a man to wear his heart on his sleeve for long. After he announced his resignation, he moved the adjournment of the House and then went to his office to ask his secretary to pack up his papers.

When he arrived home, he went straight to his upstairs bedroom. "Well, that's gone along with," he remarked casually to his wife.

"What do you mean?" she asked.

"Why, the Government has resigned," he replied. He slipped into his dressing gown and slippers, picked up two or three books from a nearby table, and stretched out on the bed.

"It's a relief to be out of it," he said. Then he opened a volume and began to read. Characteristically, he never again alluded to the subject; it was as if, to preserve his equilibrium, he had dismissed it from his mind.

The new leaders of the country did not. For most of the decade they would, on every possible occasion, taunt their opponents with the memory of the Pacific Scandal. It would influence their policies and their actions as it would influence those of the Conservatives. When, years later, a contract was finally signed for the construction of the Canadian Pacific Railway, the terms of the agreement and the choice of the principals, and indeed, their later relations with the Government, would in some degree be affected by the events of 1873.

When Mackenzie went to the country early in 1874, he was returned in a landslide. It was generally agreed that Macdonald was finished and that he would quickly resign and vanish from the political scene. The railway, it seemed, had been his nemesis. It had ruined his health, stained his honor, and wrecked his career. George Ross remembered thinking that a Macdonald revival would be a greater miracle than the passage of the Israelites through the Red Sea.

From Sir Hugh Allan, there was only silence in the years that followed the scandal. Taciturn and uncommunicative after his one terrible lapse, he left no memoir of his role in the affair, expressed no regret, delineated no hint of his emotions at the time. The closest he ever came to it was one night in his cavernous castle in Montreal when he was entertaining William Smith, a Deputy Minister of Marine and Fisheries. Warmed by Allan's hospitality and emboldened by Allan's brandy, Smith made an attempt to break through the crust of Allan's reticence.

"Sir Hugh," he ventured, "between ourselves, don't you think you made rather a mistake in mixing yourself up with John A. in that Pacific Scandal business?"

The shaggy knight of Ravenscrag stared into the fire. It was some time before he delivered himself of a definitive response. Finally . . . "Mebbe," he replied.

4

1 · *"Hurra! The jolly C.P.S.!"*

ALL THE TIME THE POLITICAL HURRICANE was gathering force in the settled East, hundreds of men were freezing, starving, sickening, and sometimes dying in the unexplored crannies of the new Canada as they tried to chart a route for the railway. On July 5, as Macdonald arrived in Toronto to launch the election campaign of 1872, a young man named George Hargreaves, deep in the rain forests of the Homathco, wrote in his diary that "there was more bad news from A Camp": two more men had been drowned, making a total of five that summer. On August 7, the day on which Allan wrote his compromising letter to General Cass, seven men perished in a forest fire in the Nepigon country north of Lake Superior. On December 27, when George McMullen was dining in the Russell House with his fellow conspirator, Senator Asa B. Foster, another survey party found itself marooned at fifty below zero on Lake Superior's frozen shores. On April 15 the following spring, when the Government was preparing the Oaths Bill for the House, Robert Rylatt, in the Athabasca country, was scribbling in his diary that "the quantity of blood discharged somewhat alarms me"; he was suffering from acute scurvy.

No life was harsher than that suffered by members of the Canadian Pacific Survey crews. None was less rewarding. Underpaid, overworked, exiled from their families, deprived of their mail, sleeping in slime and snowdrifts, suffering from sunstroke, frostbite, scurvy, fatigue, and the tensions that always rise to the surface when weary and dispirited men are thrown together for long periods of isolation, the surveyors kept on, year after year. They explored great sections of Canada. The first engineers scaled mountains that had never before been climbed, crossed lakes that had never known a white man's paddle, and forded rivers that were not on any map. They walked with a uniform stride developed through years of habit, measuring the distances as they went, checking altitudes with an aneroid barometer slung around the neck and examining the land with a practiced gaze, always seeing in the mind's eye the finished line of steel—curves, grades, valley crossings, bridges and trestles, tunnels, cuts and fills. In the first six years of the Canadian Pacific Survey, forty-six thousand miles of Canada were reconnoitered and blazed in this manner.

Twelve thousand of these miles were then laboriously charted, foot by foot, by scores of survey parties. Axmen, following the pathfinders' blazes, hacked the lines clear of brush. The chainmen who followed meticulously divided the distances into hundred-foot sections, each marked by a stake. Behind the chainmen came the transit men, calculating the angle of each bend and estimating, by triangulation, those distances which could not be measured by a chain. Behind the transits, the rodmen and levelers worked, reckoning the altitudes and inscribing them on bench marks at half-mile intervals. By 1877 there were twenty-five thousand of these bench marks and more than six hundred thousand chainmen's stakes scattered across Canada from the Shield to the Pacific. At this point the surveys had cost three and one half million dollars and the lives of thirty-eight men by drowning, forest fire, exposure, illness, and shipwreck.

Sandford Fleming, who took charge as Engineer-in-Chief in April, 1871, had by midsummer dispatched twenty-one survey parties, totaling eight hundred men, across the country. His task was not easy. A special kind of man was needed, and, as Fleming reported after the first season, it was impossible to find enough of them: "Many of those we were obliged to take, subsequent events proved, were unequal to the very arduous labour they had to undergo, causing a very considerable delay and difficulty in pushing the work."

"The leveller in party S is physically unequal to the hard work that I shall unquestionably require from all my staff," Walter Moberly, the pioneer surveyor of British Columbia, scribbled in his journal when he reached the Athabasca country in November, 1872. "He is a capital man, nevertheless I *must* have strong men for my work."

But even if enough good men could have been found, it is doubtful if Fleming would have been able to employ them. Political influences entered into the question: various sections of the country had to be considered, different nationalities and creeds had to be consulted. Then there was the problem of patronage; there was constant pressure on Fleming to appoint the friends or protégés of Members of Parliament or of Senators.

Often appointments were made over Fleming's head at Cabinet level. The Chief Engineer found he had people of whom he had never heard working for him; such appointees could not easily be fired for inefficiency. Fleming did not bother to protest. As he put it, "I knew that patronage had to be respected." Sometimes work had to be invented just to keep the political appointees busy.

One man Fleming was apparently forced to put up with for political reasons was the surly photographer-explorer Charles Horetzky, who was given his job as a result of the intervention of Sir Charles Tupper. Horetzky, after parting from Macoun at Fort St. James, had pushed on westward toward Port Simpson, "an irksome and hazardous journey." When he returned to Ottawa a fanatical advocate of the Pine Pass–Port Simpson route, which he had explored, Fleming dismissed him. Horetzky always insisted that Fleming acted out of pure jealousy: "I should have made no allusion to the Pine River route and should have known that opposition to the Chief Engineer's pet theory . . . was a signal for my dismissal." Fleming's version differed: "It was sometimes necessary to employ persons who were not adapted to the work or qualified to be chief engineers." Whatever the reasons, Horetzky ingratiated himself with the new administration and was soon back on the job again, exploring his favorite region along the northern British Columbia coast. There was nothing, apparently, that Fleming could do. In the summer of 1875, Marcus Smith, in charge of surveys in British Columbia and as irascible an engineer as ever existed, had a raging row with Horetzky at Waddington Depot near the head of the Bute Inlet. Smith arrived to find that Horetzky had been there for ten days, contrary to instructions. When Smith inquired about this, "he flew at me like an enraged tiger, defied me in my instructions and said he was going home to Ottawa." Smith had several witnesses to the scene, but Horetzky kept his job until the administration changed in 1878.

After the first year of surveys, Fleming reported that it was impossible to obtain "the class of men required." That year two crews, working through the unexplored and impenetrable country between Ottawa and Fort Garry, simply gave up the ghost. One party had had enough by late summer; the second, on learning that they would be required to stay out all winter, "suffered a few days of cold and snow and then promptly trooped in to Fort Garry." There was a seller's market in survey labor and, like it or not, Fleming and his staff had to retain incompetents.

"I wish you would find out what Walter Dewdney is doing," Marcus Smith wrote to a subordinate, Joseph Hunter, in May of 1875. "I heard last week that [he] was seen on the wagon road blind drunk and making an ass of himself." Since Dewdney's brother Edgar was Member of Parliament for Yale and a strong political power in British Columbia, the erring Walter could scarcely be dismissed.

The wonder was that anyone worked on the surveys at all. In spite of the difficulty of getting men each season, there was little long-term job security, even for experienced engineers. Crews were discharged at the end of the summer, left without winter work, and re-engaged the following spring. When the work began to diminish toward the end of the decade, there was real hardship. "There is much distress among the engineers, etc., of the staff who were dismissed last spring," Marcus Smith, then Fleming's deputy, wrote in February, 1878, to his chief, who was on leave in England. The men had been set adrift on a month's notice "and have not a shilling to maintain their families. If all the surveying staff is now dismissed there will be wholesale distress."

It was a lonely, remote existence the surveyors led in the field, cut off from news of family, friends, or the world at large, in a land where the native rites and customs were as foreign as those of an Oriental satrapy. In the spring of 1875, Henry Cambie, exploring the east branch of the Homathco, came upon Indians so removed from civilization that many of the women had never seen a beard "and would not believe that mine really grew on my chin." Jason Allard, one of Walter Moberly's men, unwittingly accepted an invitation to visit an Indian lodge on the Fiddle River and made the mistake of sitting on a bear rug next to a strapping maiden. Too late he realized that this was tantamount to an offer of marriage. In desperation he restored her to her father by giving him a handsome finger ring.

Yet out they went, year after year, men who were for the most part tough, intelligent, and uncomplaining. They drank anything they could get, and when they drank, they sang their theme song to the tune of *"Les Deux Gendarmes"*—sang it from the raveled coastline of British Columbia to the gloomy granites of northern Ontario—the song of the Canadian Pacific Survey:

> *Far away from those we love dearest,*
> *Who long and wish for home,*
> *The thought of whom each lone heart cheereth,*
> *As 'mid these North-west wilds we roam,*
> *Yet still each one performs his duty*
> *And gaily sings:*

Tra, la, la, la, la, la, la, la, la, la, la, la,
  Hurra! The jolly C.P.S.!
They're at home upon Superior's shore,
  Hurra! we'll drink to them success,
And a safe return once more.

In 1872, it was a nightmare just to reach that "home upon Superior's shore." Charles Aeneas Shaw, who was with the Canadian Pacific Survey from the beginning until the last stake was driven, graphically recalled his initiation in November of that year. Shaw, a wiry eighteen-year-old at the time, "keen to learn and a hog for work," was hired as a packer under William Murdoch, seeking to locate a line west from Prince Arthur's Landing. The trick was to try to reach the Landing before winter sealed off the lake. The group attempted it first in a cockleshell of a steamer, the *Mary Ward*. It foundered on a reef in a howling blizzard, drowning three of the party. The survivors returned to Toronto, picked up new kits, and set off again. Murdoch made his way overland to Duluth, where he offered to pay as much as twenty-five hundred dollars for a tugboat to take his men up the lake. Conditions were so desperate that no seasoned skipper would attempt the crossing. Notwithstanding, the party bought a small fishing boat and started off in mid-December, rowing and sailing to their destination. The temperature sank to fifty-two below zero—so cold that each crewman had to chip from the blades of his oars a ball of ice the size of a man's head. They crept along the shoreline, sleeping in the snow at night, existing on frozen pork and hardtack and even surviving a full-force gale. When the lake froze on New Year's Day, they finally abandoned the boat, built toboggans out of strips handsawn from frozen birch logs, and hiked with their supplies the last fifty miles to Prince Arthur's Landing.

Such hardships were commonplace. Fleming's friend J. H. E. Secretan, a man who liked his food, was reduced to eating rose hips washed down with swamp water during a survey near Lake Nepigon in 1871. In the same year seven members of a survey supply party were lost near Jackfish River as the result of a forest fire so hot that the very soil was burned away. Only one body was found. Of the remainder there was no trace, except for six holes scratched out of a nearby swamp and apparently abandoned when the smoke grew too thick.

In the same area north of Lake Superior, the problem of supplies resulted in costly delays and bitter recriminations. Henry Carre, in charge of a party working out of Lac des Îles in the Thunder Bay area, found himself in country through which no white man had ever been. He would have finished his survey had he been properly supplied but had to turn back to Prince Arthur's Landing; otherwise "I verily believe the whole party would have been starved to death." William Kirkpatrick, working near Long Lake north of Superior the same year, had to take his party away from surveying to pick blueberries. For a week the group had nothing else to eat. In 1875, Kirkpatrick headed a party of more than thirty men locating the line from Wabigoon. Winter set in but no toboggans, tents, clothing, or footwear arrived. The resourceful Kirkpatrick made forty pairs of snowshoes and thirty toboggans with his own hands, fashioned a tent out of canvas, and scrounged another one, made of skins, from the Indians.

In the Thompson River country of central British Columbia, forty miles out of Kamloops, Roderick McLennan's survey party lost almost all its pack animals in the winter of 1871. Eighty-six of them, McLennan reported to Fleming, died from cold, hunger, or overwork.

An even worse winter expedition was the exploration launched in 1875 by Edward W. Jarvis, who was charged with examining the Smoky River Pass in the Rockies. Fleming had already settled on the Yellow Head as the ideal pass for the railway, but this did not prevent him from carefully examining half a dozen others, just in case. Jarvis set off in January from Fort George with his assistant, C. F. Hanington, Alec Macdonald in charge of dog trains, and six Indians and twenty dogs.

Both Jarvis and Hanington left graphic accounts of the ordeal, illuminated by uncanny episodes: the spectral figure of Macdonald knocking on the door of their shack in forty-nine below, sheathed in ice from head to toe; the lead dog, who made a feeble effort to rise, gave one spasmodic wag of his tail and rolled over dead, his legs frozen stiff to brisket and flanks; and the auditory hallucinations experienced one night by the entire party—the distinct but ghostly sound of a tree being felled just two hundred yards away but no sign of snowshoes or axman-ship the following morning.

The party traveled light, with only two blankets per man and a single piece of light cotton sheeting for a tent. They moved through a land that had never been mapped. A good deal of the time they had no idea where they were. They camped out in temperatures that dropped to fifty-three below zero. They fell through thin ice and had to clamber out, soaked to the skin, their snowshoes still fastened to their feet. They stumbled down box canyons and found the way blocked by frozen waterfalls, two hundred feet high. They suffered from *mal de raquette*, a kind of lameness brought on by the constant need to wear snowshoes.

One day they experienced a formidable change of temperature—from forty-two below zero to forty above—which produced a strange exhaustion, as if they were suddenly plunged into the tropics. One morning, while mushing down a frozen river, they turned a corner and saw an abyss yawning before them: the entire party, dogs and men, were perched on the ice ledge of a frozen waterfall, two hundred and ten feet high; the projection itself was no more than two feet thick. One evening they made camp below a blue glacier when, without warning, great chunks of it gave way; above them they beheld "masses of ice and rock chasing one another and leaping from point to point as if playing some weird, gigantic game." A chunk of limestone, ten feet thick, scudded past them, tearing a tunnel through the trees before it plunged into the river.

By this time it was March. The dogs were dying daily. Even the Indians were "in a mournful state of despair, declaring that they . . . would never see their homes again and weeping bitterly."

On March 15, Hanington described Jarvis as "very thin, very white and very much subdued." When they had reached the Smoky Pass, some time before, Jarvis had entertained grave doubts about proceeding further, but Hanington had said he would rather starve than turn back. It began to look as if he would: "I have been thinking of 'the dearest spot on earth to me'—of our Mother and Father and all my brothers and sisters and friends—of the happy days at home—of all the good deeds I have left undone and all the bad ones committed. If ever our bones will be discovered, when and by whom. If our friends will mourn long for us or do as is often done, forget us as soon as possible. In short, I have been looking death in the face."

Jarvis described "the curious sensation of numbness, which began to take hold of our limbs," as they pushed slowly forward on their snow-shoes, giving the impression of men marking time in slow motion. Yet they made it. Hanington had lost thirty-three pounds; Jarvis was down to a bony 125. The food given them when they finally reached Edmonton produced spasms of dysentery and vomiting. Still they kept on, setting off once more across the blizzard-swept prairie for Fort Garry. All told, they spent 116 days on the trail, traveling 1,887 miles, 932 of those miles on snowshoes and 332 of them with all their goods on their backs, the dogs being dead.

Why did they do it? Why did any of them do it? Not for profit, certainly, there was little enough of that; nor for adventure, there was too much of that. The answer seems clear from their actions and their words: each man did it for glory, spurred on by the slender but ever-present hope that someday his name would be enshrined on a mountain peak or a river or an inlet, or—glory of glories—would go into the history books as the one who had bested all others and located the route for the impossible railway.

2 · *The bitter tea of Walter Moberly*

ONE MAN WHO THOUGHT HE HAD THE route and who spent the twilight of his life recalling, with increasing bitterness but not always with great accuracy, the attempts to "humbug" the route away from him, was Walter Moberly.

Moberly was working in Salt Lake City in 1871 when the news came of the pact with British Columbia. He went immediately to Ottawa, where his enemy, Alfred Waddington, was already trying to promote a railway company. Moberly hated Waddington—the verb is not too strong—for the same reason he hated anyone who tried to promote a railway route to the Pacific that did not agree with his own conception. Waddington was a fanatic on the subject of Bute Inlet as a terminus for the railway. It was "his" inlet; he had explored it. Moberly was equally fanatical on the subject of the Eagle Pass, the Fraser River, and Burrard Inlet. That was *his* inlet; he had trudged along its shores before any white man had settled there. He apparently viewed the massacre of Waddington's survey party as a salutary act, for he was incensed when some of the murderers were hanged.

Surveyors tended to fall in love with the virgin territory they explored. Moberly had fallen in love with the Eagle Pass, which he had discovered and named in the summer of 1865 as a result of watching a flight of eagles winging their way through the mountains. Moberly knew that eagles generally follow a stream or make for an opening in the alpine wall. Eventually he followed the route of the birds and discovered the pass he was seeking through the Gold Range. According to his own romantic account, he finally left his companions, after a sleepless night, and made his way down into the valley of the Eagle River, where he hacked out a blaze on a tree and wrote the prescient announcement: "This is the Pass for the Overland Railway."

Moberly had gone to school in Barrie with a tawny-haired, angular girl named Susan Agnes Bernard. In Ottawa, Susan Agnes, now Lady Macdonald, invited her former schoolmate to lunch. The weathered surveyor with the ragged beard and the burning eyes used the occasion to press his particular vision of the railroad on the Prime Minister of Canada. He insisted, with superb confidence, that he could tell Macdonald exactly where to locate the line from the prairies to the seacoast.

Not only that, but "you can commence construction of the line six weeks after I get back to British Columbia."

"Of course," Moberly added, "I don't know how many millions you have, but it is going to cost you money to get through those canyons."

Macdonald was impressed. Moberly was a fighter who came from a family of fighters. He was half Polish; his maternal grandfather had been in command of the Russian artillery at Borodino in 1812. His father was a Royal Navy captain. As a young engineer working on the Northern Railway, Moberly was fired by tales of the frontier which he heard firsthand from Paul Kane, the noted painter of Indians. The Fraser gold rush of 1858 lured him west. Eventually, he became assistant surveyor general for British Columbia. It was in this role that he discovered the Eagle Pass in the Gold Range, later called the Monashees.

When he returned to British Columbia, with the Prime Minister's blessing, as district engineer in charge of the region between Shuswap Lake and the eastern foothills of the Rockies, he was in his fortieth year, a man of legendary endurance. He had a passion for dancing, and when he emerged from the wilderness would dance the night out in Victoria. He loved to drink and he loved to sing but, as a friend recalled, "no amount of relaxation and conviviality would impair his staying power when he plunged into the wilds again."

He was as lithe as a cat and had as many lives, as his subsequent adventures demonstrated. Once, while on horseback in the Athabasca country, he was swept into a river and carried two hundred feet downstream. He seized an overhanging tree, hoisted himself from the saddle, and clambered to safety. On a cold January day he fell through the ice of Shuswap Lake and very nearly drowned, for the surface was so rotten it broke under his grasping hands. Nearly exhausted from his struggle in the icy water, Moberly managed to pull off his snowshoes, hold one in each hand, and climb to safety by spreading his arms on the ice. Another time, in a sprucebark canoe, on the Columbia River, he gave chase to a bear, cornered it against a riverbank, put an old military pistol against its ear, and shot it dead, seizing it by the hind legs before it sank—all to the considerable risk and apprehension of his companions in the frail craft.

Moberly, in short, was a character: egotistical, impulsive, stubborn, independent of spirit. He could not work with anyone he disagreed with; and he disagreed with anyone who believed there was any other railway route to the Pacific than the one that had been developing in his mind for years. Moberly had been thinking about the railway longer than most of his colleagues, ever since his explorations in 1858. Now, thirteen years later, he set out to confirm his findings. He began his explorations on July 20, 1871, the very day the new province entered Confederation.

Moberly took personal charge of his favorite area, bounded by the Eagle Pass of the Gold Range and the Howse Pass in the Rockies, just north of the Kicking Horse. Between these two mountain chains lay an island of formidable peaks, the apparently impassable Selkirks. It was in the hairpin-shaped trench around this barrier that the Columbia flowed, first northwest, then southeast again, until it passed within a few miles of its source, Columbia Lake. It was Moberly's theory that the railway would cut through the notch of the Howse Pass, circumvent the Selkirks by following the Columbia Valley, and then thread through the Gold Range by way of the Eagle Pass, which led to Kamloops and the canyons of the Fraser.

Moberly spent the next eight months in the mountains and trenches of British Columbia. He traveled down the olive-green Columbia with a crazy flotilla of leaky boats, burned-out logs and bark canoes, patched with old rags and bacon grease. He trudged up and down the sides of mountains, clinging to the reins of pack horses, accompanied always by a faithful company of Indians for whom he sometimes showed a greater respect than he did for white men. ("The Indian," he wrote, ". . . when properly handled and made to feel that confidence and trust is reposed in him, will work in all kinds of weather, and should supplies run short, on little or no food, without a murmur; not so the generality of white men.")

When winter began, he set off on snowshoes for New Westminster, a distance of more than four hundred miles, as casually as if he were heading off on a pleasant Sunday hike. He went straight over the top of the glacier-capped Selkirks, seeking a practical pass, and was almost buried by an avalanche en route. New Year's Day, 1872, found him all alone, in an abandoned trapper's hut, scrawling in his diary: "I think it . . . one of the most wretched and dreary places I ever saw . . . this was the most wretched New Year's Day I ever spent." He did not find what he was seeking: "I found there was not any practicable pass through the Selkirk Range," he reported to Sandford Fleming.

When Moberly emerged from the mountains, he had so thoroughly convinced himself that his route was the only conceivable one that he determined to take it upon himself to push forward immediately in locating the actual line through the Howse Pass. He would get permission later—he "never doubted for a moment" that Fleming would see it his way; going to Ottawa to discuss the matter would only be "a useless waste of time."

Actually he did have some communication with his superior, but in his single-mindedness he misread it. Fleming agreed that a trial line should be run through the Howse Pass, to see if it was at all practicable for a railway. Moberly had already planned something far more ambitious: "a careful location survey," which is the detailed kind that engineers make when they have finally, through exploration and trial lines, decided on the eventual route. Moberly, who had made the most cursory investigation of the pass from its summit to the Columbia, was hopelessly seduced. He seized on Fleming's telegram, "which led me to infer that the line I had taken so many years to explore and discover, and which I was quite confident would be the best to adopt for the proposed transcontinental railroad, would be adopted." He set about hiring extra men, engaging trains of pack animals, and buying thousands of dollars' worth of supplies, great quantities of which he had cached at the Eagle Pass since he reckoned his men would spend two seasons locating the line and would stay out all winter.

Four hours before Moberly and his party were scheduled to leave Victoria for the hinterland, he received a staggering blow. The Lieutenant-Governor, Joseph W. Trutch, whose brother John was a colleague of Moberly's, had a telegram for him. It was literally the eleventh hour, since Moberly's boat was scheduled to leave at 3 A.M. When Moberly tore open the message, his head must have reeled: it was from Fleming, announcing that the Yellow Head Pass had officially been adopted for the route of the Canadian Pacific Railway and that the Howse Pass survey was to be abandoned. He was to move his survey parties north by way of the Athabasca Pass and then take charge of and make a survey through the Yellow Head. All of Moberly's dreams dissolved at that moment. "His" route was not to be *the* route, after all.

Bitterly disappointed, the surveyor rushed to Portland, Oregon, where he tried to buy his way out of his costly contracts. But most of the supplies had already been dispatched to remote mountain areas where they could never be used. Seven thousand dollars' worth were abandoned forever at the Eagle Pass.

There was another problem: Moberly needed to hire pack trains to move men and supplies from the Columbia north to the Athabasca country. It was late in the season; most trains had been engaged far in advance when there was a buyer's market in renting pack animals. If the packers knew of his dilemma they would charge extortionate rates. Moberly would have to outflank the packers, who were moving toward

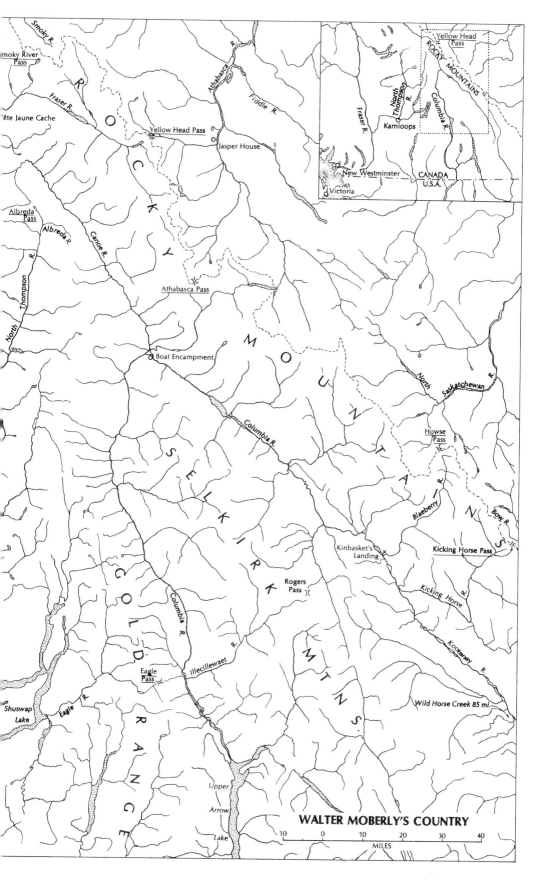

WALTER MOBERLY'S COUNTRY

Kinbasket's Landing at the foot of the Howse Pass, race ahead of them, intercept them, and re-engage the horses for the Yellow Head survey before their owners learned about the official change of plans.

He set off, first through Oregon by stagecoach (which broke down) and by steamboat (which sank), and then up through the state of Washington on horseback. He re-entered British Columbia in the Kootenay country, successfully intercepted the packers on the way, hired them all, together with four hundred horses, and then, hacking a trail as he went, reached the Columbia. With a heavy heart, he began moving his survey parties north to the Athabasca country and the despised Yellow Head Pass where Fleming had arranged to meet him on his trip with Grant from ocean to ocean. "Move" is scarcely an adequate verb to describe Moberly's transit: the pack trail had to be carved, foot by foot, out of the tangle of fallen cedars that barred the way up through the cavernous valleys of the Columbia, Thompson, and Albreda rivers.

By early September (election day had come and gone in Canada; Allan had already made the fatal pact with Cartier) Moberly had reached the Yellow Head. One day, a few miles west of Jasper House, he came upon some fresh tracks, which the Indians sneered at as those of *Moneasses*—"men of the east." A short time later, he ran into the Reverend Dr. George Monro Grant, "a long stick in his hand, driving some worn-out and very dilapidated pack animals."

In Grant's *Ocean to Ocean* there is no hint of the disagreeable encounter that took place that week between Fleming, the Engineer-in-Chief, and his errant British Columbia deputy. Moberly's "was the first face we had seen since leaving St. Ann's," Grant wrote. "To meet him was like re-opening communication with the world. . . . How welcome he was, we need not say!" That evening Fleming treated the group to a glass of punch and a cigar. Toasts were drunk to Queen and Country and Moberly put Grant in a high good humor because he had some oatmeal and the minister could, for the first time in many days, enjoy a Sunday breakfast of porridge.

Fleming waited until after the Sunday service before his interview with Moberly. It must have been painful. Fleming was taken aback at the slow progress made on the surveys and by Moberly's reckless spending. Tons of supplies left forever at Eagle Pass! "It seemed to me as if some country store had been bought out when I first saw the account," Fleming later recalled. And four hundred pack horses! The chief engineer could not understand the need for so many. At that point his impulse was to fire Moberly. He could not afford to: somebody had to take charge at the Yellow Head and push the surveys forward. But Fleming made no secret of his dissatisfaction.

Moberly's attitude toward Fleming's verbal spanking was one of disgust, not with himself but with Fleming for his own "unpatriotic action" in abandoning his pet line. To Moberly, the decision to use the other pass was little short of treason. By his own account, he was on the point of leaving the service, "which I should have done there and then had I not known the very critical position my men and animals were in on their way via the Athabasca Pass and how much they relied on me to see them safely through."

A decade later, the embittered Moberly came very close to suggesting publicly that his chief had tried to starve him in the Yellow Head by ordering all purchases stopped. "Had such an order ever reached me I should simply not have gone to the Yellow Head Pass, for I would not have taken a number of men into the mountains to starve to death when winter set in."

As Moberly took his leave of the Fleming party, he was himself plagued by worry over the slow progress of the surveys under his command. Ill fortune seemed to dog his footsteps; the survey parties were taking an unconscionable time to arrive from the Howse Pass. Actually, with Moberly so long gone they had simply settled down to wait out the winter. Moberly got them moving again: it would be touch and go if they could get through the high Athabasca Pass before the blizzards blocked it and cut them off from their work at the Yellow Head.

Another party had lost six precious weeks because its supplies had unaccountably failed to reach it from Victoria. The men, reduced to a diet of bread and tea, refused to work; the party became disorganized and spent a month and a half hunting game, at a cost of nearly eighty dollars a day in wages. "I can only say," Moberly wrote in his diary, "there has been some shameful mismanagement somewhere." It later turned out that the purveyor and accountant there—another political appointee—was incompetent. There were drafts on the department for $130,000 and vouchers for less than one-fifth of that amount. Moberly, as the man in charge, took most of the blame.

By this time Fleming had lost all confidence in Moberly. He sent him a message by Indian runner ordering him back to Kamloops. He had changed his mind, he said, about the surveys of the line: Moberly was to place the supplies and pack animals in the charge of another man in whom Moberly later related he had no confidence. Fleming was convinced that this raw tactic would force Moberly to quit the service, but his stubborn deputy decided simply to ignore the order and press on with the survey of the Yellow Head come hell or blizzard. His later explanation was that "the instructions conveyed in the letter were too childish to be followed." He would carry on the work according to his own best judgment and would obey orders "when I could see they were sensible but not otherwise. . . . I went on the survey for business, not to be made a fool of."

Fleming tried again after the new year. In another message, delivered by half-breed runner, he informed Moberly that Marcus Smith had superseded him and would be in charge of all exploratory surveys in British Columbia. To Moberly "this was joyful news . . . for I saw the way clear to get out of the distasteful occupation of making useless surveys." He did some further work for Smith, who wanted to see if there was a suitable pass up the North Thompson. Moberly reported (one suspects with a certain amount of glee) "an impenetrable wall of rock, snow and ice." Then he quit the service and left for Ottawa, where he was "very coldly received by the Engineer-in-Chief." He lingered in the capital waiting for Fleming to sign his expense accounts. Fleming rejected the first audit and passed the accounts on to a second auditor, who went over them again. They were passed at last, but not until the frustrated Moberly had been forced to borrow money to pay for his room and board.

Disheartened by his experience, Moberly moved to Winnipeg, where he soon busied himself at the comparatively prosaic job of building the city's first sewers. For the rest of his life he complained bitterly about the treatment he had received at the hands of Fleming. Eventually the railway did go south, as he said it should, but to Moberly's disgust the railway builders discarded the Howse Pass in favor of the Kicking Horse.

There was one triumph, however, of which he could not be deprived. Twenty years after he discovered the Eagle Pass, the last spike of the CPR was driven at Craigellachie, almost on the very spot where Moberly, in a moment of clairvoyance, had chalked on a blazed tree his prophecy that the overland railway would have to come that way.

3 · *That "old devil" Marcus Smith*

Marcus Smith, the man who took over all surveys in British Columbia in the spring of 1873, was without doubt the most controversial figure the Canadian Pacific Survey produced. No two men in the service seemed to agree about him. Moberly liked him. C. F. Hanington wrote that "he was a wonderful man to my mind." Thomas Henry White, another colleague, talked rather ambiguously about "the fire and sparkle of Marcus Smith's genius." Harry Armstrong, who worked first in Smith's drafting room in Ottawa and became his friend, described him as "a very crabbed and impatient man, though withal very kind of heart." Later Armstrong, by then a full-fledged engineer, ran into him on Lake Superior and recalled that he was "still the same, brusque, irritable man." Some of the men who worked under Smith used harsher terms. Robert Rylatt, a member of Moberly's Howse Pass survey party, wrote in a fury that Smith was "a hard, unjust and arbitrary wretch." In the summer of 1872, a young rodman named Edgar Fawcett, toiling in the Homathco country, called him an "old devil" and wrote in his diary that "I did not come here to be blackguarded by Mr. Smith for $45 a month." And when Smith announced he was leaving the party and moving on, another member wrote in *his* diary that it was "the best news we have heard since we left Victoria."

Smith was a pretty good hater himself. He referred to one of Roderick McLennan's traveling companions, a man named Wright, as "a Yankee sneak." Henry J. Cambie was also a sneak and, in addition, "a little toady," as was James Rowan, Fleming's assistant, and, by inference, Fleming himself. Fleming's successor, Collingwood Schreiber, was "mean and inferior," Major A. B. Rogers was "a thorough fraud," and Charles Horetzky was "a crazy, conceited fellow." Smith was suspicious of all politicians: Alexander Mackenzie was dishonest, in his view; the Governor General, of all people, he suspected of railway land speculation; and John A. Macdonald would "sacrifice anything or anybody to smooth down difficulties."

Smith reserved his choicest terms of abuse and his most withering contempt for those who dared to oppose the route to the Pacific in which he had come, by 1877, to believe. This route led from the Pine Pass southwest through Fort George, across the Chilcoten Plains to the headwaters of the Homathco, and thence down that turbulent river to its mouth at Bute Inlet. Smith quarreled bitterly with anyone who favored any other line for the railway. He fought with Fleming because Fleming continued a strong advocate of the Yellow Head Pass–Fraser River–Burrard Inlet route. He fought with Cambie because Cambie sent back favorable reports on both the Fraser River route and the northern alternative from Yellow Head to Port Simpson. He was angered by Horetzky, who also wanted the railway to keep to the north and come out to the mouth of the Kitlope. He became such a monomaniac on the subject of "his" route that, when he took Sandford Fleming's place during the latter's leave of absence, Mackenzie, who was both Prime Minister and Minister of Public Works, refused to talk to him.

Smith employed every device he knew to force the Government to accept the Pine Pass–Bute Inlet route. He wrote to Members of Parliament, dispatched secret surveys into the north, arranged for letters and articles in the newspapers, and bombarded everybody, including two Prime Ministers, with his views. He was darkly suspicious of conspiracies, which he believed were being mounted against him, and he accused Fleming of supressing his reports (as did Horetzky) out of jealousy. Fleming bore it all with remarkable equanimity, at least in public, but he did his best to get rid of Smith. At one point he thought he *had* fired him. Smith stuck around. Fleming acted as if he did not exist. Smith may have been erratic but he was a good engineer and he was a born survivor; long after Fleming himself had been eased out of the service, he was still part of the Canadian Pacific Survey, though his position was less exalted.

In 1872, when Smith first entered the long fiord of Bute Inlet and then made his way up the Homathco—"a scene of gloomy grandeur, probably not met with in any other part of the world"—it was love at first sight, as it had been with Moberly and Horetzky and all the other enthusiasts who championed a line of route, including, indeed, the Engineer-in-Chief himself. Surveyors' diaries are seldom gems of literary art. A tired man, squatting on the edge of a riverbank, scribbling with a pencil stub in a greasy notebook, is anything but poetic; but Smith, who had a habit of noting the curious trivia around him—the character of Indian communities, for instance, or the sight of a young native girl throwing off her shift coquettishly and bathing in the river—waxed positively lyrical about the region: "Scene awfully grand—the river rushing and foaming in a narrow chain between walls of rock, a frowning cliff overhanging all and the snow capped mountains piercing the clouds and hidden by curtains of glaciers glittering blue and cold in the sunlight."

Later, he wrote for an official government report an equally eloquent description of the Chilcoten meadows—"the silence of the plains only broken by the silent tread of the Indian or the sad wail of the solitary loon"—and of the Homathco canyon, "where the awful grandeur of the mountains, the roar of the waters, and the constant sense of danger kept the nerves strong and the mind active."

His description of the "charming" mile-wide valleys of the Chilcoten and Chilanko rivers had the ring of a hopelessly infatuated suitor composing a paean to his intended. He wrote of the bottom lands, ripe and mellow with bunch growth, with the clear streams meandering through them in graceful curves, of the pale, grayish green of the grasses "in agreeable harmony with the dark foliage of the spruce," and of the "picturesque irregularity of the evergreens," the whole "forming a scene of pristine beauty rarely to be met with." Compared with the spare, routine prose of some of his colleagues, Smith's on occasion seemed almost sensual.

Smith had just turned fifty-six—a stubby man with a barrel chest, tough as shaganappi and bristly as a wart hog—when he first clambered up the dripping cliffs of the Homathco. His hooded eyes, drooping mustache, and grizzled beard gave him a querulous, almost dour look. Topley, the Ottawa photographer who managed to make most of his subjects look as if they had been stuffed and mounted, did not quite succeed with Marcus Smith. There remains upon that sturdy but weather-ravaged face a fleeting expression of slight distaste. One can almost see the subject shifting impatiently in the prop studio chair and blurting out: "Look ye [a favorite expression], does it have to take so damned *long*?"

He was a Northumberland man who had been a land surveyor all his working life, first in England and Wales, then in South Africa, and, since 1850, in Canada. He had worked for Fleming on the Intercolonial, as had so many of the men on the CPS; and like so many of the others—men accustomed to fend for themselves in wild and inhospitable climes—he was totally self-confident and more than a little proud. "I have no claim for genius," he wrote at the close of his career (he lived to be eighty-nine), "but a strong love of my profession, an aptitude and energy for carrying out great works, and a determination of honesty and accuracy which I have so far carried out, that in a long practice there has never been a dollar lost to any of my employers from any blunder of mine."

He was a hard drinker. On the prairie surveys, where prohibition reigned, his keg of "lime juice" contained straight whiskey. On the Homathco, he and his subordinate, W. O. Tiedeman, broke open a case of brandy and fought and drank an afternoon away. "They would keep having a drink and a row, turn and turn about," one of the party noted. He was not an easy man to work under, for he did not tolerate incompetence, fatigue, or any kind of human frailty. Young Edgar Fawcett, the rodman on the Bute–Homathco survey, was toiling up a steep, rock-strewn hill in June, 1872, when an enormous boulder, bouncing down the slope, struck him a blow that knocked him insensible. Smith took personal affront at the mishap. He could not have children working for him, he said. "That boy who could not keep out of the way of stones would have to be sent home."

Anything that interfered with the progress of the survey distressed him, and this impatience seems to have rubbed off on his subordinates. Tiedeman, who was in charge of the Bute Inlet survey under Smith's over-all supervision, insisted on moving camp at the end of October even though it meant leaving one lost man to die in the wilderness. Anyone who got lost, Tiedeman said, in his thick German accent, deserved to die. Some other members of the party remonstrated with him and he finally consented to send out search parties. Eventually the missing man was found: he had been wandering around in circles for two days and nights without sleep or food and was so far gone he did not recognize the comrade who eventually located him. Tiedeman's reaction was an echo of Smith's: "You shall have four more days' work for losing those two days."

"Sunday morning and no one sorry for it except perhaps Old Smith who I think would like to keep everyone at work night and day and then growl and snap at anyone he came near or happened to speak to him," George Hargreaves, the leveler on the party, confided to his diary that June.

Three days later he wrote that "Old Smith came to camp about 7.30 and boiled over, accusing us of putting obstacles in his way and saying he would carry through with the survey if he had to send 5,000 miles for men."

Six days later: "Had a row with Old Smith for not bringing the levels through before stopping work. . . . Says he, 'what did you mean by saying you was through, you must be an idiot.'"

Two days later: "It appears Smith had a big row with two or three of the men and also with Bristow, the Transit. Called him a Gd. dmd. fool and Idiot, who said he would not have such language used to him that he would go home to Canada if he continued to use it, and also told Smith he was stopping the work by carrying on so. Smith told him to go back to his instrument or he would give him the G. damdist daming ever he had dam'd."

"It was most awful the way that old devil swore and went on generally," young Fawcett wrote of Smith in his own diary a week after the incident with the boulder. "He swore at me for the most ordinary things and kept us from dinner till half-past two."

Yet, Fawcett admitted, he was treated no worse than the others, for Smith made no distinctions. He barked at Tiedeman, the head of the party, and barked at transit men, levelers, axmen, and Indian packers with a fine democracy. The Indians, who could afford the luxury of independence, calmly unloaded their canoes and prepared to head off into the wilderness. Smith called in Hargreaves and asked him who had authorized the Indians to leave. Hargreaves replied that the Indians did not require authorization to do anything, a remark that seemed to astonish Smith. "He said we must talk about that, only while he was talking about it, they were going, which put him in a flutter rather." Smith asked what the Indians wanted. The Indians replied they did not want to work for Smith. Hargreaves prevented a wholesale desertion by apologizing for Smith and agreeing to pay the Indians in cash at the time of every trip.

But if Smith was hard on others, he was equally hard on himself. When he was sixty years of age, he traveled a thousand miles through the Lake Superior country by canoe, all in a single summer, making two hundred portages that varied from a few yards to four miles.

He must have seemed a superman, albeit a satanic one, to the young chairmen and rodmen who, at the end of each day, found themselves so exhausted they were ready to throw in the sponge. Some of their diary excerpts from the Bute Inlet survey of 1872, when Smith was driving them without mercy, tell the story:

> "So tired I could hardly drag myself along. After one of the hardest, hottest and longest days I had ever experienced in my life, we arrived at 'W' camp, I was so far done in I could not get up and sat down to rest."

> "Yesterday I really thought I should have to give in I felt so the loss of having eaten nothing all day but a bit of bread and fat pork in 12 hours. If this is surveying, I have had my bellyfull of it."

> "I am heartily sick of the whole business and feel like turning tail."

> ". . . legs and feet all benumbed and aching fearfully. I felt like giving up and leaving it many times but knowing it had to be done sometime, and if we left it today would have to go again tomorrow, managed to get through."

Yet here was the demonic Smith, a man twice their age, driving hard late into the evening, scaling the rocks and forging through the glacial waters with enough breath left in his barrel chest to shower curses and imprecations upon the stragglers.

The truth was that he was as exhausted as any. "Felt terribly used up," he wrote in his journal on July 9, 1872. It is a phrase that keeps recurring on those cramped pages. But he would not give up that night until he had worked out the calculations of his travels across the mountains. Four days later, when he boarded the boat to Victoria (to the immense relief of his men), he was near collapse. "Fatigue set in after a month of excessive labour and anxiety and I lay and dozed the hours away, totally unfit for anything."

Sick or not, Smith was back in the upper Homathco country a month later. He was tortured by pains and cramps in his hip and left leg and by August 11 was so ill he could not rise until noon. But rise he did, saddled a horse, and headed off across a swamp. The swamp was so bad that Smith had to leave it and make his way up the side of a hill, still on horseback. After this detour, Smith plunged into a second swamp. The horse became mired. Smith tried to spur it on. The saddle slipped off and Smith tumbled into the morass. He was too weak to resaddle the horse, but he managed to crawl all the way to the head of a lake where he found two Indians who cared for him.

He was still at it, in the same country, in the summer of 1875. He was then in his sixtieth year and he confided to Joseph Hunter, one of his surveyors, that he had "less heart for this journey than any I have undertaken. I am far from well and very weak and the mountain torrents are very high."

When he wrote that letter, Smith was planning to force his way from the Chilcoten plains through the Cascade Mountains by way of the Homathco Pass and move down to Bute Inlet. Tiedeman and Horetzky had started at the inlet and were on their way to meet him, opening up a trail and bridging the streams as they went.

Smith set off on foot with five Lillooet Indians and a Chilcoten guide, struggling for two and a half days along the dripping, perpendicular cliffs of the canyons. Sometimes it took several hours to move a few yards because they had to climb as high as fifteen hundred feet and descend again to circumnavigate the spurs of rock that jutted from the canyon face. At one point, unable to bridge a torrent (six of the largest trees, thrown across the chasm, had been swept away like chips), they were forced to detour by way of a glacier, fifteen miles long, whose sharp ridges they crossed on their hands and knees.

It was not the kind of summer excursion a doctor would prescribe for an ailing man of fifty-nine. En route to the coast Smith discovered that Tiedeman's bridges had been swept away by the mountain torrents. It took him and his men seven hours to construct an Indian fly bridge over the Grand Canyon of the Homathco. It "looked like a fishing rod and line hanging over the torrent, the butt end resting on the ground and loaded with boulders." Smith crept gingerly over this precarious filament, dropped heavily to the rocks below, and then spent six hours scrambling over tangled creepers, huge deadfalls, and masses of detached rocks before reaching the camp of division "X."

Smith's love-hate relationship with this strangely compelling land of grim canyons and smiling meadows had, to borrow his own phrase, used him up. Would all this travail be in vain? Survey parties were crawling over the rumpled face of British Columbia and probing the ragged fiords of the coastline, seeking a feasible method of reaching the Pacific. Sandford Fleming was contemplating no less than eleven different routes leading down from the mountain spine to salt water. Only two led through Smith's country. What if another route should be chosen? What if all those ghastly days in the numbing bogs and among the brooding crags should end in defeat? Marcus Smith was not a man to contemplate defeat; and he had not yet begun to fight.

5

1 · *Lord Carnarvon intervenes*

"I WILL LEAVE THE PACIFIC RAILWAY AS a heritage to my adopted country," Alexander Mackenzie is said to have declared in his dry Gaelic accent, when Donald A. Smith, the Member for Selkirk, tried to argue the merits of using a private company to build the line. Nonetheless, Smith remained in Mackenzie's camp. "He is a noble man," Smith said of him, and the voters, who returned him with a landslide early in 1874, seemed to agree.

They wanted a noble man and they got one: a high-principled Scot with honest eyes of piercing blue, clear as ice, which seemed to bore right through an adversary. Though he was in no sense immune to the pressures of nepotism and patronage, he appeared to be a man of probity. The public had reduced Macdonald's following in the House to a corporal's guard, as he himself ruefully remarked, and placed his antithesis on the pedestal. Mackenzie, with his graven features, his metallic voice, his rigid attitudes, his Baptist teetotalism, and his blunt manner, was in every possible sense, except for his Scottish heritage, the exact opposite of the rounded, soft-spoken, tolerant, and indulgent politician whom he replaced.

As Prime Minister he lacked Macdonald's conciliatory gifts and in debate he tended to continue as if he were in opposition, striking down his opponents with the blunt bullets of his words. Mackenzie could never quite let well enough alone, and his tendency to want to rub his adversaries' noses in their mistakes, real or imagined, was to affect his railway policy.

· · ·

He was a work addict who never allowed an early adjournment of the Commons if there was business to fill up the time; but he sometimes worked unnecessarily hard, for he found it difficult to separate small details from over-all plans—a stonemason's trait, perhaps. He had the body of a man who has worked hard with his hands all his life—lithe and well-proportioned without a spare ounce of flesh and not a fold of surplus tissue on his drawn face. As a stonemason he had created fortifications, canals, and courthouses. One day when he was at work on the bombproof arch at the fort, a huge piece of cut stone weighing more than a ton fell upon the lower part of his foot. He allowed no cry of agony to escape from his thin lips. For all of his political career he masked his inner tortures. He was not one to cry out in public; but then he was not one to chuckle, either.

It was remarked, wickedly, that while Mackenzie's strong point as a political leader consisted in his having been a stonemason, his weak point consisted in his being one still. That was not quite fair. The Governor General, who still yearned secretly for Macdonald, found him "industrious, conscientious and exact." Dufferin had once thought of him as terribly narrow, but he was not so narrow in his interests. In his early days in Kingston he had owned a telescope with which he used to gaze at the night sky from his log shanty. He was a lover of poetry and English literature; his speeches were seasoned with quotations from classics. He had not had much formal schooling—and he was sensitive about that—but he had managed to read everything to which his better-educated peers had been exposed and seemed to remember far more of it. Though in his younger days he had been an incorrigible practical joker, his public image was one of uncompromising sobriety. It is difficult to imagine anything but the bleakest of smiles illuminating those chiseled features. The church, to Mackenzie, was the rock on which civilization rested; scarcely a day went by on which he did not read his Bible and fall on his knees to ask his God for forgiveness and guidance.

Though the new Prime Minister had no natural gaiety, his speeches and his private conversation could be marked by a dry and often cutting wit. There was the story of his remark to William Paterson of Brantford, a fierce-faced man with a bull's voice, which was seldom restrained. Paterson, after his maiden speech, was desperate for his leader's approval. "Do you think they heard me?" he asked Mackenzie. "Aye," was the Prime Minister's only comment, "they heard you at the Russell Hoose."

As a Liberal, he stood for a retrenchment in government spending. He could not stomach the grandiose schemes of the Conservatives, which all too often seemed to him to be designed as much for profit and patronage as for empire building. He and his party opposed Macdonald's plan to build the Canadian Pacific; to them it was precipitate, rash, and spendthrift. The Tories, with their big-business connections, were temperamentally attuned to taking chances; but Mackenzie had neither the imagination nor the gambling instincts of the successful entrepreneur. His political base was in the sober farming districts and small towns of Ontario.

During Mackenzie's term of office, only a few miles of the CPR were built; but it is arguable that in those lean years Macdonald could not have done much better, though he might have handled matters with greater finesse. Mackenzie committed the worst of all political crimes: he was unlucky. Macdonald had made his rash promises when the country was caught up in a mood of extravagant optimism. It was Mackenzie's misfortune to take office just as the bubble was bursting. For the whole of his term the country was in the grip of a serious continental depression.

Like so much else, the depression was imported from the United States. It was touched off by the spectacular failure of Jay Cooke's Northern Pacific, the same company which, through a series of happenstances, had been the trigger that catapulted Mackenzie into office. But the Cooke failure was only the end product of a variety of catastrophes as ill assorted as the Chicago Fire and Franco-Prussian War. It really marked the end of the great period of railway empire building which saw the United States double its transportation machinery in eight years, exceeding for decades to come its real needs and sinking an enormous amount of capital into frozen assets. In short, there was no ready money, and though Cooke continued to feel "an unfailing confidence in God," the Deity on this occasion proved fickle. On September 17, at the very moment the royal commission was considering the implications of Cooke's secret deal with Allan, the great financial house closed its doors and the white-bearded Tycoon wept freely in public. Five thousand commercial houses followed Cooke and his allied brokers and banks into failure; railroad stocks tumbled; by midwinter, thousands of Americans were starving.

The tidal wave of the great crash washed over all of settled Canada and continued past 1878. It was an accident of economic history that it neatly bracketed the Mackenzie regime; the new Prime Minister was shackled financially. On the other hand, it is doubtful that, given prosperity, he would have accomplished any more than he did. He could gaze upon the universe with his telescope, but he did not see his country as a great transcontinental nation, settled for all of its length from sea to sea. Canada, to Mackenzie, lay east of the Shield; far off were two small islands in the Canadian archipelago: the Red River settlement and British Columbia. These were necessary nuisances.

In addition, Mackenzie seemed to be plagued with a compulsion to slash his rival's railway policy to shreds. On the hustings in 1874 and later in his public speeches, he could not refrain from the wild remarks that filled British Columbians with dismay and goaded them into retaliation. As late as 1877 he was still using the word "insane" to describe the pact with the Pacific province. The men who perpetrated that treaty, he declared, deserved "the everlasting political execration of the country." It was this kind of thing that turned Victoria, in Lord Dufferin's on-the-spot description, into a "nest of hornets."

Clearly his predecessor had saddled Mackenzie with an impossible burden. The policy was scarcely insane, but some of the terms were certainly foolhardy. A decade later George Grant recalled for *Scribner's Monthly* that in 1870 "it had come to be considered that a railway could be flung across the Rocky Mountains as easily as across a hayfield." In those roseate moments Macdonald had blithely promised the British Columbians that he would commence construction of the line in two years. *Two years!* In the spring of 1873, with the surveyors bogged down in the bewildering mountain labyrinth, Macdonald realized that he must pay lip service to his incautious pledge. A few days before the deadline he recklessly picked Esquimalt, the naval harbor on the western outskirts of Victoria, as the terminus of the Canadian Pacific Railway.

In practical terms, this meant that the railway would run to Bute Inlet on the mainland; it would then thread its way down for fifty miles from the head of the inlet through the sheer granite cliffs of the coastline and leap the Strait of Georgia, a distance of twenty-nine miles, to Nanaimo on Vancouver Island and follow the east coast of the island to Esquimalt. The work, as Fleming reported, would be "of a most formidable character." It would require eight miles of tunneling and untold rock cuts just for the right of way to negotiate those sea-torn precipices. Then the track must hop from island to island over six deep intervening channels through which the rip tide sometimes tore at nine knots; that would require eight thousand feet of bridging, and in two instances the spans would have to be thirteen hundred feet in length. That was greater than any arch then existing anywhere in the world.

But Macdonald at that moment had not been concerned with engineering. The votes were in Victoria; and Victoria, whose merchants were heavily involved in real-estate speculation, needed an economic boost. On July 19, 1873, exactly two years less a day after British Columbia's admission into Confederation, a group of dignitaries took part in the cynical fiction of turning a sod near the Esquimalt naval base. In the ensuing debate over the Pacific Scandal, Macdonald had the grateful support of the Vancouver Island Members.

This, then, was the *fait accompli* Mackenzie faced: a deadline determined, a sod turned, a terminus established, and a province militant. In this fertile ground were sown seeds for the uneasy relationship between the Pacific province and central Canada that was to be maintained into the nation's second century. Right from the beginning, the British Columbians viewed "the East" with suspicion. On its part, the East—for Mackenzie unquestionably had the support of the public at large outside British Columbia—saw the new province as greedy, shrill, and bumptious, prepared to wreck the economy of the nation for the sake of petty provincialism and real-estate profits.

During the election campaign Mackenzie had been at pains to water down Macdonald's impossible dream. He talked about a land-and-water route across the nation, with the rail line being built piecemeal. This, in effect, became Liberal policy, although the administration, beginning in 1874, made continuing attempts to entice private entrepreneurs to build the entire line by offering a subsidy of ten thousand dollars and twenty thousand acres per mile. Although that offer was considerably more generous than Macdonald's, there was no real hope of attracting private capital during the depression. If the railway was to be commenced, it would have to be built in sections as a public work. First, a line from Lake Superior to the Red River to replace the Dawson Route and, second, a branch line in Manitoba from Selkirk to Pembina on the United States border, which, it was hoped, would give the Red River its long-desired connection with the outside world. After that, as funds were available, other sections would be built—but scarcely within ten years. That was not good enough for British Columbia, whose Premier, George Walkem, jumped with both boots into the heated Battle of the Routes, which was to occupy the entire decade.

It was clear from the way the surveys were proceeding that in spite of the previous year's sod-turning ceremony, the engineers had not made up their minds about the location of the CPR terminus. At the close of 1873, Sandford Fleming was considering seven alternative routes to the coast. No fewer than six passes in the Rockies were being explored. By mid-decade Fleming was able to report on twelve different routes through British Columbia to seven different harbors on the coastline.

But as far as British Columbia was concerned, there were only two routes that really mattered. One was the ancient trail used by the fur traders and explorers through the Yellow Head Pass and down the Fraser canyon to Burrard Inlet; if chosen it would guarantee the prosperity of Kamloops, Yale, New Westminster, and all the valley points between. The mainland of British Columbia fought for this route. The other would lead probably from the Yellow Head Pass to Bute Inlet, then leap the straits to Nanaimo and thence to Victoria; it would guarantee the prosperity of the dying gold region and of Vancouver Island. The Premier, a Cariboo man who knew a political issue when he saw one, opted instinctively with the island interests for the Bute Inlet route and decided to go over the Prime Minister's head to the Crown, in the person of Lord Carnarvon, the delicate-featured Colonial Secretary, whom Disraeli called "Twitters," because he had difficulty coming to a decision. In this instance, Carnarvon was uncharacteristically expeditious. He telegraphed to Ottawa on June 17, 1874, that he was prepared personally to arbitrate the dispute between British Columbia and the Canadian Government.

Pushed hard by Lord Dufferin, the harassed Mackenzie, to his later regret, accepted the offer. Under the "Carnarvon Terms," which were to become a rallying cry in British Columbia, a railway would be built on Vancouver Island, the surveys would be pushed, and when the transcontinental line was finally launched, the Government promised it would spend at least two millions a year on its construction. In return, the province agreed to extend the deadline to December 31, 1890.

Now the stoic stonemason, who had forborne to cry out under physical pressure, began to suffer under the crushing millstone of office. He was plagued with intestinal inflammation and insomnia, both the products of political tensions. "I am being driven mad with work— contractors, deputations and so on," he told a colleague early in 1874. "Last night I was in my office until I was so used up I was unable to sleep." By 1876 the crunch of office caused him to cry out in a letter to a friend about "a burden of care, the terrible weight of which presses me to the earth." The railway—the terrible railway—a dream not of his invention, a nightmare by now, threatened to be his undoing. On one side he felt the pull of the upstart province on the Pacific, holding him to another man's bargain. On the other, he felt the tug of the implacable Edward Blake, the rallying point for the anti-British Columbia sentiment and a popular alternative as Prime Minister.

Among the flaming maples of Aurora, north of Toronto, that October of 1874, the rebellious Blake, who had left the Cabinet, delivered himself of the decade's most-discussed public speech. In a

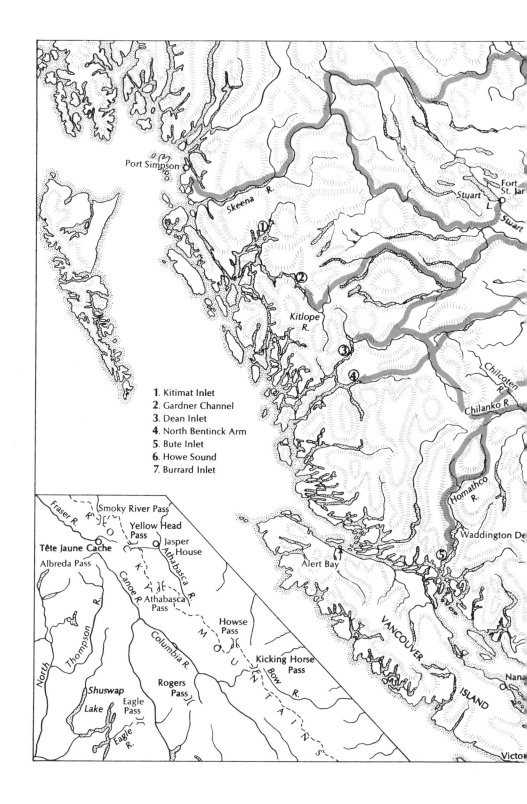

Port Simpson

Skeena R.

Kitlope R.

1. Kitimat Inlet
2. Gardner Channel
3. Dean Inlet
4. North Bentinck Arm
5. Bute Inlet
6. Howe Sound
7. Burrard Inlet

Fort St. Jar

Stuart L.

Stuart

Chilcoten R.

Chilanko R.

Homathco R.

Waddington De

Alert Bay

VANCOUVER ISLAND

Nana

Victo

Fraser R.

Smoky River Pass

Yellow Head Pass

Tête Jaune Cache

Jasper House

Albreda Pass

Athabasca R.

Canoe R.

Athabasca Pass

North Thompson

Columbia R.

Howse Pass

Kicking Horse Pass

Rogers Pass

Bow R.

Shuswap Lake

Eagle Pass

Eagle R.

MOUNTAINS

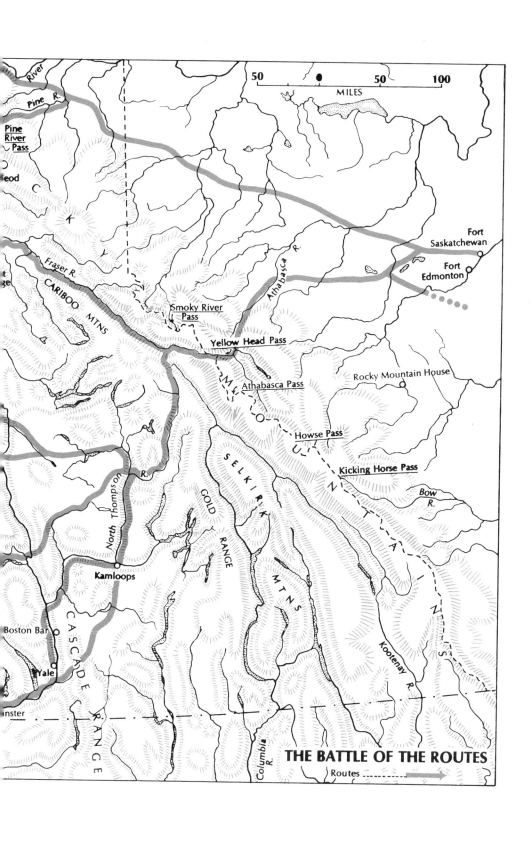

THE BATTLE OF THE ROUTES

Routes ------→

MILES

50   50   100

Pine R.

River

Pine
River
Pass

leod

Fraser R.

CARIBOO MTNS

Smoky River
Pass

Yellow Head Pass

Athabasca Pass

Howse Pass

Kicking Horse Pass

Athabasca R.

Fort
Saskatchewan

Fort
Edmonton

Rocky Mountain House

Bow
R.

SELKIRK

GOLD
RANGE

North Thompson R.

Kamloops

Boston Bar

Yale

CASCADE RANGE

MTNS

Kootenay R.

Columbia
R.

nster

section devoted to railway policy he dismissed British Columbia as "a sea of mountains," charged that it would cost thirty-six million dollars to blast a railway through it, and declared the annual maintenance would be so costly that "I doubt much if that section can be kept open after it is built."

As for the growing threats of separation: "If under all the circumstances, the Columbians should say—you must go on and finish this railway according to the terms or take the alternative of releasing us from the Confederation, I would take the alternative!"

That was exactly what the audience of hard-pressed farmers wanted to hear. They cheered him to the skies. But on the far side of the divisive mountain rampart, the name Blake became anathema—the symbol of the unfeeling East.

Mackenzie knew Blake had to be lured back into the Cabinet. Blake was willing but he had a price. The Prime Minister was forced to add a hedge to the Carnarvon Terms; they would be carried out *only* if that could be done without increasing taxes. The moody lawyer re-entered the fold in May, 1875, as Minister of Justice. Together, he and the Prime Minister worked out a compromise offer. In lieu of the island railway, the government was prepared to pay British Columbia $750,000. But the order in council was not worded that way. The money was to be advanced, it said, "for any delays which may take place in the construction of the Canadian Pacific Railway." There was that word again—"delays"! British Columbia had had nothing but delays, and now the government was practically promising more and offering hush money to boot.

But opinion in the rest of Canada had by this time swung solidly behind Blake and Mackenzie. In April, 1876, when Parliament voted on the taxation declaration that Blake insisted upon, only the island Members stood out in opposition.

The Government of Canada had resolved to go its own way in the matter of the railway and to stop trying to conciliate British Columbia. If that meant separation, so be it.

2 · *"The horrid B.C. business"*

FREDERICK TEMPLE BLACKWOOD, Viscount Clandeboye and Earl of Dufferin, was chafing with inactivity. Life in Ottawa he found so irksome that he filled his evenings reading his way through Plutarch's *Lives* in the original Greek. He longed to get away on a voyage of conciliation for which he felt his undoubted gifts as a diplomat superbly qualified him. In short, he wanted to go out to British Columbia to soothe ruffled feelings—and in a double capacity, as both a spokesman for Ottawa and an agent for Great Britain.

Mackenzie, Blake, and Richard Cartwright, the Liberal Minister of Finance, greeted His Excellency's proposal with something akin to terror—at least that was the word the Governor General used. The idea of the Queen's representative, especially this one, plunging into the most delicate problem in Canadian Dominion politics did not make them rest easily. The British Columbia government had already shown a propensity to grasp at straws. What straws would Dufferin unwittingly offer them? He loved making speeches; he made them on every possible occasion. He would undoubtedly make speeches all over British Columbia. His speeches were full of Irish blarney and could be calculated to butter up his listeners to the point of embarrassment. Macdonald, on first acquaintance, had found the new Governor General "rather too gushing for my taste." He could, said Macdonald, stand a good deal of flattery, "but he lays it on rather too thick." Would that flattery unwittingly inflate the expectations of the people to the point where a revival of understanding would be more impossible than ever? Mackenzie and his two colleagues called on the Governor General on May 26 and "there ensued a long and very disagreeable discussion." Finally, it was agreed that Dufferin would make a state visit to British Columbia but would maintain the traditional viceregal attitude of strict neutrality.

The Governor General and his handsome countess went by rail to San Francisco and there embarked by naval vessel for the "nest of hornets." Her Ladyship kept a journal, which was subsequently published, complete with sketches by her husband. They debarked from H.M.S. *Amethyst* at Esquimalt harbor on August 16, 1876, and drove through the streets of Victoria, the capital, cheered on by the entire populace: canoeloads of Indians, Chinese in pigtails, Cariboo miners, scores of little girls in private-school uniforms, old Hudson's Bay hands, and, most of all, hundreds of loyal English men and women— retired army officers, former civil servants, newly arrived immigrants.

The handsome figure in the carriage, acknowledging the cheers that engulfed him, had just turned fifty. Such was his profile that, except for the short, dark beard on his chin, he might have posed, in a later era, for an Arrow Collar ad. There was a certain haughtiness to the tilt of his head, for he was not without vanity. Long before the applause meter was invented he had devised a literary method of achieving the same effect: he used to send out verbatim reports of his speeches to the press with bracketed phrases, such as "Prolonged applause," "Great laughter," "Cries of Hear! Hear!", inserted in the appropriate places. When reading a Dufferin speech, one gets an impression of near pandemonium. But they were good speeches for all of that, the sentences nicely turned, the local allusions graceful. Dufferin, after all, came from the best literary stock. His mother—hers was the Sheridan side of his family—wrote ballads; his aunt was a poet and singer. He himself had produced an amusing book of travel. A product of the British class system, educated at Eton and Oxford, he knew all the titled families of England, but he also hobnobbed with Tennyson, Browning, and Dickens.

Coming as a stranger to the new nation, he was able to see Canada whole and not as a loose collection of self-centered and often antagonistic communities. The petty provincialism of the Canadians bothered him and he tried, throughout his term and not unsuccessfully, to encourage in them a feeling of national pride.

But in Victoria, Dufferin was dismayed to find no flicker of national feeling. The island town was in every sense a little bit of Old England. Most of the residents had been born in Britain and "like all middle class Englishmen, have a vulgar contempt for everything that is not English." The mentality was still that of a Crown Colony. Not only did Victoria consider itself separate and distinct from Canada but also from the rest of the province.

Dufferin's preconceived notions about the greed of British Columbians ("we may take it for granted, I think, that the spending of money in their neighbourhood and not the Railway is the real thing to which the British Columbia people look") were largely confirmed in the remarkable week that followed. Day after day, beginning at nine in the morning and continuing without interruption until seven at night, the representative of the Queen found himself receiving delegation after delegation to discuss the most controversial question in the country. There had never been anything quite like it before and there could never be anything like it again. He saw, in his own words, "every single soul in the place." He had not even had time to attend to his personal dispatches. His private secretary handled them for him. "Lord Dufferin," he wrote, in a postscript to a letter to Mackenzie, "bids me add that he finds great difficulty in keeping his temper with these foolish people." It was understandable. At that point, the Governor General had spent seven days, ten full hours a day, "listening to the same old story, abuse of Mackenzie, of Canada, of Sir John Macdonald and the absolute necessity of bringing the Pacific Railway via Bute Inlet to Esquimalt."

But then, Victoria was literally fighting for its life. The depression had dealt this isolated community of five thousand a staggering blow. Now it saw its chance, and its only remaining chance, to rival San Francisco as the great port of the Pacific.

"In Victoria," Lord Dufferin reported to Lord Carnarvon, "the one idea of every human being is to get the railway to Esquimalt. . . . Most of its inhabitants have wildly speculated in town lots. . . . You can therefore imagine the phrensied eagerness with which Victoria grasps at every chance of making itself the terminus of the great transcontinental railway."

When he reached the mainland, it was the same story. "The location of the Canadian Pacific Railway, and its terminus along such a line, and on such a spot as may enhance the value of his own individual town lot, or in some other way may put money into his pocket, by passing as near as possible to where he lives, is the common preoccupation of every Columbian citizen."

Yet in spite of the constant pressure upon him, he returned to Ottawa with considerable sympathy for the British Columbians. He had the feeling that Mackenzie, pushed by Blake and Minister of Finance Cartwright, was trying to wriggle out of his commitments. On his return that feeling was reinforced.

In November, "the horrid B.C. business," as Lord Dufferin was to call it, touched off an extraordinary scene at Rideau Hall. Here, for the first and only time in Canadian history, a Governor General and his two chief advisers came perilously close to fisticuffs.

Dufferin had returned from the West convinced that Lord Carnarvon should re-enter the picture. In addition, he suggested raising the $750,000 offered in lieu of the line to an even million: any reasonable sacrifice was worth while if the unity of the nation was at stake.

On Saturday, November 18, he met with Blake and Mackenzie at Rideau Hall. Both Ministers were obdurate. Mackenzie obviously regretted that he had ever consented to the British Colonial Office's interference in Canada's domestic affairs. Blake was immovable. The interview, Dufferin reported to Carnarvon, was stormy and disagreeable. They "nearly came to blows . . . Mackenzie's aspect was simply pitiable and Blake was on the point of crying as he very readily does when he is excited."

The day after this extraordinary encounter, there were expressions of regret and mutual respect all round, and a face-saving formula was evolved in which the matter was put in abeyance for eighteen months until the surveys could be completed and a route fixed; failing that, Mackenzie cautiously agreed to some sort of London meeting under Carnarvon's auspices.

With that, the importunate Dufferin had to be content. He had pushed his Ministers as hard as any Governor General could or ever would; he undoubtedly felt he had been successful; but the hard fact was that he had battered his noble head against a wall of granite.

3 · *The Battle of the Routes*

BY 1877, THE BATTLE OF THE ROUTES had reached the stage of a pamphlet war, that tried and true propaganda technique of the Victorian Age—and Sandford Fleming had still not settled on a final choice for a pass through the Rockies or a terminus along the coastline or a route in between. Some of this apparent dallying had to do with the nature of the country itself, but much of it was clearly political procrastination.

Fleming's own opinions in his massive report of 1877 are clouded in ambiguity. By 1875 there was a general understanding that Bute Inlet would probably be the terminus. Then, in November, 1876, it occurred to Fleming, rather tardily, that the Admiralty might be asked its opinion of the various harbors in British Columbia. The overwhelming opinion of the seamen was in favor of Burrard Inlet.

Fleming still could not make up his mind. He wrote that the Bute Inlet route was the only one open for selection "if it be considered of paramount importance to carry an unbroken line of railway to . . . Vancouver Island.

"If, on the other hand, the object be to reach the navigable waters of the Pacific simply by the most eligible line," then the Fraser Valley–Burrard Inlet route was preferable.

What Fleming was really saying was that the decision was a political one. And in case the politicians could not make up their minds, he had a suggestion. There was another, perhaps better, choice at the mouth of the Skeena River, a harbor five hundred miles closer to the Orient than the other two.

Fleming, at that time, was an absentee engineer-in-chief. He was a robust man who thought nothing of warding off a bear with an umbrella or unrolling his blankets in two feet of snow, as he had done on his twenty-fourth birthday, but by 1876, in his fiftieth year, he was exhausted. A Fifeshire Calvinist, who prayed aloud on the tops of mountain peaks, he had as a boy copied out a maxim from *Poor Richard's Almanack*: "Dost thou love life? Then do not squander time, for that's the stuff life is made of." Fleming loved life; he held gay parties in Ottawa and was perfectly prepared to join in an Indian dance in the wilds, a wolfskin draped over his head; he was fond of champagne and kept it by the case in his office; he loved rich food—oysters were a favorite; and he certainly did not believe in squandering time. Between 1871 and 1876 he held down two man-killing jobs: he was chief engineer of both the Intercolonial and the Canadian Pacific. Thus he could devote only half of his working day to the transcontinental line. He had taken the second job reluctantly and at no extra pay (otherwise his total salary would have been higher than that received by the Cabinet Minister over him). "I . . . felt the weight of responsibilities that were thrown upon me and I laboured day and night in a manner that will never be known," he told Charles Tupper. Poor Richard had said, ". . . the sleeping fox catches no poultry . . . there will be sleeping enough in the grave." The boy Fleming had written that down, too.

When the Intercolonial was completed in 1876, Fleming's doctors ordered a complete rest. He had suffered two accidents, one of which nearly killed him, and he was worn out. He was granted a twelve-month leave of absence and went off to England but was twice recalled by the government, once to write the monumental 1877 report and again as a result of a hurry-up call to deal with his deputy, the bristly Marcus Smith. The leave stretched out over a two-year period.

For nineteen months, between the spring of 1876 and 1878, Fleming was absent and Marcus Smith was in his place. Smith had the job but he did not, apparently, have the authority, or—as he bitterly complained—the salary. During his visits back to Canada, Fleming would countermand his deputy's instructions or disagree with his views. The personality clashes within the department seemed to be continual. More and more, as the months went by, Fleming and Smith failed to see eye to eye. Much of this was due to Smith's furious championing of the Pine Pass–Bute Inlet railway route.

Smith would not give up on Bute Inlet. The obvious impracticality of a causeway across the strait had not cooled his ardor for "his" route. "I feel confident that a steamboat properly constructed could take a railway train on board and pass safely all seasons of the year from any convenient point on Bute Inlet to a good landing on Vancouver's Island," he wrote in an appendix to the report of 1875. Originally he had thought of having the railway run to Bute Inlet through the Yellow Head Pass, which his absent chief favored, but by 1877 there had taken shape, in the back of that mysterious mind, a preference for the Pine Pass, which Horetzky had first explored. In April of 1877 in his capacity of Minister of Public Works, he wrote to Mackenzie asking permission to probe the pass with three survey parties; he added that he himself would like to go along. Mackenzie, who was trying to slash expenses in his department, turned him down, whereupon the irrepressible Smith determined to go ahead secretly without authority.

He wrote to Henry Cambie, who had replaced him as chief of surveys in British Columbia, to send Joseph Hunter to the Pine River country with two or three men and some packers. The trip was to be clandestine: "You will understand . . . that we are not pretending to favour this route but simply extending the northern exploration from River Skeena to get a geographical knowledge of the country."

Smith himself went out to British Columbia and returned full of enthusiasm for the Peace River country. The trip took on some of the aspects of a political campaign. (A friend later wrote Mackenzie of "the insolence of Marcus Smith, who . . . everywhere and most industriously spoke of your railway policy as shuffling [and] bumbling.") Back in Ottawa, he accelerated his behind-the-scenes maneuvers to get "his" route approved. He instructed Hunter that the time had arrived for him to leak some information to the press about his Pine Pass explorations "*but not official information* on my authority." With this letter, Smith actually enclosed a press release praising the Pine Pass–Bute Inlet route.

An accomplished intriguer himself, Smith was a man who saw dark plots and sinister motives everywhere he went. He lived in a cloak-and-dagger world of the mind in which he imagined himself desperately staving off, at great personal and financial risk, the forces of treason and corruption.

"I see now that the storm is going to burst as regards myself," he wrote to Fleming on December 7, 1877. "At Victoria, I found out about this Burrard Inlet mania, which is a huge land job in which the Minister and his friends are concerned—the latter certainly are from the Lieutenant Governor downwards. It was first started by Lord Dufferin in 1876." In Smith's dark view, the Governor General, cheated of a victory that "would help him much in his diplomatic career," promised the Burrard terminus to the mainland as an act of revenge.

Meanwhile, Henry Cambie in British Columbia had been caught up in the intrigue. Mackenzie, unable to budge Smith, had gone around him and wired direct to Cambie to commence the survey of the Fraser, which the Governor General had so urgently recommended on his return. Cambie, an advocate of the Fraser route, uneasily complied. When Smith returned from the West, he found himself snubbed by Mackenzie, who was closeted with Cambie, "pumping him, flattering him and getting him to show off his opinions."

At length, Mackenzie asked the reluctant Cambie for a written report on the Fraser. Cambie demurred and the strange spectacle of a

Cabinet Minister (and Prime Minister to boot) trying to circumvent his own department head in order to obtain information from a subordinate continued all that month. Mackenzie continued to ignore Smith and meet secretly with Cambie. For the wretched Cambie, the squeeze was getting tighter. He was a bearded Tipperary man, with a craggy hawk's face and a touch of the brogue in his speech, privately witty, publicly grave, a pillar of the Anglican Church and an experienced engineer who had worked on both the Grand Trunk and the Intercolonial. As a Canadian Pacific surveyor he had covered most of British Columbia from the Homathco to the Skeena. He had been in some tight fixes in his time. Just that summer he had taken a leaky boat, caulked only with leaves, for 150 miles down the rivers of the Rocky Mountain Trench, one man bailing furiously all the way. But never had he encountered a situation fraught with such tension. Cambie kept putting off his written report to Mackenzie. Mackenzie kept demanding it. He did not, however, ask for any special report from Marcus Smith. "He shall get one nevertheless whether he likes it or no," Smith remarked grimly.

Quite clearly, the Prime Minister had settled on the Burrard route. There were many reasons for that decision: the Admiralty report; the skillful advocacy of the mainland Members of Parliament; Lord Dufferin's own opinion; the new surveys by Cambie; and, finally, Smith's bullheaded intransigence. The acting chief engineer had got his Minister's back up. By March, 1878, Mackenzie had ceased to consult him or even speak to him.

On March 29, Smith sent in his own official report, as acting chief, on the progress of the surveys of the previous year. Predictably, he advocated the Pine Pass–Bute Inlet route, but suggested another year's delay to settle the final location of the line.

"It has apparently fallen like a thunderbolt," Smith wrote gleefully to a friend a month later. "It has been repeatedly asked for both in the House and Senate but kept on one excuse or another."

Smith's report presented Mackenzie with a new problem. He could scarcely settle on Burrard Inlet in the face of the direct and public opposition of his acting chief engineer. The Vancouver Islanders would pounce on that and cry foul. There was only one thing to do: without telling Marcus Smith, he sent for Fleming, who for the second time found his sick leave in England interrupted.

Fleming returned to find his department in an uproar. James Rowan, Fleming's former assistant, complained of Smith's language and treatment of him. There were also reports that Smith had stated in public that some of the department engineers were working in collusion with railway contractors—a charge calculated to infuriate the members of that proud service. Rowan reported that in Winnipeg, Smith had spent more time collecting data to be used against Fleming and Mackenzie than he had on the knotty problems connected with his own department. Smith was totally unabashed by these charges.

"He spoke to me in a way in which I had never been spoken to before by a gentleman, on several occasions," Fleming later told the Public Accounts Committee of the House. Mackenzie determined that Smith must go. He told Fleming that he no longer had confidence in him and that he, Fleming, must no longer consider Smith an officer of the department. This resulted in a curious situation: there was the peppery Smith, still fuming away in his office, still, apparently, on the staff, but stripped of his powers.

"He did not receive his dismissal but he was as good as dismissed," Fleming recounted later, "and I was not at liberty to consult him any longer, inasmuch as he was no longer a public officer." No doubt Fleming expected Smith to resign, as he had once expected Moberly to resign, but Smith hung on stubbornly, as he had once hung onto the slippery crags of the Homathco canyon. He was more than a little paranoid by this time. He explored, in a letter to a friend, the possibility that Lord Dufferin had an interest in Fraser Valley land—hence his motives in "moving Heaven and Earth" in favor of the Burrard route. Smith added that Dufferin wanted another term of office as Governor General and thus would do "any dirty work for the Canadian Government if they will use their influence to get it for him."

While Smith busied himself with his correspondence—he had nothing else to do—Fleming set about writing his own report. In this he was finally forced to a conclusion: if engineering decisions alone were to govern the selection of a route, and if that selection could not be postponed further, then the Bute Inlet route should be rejected and the Burrard Inlet route selected. He left the question of a pass open. He thought there should be more surveys in the region of the Peace River Pass in case it proved to be less expensive than the Yellow Head.

On July 12, 1878, the government settled officially on the Fraser River–Burrard Inlet route and prepared to call for tenders for the construction of the railway through the dismal canyon of the Fraser. That seemed to be the end of "the horrid B.C. business." It was not. Party lines had already been drawn around the opposing routes. The Pine Pass–Bute Inlet route, thanks in part to Marcus Smith's importuning, had become a Liberal route. As for Smith, he was still around. Two years later, in a new job and under a new administration, he would still be, in his own eyes at least, "the *Bête Noire* of the Govt."

6

1 · The first locomotive

ON THE MORNING OF OCTOBER 9, 1877, the citizens of Winnipeg were awakened by an unaccustomed fanfare —the shriek of a locomotive whistle. For the generation to follow, this would become the authentic sound of the prairie, more familiar, more haunting, more nostalgic than the laugh of the loon or the whine of the wind in the wolf willow. But on this crisp October day, with the sere leaves of birch and aspen yellowing the ground, it was something totally new. There were many there that day who had never heard a train whistle in their lives and for some of these, the Indians and métis, it was as symbolic in its sadness as it was for the white community in its promise.

George Ham, the western editor and raconteur who was there that day, recalled the scene: "A lone, blanketed Indian standing on the upper bank of the river looked down rather disdainfully upon the strange iron thing and the interested crowd of spectators who hailed its coming. He evinced no enthusiasm but stoically gazed at the novel scene. What did it portend? To him it might be the dread thought of the passing of the old life of his race, the alienation of the stamping grounds of his forefathers, the early extinction of their God given provider, the buffalo, which for generations past had furnished the red man with all the necessities of life. . . . Whatever he may have thought, this iron horse actually meant that the wild, free, unrestrained life of the Indian was nearing its end."

She was a Baldwin engine, built especially for the job, and she bore a noble name, *The Countess of Dufferin*. She came complete with six flatcars and a baggage car; but she could not arrive under her own steam. She had to be floated down the river on a flag-decked barge, pushed by the stern-wheeler *Selkirk*, because the railway to the boundary, which Mackenzie had been promising since 1873, was not finished. Even if it had been, there was nothing yet on the other side of the American border with which it could connect.

But a locomotive, even without a railway, was still a marvel, and the entire town was streaming to the dock with whistles, bells, banners, and bunting to inspect her. They gave three cheers for the massive contractor, Joseph Whitehead, who was in charge; as a boy, he had worked on railways in the old country when they were drawn by horses. Then, as the barge touched the bank, they crowded aboard and began to crawl over the little black engine with the huge smoke-stack. Two hours later, the *Selkirk* steamed to a location below Douglas Point where a piece of track had been laid to the water's edge, and here the crowds watched in awe as the little train puffed its way off the barge and ran under full steam up the bank and into St. Boniface. Whitehead, who was laying track on the line between St. Boniface and Selkirk, had imported her as a work engine. For the white community, at least, she was a promise of things to come, an end to the maddening isolation of half a century and a tangible response to the pleas for a railway, which had been issuing from the Red River since the beginning of the decade.

This isolation was real and terrible and could be translated into concrete terms. At the beginning of the decade a keg of nails, if nails were available at all, cost at least ten times as much at Red River as in Ontario—a fact of life which helps explain why Red River carts were held together with shaganappi. And it cost a dollar and a half—more than a farmhand earned in a day—to send a letter to the old country.

The steamboats, which began to arrive on the river in the late sixties, did not appreciably lower prices save during those brief, adventurous periods when rival lines fought for control. The Hudson's Bay Company held a monopoly of the Red River traffic with its rickety *International* until one spring day in 1871 when a strange vessel loaded with 125 passengers and 115 tons of freight steamed into Fort Garry. This was the *Selkirk*, operated by James Jerome Hill, a one-eyed ex-Canadian with a razor-sharp mind, now operating out of St. Paul. Hill, an omnivorous reader, had discovered an old United States law which held that all goods crossing the international border from American territories into Canadian ports had to be bonded. He quietly built the *Selkirk*, had her bonded, and persuaded the customs officials at Pembina on the border to hold up all unbonded vessels plying the river. The *International*, in short, was legally beached and Hill had a transportation monopoly of the Red River Valley. It was said that he paid off the entire cost of constructing his new steamboat with the profits of that first voyage.

Jim Hill had had the audacity to challenge the monopoly rule of the Hudson's Bay Company, which for two centuries had enjoyed the mastery of the North West. Donald A. Smith, the chief commissioner of the Company, lost no time in fighting back. He had the *International* bonded by assigning the steamer to Norman Kittson, the respected Minnesota fur trader who was the Hudson's Bay agent in St. Paul. Then he leaped into battle with Hill.

They were evenly matched adversaries and, in many respects, remarkably alike—short, fierce-eyed, muscled men, all bone and gristle, with backgrounds crammed with adventure and romance. They knew and respected one another, having met quite by chance on the bald, snowswept prairie in February of 1870.

This scene, which took place near the Elm River, north of the United States border, was a memorable one, marking the beginning of an association which would eventually launch the Canadian Pacific Railway Company. Hill, en route to Fort Garry to investigate at first hand the Red River troubles, had made a truly terrible journey from St. Paul. First, the stage out of Breckenridge, on which he was traveling, had fought its way through gigantic drifts, the passengers shoveling out the route themselves and sleeping in the snow. Hill left the stage, hired a dog team, and pushed north through the blizzard. When his métis guide became surly, Hill drove him away at revolver point and plunged on alone. The situation grew more serious: he was sleeping out by night, running behind the dogs by day, existing on a pocketful of pemmican and tea made from melted snow. He traveled this way for eighty miles until he reached Pembina. Here he hired another guide and pressed on toward Fort Garry. On his way across the white wastes of the southern Manitoba prairie he suddenly beheld, emerging from the curtain of swirling snow, the vague outline of another dog team coming south. Its passenger was Donald A. Smith, en route to eastern Canada by way of St. Paul, to report to Ottawa on his successful mediation in the Red River troubles; he had, among other things, bribed Louis Riel into exile with three thousand dollars of his own money and one thousand of the government's.

The scene deserves to be preserved on a broad canvas or re-enacted on a wide screen: the two diminutive figures, muffled in furs, blurred by the drifting snow and dwarfed by that chill desert which stretched off for a hundred and forty miles, unmarked by a single human habitation. There they stopped and shared a frozen meal together—Hill, the young dreamer, his lively mind already crammed with visions of a transportation empire of steel, and Smith, the old Labrador hand, who had clawed his way up the slippery ladder of the fur trade. Hill was thirty-two, Smith fifty; within a decade both of them would be multimillionaires as the result of a mutual association. A quarter of a century later, Smith would recall that bleak scene and say: "I liked him then and I have never had reason to change my opinion."

These were the two adversaries who, in 1871, found themselves locked in a cutthroat battle to control the Red River traffic between Minnesota and Fort Garry, where the nearby village of Winnipeg was slowly rising out of the prairie mud. Since it was axiomatic that neither would give quarter to the other, the two at last agreed to join forces in secret. On the face of it, both antagonists retired from the steamboat business and left the trade in the hands of Norman Kittson's Red River Transportation Company. In actual fact, the Kittson Line, as it was called, was a joint venture of Hill, Kittson, and the Hudson's Bay Company. The Company's shares were in Smith's name, but he agreed in advance to transfer them to whoever succeeded him as chief commissioner. The Kittson Line gave the Hudson's Bay Company a one-third discount on all river freight, and thus a commanding edge on its competitors. That, too, was part of the secret.

No sooner was this clandestine arrangement completed than the freight rates shot skyward. In the winter of 1874–75 a group of Winnipeg and Minnesota merchants, incensed at the monopoly, launched a steamboat line of their own, the Merchants' International. They built two large steamboats, the *Minnesota* and the *Manitoba*, and when the first of these, the *Manitoba*, steamed into Winnipeg on Friday morning, May 14, 1875, an impromptu saturnalia took place on her decks. Champagne flowed all that day, all that night, and again the following morning, by which time the merrymakers had broken a fair share of the vessel's glass and crockery and thrown all their hats overboard in celebration of their release from "the dreaded monopoly."

That summer seven stern-wheelers were plying the Red and another battle was in progress. Norman Kittson, who had once fought the Hudson's Bay as a free trader in Pembina, now fought on the Company's side and without giving quarter. He launched a rate war, bringing his own prices down below cost. Through friends in the Pembina customs depot, he arranged that the *Manitoba* be held indefinitely at the border. When she was finally released in July, Kittson charged her broadside with his *International*, rammed her, and sank her with her entire cargo. The Merchants' Line raised the battered craft and repaired her at staggering cost. No sooner was she back in service than she was seized for a trifling debt. The same fate awaited her sister ship, south of the border. Reeling from this series of blows, the merchants sold out to Kittson in September. Up went the rates again, as Kittson and his colleagues shared a dividend of 80 per cent and the rising wrath of the Red River community.

There was good reason for this fevered strife. The trickle of newcomers into the Red River Valley was rapidly becoming a torrent. By the mid-seventies, the immigrant sheds on the banks of the Red near its confluence with the Assiniboine were bursting with new arrivals who spilled out into a periphery of scattered tents and board shacks. Obviously, whoever controlled transportation into the newly incorporated town of Winnipeg would reap rich profits.

At the time of its incorporation in 1873, Winnipeg was still, in George Ham's description, "a muddy, disreputable village," sprawled between Main Street and the river. It had no sidewalks, no water-works, no sewerage, no pavement; but it had gumbo of such a gluti-nous consistency that for more than a decade every traveler who described the town devoted several vituperative sentences to it. Only the most perceptive of the old-timers saw that the mud was wealth. Father Albert Lacombe, the itinerant prairie oblate, once happened upon a party of immigrants so totally discouraged by Winnipeg's mud that they were planning to return to the East. Lacombe gave them a tongue-lashing: "Then go back, since you have not any more sense than to judge a country before you have looked into it. If there is deep mud here it is only because the soil is fat—the richest in America. But go back to your Massachusetts, if you want, where the soil is all pebbles, and work again in the factories."

Though the mud was not easily conquered, small signs of prog-ress began to appear as the community grew. In September, 1874, the first sod was turned on the long-awaited railway—a branch of the future CPR—that was to run from Selkirk through neighboring St. Boniface to Pembina, to connect, it was hoped, at the border with a United States line, as yet uncompleted.

The construction of the Pembina Branch moved at an unbelievably leaden pace. After the grading was completed, work stopped. There

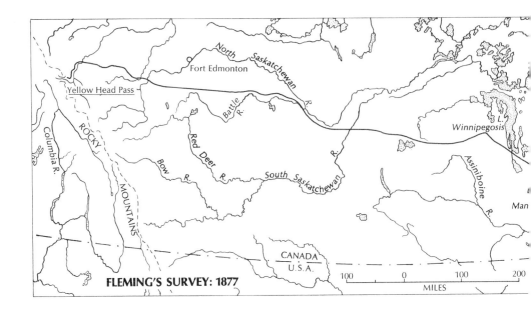

FLEMING'S SURVEY: 1877

was, after all, no point in building a railroad to nowhere—and there was as yet no connecting American line to be seen on the horizon. The contract for laying steel was not let for another three years until it became clear that the St. Paul and Pacific, reorganized and renamed the St. Paul and Manitoba, was actually going to reach the border (as it did late in 1878).

The last spike in the Pembina Branch was finally driven in November, 1878. By this time the population of Winnipeg had risen to six thousand and a gala excursion load of citizens was taken by train to Rousseau for the ceremony. It was decided that one of the ladies should have the honor of driving the final spike, but no one could decide which one. The silver-haired United States consul, James Wickes Taylor, made the diplomatic suggestion that *all* the ladies present should be allowed a whack. Each in her turn pounded away, with little success, until Taylor called over Mary Sullivan, the strapping daughter of an Irish section boss. With a single blow, Miss Sullivan drove the spike home, to the cheers of the assembly.

The cheers did not last long. The rails had been laid, but to describe the Pembina Branch as a railway was to indulge in the wildest kind of hyperbole. Under the terms of the contract, the builders had until November, 1879, to complete the job and turn the finished line over to the government. They determined, in the meantime, to squeeze the maximum possible profit out of it by running it themselves while they continued to build the necessary sidings, station houses, water towers, and all the requisite paraphernalia of a properly run railroad.

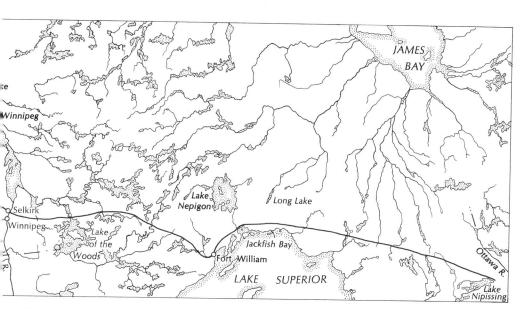

In the months that followed, the Pembina line became the most cursed length of track on the continent. Since there was only one water tank on the whole sixty-three miles, it was the practice of the engineer, when his boiler ran out of steam, to halt beside the closest stream and replenish his water supply. There was no shred of telegraph line along the entire right of way, and so the train dispatching had to be accomplished by using human runners. There were, of course, no repair shops, nor were there any fences, which meant that the train had to make frequent stops to allow cattle to cross the tracks. The only fuel was green poplar, which was piled along the track at intervals. It gave off enormous and encouraging clouds of dense smoke but supplied little energy. Under such conditions it was not easy to build up a head of steam: the passengers were often compelled to wait at a station while the unmoving locomotive, wheezing and puffing away, finally gathered enough motive power to falter off to the next one. The trip to Winnipeg was best described—and in an under-statement—as "leisurely." Passengers were in the habit of alighting to watch the perspiring crew hurling poplar logs aboard the tender. Sometimes they would wander into the woods and go to sleep in the shade. On each of these stops it became necessary to make a head count and beat the bushes, literally, for missing ticket holders. An even more ludicrous spectacle was caused by the lack of a turntable at St. Boniface. When the engine reached that point, it could not turn about but had to make the entire trip back to the border with tender foremost.

To travel the Pembina line in those days required nerves of

steel, a stomach of iron, and a spirit of high adventure. Each time a bridge was crossed, the entire structure, foundations and all, swayed and rocked in a dismaying fashion. The road was improperly ballasted, so that even at eleven miles an hour the cars pitched and tumbled about. In many places mud spurted over the tops of the ties. A man from *The Times* of London, surely accustomed to the derring-do of Victorian journalism, reported that he and his party were more sea-sick on the Pembina Branch than they had been crossing the stormy Atlantic. One of the company, so *The Times*'s man said, had not said his prayers in a long, long time but was so shattered by the experience that he reformed on the spot, took to praying incessantly, and, through sheer terror, managed to evoke some prayers that had lain forgotten in the dim recesses of his mind since childhood; the Pembina railroad shook them loose.

In Winnipeg, the citizenry could only wait and hold their breath and listen to the faint sounds of activity in the East, where, piece by piece, the railway was being built on Canadian soil from the head of Lake Superior.

2 · *Adam Oliver's favorite game*

ON THE AFTERNOON OF JUNE 1, 1875, A spirited little ceremony took place near Fort William, Ontario, on the left bank of the Kaministquia River, about four miles from its mouth on Thunder Bay, Lake Superior, in the sprawling township of Shumiah. Here was turned the first sod of the main line of the Canadian Pacific Railway. The affair was sponsored by the firm of Sifton and Ward, which had secured the contract to grade the first thirty-two miles of roadbed for a line that the government intended to build in sections between Fort William and Selkirk, Manitoba. Like so many contractors in those days, John Wright Sifton and his brother Henry were up to their side whiskers in politics, being close friends and supporters of the Prime Minister.

By two that afternoon, two steamers, "loaded with the beauty and fashion of the neighbourhood," had arrived from Prince Arthur's Landing, four miles away. With a crowd of five hundred in attendance, Judge Delevan Van Norman gained the platform.

"We have met today," he said, "for no other purpose than to inaugurate the beginning of the actual construction of the Canadian Pacific Railway."

The judge confessed his utter inability to do even a measure of justice to the occasion, but he tried manfully nonetheless, pointing out that an immigrant with his family "seeking a new home in this new world, but still under the old flag, may with celerity, safety and certainty examine the country from Cape Breton in Nova Scotia to Vancouver's Island in British Columbia, in the meantime passing over a space as vast as the great ocean that divides and separates the old world from the new."

Then Judge Van Norman told his listeners what they really wanted to hear: Buffalo had once been no larger than Prince Arthur's Landing, Chicago no bigger than Fort William! "I verily believe," the judge said, "that history is about to repeat itself."

Adam Oliver rose as the applause died. He was a bulky man with shrewd, narrow eyes and a small billy-goat beard, who hailed from Oxford County in southwestern Ontario, which he represented in the local legislature. He was known as an impassioned player of euchre, then the most popular family game on the continent. Euchre has several variations, including railroad euchre and cutthroat euchre; Oliver, as events were to prove, certainly knew something about the cutthroat aspects of the railroad game. He and his partners, Joseph Davidson and Peter Johnson Brown (a former reeve of the township), owned forty thousand acres of good timber in the Fort William area together with considerable property and a lumber mill. They already had one government contract, to build the telegraph line accompanying the railroad to the Red River, and were about to sign another for the construction of an engine house. Oliver was also a prominent Liberal.

Amid loud cheers, Oliver pointed to a pile of five hundred wheelbarrows and a thousand shovels lying ready for use.

"Looking farther still up the line you can see hundreds of men clearing the way," he cried, "while the magnificent wharf along the side of the river is rapidly approaching completion. The place on which you are now standing is destined in no distant day to form one of the most important cities in your great Dominion."

He had reason for enthusiasm. As a Senate inquiry tardily discovered, Oliver, Davidson, and Brown were planning to make a killing at the taxpayers' expense.

The story leaked out in the Opposition press in the summer of 1877. Oliver and his Liberal friends, it charged, had been selling land to the government at fancy markups. Worse than that, they had actually put up part of a building—the Neebing Hotel—on land already appropriated for the railway and had managed to sell it to the Crown at an inflated price. A Senate committee, after hearing the evidence, came to the conclusion that the charges were correct.

It was an unblushing piece of jobbery, even for those days. Oliver, Davidson, and Brown were all implicated. Lots purchased by Oliver and his partners for between sixty and ninety dollars were sold two years later to the government for as much as three hundred. And who was acting as an official government evaluator? Brown! In one instance the partners had purchased 136 acres for one thousand dollars and laid out a paper town. They sold a mere eight acres of this non-existent community to the government for four thousand dollars. Again, the valuation was Brown's.

The case of the Neebing Hotel became nationally notorious. The partners had already sold the ground on which the so-called hostelry was to be built and, in addition, had inside knowledge that the rail-road would run directly through the site of the proposed lobby. The hotel, as the Toronto *Mail* reported, was "the only structure of its kind in the world, an imaginary hostelry in an imaginary city. For this shell, unfinished, rudely and hastily thrown together, composed of refuse slabs, with not even a chimney, $5,029 was paid." Testimony showed that the builder was paid only thirteen hundred dollars to construct the hotel, and that the books were shamelessly padded. During the campaign of 1878, John A. Macdonald never failed to draw a laugh when he declared solemnly that the only punishment he wished for the government, if they were defeated, was that they be compelled to board for the next two years at the Neebing Hotel.

Just how much political influence Adam Oliver had with the Mackenzie administration came to light two years later when a royal commission began investigating various contracts awarded along the line between Fort William and the Red River. The circumstances under which Oliver and his partners secured a quarter-million-dollar contract to build the accompanying telegraph line were as astonishing as they were suspicious.

Tenders were opened in August, 1874, but nearly six months of backstage dealing took place before the contract was finally awarded. The lowest bid was passed over in a fashion that the royal commission described as "peremptory." The next two were both entered, in effect, by one Robert Twiss Sutton, who had clearly entered the contest with the hope of being bought off by his competitors, a common practice at the time. In December, Adam Oliver arrived in Ottawa to do the buying off.

The lower of the two Sutton bids was higher by twenty-five thousand dollars than the rejected tender. The other was twenty-eight thousand dollars higher still. It was in the name of Sutton and Thompson. William Thompson, of Brantford, was a mere front man,

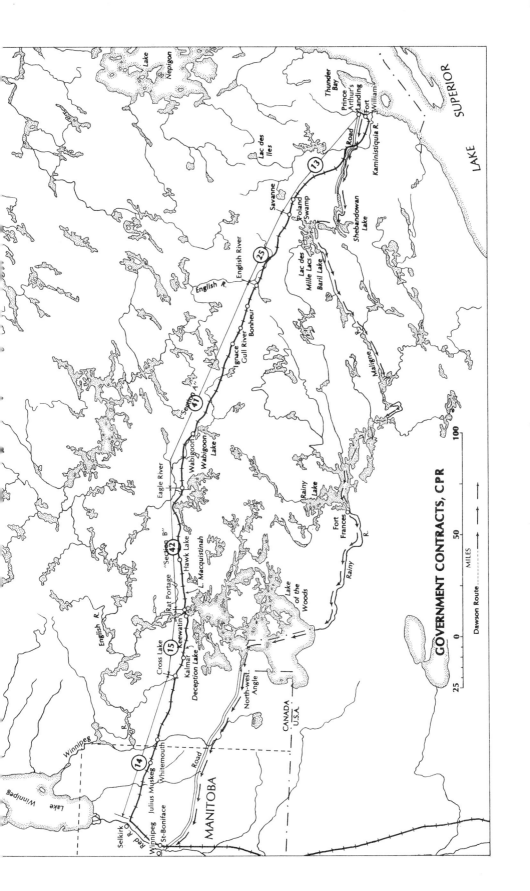

GOVERNMENT CONTRACTS, CPR

MILES

25   0   50   100

Dawson Route

LAKE SUPERIOR

LAKE WINNIPEG

Lake Nepigon

Lac des Iles

Thunder Bay

Prince Arthur's Landing

Fort William

Kaministiquia R.

Road

(13)

Savanne

Poland

Swamp

Shebandowan Lake

Lac des Mille Lacs

Baril Lake

Maligne

English River

(25)

English R.

Bonheur

Gull River

grace

Sebago A''

(41)

Wabigoon

Wabigoon Lake

Eagle River

Rainy Lake

Fort Frances

Rainy R.

"Section B"

(42)

Hawk Lake

L. Macquistinah

Rat Portage

Keewatin

Cross Lake

(15)

Kalmar

Deception Lake

Lake of the Woods

North-west Angle

CANADA
U.S.A.

English R.

Winnipeg R.

Julius Muskeg

Whitemouth

(14)

Road

MANITOBA

Selkirk

Red R.

Winnipeg

St-Boniface

brought in for a price to lend the weight of his name to the tender. Sutton, in fact, made a habit of buying Thompson's name for this purpose.

Oliver arrived in Ottawa expecting to be able to buy up the lower of the two Sutton bids. But once in the capital he discovered for mysterious and unexplained reasons that he could actually be awarded the higher one. Oliver promised Sutton a quarter of the profits; and ended up with the coveted contract. It was fifty-three thousand dollars fatter than it would have been had the lowest tender been accepted.

Apart from the cavalier treatment of the lowest bidder, there was never any explanation of how the higher of the two Sutton bids came to be accepted, rather than the lower one. But one thing did develop from the testimony. Mackenzie himself, Smith's "noble man," handled the entire business and not one of his underlings, as was the general practice. And all the dealings with the minister were in the hands, not of Robert Sutton, the official tenderer, but of Adam Oliver. To achieve the kind of financial miracle that Oliver managed required a detailed knowledge of all the tenders for the contract— information that was supposed to be secret.

In Adam Oliver's favorite game, the maker's side had to win at least three tricks to avoid being euchred. Oliver had won them all: he had got the terminus moved to Fort William, he had sold property to the government at extortionate prices, and he had gained a telegraph contract at a bonus rate. He was not quite as successful as a builder. The complaints about the state of the line were continual. Poles, badly anchored, kept toppling. Wires stretched over trees in lieu of poles strangled and killed them; the roots decayed, and the trees fell over, taking the wires with them. Sometimes it took a message as long as a month to reach Winnipeg on Adam Oliver's expensive telegraph line.

3 · *The stonemason's friends*

THE STRAINS OF OFFICE WERE BEGINNING to tell on Mackenzie's temper and health; it was the railway that was chiefly to blame. Not only was he Prime Minister, but he had also chosen to assume the burden of the Ministry of Public Works, the most sensitive of Cabinet posts in that era of railway contracts. In the spring of 1877, the ex-stonemason revealed a little of his feelings when he exploded in the House that "it is impossible for any man in this country to conduct public affairs without being subjected to the grossest political abuse. Let a political friend get a contract and it is stated at once that [it] is because he is a political friend. Let a political opponent get a contract and we are charged with trying to buy him over to the Government."

Nonetheless, more friends than opponents were awarded contracts on the various sections of the rail and telegraph lines being built along the granites of Superior and the muskegs of Manitoba. Between 1874 and 1878, the Mackenzie government awarded eleven contracts west of Lake Superior, for grading, track laying, and telegraph lines. The total amount paid, as of June 30, 1880, was $5,257,336. Eight of the largest contracts, amounting to $4,986,659, went to prominent Liberal wheelhorses, men who in every case were members of a federal or provincial Parliament, past, present, or future.

"The Mackenzie government," wrote John Willison, a journalist of the period, "like all other governments in Canada, had greedy mercenaries hanging upon its skirts, bent upon pillage and crafty beyond the wit of man in devising means to get at the treasury by devious contracts or skilful alienation of the public resources." Bogus contractors flourished—men who had no intention of grading a mile of line and whose only purpose was to enter a bid so low it had to be accepted, and then to sell the contract for a profit. Of the seventy-two contracts awarded for the construction of the Canadian Pacific Railway during the seventies, there were ten major ones from which the successful low bidders withdrew. The increases involved in awarding these contracts to higher tenderers totaled more than a million dollars. Some of the low bids were entered by men who had no intention of doing the job, others by bona fide contractors who saw a chance to make a bigger profit by pretending to drop out while actually joining forces with a higher bidder and splitting the difference between the bids. In addition, many large contracting firms that paid substantial sums to buy up a contract expected to recoup their losses by charging later for "extras" not included in the original specifications.

In 1880, a royal commission began to inquire into government spending on the CPR. It sat for more than a year and took sworn testimony from scores of witnesses—contractors, surveyors, politicians, journalists. Its exhaustive three-volume report gives a comprehensive picture of the way in which the government sections of the railway were surveyed and constructed, under both Liberal and Conservative regimes. Both were found wanting.

One leading contractor, A. P. MacDonald, himself a former Conservative Member, painted an unpleasant picture of corruption in the Public Works offices. "You do everything in your power to find out where your tender is. You offer inducements to clerks to do things that they would not [normally] do . . . you offer them bribes to get at things that are dangerous. . . . You take a clerk that gets $1,000 a year salary, and offer him $2,000 to get certain information in his office, and there is a temptation for him to break a lock and get it." Some people, MacDonald added, thought everyone in the department was corrupt.

Once a contractor secured the coveted information, he would do his best to prevent the man below him from getting the contract. One method was to try to thwart him from putting up the substantial cash security that was required once a tender was accepted. Men who supplied such surety were generally paid off by the successful tenderers with a cut of the profits, but their rivals often spread the word that the bid was impossibly low and future profits illusory. Unable to raise security money, the low bidder would have to relinquish the contract. Under this system a man who could command large sums of money tended to get the job, no matter what the original bids had been. As MacDonald pointed out, such men "can obtain more favours, etc., than the ordinary contractor could."

Political friends could also obtain special favors. For them, in instance after instance, the department found a way to depart from its rigid policy of accepting the lowest bids. One such firm was Sifton, Glass and Company, which in 1874 managed to acquire a lucrative contract for telegraph construction west from Fort Garry along the proposed right of way. The active partner in this firm was Mackenzie's friend and fellow Liberal, John Wright Sifton. The front man, who did the talking in Ottawa, was David Glass.

Glass was not a contractor at all, and certainly knew very little about building telegraph lines. He was a trial lawyer in London, Ontario, and a good one, known especially for his abilities in murder cases. A swarthy Ulsterman, he had been elected as a Conservative, only to turn against Macdonald in the Pacific Scandal debate of 1873 —the first public defection in the Tory ranks. Now he was a Liberal with a special claim to Mackenzie's gratitude.

That gratitude was not long in appearing. The complicated methods by which Sifton and Glass obtained a contract worth more than one hundred thousand dollars, in spite of the presence of lower tenders, astonished and nettled the royal commission. To put the matter simply, the firm entered a tender so ambiguous that Mackenzie, Fleming, and other members of the department pretended to misunderstand it. The partners tendered on the basis of the entire line but were awarded the contract for only part of it—the easy part;

yet they were allowed to charge for the work as if they were building the difficult parts as well. In short, they were paid an inflated price. Theirs was by no means the lowest bid: two lower bidders mysteriously dropped out and a third firm was passed over on the flimsiest of excuses.

The resultant telegraph line, which the contractors were supposed to maintain for five years, was, like Adam Oliver's, almost totally unsatisfactory. The poles were badly set, so that they often fell into the swamps and muskegs, and—since they were made of short-lived poplar (the cheapest available wood)—quickly rotted and fell away. The contractors, however, pocketed a sizable profit, having received, in the commission's words, "that to which they were not entitled." But a political debt was a political debt, and David Glass could not say that his bold support of the party in 1873 had not been recognized in the contract of 1874.

Another political friend was Joseph Whitehead, former mayor of Clinton, Ontario, and a Liberal Member of Parliament from 1867 to 1872. He was an enormous Yorkshireman with a great bald dome of a head, a vast patriarchal beard, and a big fleshy nose. He had been a railwayman since the very beginning; as a boy, he had helped drive teams of horses which pulled coaches along wooden rails before the days of steam. At the age of eleven, he had been the fireman on Stephenson's first experimental locomotive, which pulled history's first public passenger train on the Stockton and Darlington Railway in England.

Whitehead, said the *Nor'wester*, in a tribute to him while he was grading the line to Pembina, was "a plain working man, [who] knows what work is. . . . He is no kid-gloved, silk-stockinged, patent type of leather-booted, speculating, job-finessing contractor." But as an old railway hand, Whitehead knew enough to be an old political hand, too; in the seventies the two vocations were all but inseparable. He knew how to buy his way into newspapers or the good will of newspapermen, how to peddle influence, how to purchase contracts, and how to deal with politicians. The commission came to the conclusion that "he had a strong belief in the corruptibility of public men." The machinations by which he secured the contract for Section Fifteen of the Thunder Bay–Selkirk line give an insight into the relationship between politics and business in the Mackenzie years.

Section Fifteen was a thirty-seven-mile stretch of right of way that ran through muskeg country between Cross Lake and Rat Portage, near the border between Ontario and Manitoba. Whitehead tendered on the contract for grading and laying track, but when the bids were opened on September 20, 1876, his was certainly not the lowest. As the law required, the lowest tender was awarded the contract; the bidder declined to take it up because, he claimed, his prices had been based on the early completion of an adjoining piece of the line, which was well behind schedule. Accordingly the next lowest bidder, a firm called Martin and Charlton, was awarded the contract. In Whitehead's view, Charlton, a New Yorker, was a jobber "who only wanted to make some money out of it"!

Whitehead had known for some time exactly who had bid and how much had been bid. Indeed, as he later testified, everybody in Ottawa knew as soon as the tenders came in: "I know things that have not been in that department more than a couple of hours before they are known on the street." It was understandable: the sealed bids were simply shoved into an old desk drawer.

Whitehead, then, knew whom to pay off. He had no funds of his own but he did have his brother-in-law, Donald McDonald, a prominent Liberal Senator. McDonald bought off Charlton, the successful bidder, for twenty thousand dollars, charging 10 per cent interest. Mackenzie awarded the contract to the next highest bidder, Sutton and Thompson, a firm which made a practice of bidding low purposely in order to be bought out. To achieve this end, Sutton and Thompson now engaged with Whitehead in a little game of make-believe. As successful bidders they pretended that Whitehead had joined their firm. Then, for a consideration of ten thousand dollars, they dissociated themselves from Whitehead and left him with the contract. The government, however, continued to pretend that the partnership was alive.

In return for his aid, and in addition to his 10 per cent, McDonald asked for and was given an equal partnership in the firm. Since he was a Senator he could not officially be involved in railway construction, and so the industry was treated to the odd spectacle of the Senator's son Mitchell, a bankrupt who knew nothing about railways, apparently working in tandem with the veteran Whitehead.

It had been a neat gambit on Whitehead's part. He had secured a contract worth a million and a half dollars. But this, he figured, would be only the beginning: the area through which Section Fifteen would run had been subjected to the skimpiest of surveys; there would be unavoidable extra charges, not subject to competitive bidding, for which he could bill the government. Before Whitehead was through these extras, none of them officially authorized by the department, had come to $930,000. When Whitehead secured the contract he had estimated his eventual net profit at close to $200,000. He might easily have made that much had it not been for the muskegs of Cross Lake, which in the end forced him to abandon the work.

Another firm that obtained extraordinary favors in the fall of 1874 was Cooper, Fairman and Company, a hardware company in Montreal. The Department of Public Works showed an astonishing preference for this concern in its purchases of steel rails, nuts and bolts, and fish-plates, bending or breaking the rules in several instances.

What was Cooper and Fairman's secret? The silent partner of the firm was a Sarnia hardware merchant named Charles Mackenzie. He was the Prime Minister's brother. In 1873 he had put fifteen thousand dollars into the firm—more than the other two partners combined. He was to receive a third of all profits in return. There were no profits and, indeed, no losses—no business, in truth—until the government contracts began to roll in. Mackenzie left the company officially in May, 1875, after the story leaked out, but there is no doubt he was very much a part of the firm for at least a portion of the period when his brother's department was granting it extraordinary public favors.

As it turned out, not all the steel rails were really needed. They had been purchased prematurely—fifty thousand tons of them—apparently because both Fleming and Mackenzie believed they were getting a bargain. The purchase was a disaster for all but Cooper, Fairman and Company. At most, twenty thousand tons were needed for the work in progress. But having purchased that amount, Mackenzie ordered an additional thirty thousand tons, even though the price was higher. Half of this extra order was supplied by Cooper and Fairman at double the going rate. After that, to everyone's dismay, the bottom dropped out of the market. The rails rusted for years, unused, while the price of new rails went lower and lower and the interest mounted on the original investment. It was beginning to be apparent to the country at large that the government's venture into the railway business was as disastrous as that of Sir Hugh Allan.

4 · *"Mean, treacherous coward!"*

FROM HIS POPLAR-SHADED MANSION OF Silver Heights, high above the serpentine Assiniboine, Donald A. Smith was contemplating with more than passing interest the future of the Pembina Branch line. In 1875, as a Member of Parliament, he had been part of a delegation that had lobbied for the line to be built. By 1878, his interest was personal as well as political. He was a member of a syndicate which was establishing rail connection from St. Paul to

Pembina on the border. If the same group could lease the government road, it would have a through line to Winnipeg. It was left to Smith to handle the matter politically. As the man who had laid the last straw on the camel's back in the Pacific Scandal debacle of 1873, he had considerable pull with the Mackenzie government.

There was something a little frightening about Donald A. Smith. Perhaps it was the eyebrows—those bristling, tangled tufts that jutted out to mask the cold, uncommunicative gray eyes and provide their owner with a perpetual frown. At fifty-eight, his face leathered by the hard glare of the Labrador snows, his sandy locks and flowing beard frosted by the years, Smith had the look of a Biblical patriarch.

Nothing could touch him; the Hudson's Bay Company had seen to that. There is a particularly telling story about Smith's service within the Company that underlines the Spartan aspects of his character. Years before, in the heart of Labrador, he had suffered an appalling attack of snow blindness, an affliction that turns the whole world crimson and makes the victim feel as if his eyeballs are being scoured with burning grit. Accompanied by two half-breed guides, the sufferer set off from his post at Mingan, which lies on the northern coast of the Gulf of St. Lawrence, on a fearful snowshoe journey to Montreal, five hundred and fifty-five miles distant by crow's flight. Arriving at his destination, Smith hammered on the door of Sir George Simpson, the "Little Emperor," who ran the Company with a hand of iron. Simpson was not remotely concerned about Smith's plight; rather he was enraged that a servant of the Company should have deserted his post. He gave the victim a tongue-lashing: "If it's a question between your eyes and your service in the Hudson's Bay Company, you'll take my advice and return this instant." Then, after a cursory medical examination, he turned him face-about into the snows. The return journey was so harsh that the guides died before reaching their destination. Smith stumbled the remainder of the way, half dead from exhaustion, fear, and hunger. Years later when asked to describe that ghastly journey, he could not bring himself to recall it. "No, no, I can't," he told an interviewer. "It is too terrible to think about."

There is no doubt that this incident, and others like it in that bleak land which the first explorer, Jacques Cartier, said belonged to Cain, had left its mark upon him. For all his life he never complained and he never explained; that was the Company way. Few public men had more vitriol heaped upon them than Smith in his long lifetime; he bore it all without blinking as he had borne the Little Emperor's abuse. In the election of 1874, Macdonald's supporters, incensed beyond reason by his defection from their ranks, had pelted him with raw eggs until he was unrecognizable. He did not flinch. Wintry of temperament, courtly of manner, he wrapped himself in a screen of suavity which masked the inner fires, bitter furies, and hard resolution of his soul. He was unshakable in crisis, and this quality, one future day, would stand the CPR in good stead. It was impossible to panic Smith; he invested in stocks and debentures with Scottish prudence, but once he bought a stock, so legend had it, he never sold it.

In Winnipeg he was admired, hated, feared, respected, but scarcely loved. On his first visit to the North West as Macdonald's envoy in the Riel uprising, he had shown courage, tact, and diplomacy. His name was mentioned as a possible Lieutenant-Governor of Manitoba. Smith preferred the hurly-burly of political life. His active support came from the fur traders, many of whom were shunted across constituency lines at Company expense on election day. Being disciplined Hudson's Bay Company men, they knew what to do.

For all of his days in Winnipeg, Donald A., as he was called, was a figure of controversy. Seldom quoted in the newspapers, he was constantly attacked in them, especially after he shifted his political loyalties in 1873. The Laird of Silver Heights remained imperturbable, traveling daily by coach the six miles to and from his office, living his Spartan life—two meals a day, no spirits—sitting around the fire at night with visitors, recalling the old days in Labrador. His stays in Winnipeg were solitary enough, for his wife refused to join him in the North West. She was a child of Labrador and the hub of her existence had always been the fur traders' capital, Montreal. Smith had married her, in the custom of the trade, by "the rites of Labrador," i.e., without benefit of clergy, there being none available in those days. Years later, when he was about to become Lord Strathcona, it was revealed that he had no marriage certificate. This would never do: with his title in the balance, Smith agreed to a hasty wedding at the British Embassy in Paris. He was seventy-seven at the time.

The rail line to the border, which Smith and his partners coveted, was officially a branch of the almost nonexistent CPR. Early in 1878, before the branch line was completed, Smith's cousin George Stephen made several trips from Montreal to arrange with Alexander Mackenzie for a ten-year lease of the government line to the syndicate, which was building the connecting line to the border from St. Paul. On March 18, Mackenzie rose in the House to introduce a bill which would empower Parliament to lease the Pembina Branch to unspecified parties. The House would have to approve the principle first, Mackenzie pointed out, before going into the details of any contract. No mention was made of Donald A. Smith's interest; indeed, the Prime Minister was at considerable pains to conceal it from the House and the public. Smith's name was an abomination to the Conservative Opposition; he had made some bitter enemies in 1873 and one of them was Macdonald, a political leader famous for the retort that he did not want men who would stick by him when he was right, he wanted men who would stick by him when he was wrong. Smith had not stuck by him. If, in 1878, the Member from Selkirk had risen in the House to support motherhood, it is conceivable that Macdonald and his followers would have been strongly tempted to opt for matricide. They were out for Smith's blood.

When the debate began, on April 4, 1878, Macdonald and his followers were ready with sharpened claws. It had scarcely been launched when George Kirkpatrick, a locomotive manufacturer, pointed out that the group seeking the lease were proprietors of the reviled Kittson Line of steamboats, which "had ground down the people of Manitoba." A railway to Winnipeg, Kirkpatrick pointed out, would simply increase their monopoly.

Another Tory Member (and a future Prime Minister), Mackenzie Bowell, pressed the attack on Smith when he warned the Government that there might be persons connected with the St. Paul line "who had political influence which they used to their own advantage and to the detriment of this country." But in the acrimonious set-to which followed, Smith never at any time admitted to his own substantial interest in the company, even when pressed and taunted by the Opposition—though it was clear to all that he was deeply and personally involved.

Bowell put his finger on Smith's tenderest spot when he declared that the House was witnessing "the extraordinary spectacle of the champion of this proposed lease using his power and influence as a very humble and obedient supporter of the Government to secure to himself and his partners in this transaction the advantage of a lease."

Macdonald followed with a cutting attack on his old enemy: "There was seen the indecent spectacle of an honourable gentleman coming into the House as an advocate and pressing this lease in his own interest . . . he advocated more warmly and strongly this Bill, which was in his own interest, and which would put money in his own pocket, than the Minister who introduced it. The hon. gentleman admitted he was a partner in this concern, and the House should know something about it."

"I have admitted no such thing," Smith retorted; but Macdonald pointed out that he had not denied it, "and there is no doubt that, if he could have done so, he would."

It was inevitable that the bill should pass; but it was a different story in the appointed Senate, where the Tories still had a preponderance of votes. The Senate, in effect, threw the bill out and there is no doubt it did so because of Smith's involvement.

On May 9, the day before the end of the session, Mackenzie reprimanded the Senate for its actions. This allowed Macdonald to return to the attack. The Senate's actions, he said, put a stop to the Government's bargain with Smith "to make him a rich man, and to pay for his servile support."

Macdonald's sally provoked, in the closing moments of what turned out to be the final session of the Mackenzie Parliament, the most explosive and perhaps the most harrowing scene in the history of the Canadian House of Commons.

Smith was not in the House on May 9 but he read an account of Macdonald's attack in the press. The following day the House was scheduled to dissolve. The Members were in their seats at 3 P.M., awaiting the traditional knock of the Gentleman Usher of the Black Rod, when Smith, brandishing the Ottawa *Free Press* in his hand, arose on a question of privilege.

He denied that he had ever admitted being a member of the St. Paul syndicate and declared that as a Member from Manitoba, he had labored earnestly for a railway connection for two or three years; now that it had become possible, the Opposition was putting every obstacle in its way. He began to attack Charles Tupper for some remarks Tupper had made the previous summer.

Tupper, seeing the Gentleman Usher of the Black Rod at the door (the signal that the session was at an end), realized that he would have no opportunity to answer. The Cumberland War Horse had no intention of allowing that. He rose at once on a point of order, forced Smith to his seat, and asked the Speaker if it was not an abuse of the rights of Parliament to bring up an old matter, since Smith had had three months during the session to refer to it. Tupper charged that Smith's tactics were "to shelter himself from the answer he would otherwise get."

An exchange followed in which Tupper accused Smith of cowardice. He began to bellow across the floor in the face of repeated cries of "Order!" that Smith had telegraphed his support of the Government at the time of the Pacific Scandal debate in 1873. Smith denied it.

Macdonald tried to break in, but Smith kept going. More bedlam! The Liberal benches were now in full cry. "It was a sight to make sluggish blood tingle!" one eyewitness recalled. The vain knocking of Black Rod could be heard faintly at the Commons door behind the uproar; the Speaker tried in vain to answer, then resignedly resumed his seat.

Smith continued to speak, and with each new declaration the verbal contest grew more heated. As the Opposition cried "Order!" and the Government benches shouted "Hear! Hear!", Smith, over Macdonald's objections, began to recall that last evening before his speech of 1873, when the Prime Minister had received him with drunken abuse. Tupper, he said, had told him that very night that Macdonald was not capable of knowing what he said.

Now Tupper was on his feet, demanding of the Speaker whether it was "competent for a man to detail private conversations while falsifying them." Determined to turn the course of the debate into a less embarrassing channel, Tupper cried that he was prepared to prove that Smith's statement that he had never sought a favor from the Government was "as false a statement as ever issued from the mouth of any man, and he has continued with a tissue . . ." Tupper was unable to finish the sentence because of the cries for order, but he regained the attack, charging that Smith had once begged for a Privy Council post. As Smith parried the attack, the sergeant at arms managed to announce "a message from the Governor General."

The House continued in disorder and the Speaker tried to say that he had "very much pleasure in informing the House it now becomes my duty to receive the messenger." Then Tupper's powerful voice was heard, over all, bellowing "Coward! Coward!" at the imperturbable Smith.

Smith held his place.

"Coward! Coward! Coward!" Tupper boomed. "Mean, treacherous coward!"

"Who is the coward?" Smith retorted. "The House will decide—it is yourself."

"Coward!" shouted Tupper once again. "Treacherous . . ."

Smith began to speak again, but the harried Speaker interrupted him and asked that Black Rod be admitted.

It was Macdonald who got in the last word, surely the most unparliamentary expression ever to appear in *Hansard*.

"That fellow Smith," he cried, "is the biggest liar I ever met!"

The Gentleman Usher was admitted, performed his graceful triple bow, the sergeant at arms shouldered the mace, and the Speaker descended from his chair, followed by "as excited a mob as ever disgraced the floor of a Parliamentary chamber." Tupper and Macdonald and several other Tories, enraged beyond endurance, rushed at Smith, bent on physical assault. Several tried to strike him. The Speaker, without naming them, called for their arrest. Macdonald had to be pulled away from Smith, crying that he "could lick him quicker than hell could scorch a feather." The disorder was so great that the Speaker could not at once leave the House because of the throng at the door. Finally he was allowed to proceed to the Senate chamber, followed by the disheveled crowd. Thus did the Mackenzie regime come to an end, not with a whimper but a bang. It could not accommodate Donald A. Smith and his colleagues with an exclusive lease of the Pembina Branch, but it could grant running rights for ten years over the line and it did just that in August. That was one of its last official acts.

7

1 · Resurrection

SEPTEMBER 17, 1878, WAS THE DAY OF A political miracle in Canada. True to Charles Tupper's forecast, made in the dark days of '73, the Conservatives had risen again. Long before the election was called, it was clear that the party was on the rise; but nobody could be sure of the results. When they began to come in, few could give them credence.

In the election, the Liberals found themselves on the defensive, with their railway policy trenchantly supported and vehemently attacked in rival political pamphlets, some of which, it turned out, were written by the same scriveners. There is a story about Edward Farrer, of the *Mail*, walking around Parliament Hill in a brown study after a sleepless night.

"What are you doing up at this hour?" asked a friend, who encountered him.

"Thinking over my paper in defense of the Government's railway policy," Farrer told him.

"Well, are you satisfied with your work?"

"Satisfied, yes. I am so damn well satisfied that I don't see how I'm going to answer it and that's what's keeping me up." He had undertaken to write a similar campaign sheet for the Tories.

The country was on Macdonald's side more strongly than even he suspected. Macdonald was not a man to share his innermost thoughts with anyone; even his wife had no idea how he guessed the vote might go. Toward the end of July it became a necessity for her to gain some inkling, since a Conservative victory would mean a move back to the capital from Toronto, where the Opposition leader had been practicing law. She prodded her husband to give her a hint until at last he spoke: "If we do well, we shall have a majority of sixty; if badly, thirty." As it turned out, he did better than his most optimistic forecast.

Election day dawned bright and crisp in Ontario. Before the sun was up, tens of thousands of canvassers from both parties were scouring the incredibly rutted and hilly back roads for doubtful voters. The political uncertainties were compounded by the fact that this was to be the first federal secret ballot. This time no one could count noses or threaten wavering electors.

The polls closed at five, and by seven it was clear that Macdonald had suffered personal defeat in Kingston. But this news was superseded by indications of massive Conservative gains. By nine, it was apparent that the Mackenzie administration had fallen; by eleven, that Macdonald and his party had scored a landslide of unprecedented proportions. In the session just past, the Liberals had held 133 seats to the Conservatives' 73. In the new Commons, the Conservatives would have 137 seats to the Liberals' 69. Both Blake and Cartwright had gone down to defeat. For Macdonald, who would soon win a by-election in Victoria, revenge was sweet.

He was overwhelmed by the magnitude of his victory. The elections, Lord Dufferin reported to London, had "taken the entire political world by surprise." A week later both parties were still in a state of shock: "Sir John himself was as much astonished by the sweep as anybody." As for Mackenzie, he wrote a friend that "nothing has happened in my time so astonishing."

Mackenzie's railway policy had cost him the West. Worse, he had also lost Ontario. By election day he was an exhausted man, teetering on the edge of a long decline, made irritable by the tensions and travails of office. Macdonald had the ability to bounce back after defeat. Part of the secret of his long tenure of office was his refusal to worry—the gift of putting things from his mind once events had taken their course. Unlike Mackenzie, he had the capacity to delegate authority. Mackenzie attempted personally to handle the smallest details of his department, and when his subordinates disappointed him by being unable to meet his standards, he broke under the strain. He was not to lead his party for long, for in truth he was already "a dry shell of what he had been." One day on the steps of Parliament Mackenzie spoke of his depressed spirits to Macdonald, who replied: "Mackenzie, you should not distress yourself over these things. When I fell in 1874, I made up my mind to cease to worry and think no more about [it]." To which Mackenzie made the candid and illuminating reply: "Ah, but I have not that happy frame of mind."

For two years after his defeat, the Tory chieftain had kept his peace while the Liberal press continued to announce his imminent retirement. Then, during the session of 1876, Macdonald revived, and the country became familiar with, the phrase "National Policy."

By then the industrial situation in Canada was critical. United States manufacturers, protected in their own markets by heavy duties, were dumping their surplus products into the Canadian "slaughter market" at cut-rate prices. Industry after industry was forced to the wall, and still Mackenzie, the traditional free trader, made no move toward protection.

Macdonald proposed to readjust tariffs so as to support local manufacturers, mining, and agriculture, to restore prosperity to the struggling native industries, to stop the flow of Canadians across the border to the United States, and to protect Canadian interests from un-fair competition. He did not use the word "protection," which the free-trading Grits had made unpopular. Instead, at a series of political picnics, which became an established feature of the Canadian scene in the late seventies, he talked of prosperity and "Canada for the Cana-dians." In a depression-ridden nation it was an attractive slogan.

The National Policy was an aspect of Macdonald's anti-Yankee philosophy, and his speeches on the subject set the pattern for political rhetoric for another century. "We will not be trampled upon and ridden over, as we have [been] in the past, by the capitalists of a foreign country," he told an audience in the Eastern Townships of Quebec in 1877.

In 1878 the National Policy was nothing more than a euphemism for a protective tariff, but in later years it was seen as one leg of a three-cornered foundation on which the superstructure of the trans-continental nation rested. The other two legs were the encouragement of western settlement and the construction of the Pacific railway. The railway was the key: without it western settlement would be difficult; with it there would be more substantial markets for the protected industries. Macdonald himself saw this. "Until this great work is com-pleted, our Dominion is little more than a 'geographical expression,' " he told Sir Stafford Northcote, the Governor of the Hudson's Bay Company. "We have as much interest in British Columbia as in Aus-tralia, and no more. The railway once finished, we become one great united country with a large interprovincial trade and a common in-terest."

The National Policy, which won Macdonald his stunning victory in

1878 and which helped to keep his party in office for almost twenty years, was to become the policy of the country. The future would extend it to include a variety of awkward, expensive, and contentious Canadian devices which, like the railway, would continue the horizontal development of the nation that Macdonald began.

Though the two parties differed on the tariff, in 1878 there was not much difference between the new government's railway policy and that of its predecessor. Mackenzie had long since abandoned his original idea of a land-and-water route (a mixture which, Macdonald quipped, "generally produces mud") and clearly wanted to get rid of the piecemeal method of construction, which was causing so much trouble west of Lake Superior. His excuse for not proceeding faster and linking the two main sections under construction in that area was that he wanted the whole undertaking to be in the hands of a single private company.

That was Macdonald's hope, too. But in the absence of any offers from private capitalists, his administration was forced to continue Mackenzie's policy of building the line in installments: the 171-mile gap in the Lake Superior area would be completed and contracts would be let for an additional two hundred miles to run west of the Red River. The work would be accomplished without raising taxes. As Tupper, the new Minister of Railways, announced in May, 1879, the line would be paid for by selling the uncultivated land of the western plains.

Tupper also announced that the route would be lengthened to pass south of Lake Manitoba. Moreover, the selection of Burrard Inlet as the Pacific terminus was premature. The government wanted more time to make more surveys, including surveys of the Pine and Peace River passes and of Port Simpson on the coast. Marcus Smith's furious efforts had obviously not been in vain.

On the other hand, there were "the excited feelings of British Columbia in consequence of long delays." Because of these, the government felt compelled to let contracts in 1879 for 125 miles of railway between Yale, in the Fraser canyon, and Kamloops. The contracts were let in four sections. One of the bidders on all four (though by no means the lowest) was a young American named Andrew Onderdonk, the courtly scion of a prominent Hudson River family of Dutch ancestry. Onderdonk arrived in Ottawa in November, 1879, at the time the tenders were opened, his pockets stuffed with letters of recommendation from Canadian bankers and United States railwaymen.

Onderdonk went straight to see Tupper, and Tupper was impressed. Onderdonk had almost unlimited means from American financiers behind him. In the muskeg country west of Lake Superior, Canadian contractors were running into difficulties; Joseph Whitehead was teetering on the edge of financial ruin. Some of the low bidders on the four British Columbia sections looked alarmingly shaky. Obviously, a man of experience backed by solid capital could build all four sections more cheaply and efficiently than four underfinanced contractors working independently. Onderdonk was allowed to purchase all the contracts, paying a total of $215,000 for the privilege. He arrived at Yale on April 22, 1880, to a salute of thirteen guns, and by May was ready to begin construction. None of Macdonald's followers appeared to grasp the irony of a Conservative Government awarding an important section of the railway to a Yankee contractor.

Marcus Smith, who had been pronounced dead by both Fleming and Mackenzie, refused to lie down on the subject of the Pine Pass– Bute Inlet route. Indeed, he seems to have gained a new lease on life with the advent of the new administration—an administration in which Fleming's position was becoming increasingly insecure.

There is something madly magnificent about Smith's furious wind-mill-tilting at this late date. He simply refused to give up. On January 20, 1879, he sent Tupper a confidential memorandum detailing his differences with Fleming, whose reports he categorized as "an apology for a course predetermined by the Minister." He followed this up with another long memo asking Tupper to give him charge of a two-year survey of the Pine Pass section of the Bute Inlet route—scarcely a feasible suggestion in view of the clamor from British Columbia. And in May he wrote to Macdonald asking him to intercede on his behalf to reinstate him as engineer of the British Columbia division, the job he had held before becoming Fleming's deputy.

In the meantime, Henry Cambie had taken a notable party of sur-veyors and scientists right across the hinterland of northern British Columbia. They started at Port Simpson, worked their way up the Skeena, and then followed a succession of rivers, canyons, and moun-tain trails on foot and packsaddle and by canoe, raft, and leaky boat until they reached the Peace River country on the far side of the moun-tains. In all that journey they did not encounter a single human being. Cambie returned on his own with a pack train and reached the top of the Pine Pass in a raging blizzard. He made his way back to civiliza-tion down the fast-freezing Fraser, shooting the rapids of the canyon himself, without a pilot. "Sham surveys," Smith called them when Cambie returned; but on the strength of his report the Government, in October, 1879, finally gave up on the Bute Inlet route and announced that Burrard Inlet would be the official terminus after all. The Yellow Head, apparently, would be the pass through the Rockies.

Still Marcus Smith would not admit defeat. He wrote immediately to

Senator David Macpherson, attacking the whole decision, and then allied himself with General Butt Hewson, an American engineer resident in Canada, who was preparing a pamphlet advocating that the Fraser contracts be canceled and that either Bute or Dean Inlet be named as the terminus and the Pine Pass substituted for the Yellow Head.

All this pressure undoubtedly had some effect on public policy. On February 16, 1880, Tupper told the House that he still wanted more information on the Pine River–Peace River country before finally making up his mind about the choice of a pass through the Rockies. It was now the ninth year of the Canadian Pacific Survey in British Columbia, and it seemed by this time that every notch in each of the mountain ranges and all the intervening trenches had been combed as carefully as a Japanese sand garden. Moberly's men had toiled up the slopes of the Howse, Edward Jarvis had almost starved at the Smoky, Cambie and Horetzky had struggled over the Pine and the Peace, Roderick McLennan had lost all his horses probing the Athabasca, Moberly himself had braved the avalanches in the Selkirks, while Fleming, not to mention a score of others, had come through the Yellow Head.

Every pass had been checked with transit, level, and aneroid, again and again; every pass had been argued over, reported on, discarded or, sometimes, resurveyed—every pass, that is, except the Kicking Horse, which lay to the south, neglected and unsurveyed, waiting to be chosen.

2 · *"Get rid of Fleming"*

SANDFORD FLEMING'S DAYS AS ENGINEER-in-Chief were numbered. The dissensions within his own department, as symbolized by the intractable Marcus Smith; the total identification with Mackenzie's sluggish and sometimes inept railway policies; the bills coming in from Lake Superior, far in excess of estimates; the expensive surveys in British Columbia—all these were laid at his door. In the spring of 1879 he had been given a hard time as a witness before the Commons Public Accounts Committee, and it was clear that more investigations were to follow.

Macdonald intended that Fleming should go, but with as much honor as possible and with the government's blessing; one never knew when he might be needed again. Clearly, Fleming was not the man to prosecute Macdonald's aggressive railway policy. He could be maddening in his caution yet wild in his extravagances. He had, for instance, insisted on a great many instrumental surveys in British

Columbia when simple exploratory surveys would have done, for the routes were later abandoned as too expensive, too difficult, or too unwieldy. And why, for instance, did he wait five years before consulting the Admiralty about the usefulness of the various coastal harbors? A great deal of money could have been saved if these reports had been in his hands at the outset, for they made it clear that Burrard Inlet was the only really satisfactory terminus on the mainland.

Fleming, of course, had to take the blame for all the political sins of the day, including governmental delay and patronage. But Fleming also tried to do too much. When he was on the job he could give only half of his working day, admittedly a long one, to the Pacific railway; and, after 1876, when the Intercolonial was completed, he spent a great deal of time away from the job on doctor's orders, working on his concept of standard time, visiting Thomas Carlyle, hobnobbing with the Prince of Wales in Paris. Even in Ottawa a great deal of his time was taken up with preparing for and testifying before parliamentary committees of inquiry.

Overly scrupulous in the Far West, he appeared to have been unduly hasty in his eastern surveys. Here there were terrible delays and extraordinary added charges because the engineers on the job had made only cursory examinations of the ground. In every case between 1875 and 1878, the contractors arrived on the job before their work was fully laid out. Contracts were let on the basis of profile plans only, so that the estimates of the quantities of rock and earth to be removed or filled were nothing more than guesses and expensive adjustments had to be made after the fact. On four contracts tendered at a total cost of $3,-587,096 the government paid extras amounting to $1,804,830. The surveyors apparently had no idea of the kind of ground the railway builders would be working. They did not know, for instance, how deep the marshes and muskegs would go; and, because they had not studied the nature of muskeg, huge prices were paid for fill materials. Muskeg (boggy material, generally frozen) is so spongy that when it is taken from an embankment and dried out it loses about half its size. Yet the removal of muskeg, and its employment as fill, was charged for as if it were ordinary earth. On one contract, the loss from this oversight amounted to $350,000.

Often enough, Fleming, the thrifty Scot, was penny wise and pound foolish. The cost of running the railway through the gorges of the Thompson and the Fraser to Burrard Inlet seemed so high that he continued to search, diligently but vainly, for a cheaper route. On the other hand, the cost of probing the muskegs in advance seemed to Fleming so great that he decided he could not afford it; in that instance, further exploration would have paid off. In all this expensive penny-pinching, Mackenzie was Fleming's partner, but there is no evidence that the Engineer-in-Chief ever argued with him. For a good deal of the time Fleming simply was not available and his deputy, Marcus Smith, was not on speaking terms with his political master. These displays of temperament were costly and confusing. Sometimes, in fact, because of lack of communication, the work proceeded on its own momentum without authority.

The royal commission put most of the blame on Fleming's shoulders. It was not all warranted. Charles Horetzky was one of the witnesses the commissioners paid attention to. His testimony was venomous: "Mr. Fleming stands convicted of deliberate and malicious falsehood. His malevolence has been directed against me ever since I brought the Pine Pass under his notice. In doing so I unconsciously wounded his vanity, which could not brook the idea of any one but himself proposing a route."

Only a few months before giving this testimony, Horetzky had written to Fleming offering his friendship while attacking Tupper, whose protégé he had been in 1872 ("I have it in for Tupper and will follow him to the last. I shall never forget in a hurry his insulting language to my wife"). Fleming received "three extraordinary letters in which he volunteered to pledge me his lasting friendship provided I would assist in getting him the money he demanded from the Government, at the same time vowing vengeance if I failed to recommend payment."

Fleming was eased out of office in February, 1880, before the royal commission began its hearing. The government provided for him handsomely. Since the Minister of Public Works was paid five thousand dollars a year and Fleming, as chief engineer of the Intercolonial, was already receiving forty-eight hundred, it had been considered impolitic to raise his salary when he assumed the double burden. But the Government sent him on his way with an additional thirty thousand. It also offered him a titular post with the railway, but this Fleming declined; he did not care to be a figurehead.

When the royal commission finally made its report it came down very hard on the former Engineer-in-Chief, but by then the construction of the railway was proceeding apace. Fleming went off to the International Geographical Congress in Venice to ride in gondolas and deliver a paper entitled "The Adoption of a Prime Meridian." Greater glories followed. His biography, when it was published, did not mention the petty jealousies, the bursts of temperament, the political jockeying, the caution, the waste, and the near anarchy that were commonplace in the engineering offices of the Public Works Department under his rule. He survived it all and strode into the Canadian history books without a scar. The story of his term as Engineer-in-Chief is tangled and confused, neither black nor white, since it involved neither villains nor saints but a hastily recruited group of very human and often brilliant men faced with superhuman problems, not the least of which was the specter of the Unknown, and subjected to more than ordinary tensions including the insistent tug of their own ambitions.

If there is a verdict on Fleming, it is an indirect one. When the railway was finally organized as a private company, most of his surveys were discarded and an entirely new line was mapped out across the Shield, north of Lake Superior, through the southern prairies and across three mountain ranges. The matter was handled with dispatch, certainty, and even foolhardiness. William Cornelius Van Horne hustled his surveyors on, following their line of location so swiftly that they were hard pressed to stay ahead of him. It was madness, perhaps, but it got the entire job done in exactly half the time it took Fleming and his political colleagues to make up their minds about a route through British Columbia.

But, then, the times were different, the circumstances were different, the economics were different, and the men were different, too.

3 · *Bogs without bottom*

"WE BEGAN THE WORK OF CONSTRUCTION of Canada's great highway at a dead end," wrote Harry William Dudley Armstrong, a resident engineer along the half-completed Fort William–Selkirk line in the mid-seventies. It was true. One chunk of railway was begun at the Red River and run hesitantly eastward toward the muskegs on the Ontario-Manitoba border. Another was built westward from Fort William, literally to nowhere. These two pieces were useless because they did not connect. The railway builders were at work in the empty heart of Canada without rail transportation to supply them, in a country scarcely explored; they were forced to rely on steamers, flatboats, canoes, and barges to haul in supplies and construction materials. Four years later, when other contractors began to fill in the 181-mile gap between, every pound of supplies had to be taken in over the lakes by canoe and portage because the end of steel was still a good hundred miles from the water route. Steam shovels, horses, even locomotives and flatcars had to be hauled by sleigh in the wintertime over the frozen lakes, the ice-sheathed granite, and the snow-shrouded muskegs. Joseph Whitehead had a quarter million dollars' worth of machinery—steam drills, boilers, and the like—which had to be transported in this manner at prodigious cost. Indeed, some of it could not be gotten into the Cross Lake country at all until the road was in a condition to carry traffic; it lay along the line of railway out of Winnipeg for months, eating up interest charges. On Contract Forty-two, better known as Section B, eighty thousand dollars was spent just moving in supplies before a foot of road was graded or a single rail laid.

The distance between Fort William and Selkirk was only 435 miles as the surveyors plotted the line. But no one, not surveyors, not contractors, and certainly not politicians, knew the problems that lay ahead. It took seven years before through rail communication was completed from the lakehead to the Red River.

Armstrong, in a private memoir, wrote of those early days when his nearest neighbor was nine miles away, when he walked as far as fifteen miles to work and back again each day, when in the absence of any doctor he acted as midwife at the birth of his first child. Like almost everybody else who recalled those times, he remembered the mosquitoes and black flies rising from the stinking, half-frozen swamps in clouds that blotted out the sun. On one occasion, wading between the stumps of a spruce and tamarack swamp, the water four feet deep, the frozen bottom covered by a foot-thick sponge of moss, Armstrong, who was carrying a level on his shoulder, looked at the forefinger on his left hand, curled around the tripod. There, on the second joint alone, were no fewer than nine mosquitoes "with their bills sunk to the hilt on that space and they were equally thick on any exposed part of face or hands."

The land that the railway builders set out to conquer was beautiful in its very bleakness. At the western end of Lake Superior it was almost all rock—the old, cracked rock of the Canadian Shield, gray and russet, striped by strata, blurred by pink lichens, garlanded by the dark vines and red berries of kinnikinnick and sparkling, sometimes, with the yellow pinpoints of cinquefoil. From the edges of the dun-colored lakes that lay in the gray hollows there protruded the spiky points of the spruce, jet black against the green clouds of birch and poplar. Sometimes there were tiger lilies, blue vetch, briar rose, and oxeye daisies to relieve the somber panorama; but in the winter the land was an almost unendurable monochrome of gray.

As the line moved west, the land changed and began to sparkle. Between the spiny ridges lay sinuous lakes and lesser ponds of bright blue or olive green from which the yellow flowers of the spatterdock glittered. The lakes became more numerous toward the west, the bright sheets of water winding in chains between the broken, tree-covered vertebrae of granite, with here and there a chartreuse meadow of tall, rank grass. This lake country, smiling in the sunshine, gloomy in the frequent slashing rains, would one day become a tourist mecca; but in the seventies it was a hellhole for railway builders who saw their fortunes sink forever in the seemingly bottomless slime of the great muskeg swamps.

The muskegs came in every size. There were the notorious sink-holes—little lakes over which a thick crust of vegetable matter had formed and into which the line might tumble at any time. There was one sinkhole near Savanne, north of Fort William, so legend has it, where an entire train with a thousand feet of track was swallowed whole. Sometimes new sinkholes would appear in land thought to be as solid as Gibraltar. This phenomenon was partly due to an imperfect knowledge of frost conditions. During the winter the railway builders would construct enormous fills—work that looked as if it would last forever. But this would cause the frozen muskeg beneath to melt and the entire foundations would begin to heave and totter. Time and again these new holes would be filled only to reappear once more.

Worse than the sinkholes were the giant muskegs, like the Poland Swamp or the incredible Julius Muskeg, the most infamous bog of all—a vast bed of peat six miles across, depth unknown, sufficient, it was said, to supply the entire North West with fuel. From these deceptively level moss-covered stretches the naked trunks of dead tamaracks protruded, their roots weaving a kind of blanket over a concealed jelly of mud and slime. Across these seemingly impassable barriers the road was carried forward on log mattresses floated on top of the heaving bog—unwieldy contraptions of interlaced long timbers, which would sometimes run for eight hundred feet. Later on the muskegs were filled in.

Then there were the apparently placid lakes that seemed so shallow, whose bottoms consisted of solid, unfathomable muskeg—muskeg that swallowed up tons of earth and gravel fill, month after month. The problem was that there seemed to be a bottom where there was no bottom at all. The real lake bottoms were concealed by a false blanket of silt which had never been properly probed during the hasty surveys. On Section B, Lake Macquistananah devoured 250,000 yards of earth fill. Farther up the line a second lake swallowed two hundred thousand yards. On Section Fifteen the hapless Joseph Whitehead saw his dreamed-of profits slowly pouring into the notorious Cross Lake in the form of 222,000 yards of gravel at a cost of eighty thousand dollars. And still the line continued to sink.

Cross Lake was to prove Whitehead's undoing. The contractor began work on it in 1879 and was still pouring gravel into it when, with his capital used up, the government relieved him of his contract in March, 1880. It seemed a simple matter to run a line of railway across the narrows—just a shallow expanse of water through which an embankment could easily be made. Yet ton after ton of sand and gravel vanished into that black and monstrous gulf without appreciable results. Sometimes the embankment would be built up five or six feet above the water; then suddenly the lake would take a gulp and the entire mass of stone, gravel, and earth would vanish beneath the waves.

At Lake Deception—eloquent name!—James Ross's huge force of horses and freight cars moved gravel into the water, using the first steam shovel to operate on the CPR, working at top speed, but the banks slid away faster than the gravel could be poured in. Ross built massive retaining walls with rock blasted out of one of his tunnels. One day in the space of a few minutes the banks settled some twenty-five feet, pushing the protective bulwarks of rock out into the lake for almost one hundred feet "as if they had been straws," and so swiftly that the men and horses barely had time to jump clear and save themselves. Ross tried hammering pilings deep into the lake bottom, building a trestle above them, and filling in the trestle with gravel and rock. One June day, just after a work train had rumbled across the causeway, the pilings sank fifty feet. There seemed no end to the depth of these incredible swamps. In one muskeg, piles were driven ninety-six feet below the surface before any bedrock was found.

A mile from Bonheur, a construction crew believed it had filled a muskeg hole when the entire track suddenly vanished into the black mud. Trainload after trainload of gravel was dumped into that apparently bottomless pit while men sweated with timbers to shore it up. Finally a track was laid and a locomotive was able to venture across. As the engine moved, the wobbly line behind it slowly rose while the ballast beneath squeezed out on both sides like pitch from a pot. A pole driven down showed there were thirty feet of quivering muskeg directly beneath the track, which was acting as a kind of pontoon bridge floating on a sea of slime. Of the gravel there was no trace.

Even after the muskegs were conquered, the rails anchored, and through traffic established, the roadbed tended to creep forward with every passing train. When a heavy engine hauling thirty-five cars passed over the track, the rails crept about two feet in the direction the train was moving. As a result track bolts broke almost daily. An actual series of waves, five or six inches deep, rippled along the track and was observable from the caboose.

Temporary trestles were filled by dragging giant plows along a line of flatcars loaded with gravel. The plows were guided by a single rail in the center of each car and pulled by a cable powered from the detached locomotive. From each side of the bow of the plow there descended cataracts of sand, but the track was often so uneven that the plow would catch onto the end of the car, stand on end for an instant, and then topple thirty feet to the ground below. From there it would have to be dragged back by the cable to the far end of the trestle and up the bank, ready to be loaded again onto a car.

The most effective plow was the "wing plow" designed on the spot by Michael J. Haney, the colorful Galway Irishman who took over the running of Section Fifteen for the government after Whitehead's downfall. A lean, hard man with high cheekbones, cowlick, and drooping mustache, Haney was described by Harry Armstrong, the pioneer engineer, as "a rushing devil-may-care chap who did things just as he chose without regard to authority." Haney almost lost the little *Countess of Dufferin* locomotive and his own life by displaying too much daring. He had drained a lake near Kalmar, about twenty-five miles from Cross Lake, and laid a mattress of timbers across the mud bottom to carry the track over it. But when the rails were laid and the cars backed on them, the whole heaving mass began to sink. Jack Anderson, the engineer on the *Countess*, refused point-blank to take her out onto the quivering track, so Haney boldly announced he would do it himself. With the cars uncoupled he began pushing them very slowly out along the track with the locomotive. The mattress began to subside; the engine tilted wildly until it looked to bystanders as if a ten-pound weight would pull her right over and into twenty feet of ooze. Haney, realizing his predicament, started to back up gingerly toward solid ground. It was nip and tuck, since the mattress had sunk so deep he was forced to propel the locomotive up an incline that rapidly grew steeper and steeper. By using sand on the rails and all the steam he could muster, he managed to reach the top of the bank, but by then the incline was so steep that the cowcatcher, scraping against the rails, was torn from the frame. Haney astonished everybody by admitting that the move was damn foolishness. It was the only occasion in forty years' acquaintanceship, Armstrong recalled, that he had known Haney "to admit anything he did wasn't right."

Haney, though accident-prone to an almost unbelievable degree, had a feline capacity for survival. At one point he was pitched off his horse and badly injured. On another occasion he caught his foot in some wire attached to the rails and a train ran over his toes. On July 18, 1880, he was riding an engine out of Cross Lake when the tender jumped the track and the locomotive with Haney in it rolled over a twenty-foot embankment. Clouds of scalding steam poured out of the wreck, but Haney, who was in the fireman's seat, emerged without a scratch or blister. Two months later he had another close call en route from Lake Deception to Cross Lake. He had just stepped out of the fireman's seat to get a drink of water and was raising it to his lips when the engine rounded a steep curve. Haney was knocked off balance and thrown, head foremost, into a rock cut. The train was traveling at twenty miles an hour and everyone assumed Haney was dead; he escaped with a flesh wound in the forehead.

Haney's particular brand of derring-do was hard on him physically —after two years on Section Fifteen he was a sick man and his doctor ordered a complete rest—but it got results. When Whitehead finally withdrew in February, 1880, matters were in a dreadful snarl. The men had not been paid and another in what had been a series of ugly strikes was in progress. The navvies were in a black mood when Haney arrived, called them together, and told them that they would all receive their money as soon as pay sheets could be made up. Some decided to stay on the job, others to strike. Haney warned the strikers that the loyalists would be paid first. Then he set off for Winnipeg to get the needed funds. There he was besieged at his hotel by some of the strikers, demanding their money at once.

Haney was adamant: "I told you what I'd do and I'm going to do it. I told you the men who stayed would be paid first and you can bet your last dollar that they'll all be paid before any of you get a cent."

The leader of the group swore that Haney would not be allowed out of Winnipeg with a penny until the strikers got their money. Haney boldly told him that he intended to row across the river to St. Boniface, pick up an engine there at midnight, and steam back to the job. "You can do whatever you please about it," he said bluntly. He was as good as his word. With forty thousand dollars in cash on his person he set off down the track in the dead of night. It was a measure of the man that, in spite of all the threats, none dared stop him.

Back on the job, Haney found himself faced with a series of dilemmas. Whitehead's caches were bare of provisions and yet Haney had to keep four thousand men working without cessation. He and Collingwood Schreiber, Fleming's replacement, estimated that one thousand tons would be needed—and this amount had to be distributed immediately over some of the roughest country in Canada. It was March 1, with spring on its way. Soon the trails would be so rutted that a wagon would be shaken to pieces in less than ten miles. Hauling could be done only over roads made of hard-packed snow. But teams were in short supply, too; there simply were not enough horses or wagons. Schreiber figured it was impossible but Haney was not a man to cry surrender. Off he set on a voyage of importunity, moving from farmhouse to farmhouse, browbeating, cajoling, pleading, and promising. Within a few days he had hired every team in the country, and by March 15 he had accomplished the impossible.

Haney's ability to scrounge material became legendary. He was not a believer in proper channels or in red tape. When he wanted something he took it. On one occasion when Section Fifteen ran short of spikes, Haney made up his mind to seize two carloads that were, he knew, sitting on sidings in Winnipeg destined for another section. So, on one dark night, he took a light engine with a regular crew and conductor into the yards. After a considerable search, Haney located the cars, whose numbers he knew, untangled them from the array in the yard, and spirited them away behind his engine. There followed a wild night ride during which the spikes were unloaded at strategic points and the cars slipped back into the Winnipeg yards without anyone being the wiser. The incident baffled Schreiber more than anything else that occurred that year. The cars had been checked into the yards loaded and, after Haney's secret expedition, were checked out loaded; yet the spikes never reached their destination. Schreiber spent most of the summer tracing the two cars all over the continent. He finally caught up with one in Georgia and the other in Texas, but of course there was no hint of where the spikes had gone. The matter continued to prey on Schreiber's mind: How could two loads of railroad spikes suddenly dissolve out of two freight cars? The matter became so nagging that it dominated his conversation.

"What I can't make out is what became of those spikes," he said one day in Haney's hearing.

"Why didn't you ask me about it?" Haney asked.

"What in the devil would you know about it?" Schreiber snorted. "Didn't I tell you they were checked in and out of the Winnipeg yards?"

"Well," said Haney, "if you care to walk back a mile or so along the track I think I can show you every one of those spikes."

Schreiber's undoubtedly explosive retort has not been recorded but it was probably tempered with understanding. Haney's methods were unorthodox but they produced indisputable results. When he took over Section Fifteen there was a deficit on the books of almost four hundred thousand dollars. Under his management this was cleared up and a balance of eighty-three thousand dollars appeared on the black side of the ledger. Haney, of course, was a salaried man. The eighty-three thousand was paid by the government to Joseph Whitehead.

4 · Sodom-on-the-Lake

IN THE DISMAL LAND WEST OF LAKE SUPE-
rior, nature seemed to have gone to extremes to thwart the railway
builders. When they were not laying track across the soft porridge of
the muskegs, they were blasting it through some of the hardest rock
in the world—rock that rolled endlessly on, ridge after spiky ridge,
like waves in a sullen ocean.

Dynamite, patented in the year of Confederation, was as new as the
steam shovel and, though the papers were full of stories of "dynamiters"
using Alfred Nobel's new invention for revolutionary purposes, the
major explosive was dynamite's parent, nitroglycerine. This awesomely
unstable liquid had been developed almost thirty years before the first
sod was turned on the CPR but was only now beginning to replace the
weaker blasting powder, being ten times more expensive, not to mention more dangerous. It had been in regular use as a railway-building
explosive only since 1866 and had never before been used as extensively
as it was west of the lakehead in the late seventies.

The technique was to pour the explosive into holes drilled often by
hand but sometimes with the newly developed Burleigh rock drill,
worked by compressed air. The liquid was then poured into the holes,
each about seven feet deep, and set off by a fuse. In less than two years
some three hundred thousand dollars was spent on nitroglycerine on
Section Fifteen, often with disastrous results. The workmen had an
almost cavalier attitude toward the explosive. Cans of nitroglycerine
with fuses attached were strewn carelessly along the roadbed in con-
travention of all safety regulations, or carried about with such recklessness that the fluid splashed upon the rocks. Whole gangs were sometimes blown to bits in the resultant explosions, especially in the cold
weather, because the chemical was notoriously dangerous when frozen;
the slightest jar could touch it off. Under such conditions it was kept
under hot water and at as uniform a temperature as possible.

It could not be transported by wagon; the jarring along those cor-
rugated trails would have made short work of the first drover foolhardy
enough to risk it. It had to be carried in ten-gallon cans on men's backs.
The half-breed packers and the Irish navvies remained contemptuous of
it. Armstrong, the engineer, saw one packer casually repairing a leak
in a can by scraping mud over it with his knife, oblivious of the fact
that the tiniest bit of grit or the smallest amount of friction would blast
him heavenwards. Sometimes the packers would lay their cans down
on a smooth rock and a few drops would be left behind from a leak.

The engineers traveling up and down the line watched the portage trails with hawk's eyes, seeking to avoid those telltale black specks which could easily blow a man's leg off. Once a teamster took his horse to water at just such a spot. The horse's iron shoe touched a pool of nitroglycerine and the resulting blast tore the shoe from his foot and drove it through his belly, killing him and stunning the teamster.

In drilling holes for the explosive, it was the practice to fill them first with water and then pour in the heavier liquid; the water then floated to the top and acted as tamping. Often, however, some of the explosive ran out, causing secondary explosions later on when the cut was trimmed. The number of men killed or maimed by accidental explosions was truly staggering. In one fifty-mile stretch of Section B, Sandford Fleming counted thirty graves, all the result of the careless handling of nitroglycerine. Mary Fitzgibbon, on her way to homestead in Manitoba, watched in awe as a long train of Irish packers tripped gaily down a hill, each with a can of liquid explosive on his back, making wry, funereal comments all the while:

"It's a warm day."

"That's so but maybe ye'll be warmer before ye camp tonight."

"That's so, d'ye want any word taken to the Divil?"

"Where are ye bound for, Jack?"

"To hell, I guess."

"Take the other train and keep a berth for me, man!"

"Is it ye're coffin ye're carrying, Pat?"

"Faith ye're right; and the coroner's inquest to the bargain, Jim."

Mrs. Fitzgibbon wrote that in spite of the banter "the wretched expression of these very men proved that they felt the bitterness of death to be in their chests."

There were indeed some terrible accidents. A youth climbing a hill with a can of explosive stumbled and fell; all that was ever found of him was one foot in a tree, one hundred yards away. A workman in a rock cut handed a can to one of the drillers and as he did so his foot slipped: four men died, three more were maimed. One workman brushed past a rock where some explosive had been spilled; he lost his arm and his sight in an instant. At Prince Arthur's Landing, an entire nitroglycerine factory blew up in the night, hurling chunks of frozen earth for a quarter of a mile and leaving a gaping hole twenty feet deep and fifty feet across. And then there was the case of Patrick Crowley, an overmoral Irishman, who objected so strenuously to Josie Brush's bawdyhouse at Hawk Lake that he blew it up, and himself into the bargain.

Under such conditions the only real respite was alcohol. As Michael Haney recalled, "there was not an engineer, contractor or traveler who were not hard drinkers. Practically every transaction was consummated with a glass." The same was true of the navvies, and, in order to keep the work moving, herculean efforts were made to keep the camps dry. These were not notably successful. Prohibition was in effect all along the line, but this did not stop the whiskey peddlers, who had kegs cached at points along the entire right of way. "The knowing ones can obtain a bottle of a villainous article called whiskey by following certain trails into the recesses of the dismal swamps," the Thunder Bay *Sentinel*'s railway correspondent reported from up the line in the summer of 1877. He added that there were many raids on the peddlers but these were "not altogether made in the cause of temperance. Not all the whiskey was spilled on the ground."

Since a gallon of alcohol, which was sold in the cities of the East for as low as fifty cents, could, when properly diluted, return forty-five dollars to an enterprising peddler on the line, business continued brisk in spite of the vigilance of the police. The peddlers hid out in the bush or on the islands that dotted the swampy lakes, moving into the work camps in swift canoes of birchbark and darting away again at the approach of the law. If caught, the peddler generally escaped with a fine, since fines were the chief source of income for the struggling towns and villages that were springing up at the end of steel.

A few years later, when the railroad was finished, a Toronto *Globe* reporter on a visit to Rat Portage dug up some fascinating background on the good old days when, it was said, whiskey peddling was one of the chief industries: ". . . It is more than hinted that of the enormous amounts collected here in fines and costs, the Dominion Government received only a very small share, while some of the officials would have been rich men ere this had it not been for the large sums they have squandered on profligacy and dissipation. It is also stated on good authority that in some cases whiskey peddlers secured a certain immunity from the severe penalties by contributing regular stated sums, destined to appease the cravings for justice in the breasts of the officers of the Court."

Harry Armstrong, in his unpublished memoirs, set down a spirited account of one whiskey trial held in the winter of 1877–78 in which he acted as clerk of the court. The trial was held at Inver on Section Fifteen. A man named Shay was arrested with a tobogganload of whiskey and placed in charge of the local blacksmith. He was duly arraigned before two Justices of the Peace, one of whom was the government's divisional engineer, Henry Carre, and the other the contractor's engineer. It was their first case on the bench—the bench being literally a bench, since the court was held in the company mess hall.

"Produce the prisoner," called Carre, and the blacksmith entered, holding Shay by the coat sleeve and pulling at his own forelock as he announced: "The prisoner, Your Honor."

The first witness was being questioned when Charles Whitehead, the son of the contractor, acting in his role of prosecutor, "wildly suggested to the bench that it was probably in order to swear the witness." It took some time to find a Bible, but one was eventually located and the case proceeded. A further delay occurred when it was noticed that Armstrong, as clerk, was taking down the evidence in pencil. With difficulty, pen and ink were found and the evidence was retranscribed. Without much more ceremony, the prisoner was found guilty. He had formerly been employed as one of Carre's axmen and was well known to him. Obviously he had come up in the world financially, being attired in a fine suit with a fur collar—"the most distinguished looking man in the room."

"Shay," said Carre gravely, "I am very sorry to see you in this position."

"So am I, Mr. Carre," replied the convicted man with disturbing nonchalance.

"The decision of the court is that you pay a fine of twenty-five dollars."

"Well, I won't pay it. I'll appeal."

This was a disconcerting turn of events. There was no jail closer than Winnipeg and no funds to send the prisoner there, and so, after a few days of well-fed comfort in the bunkhouse, the miscreant was allowed to depart without his whiskey.

When Haney took over Section Fifteen his methods of handling the alcohol problem were characteristically his own. He made no attempt to curb the traffic himself, but when the men were put on three round-the-clock shifts, whiskey tended to slow down the work. At such times it was Haney's practice to round up the peddlers and secure from them a promise that they would not sell whiskey as long as the twenty-four-hour shift work prevailed. Generally this *sub rosa* agreement worked, but on one occasion the presence of five hundred thirsty men was too much for the entrepreneurs. Haney came to work one morning to find the whole camp roaring drunk. Work would be tied up for a week. Haney moved with his usual brusqueness. There were four officials working on the section who were technically known as whiskey detectives. He called them before him and told them that unless all whiskey peddlers were brought before him by noon, all four would be fired. The peddlers were produced in an hour and haled immediately before a magistrate who was clearly taking his orders from Haney. The law provided increased fines for each recurring offense and the option of jail on a third offense. Haney saw that the maximum fines—a total of thirty-six hundred dollars—were levied. The prison sentences were remitted but all peddlers were packed off to Winnipeg with the warning that if they returned they would be jailed. None of them ever came back.

When whiskey was unavailable on the spot, the thirstiest of the workmen tried to escape to the fleshpots of Winnipeg. Haney's best foreman was one of these: every two or three weeks he would be missing. Haney handled this matter with considerable psychology. He kept *forcing* the man to go to Winnipeg. As the compulsory trips became more frequent and the foreman grew the worse for wear, Haney continued to insist that he return. Soon the man was coming back, cold sober, on the return train, pleading to be allowed to work. As Haney later explained: "It's one thing to steal away for a few days of quiet dissipation but it's quite another to have someone else thrusting these days upon you. He didn't like anyone deciding that he should get drunk any more than he would have appreciated their efforts to prevent him from becoming so, and as long as we were on that work he was never away another day."

By the time Haney arrived on the scene, at the end of the decade, the solemn, unknown land through which Harry Armstrong had trudged on his fifteen-mile treks to the job site had come alive with thousands of navvies—Swedes, Norwegians, Finns, and Icelanders, French Canadians and Prince Edward Islanders, Irish, Scots, English, Americans, even Mennonites, all strung out over nearly five hundred miles in clustered, brawling, hard-drinking communities, most of which were as impermanent as the end of track.

Armstrong recalled, not without nostalgia, the days when "life along the railway construction . . . was like one large family. There was hospitality, helpfulness, gentle friendship, good nature and contentedness all about." He described Christmas Eve, 1876, spent in a log cabin on the right of way, with a fiddler playing for dancing couples in a room which also contained a kitchen stove and an immense bed. Everything went fine, he remembered, until someone unwittingly sat on the bed and realized that there was a baby somewhere beneath the sheets.

His account contrasts sharply with that of the postmaster of Whitemouth, a railroad community midway between Winnipeg and Rat River, also describing Christmas Eve, just four years later: "The demon of strong drink made a bedlam of this place, fighting, stabbing and breaking; some lay out freezing till life was almost extinct. The Post Office was besieged at the hours of crowded business by outrageous, bleeding, drunken, fighting men, mad with Forty-Rod, so that respectable people could not come in for their mail. . . . It is only a few days since in one of these frenzies a man had his jugular nearly severed by a man with a razor."

The very impermanence of the construction towns made any kind of municipal organization difficult. In July, 1880, when the end of track moved beyond Gull River, Ignace became the capital of Section A. All the inhabitants of Gull River moved—stores, houses, boardinghouses, a jewelry shop, a hotel, a telegraph office, a "temperance saloon," a shoemaker, and a blacksmith shop. Often, though communities changed geographical location and names, they re-elected the same public officials to govern them.

The one really permanent town along the half-constructed line and by far the largest was Rat Portage on Lake of the Woods. With true chamber of commerce fervor it called itself "The Future Saratoga of America." A less subjective description was provided by a correspondent of the Winnipeg *Times* in the summer of 1880: "For sometime now the railway works in the vicinity of Rat Portage have been besieged by a lot of scoundrels whose only avocation seems to be gambling and trading in illicit whiskey and the state of degradation was, if anything, intensified by the appearance, in the wake of these blacklegs, of a number of the *demi-monde* with whom these numerous desperadoes held high carnival at all hours of the day or night."

The town itself, in the words of one observer, seemed to have been "laid out on designs made by a colony of muskrats." Shanties and tents were built or pitched wherever the owners fancied and without reference to streets or roadways. As a result, the streets were run between the houses as an afterthought so that there was nothing resembling a straight thoroughfare in town "but simply a lot of crooked, winding trails that appeared to go nowhere in particular, but to aimlessly wander about in and out of shanties, tents and clumps of brush in such a confused and irregular manner as was extremely difficult for the stranger to find his way from one given point to another, even though they might not be over 150 yards apart."

Rat Portage, with a floating population sometimes bordering on three thousand, was the headquarters for Section B. The expense of the administration was borne by the contractors, who built the jail and organized the police force. All fines, however, went to the local government. Between April and November of 1880, six thousand dollars was collected in fines. The convictions—highway robbery, larceny, burglary, assault, selling illicit whiskey and prostitution—give a fair picture of Rat Portage as a frontier town.

With both the contractors and the government in the law business, a state of near anarchy prevailed. At one point the company constable, a man named O'Keefe, seized four barrels of illicit liquor but instead of destroying it took it back to his rooms and proceeded to treat his many friends. He was haled before the stipendiary magistrate, who fined him for having intoxicating liquor in his possession. O'Keefe paid the fine and then as soon as the magistrate left the bench arrested *him* for having liquor in his possession, an act he was perfectly entitled to perform since he was himself a policeman. He popped the protesting magistrate in jail, and when that official asked for an immediate hearing O'Keefe denied it to him, declaring that he meant to keep him behind bars for twenty-four hours because the magistrate "had treated him like a dog and now it was his turn." With the only magistrate in jail, another had to be appointed to act in his place; when this was done the hearing was held and the new magistrate fined the old magistrate one hundred dollars. In the end the local government remitted both fines.

The situation grew more complicated when Manitoba's boundaries were extended northward in 1881 and a dispute arose between that province and Ontario over the jurisdiction in which Rat Portage lay. Both provinces built jails and appointed magistrates and constables; so did the federal government. For a time it was more dangerous to be a policeman than a lawbreaker. Since there were several sets of liquor laws, the policemen began arresting each other until both jails were full of opposing lawmen. Ontario constables were kidnapped and shipped to Winnipeg. The Manitoba jail was set on fire. Anyone who wished could become a constable, and free whiskey and special pay were offered to those who dared to take the job. For a time Rat Portage witnessed the spectacle of some of its toughest characters—men who bore such nicknames as Black Jim Reddy of Montana, Charlie Bull-Pup, Boston O'Brien the Slugger, Mulligan the Hardest Case—acting as upholders of the law, or their version of the law. The situation came to a head in 1883 when both provinces called elections on the same day and two Premiers campaigned in Rat Portage with such persistence that the Premier of Manitoba actually got more votes than there were registered voters. The confusion did not end until 1884, when Rat Portage was officially declared to be part of Ontario.

By then, with the government line finished, Rat Portage had settled down to become a mild and relatively law-abiding community, but in

1880 it was the roughest town in Canada, the headquarters of the illegal liquor industry with eight hundred gallons pouring into town every month, hidden in oatmeal and bean sacks or disguised as barrels of kerosene. It was figured that there was a whiskey peddler for every thirty residents, so profitable was the business. "Forty-Rod"—so called because it was claimed it could fell a man at that distance—sold for the same price as champagne in Winnipeg from the illegal saloons operating on the islands that speckled the Lake of the Woods.

Here on a smaller and more primitive scale was foreshadowed all the anarchy of a later Prohibition period in the United States—the same gun-toting mobsters, corrupt officials, and harassed police. One bloody incident in the summer of 1880, involving two whiskey traders named Dan Harrington and Jim Mitchell, had all the elements of a Western gun battle.

Harrington and Mitchell had in 1878 worked on a steam drill for Joseph Whitehead, but they soon abandoned that toil for the more lucrative trade. In the winter of 1879–80, a warrant was issued for their arrest at Cross Lake, but when the constable tried to serve it, the two beat him brutally and escaped to Rat Portage, where the stipendiary magistrate, F. W. Bent, was in their pay. The two men gave themselves up to Bent, who fined them a token fifty dollars and then gave them a written discharge to prevent further interference from officials at Cross Lake. The magistrate also returned to Harrington a revolver that had been confiscated.

The two started east with fifty gallons of whiskey, heading for the turbulent little community of Hawk Lake, where the railroad navvies had just received their pay. They were spotted en route by one of the contracting partnership, John J. McDonald. McDonald realized at once what fifty gallons of whiskey would do to his work force. He and the company's constable, one Ross, went straight to Rat Portage, got a warrant, and doubled back for Hawk Lake.

They found Harrington and Mitchell in front of Millie Watson's bawdy tent. Mitchell fled into the woods but Harrington boldly announced he'd sell whiskey in spite of contractors and police. The two men wrested his gun from him and placed him under arrest. Harrington then asked and was given permission to go inside the tent and wash up. Here a crony, bedded with a prostitute, handed him a brace of loaded seven-shot revolvers. Harrington cocked the weapons and emerged from the tent with both of them pointed at the constable. Ross was a fast draw; as Harrington's finger curled around the trigger the policeman shot him above the heart. Harrington dropped to the ground, vainly trying to retrieve his weapons. A second constable, McKenna, told Ross not to bother to fire again: the first bullet had taken effect.

"You're damned right it has taken effect," Harrington snarled, "but I'd sooner be shot than fined." Those were his final words.

Magistrate Bent was removed from the bench the following week and the Winnipeg *Times* reported that "he is now actively engaged in the illicit traffic of selling crooked whiskey himself. He has now become an active ally [with] those whom he was at one time supposed to be at variance in a legal sense, whose pernicious vices he was expected to exterminate but did not."

It was these reports, seeping back to Winnipeg, that persuaded Archbishop Alexandre Antonin Taché of St. Boniface that the construction workers needed a permanent chaplain; after all, a third of them were French-Canadian Catholics from Manitoba. He selected for the task the most notable of all the voyageur priests, Father Albert Lacombe, a nomadic oblate who had spent most of his adult life among the Cree and Blackfoot of the Far West. In November, 1880, Lacombe set out reluctantly for his new parish.

Father Lacombe was a homely man whose long silver locks never seemed to be combed, but benevolence shone from his features. He did not want to be a railway chaplain. He would much rather have stayed among his beloved Indians than enter the Sodom of Rat Portage, but he went where his Church directed. On the very first day of his new assignment he was scandalized by the language of the navvies. His first sermon, preached in a boxcar chapel, was an attack on blasphemy.

"It seems to me what I have said is of a nature to bring reflection to these terrible blasphemers, who have a vile language all their own—with a dictionary and grammer which belongs to no one but themselves," he confided to his diary. "This habit of theirs is—diabolical!"

But there was worse to come: two weeks after he arrived in Rat Portage there was "a disorderly and scandalous ball," and all night long the sounds of drunken revelry dinned into the ears of the unworldly priest from the plains. Lacombe even tried to reason with the woman who sponsored the dances. He was rewarded with jeers and insults.

"My God," he wrote in his diary, "have pity on this little village where so many crimes are committed every day." He realized that he was helpless to stop all the evil that met his eyes and so settled at last for prayer "to arrest the divine anger."

As he moved up and down the line, covering thirty different camps, eating beans off tin plates in the mess halls, preaching sermons as he went, celebrating mass in the mornings, talking and smoking with the laborers in the evenings and recording on every page of his small, tattered black notebooks a list of sins far worse than he had experienced among the followers of Chief Crowfoot, the wretched priest was overcome by a sense of torment and frustration. The heathen Indians had been so easy to convert! But these navvies—nominal Christians all—listened to him respectfully, talked to him intimately, confessed their sins religiously, and then went on their drunken, brawling, blaspheming, whoring way totally unashamed.

Ill with pleurisy, forced to travel the track on an open handcar in the bitterest weather, his ears ringing with obscene phrases which he had never heard before, his eyes affronted by spectacles he did not believe possible, the tortured priest could only cry to his diary, "My God, I offer you my sufferings." Though hard as frozen pemmican, toughened by the harshness of prairie travel and the discomfort of Indian tepees, tempered by blizzard and blazing prairie sun, the pious Lacombe all but met his match in the rock and muskeg country of Section B.

"Please God, send me back to my missions," he wrote, but it was not until the final spike was driven that his prayers were answered. He had not changed many lives, perhaps, but he had made more friends than he knew. When it was learned that he was going, the workmen of Section B took up a large collection and presented him with a generous assortment of gifts: a horse, a buggy, a complete harness, a new saddle, a tent, and an entire camping outfit to make his days on the plains more comfortable. Perhaps, as he took his leave, he reasoned that his tortured mission to the godless had not been entirely in vain.

8

1 · Jim Hill's Folly

ON ONE OF THOSE EARLY TRIPS TO THE Canadian North West in 1870, when he was planning his steamboat war against the Hudson's Bay Company, James Jerome Hill's single eye fastened upon the rich soil of the Red River country and marked the rank grass that sprang up in the ruts tilled by the squeaking wagon wheels. It was the blackest loam he had ever seen, and he filed the memory of it carefully away in the pigeonholes of his complicated and active mind, to bring it out and caress it, time and again, and contemplate its significance. Soil like that meant settlers, tens of thousands of them. Settlers would need a railway. With Donald Smith's help, Jim Hill meant to give them one.

There was a railway of sorts, leading out of St. Paul in 1870. It was supposed to reach to the Canadian border but it had not made it that far. One of its branches ended at Breckenridge on the Red River, where it connected with the Kittson line of steamboats. Another headed off northwest to St. Cloud at the end of the Red River trail. An extension faltered north toward Brainerd, where it was supposed to connect with the main line of the Northern Pacific. But neither branch nor extension could properly be called a railroad. They had been built in a piecemeal fashion out of the cheapest materials—iron rails rather than steel, and fifteen distinct patterns of iron at that. Bridge materials, stacks of railway ties, and other bric-a-brac littered the right of way. Nobody quite knew who owned what, but the farmers along the line

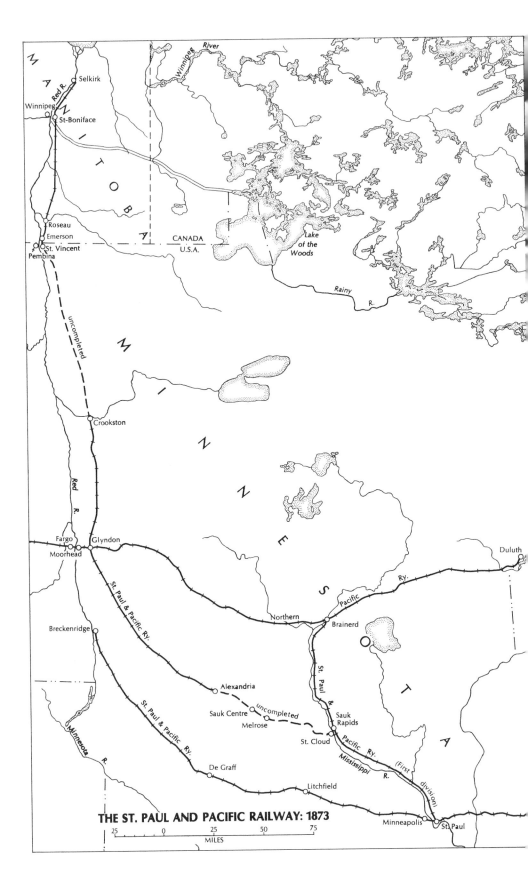

THE ST. PAUL AND PACIFIC RAILWAY: 1873

25   0   25   50   75
MILES

were helping themselves to whatever they needed to improve fences, barns, and houses. As for the rolling stock, it was best described as primitive, with the engines ancient and creaky, the cars battered and rusty.

The story of the St. Paul and Pacific Railroad is a case history in railway looting in the mid-nineteenth century, when anybody who promised to build a line of steel could get almost anything he asked. In four years of railway madness between 1853 and 1857, no fewer than twenty-seven railroad companies were chartered in the United States. One of these was the St. Paul line, first known as the Minnesota and Pacific. Its subsequent history is one of legislative corruption and corporate fraud, and the complicated tale of its financing has few equals in railroad annals.

The villain in the piece was Russell Sage, the shadowy robber baron from Troy, New York, who with a hand-picked group of "notorious lobbyists and swindlers" (to use Gustavus Myers's term) corrupted the Minnesota legislature into handing over vast land grants and bond issues, the proceeds of which they pocketed through a variety of devices, including dummy construction companies. In just five years the road was bankrupt though it had built only ten miles of line. The Sage group then coldly reorganized the bankrupt company into two new companies. By this device they rid themselves of all the former debts yet kept the land grant. They then proceeded to lobby for even more land. When they got that, they floated a bond issue of $13,800,000 in the Netherlands. They diverted some eight million dollars of this sum to their own pockets and plunged the railroad into bankruptcy again.

In the early seventies the railway consisted of some five hundred miles of almost unusable track—"two streaks of rust and a right of way," as it was contemptuously called. One of its lines—the section that was supposed to connect St. Cloud with the Northern Pacific by way of Glyndon—actually went from nowhere to nowhere, a phantom railroad lying out on the naked prairie with no town at the terminal end of iron and no facilities created to do business at the other; there was not even a siding. When Jesse Farley, the receiver in bankruptcy, arrived in 1873 to take it over, he found it in such bad condition that his train's battered old locomotive would not run over it. He had to inspect it by handcar.

Yet this was the line that Jim Hill coveted; and this was the line that would eventually make Jim Hill, Donald Smith, Norman Kittson, and George Stephen rich beyond their wildest dreams and gain them both the experience and the money to build the Canadian Pacific Railway.

In St. Paul, Hill was the town character. He was looked upon as a likable eccentric and a notorious dreamer who would talk your ear off if you gave him half a chance, especially if he got on the subject of railways—though it was admitted that he *did* know something about transportation.

Indeed he did. He seemed to know something about everything. When Hill got into a project he got in with both feet; he wrestled with any new subject until he had mastered it and he had an uncanny knack of being a little bit ahead of everyone else. When he first went to work as a shipping clerk on the levee in the days when there was not a mile of railroad in Minnesota, he used to amuse his fellow workers with wild predictions that the newfangled steam locomotives would one day replace river packets.

Hill was the kind of man who could look at a village and see a city or gaze upon an empty plain and visualize an iron highway. He took a look at St. Paul when it was only a hamlet and realized he was at one of the great crossroads of western trade. Accordingly he set himself up as a forwarding agent and began to study the movement and storage of goods. When the railway first came along Hill began to sell it wood, but he saw that coal would swiftly replace the lesser fuel and so he studied coal. He made a survey of all the available sources of coal and became the first coal merchant in St. Paul; he also sold the first bagged coal in town. That was not enough for Hill. He became an expert on fuel and energy of all kinds. He actually joined geological parties exploring for coal. Years later, when the great coal deposits were discovered in Iowa, it turned out that Jim Hill held twenty-three hundred of the best acres under lease. Until his death he was considered one of the leading experts on the continent on the subject of western coal.

But in the early seventies, no one took Jim Hill seriously. Perhaps it was because he talked so much. There he sat in his old chair in front of his coal and wood store babbling away, a stocky, powerful man with a massive, leonine head, the hair almost down to the shoulders, a short-cropped beard, a face scorched by the prairie sun, and that single black eye a glittering orb that, like the Ancient Mariner's, burned itself into the listener's consciousness.

Napoleon was his hero. He first read his biography back in Canada at the age of thirteen and nothing else that he read (and he seemed to read everything—Byron, Plutarch, More, Gibbon) made such an impression on him. From that moment, he believed that when a man set his mind to something it was already half done. Later in life, when he had built a mansion in St. Paul and stocked it with costly paintings, he began to think of himself as a Bonaparte, or perhaps a Genghis Khan. But in those early days, long before he fought his own Borodinos with Vanderbilt and Villard, he simply brought his Napoleonic determination to bear on the matter of the decrepit railroad. Hill saw it not as two streaks of rusted iron but as the nucleus of a transcontinental line. It was, everyone agreed, a crazy dream, but then Jim Hill had always been a dreamer—a "romancer," in the word of a boyhood companion. He had played hooky at the age of nine to read histories of the days of chivalry. He had sung old Scottish songs of love and derring-do while his Irish father played them on the flute. He had wild ambitions. He was going to be a doctor. He played at wild Indians until an arrow through the eye ended his medical future; but the romantic ambitions remained. He was going to be a sailor before the mast. He was going to run a steamboat line in India. He was going to conquer the world.

He was Canadian by birth and Celtic by heritage—half Scottish, half Irish. He was born in a log house at Rockwood, Ontario, and was much influenced by his teacher, the great Quaker educator William Wetherald, father of a leading Canadian poetess. Wetherald taught young Jim Hill the value of books and of study, and for all his life Hill remained a student. He studied scientific treatises, classical art, geology, finance—everything he could get his hands on. Rockwood could not hold him: at eighteen, his heart fired by the idea of adventure, he set off for the Orient.

When he got as far as St. Paul in July, 1856, it was the jumping-off place to nowhere. Hill's imagination spanned the plains in a single leap and he saw the blue Pacific beckoning. He would join a brigade of trappers and go overland to the coast, where he could find a ship bound for India. He looked at the steamboats pouring into St. Paul—three hundred in a single season—and again he began to dream. He would build a steamboat line on the Ganges, or the Hooghly, or the Brahmaputra. But he was too late; the final fur brigade had left for the season. And so Jim Hill stayed in St. Paul for a year, and then for another year —and another. Chance changed the pattern of his life, not to mention the pattern of the city he made his own.

For eight years, while he worked at a variety of jobs in St. Paul, he read and he studied; and when he was not reading he was trying his hand at painting. His first job was as a clerk on the levee and he read his way through that. He read voraciously, at all hours and in every setting. When the long five-month winter of isolation settled upon St. Paul and others found amusement in saloons, Hill read his way through that, too. One winter he took a job as a watchman on a steamboat wintering on the levee. He arrived with an armful of books, ranging from Gibbon's *Decline and Fall* to several difficult scientific treatises. When he emerged the following spring he had read and annotated them all.

By the time he decided to try his hand at business, Hill's knowledge was encyclopedic and his memory prodigious. He could repeat page after page of Byron or Plutarch. Years later, when he was wealthy enough to possess a herd of blooded cattle, he could cite the pedigrees of each one of them for generations back.

One of the things Jim Hill studied was the Toonerville operation out of St. Paul; and one of the things he learned was that whoever owned the railway could come into possession of two and a half million acres of the richest agricultural land in the American Midwest. The time would come, Hill reckoned, when the railway could be bought for a song. It was all a matter of waiting.

2 · *"Donald Smith is ready to take hold"*

IN WINNIPEG, DONALD A. SMITH HAD A similar idea. The Red River needed a lifeline to the East. If such a line could be built from Selkirk to the United States border and if the bankrupt American line out of St. Paul could somehow be revived to meet it, that connection would be effected.

Smith, like Hill, was a man who liked to look ahead: a month sometimes, a year perhaps, even a decade or more. He saw, for instance, the coming extinction of the buffalo and kept some captive animals in a corral at Silver Heights against the day when they should vanish, as they did with dramatic and almost supernatural suddenness in 1880. When he emerged from Labrador as a junior factor on his first visit to Montreal, Smith decided to learn to cook, for he saw future advantages in that art. He took a job in a bakery and another later in a restaurant to absorb culinary techniques, which at the time were nonexistent in the wilderness. He returned and gave all his employees and colleagues instruction in cooking and serving wholesome meals in order to preserve their health and sometimes their lives in the wilds. More, he picked up a knowledge of primitive medicine and learned to make an antiseptic for wounds by boiling the inner bark of the juniper tree. It was this kind of preparedness that undoubtedly saved Smith's own life on the snow-blind journey back to Mingan, and on many other occasions as well. No matter what the weather, Smith always had the foresight to carry extra warm clothing and additional provisions with him wherever he went. When a blizzard sprang up, Smith was always ready for it; he was generally ready for any eventuality.

Like Hill, he foresaw the death of the steam packet at a time when the river trade seemed to be at its height. Smith also saw the threat to the fur trade as he and his colleagues had known it, even when the fur trade seemed invulnerable. As early as 1860 he predicted that the Hudson's Bay Company could not go on forever sealing off the North West from the rest of the continent; and he realized that once the Company's charter was modified or canceled there would have to be a railway from Lake Superior to the Red River.

Thirteen years after that forecast was made, Smith contemplated the twin streaks of rust out of St. Paul. The twin railway companies (one was known as the St. Paul and Pacific, the other as the First Division of the St. Paul and Pacific) were in a terrible legal and financial snarl. One was in receivership, the other was about to go into trusteeship. There were suits and countersuits by unpaid contractors, chagrined stockholders, and swindled bondholders. It was not easy to fathom the complicated financial situation, since there were several classes of bonds for the two lines and most of these were held outside the country by Dutch investors.

In the fall of 1873, on his way through St. Paul en route from the Red River to the stormy parliamentary session in Ottawa, he dropped in on "Commodore" Norman Kittson, the Hudson's Bay representative and the president of the steamboat line which, with the Company's secret connivance, held a monopoly on the river. Smith wanted a favor: could Kittson find out everything possible about the financial and legal position of the St. Paul and Pacific Railroad, especially about the bonds held in Holland and the various prices the Dutch were asking? If the price was right, Smith thought, he might consider raising the money to help complete the line.

The project did not interest Kittson personally. He was well-to-do; he was getting on in years; it was all too rich for his blood. But he mentioned it to his other silent partner, Jim Hill, and it was as if a light had flashed on above that lion's head. Of course! For all these months Hill had been grappling with the puzzle of the bankrupt railway, wondering where the money would come from when the time was ripe to buy it. Now he had the answer: Smith was one of the chief officers of the Bank of Montreal as well as of the Hudson's Bay Company. He was wealthy in his own right. Smith was his man. From that moment on, Hill became a monomaniac on the subject of the St. Paul and Pacific.

When Donald Smith passed through St. Paul again, early in 1874, both Hill and Kittson were ready with the information he needed: most of the bonds, totaling almost eighteen million dollars' face value, were now held by Dutch investors who had formed themselves into a committee of bondholders.

The strategy was clear: buy the bonds as cheaply as possible, form a new company, force a foreclosure, buy the bankrupt railroad, complete it to the border, cash in on the resultant land subsidy, and reap the profits. But there were many obstacles. It was no use buying the railroad without being certain of getting the free land that was supposed to come with it. The Minnesota legislature, however, had passed a law (no doubt with the bitter memory of Russell Sage's plundering) making the land grant nontransferable to any new company after foreclosure. A good deal of lobbying—and perhaps more than lobbying—would be needed to get that law revoked. There was also a variety of lawsuits pending against the railway lines. Then there were the stockholders, in addition to the bondholders, to be considered. Most of the stock was held by a speculator named Edwin Litchfield, a notoriously difficult man to deal with. Litchfield was trying to get control of the railway through court action. The depression was at its lowest depth, money was hard to come by, plagues of grasshoppers were ravaging the land. For the moment nothing could be done.

"There was a time," Hill later recalled, "that everybody waited. There seemed no way to get in."

They bided their time for two full years—Smith and Hill, who were now deeply involved, and Kittson, who was reluctantly being pushed to the point of commitment by his enthusiastic partner.

During that time, Hill studied the faltering railroad in all its economic ramifications—studied its finances, studied its operation, studied the quantities and values of the various bonds and where they were held; figured out the number of acres owned by the twin companies, the number of miles completed, half completed, and still to be completed; worked out the value of the future land grants, the value of the terminals in St. Paul and in Minneapolis across the Mississippi, the value of the franchises that were granted before the state was admitted to the Union in 1858; added up the number of locomotives and freight and passenger cars; kept up with all the law cases; made friends with the legislators and lobbied for changes in the law. Within two years, it was said, Jim Hill knew more about the railway than the men involved in running it. Two things he certainly knew that few others knew: it was worth far more than it appeared to be; and it could be made to show a profit.

He made no secret of his dream. Everybody in town knew that Jim Hill wanted the railroad and hoped to get the money from Donald A. Smith. An old friend, Henry Upham, admitted that Hill "used to talk so much about this that people were a little tired of it." In the old Minnesota Club, Hill would corner fellow members and, his finger waggling in a characteristic gesture, harangue them for hours on the subject of the railway. Upham particularly remembered one evening early in May, 1874, coming across Hill in the club, gesticulating wildly in converse with Kittson, who, having had two hours of the same thing late the night before, was almost numb with fatigue. The exhausted Commodore sat immobile in front of Hill, letting his young colleague rave on and on, his own face an absolute mask. As Upham came by he caught Kittson's eye, which closed slowly and then opened again, while his face remained totally expressionless.

Hill lived and slept the railway. Indeed, he neglected his work because of it, as his partner, Edward N. Saunders, was to testify: "It seemed to occupy his mind to the exclusion of the coal business." Saunders felt injured; when Hill did turn up on the job all he would talk about was acquiring the railway.

One of the men he talked to, long and intimately, was Jesse P. Farley, an old railroad man from Dubuque, Iowa, who had been appointed receiver of the bankrupt St. Paul railroad. The twin to the bankrupt company was under trusteeship and the trustees made Farley its general manager, so that he was actually in charge of the entire St. Paul and Pacific line and its branches. As such he was supposed to keep the railroad profitable, try to get it out of trouble, and build more track. He was singularly unsuccessful, spending in three years only about one hundred thousand dollars on construction and repair. It is clear from subsequent sworn testimony that he and his assistant were on intimate terms with both Hill and Kittson, whom they saw almost daily, and that they were pleased, on occasion, to do Hill's bidding. The question, which was the subject of a prolonged series of legal battles, was whether or not the two were simply pumping Farley for information or whether Farley was in collusion with them to keep the railway in a rundown condition so that it could be bought cheaply. That mystery has never been conclusively unraveled.

But then, there are several mysteries connected with the complicated finances and eventual disposition of the St. Paul and Pacific. Another has to do with the role played by John S. Kennedy, a New York banker, who was the agent for the Dutch committee that held almost all the bonds of the bankrupt railroad. Kennedy recommended Farley as trustee. Farley, an ignorant and almost illiterate man, had previously worked for Kennedy on a small Iowa railroad and generally did what the banker told him. What was Kennedy's real role? He was officially the man charged with looking after the bondholders' interests, but he himself was to become a multimillionaire as a result of his association with Jim Hill and associates—the men who finally bought the Dutch bonds.

The bondholders in Holland appointed one of their number, Johan Carp, to visit St. Paul and look over the railway. Farley waxed pessimistic about its future. "I was induced to believe," Carp later testified, "that it would last many years before all these troubles should come to an end." Persuaded of this, he told Farley the committee was willing to sell the bonds if a reasonable bid could be obtained.

The time for waiting was over. While Farley was telling Carp that the railway would be tied up for years, Hill realized that solutions to many of the problems were at hand. Chief of these was the new legislation his political friends were pushing through the Minnesota legislature. Under the new law, companies could be sold under foreclosure and reorganized with the land grant intact. Hill had always known that the real value of the railway lay in its capacity to claim free land.

The new legislation was passed on March 6, 1876. With this huge obstacle removed, Hill left, on March 17, for Ottawa, where he told Donald Smith that it was now or never. Edwin Litchfield, the chief stockholder, was trying to reach a compromise with the Dutch bondholders which would leave him in effective control of the property and prevent foreclosure. Hill's whole scheme rested on the certainty of foreclosure. Whoever owned the bonds could foreclose if mortgage payments were in default. Then the railroad would go on the block and the new bondholders could buy it for a song. But how much did the Dutch want for their bonds? If the price was right, Smith told Hill, it was probable that the money could be raised in England.

Hill departed for St. Paul in a state of jubilation. On the train out of Chicago he ran into an old friend, Stanford Newel. "Donald Smith is ready to take hold," Hill exulted. Newel was impressed. Could it be that Hill, the voluble dreamer, had something after all?

Up to this time Johan Carp had refused to take Hill and Kittson seriously. An aging steamboat man and a garrulous coal merchant! But when he learned who Donald A. Smith was he began to pay attention.

It was now Hill's task to figure out the price at which the Dutch were prepared to sell their bonds. In January, 1877, he pretended he was ready to deal. Actually his plan was to write a letter to the Dutch committee that would sound like an offer so that he might get some idea of the actual price. He had two other purposes. He wanted to keep Carp interested and he wanted to word the letter in such a way as to convince the bondholders that the railway was practically worthless.

But since the partners had no cash, they did not dare risk outright acceptance at that moment. He and Kittson spent an entire evening working out the delicate wording and then a full morning with their lawyer rephrasing it. The letter contemplated buying the railroad property for three and a half million dollars in cash and letting the land grant go to the Dutch. But the cash was not to be paid over until the property was unencumbered, and that happy day seemed a long time distant. "We did not consider we were running much risk in making that offer," Hill was to recall.

The Dutch rejected the offer, as Hill had foreseen, but their reply contained enough information to give him a clue to the kind of deal they would accept. The time had finally come to stop dreaming dreams and playing games. The time had come to put some money on the line. The time had come to broach the subject to George Stephen, president of the Bank of Montreal, one of the keenest financial minds in Canada and a first cousin of Donald A. Smith.

3 · *Enter George Stephen*

EVER SINCE 1874, DONALD SMITH HAD been boring his cousin with talk about the St. Paul railway, in the same way that Hill had been boring his friends. George Stephen saw Smith several times a year in Montreal and listened politely to his enthusiastic accounts of the future of the North West. Stephen, like most Montreal businessmen, had a confused and inaccurate picture of the country west of the Great Lakes. "He thought of Minnesota . . . that it was at the North Pole somewhere," Smith later recalled.

Stephen cheerfully concurred in this assessment: "He [Smith] was very hot upon the matter and I was lukewarm." Stephen thought the railway scheme "an impossible thing for us to accomplish." Nevertheless he agreed to meet Hill and Smith early in 1877 to discuss the matter. Hill, armed with facts and figures, papers and documents, talking his usual blue streak, gesturing with that insistent finger, never letting up for an instant in his infectious enthusiasm, changed Stephen's attitude from one of "languid attention" to wholehearted interest; and Stephen's interests were never idle ones.

Stephen is a shadowy figure in Canadian history. The immense Rocky Mountain peak that bears his name is better known than he. His official CPR portrait, painted when the ordeal of railway building was at an end and his hair had gone white, is reasonably familiar: it shows a slender, graceful man, impeccably attired, with a long, grave Scottish face and a neatly trimmed beard. That is about all most Canadian schoolchildren know of George Stephen. Yet, apart from the politicians, he, more than any single man, was responsible for the shape and direction of the new Canada that sprang up west of Toronto after 1881.

He would have been delighted with his own historical anonymity, for he shunned the limelight. Four separate biographies of Donald Smith were published within a few years of his death, but Stephen was dead for forty-four years before he was so enshrined in 1965, and then the work was necessarily incomplete. The biographies that appeared of his colleagues provoked in him an amused contempt. He saw to it that his own personal papers were destroyed. He had no use for scribblers. He thought the newspapers printed a lot of damned nonsense. In his later years he banned the telephone from his home; it would be used, he said, for no better purpose than to spread trivialities and gossip.

Outwardly reserved, publicly reticent, and privately unassuming, he was inwardly subjected to the tugs and pressures of a mercurial psyche, reckless in its enthusiasms, magnificent in its audacities, faithful in its loyalties, consuming in its antipathies, and single-minded to the point of intolerance. He was used to the blunt directives of the business world and was maddened by the circumlocutions of the political. Unlike Macdonald, to whom he poured out his inner soul in an astonishing series of personal letters (the only real record that exists of that hidden turbulence), he indulged himself in the luxury of maintaining his animosities. As far as Stephen was concerned, you were either for him or against him. There was rarely a middle ground.

This apparently conservative business figure with the courtly manner could operate with a gambler's daring when the occasion demanded it. His sudden espousal of Hill's scheme to capture the St. Paul railroad is the first major example, but there were hints in his background. The story goes that when he was nineteen and looking for a job in London (he had been a draper's apprentice in Aberdeen) he happened past the Mansion House and was attracted by a large crowd outside; some dignitary was being accorded a civic welcome. On a sudden mischievous impulse, the brash young man moved into the ranks of the reception committee and gravely shook hands with the pear-shaped guest. It was, he discovered later, none other than Louis-Philippe, the recently abdicated King of the French.

The same audacity provided him with a business coup early in his career in the dry-goods business. As a junior partner and buyer for a Montreal firm he came under the influence, during his trips to England, of James Morrison, the most romantic business figure in the country—

a man whose swift and daring rise to fortune had inspired the phrase "Morrison's Millions."

With England on the verge of war in the Crimea, Morrison urged Stephen to buy up all the cottons and woolens he could lay his hands on and ship them across the Atlantic to Canada before wartime scarcity shot the price up. Since Stephen had no way of consulting his superiors back in Montreal, there being no Atlantic cable, he took the plunge himself. The gamble must have dismayed his senior partner, who from time to time entered into young Stephen's financial adventures with the comment "Well, it is clear George is going to ruin the firm, so it might as well come now as at a later time." But of course he did not ruin the firm. The corner he secured on cotton and woolen goods allowed him to bring off a financial coup. He eventually took over the firm, later formed one of his own, and soon found himself a member of the Montreal business establishment.

In Smith and Hill, Stephen found men like himself: shrewd in business, willing to take long risks, and, perhaps above all, wedded to the idea that a man was placed on earth to work, day and night if need be. To them, idleness was anathema and the concept of leisure almost unknown. Hill had never known an idle moment. Of Smith, an old Hudson's Bay factor recalled that he "was a wonder to work. He did not seem to take any sleep. We used to say, indeed, that he stopped up all night. No matter how late at night you looked, you would see his lamp burning in his house." Work, indeed, was Donald Smith's real religion. There is a revealing story about Smith and his secretary, a God-fearing man who refused to work on Sunday in spite of a pile of correspondence waiting for the Monday mail. Smith allowed him the Lord's Day off and then, at exactly one minute after midnight, put him to work until dawn answering the mail.

As for Stephen, "It was impressed upon me from my earliest years by one of the best mothers that ever lived that I must aim at being a thorough master of the work by which I had to get my living; and to be that I must concentrate my whole energies on my work, whatever that might be, to the exclusion of every other thing."

It was this hard ethic, so forcefully expressed by Stephen, that explains the dominance of the Scot in pioneer Canada. The Irish could loll in the taverns, sing, brawl, engage in the game of politics at ward level, and otherwise disport themselves with the religious bickering that so engrossed their time and energies. For the Scots it was work, save, and study; study, save, and work. The Irish outnumbered them as they did the English, but the Scots ran the country. Though they formed only one-fifteenth of the population they controlled the fur trade, the great banking and financial houses, the major educational institutions, and, to a considerable degree, the government. The CPR was built to a large extent by Irish laborers and Irish contractors, but it was the Scots who held the top jobs. Almost every member of the original CPR Syndicate was a self-made Scot. In the drama of the railway it is the Scots who stand out: Macdonald and Mackenzie, Allan and Macpherson, Fleming and Grant, Stephen, Smith, Kennedy, McIntyre, Angus, and Hill (who was half Scottish)—living embodiments of the popular copybook maxims of the time. *Waste not, want not.* . . . *Satan finds more mischief still for idle hands to do.* . . . *God helps those that help themselves.* . . . *A penny saved is a penny earned.* . . . *Remember that time is money.* . . . *Early to bed, early to rise.* . . . *Keep your nose to the grindstone.* . . . *See a pin and pick it up.* Stephen, it is said, got a job through following the last of these maxims. Unsuccessful in Glasgow, he had moved to London and sought work in a draper's establishment. The store was in chaos, for it was stocktaking day and no one had time to speak to him. He turned away disappointed and was halfway through the door when he stopped to pick up a pin, which he carefully stuck behind his coat lapel. The foreman, so the story goes, spotted the action, called him over, and gave him a job on the spot. Horatio Alger could not have improved upon the incident.

Stephen's idea of a spare-time activity was to make a study of banking. The hobby, if one could call it that, led him eventually to the top of the financial pyramid. His only real form of relaxation was salmon fishing, a passion which he indulged at his summer retreat of Causapscal on the Matapédia River in the Gaspé. His love of the sport almost certainly went back to his days at the parish school in his native county of Banff, a name Stephen was to make famous as Canada's best-known Rocky Mountain resort. As a young student, he came under the influence of a brilliant teacher and mathematician, John Macpherson, who rewarded his top scholars with an invitation to go salmon fishing. Stephen was certainly a top scholar in Macpherson's specialty; the schoolmaster was to recall that in thirty years of teaching Stephen was one of the three best mathematicians he had known. The salmon-fishing expeditions must have been frequent.

A mathematician must think logically and tidily; above all, he must reason creatively. Stephen had that kind of mind, able to grapple with intricate problems, to rearrange the components into a rational pattern, and then make deductions from the result. He has been called with truth "the greatest genius in the whole history of Canadian finance." His entire career is a testimony to it.

Stephen met his cousin Donald A. Smith for the first time in 1866, in a curiously chilly and awkward encounter. At this point the contrast between the two men was marked. Stephen had been in Montreal sixteen years and had climbed swiftly up the social and mercantile ladder. Smith, who was eleven years older than his cousin, had been walled off from the world in the dark and lonely corners of Labrador for more than a generation. The sophisticated Stephen was faultlessly groomed, as a good draper should be; indeed, for a time he employed a valet. Smith was shaggy and weatherworn, his sandy hair curling around his collar, his eyebrows unkempt, his beard ragged.

Smith knew very little about Stephen except that he was in the woolen trade and was a first cousin, but he decided to look him up during the course of a shopping expedition. He took along his wife and family, and en route they purchased a great, gaudy carpetbag to take back with them to Labrador; it was the sort of thing the Indians enjoyed seeing. Later, when Smith was asked if Stephen had been glad to see him, his wife burst out: "He wasn't glad at all. Why should Mr. Stephen be glad to see country cousins like us? I wish he had waited until he met Mr. Stephen before buying that red carpet bag. But he wouldn't let me carry it, and the rest of us waited outside."

It is an oddly memorable picture, this initial meeting between two men who came to be numbered among the most powerful in the country: the nervous family group on the doorstep, waiting outside like poor relations, with the rustic Smith clutching his outlandishly brilliant bag in the presence of the elegant Stephen—the country mouse and the city mouse, circling each other warily.

But Smith was no bumpkin, as Stephen was speedily to realize. He was a man of parts, who had earned the praise of a future Smithsonian director with his scientific experiments in farming at Esquimaux Bay, where in subarctic conditions he had managed to raise sheep and cattle and cultivate seven acres. His active correspondence with colleagues all over the world kept him abreast if not ahead of international affairs. More, he was an astonishing businessman. For many years his fellow officers in the fur trade had entrusted him with their salaries, thus giving him control of large sums of money. He guaranteed the fur traders 3 per cent a year and invested their money in securities. He was, in short, a kind of one-man Labrador bank and this became the basis of his fortune. One of the stocks he bought was that of the Bank of Montreal; another, of the Hudson's Bay Company. He ended up as one of the bank's largest shareholders and in total control of the Hudson's Bay Company. But, true to the copybook maxims, he was not above counting and sorting all the nails in the packing cases that were shipped to him.

When Smith met Stephen and Hill in Montreal in the spring of 1877, he was already a director of the bank. Stephen was its president. The two had become associated since that frosty meeting ten years before. Smith was moved permanently to Montreal in 1868, and he and his cousin soon found themselves co-directors and leading share-holders in several industries, including one that manufactured railway rolling stock. Bit by bit Stephen began getting involved with railways, almost by osmosis. Now, in 1877, he found himself leaning across the table while a one-eyed ex-Canadian jabbed his finger at him and talked about launching a daring financial adventure.

Stephen's precise mathematician's mind easily grasped Hill's Niagara of statistics and sorted them into a pattern. His gambler's instincts tugged at him insistently. If the coup could be pulled off—it was an immense "if"—it would be a master stroke comparable to the exploits of a Gould, a Fisk, or a Morgan. If it failed, it would literally beggar them all.

What did Stephen have to gain at this point of his career? He was president of the most important financial institution in Canada, director of innumerable companies, respected by his peers, socially impeccable. The preposterous scheme of buying into an obscure and run-down railroad somewhere off beyond the mists of the horizon could, unless it worked, bring him nothing but discredit. Perhaps if he could have seen the tortured succession of events that this venture would finally lead to, the terrible moments when he saw his world, everything that he had built and toiled for, crumbling around him, the sleepless nights when he was close to a nervous and physical breakdown, perhaps even to suicide—George Stephen might have hesitated and backed away. A decade later, after it was all over and the years hung heavy upon him, he gave more than a little indication of this when he wrote to John A. Macdonald: "Tomorrow I begin my sixty-first year, and looking back ten years I am far from being the free man I then was. . . . When I think of the misery I have suffered in these ten years I cannot help thinking what a fool I was not to end my work and enjoy the leisure which I had earned by forty years hard work. I began to earn my own living at the age of ten. 'But what maun be maun be.' It was not so ordained."

He could not resist the adventure. He sat down and began to figure, with Hill and Smith, at what price the bonds should be purchased. They worked it out together at a little more than four million dollars. If the Dutch bondholders indicated that price was acceptable, Stephen said, he thought he could raise the money in London that fall. He still

had to see the railway for himself—he was nothing if not thorough—
but from that day on George Stephen was totally captivated, body
and soul, to the exclusion of everything else.

4 · A railway at bargain rates

THE NEW ASSOCIATES HAD A GREAT DEAL
of delicate negotiating ahead of them. Before Stephen could leave for
Europe it would be necessary to make a firm and final deal with the
bondholders. Then, in order to forestall a legal battle, an attempt must
also be made to corner the stock. After that Stephen would have to
raise enough money to buy both the bonds and the stock.

Hill left Montreal for New York to see Edwin Litchfield, the man
who owned almost all the stock. He drew a blank. "The old rat," as
Stephen called him, would not even name a price. Then, on May 26,
Hill fired off a carefully worded letter to the Dutch committee. Hill,
the master letter writer, had worked at this one all night. It was so
ambiguously worded that, although it looked like an offer, it was
actually only an option. When the Dutch tried to bargain, Hill got
tough. The value of the bonds was actually decreasing, he suggested, a
grasshopper plague had caused land values to plunge, and the Northern
Pacific was threatening to build a competitive line, which would reduce
the value of the property still further.

Just before he left for Europe, on September 1, 1877, Stephen
found an opportunity to see the property for himself. He was in Chicago
on business with R. B. Angus, the bank's general manager—another
bearded, self-made Scot—and the two decided to spend the weekend in
St. Paul. Smith immediately came down from Winnipeg, and on Sunday the four associates, together with Angus and Farley, the receiver
and manager, took the pay car out along the completed portion of one
of the lines.

Stephen was dismayed at what he saw when the train chugged
past the hamlet of Litchfield and out onto the arid prairie. This was
the worst year of the great depression of the seventies. The economic
panic had been followed by drought years, which drove settlers from
the land, and—even worse—by a grasshopper plague of truly terrible
proportions. The 'hoppers came by the millions, eating everything that
grew and blanketing the roads and fences.

Passing through this ravaged country, Stephen began to shake his
head ominously: it looked for all the world like the top of a rusty stove.

The others watched in growing alarm. Would he back out now? Stephen began to ask some pointed questions: Where would the business come from in this tenantless desert? When, if ever, would there be settlers here on the parched and plundered grasslands? Then suddenly the little station of De Graff was reached. There several trails leading into the community were speckled with carts loaded with people.

"What is all this?" Stephen wanted to know.

Somebody, probably Hill, made a reply which Smith was later to remember: "Why, this is but an instance of what is to occur along the whole line of the railroad. This is a colony opened by Bishop Ireland one single year ago. Already the settlers brought in by the Bishop are counted by the hundreds and hundreds of others are coming to join them from different parts of America and Europe. This is Sunday morning and the settlers are going to Mass."

The scene made an enormous impression on Stephen: the vision of a railway tied to colonization—bringing in the very settlers who would then provide it with its future business—was limned in his mind. His old mentor, James Morrison, had always advised him: "Hold to your first impression of a bargain." Stephen's doubts evaporated and, in Smith's words, "from that moment he was won over to the new enterprise." As for Bishop Ireland, he benefited hugely from the incident. A grateful Jim Hill saw to it that his church got all the land it needed for next to nothing.

Hill had by this time made a detailed inventory of the railroad's assets and liabilities. His supple mind had grasped a point that eluded everyone else: though the net earnings of the First Division Company seemed to have dropped, they had in reality all but doubled because almost two hundred thousand dollars had been charged to operating expenses instead of to construction and equipment. This meant that the railroad was doing much better than the books seemed to indicate.

Hill knew something more: although he figured that the total cost of the bonds plus the cost of completing the remainder of the line would require some five and a half million dollars, he was able, by close reckoning, to estimate the total value of the railway, with its equipment, track, townsites, and land grants, at almost twenty millions. In short, Hill perceived that if the bondholders accepted the offer, he and his associates would get the railway for about a quarter of its real value.

By mid-September, the Dutch were ready to deal. If Stephen could raise the money, the partners could buy themselves almost eighteen million dollars' worth of bonds for slightly more than four millions. It was a fantastic bargain.

The four partners agreed to share the risks and the profits equally, each taking a one-fifth share in the enterprise. The remaining fifth went to Stephen to use at his discretion in raising a loan. At the end of September he set off for England, full of optimism.

But in London the bankers were gun-shy. The panic of 1873 had made American railway securities a bad risk, and among all the bad risks, the St. Paul and Pacific was held to be the worst. Stephen was not able to raise a shilling.

In Montreal, on Stephen's return, four bitterly disappointed men met on Christmas Day, in no mood for Yuletide merriment. The grand scheme on which Hill and Smith had been pinning their hopes for four years lay shattered. Stephen, however, had no intention of giving up. The tumblers of his precise mind were already turning over, forming new patterns. An unconventional plan was taking shape which, if accepted, would be far better than the original. Stephen decided to take the negotiations into his own hands and deal directly with the Dutch committee's New York agent.

Early in January, Stephen met John S. Kennedy for the first time. Kennedy was yet another self-made Scot, and the two swiftly became friends and, not long afterward, business associates. Stephen's plan was as bold as it was simple. He offered to buy the bonds on credit, depositing a mere one hundred thousand dollars on account and paying the balance *after* foreclosure. The payment could be made either in cash or in the new bonds of the reorganized company. The Dutch were encouraged to accept the paper rather than the money by the offer of a bonus of $250 in preferred stock for every thousand-dollar bond they took. The partners, in turn, agreed to finish the railway and put it into working order.

They were, in short, proposing to get control of eighteen million dollars' worth of bonds for a cash outlay of only one hundred thousand dollars. The Dutch bondholders were psychologically in the position of horse traders who, having had various offers dangled before them and then withdrawn, had worked themselves into a frame of mind to deal at any price. Under Kennedy's prodding, they accepted. The purchase was concluded on February 24, 1878, and the partners took control of the railway on March 13.

One of the mysteries surrounding this remarkable transaction is the disposition of the extra one-fifth share that Stephen was given to negotiate with. Did Stephen keep it for himself? If not, to whom did he give it? That it was not divided among the four partners seems clear from their subsequent court testimony, in which they appeared remarkably unconcerned and evasive about a slice of stock that came to be worth many millions.

"We showed our satisfaction and contentment in the whole matter by each of us releasing Mr. Stephen. There, with us, was the end of it," Smith said airily. "We did not ask Mr. Stephen to account for it." The agreement, as Smith recalled it under oath, was that Stephen would use the extra one-fifth "as might be necessary in getting the aid of friends or in getting the money." But what friends? Smith did not say; Stephen was not asked.

One man Stephen did *not* give the one-fifth interest to was Jesse P. Farley, the receiver in bankruptcy of one of the twin St. Paul companies and the general manager of both. Farley later sued Kittson, Hill, and the newly organized company, charging that in 1876, before the meeting with Stephen, both Kittson and Hill had promised him a one-fifth share in the enterprise in exchange for his help, co-operation, and special knowledge. It was clear that that help consisted in deceiving the courts, which had put him in charge of the property on Kennedy's advice. What Farley was saying, in effect, was that he had devised a plan and arrived at a secret agreement with Hill and Kittson to keep the line in such condition that it could be bought cheaply. The circuit-court judge who heard the case in 1882 tended to believe Farley. "The plaintiff," he said, "conceived a scheme to wreck the vast interests which it was his duty to protect"; but he threw the case out because "courts will not and ought not to be made the agencies whereby frauds are to be in any respect recognized or aided." Farley appealed and a trial was ordered. It took place in 1887, by which time Kittson was dead. This judge did not believe Farley. He said, with some sarcasm, that in his opinion Farley did not fail in his official duty "and although such conclusion carries an imputation upon his recollection or veracity as a witness, it sustains his integrity as an officer."

Farley persisted in the courts for a total of thirteen years. By the time the final judgment was read against him in the Supreme Court in 1893, he too was dead and the matter was closed. From all this testimony —two thousand pages of it in one case alone—several puzzling pieces of information emerge which do not quite fit together. It is reasonably clear that Farley *thought* he had a secret deal with Hill and Kittson. It is equally clear that Hill emphatically did not think so. It is also reasonably clear that Hill, Kittson, and Farley did a good deal of talking together about the railway, and that at a time when Farley knew that Hill wanted to buy it, he, Farley, did his best to disparage the line to the Dutch representative.

There is also the puzzling question of Kennedy's role. Farley was Kennedy's man. At the point when the bondholders were in their final negotiations with Stephen—on Kennedy's advice—Kennedy was also writing to Farley, urging him to get in on a good thing. "We think it will pay you to take an interest with K. & H. and we are glad to hear that they have offered it to you," he wrote on February 25, 1878, in a reply to a letter from Farley soliciting his advice.

All of this can be subject to innocent interpretation, but the question continues to rankle: Who got the extra one-fifth? After the St. Paul line grew into the Great Northern it was revealed that John S. Kennedy held an enormous quantity of its stock. He, Hill, and Stephen all became close friends, and when the CPR board was formed Kennedy was a director. When he died he left an estate estimated at between thirty and sixty million dollars, depending on the book value of the immense mass of railway stock he had acquired. Did Kennedy simply buy into the railway that he had urged his Dutch clients to sell so cheaply? Or was it he who was promised George Stephen's extra one-fifth during those delicate negotiations, which allowed the sale of eighteen millions in bonds for almost no cash at all?*

Perhaps Stephen himself kept the extra one-fifth, though that is hardly in character. If he did, no one could say he had not earned it. As for the Dutch, they seemed perfectly satisfied: most of them preferred to take more bonds in the new company rather than cash, a wise decision as it turned out. It was true that they had sold the railway cheaply; but it was also true that the line was worth eighteen million dollars only if and when it could be put into working order. If Hill and his associates had not come along, it is doubtful whether the bondholders would have realized anything on their original investment. As it developed, they were so well pleased that they made a gift to Stephen of a valuable bowl commemorating a great victory in which the Dutch admiral de Ruyter, in 1666, burned the best of the English fleet. Years later, when Stephen was entertaining George V of England,

---

* The Canadian historian O. D. Skelton, in his book *The Railway Builders* (Toronto, 1916), says that Stephen, Hill, Smith, and Kennedy each took one share and that Kittson took half a share, the remaining half share going to Angus after he left the service of the bank and became general manager of the railway. He gives no source for this statement, which does not square with the court testimony of the principals in 1888. Nonetheless it is a plausible suggestion: Kittson's energies were not really involved in the enterprise to the same extent as the others'; Angus could probably be lured away from the bank only on the promise of a sizable interest; and Kennedy's subsequent involvement makes it clear that he was a substantial shareholder. It is reasonably certain that Kennedy was brought into the Syndicate by Stephen at the time he convinced the Dutch committee to accept the offer.

that old sailor's eye caught sight of the trophy. The monarch was not amused at this symbol of naval humiliation.

"Why don't you destroy the damned thing?" His Majesty asked.

5 · *The Syndicate is born*

THE FOUR PARTNERS HAD POSSESSION OF the bonds but they were by no means out of the woods. A whole series of complicated problems now faced them simultaneously. Any one of these could wreck the enterprise and ruin them.

First of all, there was more money to be raised. The line had $280,000 in debts, which had to be paid immediately. Then there was the hundred-thousand-dollar deposit to the bondholders. The stock, if it could be purchased from Litchfield, would cost around half a million dollars. Finally, the railroad itself had to be completed swiftly if the land grant was to be earned.

There was only one conceivable place to get this kind of financing, and that was from the Bank of Montreal. Stephen was president and Smith was a director, and they were now proposing to borrow money personally from an institution under their care. It did not look good; there would certainly be stockholders' questions and newspaper comment, but there was no help for it.

Stephen wrote to Hill on February 10, 1878, that he and Kittson must pledge everything they owned--and he meant *everything*—in order to get a line of credit from the bank. He and Smith had already handed over "every transferable security of every kind we have got" in order to get the initial $280,000 to pay off the debts. Now it was all or nothing.

"The risks were very great," Hill later recalled, "and in case of failure so great as to entirely ruin the entire party—financially; wipe out every dollar we owned in the world and leave us with an enormous debt if the enterprise failed."

Kittson was almost sick with worry. To him, the scheme had always seemed wild; he had gone into it solely because he trusted Jim Hill. Now, if at any stage of the sensitive maneuvers that were required something went wrong, he faced the poorhouse. He kept his participation a secret, lest his friends talk him out of it. But in his old age, Norman Kittson, the erstwhile border trader, wealthy beyond his wildest visions, would be able to purchase and maintain one of the largest and finest racing stables on the continent.

Stephen's next move was to go straight to Ottawa and negotiate with Mackenzie for a ten-year lease of the Pembina Branch so that the St. Paul road, when it reached the border, would have a connection to Winnipeg. This transaction, too, was fraught with uncertainty. Smith's name was already being mentioned as a major shareholder in the company and it was impossible for him to maintain the fiction in Parliament that he was disinterested.

Almost simultaneously a new problem arose. The Minnesota legislature passed a new law setting a series of deadlines for the construction of the railroad. Two sections had to be completed by the end of the year; otherwise the land grants, franchises—everything—would be forfeited. Now it became doubly important to push the foreclosure suits. Hill was fearful that one of the twin companies might actually start making money. If that happened the new trustees would be forced to give up their control over it, since it could pay the defaulted mortgage interest with the increased revenue; and then the St. Paul terminus, among other assets, would be lost and the value of the second company's property would be reduced.

The partners were juggling several problems at once: they must lobby in Ottawa for the Canadian lease; they must raise funds to build the rest of the railway before the rapidly approaching deadline; they must haggle with Litchfield to try to get his stock in order to prevent delays in foreclosure. Finally, they must fight off the rival Northern Pacific, which was now threatening to move in with its own line to the border and launch a railway war. It seemed an impossible task, especially in view of the precarious state of their finances. If either Litchfield or the rival railway knew how badly off they were, the game would be over. This is where Stephen's control of the bank became so valuable: there would be no leaks from that source.

But there was not a million dollars available for the additional railway construction to the border. The only way to raise money was for the receiver, Farley, to get a court order permitting him to issue receiver's debentures. Thirty-five miles of railroad had to be built by August, 1878, from Melrose to Sauk Centre and another thirty-three by December (to Alexandria) in order to hold the land grant. Farley was persuaded by Hill to go to court, but the court was dubious, and the hearings were maddeningly slow. When the judge refused to issue the order, Hill himself went to see him and, using every persuasive power, managed to change his mind. The judge was impressed by Hill, but even as he signed the order he still had his doubts: he said candidly that if the associates failed to carry it out, it would destroy them and ruin him.

From this point on the financing of the railway was left to Stephen while Hill moved in to build the line. It was almost a rehearsal for the future and grander project of the CPR, when again it was Stephen's task to keep the money flowing while Hill's protégé, William Cornelius Van Horne (who later became his deadly enemy), would drive the steel.

Hill had two months in which to lay track from Melrose to Sauk Centre. He had to find rails, ties, rolling stock, and laborers in a hurry. The task took all his waking hours. By the time the men and equipment were assembled, Hill realized that he would have to lay at least a mile of track a day to make the deadline. He took charge himself, fighting mosquitoes, sunstroke, rattlesnakes, and dysentery, firing bosses on the spot if they could not maintain the mileage. When one crew rebelled at Hill's methods and quit, he wired St. Paul for replacements, taking the precaution of paying the fares in advance and hiring the toughest men he could find to guard each car door to prevent the new workers from skipping before they reached the end of track.

In the midst of this another crisis arose. The rejuvenated Northern Pacific was threatening to build a line to the Canadian border paralleling the St. Paul line. That would be disastrous.

In the American Midwest there is a particularly stubborn and obnoxious weed to which the early settlers gave the name of Jim Hill mustard. It fitted. In his battle with the Northern Pacific, Hill showed his mettle. He met the rival company head-on—the first of a series of bold encounters which would, one day, see him best a Vanderbilt. Hill was convinced that the Northern Pacific was bluffing. It was his tactic to convince his rivals that he himself was not. The Northern Pacific was at the time using St. Paul tracks. Hill threatened to cancel the agreement immediately, raise the fees for running rights, and boost the rent on the St. Paul terminal. Moreover, he would start at once, he declared, to survey a line all the way to the Yellowstone River and would ask Congress for half of the land grant that had been promised the Northern Pacific as far west as the Rockies. In the face of this bluff—it could be nothing else—the rival railroad knuckled under and an agreement was reached in November, the chief articles of which were that the Northern Pacific would withdraw from competition with the St. Paul and Pacific in return for certain running rights and terminal space in the Twin Cities. Hill had won his first corporate dogfight handily.

He met his first construction deadline with just twenty-four hours to spare and secured the vital land grant. He did not slacken his pace, for he had to finish the second stretch before December 1, 1878. The

Sir John A. Macdonald as Prime Minister.

Alexander Mackenzie as Prime Minister.

Edward Blake as Leader of the Opposition.

Sir Hugh Allan at the peak of his power.

Sandford Fleming (second from left), *with George Grant on his right, sets off on his famous trip "from ocean to ocean" in 1871. One of the party, the "rascal" Charles Horetsky, photographed the surveyors below, with their Red River carts along the North Saskatchewan.*

The Pacific Scandal was made to order for the pen of J. W. Bengough of the political weekly Grip. In a cartoon titled "Canada's Laocoon," he depicted Sir Hugh Allan, John A. Macdonald, and Francis Hincks enmeshed by the rush of events of 1873 which followed the revelations of the railway president's gifts to the Tory Party.

A second cartoon, following the Scandal disclosures, made game of Macdonald's impassioned declaration that "these hands are clean" and came down hard on his attempts to suppress or delay discussion of the charges against him.

WHITHER ARE WE DRIFTING?

Above: *End of Track on the prairies in the summer of 1882. A work train dumps its load of ties: enough for half a mile of railroad.*
Below: *The prairie contractors used 1700 teams of horses like these to build the line from Flat Creek, Manitoba, west to Fort Calgary.*

George Stephen at the time he
left the Bank of Montreal to
become president of the newly
formed Canadian Pacific.

The only contemporary photo of
William Cornelius Van Horne,
the Illinois railroader, at the
time he became general manager.

Right: *A pencil drawing of Yale, British Columbia, made on the spot at the height of the construction period in 1882. Coolies, Scots, Yankees, Siwash Indians, prostitutes, and Irish navvies caroused and brawled in front of the saloons that dominated the main street at the mouth of the Fraser canyon.*

Below left: *Without some 8000 Chinese coolies imported from Kwangtung province, the railway could not have been completed. They were paid a dollar a day to ballast the line.*

Below right: *A tent camp of coolies on the Onderdonk contract. They spoke no English, cooked their own food, and continued to wear the loose blouses and pigtails (tied here in a topknot) because they expected to return to their homeland. It was a dream that not all of them realized.*

Andrew Onderdonk, the unassuming New Yorker who blasted the line out of the granite of the Fraser's black canyon.

Four tunnels and two trestles can be seen within a few hundred yards on this section of the Fraser near Spuzzum. There were 27 tunnels on the Onderdonk contract and more than 600 trestles requiring 40,000,000 board feet of specially cut timber.

enemy was no longer the dysentery and sunstroke of the summer but the bone-chilling cold of the Minnesota prairies. Hill walked the line himself, stopping here and there to counsel one or other of the navvies —he knew them all by their first names—on the way to treat frostbite. On one memorable occasion he leaped from his private car, seized a shovel, and began attacking the snow, spelling the workmen one after another while they went inside for a dipper of hot coffee. He made his deadline well ahead of time and kept on going, for he wanted to get the full railway operating as swiftly as possible. The line would be useless until he completed the gap between Crookston and St. Vincent—across from Pembina at the Canadian border. On November 11, Hill had the satisfaction of seeing his first through locomotive arrive at Emerson, Manitoba, from St. Paul.

Stephen meanwhile was having his own problems, a whole irritating series of them. The Canadian Senate had thrown out Mackenzie's bill, making a straight lease of the Pembina Branch impossible. Mackenzie had in August given the St. Paul line running rights on the Canadian road, but the Conservatives canceled that agreement. The St. Paul group would be allowed to use the line only until the completion of the Canadian Pacific Railway. It was something, at least.

Stephen's second problem was the recalcitrant Litchfield. As long as he held the stock he could hamper the foreclosure proceedings and prevent the reorganization of the railroad company. Finally, in mid-January, Stephen went to New York and managed to secure all the stock for a half million dollars. There could be no conflicts now between stockholders and bondholders since they were one and the same.

The partners got their half million from the Bank of Montreal and moved for foreclosure. It was granted in March, 1879. In May they formed a new company, the St. Paul, Minneapolis and Manitoba Railroad Company. In June, the new firm bought up all the property at the foreclosure sale. It is said that they paid $6,780,000 for it, not in cash but in receiver's debentures and bonds. They floated a sixteen-million-dollar bond issue at once, some of which was used to pay back the Dutch. Immediately after the foreclosure sale they sold the greater part of the land grant for $13,068,887. Already they had realized an incredible profit. It was only a matter of deciding how much stock to create, and that took some time and care. Years later, Smith remembered that Hill's ideas were so big in this direction "as to cause me, a man of moderation, considerable perturbation."

Hill wanted to create fifteen million dollars' worth of stock.

"Aren't you afraid that the capitalization will startle the public?"

Smith ventured. "Isn't there some danger that we will be charged with watering the stock?"

"Well," Hill replied, "we have let the whole lake in already."

When the stock was issued, each of the original partners received 57,646 shares. Within three years, each share was worth $140, which meant that each partner had made a clear capital gain of more than eight millions. At that point—1882—the partners issued another two million dollars' worth of stock to themselves and then, in 1883, they issued to themselves ten million dollars' worth of 6 per cent bonds for one million dollars—an additional profit of nine millions. Yet at the time the railroad was still sneered at as "Hill's Folly." The attorneys who worked out the corporate structure were offered a fee of twenty-five thousand dollars in cash or half a million in stock. If they had taken the stock and held it for thirty years, they would have had in principal and interest something close to thirty millions.

From the beginning, the railroad was fabulously successful. The grasshoppers magically disappeared. The soil began to yield bumper crops. Hill had to scramble to find extra freight cars to handle the business. In 1880, the net earnings of the railroad exceeded the interest on the bonded debt by 60 per cent—an increase of one million dollars in a single year. The "Manitoba" road, as it came to be called, formed the nucleus of Hill's Great Northern, the only Pacific line in the United States that never went bankrupt or passed a dividend. Within two years its four promoters moved from the brink of disaster to a position of almost unlimited wealth.

They had also become controversial figures in Canada. The deal with the Bank of Montreal was looked at askance by press, public, and shareholders. The criticisms increased when R. B. Angus resigned as the bank's general manager in August to take a job as general manager of the new railway. Meanwhile, the partners were being attacked on another front. The new company, which operated the only trains from St. Paul to the Red River, had also taken over the Kittson Line and thus had a monopoly of all traffic to Winnipeg. That aroused the full ire of the Conservative press, to whom the name Donald Smith was still profanity. The Montreal *Gazette* called for the immediate construction of the Canadian Pacific to remove the "pernicious influence" of Smith and his associates. The Winnipeg *Times* was even more caustic. "The wily Jim Hill," it charged, "had to 'grease' other interests, legislative, judicial and private to the tune, it is said, of a million."

This was the climate in which the CPR Syndicate was eventually formed. All the controversy served to illuminate one fact: there was now available a remarkable group of successful men who had experience in both railway building and high finance. In the summer of 1880, the Macdonald government was looking for just such a group. It was John Henry Pope, the homely and straightforward Minister of Agriculture, who had first drawn his Prime Minister's attention to the St. Paul associates.

"Catch them," he said, "before they invest their profits."

9

1 · "Capitalists of undoubted means"

THERE IS SOMETHING VERY AKIN TO A sprightly look in the earlier photographs and portraits of George Stephen: the head is tilted upwards, the wide, clear eyes sparkle a little, and there is almost to be seen in those unlined features—one hesitates to use the word—a quality approaching innocence. A later well-known painting by Sir George Reid, which hangs in the CPR board room, portrays a different man. The head is sunk forward on shoulders that have become slightly bowed; the graying mustache droops, giving the bearded face a morose, houndlike appearance; the eyes, once so wide, are shrewd, knowing, and not a little sad. It is perhaps unwise to make too much of Victorian portraits; and yet all the evidence suggests that Reid did not exaggerate the change in his subject.

When the first annual report of the "Manitoba" line electrified the public in 1880, Stephen must have believed that his life's struggle lay behind him. In reality, it had only begun; the troubles he faced would be more nerve-racking than anything he had yet experienced. For when Stephen said "yes" to Jim Hill in 1877 he unwittingly catapulted himself into the great project of the Canadian Pacific.

From the moment that Stephen's success became public property, he was transformed, whether he knew it or not, into a leading candidate to build the impossible railway. Long before Macdonald again took power, Mackenzie had been seeking just such a man—a successful Canadian financier, in league with other Canadians of means, with practical experience in financing and constructing a profitable North American railway. After Mackenzie's fall, Macdonald took up the vain search. Just when it seemed impossible to find such a man, an entire group of them—Stephen, Hill, Smith, Kittson, and Angus—suddenly popped out of nowhere, loaded with credentials.

In the fall of 1879, Macdonald, Tupper, and Leonard Tilley of New Brunswick set out for England to seek an Imperial guarantee to help build the railway. The delegation was the most influential to cross the water since Confederation and the country was convinced that it would succeed. But it was all premature and overoptimistic. There was no Imperial guarantee, and no contractors willing to gamble on such a lunatic undertaking. One English financier laughed aloud when he first heard of Macdonald's plan to raise a loan to build a railway across the half-frozen continent. Years later he related to Donald Smith his impressions at the time: " 'Good Heavens,' I thought, 'somebody will have to hold these Canadians back, or they will go plunging themselves into hopeless bankruptcy before they come of age.' I felt I would as soon invest in a Yankee 'wild-cat' mine."

The government, while placating British Columbia with the Onderdonk contracts in 1880, determined to move slowly on the prairies. Its plan was to build "a cheap railway . . . incurring no expenditure beyond that absolutely necessary to effect the rapid colonization of the country." Only two hundred miles would be placed under contract and the line would not even be properly ballasted. The steel would creep across the plains, year by year, a few miles ahead of advancing settlement. After the House rose, in the spring of 1881, Macdonald told his dubious council that such a local railway was necessary to attract immigrants.

This was anticlimax after all the brave talk of a two-thousand-mile line to the Pacific built to Union Pacific standards. It did not sit well with Charles Tupper, who was more sanguine than his leader on the matter of the railway because he had learned of the incredible success of George Stephen and his colleagues. In a memo to the Privy Council on June 15, he submitted a proposition for building a through line from the proposed Canada Central railhead, on Lake Nipissing in northern Ontario, to the Pacific Coast. Tupper recommended that "authority be given to negotiate with capitalists of undoubted means and who shall be required to give the most ample guarantee for the construction and operation of the line on such terms as will secure at the same time the rapid settlement of the public lands and the construction of the work."

There was no doubt about who the "capitalists of undoubted means" were. Tupper had his eyes clearly focused on the St. Paul syndicate. But even as the Cabinet met to consider the terms it was prepared to offer—a twenty-million-dollar subsidy and thirty million acres of prairie land—it was obvious that the atmosphere was changing and that other capitalists, some substantial and some shadowy, were sending feelers to Ottawa. The depression was at an end; the previous autumn had seen a bumper harvest; the climate for railway building suddenly looked better. There was word that the principals behind Andrew Onderdonk were interested; so was Thomas Brassey's firm in England. And up from New York came a British peer, Lord Dunmore, a front man for Puleston, Brown and Company, a British financial house.

There was another offer before the government that June. It came in the name of Duncan McIntyre, who was engaged in building the Canada Central Railway from Ottawa to Lake Nipissing. It was no secret that his principals were George Stephen and the other members of the St. Paul group. The arrangement between Stephen and McIntyre was a marriage of convenience. As the virtual owner of the Canada Central, McIntyre would be a valuable ally if Stephen's group secured the contract, for McIntyre's line stopped where the CPR was to begin. The alliance could mean that the through route from Ottawa to the Pacific Ocean would be controlled by a single company. McIntyre, a heavy-browed Lowlander with a great soup-strainer mustache, was another self-made Scot who had begun life in Canada in 1829 as a clerk in a mercantile firm. Although he became a spokesman for the new syndicate in its formative period, he was always something of an outsider within the group; and when the ultimate crisis came he would be found wanting. He did not have Stephen's stamina, nor Smith's, and the day would come when Stephen could not stand to be in the same room with him.

The Stephen-McIntyre offer was a tempting one, especially as it was the only one that came from Canada, but it asked more than the Cabinet was prepared to grant: a subsidy of twenty-six and a half millions and a land grant of thirty-five million acres. The syndicate would not bargain. The subject, McIntyre told Macdonald, was closed "for the present"; but the door was obviously being left ajar. On June 29, Macdonald was emboldened to announce that there were a number of capitalists bidding for the construction of the railway and that negotiations had reached the point where a deputation of Ministers to England was indicated.

Macdonald, Tupper, and John Henry Pope, Minister of Agriculture, sailed for England on July 10. The Prime Minister intended to see both Puleston, Brown and Company and Sir Henry Tyler, president of the Grand Trunk. Alexander Campbell, the Senate leader, was left to negotiate with Onderdonk and his backers. As for McIntyre, he was sailing on the same ship—not entirely by coincidence—and, as the mail steamer touched at Rimouski on the St. Lawrence, a letter arrived for Macdonald from George Stephen at his fishing camp at nearby Causapscal. It was an odd missive, diffident yet wistful, and it opened the door a little wider.

"I am aware," Stephen wrote, "it is often impossible for a Government to adopt the best course; and it is the knowledge of that fact that makes me rather hesitate to commit myself to the enormous responsibilities involved in this undertaking. You will have no difficulty, I feel sure, in finding men on the other side, more or less substantial and with greater courage—mainly because they know less of the difficulties to be encountered but also because they will adopt measures for their own protection which I could not avail myself of."

It was a clever letter, though Stephen may not have consciously intended it as such since he himself was of two minds regarding the project. Nevertheless, he managed very subtly to damn all other aspirants to the contract while obliquely selling his own group. He pointed out the difficulties of a large bonded indebtedness in which "the real responsibility is transferred from the Company to the people who may be induced to buy the bonds . . . while the projectors pocket a big profit at the start." He suggested that any English financial organization would indulge in this kind of manipulation at great risk to Canada: "It would indeed be a disastrous affair to all concerned, if the English public were induced to invest in a bond issue which the road could not carry."

His own plan, Stephen went on, would have been to limit the borrowing to the smallest point. He would expect his profit to come from the growth of the country after the railroad was built.

"I could not be a party to a scheme involving a large issue of bonds on a road which no one can be sure will earn enough to pay working expenses," Stephen declared. He had no intention of going to England; he would be outbid there. No English or American organization could do the job as well or as cheaply, yet they would want to pocket the profits in advance while Stephen was willing to take the risk and wait.

Then, once more, the soft sell: Stephen was satisfied that he and his group could construct the road without much trouble; and if anybody could operate it successfully, they could. The line from Thunder Bay to Red River would be profitable and they would use the experience gained in Minnesota in the management and settling of the lands. The Canada Central to Ottawa and certain Quebec roads would, of course, have to be incorporated because the terminus must be at Montreal or Quebec City, not at Lake Nipissing, far off in the wilds of Northern Ontario.

It was a letter dictated from a position of strength and confidence, written when Stephen was salmon fishing with Angus; indeed, the two had discussed nothing else all week, the fishing having been poor. In the letter, Stephen played Macdonald like an angler. He had thrust the bait toward him: the Minnesota experience, the desire to take risks, the special knowledge of Canadian conditions, the unquestioned ability of his group to do the job. Then, in a final paragraph, he pulled back slightly but left the bait dangling: "Although I am off the notion of the thing now, should anything occur on the other side to induce you to think that taking all things into consideration, our proposal is better upon the whole for the country than any offer you get in England, I might, on hearing from you, renew it and possibly in doing so reduce the land grant to some extent."

It was a hard letter for Macdonald to resist, since Stephen's was the only Canadian group bidding and it was clear that he was prepared to do the job for about twenty-five millions in cash and an equal number of good prairie acres. Moreover, the other aspirants were dropping away. In August, the Onderdonk group passed: the Fraser canyon was occupying their efforts. In London, Macdonald and Tupper approached Sir Henry Tyler, the debonair and witty president of the Grand Trunk. The company was a political force in Canada and such a strong supporter of the Government that Grand Trunk employees, at election time, were given strict orders on how to vote. It was important that Tyler be given a chance, at the very least, to refuse the contract.

He did just that. Tupper reported his reaction, given in the tea room of the House of Commons, where Tyler was a sitting member: "If you'll cut off the portion of the railway from Thunder Bay to Nipissing I'll take up the project; but unless you do that, my shareholders will simply throw the prospectus into the wastepaper basket." There it was again: the terrible geography of North America conspiring against the efforts of the struggling nation to consolidate. Tupper replied that Canada could not consent to be for six months without any communication with the North West except by a long detour through a foreign land. That was that; Tyler would become an implacable enemy of the CPR and would almost succeed in smashing the line financially. The Grand Trunk's philosophy did not encompass a transcontinental nation. Sir Henry's blunt refusal, though he could not suspect it at the time, would reduce the Grand Trunk to a secondary railroad; the CPR would shortly outrank it and, in the end, outlive it. By the time the older company decided to push its own line of steel to the Pacific, it would be too late. That belated and disastrous undertaking spelled the end of the company which might have been the greatest in the nation.

The offer from Puleston, Brown and Company also dissolved. The firm could not, in the end, get the European backing it promised. It is possible the Prime Minister was relieved. A railway to the Pacific built by a British promoter with American roots using French and German money was scarcely a great national undertaking. Stephen's letter was in his pocket and McIntyre, as he well knew, was in England. He began a series of discussions with McIntyre in London. Sir John Rose, who represented one of the smaller British financial houses and had some connection with the wavering European group, was present. George Stephen, in Canada, was at the end of the cable line. By September 4, the provisional agreement was made: twenty-five million dollars and twenty-five million acres it was to be. McIntyre returned to Canada at the end of the month and so did the Prime Minister, to whom Stephen immediately wrote. He had seen "the important document," he said, and he hoped there would be no difficulty in coming to terms on all points.

He and his colleagues had taken on a job that no one else in the United States, Britain, Europe, or Canada had been persuaded to tackle. It was a huge responsibility, and already in Montreal financial circles there were murmurings that this time the reckless Stephen had bitten off more than he could chew.

". . . my *friends* and my *enemies* agree," he wrote, "in affecting to think [that it] will be the ruin of us all."

And it almost was.

2 · *Success!*

ALL DURING LATE SUMMER AND EARLY fall the newspapers of Canada were alive with rumor and speculation. During August, the *Globe*, with glee, continued to report the failure of Macdonald's mission. On September 7, the Manitoba *Free Press* also reported that on the basis of "the most positive information from London," the visit was a failure. By mid-September word of actual negotiations began to leak out. The Montreal *Daily Witness*, reporting the rumors, described the prospective deal as "utterly ruinous."

The English press, covering Macdonald's visit, was generally hostile. The all-Canadian route through the bleak Lake Superior country was universally condemned as useless. The American press was equally scathing. The New York *Herald* declared that the railway would be "constructed through a wilderness, with long stretches of absolute barrenness and in a climate of such severity that the road would be closed for four months of the year. . . . For fifty years to come it would be a sheer waste of capital to build the Canadian Pacific Railway."

Yet in spite of the hostility there was tremendous excitement when it was learned that Macdonald would be arriving at Hochelaga Station, Montreal, on the afternoon of September 27. By late afternoon people of all classes were streaming toward the station. Almost every prominent Montrealer was present, no matter what his politics. A reception committee of some fifty leading Tories was waiting on the platform; packed behind it, pushing, craning, and buzzing with anticipation, was an immense throng. Suddenly from a distance came the sharp reports of fog signals being fired as a salute along the right of way and then the train itself appeared, dead on time.

Macdonald's special car was shunted to a siding and a few moments later the Prime Minister appeared, his face wreathed in smiles. Almost everybody who knew him remarked on how healthy he appeared—"ten years younger" was the common remark. The English trip had done him good. More important, success was written on his features.

Every neck strained forward as the Prime Minister prepared to speak. It was a brief, somewhat vague statement but it was what everyone wanted to hear. The government, Macdonald indicated, had secured financing for the great railway. He could not spell out the details, for these must first be presented to the Governor General.

As was often the case, he appeared to say more than he really did, and much of what he did say was deceptive. From his short speech in Montreal and the interviews with friendly reporters that accompanied it, no one could have divined that the railway was to be built by a predominantly Canadian group. Macdonald made a good deal of the German element in the Syndicate, which was, in point of fact, very small. But it was considered politically important to get token money from Germany, which would, as Macdonald told the crowd at the station, divert the tide of migration to Canada. He mentioned no financial houses or individual capitalists, but in an interview talked about "a Syndicate composed of eminent capitalists from Frankfurt, Paris, London, New York and Canada thus forming a combination of interests in order to further emigration from all those countries." Since McIntyre had returned home on the same ship, his connection with the new syndicate was generally accepted. The United States element was played down to a point where the Conservative Winnipeg *Times* even denied its existence. But the Prime Minister was able to reassure the cheering crowd on several points: the new syndicate would finish the line in ten years, it would not build the easy portions first or save the hard ones for the last, and, finally, the road would not cost as much as Sir Hugh Allan had offered to build it for in 1872. Moreover, it would not cost the older provinces of Canada one cent: the sale of western land would pay for it all.

Before he finished, Macdonald could not resist a political gibe at his opponents. The time would come, Macdonald said, when Canada's teeming millions would remember that it was the Conservative Party that had given the country its great railway.

"I shall not be present," said the Prime Minister, "I am an old man, but I shall perchance look down from the realms above upon a multitude of younger men—a prosperous, populous and thriving generation—a nation of Canadians who will see the completion of the road."

This sobering reminder of the Prime Minister's mortality put a damper on the jollity. It was not easy to contemplate a Canada without Macdonald. Loved or hated, despised or revered, he had become a kind of permanent fixture with his silver-knobbed cane, his fur-collared coat, and his familiar Red River sash.

Almost as soon as the ministerial train puffed out of the station toward the capital, the great debate over the Syndicate, as it was now called, began. By October, the composition of the new group had leaked out even though the actual contract was not signed and the specific details had still to be worked out. The members were George Stephen and Duncan McIntyre of Montreal; John S. Kennedy of New York; James J. Hill and Richard B. Angus of St. Paul; Sir John Rose's old firm of Morton, Rose and Company, London; and the German-French financial syndicate of Kohn, Reinach and Company. Norman Kittson, who had an interest, was not named at the time: too many men with St. Paul addresses would have caused a storm in the Opposition press. There was, as well, another name far more conspicuous by its absence —that of Donald A. Smith. Smith, of course, was to be a major share-holder in the CPR; but since his name was an obscenity to Macdonald and the entire Conservative Party there was no way in which he could be publicly connected with the Syndicate.

It had been a bad year all round for Smith, politically; indeed, it marked his withdrawal from the political scene. Following his successful re-election to the constituency of Selkirk in 1878, a petition was filed in court charging that his seat had been secured through bribery and corruption. Behind this move was seen the fine hand of the Prime

Minister himself, for Macdonald was still smarting from the parliamentary skirmish of the previous spring. Smith ran in a by-election in
September, 1880, spending, as he later admitted, thirty thousand dollars. His connection with the St. Paul and Manitoba railway told against
him and he was defeated.

"Donald A., the ——— voters have taken your money and voted
against you," the secretary of his campaign committee is said to have
complained.

"You have properly expressed the situation," Smith replied quietly.

The result was scarcely known when Smith suffered a second blow
to his ego: the knowledge, imparted to him by Stephen, that he could
not be publicly associated with the greatest of all national enterprises.
The Syndicate would take his money but it did not want to be saddled
with his name. Nonetheless, his presence as a silent partner was assumed by both press and public and a great to-do resulted.

The usually imperturbable Smith briefly dropped his mask and
gave Stephen a rare private glimpse of his very human ambitions.
Stephen wrote to Macdonald that "he is excited almost to a craze and
so troublesome that I do not care if he does withdraw though his money
and co-operation would be useful, so would his knowledge and influence
in the North West." Smith did not want to withdraw his money but he
did want recognition, and so the fuss continued.

Stephen was equally exasperated with the French-German element
in the Syndicate, which Macdonald had insisted upon for entirely political reasons. The Europeans were in the Syndicate for two reasons only:
they expected to make a quick profit, and they hoped to get more
business from the Canadian government. Even at that at the last moment
the French threatened to back out unless they could get assurance either
of a speedy profit or of Stephen's pledge to buy up their shares if the
operation proved unprofitable.

In the end, Stephen told the nervous French that he would build
the railroad himself, with or without their help, and "this confidence
. . . did them good." After the contract was signed, Stephen himself
went to Paris to stiffen the Frenchmen's resolve.

It was Stephen's first venture into the periphery of politics, and the
inability to deal directly, swiftly, and conclusively with matters he considered to be purely business had already begun to torment him. The
wretched contract seemed to be taking weeks to complete, and after
it was signed Parliament would have to consider it before any company
could be formed and the actual work of building the railway could be
begun. He began to fire off letters to Macdonald urging speed. There
must be parliamentary sanction "at the earliest possible day." Stephen

was almost breathless with impatience, but nothing moved as swiftly as he hoped. He had expected to embark for London at the end of October to meet Tupper. He had to postpone his sailing date.

Among other things, the status of the Pembina Branch had to be ironed out. Stephen wanted a monopoly. If the CPR's main line was tapped at Winnipeg by rival lines running to the boundary, "no sane man would give one dollar for the whole line east of Winnipeg." Like everyone else, Stephen was reluctant to build a foot of railroad north of Lake Superior. When Macdonald insisted, he agreed—but on one condition: the CPR must have the only line running from the Red River to the United States border. On this he was adamant, and in mid-October he made it clear that he was prepared to cancel the entire contract if there was any change in this arrangement. The Pembina Branch would have to subsidize the lonely line that ran through the Pre-Cambrian desert land. Macdonald was reluctant: he saw the political disadvantages of granting a western rail monopoly to an eastern company. And yet he was caught between two unyielding points of view. He must have an all-Canadian railway; to get it he would have to concede to the importunate Stephen, who again and again in his letters was hammering home the point. Stephen feared "strangulation in the hands of our Chicago rivals hanging over our heads." The danger "is *real* and *imminent*." If any other railway except the CPR made connection with Winnipeg, the money spent east of that city "might as well have been thrown into the Lake."

Stephen had never talked so toughly, and only Macdonald knew, perhaps, how hard a bargain he was driving. For this was the basis of the "Monopoly Clause" in the CPR contract, which would turn the West against the railway and against the East and lay the basis for almost a decade of bitterness before it was voluntarily revoked. The impotence of the Manitobans in the matter of building their own railway lines became, in that province, a *cause célèbre* which was to lead to a long-term disaffection toward Ottawa and toward the railway itself. Macdonald could see that clause returning to haunt him and the nation. But there was nothing he could do.

3 · The Contract

THE CONTRACT WAS FINALLY SIGNED ON October 21, and the battle lines were drawn for the greatest parliamentary struggle since the Pacific Scandal. The comments in the Opposition press, before and after the contract was laid before the House in December, give some evidence of the virulence of the attack. The Ottawa *Free Press* referred to the whole thing as "a stupendous outrage." The Montreal *Daily Witness* cried that "one stands aghast before this Pacific Railway contract, so monstrous are its provisions and so monstrous its omissions." The Manitoba *Free Press* called it "a ruinous contract," and the *Globe*, as may be imagined, was apoplectic.

The contract was the most important Canadian document since the British North America Act of 1867 and one of the most important of all time, for it was the instrument by which the nation broke out of the prison of the St. Lawrence lowlands. It represented a continuation of the traditional partnership between the private and the public sectors, which always had been and would continue to be a fact of Canadian life whenever transportation and communication were involved. The geography of the nation dictated that the government be in the transportation business—either fully, as in the case of the canals and the Intercolonial, or in a kind of working partnership with private industry, as in the case of the Grand Trunk and the Canadian Pacific Railway. In these matters the Canadian government was to be involved far more deeply than its counterpart south of the border, and this mutual participation was to broaden and deepen as the nation developed. The express and telegraph systems, the future transcontinental railways, the airlines and the pipelines, the broadcasting networks and communications satellites— all the devices by which the nation is stitched together are examples of this loose association between the political and business worlds. Like the original CPR, they are not the products of any social or political philosophy but simply pragmatic solutions to Canadian problems.

Apart from the all-important subsidies of twenty-five million dollars and twenty-five million acres of land, the chief provisions of the CPR contract were these:

> The government would turn over to the company all the lines built with public money—the Onderdonk section in British Columbia, the Pembina Branch, and the Thunder Bay–Red River line— upon completion.
> The government would waive duty on the import of all railway materials, from steel rails to telegraph cable.
> The free land would be taken in alternate sections of 640 acres each from a strip of land forty-eight miles wide running along the right of way between Winnipeg and Jasper House in the Rockies, but the company could reject any land "not fairly fit for settlement." The company could issue up to twenty-five million dollars' worth of land-grant bonds, secured against this acreage. It must deposit

one-fifth of the bonds with the government as security, but it could if it wished sell the rest of the bonds, as the land was earned by construction, in the proportion of one dollar per acre.

The land would be free from taxation for a twenty-year period or until sold. Stations, grounds, workshops, buildings, yards, etc., would be free from taxation forever and the land for these would also be provided free.

For twenty years no other line could be constructed south of the CPR to run within fifteen miles of the United States border.

The company, in return, promised to complete the road within ten years and forever after to operate it "efficiently." That adverb was significant since it relieved the CPR of future responsibilities for unprofitable aspects of its operations—passenger service, for example.

The contract was drawn up by J. J. C. Abbott, Sir Hugh Allan's former solicitor and now solicitor to the new syndicate and eventually to the new company. It was a document free of loopholes, "one which has since borne the test of judicial scrutiny," in the words of a later CPR president.

The Ottawa *Free Press* figured out that, in one way or another, the Syndicate was being handed a gift amounting to a cash equivalent of $261,500,000. Stephen's private estimate was considerably lower, but he neglected to count such items as freedom from taxation, duty-free imports, and free land for company property. He figured the value of the 710 miles of completed government line at thirty-two millions and the cost of the work to be completed by the company at forty-five millions. The Syndicate had thirty millions in hand, including the cash subsidy, and could raise fifteen millions from its own resources. But this was a wildly optimistic piece of reckoning, as events were to prove.

The press attacked on several fronts. Even such loyal western papers as the Winnipeg *Times* found it hard to stomach the monopoly clause, especially in the light of the experience with the Kittson Line's exorbitant rates. The eastern Opposition press hit hard at the monopoly clause and also the proposition regarding duty-free construction materials; after all, Macdonald's victory had been secured by the promise of increased protection. But more than anything else, the papers harped upon the American influence in "the St. Paul Syndicate," as its opponents called it. The *Globe* cried that "all the outlets from the Canadian North West . . . will be handed over to the grasp of the St. Paul and Manitoba Railway." The Ottawa *Free Press* reported that not only the St. Paul interests "but also the railway kings of Chicago and New York"

were behind the scenes. Attacks were launched on the American influence in the shape of Jim Hill and Norman Kittson. Even Angus, a
Montreal Scot, was labeled an American, since his address was given
as St. Paul.

The editorials hit home to Macdonald. Two years before, he had
publicly called Smith the greatest liar in the world. Now he had handed
the former fur trader's closest friends—and Smith, too, by all accounts
—an enormous slice of Canada. Two years before, he had gone to the
country with a policy of protecting local manufacturers. Now he had
given the Syndicate a unique opportunity to buy on the open market.
Almost ten years before, he had boasted that he had resisted with every
atom of his being the attempts by Americans to buy into the Allan
railway syndicate. Now he appeared to be welcoming even more Americans with open arms.

These misgivings only reflected the doubts and, in some cases, the
shock of Macdonald's own followers. Some said the contract would be
the ruin of the country; the obligations were so great the credit of Canada
would be destroyed, making it impossible to borrow for other purposes.
Others saw in the contract the ruin of the party; an alarmed nation would
turn against the Tories. There were other murmurings. It was an
American syndicate whose members were either Yankees or annexa-
tionists. It was a Montreal syndicate without a single name from
Toronto or Ontario. The Manitoba Members were angry about the
monopoly clause. The Victoria Members were disturbed because there
was no mention of the island railway. As the session opened, the *Free
Press* predicted that "Sir John Macdonald cannot carry the Pacific
Railway Bill."

Already some papers, remembering '73 and seeing another political
crisis in the making, were coining slogans like "the Pacific Swindle"
and "the Pacific Disgrace."

It was an indication that the great Canadian debate, which had
been going on since 1871, was about to reach its immediate climax.
Was the country prepared to stand behind this first great national undertaking? How much did the nation care whether it was united by these
costly bands of steel? Was the price too high? Was the bargain a
fair one? Could the country afford it anyway? Was it just another piece
of railway jobbery (as the Liberals suspected) or a great nation-
building device (as the Tories proclaimed)? Could the opponents of
the great railway prolong the debate long enough to rally public
opinion, as they had in 1873, and force the Government to climb down?
Would Macdonald's own supporters stand behind him or would they
again fall away like dying leaves? The battle lines were drawn. As the

opening session approached, Macdonald, though ill once more, was reasonably confident of victory. But, unlike the impetuous and optimistic Stephen, he knew the fight would be long and consuming.

4 · *The Great Debate begins*

OTTAWA, THURSDAY, DECEMBER 9, 1880. *The weather is bitter cold: two below zero at 8 A.M., with the skies heavy, dreary, and gray. Portland and phaeton sleighs are skimming along the hard-packed roads, their occupants swathed in heavy robes of bear, wolf, and buffalo. The streets are crowded despite the cold. The town is alive with visitors, muffled in furs, steam pouring from frosted nostrils. Newspapermen and Senators are flooding into town. Backbenchers are handshaking their way through the hotels. The Russell House is preparing to accommodate one hundred and fifty dinner guests at a single sitting, all crowded together at long tables under great chandeliers and all discussing the topic of the day: the contract with the Syndicate.*

Ottawa has grown since Lord Dufferin first saw it in 1872. Then it was "a very desolate place, consisting of a jumble of brand new houses and shops . . . and a wilderness of wooden shanties spread along either side of long, broad strips of mud." Now the Russell House is adding a new wing to keep up with its enterprising opponents, the Windsor and the Union House. The former has installed grates in many of the rooms and the entire structure is lighted by gas; only the early calling of the session has prevented the building from being equipped with steam pipes. The Union House is now five stories high and it has an elevator which works by hydraulic power, as well as hot and cold running water throughout. Patent "anunciators" connect every room with the main office, making the Union House so grand that it will henceforth be known as the Grand Union. "It is safe to say," declares the Free Press, *"that Ottawa can now give as good hotel accommodation as any place on the continent."*

For lesser M.P.s there are rooms advertised with open grates on Albert Street opposite the Opera House, where Nicholas Flood Davin is about to lecture in aid of the St. Patrick's Orphan Asylum under the distinguished patronage of John A. Macdonald. Davin is one of tens of thousands whose lives and careers will be totally changed by the construction of the railway. Far out on the darkling plains lies a pile of bleached buffalo bones, the site of a future city named Regina whose voice he is to become.

It is the Christmas season. Yuletide fancies are on sale: papier-mâché brackets, glove boxes, card plates, and solitaire boards. On Sparks Street, Stitt and Company announce "novelties for the opening" —kid gloves in pale opera shades and lace jersey collars. "The Speech from the Throne is speechless about our beautiful Countess Coal Stoves," trumpets one enterprising emporium.

The newspapers, as usual, are crammed with odd and revealing trivia: the Governor General's spouse, Princess Louise, whose boredom with the capital is a matter of public speculation, has whiled away the hours writing something called "The Doctor's Galop." Police are arresting all drivers who have no bells on their sleighs. "Reprehensible" people are throwing refuse into the streets and getting an editorial slapping for it. A local youth has just accomplished the astonishing feat of drinking thirteen glasses of whiskey in as many minutes.

But the big story is the opening of Parliament and the coming debate, which all now realize is the most important in the history of the young Dominion.

Macdonald had called the session two months in advance in order to dispose of the contract before the construction season began. That may have been why the opening seemed a little short of the usual pomp. The Marquis of Lorne, a short, handsome man of thirty-five with a cow-lick and a wisp of a mustache, arrived slightly early to the usual salute of guns, but Macdonald was not there to greet him; on doctor's orders he remained in the Commons, husbanding his strength for the ordeal to come.

In the Speech from the Throne, His Excellency explained the "extra session," as some were calling it: "No action can be taken by the contractors to prosecute the work, and no permanent arrangement for the organization of a systematic emigration from Europe to the North West Territories, can be satisfactorily made until the policy in Parliament with respect to the Railway has been decided."

As he spoke, a lady in the gallery leaned forward and a red bow dropped from her hair. A young man, described as a "beau," rushed forward and pressed it close to his heart.

The pageantry was ended; it was time for the politics to begin. Macdonald was ill and so was Mackenzie, the latter an unhappy ghost in the bulky shadow of Edward Blake, who had, in effect, overthrown him as Liberal leader. Blake was full of fight; he was outraged by the contract, which he considered a national scandal, and he meant to oust the Government on the strength of it, as he had seven years before. Across from him sat the bulldog figure of Tupper, eager for the contest.

Blake's strategy was to be delay. He was totally convinced that he held in his hands a political issue as explosive as the Pacific Scandal. What he lacked in parliamentary power he felt he could make up in rising public wrath over such a massive giveaway to private capitalists. The ghost of the Scandal, which had frozen attitudes for all of that decade, still hovered over the House. The Opposition press would hit as hard as it could, opening the old sores of 1873, whipping up anti-American sentiment and linking it to the present syndicate, hinting at bribery, corruption, and shameless political handouts. The Opposition tactic was to talk forever, to speak at every stage of the debate, to propose amendments at all points, to divide the House at every opportunity and to portray themselves as the saviors of the country. They would paper the nation with tracts, engulf it with oratory, arouse it with mass meetings, and expose Macdonald's attempt to ride roughshod over Parliament with his steam-roller majority. Blake believed that history would repeat itself, that he could force an election and carry the issue of the contract to the country. If that happened, he had no doubt that he would win.

The majority belonged to Macdonald; could he keep it in line? The job of maintaining party discipline would not be easy. Stephen, who was already convinced that what was good for the CPR was good for the country, naïvely supposed that the business would be disposed of by Christmas. Macdonald knew better. "Surely," Stephen wrote, "the Opposition will not be foolish enough to take a line to damage us in the country, too." But the Liberals' whole strategy was to save the country from Stephen.

The debate, which began in early December and ran until the end of January, was the longest ever held until that time and one of the longest in all the history of the Canadian Parliament. During that period, more than one million words were uttered in the House of Commons on the subject of the Canadian Pacific Railway contract—more words by far than in both the Old and the New Testaments. Though the proceedings were not immune from the kind of bitter, personal invective that marked the polemics of the period, there was a very real sense of the importance of the occasion. Tupper, when he put the resolution to the House, called it "the most important question that has ever engaged the attention of this Parliament," and speaker after speaker on both sides echoed these words when it came his time to stand up and be counted. They realized, all of them, that once the contract was committed, the small, cramped Canada they knew could never again be the same. Some felt the nation would be beggared and ruined, others that it would blossom forth as a new entity. All understood that a turning point had been reached.

Meanwhile, the misgivings among Macdonald's followers had to be met head-on. This became Tupper's task. The party caucused in the Railway Committee room on Saturday, December 11, in a session that lasted all day. According to George Ross, "the caucus was so shocked and overwhelmed at the enormous concessions made by the Government that not a single member of the party expressed approval." Tupper let them talk, and they talked all day. Then, in a forceful speech, he brought them round. His most telling argument was not nationalistic but political: the construction of the railway would give the party such éclat throughout the nation that they would be rendered invincible in the next election. After this coldly pragmatic assessment, they gave him a unanimous vote of confidence.

In Parliament there were two days of minor infighting around the Speech from the Throne before Tupper put the resolutions regarding the subsidy and the land grant before the House.

He rose that Tuesday, December 14, heavy-jowled and solemn-eyed, and launched into an exhausting speech, one of the best of his career. On and on he went, hour after hour, pausing for the dinner period and then taking up the cause again until he had spoken for almost six hours. He wound up passionately: "If I have no other bequest to make to my children after me, the proudest legacy I would desire to leave was the record that I was able to take an active part in the promotion of this great measure by which, I believe, Canada will receive an impetus that will make it a great and powerful country at no distant date."

The following day was Blake's. His speech was almost as long as Tupper's—indeed, in that great debate any speech of less than two hours' duration would be called short. It seemed much longer. Though the galleries had been full and the House, too, at the outset, there was a dwindling as Blake droned on and on. Macdonald was not present;

his illness kept him out of the House for most of the week. Mackenzie, whose own ailments would soon force him to his bed, seemed half asleep. It was an elaborate speech, designed to show that the contract would "prove disastrous to the future of this country"—but it was a little too elaborate.

In his speech Blake had hinted darkly at corruption. When Richard Cartwright rose, he brought the hint out into the open in the most shameless fashion, twisting Tupper's closing remarks in such a way as to cause a verbal Donnybrook. Of Tupper he said: "If I understand him aright, the fact of his being a permanent party in conducting this negotiation would enable him to leave a substantial legacy to his children."

Tupper, red-faced, jowls quivering, leaped to his feet; he had, he cried, insinuated nothing of the kind. Cartwright retracted his remark: if it was only a legacy of fame and not a substantial legacy, he was sorry for his mistake and also for the children.

Such remarks did not advance the Liberal cause. The Montreal *Daily Witness*, a Liberal paper, found it "objectionable in tone as well as in subject matter." The Commons settled down after that and the speeches were more moderate.

By December 21, the Opposition was itching for a Christmas recess. It needed as much time as possible to take the case to the people through public meetings and to appeal to Macdonald's supporters through massive petitions from constituents opposed to the deal with the Syndicate. But Macdonald did not intend to give it any more time than necessary. The House did not adjourn until December 23.

For most of the Members it would be a busy Yule season. Macdonald had called them back for January 5, the first Wednesday after the New Year. That left Blake with less than two weeks in which to rouse the nation.

5 · The "avenging fury"

As the session closed, the Conservatives caucused again. Macdonald's following, rallied a fortnight before by Tupper's eloquence, had grown alarmingly shaky. A new attempt was made to persuade the Prime Minister to modify the contract terms. Resolutions were read from the Manitoba Tories and the Manitoba legislature urging that the monopoly clause be changed. Macdonald knew how impossible that was. Several other prominent members rose to press for the abandonment of the promised tax exemption on railway materials. Others pooh-poohed the idea of building the railway through the rock of Superior. The Quebec contingent offered to vote for the contract, but only if the Dominion government promised to purchase the province-owned white elephant—the Quebec, Montreal, Ottawa and Occidental Railway along the north shore of the St. Lawrence, presumably at an inflated figure. Nonetheless, the party leadership stood firm, and Tupper, in a three-hour speech to the dissenters, held them, for the moment, in line.

Meanwhile, the Opposition was in full cry across the country. Blake's five-hour speech in the House was printed as a pamphlet and the Liberals were smothering the nation with it. The Conservatives replied with a similar blizzard of tracts reprinting Tupper's speech. Christmastide or not, every Liberal member was under orders to call a series of public meetings, to attack the Syndicate and the contract, and to force through a series of resolutions to be forwarded to Ottawa. Coincident with this, petitions were to be circulated on the same theme so that hundreds of thousands of signatures would fall like a storm upon the capital by the time Parliament sat again.

The Conservatives' strategy was to initiate no meetings of their own but to have a man of stature at every Liberal gathering to challenge the speaker. The meetings were lengthy, well attended, and often full of surprises. In East York, one meeting was convened at two in the afternoon and continued until nine. The Liberal chairman tried to break it up for supper but the farmers insisted on hearing both sides of the question and agreed to forgo their evening meal and continue the discussion. The Liberal orators retired anyway, whereupon the farmers voted another man into the chair, a move that brought the Liberals scurrying back, their suppers untasted.

The speaker most in demand was Edward Blake. Tupper offered to attend Blake's meetings if Blake would grant him half the time for speaking, an offer which the wordy Liberal leader rejected because he would require an entire evening for his own statement of the case. Blake's meetings opened at 8 P.M. and were rarely finished until long after midnight.

Tupper determined on a change of tactics. He detailed a man to attend every Blake meeting to announce that he, Tupper, would reply to Blake, point by point, the following night. The nation was treated to the dramatic spectacle of "the Honourable Member for Duluth," as one Tory Member called Blake, "flying from city to city, pursued by the Honourable Minister of Railways as though he were an avenging fury."

It made for exciting holiday fare in an era devoid of electronic entertainment, and both Blake's and Tupper's meetings were jammed.

It was slowly becoming apparent that the great wave of public opprobrium which Blake had so confidently expected was largely non-existent. Though there were misgivings about certain clauses in the contract, the people manifestly wanted the railway question settled. Canadians had been hearing about the railway now for almost a decade. In 1871 it had been a new and frightening idea. Ten years later they had come to accept it as a probability.

Nor were they put off by the cries of scandal. The shrill press had made them cynical of such red herrings. If there was scandal, the people wanted proof and there was no proof. The Syndicate might be controversial, but anyone could see that it was possessed of the kind of boldness that, after a decade of vacillation, could only be refreshing. In vain the *Globe* called for the people to rise up and smother Ottawa with their signatures; the *Globe* had cried wolf too often. A total of 266 petitions arrived at Ottawa, of which 256 came from Ontario. They contained 29,913 signatures, scarcely the avalanche that Blake and his followers had envisioned. Moreover, a suspicious number seemed to be in the same handwriting, and at least one signature, in Sir Richard Cartwright's riding, belonged to a corpse. "Generally speaking," the *Bystander* reported, "the attempts of the Opposition leaders to fire the heart of the people were not very successful."

But Blake and Cartwright had no intention of giving up. They had almost a month left to fight and one more major card to play.

6 · *Macdonald versus Blake again*

EARLY IN JANUARY, AS THE SESSION BE-gan, there was a kind of insistent buzzing in Liberal circles in Ottawa and Toronto that something big was being planned: the Syndicate, the contract, and the Government were about to be challenged in a dramatic and decisive fashion. On Friday, January 7, Macdonald, over Opposition protests, ruled that the contract debate would have precedence over everything except routine proceedings: "I believe that the settlement of the North West will be greatly retarded by delay." But the delays continued. That day the House sat until after midnight, but such was the duration of the speeches that only five members were accommodated. On Monday the House sat until three-thirty the following morning, yet there were only four speeches that day. George Ross's took four and three-quarters hours. Years later he admitted in his memoirs that he had spoken at "unpardonable length."

Macdonald had a reasonably clear idea of what his adversaries were planning, but he was more concerned with the troubles he faced from his own supporters. Two days before, he had received a letter from a faithful Tory, John Haggart, regretting that he could not vote for the Government on the Pacific Railway resolution.

From Halifax came word that some of Macdonald's leading supporters there were expressing grave doubts about the railway; they felt the party would be crushed under the financial load it was imposing on the country.

The Premier of Quebec, Joseph Adolphe Chapleau, had been in town for a week trying to sell the votes of his federal followers in exchange for a fancy price for the Quebec-owned railway. Macdonald had to put him off with evasions.

The Manitoba Members had an interview with both Macdonald and Tupper intimating that they could not support the bill unless it was modified; Macdonald did not yield. He was sixty-seven years old and he was ill with a complaint the doctors eventually diagnosed as "catarrh of the stomach"; the Opposition papers were slyly insinuating that he was drunk again; some of his friends feared that he had cancer. But ill or not, on this issue Macdonald intended to stand firm as a rock. There would be no modification of the contract and no compromise. When the vote came, he meant to regard it as a vote of confidence. Let his supporters betray him at their peril! If the bill failed to pass, he intended to resign.

On the night of January 11, when the resolution was finally taken out of committee, the Government whips were busy, and at 1:30 A.M. Macdonald's supporters trooped in, filling all the ministerial benches. The Opposition, so the *Mail* reported, was startled by this "sudden display of spontaneous force."

The following day the ailing Mackenzie, who had been absent from his seat for all of that session, made his first speech as the bill was read for the first time. He referred to "public reports that eminent men on both sides of politics are, at this moment, preparing offers to the Government of a much more favourable character than those that are now before it." Mackenzie did not need to get his information from public reports. He knew better than most what was afoot. This was the Opposition's final tactic—to mount a rival syndicate, which would offer the Government a much better proposition divested of all the objectionable clauses in the original contract and at a cheaper price. If the Government refused this offer, the Opposition believed, it would be shown to be in league with the "monstrous monopoly," as Cartwright called it. On the face of it the gambit was irresistible.

Even as Mackenzie spoke, the new syndicate was meeting to draw up a tender. The Liberal newspapers revealed the general terms of the new syndicate's bid: they would ask only twenty-two million acres of land and twenty-two million dollars in cash. There would be no monopoly clause. They would ask no exemptions from the tariff on railway materials. They would ask no exemptions from taxation on either land or railway property. On the matter of the construction of the line, they were equally obliging. They would be willing to postpone the building of both the Lake Superior and the mountain sections and would cheerfully release the government from the liability of building the difficult Fraser River section from Emory's Bar to Port Moody on salt water. They would also be willing to construct a line to Sault Ste Marie to connect with the U.S. railhead in return for a bonus of twelve thousand dollars a mile.

Such was the Opposition's ploy—to paint the new syndicate as totally nonpartisan and totally businesslike; to convince the country that all objectionable clauses in the contract were unnecessary. First, however, the tender had to reach the government; more delays would be needed.

Macdonald had determined to push the bill through its first reading. Accordingly, on January 13, he moved that the House waive the motions on the agenda and continue the discussion on the contract. The Liberals, of course, opposed him and the debate on this bit of procedure dragged on until 1:25 the following morning.

Later that day Tupper revealed, on a question from Blake, that the new tender had reached him about an hour before the House sat. He had not had time to consider it. The atmosphere grew more acrimonious.

Macdonald was too weak that day to attend, but he knew what he must do. The talk about the new syndicate was having its effect. It had raised the morale of the Opposition and it had caused new murmurings among his own followers in both House and Senate. He saw that he must kill the new syndicate—slay it so thoroughly that no man would ever dare to mention it again.

He rose on Monday, January 17, as soon as Tupper laid the new tender before the House. Blake, he knew, would follow the next day, with one of those earnest, perfectly constructed, and brilliantly contrived orations for which he was so well known and for which he was preparing himself with his usual meticulous labor. There was a strange feeling of repertory about it all: the same chamber and the same adversaries of 1873, the same charges of scandal, corruption, and dictatorship, the same feeling of age and infirmity (though not from drink this time), and the same subject—the railway. In a sense Macdonald was back where he had started, fighting for the contract as he had fought eight years before. But it was not quite the same; this time Macdonald had no apologies to make.

He had to be helped to his feet, but his words carried all the force of a pile driver: the road *would* be constructed. Period. "Notwithstanding all the wiles of the Opposition and the flimsy arrangement which it has concocted, the road is going to be built and proceeded with vigorously, continuously, systematically and successfully"—the adverbs fell like hammer blows—"until completion and the fate of Canada will then, as a Dominion, be sealed."

Now the time had come for him to scuttle that "flimsy arrangement": "I may say it is too thin. It won't catch the blindest. It won't catch the most unsuspicious. No one of common sense, no man who can say two and two make four, will be caught for one moment. . . . It was concocted here. It was concocted in Ottawa. It was concocted as a political engine."

Seven of the signatories to the document, Macdonald pointed out, were disappointed or defeated Liberal candidates in former elections. "No man, be he ever so simple, who is fit to be elected, can read else on these papers than that it is a political trick."

He had to pause for a moment. "I am speaking at some disadvantage," he said, "because I am not well. But I will make myself heard."

He gathered his strength and continued. The joker in the pack was the optional clause in the proposed contract which suggested that the new syndicate had no real intention of building anything but the easiest section of the railroad. The first clause, Macdonald showed, did away with the Superior section, the second provided for a rail line to Sault Ste Marie and the United States, the third provided for the government to abandon the British Columbia section, and the fourth gave up building anything west of the Rockies. The scheme, then, was nothing more than "an impudent offer to build the prairie section and to do it by means of political friends." Connecting with the Yankee railways at the Sault would be "to the utter ruin of the great policy under which the Dominion of Canada has been created, the utter ruin of our hopes of being a great nation. . . .

"They would be relieved from running any portion of the road that would not pay. Canada might whistle for these connections . . . but the people would gradually be severed from each other; and we should become a bundle of sticks, as we were before, without a binding cord, and then we should fall, helpless, powerless and aimless, into the hands of the neighbouring republic."

He fought next for the Monopoly Clause; and here all his passionate distrust of the American colossus came to the fore. The Rhine, he said, had a miserable, wretched end, "being lost in the sands of the approaches to the sea; and such would be the fate of the Canadian Pacific Railway if we allowed it to be bled by subsidiary lines, feeding foreign wealth and increasing foreign revenue by carrying off our trade until, before we arrived at the terminal points of Ontario and of Montreal, it would be so depleted that it would almost die of inanition."

What chances, Macdonald asked, would an infant country of four millions have against the whole of the United States' capitalists? He had some facts and figures dealing with United States railway wars: "The road would become shrunken, shrunken, shrunken, until it fell an easy prey to this ring. We cannot afford to run such a risk."

He was almost finished, but he wanted to nail down in the clearest possible language his vision of the railway and his vision of the nation. He wanted, he said, an arrangement "which will satisfy all the loyal, legitimate aspirations, which will give us a great and united, a rich and improving, developing Canada, instead of making us tributary to American bondage, to American tolls, to American freights, to all the little tricks and big tricks that American railways are addicted to for the purpose of destroying our road."

He had spoken for two hours and a half and he had made his point. The *Canadian Illustrated News*, which was less partisan than the daily press, reported that his criticism of the new syndicate "was so searching that he practically killed it, even in the eyes of the Opposition members themselves."

The morrow would be Blake's, but first there was a respite. Parliament adjourned at six so that the Members would attend the Governor General's reception held that evening in the Senate chamber. Sick or not, Macdonald had to be in attendance in Windsor uniform. Friends and foes mingled and murmured pleasantries, the Members dressed in swallowtail coats and sporting white kid gloves, the ladies in satin, feathers, silk, and velvet. The air was fragrant with the perfume of half a hundred bouquets and with the music of a spirited military band, which obliged with waltzes, galops, marches, and quadrilles.

The following day the Commons got down to business again. Blake had been waiting for this moment. He had not been at ease during the debate. The Government speakers, knowing his uncommon sensitivity, had baited him continually. When thus attacked he found himself unable to stare his opponents down but instead would pick up a book and pretend to read. Macdonald had challenged him the previous day, asking him to get on his feet and say that he could approve, on the basis of his past declarations, some of the essential features of the new tender.

He could not rise to that challenge, but now, on this afternoon on January 18, he was prepared to deliver another five-hour speech, crammed with facts and figures to prove why the contract was a disaster and why, indeed, the whole concept of the Canadian Pacific Railway was, as in his view it had always been, insane.

The arguments were familiar; they had not changed greatly since 1871; nevertheless, they were often telling. For instance, Blake made a hash of Macdonald's figures, which had been changing from year to year, showing the sums which the government expected to receive from the sales of raw prairie land. Indeed, on almost every point Blake was convincing. The idea of the railway *was* insane, if you thought in terms of an undivided continent; it *was* perfect madness to try to punch it through that sea of mountains and across those rocky Pre-Cambrian wastes. Immigration would not come as swiftly as the Government implied, and events were to prove Blake right on that point. The land sales would not pay for the railway. It would be easier and cheaper for everybody to go west by way of the United States, at least in the foreseeable future. Logic, then, was on Blake's side.

The key to Macdonald's argument was emotion: the only way Canada could hold onto British Columbia—and thus the land in between —was to build the railway; that was the point he continued to hammer home. British Columbia would not wait, or at least that was what the British Columbians were saying; the Premier, George Walkem himself, was in Ottawa in December making secessionist noises. Meanwhile, the reorganized Northern Pacific was creeping west again; with no parallel line on the other side of the border, that great artery would drain off all the commerce of British North America.

Blake's speech was a model of earnest, logical argument. On a previous memorable occasion he had used earnestness accompanied by pitiless fact to bring Macdonald down. In this contest between logic and passion, would logic win again? Blake, the nineteenth-century liberal, was properly suspicious of the "big interests," critical of business speculation, and committed, philosophically at least, to the one-world concept of free trade and all that it connoted. But the climate of the times was not conducive to this kind of idealism, especially in Canada, where free trade could mean economic strangulation. Macdonald, the pragmatic politician and hard-nosed Conservative, was in tune with his era—an era which saw the commercial interests working hand in glove with the politicians to develop, exploit, or consolidate the nation (one could use all those verbs) for personal profit, political power, and (sometimes incidentally) the national interest. Given the political morality of the day and the prevailing public attitude, this traditional Conservative partnership with business was probably the only way in which the nation could be constructed in a hurry. To Blake, with his literal, legal mind, Macdonald was all bombast and humbug. He himself never stooped, in the House or out of it, to the kind of witty sallies, gossipy small talk, or passionate declarations that were among the Prime Minister's trademarks. Macdonald, though a cynic, was also an optimist and a gambler. Blake, though an idealist, was a pessimist by temperament as well as by conviction. He could see the pitfalls in Macdonald's program—and they were real enough. He himself understood the value of a dollar: when younger he had vowed to make one hundred thousand dollars so that he would have personal security (and moral security as well) before entering the political lists. The wild extravagance of the railway appalled him. But Macdonald had thrown aside all personal security and bankrupted himself in order to enter and remain in politics.

Blake, the man of ideals, had a strong political philosophy and little imagination. Macdonald, the practical politician, whose only real philosophy was expediency, was endowed with a lively imagination. That, really, was where Blake foundered in the matter of the railway. He could not see the new Canada as Macdonald could see it; nor would he ever see it. Long after Blake had left the country expressing the gloomiest of forebodings, the political analysts continued to discuss the mystery of why he had never quite fulfilled his early promise. But there was really no mystery. Canada in the seventies was an imaginative dream more than a nation. Blake lacked both the imagination and the daring (he thought of it as recklessness) to lead in the development of that dream. If Macdonald's political gamble had failed, if, after all the passionate talk in the House, the railway had foundered, then Blake might have been hailed as a Cassandra and have gone on to become the leader of his country—the very epitome of a sober, sensible, frugal Canadian Prime Minister. But that was not to be.

7 · *The dawn of the new Canada*

THE LONG, EXHAUSTING DRAMA WAS drawing to its close but it was not quite over. It was not until January 25 that word spread about Ottawa that Parliament was to see the end of the longest debate in history. The galleries began to fill up with the wives of Senators and M.P.s as well as members of the general public. Macdonald meant to force a vote through even if he had to keep the House in session all night. The debate droned on while the Members, many of them gray with fatigue yet bolstered by the excitement of the evening, moved out into the corridors and smoking rooms in small buzzing clusters. From one smoking room came the faint strains of several Quebec Members singing "*La Marseillaise*," while an Irish jingle rippled from the parliamentary restaurant. Several card games were in progress throughout the building.

It was time for a division on the first amendment to the resolution, offered by the Opposition leader. The amendment was typical of Blake, being the longest ever offered in Parliament to that moment. It covered three and a half pages of *Hansard*'s small type and raised fifty-three distinct objections to the proposed legislation.

This was the moment of truth. Macdonald had told his wavering supporters in the bluntest terms that if the bill was lost the Government would resign immediately and they would be forced to go to the country with all the opprobrium of a parliamentary defeat hanging over them. The threat was enough: the first amendment was defeated by a vote of 140 to 54. The House adjourned that morning, January 26, just before six.

It was not yet over. The Opposition had twenty-three more amendments and it proposed to move them all. The galleries were thin later that day; all the old habitués were asleep. The House reconvened at three and sat until eleven that night. Five more amendments were defeated.

The long nights and the grueling verbal skirmishes were taking their toll. Macdonald, Mackenzie, Tupper, and Pope were all seriously ill. Others, the press reported, were breaking down under the strain. And still Macdonald drove them on. Illness of some sort seemed to be a chronic condition of the political leaders of the day; Macdonald's letters and those of his Cabinet colleagues are full of earnest inquiries about each other's health, reports of doctors' advice, and descriptions of their own symptoms. On Government leaders, such as Macdonald, the work load was crushing. Although the business of government was relatively uncomplicated compared to that of a later century, there were few executive short cuts. One could not pick up a telephone to transact a piece of business with dispatch. A rudimentary typewriter had been invented but it was rarely used; Macdonald considered it almost an insult to employ it in a letter of any substance. Though he did have a single secretary, he wrote almost all of his vast personal correspondence himself—thousands and thousands of letters in a lazy, angular hand. The wonder was not that he was ill; the wonder was that he was alive. The secret lay in his ability to relax totally after a harrowing parliamentary session—to push the fevered events of the day out of his mind, for an hour, a day, or, as in the case of the Pacific Scandal, forever. One of his methods was to devour cheap yellowbacks, novels of blood-curdling horror that were the popular mass reading of the day.

Now, ill and exhausted, he was nevertheless determined that, though there be a thousand amendments, the first reading of the bill should be voted on before the end of next day's sitting starting January 27.

He kept his word. The House sat from three until six, recessed briefly for dinner, and then remained in session for twelve hours without a break while amendment after amendment was offered and voted down. It had become a game, nothing more, and because it had become a game, a kind of gay lunacy settled over the House of Commons. The bitterness drained away, and as each amendment was offered, it was greeted with cheers by both sides. The speeches were mercifully short, but even these were interrupted by whistles, chirps, and desk pounding. Paper pellets were flung about and caps placed over the heads of slumbering members. As evening gave way to night and night to morning, a choir was organized, and the members began plaintively to sing "Home, Sweet Home." Josiah Burr Plumb, known as the poet laureate of the Tory Party, led one group in singing "When John A. Comes Marching Home." Dr. Pierre Fortin, from the Gaspé, led the French members in the traditional voyageur song, "*En Roulant, Ma Boule, Roulant.*" The dapper James Domville, from King's, New Brunswick, arrived at 6 A.M. after an all-night dinner party and commenced what the *Globe* referred to delicately as "most unseemly interruptions."

There were other diversions. While one French Canadian was speaking, a dummy telegram was thrust into his hand; he asked the indulgence of the House to pause and read the contents, which were unprintable. Auguste-Charles-Philippe-Robert Landry, a young gentle-man farmer from Montmagny, devised an original jape. Landry, who was known as the most mischievous Member in the House, went to a hairdresser about midnight and had his hair and mustache powdered iron gray; then he donned an old pair of green goggles, turned up his coat collar, and took his seat at the back of the ministerial benches. The deputy sergeant-at-arms, not recognizing him, tried to throw him out; Landry refused to go. When the votes were being recorded on the latest amendment, the strange figure, gesturing ludicrously, stood up to be counted amid cheers and laughter. The clerk, whose duty it was to name each Member as he voted, did not recognize Landry, looked again, puzzled, hesitated and blushed, then looked again and again until at length he pierced the disguise.

Finally, the last amendment was voted down and the main divisions on the two resolutions—the first on the land and the second on the cash subsidy—were carried. In Tupper's absence, Macdonald introduced the bill founded on these resolutions respecting the Canadian Pacific Railway. Not until it was read for the first time did he allow the weary, punch-drunk House to adjourn. By then it was eight in the morning on January 28.

The Ottawa social season, held back for some weeks by the dike of the great debate, had already burst out like a flood. "Balls, dinners, routs of all kinds, extravagant dressing and fashionable follies, in which half a dozen ministers are the moving figures, and foolish civil service clerks the puppets, are the order of the night at Ottawa," the Saint John *Globe*'s correspondent reported primly. "The social world is full of unhealthy excitement." Sir Leonard and Lady Tilley's grand ball in the Geological Museum was "the social event of the season," according to the Ottawa *Free Press*, which devoted four solid columns to a description in which every minuscule detail of décor, dress, and deportment was lovingly detailed.

It must have astonished and perplexed many a visitor from London or Washington to encounter such a glittering assembly within the make-believe palaces of what was, in many respects, still a brawling backwoods village. Every midwinter the city was a battleground for Irish lumberjacks who drank, fought with bare knuckles, roamed the streets in gangs, smashed entire saloons, toppled buggies, and sometimes even blew up houses. Only, perhaps, in Canada could such a town become the federal capital—selected for no other reason than that it neatly straddled the boundary between the two founding cultures.

To one American lady visitor, reporting back to a home-town paper, the Cleveland *Herald*, Ottawa at the time of the great debate was "a city of frightful contrasts." If the booted lumberjacks were hooligans who gave no quarter when they met in sodden combat, the parliamentarians, engaged in their own verbal Donnybrooks over the future of the nation, were little better: "To the fair-playing average American, it is shocking to hear the way the rampant party in Parliament heaps insult and blatant invective on the minority party. There seems to be not the slightest sense of honour towards the mighty fallen. I doubt if in all the annals of the American Congress such indignities were ever offered to the party out of power even by a Democrat."

Yet the Donnybrooks would have to continue, for the game was not yet played out. There were two more readings to go through before the bill could become law. The first of these was a clause-by-clause consideration of the full text, and this was bound to take time. Even the Governor General's fancy-dress ice carnival on January 31 could not lure Macdonald from his duties in the House. At 12:30 that night, while

Lord Lorne and his costumed guests were skating in the glare of two locomotive headlights beneath flag-draped arches, festoons of evergreens, and Chinese lanterns—"an overhanging panorama of grotesque and fanciful figures"—the bill passed its second reading.

The following day, February 1, just before midnight, the bill was given its final reading. The formality of Senate assent was still needed, but it was now as good as law and the Canadian Pacific Railway Company was a reality.

Finally, it was over. It had been ten years, almost to the month, since the subject of a railway to the Pacific had first been broached to the House of Commons. For all concerned it had been a desperate, frustrating, and often humiliating decade; yet it had also been exhilarating. Macdonald was ill with fatigue, stomach trouble, and nervous tension—so ill that it would take him six months to recover; but he was triumphant. The railway, which had hurled him into the abyss of despondency, had now hoisted him to the pinnacle of victory. It had consumed many of the men who were closely allied with it. Mackenzie was a political has-been. Blake was in retreat. Sir Hugh Allan had never lived down the events of the Pacific Scandal. Fleming had been driven back to England. Moberly had quit his profession. Marcus Smith hung grimly on but in a minor post. Joseph Whitehead was out of business. In every instance, the railway had changed and twisted their future, as it had Macdonald's, as it had the nation's.

Far out beyond the Red River, the prairie lay desolate under its blanket of shifting snow, still void of settlers. In just twelve months, as Macdonald knew, all that would have to change. Before the present Parliament was dissolved, cities yet unnamed would have their birth out on those wind-swept plains, passes yet uncharted would ring to the sound of ax and sledge. Within one year an army of twelve thousand men would be marshaled to invade the North West. Other armies would follow: ten thousand along the Fraser, twelve thousand attacking the mountain crevasses, fifteen thousand blackening the face of the Shield. Nothing would ever be the same again. The tight little Canada of Confederation was already obsolete; the Canada of the railway was about to be born. There was not a single man, woman, or child in the nation who would not in some way be affected, often drastically, by the tortured decision made in Ottawa that night.

The future would not be easy, and all the cries of dismay that had echoed down the corridors of the seventies would return to haunt the eighties. The granite Shield of Canada had to be cracked open to let the railway through. The mountain barrier had to be breasted and broken. There would be grief aplenty in the years to come—frustration, pain, hard decisions, and, as always, bitter opposition.

But the great adventure was launched. Tomorrow would take care of itself, as it always did. At last the dream was about to become a reality. The triumph lay just a few short years ahead.

10

1 · The end and the beginning

THE CANADIAN PACIFIC RAILWAY COM-
pany was officially launched on a crisp winter afternoon in an office
near Dominion Square in Montreal. The date, February 17, 1881,
marked a change in the fortunes and the future of the Canadian
frontier. For the next half century, this single corporation would be
the dominant force west of Ottawa. The CPR station would be the
hub around which every prairie community revolved. CPR spur lines
would mean instant prosperity; a change in their route would spell
ruin. CPR hotels would shortly become the social and business centers
of every western city along the main line. Even the lowly prune
would soon be known from Vancouver to Toronto as a "CPR straw-
berry."

Already the initials CPR had entered the national lexicon; soon
they would be as familiar to most Canadians as their own. In the
decades to follow they would come to symbolize many things to
many people—repression, monopoly, daring, exploitation, imagination, government subsidy, high finance, patriotism, paternalism, and
even life itself. There were few Canadians who were not in some
manner affected by the presence of the Canadian Pacific; indeed, no
other private company, with the single exception of the Hudson's
Bay, has had such an influence on the destinies of the nation. Nor
has any other come so close to ruin and survived.

When the great debate came to an end, Ottawa settled into a
kind of doldrums—after two months of verbal pyrotechnics in the

House everything else seemed to be anticlimactic. The glittering social season burned itself out, the session limped to its close, and the capital reverted to the status of a backwoods lumber village. When the young Governor General, Lord Lorne, arrived to prorogue Parliament on March 21, there was hardly anybody left in the House.

The rigors of the debate had wrecked the health of Macdonald, Tupper, and Pope. The Prime Minister seemed to be desperately—perhaps fatally—ill. The post-midnight sessions had sapped his strength so sorely that he could not be present when the Governor General finally approved the bill for which he had worked so hard. A few days before the session ended, he broke down completely: his pulse dropped to forty-nine and he was in an agony from bowel cramps. His physician was alarmed at his haggard appearance and his friends were aghast for he looked old before his time. He was dispatched to England in May with the unspoken fear that he was suffering from terminal cancer, and it was generally assumed that he would soon resign. As for Tupper's condition, it was described by the press in February as "critical," while John Henry Pope, in Tupper's words, was "in a sad condition which promises little for the future."

Remarkably, all three of them recovered. Tupper's doctor told him that he had been "strained but not sprung." His condition was diagnosed in August as "catarrh of the liver" and Macdonald's not as cancer but as "catarrh of the stomach," phrases that doctors used when they could not explain an illness. "Sir John still suffers from languor and a sense of prostration," the Ottawa *Free Press* reported from London that summer. Obviously, the problem was exhaustion from overwork.

In contrast to the lassitude of the capital, Winnipeg, a thousand miles to the northwest, was all bustle and turmoil. Tupper was preparing for an autumn visit to the country through which the railroad would run and so was the Governor General. The great North West boom was about to begin.

Within a fortnight of its formation, the CPR company was established in Winnipeg in temporary headquarters pending the completion of the new Bank of Montreal building. Fourteen new locomotives were on their way—all samples from various makers in the United States, sent up on trial for the company's inspection. Contracts had already been let for half a million railroad ties, six thousand telegraph poles, and fifty thousand feet of pilings. Mountains of timber were heaped in the yards waiting to be moved to the end

of track. The great triple-decker construction cars were rolling westward and workmen were pouring into town by the hundreds from
Montreal and Minneapolis. Five hundred teams of horses had already
been hired to move construction supplies. A trickle of new settlers
was seeping through town.

There were other signs of the swiftly changing character of
the old North West. The Ogilvie Milling Company had abandoned
millstones and introduced steel rollers to cope with the hard northern
wheat. The Manitoba Electric and Gas Light Company was planning
to light the entire city by gas. There was talk of a street railway to
run the whole length of Main. And the Red River cart was all but
obsolete; ingenious Winnipeg wheelwrights were working on new
wagons with iron axles and iron tires to compete with the railway.

The railway builders estimated that they had close to two thousand miles of trunk line to construct.* It could be divided into three
sections:

In the East, some six hundred and fifty miles, between Callander
on Lake Nipissing and Fort William at the head of Lake Superior,
all heavy construction across the ridges of the Pre-Cambrian Shield.

On the prairies, some nine hundred miles from Winnipeg across
the rolling grasslands to the Rocky Mountains.

In the West, some four hundred and fifty miles of heavy mountain construction.

In addition, the railway company was to be presented, as a gift,
some seven hundred miles of line built as a public work. There were
three of these publicly built lines:

First, there was the sixty-five-mile Pembina Branch from Winnipeg to the Minnesota border, already completed, which gave the CPR
a freight monopoly on goods and grain leaving Winnipeg for the
East.

Second, there was the line between Fort William and Selkirk,
near Winnipeg—433 miles long—still under construction but slated
for completion in the summer of 1882.

Third, there was the 215-mile stretch that led from Savona's
Ferry on Kamloops Lake through the Fraser Canyon to Port Moody
on Pacific tidewater. Construction had begun on this line under
the contractor, Andrew Onderdonk, in the spring of 1880, but very
little had yet been built.

Construction would proceed in four major stages:

First, the surveyors would locate the actual line, laying out the

---

* After the line was shortened, the figure was eighteen hundred miles.

curves and gradients and driving stakes along the center line as a guide to navvies who followed.

Next, the road would be graded, ready to lay steel. This was the most important operation of all. A swath sixty-six feet wide would be chopped out of bushland and forest. Tunnels would be drilled through mountain barriers and galleries notched into the sides of cliffs. Bridges of various designs would be flung across coulees and river valleys. Cuts would be blasted out of rock and the broken debris thus obtained would be "borrowed" to fill in the intervening gorges and declines so that the grade might be as level as possible. Swamps and lakes would be diked or drained. On the plains, huge blades drawn by horses would scrape the sod into a ditched embankment four feet high and nine hundred miles long so that the trains could ride high above the winter snowdrifts.

The third operation was to lay the steel. Ties would be placed at right angles across the grade at exact distances. Parallel rails would be laid on top of them and spiked to the ties. Fishplates would connect one rail to the next.

Finally, the line would be ballasted—the space between the ties filled with crushed gravel so that the line would not shift when the trains roared over it.

In addition, all the varied paraphernalia of an operating line— stations, sidings, water towers, turntables—would have to be installed before the railway could be said to be complete. Later on, branch lines to serve neighboring communities would connect with the main trunk so that the railroad would resemble an intricate tree more than twenty-five hundred miles long, coiling through all of western Canada.

Almost twenty years before, Sandford Fleming had reckoned that such a trunk line would cost about one hundred million dollars to construct. That rough estimate was probably in the minds of the men who had contracted to build the railway. In addition to its twenty-five-million-dollar subsidy, the Syndicate hoped to turn the land grant into an additional twenty-five million as quickly as it was earned by mortgaging it, at the rate of one dollar an acre, through the issuance of "land grant bonds." It could also mortgage the main line at the rate of ten thousand dollars a mile, and issue capital stock up to twenty-five million dollars. Unlike other North American railway companies, the CPR shunned the idea of bonded indebtedness and heavy stock promotions. It expected—naïvely, as it developed— to build the railway with the subsidy, the proceeds of the land sales, the operating profits, and a minimum of borrowing. The first stock issue was fifty thousand shares at a par value of a hundred dollars a share; almost all of the five millions was subscribed on February 17, 1881, by the members of the original CPR Syndicate. By March 3, an additional $1,100,000 had been subscribed; that was the extent of the original stock sale.

The hustle in Winnipeg, that spring of 1881, was in strong contrast to the vacillations of the previous year, when the railroad was being built as a public work. Though the Government had let contracts for two hundred miles beginning in 1879, only about seventy miles had actually been laid to Portage la Prairie.

This flimsy section of the colonization line, which the CPR, under the terms of the contract, purchased from the government, was virtually useless; the company determined to rebuild it entirely to better specifications and relocate most of it. A different mood had settled upon railway construction in Canada. For the first time in the long, tangled history of the Canadian Pacific, the rails were being laid under the supervision of the same men who would eventually operate the road; it would not profit them to cut corners.

On May 2, 1881, the company was ready to begin. At the end of track, the little community of Portage la Prairie clattered with activity. Strange men poured off the incoming coaches and elbowed each other in the mire of the streets, picking their way between the invading teams of snorting horses. Great heaps of construction materials transformed the railway yards into labyrinths. An army of plows and scrapers stood ready to rip into the unbroken prairie. Like soldiers poised on the start line, the navvies waited until the company's chief engineer, General Thomas Lafayette Rosser, a one-time Confederate cavalry hero, ceremonially turned the first sod. Then the horses, the men, and the machines moved forward and began to fashion the great brown serpent that would creep steadily west, day after day, toward its rendezvous with the mountains.

2 · *How John Macoun altered the map*

CANADA IS DECEPTIVELY VAST. THE MAP shows it as the second largest country in the world and probably the greatest in depth, extending through forty degrees of latitude from Ellesmere Island in the high Arctic to Pelee Island in Lake Erie, which is on the same parallel as Rome. It is almost twice as deep as the United States and considerably deeper than either China or the Soviet Union. Yet for practical purposes Canada is almost as slender as Chile. Traditionally, half of its people have lived within a hundred miles of the United States border and 90 per cent within two hundred miles. It is a country shaped like a river—or a railway —and for the best of reasons: in the eastern half of the nation, the horizontal hiving of the population is due to the presence of the St. Lawrence; in the western half to that "sublime audacity," the Canadian Pacific.

The CPR was the natural extension of the traditional route used by the explorers and fur traders on their passage to the West. If that natural extension had been continued as was originally planned through the Fertile Belt of the North Saskatchewan, Canada might today have a different dimension. But in the spring of 1881 a handful of men, gathered around a cluttered circular table in an office in St. Paul, Minnesota, altered the shape and condition of the new country west of Winnipeg.

That decision affected the lives of tens of thousands of Canadians and ensured the establishment of cities close to the border that otherwise might not have existed for another generation, if ever. It affected aspects of Canadian life as varied as the tourist trade and the wheat economy. In addition, it gave the railway company something very close to absolute control over the destinies of scores of embryonic communities along the right of way.

The decision to change the route was made by three members of the four-man executive committee of the CPR—George Stephen, James J. Hill, and Richard Angus. Only Duncan McIntyre was absent that day in St. Paul. The catalyst was John Macoun, the same botanist who had accompanied Fleming and Grant on their memorable trek from ocean to ocean a decade before.

Macoun had come to St. Paul at Hill's behest because he was familiar with so much of the southern prairie. As a result of his trip with Fleming and Grant he had become enamored of the North West. In 1879 and again in 1880, the Canadian government sent him out to explore as far as the Bow River valley in the foothills of the Rockies. These investigations confirmed a belief that had been taking form since 1872 and had by this time become a kind of religion with him. He was convinced that the southern plains were not the desert that almost everybody thought them to be.

In spreading this dogma, Macoun was flying in the face of previous scientific reports by John Palliser and Henry Youle Hind. Macoun resorted to the public platform as well as to the printed page to discredit both explorers, and his infectious enthusiasm drew large crowds. He rarely gave the same speech twice. "I was so full of the question," he recalled, "that I could talk for a week without stopping." His estimates of arable prairie soil were far in excess of anyone else's and helped confirm John A. Macdonald's conviction that profits from the sale of prairie land could underwrite the cost of the railway subsidy. Since few Canadians wanted to pay higher taxes for the sake of a railway, this was a telling point with Parliament as well as public.

Both Macdonald and his Minister of Railways, Sir Charles Tupper, were a little wary of Macoun, and not without reason. He was a man with a fixed idea, which had come close to being an obsession. The evidence suggests that he was prejudiced in advance. Long before he actually visited the southern prairie, he was making pronouncements about its riches. After he did see it, in 1879, he "fearlessly announced that the so-called arid country was one of unsurpassed fertility, and that it was literally the 'Garden of the whole country.' "

How could one explorer have seen the plains as a lush paradise while another saw them as a desert? How was it that Macoun found thick grasses and sedges where Palliser reported cracked, dry ground? The answer lies in the unpredictability of the weather in what came to be called Palliser's Triangle. Palliser saw the land under normal to dry conditions; Macoun visited it during the wettest decade in more than a century. If Palliser was too pessimistic, Macoun was too enthusiastic.

Macoun was brought to St. Paul by the Syndicate to bolster the growing conviction that a more southerly route to the Rockies was practicable. Hill and the others were already partially convinced. Early in November, 1880, Angus wrote to the American consul in Winnipeg, James Wickes Taylor, inquiring about the possibilities of a more southerly route. Taylor enthusiastically cited several Hudson's Bay Company reports to back up his belief that such a route was feasible and he quoted John Macoun, who had told the press that "the roses were in such profusion that they scented the atmosphere" and that water could be found in any part of the Palliser Triangle by sinking shallow wells. Taylor had also talked to Walter Moberly, the surveyor, who had long been a trenchant champion of a more southerly route through British Columbia; in his correspondence with Angus he made light of the problem of the three mountain ranges that barred the way to the Pacific.

Immediately after the new company was formed, in February, 1881, Jim Hill hired an American railway surveyor, Major A. B.

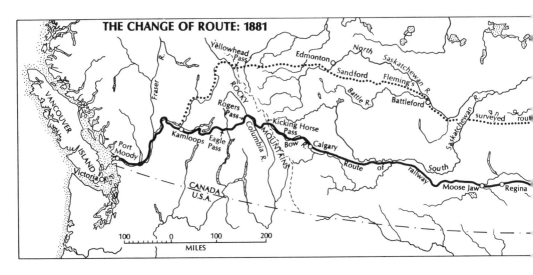

THE CHANGE OF ROUTE: 1881

Rogers, and sent him off to the Rocky Mountains, which Rogers had never seen, with orders to examine the four most southerly passes, three of which—the Kicking Horse, Vermilion, and Kootenay—had been ignored by the government's survey teams. The fourth, Howse Pass, had been rejected by Sandford Fleming after a cursory examination. Rogers, a profane, irritable, tobacco-chewing Yankee, arrived in Kamloops late in April, prepared to start work. His presence raised the hackles of more than one Canadian nationalist. "We are not inclined to credit the Yankee employees of the Syndicate with all the prodigious engineering feats that they promised to perform," the Toronto *Globe* editorialized with some asperity on May 3. After all, the Canadians had spent ten years examining no fewer than seven passes in the Rockies before settling on the Yellow Head. Who were these Americans to suggest they were wrong?

But Hill and his colleagues were already leaning strongly toward a more southerly route. The only stumbling block was the historical belief that the land it would pass through was semi-desert. All they needed was Macoun to convince them that Palliser and Hind were wrong, and it did not take the voluble naturalist long to effect their conversion. The three old friends, Stephen, Hill, and Angus, together with Rosser, the new chief engineer, sat around a table littered with maps of the Canadian North West while a torrent of words poured from the lips of their enthusiastic guest. After he was finished, a brief discussion followed. Then Hill, according to Macoun's own account, raised both his hands and slammed them down on the table.

"Gentlemen," he said, "we will cross the prairie and go by the Bow Pass [Kicking Horse], if we can get that way." With that

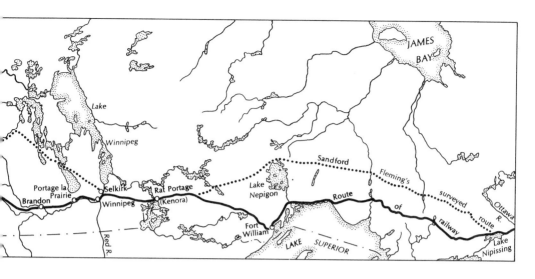

statement, ten years of work was abandoned and the immediate future of the North West altered.

Why were they all so eager to push their railroad through unknown country? Why did they give up Fleming's careful location in favor of a hazardous route across two mountain ramparts whose passes had not yet been surveyed or even explored? If the Kicking Horse was chosen it would mean that every pound of freight carried across the mountains would have to be hoisted an additional sixteen hundred feet into the clouds. Even more disturbing was the appalling barrier of the Selkirk Mountains, which lay beyond the Rockies. No pass of any description had yet been found in that great island of ancient rock; the general opinion was that none existed. Yet the company was apparently prepared to drive steel straight through the Rockies and right to the foot of the Selkirks in the hope that an undiscovered passage would miraculously appear.

The mystery of the change of route has never been convincingly unraveled. A variety of theories has been advanced, some of them conflicting. Even the CPR's own records do not provide any additional clues as to the real or overriding reasons for the decision that was made in May of 1881.

The chief reason given by Sir Charles Tupper in Parliament a year later was that it would shorten the line by seventy-nine miles and give it a greater advantage over its American rivals. Certainly this factor would have appealed to Hill, with his knowledge of transportation, and to Stephen, whose mind moved in logical lines, straight from Point A to Point B. Yet if no pass in the Selkirks could be found, then the railway would have to circumvent these mountains by way of the hairpin-shaped Columbia Valley and almost all the ad-

245

vantage over the northern route would be lost. Moreover, in changing the line of route along Lake Superior the company had actually lengthened that section of the railway.

It is unlikely that the shortening of the line was the chief reason for adopting a new route. Subsequent accounts have generally attributed the move to fear of competition from American lines, which could send feeders into the underbelly of the country if the Canadian Pacific trunk line ran too far north.

Stephen, certainly, was concerned about American encroachment in the shape of the Northern Pacific. It had reached no farther than North Dakota by 1881, but its new president, the brilliant if erratic journalist and financier, Henry Villard, had already succeeded in buying control of a local Manitoba line, the Southwestern. Villard was planning to cross the Manitoba border at three points. If he did he would siphon off much of the Canadian through trade and make the CPR line north of Lake Superior practically worthless.

On the other hand, Stephen had the controversial "Monopoly Clause" in the CPR contract to protect him. Under its provisions, no competing federally chartered Canadian line could come within fifteen miles of the border; Macdonald was prepared to disallow provincial charters for similarly competing lines. No doubt Stephen felt that the more southerly route provided him with extra insurance against the Northern Pacific and against other United States railways (not to mention rival Canadian roads that might be built south of the CPR) when, in twenty years' time, the Monopoly Clause would run out. Undoubtedly this was a consideration in adopting the new route.

Was it the chief consideration? Perhaps—the hindsight of history has made it appear so. Yet Hill himself was already dreaming dreams of a line of his own to the Pacific, springing out of the St. Paul, Minneapolis and Manitoba road. Stephen and the other major CPR stockholders all had a substantial interest in that American railway. If the frustration of United States competition was the reason for the decision of 1881, why was Hill the man who made the decision to move the route south?

Hill did give his reason for changing the route when he banged on the table and made the decision. Macoun, in his autobiography, quoted it: "I am engaged in the forwarding business and I find that there is money in it for all those who realize its value. If we build this road across the prairie, we will carry every pound of supplies that the settlers want and we will carry every pound of produce that the settlers wish to sell, so that we will have freight both ways."

This was Hill's basic railroad philosophy—a philosophy he had expounded over and over again to Stephen in the days of the St. Paul adventure: a railroad through virgin territory creates its own business. It was for this reason that Hill was able to convince Stephen that the CPR should not attempt to make a large profit out of land sales but should, instead, try to attract as many settlers as possible to provide business for the railway. The philosophy, of course, would have applied to a considerable extent to the original Fleming line. On the other hand, that line ran through country where some settlement already existed and where real-estate speculators expected to make profits out of land adjacent to the right of way. It undoubtedly occurred to the railway company that it would be easier to control an area that had never known a settler and where there were no established business interests of any kind. Why should the road increase the value of other men's property? Why should the CPR become involved in warfare between rival settlements? The unholy row between Selkirk and Winnipeg was still fresh in the minds of both Hill and Stephen. Winnipeg businessmen had forced a change in the original survey to bring the main line through their community. In striking comparison was the CPR's founding of the town of Brandon that spring of 1881. The company arbitrarily determined its location in the interests of real-estate profit, and the company totally controlled it.

That was to be the pattern of future settlement along the line. For Regina, Calgary, Revelstoke, and Vancouver, to mention the most spectacular instances, it was the company that dictated both the shape and the location of the cities of the new Canada—and woe to any speculator who tried to push the company around! The company could, and did, change the center of gravity by the simple act of shifting the location of the railway station. For it was around the nucleus of the station that the towns and villages sprang up. The contract stipulated that if government land was available it would be provided free for the company's stations, station grounds, workshops, dock grounds, buildings, yards, "and other appurtenances." With a scratch of the pen the company could, and did, decide which communities would grow and which would stagnate; the placing of divisional points made all the difference. Since some eight hundred villages, towns, and cities were eventually fostered in the three prairie provinces by the CPR, the advantages of total control were inestimable.

Thus, for better or for worse, the die was cast, though an act of Parliament was required before the change could become official.

Few single decisions by a private corporation have had such wide-spread public repercussions. As a result, and quite by accident, the most spectacular mountain scenery in North America was opened up in the early eighties; Canada gained a new image as a tourist attraction: Banff, Lake Louise, Glacier, and Yoho parks were all by-products of Jim Hill's table pounding. So was a whole series of prairie communities strung out like beads on a string between Brandon and Calgary. So were the costly locomotives that had to be harnessed to haul the trains over the Great Divide. So were the miles of snow-sheds in the Selkirks and—after many deaths from avalanches and snowslides—the costly diversions of the "spiral" and Connaught tunnels. In later years it became railroad cant that the Canadian Pacific had the scenery but the Canadian National had the grades; from the company's point of view, it remains to this day a toss-up whether the change of route was really an economically sensible decision. There are too many imponderables to render a judgment. Who can say how important the mountain scenery was to a once profitable passenger trade? Who can estimate whether the profits on townsites and the advantages of a shorter line canceled out the increased construction costs and additional carrying charges over the mountain peaks?

From the point of view of the nation, a better guess can be hazarded. It is probable that the switch to the southern route was one factor in delaying the settlement of the North West for twenty years and thus partially frustrating John A. Macdonald's dream of filling up the empty plains. The settlers tended to take up land as close as possible to the railway; and often enough they were driven off it by drought.

Significantly, it was the CPR itself that implicitly debunked Macoun's enthusiastic reports of almost unlimited arable land by refusing to accept a great deal of the acreage that had been set aside for it in the forty-eight-mile belt between the Red River and the Rockies, along the route of the railway. The land subsidy in the CPR contract was unique. In effect, it allowed the railway to pick and choose the best available acreage anywhere on the prairies. In 1882, the company's most generous estimate of "fit" land within the belt stood at six million acres; later that estimate was reduced to five million acres. Clearly, the CPR was saying that the land could *not* be settled. To keep its bargain with the railway, the government was forced to give it land elsewhere; much of this substitute acreage was found in the Fertile Belt, along the original line of route. If the railway had followed the valley of the North Saskatchewan, it is probable that much more land would have been taken up because of the attractive combination of good soil and easy access by rail and the pattern of settlement would have been changed.

The CPR rejected tens of thousands of acres in the dry country west of Moose Jaw; and, in spite of the heavy immigration to the plains in the early 1880's, very few settlers were prepared to occupy land in that portion of Palliser's Triangle. By 1885, the year the railway was finished, only twenty-three homesteads had been taken up along more than four hundred miles of railway between Moose Jaw and Calgary.

The settlers, used to eastern Canadian conditions, were not prepared to cope with the special problems of prairie agriculture, especially in dry country. The hard-baked sod required a heavier plow. The dry land demanded new methods of cultivation and cheap windmill-powered pumps. Fuel, timber, and fencing had to be imported into the vast treeless areas. There was also the necessary shift from fall to spring planting in a land where the winters were long and harsh and the growing season alarmingly brief. Some of these conditions would have existed no matter which route the railway followed. The choice of the southern route accentuated them.

The wet cycle, which had such an effect on Macoun in 1879 and 1880, continued through 1881 and 1882. Then, in 1883—the peak year for immigration—the dry cycle returned. By 1886 the land was so dry in many places that cracks a foot wide opened up in the parched soil. Immigration figures in the North West, which reached a record 133,624 in 1883, began to decline with three successive years of crop failures. It was twenty years before they again climbed above the hundred thousand mark. There was an equally spectacular drop in homestead entries: in 1884 they were halved. Thousands abandoned the embryonic farms they had so eagerly taken up. By 1896, half of all contracts entered into with the railway by the various colonization companies had been canceled; a total of 1,284,652 acres reverted to the CPR.

With the acceptance of the disk plow and more adaptable farming methods, the prairie country became, after the turn of the century, the granary of the world; Regina, which might not have existed had the northerly route been chosen, was found to be in the very heart of the richest grain-growing soil on the continent. In those portions of Palliser's Triangle where cereals would not grow, a healthy ranching economy developed. But the cycle of drought continued. The undue optimism of the seventies and early eighties was replaced in the decade from 1884 to 1894 by an extreme pessimism. So many farms were abandoned that the Canadian government began to entertain doubts about the future of the West. Once again, John Macoun was dispatched to the southern prairies to report on the seriousness of conditions and once again, just as he arrived on the scene, the rains came and Macoun was able to predict the end of the drought. The vast wave of immigration that filled up the prairies in the following years appeared to vindicate him. When he died in 1922, his friends triumphantly published his autobiography with a flattering foreword by Ernest Thompson Seton. It was not until the desperate years of the 1930's, when the rains ceased once more and the grasshoppers and the cutworms and the hot, dry winds returned, that there took place a rueful reassessment of his strange role in the shaping of the nation.

3 · The first of the CPR towns

GENERAL ROSSER'S NEWLY SURVEYED route led out of Portage la Prairie toward Grand Valley on the Assiniboine, and then through the Brandon Hills to Flat Creek (later known as Oak Lake). It was near the crossing of the Assiniboine that Brandon, the first of the CPR towns, sprang up. The method of its selection by the general provided an object lesson for the company in the value of establishing its own communities instead of building on existing ones.

Rosser was a Virginian gentleman of the old school—tall, handsome, and popular. A West Point chum of General Custer, he had fought opposite him as a guerrilla officer during the Civil War. After the war he had risen to become chief engineer of the Northern Pacific—his workmen protected by Custer's troops—laying out the route along the Yellowstone River in Montana. Later, as a railway contractor, he had helped build part of Jim Hill's St. Paul, Minneapolis and Manitoba line. He was, according to the Winnipeg *Times*, "known as one of the most pushing men on the American continent." Hill, who hired all the key CPR personnel that year, was as partial to pushers as he was to Americans.

Rosser was a man of precipitate action, as events were shortly to prove. During the Civil War he had risen from lieutenant to major general. He had refused to surrender with Lee at Appomattox, preferring instead to charge the Federal lines with two divisions of cavalry. When he was finally captured, some time later, he was trying to reorganize the shattered remnants of the army of Northern

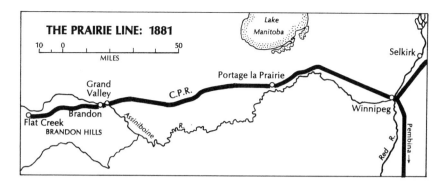

THE PRAIRIE LINE: 1881

Lake Manitoba

Selkirk

Portage la Prairie

Grand Valley

C.P.R.

Brandon

Flat Creek

BRANDON HILLS

Assiniboine R.

Winnipeg

Red R.

Pembina

MILES

10   0   50

Virginia for a final dramatic stand. His subsequent civilian record was equally dashing. He had begun as an axman and again worked his way up through the ranks from rodman to scout to chief surveyor. He was surrounded by an aura of legend—a record of hairbreadth escapes in war and peace. On one occasion, when surprised by Yankee cavalry and wounded above the knee by a bone-shattering bullet, he had ridden all night to safety with the broken limb swinging back and forth and the enemy hard on his tail. A decade later, near Bismarck, North Dakota, a party of Sioux had cut him off. One crept up behind a tree, used it as a shield, and began taking pot shots at him. Rosser coolly waited until the Indian poked his head around the trunk to take aim, shot him squarely between the eyes, heaved his corpse onto a pony, and again galloped safely away. In 1881, as chief engineer of the CPR, he brought the same dash and impulsiveness to the establishment of townsites.

A fortnight before the first sod was turned, rumors of a great new city west of Winnipeg began to fly. Survey parties started to move out of Portage la Prairie in the last week of April, locating the new route. Everyone knew that the railway would require a divisional point about one hundred and thirty miles west of Winnipeg. That fitted almost to a mile the location of the little settlement of Grand Valley, clustered on the banks of the Assiniboine at the exact spot where the railway was to cross the river. Tents and shacks began to spring up in the vicinity as land speculators poured in. The excitement increased day by day. Two men from Perth, Ontario, arrived with fifteen tons of dry goods and groceries to set up a general store. Two more began to erect a sawmill. Another opened a "hotel" of canvas spread over wooden frames. Dugald McVicar, the pioneer resident, whose wife was the local postmistress, began enlarging his home and warehouse. His brother John followed suit. The McVicar brothers were humble, illiterate men who had come west in 1879 from Quebec, to build the first sod dwelling in the region. The little town grew around the site of their original homestead, and the McVicars expected to get rich from the Grand Valley boom.

In April, General Rosser paid a visit to John McVicar and made him an offer for his property as a future townsite for the CPR's divisional point. The accounts of exactly what took place are conflicting. One of the CPR's surveyors, J. H. E. Secretan, said that Rosser, having settled on Grand Valley as the divisional point, offered McVicar fifty thousand dollars for his property. The farmer could scarcely believe that that much money existed. A discussion followed and some " 'wise guys' of neighbours and relations," were invited in. Around dawn, McVicar was persuaded by his friends to demand sixty thousand. Charles Aeneas Shaw, another of Rosser's engineers, gave a different version. He wrote that Rosser empowered *him* to buy the McVicar land for thirty thousand dollars. Shaw had dinner with McVicar but "some speculators had got hold of him, and he would not hear of anything less than eighty thousand dollars." Beecham Trotter, a Brandon pioneer, reported that Rosser offered McVicar twenty-five thousand but McVicar immediately demanded fifty thousand dollars down and a half interest in all future sales. Whereupon Rosser is said to have retorted: "I'll be damned if a town of any kind is ever built here."

Whatever the details of the legendary incident, one thing is clear: when McVicar, goaded by speculators, tried to bargain with the railway, the railway simply moved the site of its station two miles farther west. This would be the pattern in all future dealings when private individuals tried to hold up the company for speculative profits.

The new site in the Brandon Hills cost the CPR a small fraction of the Grand Valley price, and its choice marked the end of Grand Valley as a viable community and the beginning of the town of Brandon. What was not realized at the time was that Rosser and his immediate superior, Alpheus B. Stickney, the general superintendent of the western division of the CPR, were themselves speculating in real estate, using the inside knowledge that their positions provided them.

The main street was named after General Rosser, who decreed that the lots should be small, since more money could be made from the land in that way. The survey took until mid-August but the lots went on sale long before it was completed. Once the location of the new town was known, people began to appear and tents to blossom all along the high bank of the Assiniboine.

After the land agent, the first businessman on the scene, not unnaturally, was a lumber merchant: Charles Whitehead, the son of Joseph Whitehead, the railway contractor. Whitehead, whose descendants would own the Brandon *Sun*, purchased the first parcel of land sold by the CPR.

On Whitehead's heels, in late May, came a doctor, a grocer, and a hotelman. The grocery store was the one that had been erected the previous month at Grand Valley; when it became clear that the original settlement was dying, the proprietors moved it in sections by barge to the new townsite. The McVicar brothers were stubbornly trying to sell lots on the old site in the wistful hope that the CPR might locate a station on their land, but their neighbors were less sanguine. By June, two more stores and a billiard hall had been moved to Brandon.

The CPR's clear intention was to destroy Grand Valley as a community. Lots on both townsites were advertised in mid-May and went on sale at the end of the month. The Brandon lots sold swiftly at prices that ranged from $63 to $355. Grand Valley lots went badly and sold for an average price of $33. The original community was clearly doomed by the decision to move the station two miles west.

The first newcomers had great difficulty finding Brandon at all. James Canning, who had trudged across the prairie from the end of track looking for work, arrived at the corner of Tenth and Rosser and asked a man who was helping to erect a new building where the town was.

"Right here," came the reply.

Canning climbed up on a window sill of the half-completed structure and looked around him. There was only one other building in sight.

"I don't see any town," Canning said, as he climbed down.

"Well, it is only a paper town yet," his acquaintance replied.

The paper town blossomed swiftly into a tent community. The first post office was nothing more than a soapbox with a slit in it placed outside the tent of L. M. Fortier and his bride. The first restaurant was a plank laid across two barrels on the trail that was to become Pacific Avenue. The proprietor was an eccentric white-bearded cockney named Tom Spence whose entire stock consisted of a keg of cider, a bottle of lime juice, a couple of pails of water, and two drinking glasses. To attract trade, Spence had chained a live badger to a nearby post, "just far enough from the counter to be unable to bite the customers."

The first church service was held out of doors in a driving rainstorm in June by the Reverend Thomas Lawson, a Methodist. The local harnessmaker held an umbrella over the minister's head while the congregation, composed entirely of young men, sang lustily, oblivious of the downpour. Lawson was able to move his service indoors thanks to the hospitality of a Mrs. Douglas, "a motherly lady of no mean proportions," who operated one of the two tent hotels. The beds of this "pretentious hostelry" were built double-decker fashion along one side of the tent, screened by Pullman-style curtains. A lean-to at one end served as a kitchen. The rest of the tent did duty as dining room and lobby and, on Sundays, as a church. An early Brandon settler, J. A. Smart, who was a regular attendant, remembered noticing with some amusement the ample landlady accompanied by her daughter emerging silently from a corner of the tent, "dressed in her most stately attire, not omitting bonnet, coat and gloves," creeping out the back flap through the kitchen, maneuvering around to the front, entering through the front flap, and marching up before the congregation "in high reverential style" to a front seat a few feet from the curtained bunks from which they had just emerged.

In that golden summer of 1881, the pattern of the new Canada began to take hesitant shape along the line of the railway. Brandon was the beginning—the first of the scores of raw communities which would erupt from the naked prairie. Its birth pangs would be repeated over and over again as the rails moved west. There was a kind of electric feeling in the atmosphere—a sense of being in on the start of a great adventure—which those who arrived in Brandon that summer would never forget. In future years, when recollections of later events became blurred, they would still retain unclouded the memory of those first months when the sharp, spring air was pungent with the incense of fresh lumber and ringing with the clamor of construction; when lasting friendships were forged among the soiled tents on the riverbank; when every man was young and strong and in love with life; and when the distant prairie, unmarked by shovel or plow, was still a mysterious realm waiting to be claimed. Some forty years later, J. A. Smart, who had stood out in the rain during that first church service, wrote about those days "when the world, full of opportunity and hope," lay before him. "No small town in Canada or elsewhere," he wrote, "could possibly have contained a happier army of young men than did Brandon in its earliest years."

For the newcomer who planned to stay and grow with the community, the opportunities were almost unlimited. Of the first seven lawyers who arrived, four became Ministers of the Crown, and one the Leader of the Opposition in the Manitoba legislature. The first organist in Thomas Lawson's new frame church (the seats were two-by-ten planks without backs) became mayor of the city four times running. Douglas Cameron, from grading the bumps out of Sixth Street, rose to be Lieutenant-Governor of his province. And a jovial young Irish plowboy from Kirkfield, Ontario, named Pat Burns, who broke sod on J. W. Sifton's farm at six dollars an acre, went on to become the meat-packing king of the Canadian West. Sifton's own sons, Arthur and Clifford, became, respectively, Premier of Alberta and Minister of the Interior in the federal government.

By October 11, when the first official passenger train pulled into the new station, an epic boom was in full swing. The coming of the railway was already transforming the West, and the changes were spectacular enough to set the continent buzzing.

In April, J. H. E. Secretan, whose tent was the only habitation on the site, had encountered a young Englishman who wanted to be a farmer. Three months later Secretan returned to find Brandon seething with activity—hundreds of tents, billowing in the prairie wind, lined geometrically along what would some day be streets and avenues. He ran into his English acquaintance, who was bemoaning the fact that he had sold his homestead to a land shark for a piebald pony, a secondhand meerschaum pipe, a broken German-silver watch, and $7.25 in cash.

Since no transfer papers had been executed, the surveyor was able to get the tenderfoot's homestead back for him. He did not return to Brandon again until Christmas, by which time the rails had passed through "and a real live town was in full swing." Alas, the young homesteader had grown homesick and had again sold out, this time for three pairs of navy-blue socks, a secondhand concertina, six packages of cigarettes, eighteen dollars in cash, and steerage passage to Liverpool. Shortly afterwards, Secretan discovered, that little piece of land was purchased for eighty thousand dollars.

As for Grand Valley, which might have been the new metropolis, it lapsed into decay. In September, the McVicar brothers vainly offered Robert Adamson, a Winnipeg banker, a half interest in the site if he could persuade the CPR to build a station on their property. In January, the McVicars offered eight hundred acres of their land free to two lumber merchants if they could persuade the CPR to put in a station by May, 1882. But the trains went roaring through without stopping and the McVicars eventually sold out their townsite for fifteen hundred dollars. When Beecham Trotter passed through, early in 1882, "Grand Valley was a living corpse." Some years later, Charles Aeneas Shaw happened upon John McVicar plowing in the vicinity with a team of mules. The farmer ran out onto the road. "Oh,

Mr. Shaw, I was a damn fool. If I had only taken your advice, I would have been well off now!"

For future speculators in townsites, the fate of the little community on the Assiniboine was an object lesson in how not to deal with the Canadian Pacific Railway.

4 · The "paid ink-slingers"

SIR HENRY WHATLEY TYLER WAS THE kind of man who, on his visits to the United States, enjoyed riding conspicuously on the cowcatchers of locomotives. He had been, variously, a captain in the Royal Engineers, a British railway inspector, and a Member of Parliament. Since 1876 he had been president of the Grand Trunk Railway of Canada, an enterprise that was directed from England. He might also have been president of the Canadian Pacific, but he could not stomach the idea of an all-Canadian route over the barren desert of the Canadian Shield. Like most Britons and many Canadians, including perhaps half of Sir John A. Macdonald's Cabinet and several directors of the CPR, he believed it an act of incredible folly to build seven hundred miles of line across country incapable of settlement. His own road ran south of the Great Lakes on its route from Sarnia to Chicago. That, clearly, was the sensible route to take. Macdonald was one of the few public figures who believed otherwise. Even George Stephen, in the early months, was unconvinced.

A handsome and debonair man with a military bearing, Tyler was noted for the brilliance of his conversation and his effectiveness at repartee. Shareholders' meetings held no terrors for him; he apparently enjoyed being baited. His sense of humor was infectious and his wit often ironic. He could hold his own in any verbal battle. Behind the sophisticated façade there was a will of steel. With the help of his shrewd general manager, Joseph Hickson, he had beaten the Vanderbilt interests and pushed his railway into Chicago, consolidated several lines in the New England States, and made the Grand Trunk one of the great railway systems of North America. But was it a Canadian system? Its ownership and its direction were largely British. Its main purpose seemed to be to link the American Midwest with the U.S. Atlantic Coast, using the St. Lawrence lowlands of Canada as a convenient route between Chicago and Portland, Maine. Its directors clearly did not grasp the significance of the Canadian North West.

Tyler had never thought of the CPR as a competitor. Indeed, until the contract was signed in 1880, he considered the entire transcontinental railway scheme an elaborate political pipe dream. Even if it was built it would never threaten the Grand Trunk. It would start at Lake Nipissing in the wilds of Ontario and terminate at Port Moody in the wilds of British Columbia. It did not, apparently, occur to Sir Henry that a railway of that length, built at enormous cost, would have to continue on into the settled East. If the CPR had stopped at Callander it would, of course, have become a valuable feeder for the Grand Trunk. But it is clear from the CPR charter that the Syndicate intended from the very outset to establish a complete transcontinental system.

In the midsummer of 1881, Tyler woke up to the fact that the Canadian Pacific was to be a major competitor. The first CPR shareholders' meeting, held in London on May 31, had approved the amalgamation of the new company with the government-subsidized Canada Central, whose president, Duncan McIntyre, was also vice-president of the CPR. The Canada Central linked Lake Nipissing with Ottawa. On July 20, the CPR moved to extend its operations further into Grand Trunk territory. Stephen and McIntyre were elected directors of the Ontario and Quebec Railway, a company that held a charter to build from Montreal to Toronto. It shortly became apparent that the CPR intended to swallow this line. The CPR, through Stephen, also had an interest in the Credit Valley Railway, which connected Toronto with Georgian Bay. In addition it had announced a branch line to Sault Ste Marie to connect with another line on the United States side being taken over by Jim Hill. The new company was not yet six months old and already it was posing a serious threat to the older railway.

Thus was the scene set for a battle between the two roads—a battle that was to run unchecked for the whole of the construction period and for many years after. The Grand Trunk's strategy was to discredit the CPR in public while crippling it financially behind the scenes in London and New York. In his campaign of attrition, Tyler had some powerful allies. Two great financial houses, Baring Brothers and Glyn, Mills, were on his side; they had originally financed the Grand Trunk. So were a large number of newspapers on both sides of the water, including most of the financial press, many of them enjoying the largesse of Grand Trunk advertising. Joseph Hickson, Tyler's general manager in Canada, was on friendly terms with Sir John A. Macdonald—the two were pen pals; and the Grand Trunk could always be depended upon to deliver the vote of its employees to the Conservatives in federal elections. These links with the Canadian government were not decisive ones, but they might serve as a brake on the ambitious plans of George Stephen.

The Grand Trunk's English shareholders had some cause for

righteous discontent. The railway's stock had not been the profitable investment they had hoped for. For the best part of thirty years, the company had teetered on the edge of financial disaster. Now, under sounder and bolder management, its prospects seemed much brighter. Suddenly the new railway came along to dampen that future. No wonder the overseas investing public looked with jaundiced eye on the CPR: the Canadians, having asked the Englishmen to pump millions into one faltering railway, were now asking them to pour more millions into its chief competitor! The Grand Trunk propaganda to discredit the CPR in the British market found fertile ground.

All that summer and fall, the Canadian Pacific Railway and the Canadian North West were subjected to a torrent of abuse in the press of Canada, the United States, and Great Britain.

The American attitude was summed up in a brief interview in the New York *Herald* with the taciturn Jay Gould, the American railroad financier, shortly after the CPR was formed:

REPORTER: There is a great project underway up in Canada?

GOULD: The Canadian Pacific Railroad?

REPORTER: Yes; what do you think of it?

GOULD: Visionary.

REPORTER: No dividends?

GOULD: Perhaps in one hundred years. It will be a good excursion line for English tourists and Canadian statesmen when Parliament adjourns.

REPORTER: But they say there are great possibilities. How about the great agricultural resources . . .?

GOULD: One, the chief one, of the successful agricultural conditions is not there.

REPORTER: Which is?

GOULD: Population.

A large section of the British press, led by *The Times* of London, had convinced would-be immigrants that Australia was a far better prospect than the forbidding Canadian plains. The Governor General, Lord Lorne, the handsome and poetic son-in-law of the Queen, determined to remedy this impression by a personal tour of the railway's route to the Rockies. He invited four British journalists, including a man from *The Times*, to accompany him at his personal expense. Singlehandedly, the young marquis had decided to change the minds of his countrymen about the new Canada.

It was a colorful excursion. No British writer could resist the ceremony of a Blackfoot powwow, nor could he fail to be impressed by the unbroken ocean of grass or by Lorne's own enthusiastic speeches along the way. The coverage was good, and *The Times* changed its editorial line and ceased to thunder against Canada.

But the gibes from other British newspapers and journals continued. The most memorable, entitled "The Canadian Dominion Bubble," was published in *Truth* on September 1, 1881. The author was Henry Labouchère, a forthright journalist, financial critic, and Liberal M.P. whose uncle and namesake had been Colonial Secretary in 1857 when Captain John Palliser made his gloomy report on conditions in the Canadian North West.

Labouchère said flatly that the floating of a Canadian Government bond issue in England and ten million dollars' worth of CPR land-grant bonds in New York and Montreal that fall was a fraud. New York investors, he declared, would never be such fools "as to put their money into this mad project. I would as soon credit them with a willingness to subscribe hard cash in support of a scheme for the utilization of icebergs." As for the Canadians, they were "not such idiots as to part with one dollar of their own if they can borrow their neighbours'. The Canadians spend money and we provide it.

"The Canadian Pacific Railway will run, if it is ever finished, through a country frost bound for seven or eight months in the year, and will connect with the eastern part of the Dominion a province which embraces about as forbidding a country as any on the face of the earth." British Columbia was "a barren, cold, mountain country that is not worth keeping." It would never have been inhabited at all had it not been for the mining boom: "Fifty railroads would not galvanize it into prosperity." As for the CPR, it was "never likely to pay a red cent of interest on the money that may be sunk into it."

This broadside and others that followed had their effect on the British money market. They were accompanied that fall by the first of the anti-CPR pamphlets, said to have been written by the Grand Trunk's "paid ink-slingers," as Stephen called them.

There was no doubt in George Stephen's mind about who was behind the press attack. "The G.T.R. is bound to do all the harm they can," he wrote to Macdonald. In Stephen's view, those who were not passionately devoted to the cause of the railway were seen to be enemies, traitors, blackguards, and cowards. Such terms cropped up constantly in his astonishingly garrulous correspondence with Macdonald, almost all of it scrawled in Stephen's own sloping hand.

Stephen saw himself beset by other formidable forces intent on crushing the CPR. One of these was the Northern Pacific, whose dynamic new president, Henry Villard, seemed determined to thrust his rapidly expanding railway into the Canadian North West. Villard was one of those phenomenal business successes thrown up by the yeasty society of nineteenth-century America. A Bavarian immigrant, he had arrived in New York at the age of eighteen and eked out a living working as a reporter for German-American newspapers. He had shot up swiftly in both the journalistic and the financial fields. As a reporter for leading United States dailies, he had covered the Lincoln–Douglas debates, the Pike's Peak gold rush, and the Civil War. Beginning as an agent for German bondholders, he moved into railway finance and helped reorganize an Oregon railroad and steamship line. By 1881, at the age of forty-six, he owned the *Nation* and the New York *Evening Post* and controlled the Northern Pacific, whose construction he was pushing westward with a reckless enthusiasm that took little account of rising costs.

In Manitoba two private railways were being built toward the United States border. The Northern Pacific had bought control of one and was ready to buy control of the other, believing, in Stephen's words, that "they can force a connection at the boundary and so strangle the Canadian Pacific; which they are determined to do if they can."

All that fall of 1881, Stephen kept up continual pressure on the Prime Minister to disallow by federal decree any provincially chartered lines that came within fifteen miles of the border. Again and again he made the point that a "Yankee line" into Manitoba would make it impossible to operate or even to build the Lake Superior section of the CPR. With such American competition, no one could prevent the products of the North West being drawn through the United States to Chicago, whose attraction as a market for wheat was almost irresistible. Stephen used every argument in his power to persuade Macdonald to disallow the Manitoba charters: it would, he told him, mean the disgrace not only of the railway but also of the Conservative government itself, since the country would not stand for the enormous expense of the Lake Superior line if it turned out to be worthless. "It would be a miserable affair to find that the benefit of all our efforts to develop the North West had by our own acts, fallen into Yankee hands."

Many of Macdonald's followers, especially those in Manitoba, were eager to subvert the spirit of the contract which protected the railway through its Monopoly Clause. Because of the British North America Act, the clause did not prevent the provinces from chartering lines to the border in competition with the transcontinental railway. This was Stephen's fear. There is no doubt that Macdonald intended to back Stephen up, but there is also no doubt that the Monopoly Clause was already causing him grave political uneasiness. To ride roughshod over the legitimate desire of Manitoba settlers for more railways to serve their communities was to alienate politically an entire province. From the beginning he had seen the railway as a device to unite the nation—to tie the settled East to the new country beyond the Shield. Now in the very first year of its construction the railway had become a divisive force, antagonizing the very people it was supposed to link together. The Prime Minister gave vent to his view in the presence of some of Stephen's colleagues on the subject of the "cussed" Manitoba charters, and Stephen wrote to him in alarm that "they have all come back more or less full of misgivings and fears lest in some way the 15 mile Yankee barrier will not be maintained."

There was another threat on the horizon. The ubiquitous Northern Pacific was about to purchase the railway owned by the Quebec government—or so the Premier, J. A. Chapleau, kept insisting. This was the Quebec, Montreal, Ottawa and Occidental and its eastern section, familiarly termed the North Shore Line. Quebec had been trying to unload this white elephant ever since the days of Sir George Étienne Cartier, who had promised to make it part of the CPR. The previous winter, Chapleau had tried to make the purchase of the partially completed railway a condition of French-Canadian support for the CPR contract.

Macdonald had managed to evade such an out-and-out promise. But now he was again facing the same kind of political blackmail. If the aggressive Henry Villard came to the rescue of Quebec by buying up the railway, it would give him a threefold advantage in his drive to tap Canada for the Northern Pacific's profit. With one stroke he would occupy a key position between the government-owned Intercolonial on the east and the Canadian Pacific on the west. Secondly, it was clear that he meant to link the Quebec line with the Northern Pacific at Sault Ste Marie; thus the country faced the possibility of a Yankee transcontinental railway mainly on Canadian soil. But there was more: by taking the faltering railway off the hands of the Quebec government, Villard would be buying considerable political leverage in that province and, consequently, in Ottawa. Macdonald feared that he would use this new political strength to persuade the Quebec Members to vote in a bloc against federal disallowance of the Manitoba railways. If Villard's gambit succeeded, he would have a through line from Quebec City to Winnipeg by way of Sault Ste Marie and Duluth; and Macdonald's dream of an all-Canadian route would be shattered, perhaps forever.

The Prime Minister confessed to Stephen that he was "very uneasy." If the rumors were true, "it means danger ahead." A Quebec election was coming up. The president of one of the Manitoba lines was tactlessly predicting that the Northern Pacific would be a factor in that election. If Stephen was to act at all, Macdonald urged, then he must act at once. The CPR president decided he must make an offer for the section running west to Ottawa from Montreal in order to head off the American attempt to control Canada's transcontinental transportation system.

Stephen, who had once thought the idea of building the line north of Lake Superior "great folly," was becoming an enthusiastic champion of an all-Canadian route. In August, 1881, he confessed to the Prime Minister that "all misgivings I had last year . . . have disappeared with a better knowledge of the position of the whole country. I am now satisfied that the C.P.R. without the control of a line to the *Atlantic* seaboard would be a *mistake*. If for instance, it terminated like the Northern Pacific, at Lake Superior it never could become the property it is certain to be having its own rails running from sea to sea. I am sure you will be glad to hear this from me because I do not think but for your *own* tenacity on that point, would the line North of the Lake *ever* have been built, events have shown you were right and all the rest wrong."

Some of this was flattery and some of it was close to being black-mail. Stephen had been aware, from the outset, of Macdonald's obsession with an all-Canadian railway. The Prime Minister was made to under-stand that he could not have that without the Monopoly Clause. If the CPR was to pay through the nose for an unprofitable line through an uninhabitable wilderness, it must receive compensation. Stephen might argue that this was merely an extension of the Conservative Party's National Policy of protection, but that protection was paying big dividends for the proprietors of the CPR and of the St. Paul, Min-neapolis and Manitoba Railway, whose directorates interlocked. The contract gave them a monopoly of all traffic out of Winnipeg into the United States and they made the most of it.

At the time he wrote that letter, Stephen had an additional reason for his enthusiasm. He had just returned from Winnipeg, where he discovered that the white elephant might not be as unprofitable as he and his colleagues had believed. Lumber from Ottawa could be laid down in the Manitoba capital at ten dollars a thousand less than the city was paying elsewhere. He confided to the Governor General that the company would not give up the controversial portion of the line "even if the Government wished us."

Again, as in the case of the prairie and mountain sections, Stephen and his colleagues had rejected Sandford Fleming's surveys. The Fleming line took the easiest route, well to the north of Lake Nepigon, but Stephen wanted to adopt a new location that would hug the granite-ribbed shores of Lake Superior. "The line north of Nipigon would be easy of construction and operation too, but it *never* can support settlers, there is absolutely no *land*, nothing but bare rocks and pools of water." Moreover, by building close to the lake the contractors could be supplied by water transport. Stephen argued that because of this, construction time would be cut, perhaps in half. "Do not forget," he told Macdonald, "that its adoption means the completion of the road in 5 years." The Prime Minister, by mid-November, 1881, had become a convert.

Though Stephen thought the new route along the lake ought to be most acceptable to Ontario, he had no illusions about the attitude of the Toronto *Globe*, which he believed was "conspiring with the Northern Pacific to strangle Canada's national road." It was "simply disgusting" to have to swallow the "lying charges" of such newspapers. The best answer was "to take care to avoid anything that even looks like a breach, or even an evasion, of the terms of the contract. It will be the duty as well as the interest of the Company to ask nothing of the Government savoring of a favoritism not provided for in the contract, and you may be sure, that so far as I know, I will be guided by this principle. Acting in this way and pushing our work with the utmost energy and especially that part of the contract which the *Globe still insists we mean to shirk*."

Few railroad executives in North America had ever talked this way before, but then Stephen was not cast in the traditional mold of the railway entrepreneur. Among his own colleagues he was unique. Certainly Jim Hill had no intention of blasting a railroad out of the black scarps that frowned down on the slate waters of the great lake. Hill pinned his hopes on the branch line that Stephen had announced would be built to Sault Ste Marie to link up with Hill's road from St. Paul. Like Villard of the Northern Pacific, Hill saw Canadian freight being diverted south of the lake and up through the underside of Manitoba. One of his chief reasons for joining the CPR Syndicate was that his St. Paul road would get all the construction traffic for the line being built west of Winnipeg. The line across the Shield, he was convinced, "would be of no use to anybody and would be the source of heavy loss to whoever operated it."

In the fall of 1881, Hill picked the best railway man he could find to look over the Pre-Cambrian country to the north and west of Lake Superior. According to William Pearce of the Dominion Land Department—a man privy to a good deal of CPR gossip—Hill's plan was to have the visitor damn the all-Canadian route as impractical. He chose for this task the dynamic young general manager of the Chicago, Milwaukee and St. Paul Railroad; though no one yet realized it, his influence on the future of the young nation was to be tremendous. His name was William Cornelius Van Horne.

5 · *Enter Van Horne*

THE NEW MAN WAS BEING CONSIDERED for something more permanent than a mere report on the Lake Superior route. The CPR badly needed a new general manager. Alpheus B. Stickney, as general superintendent of the western division, had managed to build only one hundred and thirty miles of railway that season; moreover, he was under a cloud because of his land speculations.

As usual, George Stephen turned to Hill, who had done the major share of the hiring for the top echelons of the company that year. Hill recommended Van Horne. Of all the men he knew, Van Horne was the best equipped mentally for the job, and in every other way as well. A pioneer was needed, Hill told Stephen, "and the more of a pioneer, the better."

"You need a man of great mental and physical power to carry this line through," Hill said. "Van Horne can do it." He added a word of caution: "But he will take all the authority he gets and more, so define how much you want him to have."

Stephen undoubtedly recognized the type; he had seen it once before in his career when he was fighting to turn a bankrupt railway into a profitable business. Hill in those days had been the pioneer, a man of seemingly inexhaustible mental and physical power. Now Stephen was being offered a second Jim Hill. It was small wonder that he was prepared to pay Van Horne the largest salary ever dangled before a railroad man in the West—a princely fifteen thousand dollars a year.

In the two-volume authorized biography of James Jerome Hill there is not, in all of 957 pages, a single reference to his remarkable protégé. Physically and temperamentally, Hill and Van Horne were very much alike; that similarity may help to explain the unyielding antagonism that developed between them over the rival interests of the Great Northern and the Canadian Pacific—two parallel transcontinental lines that fought for business. They were both powerful men with big chests and huge heads sunk on massive shoulders. Their strong faces were half hidden by short beards, which tended to mask the expression of their mouths. The eyes differed: Hill's single eye was like a smoldering coal; Van Horne's, impassive and ice-blue, were the product of his Dutch-

German ancestry. If you removed Van Horne's beard, cropped his hair, and gave him a Bismarck mustache, he could have been mistaken for a Junker general. Indeed, it was often remarked that the CPR's gain was the military's loss. After all, like Hill, he was used to controlling armies of men—"the ablest railroad general in the world, all that Grant was to the U.S.A.," in the admiring phrase of a fellow railroader, Jason C. Easton, president of the Chicago, Milwaukee and St. Paul.

Van Horne's speech was military in its decisiveness—blunt, direct, and simple. So was Hill's; the ex-Canadian hated adjectives, preferred short, pungent words, and often spoke of *Pilgrim's Progress* as a model of style. Both men had the ruthlessness of great generals and great statesmen. Both were singleminded to the point of obsession in any cause they served. Both knew how to seize and hold power. Hill, the Canadian turned American, and Van Horne, the American turned Canadian, would both push their railroads through to the Pacific. It was inevitable that when their interests clashed they would find themselves locked in battle. It was also understandable that, given their temperaments, they would be hard to reconcile. The sophisticated Stephen remained Hill's mentor and was called on more than once to act as arbiter between the two strong men who were both his closest friends and business associates.

On October 7, Hill brought Van Horne into Winnipeg to look over the CPR's prairie construction and also the government line still being built between the Red River and Fort William. Winnipeg was then locked in the throes of a great real-estate boom, which had been touched off by the railway and which was to astonish the nation and cause a ferment in the North West for more than a year. It was a city of contrasts—buildings springing up everywhere; "the streets full of garbage, egg shells, rinds of lemons and other forms of refuse cast out in broad daylight"; stray horses prowling around the suburbs where they "mangle shade trees, stamp around at nights and make a nuisance of themselves generally"; tents blossoming so thickly in St. Boniface along the Assiniboine that the police tried to burn them out; workmen and settlers jamming the broad, muddy avenues. Arthur Rowe Miller, a young music student from England on his way to join a survey party, noted in his diary that the town was "just old enough to be dirty, and smells dreadfully."

Nonetheless it was beginning to acquire a patina of culture. The Nathal Opera Troupe performed at the city hall on the very day Hill and Van Horne arrived. "Miss Louise Lester . . . was particularly effective, her performance in the wine drinking scene being most artistic in every respect." The wine drinking was not confined to the stage: "This city," the *Free Press* had complained the previous month, "is suffering from drunken Indians. They are to be met on almost every street at almost every hour. They seem to have no difficulty in procuring whiskey."

The white population was as addicted to drink as the Indians. The opening that August of Winnipeg's pride, the Louisa Railway Bridge, had been accompanied by an "incarnal orgy . . . a great, hilarious, illimitable guzzle," in which small boys quaffed glass after glass of free champagne and beer, provided by the city, "with the easy nonchalance of veterans," and the crowd, on learning that the liquor was cut off, "acted generally more like wild beasts than rational creatures," tearing down the ceremonial tent, appropriating the forbidden stock of spirits, and indulging in a "debauch . . . the largest and most varied the city has seen for many a day."

Hill, Van Horne, and Hill's two sons, who had come along for the excursion, stayed overnight in Winnipeg and then went west through the booming community of Brandon, and on to the end of track. The trip impressed Van Horne: the quality of the grain in the fields was good, the vegetables unusually large, the crops abundant. The following day, the party headed east along the still unfinished line to Thunder Bay.

It must have been a stimulating two days. Both Van Horne and Hill were insatiably curious. Hobbies with them became obsessions. Van Horne was an amateur geologist who constantly chipped away at rock cuts in his search for new fossils, nine of which carry to this day the descriptive suffix "Van Hornei." Once, in Alton, Illinois, he had been tantalized for several weeks by the spectacle of a fine trilobite embedded in a slab sidewalk until, unable to resist the impulse, he had smashed at the pavement with his hammer and borne the trophy away.

Of the two, Van Horne was the broader in his interests. Hill usually made his curiosity work for him in a business sense; transportation, fuel, and forwarding attracted him. But Van Horne indulged his varied fancies for the sheer love of it. He was a first-rate gardener (roses were his specialty); he was a caricaturist; he was a conjuror; he was a mind reader; he was a violinist; he was a practical joker; he was a gourmet; he was a marthon poker player.

He was also the more sybaritic. Both Hill and Van Horne were furious smokers, but the latter's long Havana cigars were to become such a trademark that a brand was named after him, his likeness on every band. All his appetites appeared to be gargantuan. He ate prodigiously and was known as a man who fed his workmen generously. He could sit up all night winning at poker and go to work the following morning without showing a trace of fatigue. He liked his cognac, his whiskey, and his fine French vintages, but he did not tolerate drunkenness in himself or others. Inebriates were fired out of hand. So were slackers, dunces, cravens, cowards, slowpokes, and labor organizers. Van Horne did not suffer laziness, stupidity, inefficiency, or revolt.

He was probably appalled by what he found between Winnipeg and Thunder Bay. Later Van Horne was to describe a section of the desert east of Fort William as "200 miles of engineering impossibilities." It may be that at this juncture he shared Hill's belief that it would be madness to try to push a railroad across the Shield. Did he actually damn the Lake Superior route, as Hill wanted him to? William Pearce, the land commissioner, believed that he did. "I have no doubt he carried out what he was asked to do," he wrote in a memoir years later. But Van Horne at the time was not a committed officer of the company, nor had he yet fallen under the spell of George Stephen.

Events, however, were moving rapidly. The pressure was on him to leave his job in Milwaukee and take over the Canadian railway. It was an enormous risk. His prospects south of the border were as bright as those of any rising young railway executive in the country. He could, almost certainly, have had the pick of half a dozen sinecures; yet he chose the CPR. Certainly the salary that Hill was dangling before him was attractive, but it was not really the money that turned William Cornelius Van Horne into a Canadian. The Canadian Pacific Railway company was launched on a breath-taking gamble. The steel was creeping across the prairie like an arrow pointed at the successive bulwarks of the Rockies and the Selkirks. At that moment, no one knew exactly how the rails were to penetrate those two mountain series or, indeed, if they could get through the Selkirks at all. The railway's future depended on that eccentric little wisp of a surveyor, Major A. B. Rogers, who, all that summer, had been clambering over the naked peaks looking for a notch in the rampart. Few Canadian engineers believed he would find what he was seeking, but Van Horne, the poker player, had talked to Rogers. The gamble, the challenge, the adventure, the desire "to make things grow and put new places on the map," were too much for a man of his temperament to resist.

Van Horne's appointment was confirmed on November 1. He began work on January 2, 1882, in the CPR offices in the new Bank of Montreal building. By that time the astonishing real-estate boom, which swept across all of western Canada from the Red River to Fort Edmonton and electrified most of the continent, was at its height. The smell of money was in the air. For the past several months, ever since the founding of Brandon, the people of Manitoba had seemed to be going stark, raving mad over real estate. When Van Horne arrived the insanity had reached a kind of crescendo. It would continue unabated until the snows melted and it was snuffed out by the angry floods of spring.

11

1 · The great Winnipeg boom

VAN HORNE'S FIRST OFFICIAL ACT WAS
to place a small advertisement in the Winnipeg newspapers cautioning
the public against buying lots at prospective stations along the line
until he had officially announced their locations. All but five sites, he
pointed out, were still temporary. Future townsites would be chosen by
the company and by the company alone, "without regard to any private
interest whatever."

This clear warning to real-estate speculators that they could expect
no aid or comfort from the CPR fell largely on deaf ears. The little ad
was almost lost in an ocean of screaming type, trumpeting unbelievable
bargains in lots on townsites many of which were nonexistent and in
"cities" that could scarcely be found by the most diligent explorer. Such
ads had fattened Winnipeg's three dailies, the *Free Press*, the *Times*,
and the *Sun*, for all of the latter half of 1881; they would continue to
dominate the press for most of the first half of 1882. MAKE MONEY!
the advertising shrieked. GET WEALTHY! GOLDEN CHANCES! GOLDEN
SPECULATIONS! MILLIONS IN IT!

The boom had been launched the previous June with the opening
sale of lots in Brandon. By January, the value of those lots had tripled,
the town had been sold seven or eight times over, and the price was
said to be rising at a rate of one hundred dollars per lot per week. In
March, lots on Brandon's main street were selling at $140 a front foot.
In Portage la Prairie the price was $230 a front foot. In Winnipeg, on

Main Street the price rose as high as $2,000 a front foot for choice locations. This meant that downtown real estate in Winnipeg was more expensive than it was in Chicago. An idea of the inflated values of that spring may be gained from a study of modern real-estate prices in the same city. By 1970, real estate at the corner of Portage and Main was again worth $2,000 a front foot; but the 1882 dollar was worth at least four or five times its 1970 namesake. In short, the cost of land in Winnipeg was never higher than when the city was in its infancy.

The town was said to have been surveyed into city lots for ten miles—enough real estate to support a population of half a million. In three years, farm land in the vicinity had soared from twelve to one hundred dollars an acre. By April, when the boom began to decline, it was estimated that fifteen million acres had changed hands. To eastern ears this was little short of miraculous. In all of southwestern Ontario, which had a population seventeen times that of Manitoba, there were only eleven million acres.

Winnipeg, with a population of some sixteen thousand, supported no fewer than three hundred real-estate dealers. Its population had doubled in a year. Buildings were popping up like toadstools. Accommodation was at such a premium that the smallest building—a story-and-a-half structure, thirty feet by thirty—could rent for five thousand dollars a year before it was completed.

The news from Winnipeg caught the imagination of the continent. On March 7, the New York *Graphic* devoted two full pages to "the wondrous city of northwestern Canada." "Think of $1000 a front foot!" exclaimed the Fargo *Argus* over in Dakota Territory. "If you haven't a lot in Manitoba you had better buy one at once," cried the London, Ontario, *Herald*. The Thunder Bay *Sentinel* editorialized that in Winnipeg there was "more money to the square inch than in any other city on the continent double or quadruple the size."

The Toronto papers were crammed with advertisements from Winnipeg real-estate men who had come east offering lots. The *Globe*, noting that auction rooms dealing exclusively in Manitoba lots were springing up in towns and cities all over Ontario, warned its readers of "the necessity of receiving with very heavy discount the rose-coloured descriptions and prognostications of interested agents."

The eastern press covered the Manitoba boom as if it were a war, sending correspondents into the front lines, some of whom stayed to speculate themselves. "I have yet to hear of any one who has not made money," the reporter for the St. Catharines *Journal* exclaimed at the end of January.

Stories of fortunes made and lost excited the nation. There was, for instance, the tale of one elderly man who owned a parcel of fifty-four acres on the outskirts of the city. In 1880 he had tried, unsuccessfully, to sell it for seven hundred dollars. He moved to Toronto and tried to sell it there, again without success. In 1881 he returned to Winnipeg, intending to pack up and leave the country. Soon after his arrival two strangers knocked on his door and asked if he wanted to sell his land. The old man was afraid to ask seven hundred dollars for fear of driving them away. Seeing him hesitate, the visitors jumped in with an offer of forty thousand dollars. The old man, concluding that he was in the presence of lunatics, shooed them off his property and then went to his lawyer with tears in his eyes and told him that a couple of scamps had been poking fun at him. It was some time before he could be convinced that the offer was genuine. By the time he had been persuaded to sell, the price had risen by another five thousand dollars.

A newspaperman from St. Catharines purchased several lots on Portage Avenue well before the boom. In September, 1881, a friend dropped in and offered him twenty-five hundred dollars for one lot. When the reporter hesitated, the friend increased the offer to three thousand. The news of the available property traveled swiftly. The following morning, as the St. Catharines man walked down the street he was besieged with offers that seemed to increase block by block. An acquaintance rushed up to him and offered to buy all his lots at three thousand apiece. A few hundred yards farther along, a man popped his head out of the window and raised the price to thirty-five hundred. Another few hundred yards and he was stopped by a stranger who offered four thousand dollars per lot. He had scarcely moved another block before the figure had reached six thousand.

Harry Armstrong, who had helped survey the government line between Thunder Bay and Red River and who was working in the CPR's engineering department in Winnipeg early in 1882, managed to buy a lot on Portage Avenue for fifteen hundred dollars before the boom began. He sold it late in 1881 for ten thousand dollars. A short time later it was resold for forty thousand.

Such tales crowded the world news out of the papers. Even the exploits of Billy the Kid and the revelations of Robert Ford, the man who killed Jesse James, were overshadowed by more piquant items:

"W. J. Ovens used to sell nails for a cent in a hardware store in Yorkville four years ago but he can draw his check for $100,000 to-day."

"A man who worked on the street here last spring, wore a curly dog-skin coat this spring, smokes 25 cent cigars and talks with contempt about thousands."

"Mr. Wm. J. Twigg, of Thompson, Twigg & Co., Real Estate, has retired from business after making one hundred thousand dollars."

It puts matters in perspective to realize that twelve hundred dollars a year was considered, in 1882, to be a very good income and that a hundred-thousand-dollar profit then could keep a man and his family in luxury for life. But many of these fortunes were paper ones. George Ham was staying that winter in Winnipeg's Queen's Hotel along with La Touche Tupper, a government employee who was deeply involved in land speculation. "He was a fairly good barometer of the daily land values," Ham recalled. "Some days when he claimed to have made $10,000 or $15,000 everything was lovely. The next day, when he could only credit himself with $3,000 or $4,000 to the good, things were not as well, and when the profits dropped, and some days they did, to a paltry $500 or $600, the country was going to the dogs. We faithfully kept count of La Touche's earnings, and in the spring he had accumulated nearly a million in his mind."

In mid-February, one minister preaching a sermon about Lot's wife had to make it clear to his congregation that it was not his intention to talk about real estate. A performer at a skating carnival that same week costumed himself as a coffin on which was inscribed: "Talked to death by a real estate agent. Lots for sale." In Brandon, the first wedding was precipitated by an offer from the municipal council of a free lot to the first bride and groom. A man named Robbins immediately proposed to a woman popularly known as English Nell. One old-timer recalled that "no questions were asked whether it was a love match but most folks were satisfied it was principally to get the city lot." The nuptials were celebrated at the city hall and then the entire congregation, singing "One More River to Cross," followed the newlyweds across the Assiniboine, where the city fathers delivered up to them the certificate and title.

Children and teen-agers were caught up in the speculative fever. "Little girls gamble in lots for doll-houses," the astonished representative of *The Times* of London reported, "and when two youthful partners begin whispering earnestly in the intervals of a dance, the chances are that their theme is not love, but land." In Selkirk, in February, an old resident, Major Bowles, was so inspired by a local real-estate boom touched off by rumors of additional railroad facilities that he christened his infant son "Selkirk Boom Bowles" in honor of the event.

Everybody from the lowest tradesman to the leading citizen of the province was involved in land speculation. The chief commissioner of the Hudson's Bay Company, James A. Grahame, and his land commissioner, Charles Brydges, together with the company solicitor, all of whom had inside knowledge, bought fifty-six of their company's lots at Fort Garry for $280,000 and within eleven days sold eleven of them for $275,000. The Company's surveyors speculated in land as did ordinary clerks, all of them privy to information regarding Hudson's Bay property that had not yet been advertised to the public.

So all-pervasive was the talk about real estate that it did not occur to the average citizen that there could be any other topic. In January, a stranger seeking a church service inquired of "a respectable elderly gentleman" where the town hall might be, since it did double service as the Presbyterian meeting place. The Winnipegger jumped to the obvious conclusion that the stranger wanted to buy the property and informed him that it had already been sold at eight hundred dollars a front foot. He "was unable to realize the possibility of any one coming to Winnipeg for any other purpose than to learn how real estate was going."

Certainly, the dividing line between God and Mammon was blurred that hectic winter. Early in February, the trustees of Knox Presbyterian Church succumbed to the craze. The church occupied a desirable corner lot at the junction of Fort and Portage and the trustees announced that the building would be auctioned off on February 18, 1882, to the highest bidder. Not surprisingly, the crowd that attended in the basement formed the largest congregation the church had ever known. An eyewitness called it "the wealthiest, as well as the most intelligent, audience that ever gathered in any similar building in Canada," and added that no one removed his hat. "The puffing cigars held in several hundred mouths soon rendered the atmosphere of the sacred edifice disagreeable in the extreme."

The church had been built at a cost of $22,000 and the land secured for a few hundred. It was knocked down for $126,000. The syndicate who bought it resold the church, realizing a cash profit of fifty thousand dollars. The first tenants included the Bank of Montreal and the Canadian Pacific Railway.

The Anglicans were not far behind the Calvinists. (The Methodists were already renting out their Wesley Hall as a theater, of all things, on week nights.) On February 26, the congregation of Holy Trinity learned from their rector that a meeting was being planned "for the purpose of considering whether it was advisable to sell the church." That was too much for one aggrieved parishioner. "To what are we tending?" he cried, and then he quoted St. Paul's familiar dictum about the love of money being the root of all evil—an admonition which for all that winter had been ignored by Christian and heathen alike. Few paid him any attention.

2 · Fool's paradise

"IF THERE EVER WAS A FOOL'S PARADISE," wrote George Ham, "it sure was located in Winnipeg. Men made fortunes—mostly on paper—and life was one continuous joy-ride."

The joy ride lasted from June, 1881, until mid-April, 1882. For all of those eleven months, the business section of the city resembled a giant carnival. Almost every visitor remarked on the immense crowds jostling each other on the streets, on the general air of wealth, on the feeling of hustle and energy, and on the smell of money. A contemporary essayist, J. C. McLagan, talked of cabmen and bus drivers "plying their vocation with lusty lungs," of immense piles of baggage blocking every available space, of conveyances of all descriptions clogging the winding streets, "magnificent turnouts with coachmen and footmen fully equipped," ox sleds laden with lumber and produce, dog trains of great length yapping their way through the throngs, farmers, newly rich, driving spanking teams. "Men, old and young, hurry along with anxious looks—eagerly intent on business—and, as a rule, a roll of plans under the arm or a notebook in the hand."

Two-thirds of those on the streets were men. "I doubt if to-day any other city on the continent, according to its population, can boast of so many wealthy, young and middle-aged men," one eyewitness wrote in March. "In physique and general appearance no place can produce their equal. This is the general theme of conversation indulged in by all newcomers, who stand in utter amazement admiring the busy throng as they pass by. Eagerness and determination are depicted on every countenance."

Samuel Benfield Steele, one of the original detachment of North West Mounted Police that went west in 1874, saw Winnipeg in its flush times and recalled them in his memoirs: "People were ready to buy anything. The hotels did a roaring trade and the bars made profits of hundreds of dollars a day. . . . In the forenoon the speculators were at their writing tables going through their correspondence; the city was quiet, though crowded with men. At noon there was the usual hearty luncheon; at 3 p.m. the fun began, and was kept up until a late hour. Those who had made money were ready to re-invest it, and the real estate offices were crowded with men ready to buy or sell lots."

The "king of the land," in the Winnipeg *Sun*'s phrase, was thirty-six-year-old Arthur Wellington Ross, M.P., a real-estate agent who had been first on the scene at the founding of Brandon and who had secured that townsite for the CPR. A small, thin man with a dark spade beard, Ross was reputed to be worth half a million dollars at the height of the boom, owning for a period almost all of the Fort Rouge subdivision, where he was constructing one of the most palatial residences in the West. Ross was an opportunist. He had begun life as a schoolteacher and was later a school inspector in Ontario but had gone back to school himself to study law. After he moved to Winnipeg he became a solicitor for the Mackenzie administration, but in 1882 he switched his allegiance to the party in power. By 1882, he held the federal seat of Lisgar. He was a man who clearly made it a practice to be in with the right people. He also had a shrewd eye for land. As early as 1878 he was buying lots in St. Boniface for three hundred dollars an acre; within three years their value had increased eightfold. He always seemed to know where opportunity lay; wherever the CPR went, there was Arthur Wellington Ross, quietly moving ahead of it, buying up property, always unobtrusively. He was, the *Sun* declared, known for his tact. He was also known for his Calvinist principles: "While others played, he worked. While others were enjoying themselves in social festivities, he was thinking and working and he has only himself to thank for his present success."

Ross's real-estate advertisements overshadowed the slender columns of news on the front pages of the Winnipeg papers from the very first day of the boom, when his firm put the CPR's original Brandon subdivision on the market. Shortly thereafter two other names became household words in Manitoba—those of the colorful real-estate auctioneers Jim Coolican and Joseph Wolf. Wolf, "portly and indefatigable," sold half a million dollars' worth of real estate in the first six months of the land fever. He was known as the "Golden Auctioneer" because he operated from the Golden Hotel and Real Estate Exchange. When the CPR decided to place a second Brandon section on the market in February, it was Wolf who was chosen to handle the bidding. The crowds were so huge that the city hall itself was transformed into a real-estate office. Wolf worked for three nights in a row and sold $133,000 worth of North Brandon lots. His personal fortune was estimated at two hundred thousand dollars, but his exertions were so great that he suffered a collapse in the late spring and was ordered east by his doctor for a five-week rest.

Coolican, "the Real Estate King," was perhaps the most ebullient and resourceful real-estate man in Winnipeg. A rotund and florid Irishman with a black soupstrainer, his plump fingers and silk tie glittered with "real diamonds," in the phrase of the day. At work he wore a snappy black-velvet jacket; on the streets he sported the status symbol of the city—a five-thousand-dollar sealskin coat with matching cap. He too was building what was described as a "palatial residence" on the Assiniboine, to which he was conveyed in an English state coach, the first of its kind ever brought into the North West.

Coolican's advertisements for the paper towns he auctioned off— often a half or a full page in size—were masterpieces of hyperbole, studded with exclamation marks and superlatives rendered in heavy type. In a single fortnight in February he spent four thousand dollars on newspaper advertising. It was worth it; in the same period he auctioned off almost a million dollars' worth of property. He did his business at the very hub of the city, in the Exchange at the corner of Portage and Main, which he was forever enlarging to handle the crowds, "a transformation more wonderful than anything experienced in the Arabian nights."

He was an expansive and popular figure about town. One night when lots were selling particularly well, he bought out the entire stock of a passing apple vendor and scattered the fruit "promiscuously amongst the audience." The next night he gave away seven hundred cigars to his customers. This was in mid-February, when Coolican had placed the entire "city" of Cartwright on the market. "Cartwright Leads Them All!" his ads screamed. "Unquestionably the Best Situated Rising Town in the Province." Coolican's silver tongue moved Cartwright lots at the rate of twenty thousand dollars a night. The town itself, as the investors discovered, consisted of a single building, a general store that also did duty as a post office. Everything else—the advertised shops, mills, schools, and churches—were, as one investor ruefully put it, "the merest castles in the air."

In Winnipeg that winter, there was a liquor store or a saloon for every two hundred permanent residents. Champagne replaced whiskey as the class beverage. On the same day that Coolican auctioned off the Cartwright lots, an entire carload of champagne arrived in town in specially heated cars. Lucky speculators spent a hundred dollars a week and more on champagne suppers, to the point where the city's supply gave out and a fashionable wedding had to be celebrated without it—

a disaster grave enough to be reported as news. One man actually bathed in champagne. He was Captain Vivian, a monocled English aristocrat who had arrived in the summer of 1881 with a thousand pounds in his pocket. Vivian sank the entire sum into a 160-acre homestead in the Brandon district, which he proceeded to sell at inflated prices. By February he was said to be worth four hundred thousand dollars. Unable to drink up all the champagne he had purchased, he filled a bathtub with it and invited his friends to watch him splash about. The affair cost him seven hundred and fifty dollars.

The scene is no more unreal than Winnipeg itself was that winter and spring. It seemed as if all belief had been temporarily suspended, all rational conjecture swept aside. A young lawyer from Hamilton named William White who moved through the town early in 1882 wrote that money meant nothing: "Everything was 'jake' to use a Western expression denoting perfect satisfaction with life generally."

Coolican and Ross were not the only *nouveaux riches* who indulged themselves with mansions and carriages. One Easterner wrote home that "women, who a few years ago were cooking and washing in a dirty little back kitchen, now ride about in carriages and pairs, with eccentric looking individuals for coachmen sitting in the back seat driving, the mistress looking as if the world were barely extensive enough for her to spread herself in." But it was not easy to secure such servants. *The Times* of London reported that "you find that your hackney coachman is a landowner, and cease to feel surprised at this when he declines to drive you five miles for less than $4 or to drive you at all at any but his own pace."

It was a winter of conspicuous extravagance. Diamonds became baubles on scores of fingers; Coolican's sealskin coat was widely copied. "Twenty gold pieces were just nothing." Next to the advertisements for lots were others for crystal ware, mantel ornaments, music boxes, choice gas fixtures, fine Etruscan jewelry, India and China tea, Weber pianos, cornice poles, and "beautiful dado hand painted shades." The Palace Hotel advertised quail on toast, and no luncheon could be considered complete without the customary dozen oysters on the half shell. Woltz, "the princely Toronto jeweler," set up shop in March. "Even if you buy nothing," the *Sun* told its readers, "the rich splendor of his wares will feast you with the artistic and educate you in the beautiful."

Woltz pressed a gold watch as a gift upon the reporter who wrote that embroidered prose. He accepted it with alacrity and boasted about his good fortune in print. In Winnipeg that year, the accumulation of sudden and unexpected wealth was looked upon with favor and greeted with applause. Speculators were heroes, profiteers were the new nobility.

Normally reticent businessmen boasted openly about their killings and gave interviews to newspapers detailing their worth. The *Sun*, revealing some of the largest of the new fortunes, reported that the mayor himself led the list with an accumulation estimated at three hundred thousand dollars. Cabinet Ministers, backbenchers in both parties, and the Queen's representative were all speculating in real estate in the most open manner possible. It was publicly reported, with approbation, that the Lieutenant-Governor of Manitoba had cleared a million dollars out of his knowledge of North West speculations.

Clearly, it was a mark of considerable status to have made a fast dollar. M. C. Cameron, one of the powers in the Liberal Party, made a seventy-five-thousand-dollar killing in Winnipeg real estate and cheerfully gave the details to the newspapers. The property was quickly resold for one hundred thousand, but Cameron announced that he was perfectly satisfied with the lower figure, "having got the price he asked." The point was implicit: no one had put anything over on M. C. Cameron. Shrewdness was more highly prized than virtue during the boom.

The *Globe*'s man in Winnipeg, himself caught up in the land craze, ventured to admit that "the moral aspect of this real estate fever is a cause for considerable anxiety," but hastened to reassure his Ontario readers that nothing could be further from the truth: "I would be very sorry to countenance gambling in any way, but I look on speculation here, when legitimately conducted, as perfectly safe and proper. If one can grasp the magnitude of this North-West and believe in its rapid development he can invest his money in city or farm property without any anxiety or chidings of conscience."

Everybody in Winnipeg, it seemed, was affluent—or believed himself to be. Visitors remarked on the absence of beggars in the streets and the total lack of copper coins. The Winnipeg city council, in 1881, had not found it necessary to distribute so much as one hundred and fifty dollars for charity.

The signs of prosperity were everywhere. By March, one hundred and eighty of Alexander Graham Bell's newly developed telephones were in operation. Gas street lighting, hailed the year before, was already becoming obsolete. On June 13, three sample electric lights were installed on the grounds of the CPR station at the head of Main Street, which was "illuminated as if by sunlight. . . . Books and newspapers could be read with ease."

In eastern Canada, thousands of adventurers were preparing to set out for "the New Eldorado," as the Winnipeg *Times* dubbed the North West. The press talked of "Manitoba Fever," and the irreverent *Sun* insisted that Phineas T. Barnum, then at the peak of his fame, was advertising in Ontario for a man who was *not* going to Manitoba to travel with his show as a companion curiosity to the Most Beautiful Woman in the World. The paper solemnly added that the showman had not been able to find such an oddity.

By early April, every train from St. Paul was bringing in hundreds of immigrants from eastern Canada and from every part of the world. One traveler taking an immigrant train from Toronto to Winnipeg described the scene, with the men, women, and children crowding aboard at every stop with their kits and baggage and all their household goods, "their faces beaming with satisfaction at being at last on the way to Manitoba." During the journey, "nothing was talked of but Manitoba and the North West." Everybody who was anybody, it seemed, was heading for Winnipeg and beyond—from Peter Redpath, "the sugar king," to Captain Charles Boycott, the unfortunate British land agent in Ireland whose name had gone into the language.

The influx of newcomers created an unprecedented demand for space to which the overcrowded community was unequal. Since the previous May, Winnipeg's hotels had been scandalously overtaxed. By the spring of 1882 they were so crowded that every available space was used for sleeping accommodation, including parlors, corridors, and lobbies. Beecham Trotter, who lived in Winnipeg during the boom, put up at a "miserable hotel" on Main Street, where he paid two dollars to spend a night in a chair. Even a chair was a rarity that winter and spring, and the same was true in the outlying towns. At a Brandon boardinghouse a clergyman and his wife were turned away in thirty-below-zero weather. When they returned, unable to find any room in town, the proprietor took pity on them and found them each a space on the crowded floor.

One mathematically inclined newcomer to Winnipeg figured out that in the house where he was boarding each occupant had exactly twenty-eight square feet of floor space for his own use, compared to an average of between two hundred and fifty and three hundred square feet in Ontario. Mealtimes, by all accounts, were savage: ". . . Long ere the dining rooms doors are thrown open, a crowd gathers, eager to charge the tables and anxious to satisfy the cravings of the inner man. Frequently weak men are seriously injured in these jams. The tables have to be cleared and re-set several times ere the guests are all dined." At one of the leading hotels the crush was so great that one diner suffered a broken arm.

Several "mammoth hostelries" were being planned for the city, but this was cold comfort to those who tumbled off the cramped trains into the snow without a hope of accommodation. During one fearful blizzard in early March, when the wind reached hurricane force and it was impossible to see half a dozen yards in any direction, several immigrant parties had to be lodged temporarily in the CPR's passenger depot. During that month the National Manufacturing Company of Ottawa rushed fifteen hundred heavy cotton tents to Winnipeg. On the outskirts of town, canvas boardinghouses began to rise in rows. These gargantuan marquees were large enough to accommodate within their folds a cluster of smaller tents, each capable of sleeping eight men. By May, the ever-alert Arthur Wellington Ross was importing portable houses from an eastern manufacturer. Space was at such a premium that he was able to rent them all before they arrived.

That social phenomenon, the Winnipeg boardinghouse, had its birth that year. It was unique—"a style to be found nowhere else in the Dominion," in the words of a man who endured one. Architecturally it was a hybrid—half tent, half ramshackle frame. Entirely unpartitioned, it served as a combined dormitory, dining room, scullery, and den.

"You open the door," one observer wrote, "and immediately there is a rush of tobacco smoke and steam mingled with indescribable results which makes you want to get outside and get a gulp of fresh air. You go to the counter and get tickets from the man behind the desk for supper, bed and breakfast. There are no women about and no children. Nor are there any elderly people—they are all young men. You have no time to study them for through the mist of smoke in the great room there breaks the jangling call of a bell and a terrible panic seizes the crowd. It is not an alarm or fire nor is there any danger of the building caving in, neither is it a fight nor a murder—it is only supper."

Supper consisted of a plate of odorous hash, flanked by a mug of tea and a slab of black bread, served up by a number of "ghastly, greasy and bearded waiters with their arms bare to their elbows and their shirt bosoms open displaying considerably hairy breast." The meal was devoured in silence, the only sound being "a prodigious noise of fast-moving jaws, knives, forks and spoons."

The boarders themselves were a motley lot: "Men who were at one time high up in society, depraved lawyers, and decayed clergymen brought down by misconduct and debauchery, but still bearing about them an air of refinement . . . carpenters smelling strongly of shavings, mill hands smelling of sawdust and oil, teamsters smelling of horse, plasterers fragrant with lime, roofers odorous with tar, railway laborers smelling of whiskey, in short all sorts and conditions of men."

At night, when the tables were cleared and the occasional drunk subdued with a club, a man at the end of the building picked up a ladder, planted it against the wall, and told the inmates to clamber into their bunks among the gray horse blankets that served as bedding.

For such accommodation, new arrivals were happy to pay double the rates at better-appointed eastern hotels. Wages were the highest in the land. Day laborers got as much as three dollars a day, triple the Ontario rate. As one immigrant wrote back home, however, since there was such a shortage of accommodation "mechanics are spending what they earn in trying to live."

Still the immigrants poured in. Often their enthusiasm was dampened when they reached the city. One carpenter, arriving in March, found he could get no work because his employer had no shop. Moreover, the station platform was covered with toolboxes and he realized that his fellow artisans, arriving by the score, would make his services a drug on the market. In St. Paul that same week, an un-named Canadian uttered one of the few murmurs of gloom voiced about the prospects in Manitoba. "When the tumble comes in Winnipeg it's going to be something awful," he said. But among the swirling crowds in the auction rooms of Main Street, bidding higher and higher for lots in towns and "cities" like Emerson, Shoal Lake, West Lynne, and Minnedosa, there was still no hint of the reckoning to come.

3 · "*Towns cannot live of themselves*"

THE WINNIPEG LAND BOOM CAN BE divided into two parts. The euphoria of 1881 was followed by a lull in late January and February before the spring upsurge of 1882 began. The weather in mid-February was as fickle as the market, being warm and sunny one day, chill and gusty the next. On February 16, the city fell under the lash of one of the worst storms it had yet known, a truly blinding blizzard that brought all movement to a stop. Speculators who had come into town from outlying points found themselves im-prisoned by the cold. Even the CPR trains were unable to travel west to Portage la Prairie and Brandon; although the track had been built high and ditched carefully to prevent just such a calamity, the roadbed was effectively blocked by a wall of packed snow.

February, it was said, would test the stability of the boom. At first the storm seemed to act as a depressant; the demand for city property ebbed. Undismayed, the entrepreneurs began to boost other Manitoba "cities" to the point where those who held property on Winnipeg's out-skirts tried to sell out in order to take advantage of more attractive bargains. In most cases they found they could not sell. The boom had moved on to a score of unfamiliar communities where, it was whispered, new railroads would soon be built.

As a result, extraordinary efforts had to be made to sell outlying lots in the immediate Winnipeg area. Curiously, the prices of these lots did not go down; rather, they rose. Properties many miles from the center of town, which could have been purchased the previous fall for fifty dollars an acre, carried, in late February, price tags ranging from two hundred and fifty to one thousand dollars.

The asking prices were so high, in fact, that it was doubtful whether any purchaser would be able to make more than the down payment. Apparently it did not matter. Real-estate speculation in Winnipeg that spring resembled very much the dime chain-letter crazes and the pyramid clubs of a later era. Everybody reasoned that the real profits would be made by those who moved in early and got out swiftly; every man expected that somebody would eventually be left holding the bag; but no one was so pessimistic as to believe that he would be caught with worthless property.

The sellers had so little confidence that the prices would be maintained that they tried to get the largest possible down payment and the shortest terms. The new purchasers, in turn, arranged at once with a broker to have their interest transferred to a syndicate at a handsome advance. The syndicates, in their turn, hired groups of smart young men to extol the virtues of the property as "the best thing on the market." Because it was difficult to move properties that could not be shown on the latest map of Winnipeg and its environs, the land sharks resorted to subterfuge. Maps were cut and pasted so that outer properties seemed to be much closer to town than they really were. But the real action was taking place in the smaller communities of Manitoba.

The safest investments were to be found at Brandon and Portage la Prairie, for these were established centers on the main line of the CPR. The boom in Brandon had not abated since the summer of 1881. "Nobody who saw Brandon in its infancy ever forgot the spectacle," Beecham Trotter wrote. Trotter nostalgically recalled a variety of sights and sounds: the hillside littered with tents, the symphony of scraping violins playing "Home, Sweet Home" and "The Girl I Left Behind Me," the cries of the auctioneers: "All wool from Paisley; and who the hell would go naked?" Brandon lots were still rising in price. So all-embracing was the real-estate fever in Brandon that when the town was laid out no provision was made for a cemetery. The dead had to be brought to Winnipeg for burial.

Portage la Prairie, advertised in March as the "Greatest Bargain of this Spring Boom!", was in a perfect frenzy of speculation. "A craze seemed to have come over the mass of the people," an early chronicler recounted. "Legitimate business in many cases was thrown aside, and buying and selling lots became the one aim and object of life. . . . Carpenters, painters, tailors, and tradesmen of all kinds threw their tools aside to open real estate offices, loaf around the hotels, drink whiskey and smoke cigars. Boys with down on their lips not as long as their teeth would talk glibly of lots fronting here and there, worth from $1,000 to $1,500 per lot." The Portage, at that time, had a population well below four thousand. Of the 148 business institutions, fifty-eight were involved in some way with real estate.

"Men who were never worth a dollar in their lives before, nor never have been since, would unite together, and, on the strength of some lots, on which they had made a small deposit, endorse each other's paper, and draw from the banks sums which they had never seen before, only in visions of the night."

The Portage boom was at least understandable, since this was a prominent station on the main line of the railway. The Rapid City boom was more mysterious. The town was one of the most remarkable paper communities in the province: although its population was well under four hundred, the city was laid out with intersecting streets for eight square miles. The fever persisted in the face of the obvious fact that the CPR had passed Rapid City by. The road between Brandon and Rapid City to the north was lined with wagons loaded with speculators, settlers' merchandise and effects, and horses, cattle, and sheep. Every hotel and every stable in town was overcrowded. Vacant land was being snatched up so swiftly that two or three men would sometimes arrive at the land office within minutes of one another, each intent upon grabbing the same section.

As late as May 30, a Rapid City doctor reported that "Rapid Cityites are not at all despondent over the change of route of the CPR but confidently expect having a railway connection with some place or other before twelve months—even if the people have to build the line themselves." Advertisements in the Winnipeg papers boasted that *six* railways would soon run through the community.

In that demented winter people no longer asked what the land could produce, only what it would sell for. "People seem to have forgotten," the Edmonton *Bulletin* wrote, "that towns cannot live of themselves." In Winnipeg scarcely a week passed that did not see a new community extolled in print. Towns that did not exist, such as Garfield, were given nonexistent suburbs such as North Garfield. "It Stands," Coolican's huge advertisement disclosed, "Upon An Eminence From Which The Land Slopes Gradualy [*sic*] Down To Garfield Itself."

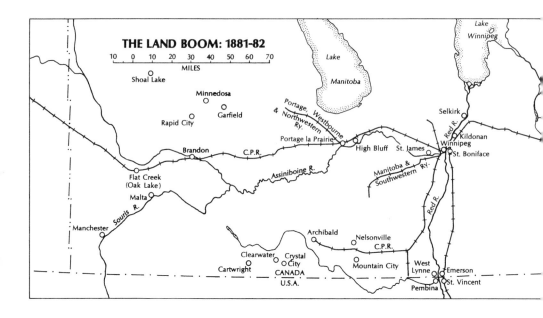

THE LAND BOOM: 1881-82

MILES
10 0 10 20 30 40 50 60 70

Shoal Lake

Minnedosa

Garfield

Rapid City

Brandon   C.P.R.

Flat Creek
(Oak Lake)

Malta

Manchester   Souris R.

Portage & Northwestern Ry.

Portage la Prairie

Assiniboine R.

High Bluff   St. James

Manitoba & Southwestern Ry.

Lake Manitoba

Lake Winnipeg

Selkirk

Kildonan
Winnipeg
St. Boniface

Red R.

Archibald

Nelsonville
C.P.R.

Clearwater   Crystal
Cartwright   O City
CANADA
U.S.A.

Mountain City

West Lynne
Pembina

Emerson
St. Vincent

One series of lots purporting to be in the West Lynne subdivision (on the banks of the Red River just opposite Emerson near the border) sold for ten thousand dollars. Actually the property was two miles away, far out on the empty prairie.

For the moment at least, the railway was king; it seemed to bring the Midas touch to the smallest shack towns. Like a golden highway, the CPR had brought prosperity to Manitoba beyond the wildest dreams of the most optimistic pioneers. The very whisper of a railway —any railway, real or imagined—drove people to greater and greater financial excesses. Local councils offered fat bonuses for CPR branch lines to their communities; rumors of newly formed railway ventures were greeted with the greatest enthusiasm and a resultant rise in real-estate prices. The day would come when the people of Manitoba, in their grief and disappointment, would turn against the railway; but in the early months of 1882, the CPR could do no wrong.

Emerson, the customs point on the Pembina Branch of the CPR, confidently expected that it would be *the* great railway center of the North West, the metropolis of western Canada, easily outdistancing Winnipeg, since it had been for some time the only point of entry into Manitoba. It had two newspapers and a population of fourteen hundred; it appeared to be the logical gateway to the rich farm lands of southwestern Manitoba, "the great country whose fame is now the theme of almost every tongue," as one eastern visitor described it. "Nothing is to be heard but 'boom,' 'boom,' 'boom,' in every hamlet you pass; 'boom' in every person's mouth. In fact the excitement is fully as great as if a mountain of gold had been discovered near Toronto."

That was in the first week of January, 1882. Three weeks later it was Selkirk's turn. The excitement stemmed from a new bylaw guaranteeing a bonus of seventy-five thousand dollars to the CPR, which ran only a few miles to the south, to construct a branch line into the community. The news instantly raised real-estate prices in Selkirk and reporters on the scene could hardly contain themselves: "In the carrying out of this the owners of lots in Selkirk see a great city rising to rival, and possibly eclipse, Winnipeg."

In the same weeks, lots in a semi-mythical "Manitoba City" began to boom with the news that the terminus of the Pembina Mountain branch line of the CPR had been settled upon. Minnedosa, "the railway centre of the North West," had also been by-passed but it was booming anyway. In mid-February it experienced a new flurry of excitement on the strength of a report that it would be the seat of a judicial district. "Thank fortune, the 'boom' has also struck Minnedosa!" the *Times*'s resident correspondent burbled. "Happy name! High flown and sweet sounding. A place with such a name and such a vicinage, and, shall I say it? such people, could not but boom. Again, I say, the boom has struck Minnedosa."

Though Manitoba's population in 1882 was only sixty-six thousand, a casual newspaper reader in a foreign country, perusing the advertisements, might have believed it to be the crossroads of the continent, teeming with people and jammed with great cities. There was Crystal City, "the featured great city of Manitoba"; Mountain City, "the embryo city"; Dobbyn City, "the future great manufacturing city of the Souris district"; St. Vincent, "one of the leading cities of the Great North West . . . booming beyond imagination"; Manchester, "the future great manufacturing town of the North West"; Clearwater, "the Brandon of Southwestern Manitoba"; Nelsonville, "the largest town in Southwestern Manitoba"; Kildonan, "the Yorkville of Winnipeg"; Rapid City, "the Minneapolis of the North West"; Malta, "situated in the garden of the North West"; Cartwright, "unquestionably the best situated and rising town in the province"; Pembina Crossing, "the most prosperous town in Southwestern Manitoba"; and High Bluff, "the best chance of the season."

As the frenzy continued unabated, the advertisements became larger and shriller, the methods used to peddle property wilder and more unscrupulous, and the paper communities more ephemeral. William White, in his brief stay in Winnipeg, recalled walking into one auction room and being attracted by the sale of lots in "Minnedosa the

Beautiful." An immense map of the community covered an entire wall. "It had to be large in order that the river flowing through the town, called the Little Saskatchewan, should be properly displayed." Majestic steamers were shown sailing down the river or moored at handsome landing docks. White decided to visit Minnedosa the Beautiful and was glad that he had done so before speculating in lots there. The Little Saskatchewan was so little that in midsummer a man could jump across it. There were no steamers to be seen and the only landing docks were the ones painted on the map. The town itself was a hamlet.

The land sharks used transparent devices to victimize the new-comers. Two men from Barrie, Ontario, were persuaded to buy, sight unseen, for sixty thousand dollars, a piece of swamp five miles from Winnipeg. The sellers played upon their greed: as the easterners were mulling over the deal, a third man came up and, pretending to believe that the transaction was closed, offered them eighty thousand dollars for the property. It did not occur to the two that the new buyer was operating as a shill. They handed over the money cheerfully and ended up in possession of the slice of swamp.

Such tales filtering back east helped to drive a wedge between settled Canada and the new North West. "At this moment Winnipeg is filled with thousands of the vilest villains," the Bobcaygeon, Ontario, *Independent* declared in an editorial in late March, "and it is possible that never before on this continent was there assembled together so large a congregation of scoundrelism. Leadville [Colorado] may, per-haps, in its early days, have approached Winnipeg in the number and intensity of its rascality, but it never quite equalled that which now exists in Winnipeg. It is a saddening spectacle to observe the uni-versality of this disgusting degradation. It is confined to no class. You read on the walls notices of pastors selling off to go to Manitoba, just as you hear of Tom, Dick and Harry starting off for the same purposes of fraud and swindling. . . . It is an outbreak of the worst passions of human nature. . . . The business of men's lives in Winnipeg . . . is the gratification of that vile lust of gold which completely overpowers the moral sense, extinguishes reason, annihilates the sense of responsibility, renders crime no longer repulsive, and unfits the miserable and wretched beings for any other companionship than that of themselves and the devil."

To this Victorian invective, the Winnipeg *Times* made a scoffing reply: "Listen to the sage of Bobcaygeon," it sneered, "—and laugh." One of its own editorial writers, C. R. Tuttle, had himself become a leading Winnipeg speculator.

The Toronto *Globe*'s man in Winnipeg described his own experience with land sharks. An old Ontario friend had approached him about "a big thing" in the wind. When the reporter showed his interest he was introduced to the organizer of a new syndicate, who pulled from his pocket a preliminary agreement in the form of a soiled half sheet of foolscap purporting to be a legal instrument whereby the owner of a certain half section agreed to transfer his rights for $2,880. The broker proposed a syndicate of no less than 90 shares at $32 each. The 320 acres were to be chopped up into 32,000 lots to be peddled in Ontario at $20 a lot. An attractive name had already been settled upon, surveys were to be undertaken immediately, and great store would be set on the report that a railway would run through the property, "but the other fact that the railway in question had been abandoned in favour of a shorter cut, through better country, was to be studiously concealed."

In spite of all this, the *Globe*'s man admitted that he had bought a share in the syndicate. But by this time it was early April; there was a feeling of letdown in Winnipeg; the share was clearly worthless. "Our eyes have been open," he wrote, "and we have seen silly fish ready to jump at every fly, and the fish have been tempted and landed on the banks. We now perceive that the pool is nearly empty, and we have returned to legitimate business."

4 · *The bubble bursts*

TWO EVENTS, ONE MAN-MADE AND THE other natural, following hard upon each other in mid-April, killed the great North West boom. The first was the sale of Edmonton lots beginning April 12, which soured the most optimistic speculators. The second was the three-week rampage of the Red River which began a week later, causing the most serious flood in memory, drowning the railway line, and cutting off the city from the outside world.

Edmonton lay on the very rim of the unknown. Perhaps for that reason it caught the fancy of the Winnipeg land buyers. The word was that the Hudson's Bay Company had surveyed the environs of the old trading post into town lots and was about to throw them onto the market. On April 12, the news was made public in gigantic advertisements by Arthur Wellington Ross. EDMONTON! EDMONTON! the ads screamed, EDMONTON AT LAST! The settlement—it contained scarcely five hundred souls—was referred to in the press as "the future Golden City of the Dominion" and was described in block letters as the country of "GOLD, COAL, TIMBER, MINERALS, AND WHEAT . . . Bounded on the South by the grazing land of the Bow River District, on the North by the Peace River and on the West at a distance of seventy miles by an uninterrupted forest of timber."

The lots went on sale immediately and Ross's office was jammed with purchasers. The previous fall, lots in Edmonton had been sold for an average of twenty-five dollars; now three hundred went in a single night at prices ranging between two hundred and four hundred. But a strange thing happened. On April 13, scores of speculators poured into Ross's office, waving marked checks for thousands of dollars, intent on picking up Edmonton lots. The following day, almost all of them tried to sell the lots at a profit, but there were no buyers. The boom was collapsing, though nobody would yet admit it.

Coolican, the auctioneer, tried to resuscitate the good times. On April 14, the day of the Edmonton collapse, he engaged a private train for himself and a group of Winnipeg businessmen and steamed off to St. Paul to sell Manitoba lots. It was a gala excursion, a kind of last gasp by Winnipeg's leading speculators. Coolican was promising to turn St. Vincent into a great "International City" straddling the border and including within its limits all of Pembina, Emerson, and West Lynne. He took St. Paul by storm. "There is a smack of enterprise, push and dash in the Winnipeg boomers . . . which commands admiration," a local editor wrote. It was strange to see such phrases applied by Yankees to Canadians; for years it had been the other way around. In Sherman's Hall, St. Paul, Coolican sold a hundred thousand dollars' worth of Canadian border lots.

There was only one problem: the boomers could not get back to Winnipeg. The Red River was on the rise. Bridges were being ripped away before the onslaught of mountains of water. Entire communities listed the previous week as attractive buys were half submerged. Many of the lots sold in St. Paul had turned to lakes, and the CPR line between Minnesota and Winnipeg was washed out. For the so-called International City, the result was catastrophic. The bridge at Emerson was swept away on April 16. By April 19, West Lynne had almost disappeared beneath the waves. Across the river, Emerson's citizens were forced to live for weeks on their second floors. The steamer *Cheyenne*, pushing a bargeload of lumber, steamed right up the main street and unloaded its cargo at the steps of the Presbyterian church.

The crest hit Winnipeg on April 19. The water had been rising steadily all night, and when a field of ice, acting as a dam, broke away it rose another three feet. Shortly after one o'clock that afternoon, the Broadway Bridge, nine hundred feet long, began to surge and sway until it plunged down the river on the breast of a six-mile current, its piers toppled by tumbling ice floes. Hundreds thronged the banks to watch the dazzling spectacle of a river out of control—a seething mass of ice, boiling, twisting, and writhing, the bright sunshine glistening on the huge blocks "with all the prismatic hues of the diamond."

By April 23, train service to and from St. Paul was suspended because of washouts along the line. Thousands found themselves stranded at St. Paul. Winnipeg was like a morgue. Mail failed to arrive. Freight was at a standstill. Some immigrants managed to reach the city by barge and boat, but since no food was carried, shortages began to drive the prices higher and higher. Bread went up to fifty cents a loaf—half a day's pay for a Toronto workingman. Building operations came to a stop, there being neither nails nor lumber available. Trade fell off because the merchants had no spring goods to sell. People were wary of placing orders for fear they would not be filled until late summer. Mechanics arriving by boat, expecting high wages, found there was no work for them at any price. On May 4, the river crept to within eighteen inches of the Assiniboine Bridge. That same day, one of the two newspapers in Emerson, the *International*, was forced to suspend publication.

By the time the floods subsided, the boom was finished. The railway blockade lasted for three weeks and did irreparable harm to Winnipeg's business community. The gigantic advertisements vanished from the newspapers as swiftly as the snows. Coolican, who finally managed to get back to Winnipeg by boat on April 28, took one last advertisement on the front pages headed: "COOLICAN'S RETURN! and the Boom Returns Also!" But the boom did not return. When Coolican tried to auction off lots in Prince Albert a month later, there were no takers. In vain real-estate dealers announced: "No paper cities! No humbug! A new boom in a new quarter!" The public was not buying. Coolican was reduced to auctioning carpets and tapestries.

Arthur Wellington Ross also tried again, offering lots at Port Moody, British Columbia, the terminus of the CPR. Ross, too, was at the end of his financial rope. When real-estate values plunged, he lost most of his huge fortune. He was forced to give up his landholdings— he owned hundreds of acres in the northern and western portions of the city—for taxes. It is said that seven thousand dollars would have cleared the property, but once the boom was over, seven thousand became an impossible figure. Ross did not have it and his credit was exhausted.

By this time the CPR had moved against the speculators by changing its regulations for the sale of prairie lands. The nominal price was raised from $1.25 to $5 an acre, a quarter of which had to be paid at the time of sale and the balance in five years without interest. But the rebate for land placed under cultivation was also raised to three-quarters of the original five dollars. Thus bona fide settlers who were prepared to work the land actually got it for $1.25 an acre. Those who bought land in the hope of a quick turnover paid four times as much.

Of those who speculated in land in Manitoba in 1881 and 1882, it was estimated that only about 5 per cent made any money at all. The lucky ones broke even. The less fortunate ended their days in destitution —like Harry Armstrong's Toronto friend Helliwell, "who cleaned up sixty thousand dollars, put it in his pocket, went broke and walked the streets till he died," or a Brockville man named Sheppard, whose obituary appeared in the dying days of the boom: "The rumour current Sunday evening was that he had lost $30,000 in speculating and hanged himself in consequence."

As a result of the bubble's sudden collapse, Winnipeg and, to a lesser degree, Manitoba entered into a period of recession which had far-reaching effects. Confidence in the North West was badly shaken. The international financial world began to look askance at any venture in the new Canada; the CPR would feel the pinch especially. The breach between West and East widened; the depression left by the boom prepared the climate for the agrarian agitation that followed, with all its attendant bitterness. People who had once extolled the railway as a bearer of gifts now looked on it darkly as the source of their misfortunes.

The immediate effects were devastating. Seventy-five per cent of the business institutions in the province wilted away. Robert Hill, Manitoba's pioneer historian, wrote eight years later that men "once deemed honest and good for any amount, were turned out of house and home, their goods and chattels liened on and sold by the sheriff, in many cases not bringing the latter's fees." The wide-open credit system, which saw properties sold for small down payments, was the real culprit. People had been speculating with money they did not have. Buggies, buckboards, and wagons were shipped to Manitoba in wholesale lots by Ontario manufacturers and sold to anyone who would buy them on time. So extravagant was the spirit of optimism engendered by the coming of the railway that any newcomer who claimed to have taken up a farm or who said he had come to stay was granted almost instant credit as a safe risk; indeed, it was considered well-nigh an insult to turn him down. As a result of this reckless policy, scores of farms and even entire townships fell eventually into the hands of the loan companies. Worse, bona fide settlers, hacking away at the tough prairie sod, found they could get no further loans for stock, farm equipment, or seed. The boom collapsed just as the first great wave of immigration reached the prairies. The newcomers ran squarely into a wall of pessimism. The financial hangover that followed was one of the reasons so many were forced to leave their new-found homes and retreat to the East and why the immigrant tide, which seemed to be unending during that roseate spring, eventually slowed to a halt for another generation.

In the years that followed, the pioneers of Manitoba looked back upon those bizarre months and wondered how they could have been so foolish. There was the case of J. A. Little, a blacksmith from Portage la Prairie who threw up his job in 1881 to sell real estate—so successfully that he soon became an acknowledged authority on the value of property. Little made a hundred thousand dollars during the boom. He was so flushed with success that he resolved to build a residence elaborate enough to eclipse any similar structure in the North West. He had completed the stable and the cellar when the end came. All the remaining years of his life were spent trying to earn enough money to pay back his crushing debts. He did not quite succeed. Shortly before he died in 1890 the stable was sold to a livery company, and the great cellar, the last remaining testament to his folly, was filled in.

There was also the tale of Roderick McLeod, who owned a river lot of two hundred and forty acres. He sold it for fifty thousand dollars, of which fifteen thousand was the down payment. When the boom burst, the purchaser, unable to pay the balance, offered to return the land. Such was McLeod's avarice that he refused and the case went to court. In the soberer climate of a later period, the judge saw that the land had been overvalued. McLeod did not receive a nickel more for his inflated property; worse, the legal expenses gobbled up all of his original fifteen thousand and his homestead as well. Perhaps he contemplated, ruefully, the irony of his stand. Stretching off from that disputed parcel of real estate, in every direction, were millions of acres of prime farm-land, available for homestead or pre-emption, all free for the asking.

The boom had a sobering effect on Winnipeg. All during the decade of the seventies it had been a lusty infant of a village. In one incredible winter it had reached its adolescence and sown its wild oats. By the fall of 1882, it had matured to become a sadder and wiser city. As men recall their lost youth, old-timers recalled wistfully those halcyon days before the bubble broke. One of these was George Ham, who wrote in 1921 that "since the boom of 1882, the soul of Winnipeg has never been what it was before."

"The later Winnipeg may be a better city," Ham admitted, but he regretted the good old days. "It was a short life from '71 to '82, but while it lasted, it was a life with a 'tang' to it—a 'tang' born of conditions that cannot be repeated and therefore cannot be reproduced."

12

1 · The new broom

WILLIAM CORNELIUS VAN HORNE AR-
rived at Winnipeg that January with a considerable reputation among
railwaymen. The previous year, the *Railway Journal* had called him
"a man of wonderful power and shrewdness." He was known, too, as a
railway iconoclast, "an idol-smashing heathen" who had no respect
for the rigid dogmas of a tradition-ridden business. In Chicago he had
astonished his contemporaries by the amount of trackage he had managed to work into a limited area in the yards. He used locomotives to
their fullest capacity over the protests of engineers who wanted to treat
them like horses and let them rest quietly in the shops. He was credited
with doctoring sick railroads until they were made to pay. He was also
known as a fighter: he had fought the grasshoppers, he had fought the
labor unions, he had fought the encroachment of other railroads, and
always he had won.

He seemed to know a terrifying amount about railroading. He knew
all about yards and repair shops. He understood the mysteries of accounting. He could work out a complicated system of scheduling in his
head while others sweated laboriously with pins and charts. He could
comprehend the chatter of the fastest telegraph key. He could operate
any locomotive built. He had even redesigned, with grace and taste, that
ugliest example of nineteenth-century American architecture, the railroad station.

He was a true Renaissance man, the most engaging and versatile
immigrant that Canada ever enticed across its borders and one of the

few larger-than-life figures in the Canadian story. It is interesting to speculate on what he might have been in another era: a prince of the Church in the Middle Ages? the ruler of a dukedom in the sixteenth century? a Roman conqueror? In any age Van Horne would have fitted his times exactly. In a century when railways were venerated above all else—when a private railway car had equal status with a yacht, when entire magazines were devoted to news and opinions about railways, when railway financiers were numbered among the real rulers of the land—it was ordained that Van Horne would become a railway man. He was probably the greatest that the continent ever produced.

There are a great many adjectives that apply to him: buoyant, capable, ingenious, temperamental, blunt, forceful, boyish, self-reliant, imaginative, hard-working, ruthless, puckish, courageous; but the word that best sums him up, and the one that his contemporaries used more than once, is "positive." He exuded confidence. J. H. E. Secretan, who worked for him as a surveyor, recorded that "the word 'cannot' did not exist in his dictionary." Was he ever bedeviled by doubts of his own or haunted by fears of private failure? If he was, he hid his emotions well behind the grave mask of his face and those unrevealing eyes of penetrating blue. Even when the mask slipped a little to reveal the sensitive man behind it, the approach was characteristically direct. Once, in Milwaukee, when he had been given a job that seemed to be far beyond his years, he sensed hostility all around him. He went straight to one of the clerks and asked him point-blank: "Why are you prejudiced against me?" Startled, the man replied that he was not prejudiced, "and, now that I come to think of it, I have no reason to be against you at all."

Van Horne believed in coming to the point swiftly, with an economy of words. It was the same with railway lines. The best-run railways were the ones that achieved their destinations with an economy of mileage. One of Van Horne's first tasks was to ensure that the CPR would reach Pacific tidewater by the shortest possible route.

He had not yet met George Stephen, but he had encountered Major A. B. Rogers, "the Railway Pathfinder," a gnarled little whippersnapper of a man, notorious for the length of his white Dundreary whiskers, his astonishing profanity, and his apparent ability to exist for days on little more than hardtack. After a summer in the mountains, Rogers (though he harbored some secret doubts) had decided to announce that the Kicking Horse Pass in the Rockies was feasible. In the second week in January, 1882, he and Van Horne went to Montreal to meet Stephen, Duncan McIntyre, and Richard B. Angus to discuss the matter.

The meeting took place on January 13 and resulted in two major decisions. The first was communicated to the press by Van Horne himself, with characteristic bluntness.

"We have changed the point," he said, "at which the road will enter the Rockies." The Kicking Horse Pass, still unsurveyed, had officially been chosen, confirming the tentative decision of the previous year. Although, as the *Globe* pointed out, only the Dominion government could "change the point," it had in fact been changed almost without that authority.

The second decision was that there would be a change of route between Lake Nipissing, the official start of the railway, and Fort William, to allow the line to hug the shore of Lake Superior, something Stephen had suggested to Macdonald months before. In addition, a branch line contemplated from Lake Nipissing to Sault Ste Marie would be greatly shortened, placing the Sault virtually on the main line, a change that caused some lengthening of the road.

This announcement was significant because it underlined the company's intention of proceeding with the Lake Superior section. Up to that point, several of the directors—certainly James J. Hill and his friend John S. Kennedy, the New York banker—had not contemplated building the line across the Pre-Cambrian Shield. Their plan was to divert it from Callander Junction, on Lake Nipissing, by way of the Sault, to join up with a branch of Hill's road, the St. Paul, Minneapolis and Manitoba, in which Stephen, Donald Smith, Angus, and Kennedy were all leading shareholders.

From a business point of view, the plan made great sense. Had it been adopted, it is conceivable that the CPR might have become part of the railway empire that the ambitious Hill was constructing—a Canadian feeder line for the Great Northern, which was to grow out of the original St. Paul railway.

It is probable that Stephen himself felt originally that the Sault branch would for many years carry Canadian passengers and freight south of the Shield through American territory into Manitoba and thence west before any all-Canadian line could be successfully undertaken. But by 1881, Stephen had changed his mind and he now had an ally in Van Horne, who helped to swing the issue in Montreal. The new general manager became that year the most trenchant advocate the Lake Superior line had. His railway sense rebelled against a connection with another railroad. He wanted a through line, independent of local traffic; and there is little doubt that he saw more clearly than the others the consequences to the CPR of linking up with Hill's road. The railway would become Hill's railway and there was no room in one company for two practical railway men as ambitious and as strong-minded as

Jim Hill and W. C. Van Horne. It was the start of a memorable antagonism. When Hill heard of Van Horne's opposition to his plan, he burst out that he would get even with him "if I have to go to Hell for it and shovel coal."

No doubt Hill ruefully recalled his advice to Stephen that Van Horne would take all the authority he could. The new general manager was a man of towering ambition whose love of power had its roots in his childhood and youth. At the age of eighteen, he had breathlessly watched the arrival of the general superintendent of the Michigan Central—an awesome figure to a young telegraph operator—coming forward to meet his assistants with, as he later put it, "that bearing of dignity and importance which consciously or unconsciously attends the great majority of men who have long been accustomed to command." When the "mighty man," as Van Horne called him, moved away, the youth walked around the official car and gazed on it with awe. He found himself wondering if he might not someday attain the same rank and travel about in a private car of his own. "The glories of it, the pride of it, the salary pertaining to it, all that moved me deeply," he told his grandson many years later, "and I made up my mind then and there that I would reach it." He did, in just ten years; at twenty-eight he became the youngest railway superintendent in the world.

To achieve that end he had "avoided every path however attractive that did not lead in its direction." Now, with a new railway in his grasp —the longest in the world and potentially one of the mightiest—he had no intention of sharing his power with any man.

He could get along quite easily with George Stephen, for Stephen was a financier, not a railroad man. Stephen had been persuaded to head the CPR on the condition that he was to have nothing to do with the actual building of the line. With the advent of Van Horne, Hill's influence began to fade. Van Horne would build the road; Stephen would look after the money.

The two men hit it off from the beginning, though their backgrounds were dissimilar. Stephen, the Highland Scot with the mathematician's brain, was single-minded in his interests, passionate in his loyalties and hatreds. The stocky Van Horne was a mixture of Dutch, French, and German; in his drive and hustle he was the epitome of the American businessman so despised by Canadian merchants and politicians. Macdonald, in fact, once called him "that sharp Yankee." He had already rubbed his subordinates in Winnipeg the wrong way. On the very day he arrived in Montreal, the *Globe* published a rumor that he did not like his new position and that the Chicago, Milwaukee and St. Paul was holding his old post open for him. His cronies, hearing of the chill in Winnipeg, urged him to leave his crusty colleagues to "build their own road and come back here to your friends."

But Van Horne was not a man to quit something he had scarcely tackled. There was a quality of enthusiasm about him that Stephen must have admired, for Stephen had it too. When Stephen threw himself into a project he went all the way; so did Van Horne. Once he became general manager of the CPR, he was a Canadian railwayman through and through. The difference was that Van Horne, unlike Stephen, seemed able to switch from one pursuit to another and make himself master of all of them.

He threw himself into half a dozen hobbies. As a gardener he thought nothing of traveling for miles to seek out and dig his own leaf mold for roses. He studied fertilizers and soil mixes and bred new varieties—a triple trumpet flower, for example, and a perfect hyacinth. As an amateur geologist he was not content to pore over the works of Louis Agassiz; he must meet the great man himself and correspond with him; he must discover and name new trilobites and brachiopods. Old railway men working in quarries along any line of road with which Van Horne was connected knew that he was a sure market for fossils; the slightest hint of a discovery would send him speeding toward the source with his hammer and sample box. He carried his rock collection about with him as other men carried a dispatch case.

Like Stephen, Van Horne had been raised in poverty, born literally in an Illinois log cabin. Like Stephen, he revered his mother, "a noble woman, courageous and resourceful." His father had died when he was eleven; at fourteen he had been forced to leave school to support his family. Again like Stephen, he had worked hard all his life to achieve his ambitions. In his ten-year drive to the top he had never known a day or even an evening off. When others sought respite, the young Van Horne cheerfully assumed the burden of their tasks; that was how he learned so much about railways, haunting the repair shops, mastering the use of every tool, watching the engineers building bridges, learning line repairs from trackmen and section hands, studying accounting and figures.

As a train dispatcher in Alton, Illinois, Van Horne's official workday was twelve hours, but when it was over he did not go home; instead, he lurked about the yards, shops, and offices, soaking up the railroad business. He was convinced that "an object can usually be attained through persistence and steadiness of aim," and in all his activities— from tracklaying to poker—he held fast to that credo.

Van Horne had been in office only one month and was still in Montreal when he fired General Rosser, the courtly and popular chief engineer of the western division of the company. Long before he came to Canada, the new general manager had cultivated the reputation of being able to smoke out incompetence, dissent, and dishonesty in an almost supernatural fashion. A good deal of this sprang from his ability to read a telegraph key and thus listen in to the gossip and sometimes disgruntled small talk that clattered over the wires and into the railway offices through which he wandered. On one occasion he discovered by eavesdropping on a key that a group of trainmen had appropriated the cushions from a first-class passenger car and were making themselves comfortable in the baggage car playing poker. When Van Horne reached a station farther down the line, he shot off a message that the cushions were to be returned and that poker playing was not allowed on CPR time. (He clearly did not include himself and his cronies.) For all their lives the men thus caught in the act were mystified as to how the general manager found them out.

But it required no such arcane ability to learn that Rosser was using inside knowledge of future railway locations to speculate in real estate; he appeared to regard it as part of the compensation for the job.

In January, Van Horne came across a letter in which the general had revealed to a railway contractor, John Stewart, the exact location of the terminus of the CPR's Pembina Mountain branch. This was valuable and privileged information. On February 1, Van Horne wired to Rosser that he had seen the letter and on account of his "unwarranted and unauthorized action on this and other matters" he was notifying him that his services were no longer required.

Rosser was not an easy man to dismiss. The wire had come at an extremely awkward time. He was about to leave for the western foothills on an ambitious twelve-hundred-mile reconnaissance, which had already received considerable publicity. In making this "difficult and hazardous journey," Rosser told the newspapers, he and his assistant would be provided with Arctic outfits, such as rabbitskin robes and Eskimo clothing, "prepared to resist any eccentricity of the season and the high latitude." They planned to cover forty-five miles a day, using Husky dogs "with wolf blood in their veins" hitched Eskimo fashion eight to a sled, each team pulling eight hundred pounds.

This romantic odyssey, which would have provided the chief engineer with priceless information about the future location of western townsites, was quashed by Van Horne's peremptory telegram. Rosser was forced to postpone his journey. He rushed to St. Paul, where he planned to intercept Van Horne, who was returning from Montreal. Meanwhile he denied the inevitable rumors.

But matters could not be adjusted. In Van Horne, Rosser was up against an unyielding obstacle. The two met on February 10; Rosser asked the general manager to reconsider; Van Horne gave him a blunt "No." He added that he was not disposed to do anything that would unnecessarily injure the reputation of the old cavalryman; on reaching Winnipeg, Rosser would be allowed to resign. Rosser did so on February 13, asking that his resignation take effect March 10. Again, Van Horne was blunt: he wanted him out immediately, with his desk cleared, that very day. Indeed, he had already replaced him temporarily with his wife's cousin, Samuel B. Reed of Joliet, Illinois.

Rosser's dismissal was followed shortly afterward by that of his entire engineering staff. On March 13, a fire destroyed the new Bank of Montreal building, in which the CPR had its offices. During the transfer of some of the engineering department's documents to temporary quarters in the Knox Church, it was discovered that some were missing. These included plans and profiles of the contemplated westward route of the railway. Van Horne told Reed to find the leak, and if he could not, to fire the whole staff on the spot. At the same time, Reed made an accusation against his predecessor, charging that Rosser, "by falsely pretending that he was acting for the C.P.R.," had fraudulently obtained the profiles of the line extending all the way to Calgary.

In the end, the CPR dropped the case. When it came to court on June 1, the company's solicitors declined to appear and Rosser was acquitted. That might have been the end of the matter had Rosser not accidentally encountered Van Horne on a hot July evening in the Manitoba Club. Van Horne was no man to back away from any encounter— as a child in Joliet he had taken on every boy in school. In the Winnipeg *Sun*'s spirited account of the affair, "their slumbering anger broke out in words, and the words would have ended in more than blows had it not been for the interference of a couple of peacemakers." Winnipeg, in fact, almost witnessed its only Western-style gun fight. Rosser and Van Horne both drew pistols, and a serious battle was averted only when "the better counsels of cooler heads prevailed, and the belligerents were separated before their passions were cooled in gore."

2 · *Five hundred miles of steel*

WHEN VAN HORNE MET THE CPR DIRECtors in Montreal, he was able to convince them that he could lay five hundred miles of track during the 1882 season. That was what Stephen wanted to hear: he had already told Macdonald that the company was planning to finish the railway in half the ten-year period allowed by the

contract. It was, indeed, essential that the through line get into operation as swiftly as possible, since for many years there would be very
little local traffic. The CPR would stand or fall on its transcontinental
trade—shipments such as silk, for example, that demanded speedy
dispatch. The Canadian road was far shorter than any United States
transcontinental route—the company expected to have a tremendous
advantage in that respect—but it could not turn a dollar of profit on
its through line until the last spike was driven.

Van Horne's announcement was greeted with considerable skepticism. He seemed to be promising the impossible, but he gave no hint
that he was embarked on anything remarkable. Back in Winnipeg in
mid-February, 1882, he told Secretan that he wanted "the shortest commercial line" between Winnipeg and the Pacific Coast. He added that
he would not only lay five hundred miles of track that summer but
would also have trains running over it by fall. Secretan, a great, bulky
Englishman with a waxed mustache, took a rather lofty view toward
his fellow men. He ventured a modicum of doubt, whereupon Van
Horne declared that nothing was impossible; all he wanted his engineers
to do was to show him the road; if Secretan could not do that, then
he would have his scalp.

The general manager did not care much for engineers. He resented,
as Secretan noted, their professional interference; it clashed with his
own dictatorship. "If I could only teach a section man to run a transit,"
he once remarked, "I wouldn't have a single damned engineer on the
road." Secretan himself, as his memoirs reveal, was as snobbish an
engineer as ever took a level; but he admired Van Horne, "the most
versatile man I have ever encountered."

Secretan noticed that as Van Horne talked he had a habit of making
sketches on blotting pads, "well worth framing," which he tore up as
fast as he drew them. All his life, since he had been old enough to
handle a slate, the artist in Van Horne had struggled to be released;
indeed, in another age and another climate the artist might have won
out over the hardheaded man of action. As a very small boy, unable
to afford paper, he had covered the whitewashed walls of his house with
drawings. One of the most telling incidents in his biography is the story
of how he fell so much in love with Edward and Charles Henry Hitch-
cock's *Elementary Geology* that he determined to use his copyist's skill
to make it his own. Night after night by candlelight the determined
child copied the book in ink onto sheets of foolscap—copied every page,
every note, and every picture right down to the index. It did great things
for him, as he later pointed out: "It taught me how much could be
accomplished by application; it improved my handwriting; it taught me

the construction of English sentences; and it helped my drawing materially. And I never had to refer to the book again."

In later life, Van Horne the amateur painter attacked great canvases as he attacked the building of the railway—with huge brushes and considerable spontaneity; he believed that work was best done when it was done as rapidly as possible. Not surprisingly, his art was meticulously literal. His drawings were so real that they could be, and sometimes were, mistaken for actual engravings by other artists. Once he managed to purloin a copy of *Harper's Weekly* before it reached his mother. With great care, Van Horne transformed a series of portraits of American authors into bandits—and did his work so well that they did not appear to have been altered. His mother complained to the mystified editor about his apparent policy of desecrating the images of great Americans. The baffled illustrator, Wyatt Eaton (who was commissioned to paint Van Horne's portrait), was equally indignant when shown the same copy some years later. The issue became a collector's item.

This was the puckish side of Van Horne's nature. He was thirty-one years old when he tampered so expertly with his mother's copy of *Harper's*. A colleague described him at the time (he was about to become president of the Southern Minnesota Railroad) as grave and thoughtful: "His constant manner was that of a person preoccupied with great affairs." But behind that poker face—so useful to him in his swift climb to the top and in those all-night card games along the line of the CPR—lurked the curiosity, the high spirits, and the ingenuousness of a small boy. Thomas Shaughnessy in his valedictory of Van Horne said truly that "he possessed the splendid simplicity of grown up boyhood to the end."

His reputation as a hustling Yankee had a reverse side. It was generally held, with good reason, that he was favoring Americans— or "sour mash" as they were called—over Canadians when new employees were hired for the CPR. This was especially true in the key jobs.

It was not in Van Horne's nature, however, to take notice of such criticism. In the summer of 1882, he was doing his best to lure another American into the fold, a Milwaukee Irishman named Thomas Shaughnessy, who had once been on his staff in the United States. Van Horne needed Shaughnessy to act as quartermaster general for the vast army he intended to throw into the West once the floods subsided that spring. Shaughnessy required some persuading and did not arrive until late in the year, "a fashionably-dressed, alert young man, sporting a cane and giving general evidence of being what we call a live wire," in the words of Van Horne's private telegrapher, E. A. James.

It is an irony that from the very beginning the CPR, that most nationalistic of all Canadian enterprises, was to a very large extent managed and built by Americans. The government section in British Columbia, from Kamloops Lake to Port Moody, was contracted to an American engineer, Andrew Onderdonk, backed by a syndicate of American financiers. On the prairies another American company, Langdon and Shepard, held the prime contract. The remainder of the railway, involving the most difficult work of all—the mountain section and the section north of Lake Superior—was given to a third American concern, the North American Railway Contracting Company of New Jersey. This firm was to be paid partly in cash and partly in CPR stock; in November, 1883, after the shares tumbled on the New York exchange, the company backed out and the CPR took over construction in the mountains and across the Shield. On both these sections most of the subcontractors were Canadians, several of whom went on to become internationally famous entrepreneurs.

But in the eighties, most of the experienced railway talent was American. No major trunk line had been built in Canada since the Grand Trunk, almost thirty years before. It was natural that Van Horne, like Jim Hill before him, should employ men he knew something about and felt he could depend upon. Many of these came from the Chicago, Milwaukee and St. Paul Railroad—executives like his old colleague John Egan, who became general superintendent of the CPR's western division, or his home-town in-law from Joliet, S. B. Reed. Neither was popular with Canadians. By July, 1884, the Prime Minister himself was complaining to George Stephen about Egan's reputation for dismissing Canadians and hiring Americans. A friend, "on whose calmness of judgment I can rely," had called the western superintendent "a low down blasphemous Yankee Fenian." Macdonald reported to the president that Egan's policies in Winnipeg had, rightly or wrongly, "made the CPR so unpopular that the feeling amounts to hatred." But Van Horne stuck by his friend.

The presence of so many Americans at every level in the CPR's hierarchy was the subject of bitter complaint throughout the construction period. But the brain drain to the United States, about which Canadians had complained for more than a decade, was being partially reversed by the great project of the railroad. Many of the "sour mash" became dedicated Canadians; as someone remarked, the building of the CPR would make a Canadian out of the German Kaiser. It certainly made Canadians out of Van Horne, Shaughnessy, and Isaac Gouverneur Ogden, the company's western auditor, who, after he became vice-president, was known as the Finance King of the CPR. These men, and many lesser executives, turned their backs on their native land forever when they joined the railway. Business dictated that they must, since their chief rivals were the transcontinental Yankee lines. Shaughnessy, the policeman's son who became a baron, was an Imperialist's Imperialist, a staunch supporter of Monarch, Empire, and Nation—so British in outlook that he was offered a Cabinet post (which he declined) in the Asquith government. As for Van Horne, he was more Canadian than any Canadian. "I am a Chinese-wall protectionist," he told a reporter shortly before his death. "I don't mean merely in trade. I mean —everything. I'd keep the American idea out of this country."

But in the late spring of 1882, Van Horne was more concerned over floods than he was with "sour mash." The high water had already thrown his careful schedule off balance by postponing construction for nearly a month. The *Globe*, which seized every opportunity to belabor the Syndicate in general and Van Horne in particular, ignored the unseasonable weather and laid the blame at the feet of the general manager. On June 23, it reported that "Van Horne's men have not laid one solitary rail upon the grading done under his regime." The paper dug up "a well known track-layer who has been in the business out west for 20 years" who was quoted as saying that "the idea of Van Horne talking about laying 500 miles of track this year, after the way time has been frittered away, is preposterous," and that there was "more construction in [Alpheus] Stickney's little finger than in Van Horne's body."

Nonetheless, the general manager was making his presence felt. He was positively indefatigable, an iron man who never knew a moment's sickness and did not seem to require any sleep. Years later, when asked to reveal the secret of his stamina, he summed it all up with characteristic candor: "I eat all I can; I drink all I can; I smoke all I can and I don't give a damn for anything."

"Why do you want to go to bed?" he once asked Secretan. "It's a waste of time; besides, you don't know what's going on." He could sit up all night in a poker game and then, when seven o'clock came, rub his eyes, head for the office, and do a full day's work. He loved poker and he played it expertly. It was not a game, he would say, but an education. He enjoyed all card games and he was good at them all. James Mavor, the Toronto professor who knew him well in later years, thought this was his secret—his ability to "turn rapidly from one form of activity to another and to avoid overanxiety about any one of his enterprises."

Many colleagues were to remark upon this trait of Van Horne's. When he had done his work he was free to play games, to eat a good supper, to smoke one of his gigantic cigars, to pore over his collection of Japanese porcelains, to work with his rock specimens, or to best a colleague at billiards or chess. Chess fascinated him; he kept a set of chessmen in his private car and would challenge anyone—private secretary or merchant prince—to a game.

He loved to play and he loved to win. He was reluctant to leave any poker table when he was losing. He liked to dare his associates to duplicate the feats of memory with which he astonished acquaintances and utter strangers. His memory for obscure detail was quite remarkable and he reveled in it. Harry Armstrong, the engineer, had one experience of it that remained with him all his life. Early in 1882 Van Horne told him to substitute nine-inch discharge pipes for the seven-inchers on a water tank in order to save six minutes' time. Armstrong did not receive any nine-inch pipe before he and his fellow workers were dismissed. Two years later, when he was once again working for the CPR, he received a note from Van Horne, naming the date on which the order had gone out. "I told you to have those goosenecks made 9 inches," Van Horne wrote. "Why wasn't it done?"

By June, Van Horne had become the terror of the railway, a kind of superman who had an uncanny habit of always turning up just when things went wrong. The *Sun*'s uninhibited columnist, R. K. Kerrighan, who signed himself "The Dervish Khan, the Screamer of Qu'Appelle," had been dispatched to Flat Creek—or Flat Krick, as he invariably called it—the transitory community at the end of track. There he watched, with a mixture of awe and amusement, the descent of Van Horne upon the unsuspecting settlement:

"The trains run in a kind of go-as-you-please style that is anything but refreshing to the general manager. But when Manager Van Horne strikes the town there is a shaking up of old bones. He cometh in like a blizzard and he goeth out like a lantern. He is the terror of Flat Krick. He shakes them up like an earthquake, and they are as frightened of him as if he were the old Nick himself. Yet Van Horne is calm and harmless looking. So is a she mule, and so is a buzz saw. You don't know their true inwardness till you go up and feel of them. To see Van Horne get out of the car and go softly up the platform, you would think he was an evangelist on his way west to preach temperance to the Mounted Police. But you are soon undeceived. If you are within hearing distance you will have more fun than you ever had in your life before. He cuffs the first official he comes to just to get his hand in and leads the next one out by the ear, and pointing eastward informs him the walking is good as far as St. Paul. To see the rest hunt their holes and commence scribbling for dear life is a terror. Van Horne wants to know. He is that kind of man. He wants to know why this was not done and why this was done. If the answers are not satisfactory there is a dark and bloody tragedy enacted right there. During each act all the characters are killed off and in the last scene the heavy villain is filled with dynamite, struck with a hammer, and by the time he has knocked a hole plumb through the sky, and the smoke has cleared away, Van Horne has discharged all the officials and hired them over again at lower figures."

As a Van Horne admirer, the Wisconsin banker and railway president Jason Easton, remarked, "Van Horne was one of the most considerate and even-tempered of men, but when an explosion came it was magnificent." Yet he rather enjoyed it when somebody stood up to him. In June he finally managed to secure the services of Michael Haney as superintendent of both the Pembina Branch and the Rat Portage divisions, both of them originally built under government contract. It was inevitable that sooner or later Haney and Van Horne would clash.

Haney had already tangled with Van Horne's western superintendent, John Egan, and won. Egan, on an inspection tour, discovered what he considered to be a shortage of railroad ties; since Haney was in charge of the delivery of construction supplies, he sent him a memorandum telling him to ship every tie available and in the future to attend to his work more closely. The irate Haney went straight to Winnipeg, gathered up every unemployed man he could find around town, and shipped them out along the line on flatcars. At every point where spare ties were available, Haney and his crew loaded them onto the cars and moved forward. In two days, Haney had loaded one hundred and forty cars and blocked every siding between Rat Portage and the end of track. A heated wire arrived: "What in hell are you doing?" Back came Haney's laconic answer: "Filling orders, send more flat cars and will double quantity in 24 hours." It was the last time the chastened Egan sent Haney any kind of blanket instruction.

Haney was in the Winnipeg freight yard one day when his secretary came hustling down the track to warn him that Van Horne was on the warpath.

"He's hot enough to melt the rails," Haney was told. "If you've got any friends or relatives at home who are fond of you I'd advise you to hunt a cyclone cellar."

As Haney recalled it many years later, he was feeling pretty hot himself at the time. Everything seemed to have gone wrong that day. Jobs had been held up by a shortage of materials. He was, as he put it, in a humor to look for somebody with trouble. Instead of getting out of Van Horne's way, he stalked resolutely down the yards to meet him.

Van Horne began an exhaustive recitation of the system's defects, punctuating his remarks with a colorful selection of profanity. Haney waited until the general manager stopped for breath.

"Mr. Van Horne," he said finally, "everything you say is true and if you claimed it was twice as bad as you have, it would still be true. I'm ready to agree with you there but I'd like to say this: Of all the spavined, one-horse, rottenly equipped, bad managed, badly run, headless and heedless thing for people to call a railroad, this is the worst. You can't get anyone who knows anything about anything. You can't get materials and if you could it wouldn't do you any good because you couldn't get them where you wanted them."

Haney followed up this outburst with a list of countercomplaints far more complete than Van Horne's, since he was in closer touch with the work. His tirade made Van Horne's explosion "sound like a drawing room conversation." The general manager waited patiently as Haney unleashed his torrent of grievances; by the time Haney had finished he was grinning.

"That's all right, Haney, I guess we understand one another," he said. "Let's get to work."

3 · *End of Track*

THE CONTRACT TO BUILD THE PRAIRIE section of the Canadian Pacific Railway was probably the largest of its kind ever undertaken. Tenders were called for in the third week of January, 1882, and the prize was awarded the following month to the partnership of General R. B. Langdon of Minneapolis, a onetime stonemason of Scottish heritage, and D. C. Shepard of St. Paul, a former engineer who had helped build the Chicago, Milwaukee and St. Paul Railroad. The firm undertook to build six hundred and seventy-five miles of railroad across the plains from the end of track at Flat Creek to Fort Calgary on the Bow River. This was a formidable task—just fifteen miles short of the entire length of the Central Pacific. In spite of the *Globe*'s remarks about sour mashers, it is probable that no Canadian company existed that could tackle a job of such magnitude.

Shepard, an extremely shrewd contractor and an old friend of James J. Hill's, was aware of this. Hill knew it too, but he also felt that Shepard, operating from a position of strength, had set his bid unreasonably high.

A day or so after Shepard and his partner had submitted their bid he called, according to habit, at Hill's office. Lying face down on the desk, where he could not fail to notice it, was a telegraph form. Ostensibly it contained a lower bid from a large firm of contractors in the Middle West. Hill made an excuse to leave his office. When he returned a few minutes later, Shepard, apparently unconcerned, was seated in the same position. There was some small talk and then Shepard took his leave. But the next day he and Langdon submitted a revised bid which was somewhat lower than the one in the telegram—a telegram that Hill, of course, had concocted. The new terms suited Hill, who accepted them on behalf of the CPR. In later years he used to joke about the incident with Shepard, who never betrayed by so much as a lifted eyebrow that he knew what Hill was talking about.

On the day after the contract was signed, Langdon and Shepard advertised for three thousand men and four thousand horses. The job they faced was staggering: it would require no fewer than three hundred subcontractors. Between Flat Creek and Fort Calgary the partners would have to move ten million cubic yards of earth. They would have to haul every stick of timber, every rail, fishplate, and spike, all the pilings used for bridge construction, and all the food and provisions for 7,600 men and 1,700 teams of horses across the naked prairie for hundreds of miles. Just to feed the horses it would be necessary to distribute four thousand bushels of oats every day along one hundred and fifty miles of track. It was no wonder that Van Horne's boast about building five hundred miles in a single season was openly derided.

Winnipeg was transformed early in that spring of 1882 into a gigantic supply depot. Stone began to pour in from every available quarry, railroad ties from the Lake of the Woods, lumber from Minnesota, and rails from England and from the Krupp works in Germany. Since the St. Lawrence would still be frozen well into the construction season, Van Horne had the steel shipped to New York and New Orleans and dispatched to Manitoba by way of St. Paul. Whole trainloads of material destined for the Canadian North West were constantly passing through American cities, where hundreds of checkers reported on them daily so that the exact moment of their arrival could be plotted. As fast as the supplies arrived they were hauled away to the end of the track. Long trains loaded with rails, ties, fishplates, and provisions rattled westward to Flat Creek, dumped their loads, and returned empty.

No newly completed line of steel had ever known such activity in the first year of its construction.

The floods of April put a halt to all this activity. Almost all work on the railway came to a standstill. Flat Creek, which seemed to be "the repository of more railway material than the whole world contained," was a quagmire. Tents of every shape and size, some brand new, some filthy and tattered, stretched out in all directions on a gloomy expanse of swamp. For any but the strongest, the community could be a death trap. There was no place to sleep and the food was of the very worst and sometimes nonexistent. Men were "herded together like rats in a hole, [and] . . . given food which a well kept dog wouldn't eat." Perhaps fortunately, Flat Creek had a brief life. When the railroad blockade ended and the tracks began to creep west once more to the newer community of Broadview, the town virtually disappeared. Even the name was changed to the pleasanter one of Oak Lake.

By the time the floods ended, scores of would-be homesteaders were ready to quit the North West. In Brandon, building was at a standstill because the CPR was rushing all available construction materials to the front; even before the floods began, hundreds of men were idle. The railway yards "looked like a great country fair." Trunks were piled along the grade like cordwood, as high as men could throw them, but many of their owners were already trying to sell their outfits and leave.

In late May a blizzard struck, destroying scores of tents and causing great suffering. Fuel was at such a premium that men resorted to stealing lumber, piece by piece, while others held them off at gunpoint. People began to tell each other that it would be better to leave the land to the Indians."'Why should we take such a country away from them?' was heard on all sides." The first passenger train to leave Brandon for Winnipeg after the flood pulled three coaches loaded to the doors with men and women quitting the North West, never to return.

At last the waters subsided, the blizzards ended, and the sun appeared to warm the frigid plains. The prairie evenings grew mellower and soon the sweet incense of the wolf willow drifted in from the ponds and marshes to mingle with the more familiar odors of salt pork, tamarack ties, wood smoke, and human sweat. The early spring blossoms—wild pansies, strawberries, and purple pasqueflower—began to poke their tiny faces between the brittle grasses. Then, as a flush of new green spread over the land, the oxcarts started west again until they were strung out by the hundreds ahead of the advancing line of steel.

As soon as the waters ebbed, a mountain of supplies descended upon Winnipeg. With the freight came people. By June, three thousand immigrants were under canvas in Winnipeg, all buoyed up by the expectation of an entirely new life on the Canadian prairies.

Though few people believed it would be possible for the CPR to achieve its season's goal or anything close to it, Van Horne was immovable. The general manager made it clear that he would cancel the contract if Langdon and Shepard did not live up to their obligations.

The contractors responded by increasing their army of men and horses, by adding an extra shift to the track laying, and by lengthening the total workday from eleven hours to fifteen. "The iron now is going down just as fast as it can be pulled from the cars," Shepard announced, "We shall show a record at track-laying which has never been surpassed on this continent."

There followed a whirlwind of construction that was, in the words of the *Quarterly Review*, "absolutely without parallel in railway annals." The grade, winding snakelike across the plains, moved so swiftly that Secretan and his surveyors were hard put to stay ahead. Sometimes, indeed, they were awakened at night by the rumble of giant scrapers being dragged past their tents. "We had never seen the like in Canada before," Secretan wrote.

The prairie section of the CPR was built telescopically from a single base—a feat that a leading London journal, commenting on a projected British road in the Sudan, declared to be impossible. Winnipeg was the anchor point: from there the steel would stretch for a thousand miles into the mountains; there would be no supply line for the railway builders other than the rails themselves.

The previous year's operations had seen small knots of men with loaded handcars, pushing the track forward at about three-quarters of a mile a day. Van Horne determined to move at five times that speed. This would necessitate the kind of timing that divisional commanders require of troops in the field when an assault is launched. Van Horne's army worked that summer with a military precision that astonished all who witnessed it. "Clockwork" was the adjective used over and over again to describe the track-laying technique.

The pulse of the operation was at "End of Track," that unique community that never stayed in one place for more than a few hours at a time. The nerve center of End of Track was the line of boarding cars —eight or nine of them, each three stories high—that housed the track-laying crews. The ground floors of these cars served as offices, dining rooms, kitchens, and berths for the contractors and company officials; the two stories above were dormitories. Sometimes there were even tents pitched on the roofs. These huge cars formed part of a long train which contained smaller office cars for executives, a cooking car, freight cars loaded with track materials, shops on wheels, and, on occasion, the private car of the general manager himself. Van Horne was continually to be found at End of Track, spinning yarns with the workmen, sketching buffalo skulls, organizing foot races and target shooting at night, and bumping over the prairie in a buckboard inspecting the grade. Every day some sixty-five carloads of railroad supplies, each carload weighing eighteen tons, were dumped at End of Track. Most of these supplies had been carried an average of a thousand miles before reaching their destination.

To a casual visitor's first glance the scene was chaotic: cars constantly being coupled and uncoupled, locomotives shunting back and forth pushing and pulling loads of various lengths, little handcars rattling up and down the half-completed track at the front, teams of horses and mules dragging loaded wagons forward on each side of the main line—and tents constantly rising like puffballs and vanishing again as the whole unwieldy apparatus rolled steadily toward the Rockies.

The apparent anarchy was illusory, for the organization was meticulous, down to the last railway spike. Each morning two construction trains set out from the supply yards, far in the rear, for End of Track. Each was loaded with the exact number of rails, ties, spikes, fishplates, and telegraph poles required for half a mile of railway. One train was held in reserve on a siding about six miles to the rear; the other moved directly to the front where the track-laying gang of three hundred men and seventy horses was waiting for it.

The tracklayers worked like a drill team. "It was beautiful to watch them gradually coming near," one observer wrote, ". . . each man in his place knowing exactly his work and doing it at the right time and in the right way. Onward they come, pass on, and leave the wondering spectator slowly behind whilst he is still engrossed with the wonderful sight."

The ties were unloaded first, on either side of the track, to be picked up by the waiting wagons and mule teams—thirty ties to a wagon —then hauled forward and dropped all the way along the graded embankment for exactly half a mile. Two men with marked rods were standing by, and as the ties were thrown out they laid them across the grade, exactly two feet apart from center to center. Right behind the teams came a little truck hauled by two horses, one on each side of the grade, and loaded with rails, fishplates, and spikes. Six men marched on each side of the track, and when they reached the far end of the last pair of newly laid rails, each crew seized a rail among them and threw it into exact position. Two more men gauged these two rails to make sure they were correctly aligned. Four men followed with spikes, placing one in each of the four ends of the rails. Four others screwed in the fishplates and another four followed with crowbars to raise the ties while the spikes were being hammered in. All worked in a kind of rhythm, each man directly opposite his partner on each separate rail. More men followed with hammers and spikes to make the rails secure, but by this time the truck had already moved forward, passing over the newly laid rails before the job was complete. W. Henry Barneby, an Englishman who watched this operation when it had reached a peak of sophistication, noted that "all the men must keep in their places and move on ahead, otherwise they will be caught up by those behind them."

As each construction train dumped its half mile of supplies at End of Track, it moved back to the nearest siding to be replaced by the reserve train. There was no time lost. As the track unfolded, the boarding cars were nudged ahead constantly by the construction-train locomotive so that no energy would be wasted by the navvies in reaching their moving mess halls and dormitories.

The operation was strung out for hundreds of miles across the open prairie. Up ahead were the survey camps, followed by the grading gangs and the bridge builders. Far to the rear were other thousands—saddlers and carpenters, cooks and tailors, shoemakers, blacksmiths, doctors, and provisioners. Vast material yards were established at hundred-mile intervals between Winnipeg and End of Track. The supply trains moved west on schedule, unloading thousands of tons of goods at the yards; here the material was sorted daily into train lots and dispatched—as many as eight trains a day—to the front.

The organization left nothing to chance. In case the track laying should proceed faster than expected, reserves of supplies were held on the sidings and in the yards themselves. There were always rails available for three hundred miles and fastenings for five hundred, all within one hundred miles of End of Track. When the steel moved past the hundred-mile point, the yards moved too. An entire community of office workers, sorters, dispatchers, trainmen, laborers, and often their families as well could be transported a hundred miles in a single night without the loss of an hour's work, because the houses were all portable and could be fitted easily on flatcars.

Right behind the track-laying gang came the telegraph teams. The telegraphers camped in tents and moved their gear forward every afternoon on handcars. The construction trains that brought half a mile of track supplies also brought half a mile's worth of poles, wires, and insulators to the front. One hour after the day's track was laid, End of Track was in telegraphic communication with the outside world.

Far out on the barren plains, miles to the west of End of Track, were the bridging teams, grading units, and surveyors, all driven forward by the knowledge that the tracklayers were pressing hard behind them. Although the work was broken down into subcontracts, the organization was so arranged that no weak link could hold up construction. The head contractor had a flying wing of his own men standing by, prepared to complete immediately any work that seemed unlikely to be ready in time for the "ironing" of the track. This work was, of course, charged against the subcontractors; it served to force the pace. When the flying wing was not needed for this purpose, it was employed in completing the ballasting of the line, which was laid so rapidly that it was necessary to go over it again with great care. In addition, the flying wing built the sidings which were required at six-mile intervals across the prairies.

The grading was accomplished by immense scrapers pulled by teams of horses. Their task was to build an embankment for the railway four feet above the prairie and to ditch it for twenty yards on either side. This was more than the original contract had called for; but Van Horne, who always looked ahead, knew that in the long run a solidly built line—the standards here exceeded those of the Union Pacific—would pay off. At that height the rails would be protected from blizzards, and costly delays from snow blockage would be avoided.

The bridgers worked in two gangs, one by day and one by night. Every sliver of bridging had to be brought from Rat Portage, one hundred and forty miles east of Winnipeg, or from Minnesota; for this reason the bridge builders were seldom more than ten miles ahead of the advancing steel. The timbers were unloaded as close to End of Track as possible and generally at night so as not to interfere with other work. "Sometimes," one eyewitness reported, "not a stick of timber nor any preparation for work could be seen one day, the next would show two or three spans of a nicely finished bridge. Twenty-four hours afterwards the rails would be laid, and trains working."

"The history of the world offers no such evidence of push as the work of this year has done," R. B. Conkey, Langdon and Shepard's general manager, declared at Winnipeg in August. "Sherman's march to the sea was nothing to it. When the road is completed there will be nothing in history to compare with it."

The nation was electrified by the speed with which the railroad was being forced across the plains. One man on the scene noted that it seemed to move as fast as the oxcarts of the settlers who were following along beside the tracks. Alex Stavely Hill, a visiting British Member of Parliament, going in for lunch on one of the boarding cars around eleven one morning, noted, on emerging at two that afternoon, that a wagon that had been parked beside the car was already two miles to the rear. William White, homesteading near Pile o' Bones Creek, left his camp one morning to bring in wood from a thicket six miles away. When he departed there was no sign of construction for two miles to the east. When he returned, he and his companions had to cross a newly completed track.

The North West of Canada, once so haunting and so mysterious, was being transformed by the onslaught of the rails. A single incident illuminates that change: a young homesteader and his sweetheart eloped successfully in the face of parental obduracy by commandeering a handcar and speeding toward Winnipeg along the line of steel, thus throwing off their pursuers.

One railway employee, A. C. Forster Boulton, who came from a notable Toronto family, wrote that the progress of construction was so swift that antelope and other game migrating north were cut off on their return that fall by the lines of rails and telegraph posts, "and terrified by the sight . . . gathered in hundreds on the north side, afraid to cross it." It was probably the last summer in which herds of buffalo and antelope freely roamed the prairie.

Father Albert Lacombe, the voyageur priest who had served his time as chaplain to the navvies of Rat Portage and was now back among his beloved Blackfoot nation, watched the approach of the rails with both sadness and resignation:

"I would look in silence at the road coming on—like a band of wild geese in the sky—cutting its way through the prairies; opening up the great country we thought would be ours for years. Like a vision I could see it driving my poor Indians before it, and spreading out behind it the farms, the towns and cities. . . . No one who has not lived in the west since the Old-Times can realize what is due to that road—that C.P.R. It was Magic—like the mirage on the prairies, changing the face of the whole country."

The Indians also watched in silence as the steel cut through their hunting grounds. They would arrive suddenly, as if from nowhere, squat on their haunches in double rows, and take in the scene with only the occasional surprised grunt. To them the engines were "fire wagons." They were a little puzzled by the lack of white squaws and papooses. Why would men want to work in a wilderness without women and children? But if they realized that their wild, free existence was at an end they gave no sign.

Onward the track moved, cutting the plains in two. It moved through a land of geese, snipe, and wild ducks, whose eggs were prized by those who took the trouble to search them out. It moved through a land fragrant in the soft evenings with the scent of willow and balsam. It cut across acres of yellow daisies, tiger lilies, purple sage, and briar rose. It bisected pastures of tall buffalo grass and skirted green hay meadows which in the spring were shallow ponds. As it traveled westward it pushed through a country of memories and old bones—furrowed trails fashioned decades before by thousands of bison moving in single file toward the water, vast fields of gray and withered herbage, dead lakes rimmed with telltale crusts of alkali. Day by day it crept toward the horizon, where, against the gold of the sunset, flocks of fluttering wildfowl, disturbed by the clamor of the invaders, could be seen in silhouette; or where sometimes a single Indian, galloping at full speed in the distance, became no more than a speck crawling along the rim of the prairie. This had been the Great Lone Land, unfenced and unbridged, which explorers like Palliser, Butler, and Grant had described as if it were on the dark side of the moon. The line of steel made Butler's phrase obsolete, for the land would never again be lonely. All that summer it reverberated with the clang of sledge and anvil, the snorting of horses and mules, the hoarse puffing of great engines, the bellowing of section bosses, the curses of thousands of sweating men, and the universal song of the railroad work gangs: "Drill, Ye Tarriers, Drill!"

History was being made, but few had time to note that fact. Beecham Trotter was to write, a little sheepishly, that "few, if any of us were historically minded enough to think of the interest that might attach to a running diary of what was seen, and said, and done, from day to day." Nor did William Oliver (a future mayor of Lethbridge, Alberta) in his oxcart heading west, almost always in sight of the railway grade, watching idly the straining mules and men, consider the significance of what he saw: "It never came to my mind in watching the building of the railway . . . that in the next fifty years it would play so important a part in the commerce of the country and in fact of the world. . . . We were more interested in our own affairs and the prospects of a future home."

But the spectacle of the steel-laying gangs remained in Oliver's memory all his life. They were "a sight never to be forgotten. . . . Ties to the Irish and Swede giants were like toothpicks, steel rails like crowbars. They were soon gone and out of sight."

They were a mixed lot, these railroad navvies. Charles Alfred Peyton, walking down the track and looking for work, came upon a gang of Italians who "looked like guys who would cut your throat for a dime." A few miles farther on, however, he joined a team of young Englishmen, "a very nice bunch of lads," and went to work for $1.25

a day. Stavely Hill, who was a barrister, encountered a man ploughing, "throwing almost as much strength from himself into his work as he was getting out of his horses." It developed that he was a former doctor. That night, the man who cooked his dinner in the boarding car turned out to be a solicitor's clerk who had once visited his London chambers with briefs.

R. K. Kerrighan was introduced to one track-laying gang by a section boss who identified some of them: "Do you see that person yonder, that man can read and write Greek and is one of the most profound scholars on the continent; that man next him was once one of the foremost surgeons in Montreal, and that man next him was at one time the beloved pastor of one of the largest congregations in Chicago."

The general run of railroad navvies was far rougher. One eastern reporter found them "ill-bred and offensive in their manners, applying the most obscene epithets to every passerby, jostling with their heavy teams every traveller they meet upon the trail, and in all respects making themselves as disagreeable as they know how to be. In their personal habits they are much more uncleanly than the poorest and most degraded of Indians, and in all respects they fairly represent the class from which they were drawn, that is, the scum and offscourings of the filthiest slums of Chicago and other western cities."

They were paid between $2 and $2.50 a day, which were good wages for the era, and often enough after they had made a little money they quit. Of the twenty-eight men who left Winnipeg in the spring in Beecham Trotter's telegraph gang, only half a dozen remained by fall. Swedes who had learned how to lay track in the old country were highly prized. One Broadview pioneer claimed that "if they were given enough liquor they could lay two or three miles of tracks a day." Liquor, being prohibited by law in the North West, was hard but not impossible to get; it existed in private caches all along the line. "If I were not a total abstinence man," the Khan wrote in his *Sun* column, "I could get more whiskey in Flat Creek this blessed minute than would float this pork barrel on which I pen these immortal lines from here to Hong Kong." No law, the Khan believed, would succeed in driving the whiskey peddlers away. Not even the threat of execution or torture with red-hot irons would do it. "Inside of ten hours a daredevil would be selling budge on the sly." The liquor itself was described as "a mixture of blue ruin, chain lightning, strychnine, the curse of God and old rye."

As autumn approached, the pace of the railway quickened still more. At the end of August one of the superbly drilled crews of Donald

Grant, the seven-foot-tall track boss, managed to lay four and a half miles of steel in a single day. Next day they beat their own record and laid five miles. It was all horribly expensive, as a worried Stephen reported to Macdonald in September: "This so called prairie section is not a prairie at all in the sense that the Red River valley is a prairie. The country west of Portage la Prairie is broken rolling country, and the amount of work on our road bed is more than double what it would have been had it run along the valley. In short the road . . . is costing us a great deal more than the subsidy and a great deal more than we expected. We are just about even with the world at the moment, but to reach this position, we have had to find 5 million dollars from our resources. *To enable me to make up my quota I had to sell my Montreal Bank stock*."

There were those who thought that Van Horne "seemed to spend money like a whole navy of drunken sailors." Actually he counted every dollar. In the interests of both speed and economy he allowed steep grades and tight curves, which he planned to eliminate once the line was operating. In the rolling country to which Stephen referred, the road in places was like a switchback; it remained that way until the end of the century.

The contractors did not reach Van Horne's goal of five hundred miles; the spring floods had frustrated his ambition. By the end of the season, however, they had laid four hundred and seventeen miles of completed railroad, built twenty-eight miles of siding, and graded another eighteen miles for the start of the following season. In addition, Van Horne had pushed the Southwestern branch line of the CPR in Manitoba a hundred miles and so could say that, in one way or another, he had achieved the aggregate he sought.

As far as the general public was concerned, he had wrought a miracle. Only the waspish *Globe* refused to be impressed. The paper, which had earlier attacked the company for the lethargy of its progress, now hit out at it for the opposite reason: "The public has nothing to gain by this breakneck speed. . . . If . . . a southerly pass had been found across the Rocky Mountains, there might be some object in making haste across the plains. But from present appearances, the entire Prairie section will be crossed long before it is positively known whether or not there is a better crossing than the Yellowhead Pass. . . . We are satisfied that the public good would have been better served if the Company had built about 200 miles only of its plains line every year, and had put some of its superfluous energy upon the Eastern Section."

There was some validity in the *Globe*'s carping. In the heart of the Rocky Mountains that summer, Major A. B. Rogers was still plagued with doubts about the feasibility of the Kicking Horse Pass as a railway route. Equally serious was the whole question of the barrier of the Selkirks. The plain truth was that Van Horne and his men had been driving steel all summer at record speed, straight at that double wall of mountains, without really being sure of how they were going to breach it.

4 · *Edgar Dewdney's new capital*

THE HONOURABLE EDGAR DEWDNEY, Lieutenant-Governor and Indian Commissioner of the North West Territories, was a handsome giant of a man. With his fringed buckskin jacket and his flaring muttonchop whiskers (which won for him the Indian name of "Whitebeard"), he made an imposing figure as he stalked about accompanied by his two gigantic Newfoundland dogs, the gift of the Marquis of Lorne. It was not difficult to spot Dewdney at a distance—he stood "like Saul, head and shoulders above most men." In the late spring of 1882 there were a good many who wanted to keep him in view: the Lieutenant-Governor had been charged with staking out the site for the new capital of the Territories. No more profitable parcel of real estate could be imagined.

Battleford had been the original capital, but Battleford was no longer on the route of the CPR. The location of the railway would determine the site of Battleford's successor—clearly the most important city between the Red River and the Bow—and, though Dewdney could recommend its site, the owners of the railway would have the final word in its selection.

For all of the winter of 1881–82, Winnipeg speculators, knowing that the seat of government was about to be changed, had been dispatching platoons of men to squat on every promising location. It is fairly clear that General Rosser himself had his eye on land profits in the vicinity of the new capital; that was one reason why the preliminary survey of the line in Saskatchewan was altered and the location moved about six miles to the south.

A likely townsite along that preliminary survey had been at the crossing of the Wascana or Pile o' Bones Creek, along whose banks the bleached bones of thousands of buffalo lay in heaps. Because water was so scarce, the riverbank seemed a probable site; there was a well-wooded area at one point; it was here that the speculators squatted and it was here that the original line crossed the creek. When the railway location was moved half a dozen miles to the south, across an absolutely treeless plain, the land sharks were left out in the cold.

Most Canadians familiar with the country felt that the only possible site for a capital city of the plains lay a few miles to the northeast near Fort Qu'Appelle in the broad, wooded valley of the Qu'Appelle River, perhaps the loveliest spot on all that sere steppe. Here were the necessary requirements for a townsite: an established community, sweet water, sheltering hills, good drainage, and timber for fuel, lumber, and shade.

The railway, however, was designed to skirt Fort Qu'Appelle. The reason given was that the steep banks of the valley would make construction difficult and costly. An equally strong motive was undoubtedly the company's policy of by-passing established communities in the interest of greater land profits.

There was another factor to be considered, although it was mere rumor at the time. Governor Dewdney had a secret interest in the land surrounding Pile o' Bones crossing. He and several friends, most of them leading politicians and public officials, had formed at least two land syndicates earlier that year. One, in which Dewdney had a one-eleventh interest, owned four hundred and eighty acres (purchased from the Hudson's Bay Company) on the very spot that Dewdney selected as the site of the future capital. It was to the advantage of the members to have their names kept secret, for most were well known and several could have been accused of a conflict of interest—Hudson's Bay Company, North West Mounted Police, and Government officials plus five politicians and a future Manitoba judge.

By late June rumors were flying in the Qu'Appelle Valley about the choice of a new capital. More tents were rising. At the Fort, the speculators were keeping a careful watch on Dewdney's movements. It was not expected that he would leave the community during the July 1 Dominion Day festivities. Dewdney took advantage of this conviction to slip quietly away. Late in the afternoon of June 30 he posted a notice at Pile o' Bones Creek reserving for the government all the land in the vicinity. The syndicate property, in which he had an interest, adjoined the Government reserve directly to the north. Thus was the city of Regina, as yet unnamed, quietly established.

Squatters began to pour toward the embryo city. Dewdney reported to the Prime Minister, four days after the site was chosen, that most of them were paid monthly wages by Winnipeg speculators to hold land "until it is found out where the valuable points are likely to be." By fall, they held most of the available homesteads in the area of both Pile o' Bones and Moose Jaw Bone creeks. As Dewdney described it, "when a settler comes along looking for a homestead he is met by these ruffians who claim it." Genuine settlers, who were supposed to get homesteads for nothing, found themselves paying up to five hundred dollars for them. The speculators used a variety of devices to swindle the newcomers. One method was to use a bogus lawyer to confuse settlers about their pre-emption rights to quarter sections adjacent to their homesteads. If that failed, Dewdney noted in an interview that fall, "a revolver is produced."

The matter of the capital was settled on August 12. Lord Lorne, consulted about the name, left the matter to his wife, Princess Louise, who chose Regina in honor of her mother. There was an instant adverse reaction. Princess Louise was not popular; her boredom with Ottawa was the subject of public comment. The Manitoba *Free Press* declared that the name was "enough to blight the new city before it gets out of its swaddling clothes."

The choice of the site provoked even greater controversy. Some of this resulted from a Canadian Press Association visit to the townsite in August. The eastern reporters, used to the verdant Ontario countryside, were dismayed to find nothing more than a cluster of tattered tents, huddled together on a bald and apparently arid plain. The London *Advertiser* called it a "huge swindle," the Brandon *Sun* said it should have been named Golgotha because of its barren setting, and the Toronto *World* declared that "no one has a good word for Regina."

Early visitors were astonished that such a bleak plain should have been preferred over the neighboring valley. Beecham Trotter, the telegraph-construction man, stringing copper wire across it early in July, thought of it as a lifeless land: ". . . there was not a bush on which a bird could take a rest. . . . Water was invisible for mile after mile." One of Trotter's companions remarked "if anybody had told us that the middle of this billiard-tabled, gumboed plain was the site of the capital of a territory as big as France, Italy and Germany, we would have thought him daft." Marie Macaulay Hamilton, who arrived as a child, remembered the embryo capital as "a grim and dismal place"; to Peter McAra, who later became its mayor, Regina was "just about as unlovely a site as one could well imagine." Even George Stephen was dubious. He would have preferred Moose Jaw.

Dewdney stuck to his stated conviction that he had chosen the best possible location. He publicly declared that the site had been

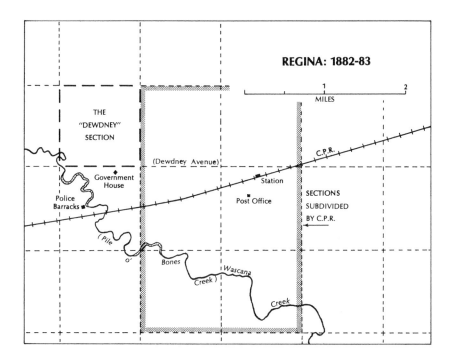

REGINA: 1882-83

THE "DEWDNEY" SECTION

(Dewdney Avenue)

Government House

Police Barracks

C.P.R.

Station

Post Office

SECTIONS SUBDIVIDED BY C.P.R.

Pile O' Bones Creek

Wascana Creek

1 2
MILES

selected because "it was by all odds the most favorable location for a city on the main line of the Canadian Pacific . . . it was surrounded by the best soil, it has the best drainage, and the best and greatest volume of water, of any place between the Assiniboine and Swift Current Creek." He told Macdonald, quite accurately as it turned out, that the new capital was in the very heart of the best wheat district in the country. But in the light of Dewdney's personal interest in Regina real estate (at 1882 prices, he and his partners stood to make a million and a half dollars from their property if they could sell it), these statements were greeted with jeers.

Dewdney's Regina interests inevitably led to a clash with the CPR. The railway was already hard pressed for funds and its main asset was townsite land. It did not intend to share these real-estate profits with outsiders. In Regina, its interests were identical with those of the Government, for here, as elsewhere, the two had pooled their land interests, placed them under joint management, and agreed to share the profits equally. That summer the railway, in order to raise funds, agreed to sell five million acres to a British-Canadian syndicate, the Canada North-West Land Company, for $13,500,000. The syndicate's job was to manage townsite sales, for which the railway would receive half of the net profits. Thus, in Regina, one quarter of the land profits went to the railway, one quarter to the land company, and one half to the government. Since, in Stephen's phrasing, the land company was "practically a branch of the Land Department of the C.P.R." the railway controlled all of the Regina land except for that held by the Dewdney syndicate.

A struggle now ensued between William Scarth of the land company and John McTavish, the CPR's land commissioner, on one side and Dewdney on the other over the exact location of Regina's public buildings. The former wanted the nucleus of the new capital on the railway- and government-owned sections; Dewdney wanted it on his property. The struggle moved to Winnipeg, where the rival properties were "boomed," as the locution of the day had it, in huge competing advertisements.

The railway won. Scarth sold some half a million dollars' worth of Regina real estate that winter; the rival sales were negligible. A further struggle, however, developed over the location of government buildings. Dewdney wanted them on the river, where, as he pointed out, the drainage was good (and also where they would be next door to his syndicate's land); Stephen and Scarth wanted them near the station, where, they contended, the government as well as the railway would profit. In the compromise that followed, Prime Minister Macdonald tried to placate all his Conservative friends by scattering the locations of the public buildings. As a result the queer community straggled for two and a half miles across the prairies, the various clusters of official buildings standing like islands in the prairie sea. Regina was a city without a center.

In all the wheeling and dealing over land profits, no one ever bothered to consider the interests of the people who would build the Queen City of the Plains and make it their home. Ottawa ignored the settlers who pleaded that the public buildings be concentrated in one area. The CPR and the land company were equally culpable; together they had contrived to split the community in two. The settlers had an awkward town plan imposed upon them by men from eastern Canada, few of whom had any intention of making Regina their home.

Bona fide settlers who had arrived on the scene early, taken up land, and built homes found that they were given no special consideration. Arbitrary prices were placed on such parcels by the land officials not only in Regina but also elsewhere. This led to bitter recriminations against "the East," the echoes of which lingered for decades. It was typical of eastern indifference to local North West interests (an indifference that would have bloody results in 1885) that when the first train arrived on August 23 with a carload of officials to christen the town, the settlers themselves were given no part in the ceremony. They had trekked across the prairie by oxcart, buckboard, horseback, and construction train; one, at least, had walked all the way from Rapid City, two hundred miles to the east. But no one thought to ask any of them to participate in the official beginning of the new town; in fact, when Regina's lots went on sale, these first settlers were forced to pay exactly the same rate as everybody else for the property they had vainly tried to appropriate as their own. One of their number wrote half a century later that since most of them had been living under canvas for two or three months, "our work clothes were not considered in good enough condition to appear among the well-dressed people from the East."

The ceremony took place in Van Horne's private car. The assemblage was a glittering one, representative of the most powerful interests in the Dominion. Van Horne, Donald Smith, Duncan McIntyre, and John McTavish of the CPR were all present, along with the company's solicitor, J. J. C. Abbott. Both the Hudson's Bay Company and the Bank of Montreal were represented on the highest level. (Only George Stephen was absent; he had come as far as Winnipeg, then hastened back to Montreal to deal with the Company's growing financial crisis.)

In retrospect, it makes an ironic little scene: there are the eastern dignitaries in their dark suits, wing collars, and striped trousers, lounging on the rear platform of the private car with their well-bustled wives; and there are the first families of Regina in their shapeless clothing, peering curiously out from behind the protection of the canvas flaps. Among the onlookers that day were at least three future mayors and one future chief justice; in the years that followed they and their fellows would help to shape the destinies of Saskatchewan and perhaps to nurture the seeds of dissidence sown in those formative months. But none of this occurred to the gentlemen on the train, sipping their French champagne and squinting across the parched prairie, flat as a board, where the little tents stretched off in ragged clusters to the distant river.

5 · *The Grand Trunk declares war*

FROM HIS VANTAGE POINT AT WINNIPEG, George Stephen must have contemplated the astonishing progress of the railway with mixed feelings. Certainly his strategy, and Van

Horne's, was working; but the company itself was in a desperate cash position.

The strategy had been to get the prairie section of the CPR operating as swiftly as possible. In that way a great chunk of the subsidy, which was paid to the company on the completion of each twenty-mile section, could be gained. Equally important, the paying portion of the line could go into operation and begin to show a profit at once.

Critics might carp that the company was building the easy part of the railway first, but Stephen's strategy was dictated as much by necessity as by guile. The mountains could not be tackled until there was a line of steel to bring supplies to the passes. As for the Lake Superior section, there were new surveys to be completed before the roadbed could be graded. The Opposition press—and some Government newspapers, too—charged the company with dragging its feet on the section between Callander Junction and Fort William. The Prime Minister, pushed by some of his Cabinet colleagues, was uneasy about the lack of progress in the East for political reasons. After all, he had staked his career on an all-Canadian route. He urged that an immediate start be made that summer of 1882 at Thunder Bay. That fall, he wanted to hold back payments unless the company complied. John Henry Pope, the Minister of Agriculture, balked at this. He had already "talked very sharp" to Stephen and his colleagues and believed they were doing all they could. Pope felt strongly enough about the matter to offer his resignation. He knew the CPR's precarious financial position and urged the Prime Minister not to delay payments.

Macdonald wrote Stephen a mollifying letter: "All I want is to be able to brag a little next Session as to the progress of the Eastern Section." Obviously, a start would have to be made by 1883; the Opposition had predicted all along that the Lake Superior section would never be built. Neither Macdonald nor Stephen could afford to allow Blake to gloat, "I told you so!" Any lingering hopes by Syndicate members that the project could be postponed until the CPR began to make money were dashed. Somehow the money would have to be found.

All that year the financial climate in London and New York had been bad for railway stocks and bonds in general and Canadian Pacific bonds in particular. As far as English investors were concerned, Canadian railways were the most disappointing foreign investment of all; they earned only a quarter as much, on an average, as other overseas holdings. Since the British had already sunk two hundred million dollars into various Canadian railroad schemes, the arrival of the Canadian Pacific on the financial scene was not propitious. That was one reason Stephen made no effort to place CPR securities on the London market, though he hoped to interest British investors in ordering land-grant bonds from Montreal and New York.

There was a kind of lassitude in England about Canada—an indifference that infuriated a man like Stephen, who in February, 1882, noted with disgust that P. T. Barnum's most recent acquisition, the huge elephant Jumbo, was "a matter of ten times more interest to London than twenty colonies." The emigrants might be flocking toward the new land but this did not make those at home feel any happier. ". . . the genuine insular Britisher hates all emigration efforts and would rather have people remain to struggle and sometimes starve than emigrate."

The market was so bad that when the CPR was driven to issue the remainder of its authorized stock in May, 1882—about 190,000 shares with a par value of $19 million—the best price it could get was twenty-five cents on the dollar. Stephen was loath to issue any stock at all; from the outset he had tried to desist from the normal practice of floating large issues of shares and bonds, a technique employed over and over again—usually with lamentable results—by North American railways, ostensibly to raise money for construction. As often as not, the proceeds were siphoned into the pockets of promoters through such devices as dummy construction companies. Stephen was no longer a promoter. He had already made an immense fortune out of watered stock of the St. Paul railway. In Canada he was not as interested in personal profit as he was in the adventure of actually building a transcontinental line and making it run.

He had promised Macdonald that there would be "no financial fire works." Before issuing stock to the public he wanted to prove that the CPR was a paying proposition. For that reason the company had issued only sixty-one thousand shares of its stock at par value in 1881. But in 1882 Stephen had to find $4,300,000 to buy up the western section of the Quebec government railroad and its branch lines in order to give the CPR access to Montreal. To raise the money he was forced to sell four times as much stock as he had originally reckoned on.

One of the unforeseen problems lay in the manner in which the twin subsidies—cash and land—were paid by the government to the railway. The money was advanced in equal installments after each twenty-mile section was completed. This worked very well on the prairie section, where the track was advancing at the rate of twenty miles a week. But Stephen realized that he would shortly be faced with the two mountain barriers and the Canadian Shield. There, men would have to struggle for months to complete twenty miles of track. Cash from the subsidy would not be available to the company until long after the actual outlay. The CPR had already spent more than the subsidy on the prairie section. Where would it get the money to pay for labor and materials on the more difficult stretches of the road?

The matter of the land subsidy was even more complicated. On paper it all sounded simple. Every time the railroad moved twenty miles, it was to be given a proportionate number of acres from the land grant of twenty-five millions. The only crown land available was situated on the prairies between Winnipeg and the Rockies, but even if every alternate section in the forty-eight-mile belt across the plains had been fit for settlement, it would have been impossible to locate all of the twenty-five million acres in that strip. Some of it had already been sold, and some of it belonged to the Hudson's Bay Company; moreover, the CPR had rejected a great deal of it. Clearly the government would have to be persuaded to set aside four-fifths of the grant in tracts elsewhere in the North West. It would be harder to sell, but it could stand as security for the land-grant bonds that the company was issuing as fast as the land was located. The trouble with governments, as Stephen was discovering, is that they do not move very swiftly.

As the fall of 1882 wore on, Stephen's letters became increasingly importunate. By the end of the season, he realized, the company would have earned ten million acres of land; but there were only three million available along the completed right of way. Where would the rest come from? The Government itself was selling land as fast as it could in the North West. It began to look as if there would not be enough left for the CPR. ". . . we shall need every acre of the grant to enable us to find the money," Stephen wrote. ". . . delay will be fatal to us—we cannot wait."

But of course he had to wait. A hint of panic crept into the letters that arrived, sometimes daily, on the Prime Minister's desk: "I . . . cannot move until I have the patents for the lands earned, up to this time." ". . . The demand on us for money is something appalling. *$400,000* went to Winnipeg last week and one million more to be there on the 10th."

Old Tomorrow, however, was not to be pushed. "Let us go by degrees in what we do," he wrote in October. "We are endeavouring to discover some plan for the issue of the patents speedily, but I fear that will need legislation." Stephen was beside himself. He began to underline words with great slashes of his pen: "It is most *essential* it should be settled *where* we are to get these lands." The CPR's account at the Bank of Montreal was badly overdrawn. Without the land it had no hope of raising further cash. "Our pinch is *now*," he wrote in frustration at the end of November. Bit by bit the Canadian Pacific Railway got its land, but it was another twenty-two years before the last acre was finally set aside for the company.

Even the acreage the company received at the time did not produce the hoped-for revenue; the land-grant bonds were not selling. The only other possible source of ready cash was stock. In December, 1882, the company increased its authorized capital stock from twenty-five million dollars to one hundred million. Stephen, in New York, persuaded a number of leading American financial houses (including that of his friend and fellow director, John S. Kennedy) to form a syndicate to take a potential thirty millions in three equal installments over a nine-month period. To get cash, Stephen had to offer a substantial discount: he sold the stock at slightly better than half price. Moreover, the purchase of the second two installments was conditional on the successful sale to the public of the first. Stephen set off immediately for London to attempt the impossible: to find buyers for the new issue in a market which, as Macdonald's confidant, the British financier Sir John Rose, cabled, was "practically shut against Canada Pacific."

But Stephen succeeded. He persuaded financial houses in London, Amsterdam, and Paris to purchase blocks of the stock from the Americans (CPR shares were listed on the New York exchange but not in London)—a notable piece of financial legerdemain, in view of the business climate. As of October 28, 1883, when the final installment was taken up, 50.3 per cent of all CPR shares were held in the United States.

This did not mean, however, that Americans controlled the Canadian Pacific Railway. The American-held stock was spread among 320 investors. Another 30 per cent was held in Britain and Europe by 157 shareholders. The remainder—just under 20 per cent—was controlled by a tight group of forty-two Canadians. All but a few thousand of these Canadian-held shares was in the hands of four men—Stephen, Angus, McIntyre, and Donald Smith—or their friends. This Canadian control of the CPR was even more pronounced at stockholders' meetings. At the general meeting of March 3, 1884, sixteen Canadians by their presence or by proxies voted 96,141 shares. By contrast, the forty-two Americans voting could muster only 90,212 shares.

This tight ownership of a substantial slice of the company by a Canadian group was one of the reasons for the continuity of management that endured well into the following century. For almost thirty years, the CPR was run by members of the original Stephen–Angus–Van Horne–Shaughnessy combination which built it. The dynasty was continued when Baron Shaughnessy stepped down in 1918. His successor, Edward Beatty, was the son of Henry Beatty, a charter member of the original syndicate of 1880 who was placed in charge of the company's lake transportation division in 1882.

But even in 1883 it would have taken a major proxy battle to have ousted the Canadians from control of their own railway. Such a move was unthinkable; the shareholders had every confidence in Stephen, and with good reason. His earnestness and force of character, his passionate devotion to and belief in the Canadian Pacific Railway and the Canadian North West, had persuaded the businessmen of four capitals to take up his new stock issue. "I have never had misgivings about eventual success in spite of all opposition," Stephen declared, "but sometimes it has taken some courage to keep weak-kneed associates from wilting."

By "opposition," Stephen meant the Grand Trunk, whose forceful general manager, Joseph Hickson, was no minor adversary. He was a Northumberland man who had been involved with railways since boyhood, working his way up from apprentice clerk to chief accountant and finally to the very top. "A straightforward and fair-dealing man," a contemporary biographer called him, punctual as a conductor's watch and tough as a rail spike. He was known as a shrewd negotiator, patient and tenacious. His brain moved like quicksilver: he had a habit of sizing up a situation almost instantly, recognizing its potentialities, and acting with dispatch. He had the kind of supple mind that grasps the significance of statistics and turns them to account. He could, said one admirer, make pounds, shillings, and pence, traffic miles and ton-miles, dance in sarabands. In Canada he was a power in both the political and the financial worlds. Married to a member of the Dow brewing family, he was a long-time crony and supporter of Sir John A. Macdonald.

During his tenure of office, Hickson had been creating a route for the Grand Trunk through Ontario and into the American Midwest. After saving the railway from bankruptcy in the seventies, he had, in a "master-stroke of railway tact, ability and diplomacy," managed to dump the unprofitable section of his road onto the Canadian government's lap and use the proceeds of the sale to seize control of a direct line into Chicago. He did not intend to stand idly by and watch a new railway destroy his creation. As long as the CPR stayed in the North West of Canada, Hickson and his president, Sir Henry Tyler, had no quarrel with it; but now it had invaded Grand Trunk territory, buying up a link with Montreal and controlling the Ontario and Quebec Railway out of Toronto. Van Horne considered this move essential. Had the CPR stopped at Lake Nipissing, it "would have existed only as a sickly appendage of the Grand Trunk." It would be like "a body without arms . . . dependent . . . upon the charity of a neighbor whose interest would be to starve it." Over the next several years, the two rival general managers, both men of stubborn courage and determination, would be at loggerheads.

In the election of 1882, Macdonald found himself caught between the Canadian Pacific and the Grand Trunk. He confidently expected that his railway policy would win him the election. On the other hand, he needed Grand Trunk support, especially in Ontario, where he faced a hard fight. The older railway's political muscle in that province was considerable. Among other things, it told its employees exactly how they must vote.

The Prime Minister did not hedge. He openly solicited Hickson's political assistance. "I have, as you know, uniformly backed the GTR since 1854 and won't change my course now," he reassured him in February, 1882, as the campaign started to warm up. In May he was writing to ask him to "put your shoulder to the wheel and help us . . . in the elections." Four days later he was naming specific candidates he wanted the Grand Trunk to back.

Hickson appeared happy to comply: he put a private car at Macdonald's disposal for four weeks for the campaign; but he was determined to exact a price for his support. On the very eve of the election he asked the Prime Minister to put a stop to the CPR's invasion of Grand Trunk territory in Ontario.

Here was a delicate matter for a party leader to face on election eve. Macdonald, who liked to seek refuge in delay, wired Hickson that he could not reply by telegraph but would write by the next mail— "meanwhile you may depend on my exertions to conciliate matters." In a later wire he was a little more specific: "Government not committed to any adverse line you may depend upon what I can possibly do personally to meet your views." With that fuzzy promise Hickson had to be content. Later Macdonald told him that he was overrating the Government's influence with the CPR; "they are quite independent of us." Hickson scarcely believed that convenient remark. Macdonald, he declared, had created a power which believed itself to be stronger than either the Government or the rival railway. "The result will be serious trouble in a good many quarters in the near future." The Grand Trunk was moving into the Liberal camp.

Meanwhile, Hickson was attacking on a second front. The Grand Trunk's chief rival in southwestern Ontario was the Great Western, which operated a network of lines between Toronto, London, Hamilton, and Windsor. Hickson, by aggressive competitive tactics, brought the

Great Western to its knees and forced an amalgamation in August, 1882, outbidding the CPR, which also wanted to acquire the line. Hickson now controlled every rail approach to the United States. If he linked up with the Northern Pacific at Duluth, he would shortly be part of a transcontinental through line that could undercut the Canadian Pacific.

Hickson struck again in Quebec. The CPR had bought half of the Quebec, Montreal, Ottawa and Occidental Railway—the section between Montreal and Ottawa. Hickson, in a swift coup, bought the other half, the "North Shore Line," to prevent the CPR from getting into Quebec City.

In London, a propaganda barrage aimed directly at the CPR continued. "The attacks here on the country as a place for settlers to go are abominable," Stephen reported to Macdonald in January, 1883, "and everything that the G.T.R. people in Canada can find in any wretched sheet against the country, is sent over here for republication. The worst feature . . . is that there is hardly a newspaper in the whole country which is in a position to say a word against the G.T.R. no matter what it may say or do against the country—without losing Hickson's advertising. . . . I will yet pay off Hickson and his road for the unfair weapons they have used against me."

The "enemy," as Stephen was now calling them—"because no other word expresses their opposition"—was producing a stream of pamphlets declaring that the Canadian Pacific could never pay its investors but must inevitably lose money. The pamphlets harped especially on the foolhardiness of crossing the country north of Lake Superior. A letter planted in the *Money Market Review* declared that "no more hopeless project than that line, or a more baseless speculation than its land grant . . . was ever started to enveigle the British public."

Meanwhile the Canadian Pacific moved to acquire more lines in Ontario and Quebec. Van Horne said bluntly that he would match Hickson foot for foot if necessary. But if the newspapers and general public, who watched the battle of the two giants like spectators at a prize fight, had been privy to some of the general manager's private correspondence with his adversary, they might have viewed the contest with more cynicism.

For in the matter of passenger and freight rates, business was still business and profits were still profits. Much of Van Horne's invective against Hickson in the years that followed was confined to charges that Grand Trunk personnel were breaking rate-fixing agreements which the two companies, in spite of their public enmity, had secretly entered into in eastern Canada. Such rate cuts, in Van Horne's words, were "simply idiotic." He gave orders that any CPR agent who dropped rates below those established by the two companies should be subject to instant dismissal—and he wanted the same understanding from his rival.

In areas where direct revenue was not concerned, Van Horne continued to do battle with Hickson. When the Grand Trunk played down the CPR's route in its own folders, Van Horne instructed Alexander Begg, the company's general emigration agent, to strike back with a map of his own. He told Begg to show the GTR's Toronto–Montreal road as a faint line and to drop out their Toronto–Chicago line entirely. In the matter of cartography, the general manager was quite prepared to smite his rivals; but free enterprise in the nineteenth century did not extend to the costly competition of a rate war.

13

1 · *"Hell's Bells Rogers"*

ONE OF JIM HILL'S SEVERAL EXECUTIVE strengths was an ability—it verged at times on the uncanny—to settle upon the right man for the right job at the right moment. His choices, however, were not always obvious ones. Certainly his decision to employ a former Indian fighter to find a practicable railway route through the Rockies and Selkirks must have seemed totally outrageous. For one thing, Major A. B. Rogers had never seen a mountain; he was a prairie surveyor, used to the rolling plains of the American Midwest. Yet Hill was sending him off to British Columbia to explore the most awesome peaks in the cordilleran spine of the continent and expecting him to succeed where dozens of more experienced engineers had failed! For another thing, Rogers was perhaps the most heartily disliked man in his profession. Few were prepared to work under him for more than one season and many quit his service in disgust or fury before the season's end. He fed his workmen wretchedly, drove them mercilessly, and insulted them continually. There were some who considered him and out-and-out sadist; all agree that he was, to put it mildly, eccentric. Admittedly, he was honest; he would have scorned to engage in the kind of real-estate profiteering that had attracted General Rosser and he pared corporate expenses with a fealty that almost amounted to fanaticism. He was also ambitious, not for money but for fame; and it was this quality that clearly attracted Hill when he called him into his office in February, 1881, and proceeded, with great shrewdness, to dangle before him a chance at immortality.

Hill liked to study men thoroughly, in the same way he studied transportation, fuel, or the works of Gibbon. Undoubtedly he knew a good deal about Rogers's background—that he had gone to sea as a youth, that he had begun his adult life as an apprentice to a ship's carpenter, that he had studied engineering at Brown University and then entered Yale as an instructor. Though Rogers was a Yale graduate, with a bachelor's degree in engineering, it is impossible to think of him as a "Yale man," with everything that phrase connotes. In a profession remarkable for its individualists, he was unique. He was short and he was sharp—"snappy" was an adjective often used to describe him—and he was a master of picturesque profanity. Blasphemy of the most ingenious variety sprang to his lips as easily as prayer to a priest's. Because of this he was saddled with a variety of nicknames, such as "the Bishop" and "Hell's Bells Rogers." The young surveyors who suffered under him generally referred to him as "the old man." He was fifty-two when he set off into the mountains, but he must have seemed more ancient than time—a crotchety old party, seemingly indestructible and more than a little frightening. Small he may have been, but his mien was forbidding: he possessed a pair of piercing eyes, blue as glacial ice, and a set of white side whiskers that were just short of being unbelievable; they sprouted from his sunken cheeks like broadswords, each coming to the sharpest of points almost a foot from his face.

He had won his military title by displaying a quick mastery of bush fighting in the Sioux uprising of 1861 and gained his professional reputation as "the Railway Pathfinder" while acting as a locating engineer for the Chicago, Milwaukee and St. Paul Railroad. In the field he carried a compass, an aneroid barometer slung around his neck, and very little more. Generally he was to be seen in a pair of patched overalls with two pockets behind, in one of which he kept half a plug of tobacco and in the other a sea biscuit. That, it was said, was his idea of a year's provisions.

The tobacco he chewed constantly. Secretan, who did not care at all for Rogers, paid tribute to him as "an artist in expectoration." There were many who believed that he was able to exist almost entirely on the nutritive properties of chewing tobacco. "Give Rogers six plugs and five bacon rinds and he will travel for two weeks," someone once said of him. Everyone who worked for him or with him complained about his attitude toward food; he was firmly convinced that any great variety—or even a large quantity of it—was not conducive to mental or physical activity.

His own diet was supremely Spartan. Harry Hardy of Chatham, Ontario, who was with him in 1883, recalled that "he was stingy with the Company's money, but generous to a fault with his own. . . . It was

beans—just ordinary beans—that he carried. He used to eat them raw."
A. E. Tregent, who was with him that first year in the mountains,
agreed: "His idea of a fully equipped camp was to have a lot of beans.
He would take a handkerchief, fill it with beans, put a piece of bacon
on top, tie the four corners and then start off." John F. Stevens, who
worked with him as an assistant engineer, described Rogers as "a monomaniac on the subject of food." The major once complimented Stevens
on the quality of his work but then proceeded to qualify his remarks
by complaining that he made a god of his stomach. Stevens had dared
to protest about the steady diet of bacon and beans which, he said, were
the camp's *pièce de résistance* three times a day. His demands for more
varied fare marked him in Rogers's eyes as an "effeminate gourmet."

Van Horne tried constantly, and with only intermittent success, to
get Rogers to provide more appetizing food in larger quantities for his
men. On one occasion, while visiting his camp, he challenged the major
on the subject.

"Look here, Major, I hear your men won't stay with you, they say
you starve them."

" 'T ain't so, Van."

"Well, I'm told you feed 'em on soup made out of hot water flavored
with old ham canvas covers."

" 'T ain't so, Van. I didn't never have *no hams!*"

Van Horne, so the story has it, moved hurriedly on to James Ross's
mountain camp, where plenty of ham was available. It is small wonder
Rogers had trouble keeping men working for him.

Outwardly he was a hard man—hard on himself and hard on those
who worked for him. Only a very few, who grew to know him well,
came to realize that much of that hardness was only an armor that
concealed a more sensitive spirit. The profane little creature with the
chilly eyes and the rasping voice was inwardly tormented by intense
emotions, plagued by gnawing doubts, and driven by an almost un-
governable ambition. "Very few men ever learned to understand him,"
his friend Tom Wilson wrote of him. Wilson, a packer and later a
Rocky Mountain guide, was one of those few. Rogers, he said, "had a
generous heart and a real affection for many. He cultivated a gruff
manner to conceal the emotions that he seemed ashamed to let anyone
sense—of that I am certain. His driving ambition was to have his name
handed down in history; for that he faced unknown dangers and suffered
privations."

James Jerome Hill understood those ambitions when he offered
to put Rogers in charge of the mountain division of the CPR. Rogers's
main task would be to locate the shortest practicable route between

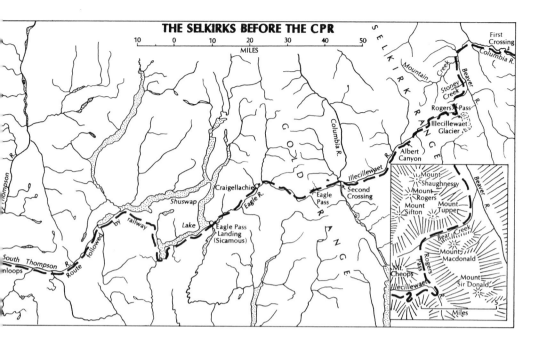

Moose Jaw Bone Creek, west of Regina, and Savona's Ferry in British Columbia, where Andrew Onderdonk's government contract began. That meant finding feasible passes through the southern Rockies and also through the mysterious Selkirks in British Columbia. There were several known and partially explored passes in the Rockies, including the Vermilion, Kootenay, Kicking Horse, and Howse, but no one had yet been able to find an opening in the Selkirk barrier. Hill made Rogers an offer he knew he could not refuse: if the major could find that pass and save the railroad a possible hundred and fifty miles, the CPR would give him a check for five thousand dollars and name the pass after him.

Rogers did not care about the cash bonus. But to have one's name on the map! That was the goal of every surveyor. He accepted Hill's offer on the spot and, from that moment on, in Tom Wilson's words, "to have the key-pass of the Selkirks bear his name was the ambition he fought to realize."

Rogers's first move was to read everything that was available about the mountain country, including the journals of Walter Moberly. An entry in the surveyor's journal of 1866, published by the British Columbia colonial government, immediately caught his eye:

"*Friday, July 13th*—Perry returned from his trip up the east fork of the Ille-cille-waut River. He did not reach the divide, but reported a low, wide valley as far as he went. His exploration has not settled the point whether it would be possible to get through the mountains by this valley but I fear not. He ought to have got on the divide, and his failure is a great disappointment to me. He reports a most difficult country to travel through, owing to fallen timber and underbrush of very thick growth."

Rogers determined to complete Albert Perry's exploration. With his favorite nephew, also named Albert, he set off at the beginning of April for Kamloops. It took him twenty-two days to reach the town by way of San Francisco and Victoria. When he arrived, he engaged ten "strapping young Indians" through a remarkable contract made with their leader, Chief Louie. Its terms rendered them up to Rogers as his virtual slaves, to work "without grumbling" until they were discharged. If any of them came back without a letter of good report, his wages were to be forfeited and the chief agreed to lay one hundred lashes on his bare back. The Indians were all converted Christians, but the local priest did not complain about this barbarity; rather he was a party to it, for he was the man to whom the letters of good report were to be addressed, and his church was to be the beneficiary of the forfeited wages. It is perhaps unnecessary to add that, in spite of the hardships the party encountered, no murmur of complaint ever escaped the Indians' lips.

Rogers did not have a very high opinion of Indians, possibly because they ate too much. "Every Indian," he once declared, "is pious and hungry. Their teachings and their stomachs keep them peaceably inclined. Any one of them can out-eat two white men, and any white man can out-work two Indians." The major spent eight days in Kamloops trying to find out how far an Indian could travel in a day with a hundred-pound pack on his back and no trail to follow, and how little food would be required to keep him alive under such conditions. He concluded, wrongly, that the expedition's slim commissariat could be augmented by game shot along the way and so set off with a minimum of supplies. He was to regret that parsimony.

The twelve members of the party headed east from Kamloops on April 29, 1881. It took them fourteen days to cross the rounded peaks of the Gold Range, now called the Monashee Mountains. They proceeded down the Columbia by raft, with the unfortunate Indians swimming alongside, until, about May 21, they reached the mouth of the Illecillewaet. Here Rogers found himself standing on the exact spot from which Moberly's assistant, Perry, had plunged into the unknown, fifteen years before.

It must have been a memorable moment. The little group, clustered on the high bank of the Columbia, was dwarfed by the most spectacular mountain scenery on the continent. Behind them the rustling river cut an olive path through its broad evergreen valley. Above them towered the Selkirks, forming a vast island of forest, rock, ice, and snow three hundred miles long, cut off from the rest of British Columbia's alpine world by two great rivers, the Kootenay and the Columbia.

Now began a terrible ordeal. Each man, balancing a hundred-pound pack on the back of his neck struggled upward, picking his way over mudfalls, scaling perpendicular rock points, wading through beaver swamps dense with underbrush and the "villainous devil's clubs," whose nettles were almost inescapable. Albert Rogers later wrote that without the fear of his uncle's dreadful penalty, all the Indians would have fled. Recalling the journey two years later, he remarked that "many a time I wished myself dead," and added that "the Indians were sicker than we, a good deal."

In the gloomy box canyon of the Illecillewaet (later named for Albert Rogers) the snow was still several feet deep. Above them, they could see the paths of the avalanches—the timber crushed to matchwood in swaths hundreds of feet wide. Sometimes, unable to move farther on one side of the river, they were forced to crawl gingerly over immense snow bridges suspended a hundred and fifty feet above the frothing watercourse. At this point the toiling men, bent double under the weight of their packs, were too concerned with the problems of terrain to marvel greatly at the beauty around them; that luxury would have to await the coming of the railway. But there was a touch of fairyland in those shadowed peaks. The music of running water was everywhere, for the torrents of spring were in full throat. Through the clouds they could catch glimpses of an incredible wedge-shaped glacier, hanging like a jewel from the mountain pinnacles. Before many years passed, the Illecillewaet Glacier would become one of the CPR's prime tourist attractions.

The Indians could no longer carry packs weighing a hundred pounds. When the fish and game the major had expected to garner along the way proved to be nonexistent, the party was forced to go on short rations. They were seldom dry. The heavy rains and wet underbrush, the continual wading in glacial waters and soft deep snow, the lack of proper bedding at chill altitudes (a pair of blankets per man was all that Rogers allowed)—all these ordeals began to take their toll.

They held cautiously to the lee of an obelisk-shaped peak, which would later be named Mount Sir Donald, after Donald A. Smith. Here, in the cool shadows, there was still a crust on the snow which allowed them to walk without floundering. At four one afternoon they came upon a large level expanse that seemed to them to be the summit. They camped there, on the edge of timber, out of range of the snowslides.

When the sun's rays vanished and the crust began to form again, they made a hurried trip across the snow field. At the far end they heard the sound of gurgling water and to their satisfaction saw that it separated, some of it running westward, some to the east. They had reached the divide; was this the route the railway would take?

Mountains towered all around them. A smear of timber extended halfway up one slope between the scars of two snowslides, and they determined to make their ascent at this point. Each man cut himself a stick of dry fir and started the long climb. "Being gaunt as greyhounds, with lungs and muscles of the best, we soon reached the timber-line," Albert Rogers recounted.

Here the going became very difficult. The party crept around ledges of volcanic rock, seeking a toehold here, a fingerhold there, staying in the shade as much as possible and kicking steps in the crust. Several feet above the timber line, the route followed a narrow ledge around a promontory exposed to the sun. Four of the Indians tied packstraps to each other's belts and then the leader crept over the mushy snow in an attempt to reach the ledge. He fell back with such force that he lost his footing and all four men plunged thirty feet straight down the dizzy incline, tangled in their packstraps, tumbling one over another until they disappeared from sight. The others scrambled down after them; miraculously, none was injured.

It was late in the day when the twelve men reached the mountaintop, but for Albert Rogers, at least, it was worth the ordeal: "Such a view! Never to be forgotten. Our eyesight caromed from one bold peak to another for miles in all directions. The wind blew fiercely across the ridge and scuddy clouds were whirled in eddies behind great towering peaks of bare rocks. Everything was covered with a shroud of white, giving the whole landscape the appearance of snow-clad desolation. Far beneath us was the timber line and in the valleys below, the dense timber seemed but a narrow shadow which marked their course."

The major was less poetic, though he read a great deal of poetry and loved it. On occasions such as this it was his habit to doff his hat, ruffle his long hair, and say reverently: "Hell's bells, now ain't that thar a pretty sight!"

The party had neither wood for a fire nor boughs for beds. They were all soaked with perspiration and were wolfing great handfuls of snow to quench the thirst brought on by their climb. "But the grandeur of the view, sublime beyond conception, crushed out all thoughts of our discomfort."

They were in a precarious position, perched on a narrow ridge where a single false move could lead to their deaths. They crawled along the razorback on all fours until they encountered a little ledge in the shadow of a great rock, which protected them from the wind. Here they would have to wait until the crust formed again and the morning light allowed them to travel.

It was a long night. Wrapped in blankets, nibbling on dried meat and stamping their feet continually in the snow to keep their toes from freezing, they took turns flagellating each other with packstraps to keep up the circulation. At two o'clock, the first glimmer of dawn appeared. They crept back to the ridge and worked their way down the great peak to the upper south fork of the river. It seemed to Rogers that this fork paralleled the valley on the opposite side of the dividing range through which, he concluded, the waters of the Beaver River emptied into the Columbia on the eastern flanks of the mountain barrier. If that was true, then a pass of sorts existed.

Unfortunately, he could not be sure. There were eighteen unexplored miles left, but by this time the party was almost out of food. Rogers's notorious frugality had destroyed all chances of finding a pass in the season of 1881; he did not have supplies enough to allow him to press forward and so was forced to order his men to turn their backs on that tantalizing divide and head west again. He must have been bitterly disappointed. It would be at least another year before he would be able to say for certain whether a practical route for a railway led from the Beaver to the Illecillewaet. By that time the rails would be approaching the valley of the Bow, and he still had not explored the Kicking Horse Pass in the Rockies, which had scarcely been glimpsed since the day when James Hector, Palliser's geologist, first saw it in 1858.

Rogers sent all but two of his Indians back to Kamloops. The others guided him down the Columbia and across the international border to Fort Colville in Washington Territory. There he hired a pack train and saddle horses and made his way by a circuitous route back into the Kootenay country to the mining camp at Wild Horse Creek.

The major had a long trek ahead of him. That spring he had dispatched the main body of his survey party from the East to Montana Territory, with directions to enter Canada from the south and proceed toward the eastern slopes of the Rockies by way of the Bow Valley in what is now Alberta. He planned to join them by crossing the Kootenay River, hiking over the Brisco Range, and then working his way down the Spray to the point where it joined the Bow. It was wild, untraveled country, barren of human habitation, unmarked by trails or guideposts; but short of going back to San Francisco and across the American West by train, it was the best route available to Rogers if he was to link up with his men on the far side of the mountains.

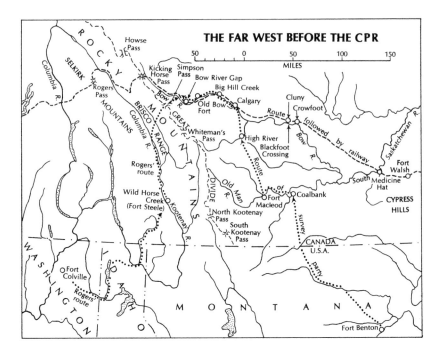

THE FAR WEST BEFORE THE CPR

He did not take his nephew with him. It was late June by this time, and it was imperative that somebody explore the Kicking Horse Pass from its western approach. Rogers decided that Albert must take the pack train to the mouth of the Kicking Horse River and from that point make his way to the summit of the continental divide. Only one white man, James Hector, had ever come that way before; but he had descended from the summit. Even the Indians shunned the Kicking Horse whose terrible gorge was considered too difficult for horses. On his first trip into the Rockies, young Albert, aged twenty-one—"that little cuss" as the major fondly called him—was being asked to attempt a feat that no human being had yet accomplished.

2 · On the Great Divide

MAJOR ROGERS AND HIS MEN WERE ADvancing on the Rockies from three directions that spring of 1881. While Albert worked his way toward the unknown slopes of the Kicking Horse and his uncle guided his packhorses over the Brisco Range, the main body of surveyors, most of them Americans, were heading westward from St. Paul toward Fort Benton, Montana, the jumping-off point for the eastern slopes of the Canadian Rockies. Waiting impatiently for them at the steamboat landing was a twenty-two-year-old from Ontario. His name was Tom Wilson and he was positively lusting for adventure.

For many eastern Canadian farm boys in the 1870's, the lure of the North West was impossible to resist; it got into their blood and it remained in their blood all their lives. They were raised on Butler and Grant and the tales of soldiers back from the Red River expedition of 1870. The North West Mounted Police, formed in 1873, were already forging an authentic Canadian legend in the shadow of the Rockies. To any healthy youngster, confined to the drab prison of farm and village life, the Great Lone Land spelled freedom.

Tom Wilson was one of these. He was a rangy youth with a homely Irish face. His long jaw, high cheekbones, and prominent teeth gave him an appropriately horsy look, for he would work with horses all his life. Later he would grow the shaggy mustache that was almost a trademark of Rocky Mountain packers. He was easygoing, industrious, good-humored, and incurably romantic. In 1875, at the age of sixteen, he quit school, bade good-by to his family, and set off through Detroit and Chicago for the Canadian North West. But at Sioux City he was overcome by a bout of homesickness and went back to Ontario.

Four years later he tried once more, and this time there was no turning back. He joined the North West Mounted Police and was stationed at Fort Walsh, not far from the present town of Maple Creek, Saskatchewan. There was adventure in the air. The Sioux, who had moved into Canada under Sitting Bull following the Custer massacre, posed a constant threat. The Blackfoot bands and their traditional enemies, the Crees, were held in uneasy check. Those curious geological formations known as the Cypress Hills, a spur of desert complete with cacti and rattlesnakes, lay just to the south—the scene of a notorious massacre of Indians by Yankee traders. Most important of all, it seemed likely that a railroad would soon be pushed across the parched coulees directly into the heart of the mountains.

In April of 1881, when it became clear that a private company was actually embarked on the CPR's construction, Wilson could stand it no longer. He had to be part of the action, and so he wangled a discharge, made his way south with a freight outfit, and reached Fort Benton, Montana, one week before Major Rogers's survey crew—a hundred men in all—disembarked from the steamer. He was the youngest man to be hired by Rogers's deputy, a stickler of a civil engineer named Hyndman, whose rules were so strict they were promptly dubbed "Hyndman's Commandments." Three aroused the special ire of the men:

Not a tap of work to be done on Sunday.

Men caught swearing aloud to be instantly discharged.

Men caught eating, except at the regular camp meal, to be instantly discharged.

The surveyors, whose task it was to find a route through the southern mountain chains, had come by way of the United States because that was the only existing route leading to the Canadian foothills. The traffic moved north and south between Fort Benton and Fort Calgary, as it would until the coming of the railway confirmed the lateral shape of the new Canada. The only evidence of an international border was a small cairn placed along the wagon trail. It was unsettled country, populated largely by roving bands of Indians—Blackfoot, Piegans, and Bloods—and an occasional trader, priest, and Mounted Policeman. The party reached its rendezvous at Bow River Gap several days late, but when they arrived there was no sign of Rogers.

About a week later, July 15, Tom Wilson was sitting on a narrow Indian trail west of the camp when a mottled roan cayuse appeared around a curve carrying a man wearing an old white helmet and a brown canvas suit. The rider, accompanied by two Shuswap Indians, was more than trail-worn. "His condition—dirty doesn't begin to describe it," Wilson remembered. "His voluminous side-burns waved like flags in a breeze; his piercing eyes seemed to look and see through everything at once. . . . Every few moments a stream of tobacco juice erupted from between his side-burns; I'll bet there was not many trees alongside the trail that had escaped that deadly tobacco juice aim."

Wilson realized at once that the tattered creature on the scarecrow horse must be the notorious Major Rogers.

"This Hyndman's camp?" the major asked in his jerky manner.

Wilson nodded and guided Rogers to Hyndman's tent. Hyndman stepped out, but there was no word of greeting from his chief.

"What's your altitude?" he shot at Hyndman. The engineer stammered that he did not know.

"Blue Jesus!* Been here several days and don't know the altitude yet. You ———!" There followed what Wilson described as "a wonderful exhibition of scientific cussing [which] busted wide all of Hyndman's 'Holy Commandments' and inspired delighted snickers and chuckles of admiration from the men who had quickly gathered around."

---

* Tom Wilson's memoirs, written in the still strait-laced thirties, reproduce the major's favorite bit of profanity as "Blue ———!" Since it is doubtful that he would have censored so mild a word as "blazes" (and equally doubtful that the major himself would have lapsed into such a euphemism), I have filled in the blank with the most obvious expletive.

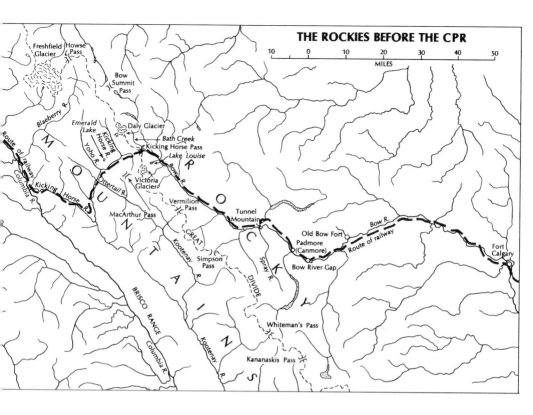

Rogers told the men that the utmost speed was essential if the survey was to keep up to schedule, since the season was late and the work well behind. One party left the following morning for the Kananaskis summit of the Bow; the others worked their way westward, widening the Indian trail as they moved.

Three days later Rogers announced that he intended to set off on his own to do some exploring, but when he asked for a volunteer to accompany him, the request was greeted by absolute silence.

There was good reason. As Wilson put it: "Every man present had learned, in three days, to hate the Major with real hatred. He had no mercy on horses or men—he had none on himself. The labourers hated him for the way he drove them and the packers for that and the way he abused the horses—never gave their needs a thought." In spite of himself, Wilson thought he might as well take a chance and follow Rogers.

The parties began to peel off from the main force on their various assignments, Rogers and Wilson accompanying one up toward the head of the Bow Valley. The major was clearly worried about the fate of his nephew, whose task it was to come directly across the mountains by the Kicking Horse and Bow rivers.

"Has that damned little cuss Al got there yet?" was his first question on riding into camp one afternoon after an exploration. It was some time before Wilson came to understand that Rogers's manner of speaking about his nephew was part of an armor he affected in order to conceal an inner distress.

When Rogers learned that there was no sign of Albert, he began to prance around and shout.

"If anything happens to that damn little cuss I'll never show my face in St. Paul again," he kept saying. The fact that he had given a twenty-one-year-old a task that the Indians themselves would not tackle did not seem to have occurred to him; obviously he expected the impossible.

Rogers decided to search for his nephew in the mountains south of the Bow, and shortly he and Wilson turned their horses down the great valley.

It was a searing day in late July, a day in which the melting glaciers had turned the gentle streams to torrents. They reached an unnamed creek pouring out of the ice field on Mount Daly and found it terribly swollen, the current tearing at top speed around enormous boulders. Wilson knew that all glacial streams begin to rise in the afternoon after the sun melts the ice in the mountains. He suggested they halt for the night and cross over when the water had subsided in the cool of the morning. Rogers swore a blue oath.

"Afraid of it, are you? Want the old man to show you how to ford it?"

He spurred his horse, forged into the current, and was immediately caught by the racing stream. The horse rolled over and the major disappeared beneath the foaming, silt-laden water. Wilson seized a long pole, managed to push it toward the spot where the struggling form had disappeared, was rewarded by an answering tug, and proceeded to pull his bedraggled chief to the safety of the bank. Rogers gave him a funny look.

"Blue Jesus! Light a fire and then get that damned horse. Blue Jesus, it's cold!"

In such a fashion did Bath Creek get its name. The story was soon all over the mountains. In the flood season, when the creek pours its silty waters into the larger river, the normally pristine Bow is discolored for miles; and for years when that happened veteran surveyors would mutter sardonically that the old man was taking another bath.

A further day of searching failed to locate the missing Albert. When Rogers and Wilson returned to the summit, hoping for word of him, there was only silence. The major grew more and more excitable. He tried to rout the men out to search in the moonless night, but they sensibly refused. "How the Major put in that night I do not know," Wilson confessed, "but I do know that at daybreak next morning he was on the warpath cursing about late risers." The members of the summit party were dispatched in all directions to fire revolvers and light signal fires if the lost should be found. Somewhere down below, on the tangled western slope of the Rockies, wrinkled by canyons and crisscrossed by deadfalls, was the missing man—dead or alive, no one could say.

Down that western slope, Tom Wilson and a companion made their way through timber so thick they could not see a yard ahead and over carpets of deceptive mosses that masked dangerous crevices and deep holes. Finally they reached the mouth of a glacial stream later to be called the Yoho. There they made camp. They had scarcely finished their meal when a shot cracked out in the distance. They sprang to their feet and began clambering down the stream bed, shouting as they went; rounding a curve, they came upon the missing man. Albert Rogers was starving and on the point of mental and physical exhaustion. His rations had long since been used up and for two days he had had nothing to eat but a small porcupine. He had picked it clean, right to the quills.

The reascent of the Kicking Horse, which the trio made the following day with Albert Rogers's two Indians, was so terrible that half a century later Wilson insisted that it could not be described. Nearing the summit, they discharged a fusillade from their revolvers and a moment later the little major came tearing down the trail to meet them. He stopped, motionless, squinting intently at his nephew; and then Wilson was permitted, for a moment, to glimpse the human being concealed behind that callous armor of profanity.

"He plainly choked with emotion, then, as his face hardened again he took an extra-vicious tobacco-juice-shot at the nearest tree and almost snarled . . . 'Well, you did get here, did you, you damn little cuss?' There followed a second juice eruption and then, as he swung on his heel, the Major shot back over his shoulder: 'You're alright, are you, you damn little cuss?' "

Al Rogers grinned. He understood his uncle. "He also knew that, during the rest of the walk to camp, the furious activity of his uncle's jaws and the double-speed juice shots aimed at the vegetation indicated our leader's almost uncontrollable emotions."

There was an eerie kind of undercurrent drifting about the Rogers camp that evening. As twilight fell, purpling the valleys and making specters of the glacial summits, the men began to gather around the fire, sucking on their pipes and gazing off across the unknown ocean of mountains. Albert Rogers, still shaky from his ordeal, was present; so was Tom Wilson, together with eighteen others—axmen, chainmen, packers, transit men, and the cook. Only the major, toiling in his tent, was absent.

They were perched on the lip of the Great Divide—the spine of the continent—and they were conscious of both the significance and the loneliness of their situation. The feeling of isolation that descends on men who find themselves dwarfed by nature in an empty land was upon each of them. In all of that vast alpine domain there was scarcely another human soul. The country was virtually unexplored; they themselves had trudged through forests, crossed gorges, and crept up slopes that no man, white or native, had ever seen. What nameless horrors did these peaks and ridges hold? For all they knew (as Wilson was to write), ferocious animals of unknown species or fearful savages lurked somewhere beneath them in those shrouded hollows. To many it was inconceivable that the mountains would ever be conquered or the chasms bridged.

One man declared emphatically that no railroad would ever get through such a God forsaken land, and several grunted agreement. Others argued that the success of the project depended on Major Rogers's ability to discover a pass in the Selkirks.

"Wonder where we will all be this time next year," someone said.

"Not here! No more of this for me!" another responded. He wanted to go where there was decent grub and "not seven days work a week, wet or dry." A chorus of approval greeted this remark. For weeks they had all existed on dried salt pork, boiled beans, and tea. They had seen no butter, eggs, vegetables, or fruit; and there was no time to hunt for the game that abounded. The monotonous diet and the need to be one's own bootmaker, tailor, barber, and laundryman was beginning to tell. "Let me get back to the settlements and this damn country won't see me again," one man declared.

Again they discussed the railroad, and again, when one of the party remarked that no line of steel could get through the Kicking Horse— that if a railway ever reached the west coast it would be by way of Fort Edmonton and the Yellow Head Pass—a majority of heads nodded in agreement.

There followed a strange and moving scene. The fire crackled. The peaks above stood out like ghostly shadows against the night sky. The men pulled on their pipes and stared into the flames. Nobody spoke for some time. At length one man broke the silence: "Let's make a deal. Let's promise to keep in touch with each other at least once a year after we get out of here."

The twenty men got to their feet and, without further prompting, took part in a solemn ritual. Each one raised an arm to the sky, and all gravely vowed to keep the Pledge of the Twenty, as it came to be called. In the years that followed, almost all were faithful to it.*

Wilson resumed his job as personal attendant to Major Rogers. A creature of whim and hunch, the major had pinned his hopes on the Kicking Horse, with the Bow Summit as his second choice. In this stubborn espousal of a single route, Rogers resembled most of the other leading railway surveyors, each of whom embraced the cause of a piece of real estate almost as if he were married to it.

Near the end of the season Rogers played one hunch that was to cause him a good deal of mental anguish during the months that followed. He and Wilson were not far from the survey gang working at the headwaters of the Bow River, trying to find whether a possible railway route led from that point over the Howse Pass. Rogers abruptly decided not to proceed further with the survey. Though he knew nothing about the Howse Pass, he had come to the sudden conclusion that it was not a feasible route and was not worth bothering with. As Wilson noted, "always the Kicking Horse ruled his mind, and although at times he had doubts regarding it being the best route, yet those fears never lasted long." But his sudden decision that morning caused him many misgivings the following summer, long after the Kicking Horse Pass had been officially chosen by the CPR's board of directors and agreed to by Parliament.

Wilson, also on a hunch, quit Rogers at this juncture and so saved himself a good deal of hardship. The survey crews lingered too long in the mountains. They did not emerge until late October, and by the time they reached High River they were frozen in. Indians robbed them of their food and some clothing. Half starved and freezing, the party managed to trudge to Blackfoot Crossing, where they were given some assistance. Then they began the long, sub-zero trek across the prairies, through the snowstorms and blizzards, to the end of steel near Flat Creek, Manitoba.

J. H. E. Secretan encountered the party, starving and in rags, on the high bank of the South Saskatchewan. The sight of them offended the fastidious Englishman, who believed, above all else, in cleanliness, good order, and discipline (he even had gunny sacks sewn together to

* After forty-five years only two of the originals were left alive. The last letter linking the men of the Great Divide was scribbled in pencil by Al Rogers in Waterville, Washington, on two report sheets of the Seattle Grain Company. It reached Tom Wilson in Banff late in February, 1929. "Dear Old Tom," Rogers had written, "you are as loyal soul as ever lived and I love you for it." Three months later Rogers, too, had gone, leaving Tom Wilson as the sole survivor of the group that had sat around the campfire and talked about the impossible railway on that haunting night in the mountains.

carpet the floors of his tents). Rogers he later described as "the worst looking, long haired ruffian of them all."

An avid sportsman, Secretan had been living all summer on ducks, prairie chickens, geese, cranes, and other game, which he shot himself. Rogers was as horrified by such Lucullan fare as Secretan was horrified by Rogers's appearance. The two did not get along, but Rogers had his revenge—or thought he did. When he reached Winnipeg he informed General Rosser, who was then in command, that Secretan "was living like the Czar of Russia [with] tents carpeted with Brussels carpet [and] living upon roast turkeys and geese and other expensive luxuries unheard of in the cuisine of a poor, unsophisticated engineer."

"Thus," wrote Secretan, "did the Major bite the hand that fed him."

3 · *The major finds his pass*

BY THE TIME ROGERS REACHED WINNIpeg, late in 1881, Van Horne's appointment had been announced. The new general manager took Rogers with him to Montreal in January, 1882, to convince the CPR directors—the Syndicate, as the press and public still called them—that the Kicking Horse route was practicable with grades of 2.2 per cent and that there appeared to be a feasible pass through the Selkirks.

Rogers had not fully convinced himself, though his pronouncements to the board exuded confidence. In truth, he had discovered only half a pass. To confirm his findings he would have to scale the eastern wall of the Selkirks and make sure that the gap he thought he saw from the Illecillewaet actually pierced the mountain barrier.

Tom Wilson had sworn that he would never return to the mountains. Rogers thought he knew otherwise: "You may think you're not coming back but you'll be here next year and I'll be looking for you," he told him when they parted. Wilson rode off, muttering to himself that Rogers would have to look a long time. He spent the winter hunting and trapping in Montana, but as the snow began to melt, "longings for the unexplored solitudes of the far-away Canadian Rockies assailed me, nor could they be cast out." The first of May, 1882, found him once again at Fort Benton impatiently awaiting the arrival of the survey parties from the East.

Two of the routes explored the previous year—the Kananaskis and the Simpson Pass—had proved unsuitable. Rogers, on a whim, had also rejected the Howse Pass. That left only the Kicking Horse. The entire party immediately pushed full speed for the summit to try to locate a line of railway through the Rockies.

In the meantime, Major Rogers once again was attacking the Selkirks. On May 22, he decided to try to reach the summit and complete his exploration of the previous year. No detailed account of that abortive journey remains, but it was clearly an ordeal. Swollen torrents, coursing down from the snow fields above, heavy timber, and a dense undergrowth of vinelike alders, nettles, and devil's-clubs frustrated their movement. Once again Rogers had failed to bring along enough supplies. He put his grumbling men on half rations, relenting only on his birthday, when he allowed them a little sugar to sweeten their tea in celebration. Only the discovery of an old canoe, which brought them swiftly back to camp, prevented the entire party from starving to death.

On July 17, Rogers tried again, taking two white men and three Indians with him and setting off from the point where the Beaver flows into the Columbia. Here, before the railway builders helped destroy it, was some of the loveliest scenery to be found in the mountains. There was a softness about it all—the river, pale milky green, winding through the golden marshland, the shining ponds winking through the dark spruces, the cataracts traced like tinsel strands on the crags above. Farther up the trail, the river knifed through the shaggy forest, boiling and frothing over shale steps and winding through carpets of ferns and thick tangles of saskatoons and raspberries. The timber was stupendous: the cedars were often ten feet or more in diameter; sometimes they rose two hundred feet above the matted forest floor.

Through this unknown country Rogers and his party climbed for hour after hour along a spectacular route that millions would one day traverse in comfort. They followed the Beaver through its canyon and then cut up a smaller tributary, the Bear, turning off again on a smaller stream that branched away to the south. The brush was so dense that they could make little more than two miles a day. Rogers suffered severely from blackflies and mosquitoes. His forehead swelled and his ears puffed up so badly that they swayed as he walked and he remarked that they felt like pieces of liver. "Not one engineer in a hundred," his friend George Monro Grant later remarked, "would have risked, again and again, health and life as he did."

Above them loomed glaciers fifty feet thick and mountains that would one day bear the names of famous Canadians—Shaughnessy, Sifton, Tupper, Macdonald—and of Rogers himself. The lower mountain slopes were flawed, each forested flank scarred by the paths of snowslides, the trees snapped off dozens of feet from the base. These mountains—conical, pyramidal, serrated—looked familiar to Rogers, for he had seen them all the previous year from the opposite side. There, before them, was the very peak on which he had stood in the summer of 1881, and over there was the same broad meadow that he had spied from his vantage point. He and his party had reached an altitude of forty-five hundred feet and were standing in a valley that seemed completely enclosed by mountains. Ragged black precipices (later named for Macdonald and Tupper) stood guard at the entrance, apparently forming an impassable wall between them. To the north and west the black smudge of timber rose to blend with sloping meadows, the soft grasses flecked with wildflowers. Beyond these spangled pastures were glacial fields of glistening white, tilting upward to curved ridges which, in turn, led the eye higher to frosted peaks. A sharp-cut pyramid (it would later be named Cheops) was silhouetted against the sky. To the southwest more mountains stretched off into a haze of misty blue. Somewhere in the distance a brook gurgled above the sound of the wind in the swaying spruces. Here the waters flowed in opposite directions, spilling down both sides of the Selkirks. Now the major realized he had found at last the long-sought passage through the barrier. In the face of formidable hardship and some foolhardiness, he had succeeded where others had failed and done what his detractors had said was impossible. There *was* a way through the Selkirks after all, and its discovery would make him immortal. Almost from this moment, this smiling, mountain-ringed meadow would bear the name of Rogers's Pass. The date was July 24, 1882, and Rogers, after searching vainly for an alternative pass, lost no time in retracing his steps so that he might let the world have the news of his discovery.

Tom Wilson, meanwhile, was engaged in transporting supplies from Padmore in the foothills to the summit of the Kicking Horse in the Rockies. One day in August he ran into a small band of Stony Indians and asked them about the roar of avalanches which was clearly audible in the distance. One of the band, a man known as Gold-seeker, told him that these slides occurred on "snow mountain," which Wilson later identified as Victoria Glacier. This mountain of snow, the Indian told him, lay high above "the lake of the little fishes," whose source it was.

Something about the Indian's description intrigued Wilson, and he asked him to guide him to the lake. It was not a difficult passage on horseback and it was well worth the trip. The two men burst out upon a small emerald gem, framed by a backdrop of dark evergreens, a dazzling white glacier, and a curtain of blue mountains.

"As God is my judge, I never in all my explorations saw such a matchless scene," Wilson recalled. He sat down, pulled out his pipe, and, as he smoked, gazed for a long time on that mirror of blue-green water, soon to become one of the most famous tourist attractions on the continent. It was noon, and the sun, directly above him, shone down upon the pool around which mountains and glacier formed an almost perfect horseshoe. Forests that had never known an ax seemed to grow directly out of the shining surface. A mile and a half beyond, the backdrop of the scene was divided into three distinct bands—white, opal, and brown—where the glacier merged with the water. Wilson decided to name it Emerald Lake, and so it appeared on the first geological map of the Canadian Rockies. But even as the map was published the name was changed to Lake Louise in honor of the Governor General's lady. (Wilson that same season discovered a second gem of a lake, which he also named Emerald Lake; this time the name stuck. So did that of the Yoho Valley, which he also discovered and which was to become a national park.)

Later that afternoon—the date was August 21—Wilson arrived at one of the survey camps and ran into Major Rogers.

"Blue Jesus!" roared the major. "I knew you'd be back. I knew you'd be back. You'll never leave these mountains again as long as you live. They've got you now." As it turned out, Rogers was absolutely right.

Rogers confided to Wilson that he still had doubts about his choice of the Kicking Horse Pass. Perhaps the Howse Pass, after all, was an easier grade. Both passes led to adjacent points on the Columbia; both were about the same length. What if, after the road was built, Rogers should be proved wrong?

Very little was known about the Howse Pass. Years before, it had been used by Hudson's Bay packers moving to and from the Columbia. James Hector had climbed the eastern slope in the days of the Palliser expedition more than fifteen years before. Walter Moberly and his men had ascended the western side and made a preliminary survey down from the summit to the Columbia in 1871. Moberly had been convinced that the pass was the best possible route for the railway to follow. What if Moberly should be proved right after the fact? He was not the sort of man who would ever let Rogers forget it.

"Tom," the major said as the two men sat outside his tent that evening, "I mustn't make any mistakes and I am not quite easy in my mind about the Howse Pass. It might be an easier one than this and I must be sure about it. I'd like to take a trip over it and I'd like you to go with me."

The two set off with packhorses the following morning, struggling through muskegs and over fallen timber and chopping their way through trails blocked by deadfalls. After the second day they found they had traveled only half the distance they had planned. Rogers began to fret.

"Blue Jesus! We won't get through here to the Columbia in two weeks at this rate. A man carrying a pack on his back could travel twice as fast as we are going. I'll give you a fifty dollar bonus if you'll go through alone on foot. . . . You ought to do it in ten days easy."

Rogers promised to meet Wilson in ten days' time on the far side of the Rockies where the Blaeberry, flowing down from the Howse Pass, empties into the Columbia. Then he went off with the horses, leaving Tom Wilson to face the most terrible ordeal of his career.

There was no trail. He groped his way through a forest of eternal night—the trees and underbrush packed so tightly that he could get his bearings only by glimpsing the tips of the mountains above. Bear Creek (another Bear Creek), its banks walled in by an impenetrable mass of tangled willows, was in flood and he used it as a guide. It proved to be a fickle ally. At one point he broke out of the gloomy labyrinth of the evergreens only to find his way blocked by an immense wall of ice, the Freshfield Glacier. He had taken the wrong fork and lost a day.

He kept plugging along like a blind man, following the racing waters, which led him ever upward. This was virgin country; there was no sign that any human being, white or native, had passed this way before. Then, when he seemed to have penetrated to the very core of the wilderness, he saw on the trunk of a tree a scar that could only have been made with an ax; it was gray with age and he realized that this must be a surveyor's blaze, left by one of Moberly's men a decade before. He had reached the summit of Howse Pass.

The descent was even more difficult than that of the Kicking Horse. Nature appeared to have devised a series of obstacles to frustrate all human passage. Wilson's account of his odyssey is reminiscent of those medieval tales in which an invisible wizard bestrews the hero's path with frightening examples of his sorcery. Wilson faced mile upon mile of deadfalls—great trees torn up and tossed helter-skelter, as if by an unseen hand, forming an apparently unending series of eight-foot barriers over which he had to scramble. There were other pitfalls. A canyon barred his way at one point; he was forced to scale a mountain wall to circumvent it. Later he faced a vast slide—an unstable desert of shattered rock. There was no way around, and so he was forced to strike out directly across it, like a man on shifting ice, knowing that a single slip or even the displacement of a loose piece of shale could send the whole mass roaring into the depths below.

There were more canyons and more delays, and because of the delays, the greatest obstacle of all came to be hunger. After twelve days of exhausting travel—sometimes he could cover no more than a mile in an hour—Wilson was down to a half a bannock. Every mile began to count, but every mile was crisscrossed with uprooted tree trunks. His pace grew slower and slower and for the first time he began to grow alarmed. Would he die in this maze of fallen timber? He decided, at last, on a desperate gamble. After a night's sleep he cast aside every scrap of equipment except for his ax and made for the Columbia as swiftly as he could. Late the following day, as fatigue dragged his movements to a crawl, he ran into Major Rogers.

"Blue Jesus! What kept you so long?" was Rogers's only greeting. Then he snorted, turned on his heel, and uttered no further word until Wilson had been fed. The others in the camp later told the packer that the old man had paced up and down for hours like a caged lion, crying over and over again: "If that boy don't show up what in hell will I do? No-one but a fool would send a lad on such a trip alone, and no-one but a fool would try to make it alone." Wilson's journey served to confirm Rogers's original hunch that the Kicking Horse provided a better route for the railway than the Howse.

By early fall Rogers was ready to leave the mountains. He wanted to carry the news personally to Montreal. Wilson, who had departed earlier, encountered him on the prairies one Sunday morning in an open wagon drawn by four horses, galloping toward the end of steel and "feeling jubilant, for his ambitions were promising realization."

At Blackfoot Crossing, Rogers met the saintly Father Lacombe and, in the presence of the oblate missionary, made a Herculean effort to avoid any blasphemy.

"Blue——," he began, and checked himself as he paid for his provisions. He stared at the bills remaining in his hand and then turned to the priest, who had just finished conducting Mass.

"You've got a mission here, haven't you?" he began, speaking slowly and carefully, watching every word.

He handed the priest the rest of the money: "This is no use to me until I get to the end of steel where I can get lots more. Here, take it—you've got some sort of school, haven't you?"

Lacombe, who had become used to profanity during his Rat Portage days, appeared to hesitate. Wilson, who was present, was certain that the priest was trying to make Rogers lose control of his tongue. The major became embarrassed and "with what looked like a do-or-die attempt," pushed the money into Lacombe's hands.

"Here, take it," he burst out. "If you can't use it that way then buy yourself some cigars. Blue Jesus, what in hell's the use of me toting it across these damnation prairies?"

Lacombe, Wilson noted, uttered a guffaw that could be heard at Fort Calgary.

Some time later, George Stephen, faultless in white tie and tails, was entertaining guests in his home in Montreal. His butler was taken aback to discover on the doorstep a wiry little man, roughly dressed and sporting a set of the largest Dundreary whiskers he had ever seen. The butler protested that Stephen could not be disturbed, but the little man was adamant. The CPR president reluctantly came to the door and instantly recognized the major. He ordered the butler to dress Rogers in suitable style and then bring him down to dinner. There he heard at first hand the tale of the discovery of the pass through the Selkirks.

True to Jim Hill's promise, the railway presented Rogers with a check for five thousand dollars. To the frustration of the CPR's accounting department, he refused to cash it. A year later Van Horne tried to remonstrate with him on the matter.

"What! Cash that check?" Rogers cried. "I would not take a hundred thousand dollars for it. It is framed and hangs in my brother's house in Waterville, Minnesota, where my nephews and nieces can see it."

"I'm not here for money!" the major added. It was an unnecessary comment—but one which must have given considerable satisfaction to James J. Hill, the man who originally made that puzzling decision to send a prairie surveyor into the unknown Selkirks.

4 · *The Prairie Gopher*

ROGERS'S DISCOVERY OF A FEASIBLE PASS through the Selkirks intensified the Canadian-American rivalry, which was a feature of railway location and construction in the West. How could a Yankee engineer, with no mountain experience, succeed where seasoned Canadians had been forced to admit defeat?

The Opposition press was skeptical of Rogers's report. ". . . on the face of it, the story appeared highly improbable," the Edmonton *Bulletin* wrote in February, 1883. It published a rumor that the route was a failure and that Rogers was to be dismissed. The *Bulletin*, of course, had a vested interest in the failure of the southern route, which had doomed Edmonton to the status of village for the foreseeable future. The fact was, however, that although Rogers had found a pass, there was not much hard evidence that it was a practicable one. He had measured it with his eye alone. No one had put a surveyor's chain on a foot of the Selkirk Mountains. No human being, white man or Indian, had succeeded in making a continuous passage from west to east along the route that he was recommending.

Stephen was himself concerned about Rogers's credibility. Could that strange, tobacco-chewing little man really be trusted? The president decided that a disinterested party of proven ability and integrity must be engaged to check up on him. The choice fell, obviously, on the former Engineer-in-Chief, Sandford Fleming, who had been living in England since his dismissal in 1880.

Van Horne also had some reservations about Rogers and was planning a second expedition to check up on him. He liked Rogers and respected his ability; but he was not happy about the location survey over the Kicking Horse, he was not certain about the practicability of the Selkirk Pass, and he was greatly concerned about Rogers's penchant for economizing on food and pay.

"We cannot expect to get good men for that work at as low or lower rates than are paid further East and we must feed the men properly in order to get good service," he told the major early in 1883. "It will be cheaper for the Company to pay for twice the amount of supplies actually necessary than to lose a day's work for lack of any."

But to a New York businessman, one of those who reported rumors "tending to discredit our work," Van Horne defended Rogers as capable and honest. He admitted that most of the men under Rogers were "utterly useless" but pointed out that the shortage of good engineers was so great he had to take chances in his hiring. He also admitted that "it may be that his work in the Selkirks will not turn out as well as his reports would lead us to believe." He planned to send "two competent and disinterested engineers" over the work in the early spring to make sure of it.

The two "competent and disinterested engineers" were Charles Aeneas Shaw, who had spent more than half his thirty years working at his profession, and James Hogg, a cousin of James Ross, the man in charge of mountain construction. Competent they were; disinterested they were not. No surveyor was disinterested in those days. They were ambitious, often blindly stubborn and jealous of their fellows, brave to the point of being foolhardy, and sometimes temperamental; but they were never disinterested. The petty hatreds and suspicions in the early days of the Canadian Pacific Survey were legendary. Such passions did not cool when the railway passed into private hands. Shaw could not stand Secretan, whom he called "selfish" and "disagreeable." The snobbish Secretan took every opportunity to denigrate Shaw. Shaw despised Hogg, who was to be his companion in the mountains. And all three men had very little use for Rogers.

The conditions of the surveyors' existence make much of this understandable. They were thrust into one another's company far from civilization for months and sometimes years. Perhaps most important, they were, for a great portion of their lives, without the company of women. They were also a garrulous lot, much more so than the contractors, many of whom went on to public fame and private fortune without leaving behind a scrap of memoir. If the contractors were consumed by petty jealousies, they kept it a secret, but the surveyors told all. They were used to spinning yarns around the campfire and so developed a flair for anecdote, both witty and malicious. Moreover, it was part of their job to keep a journal. In the diaries and memoirs they left behind, full of conflicting evidence, each writer tends to play the hero, fighting off his villainous colleagues. They were egotistical, as their memoirs show, craving public notice far more than money, as Jim Hill guessed when he made Rogers his original proposition. Rogers was equally well aware of this trait in his colleagues. On his second attempt to scale the Selkirks, he was able to persuade a reluctant transit man to climb a distant peak, even though the party was down to its last bannock, by offering to name the mountain after him. The starving surveyor eagerly leaped to his feet and headed for the crags.

Charles Shaw first tangled with Rogers, by his own account, in Winnipeg early in March of 1883. James Ross, then in charge of all engineering on the railroad's western division, outlined the plans for the coming season and then asked Shaw to look over the profile of Rogers's final location line between Calgary and Bow Gap—a distance of some sixty miles: "It's a nightmare to me and I'm afraid it will hold us back a year."

Shaw examined the plan and announced at once that he could get a far better line. A stranger working near by sprang to his feet and cried out: "That's the best line that can be got through the country. Who in hell are you, anyway?" It was Rogers. Shaw told

Ross that he was prepared to relocate the major's line, and "if I don't save at least half a million dollars over the estimated cost of construction of this line, I won't ask any pay for my season's work."

A fight threatened to break out between Shaw and Rogers. Ross calmed both men down, but at a later meeting he asked Shaw to go ahead.

Van Horne in the meantime was examining Rogers's profiles and plans out of Fort Calgary and was not happy. He called in Secretan, and a memorable encounter, which became part of the Van Horne legend, ensued.

"Look at that!" the general manager exclaimed. "Some infernal idiot has put a tunnel in there. I want you to go up and take it out."

"But this is on the Bow River—a rather difficult section. There may be no other way."

"Make another way."

Secretan hesitated, whereupon Van Horne hurled a question: "This is a mud tunnel, isn't it?"

Secretan nodded. Engineers shunned mud tunnels; it was impossible to keep the track in line because the bank tended to move constantly.

"How long would it take us to build it?"

"A year or eighteen months."

Van Horne swore and banged his fist on the desk.

"What are they thinking about? Are we going to hold up this railway for a year and a half while they build their damned tunnel? Take it out!"

Secretan picked up the profile and studied it as he headed for the door. He turned back for a moment. "Mr. Van Horne," he said in his sardonic way, "those mountains are in the way, and the rivers don't all run right for us. While we are at it we might as well fix them, too."

But Van Horne insisted that Secretan personally "take that damned tunnel out. Don't send anybody else." The engineer was spared the trip, however, when Shaw found a route around the offending hill by way of a small creek valley, which actually shortened the main line by a mile and a half.

By the end of June, when Shaw had finished his task of relocation, James Ross arrived and assigned him to relocate the rest of the line to the summit of the Rockies.

At the summit, Shaw was met by James Hogg, who had arrived with instructions from Van Horne: he and Shaw were to examine and report on the pass through the Selkirks because, in Shaw's words, "Rogers's reports were very unsatisfactory and inconclusive." They set off down the difficult incline of the Kicking Horse on the zigzag pathway, which the survey crews had already christened "the Golden Stairs" because it was the most terrifying single stretch of trail on the entire route of the railway. Actually it was little more than a narrow ledge, less than two feet wide, cut into the cliffs several hundred feet above the foaming river. It was so frightening that some men used to hang onto the tails of their packhorses and keep their eyes tightly shut until they had passed the most dangerous places. Shaw had one horrible moment when his horse ran into a nest of hornets and another when he met two men with a packhorse coming from the opposite direction. Since it was impossible for anybody to turn around, they simply cut the lashings off one of the horses and pushed the wretched animal over the cliff.

At the base of the Golden Stairs, on the banks of the Columbia, they ran into Rogers. Shaw noticed that the seat of his pants was patched with a piece of buffalo hide that still had the hair on it. Apparently the major did not recognize his antagonist of the previous spring.

"Who the hell are you, and where the hell do you think you're going?" was Rogers's greeting.

"It's none of your damned business to either question," Shaw retorted. "Who the hell are you, anyway?"

"I am Major Rogers."

"My name is Shaw. I've been sent by Van Horne to examine and report on the pass through the Selkirks."

Shaw recalled that Rogers practically frothed at the mouth when he heard the name.

"You're the ————— Prairie Gopher that has come into the mountains and ruined my reputation as an Engineer." A stream of profanity followed.

Shaw, a big man with a high intelligent forehead and an all-encompassing black beard, was not inclined to take this sort of abuse. His Scottish ancestors were all notorious fighters—chiefs of the Clan Chatten in the Inverness country. His grandfather had fought at Waterloo, and his father against the Papineau rebels and the Fenian raiders. Since the age of fourteen Charles Shaw had been doing a man's work, first as a farmhand and later as a surveyor. He was as hard as nails and would live to his eighty-ninth year. Before Rogers was finished, Shaw had leaped from his horse and seized him by the throat; in his own words, he "shook him till his teeth rattled."

"Another word out of you," said the infuriated Shaw, "and I'll throw you in the river and drown you."

Rogers immediately apologized for losing his temper and said that the engineers in charge of the relocated section had let him down badly. He offered to guide Shaw to the pass in the Selkirks.

"That will be all right," Shaw told him, "as long as you keep a civil tongue in your head."

The trip to the mouth of the Beaver could not have been very pleasant, since Shaw kept up a continual barrage of criticism regarding the line that Rogers had located along the east bank of the Columbia, insisting that it was on the wrong side of the river. As a result, "relations between us were strained for the rest of the day." In this instance, however, Shaw's advice was ignored by the CPR and the railway followed Rogers's location.

Shaw's version of the scene at the pass, along with the "Prairie Gopher" incident, which clearly rankled, was told and retold by him in his old age, half a century later. He recounted it in letters to various editors, in newspaper interviews, in an article in the CPR's staff publication, and in his memoirs, which were set down in 1936 but not published until 1970, twenty-eight years after his death.

According to Shaw, Rogers, "in his usual pompous manner," after gazing up at the great Illecillewaet Glacier, turned to him and remarked: "Shaw, I was the first white man ever to set eyes on this pass and this panorama."

Shaw walked over to a small spring to get a drink and there, he related, he found the remains of a fire, some partly rotted poles, evidently used for a tent, and a couple of badly rusted cans. He called Rogers's attention to these.

Rogers's reaction, as quoted by Shaw, was astonishment: "How strange! I never noticed those things before. I wonder who could have camped here."

"These things were left here years ago by Moberly when he found this pass!" Shaw claimed he replied.

It was the repetition of this story that helped convince Canadian engineers and journalists that Major Rogers was a fake and that the credit for discovering the pass rightfully belonged to Walter Moberly. Even Moberly began to believe it in his declining years, as his imperfect reminiscences reveal, though he was generous enough at the time. In 1885 he wrote: "I cannot . . . but pay a high tribute to the dauntless energy and untiring zeal that has characterised and, I am glad to say, crowned with success the unwearying struggles of my successor in the mountain surveys, Major A. B. Rogers." Thirty years later he was insisting that Rogers had not seen the pass named after him until the railway had gone through it, and that it should have been named the Perry Pass after his assistant, who, Moberly came to believe, actually *had* seen the pass. The memoirs of aging surveyors are not very good evidence when set against words actually written on the spot at the time. Moberly's journal of 1866 makes it clear that the campfire Shaw said he found did not belong to his party.

Then who left those relics? Certainly they could not have been as old as Shaw thought they were. The snow on the top of the Rogers Pass reaches a depth of fifty feet or more in the winter; it is scarcely credible that the remains of a small fire could have survived for seventeen years. It is more likely that (assuming that Shaw was not indulging in a pipe dream) the camp was left by Rogers himself the previous season or by his men, who had hacked a road to the summit and were working on the western slopes of the pass at that very time.

5 · *"The loneliness of savage mountains"*

ON THEIR WAY BACK TO THE SUMMIT OF the Rockies, on the Kicking Horse Trail, Shaw and Hogg ran into the second party dispatched by the CPR to check up on Major Rogers: Sandford Fleming, at the invitation of George Stephen, was also heading for the Selkirks, accompanied by his son Frank and his old comrade the Reverend Dr. George Monro Grant.

Shaw informed Fleming that he and Hogg had gone as far as it was possible to go and that no one had been through to the western slope of the Selkirks. This was the second such report that Fleming had received from Canadian surveyors. Earlier, two others had told him that Rogers had not been able to pass over to the far side of the mountains and that "it was questionable if it were possible to find a route which could be followed." Fleming took it all with a grain of salt: "I had some very serious reflections on what I heard from these gentlemen."

Nonetheless, the Selkirks remained a mysterious, unknown land for some time. Morley Roberts, a British adventurer and novelist who worked on the railway the following year, wrote: "I could find no one who had been on the journey, and the reports about it were so contradictory that in the Kicking Horse Pass it was impossible to find out how far it was across the Selkirk Range, whether it was 60 or 120 miles or even more. There was a halo of romance thrown over the whole place west of us, and when we passed in imagination the Columbia for the second time all beyond was as truly conjectural as El Dorado or Lyonesse." James Ross himself, who kept sending

Indian couriers out to the Selkirks, had only the vaguest idea of what lay ahead.

Fleming and Grant were far more concerned about the terrible descent down the Golden Stairs of the Kicking Horse. It was almost a dozen years since these two companions had set out, in the prime of life, to breast the continent. Now the years were beginning to tell. Fleming, though a superb physical specimen, was fifty-six. For the past three years he had been leading an eventful but sedentary life in England with side visits to various European capitals, attempting, without much success, to interest the Royal Society in his proposals for standard time and engaging in such mild adventures as a gondola ride in Venice and a trip in a hot-air balloon. Grant, who was forty-seven and inclined to a paunch, had quit his ministry in Halifax for the principal's chair at Queen's. Now these middle-aged explorers were forced to negotiate a trail that terrified the most experienced mountaineers.

Fleming dared not look down. To do so "gives one an uncontrollable dizziness, to make the head swim and the view unsteady, even with men of tried nerve. I do not think that I can ever forget that terrible walk; it was the greatest trial I ever experienced."

At that point the members of the party found themselves teetering on a ledge between ten and fifteen inches wide, eight hundred feet above the river. There was nothing to hold onto—not a branch or even a twig. Grant, who had lost his right hand in childhood, was especially vulnerable: "It seemed as if a false step would have hurled us to the base, to certain death." The sun, emerging from behind a cloud, beat down upon them until they were soaked with a perspiration that was accentuated by their own state of tension. "I, myself, felt as if I had been dragged through a brook, for I was without a dry shred on me," Fleming admitted. It was an exhausted party that finally arrived that evening at Rogers's camp on the Columbia.

Rogers's men were highly amused at the idea of the hard-swearing "Bishop" entertaining a man of the cloth. They warned Grant of the major's roughness of speech and attitude: "He can blow, he can swar, and he can spit tobacco as well as any man in the United States."

Because Grant was addressed as "Doctor," Rogers at first believed him to be a medical man. When, on the following morning—a Sunday—Fleming proposed that his companion hold a service, Rogers thought the idea was a practical joke. He indulged in a good deal of jubilant profanity and bustled about, drumming up his men for the event, until the truth dawned upon him.

Grant was no mean preacher, and, as always when he had a

captive and willing audience, he preached at great length. Slowly he brought the subject around to profanity and, being careful not to single anyone out, pointed out that it was a useless device and one not generally heard any longer in the conversation of gentlemen. Grant was a shrewd judge of character. He had grasped an essential aspect of Rogers's motivation: above all, the little engineer wanted to be thought of as a gentleman. Then and there Rogers resolved to abstain from swearing. He was not always successful; at one point, when something went wrong with the canoes and Rogers tried desperately to suppress his normal vocabulary, Grant took pity upon him. The major was standing with his mouth open, struggling to force the words back. The minister laid a hand on his arm: "Major, hadn't you better go behind a tree and say it?"

That Sunday evening, Grant and Fleming climbed to the benchland five hundred feet above Rogers's camp to ponder the "noble landscape" and to meditate on the future of the virgin country that stretched off below them.

The scene was like a painted backdrop—the great river winding its slow way through the forested valley; the evergreen slopes of the foothills rising directly from the water; a line of blue mountains, sharp as sword blades, limned behind the dark hills; and behind them another line of peaks, stark white, chiseled into the blue of the evening sky.

"I asked myself," Fleming wrote, "if this solitude would be unchanged, or whether civilization in some form of its complex requirements would ever penetrate this region? . . . Will the din of the loom and the whirl of the spindle yet be heard in this unbroken domain of nature? It cannot be that this immense valley will remain the haunt of a few wild animals. Will the future bring some industrial development: a future which is now dawning upon us? How soon will a busy crowd of workmen take possession of these solitudes, and the steam whistle echo and re-echo where now all is silent? In the ages to come how many trains will run to and from sea to sea with millions of passengers?"

The following day he and his son, with Grant, Albert Rogers, and the major, set off up the valley of the Beaver for the pass. Grant thought that it "was like riding through a deserted garden." The trail was bordered with half a dozen varieties of ripe fruits and berries, which the travelers could pick and eat without dismounting. Refreshed by such luxuriance, they emerged from the forest and into the saucer-shaped meadow where Rogers had planted a yew stake to mark the actual summit.

Fleming had had the foresight to bring along a box of cigars, and these were smoked as the group sat down on natural seats of moss-covered rock and listened to the major tell the story of how he discovered the pass. The whole company was in high spirits. To show that they were still young and unaffected by the journey, Fleming proposed a game of leapfrog, "an act of Olympic worship to the deities in the heart of the Selkirks!"

The following day the major returned to the Columbia, while the others, with Albert Rogers as their guide, set off down the western slope. Twenty-four miles from the summit, the freshly cut trail came to an end, and from this point on the party bade farewell to all civilization. It was to be Grant's last journey. After it was over he vowed that he would never attempt to pioneer through a wilderness again. "In all my previous journeyings," he later wrote, "other men had been before me and left some memorial of their work, a railway, a Macadamized or gravel road, a lane, a trail, or at least, blazed trees to indicate the direction to be taken. Now we learned what it was to be without benefit of other men's work. Here, there was nothing even to guide, save an occasional glimpse of the sun, and the slate-coloured, churned-up torrent . . . hemmed in by cañons, from which we turned aside only to get mired in beaver dams or alder swamps, or lost in labyrinths of steep ravines, or to stumble over slides of moss-covered rocks that had fallen from overhanging mountains."

The nettles of the devil's-club were so bad that long after reaching civilization again, at Kamloops, the travelers felt the effects of them; their hands had to be wrapped in oatmeal poultices, and even then the pain was so severe that one member of the party was unable to sleep.

All this time James Ross had been worrying about the suitability of the Kicking Horse Pass. Like Rogers before him, he began to wonder whether every other method of crossing the Rockies had been considered. The terrible descent from the Great Divide by way of the Kicking Horse River bothered almost everybody: if grades of 2.2 per cent were to be maintained, as the contract stipulated, construction costs would be very heavy. But if steeper grades were agreed upon, maintenance and running costs would be vastly increased and the government would probably not pay a subsidy on any part of the line that did not adhere to the contract.

Ross asked Shaw to explore the headwaters of the Bow and the Howse Pass—the very region which Tom Wilson, the packer, had reported on to Rogers the year before. If Shaw found a better pass, Ross was prepared to move swiftly. Shaw was instructed to run an immediate trial line from the summit without waiting for further orders while Ross stood ready to rush a survey crew to the spot. There was not a day to be lost; the rails had moved across the prairies at record speed and were now inching into the mountains.

Ross, meanwhile, decided to move over the summit, down the Kicking Horse, and then down the Columbia to the foot of the Howse Pass. He took James Hogg with him; en route he picked up Major Rogers and Tom Wilson.

Rogers was desperately worried when he learned that another attempt was being made on the Howse. Would "his" pass be rejected after all? Was Wilson's report of the previous year accurate? He stoutly defended it, but he was reminded that "Wilson is not an engineer so what does he know about grades?" Ross was inclined to agree with Wilson and abandoned his idea of climbing to the top of the Howse Pass to rendezvous with Shaw. Hogg, however, was determined, in Wilson's words, "to prove that my report was wrong." He insisted on heading up the mountainside with only a day's rations in his pack. It was almost the end of him. Shaw found him, quite by accident, crouched over a dying fire, insensible from exhaustion and frostbite, with most of his clothing burned away.

It was late October by this time; already the snow was falling thickly. Rogers left the mountains without knowing the results of Shaw's explorations. By now Tom Wilson had become his friend and confidant and he revealed to him something of his feelings. He was in a state approaching despondency. All his work, he felt, had been for nothing: the contractors wanted to circumvent his pass in the Selkirks by taking the long way round, using the hairpin valley of the Columbia, "and if they did that he would be robbed of his ambition." The Kicking Horse was also in doubt. If it were rejected, too, there would be nothing in the mountains to mark his passing. "Are you sure you're right about the Howse Pass, Tom?" he asked time and time again.

In Calgary, to his great relief, the major learned that Shaw and Ross had rejected the rival pass. The gradient was easier but the summit was one thousand feet higher than that of the Kicking Horse, and its employment would lengthen the railway by thirty miles. For better or for worse, the route which he had so enthusiastically and so profanely endorsed would become the main line of the CPR, and the name of Rogers would go down in history.

14

1 · Onderdonk's lambs

ALMOST EVERY LEADING FIGURE CON-
nected with the building of the great railway—with one notable exception—achieved the immortality of a place name. The map of western
Canada is, indeed, a kind of coded history of the construction period.
The stations along the way (some of them now abandoned) tell the
story of the times: Langevin, Tilley, Chapleau and Cartier, Stephen and
Donald, Langdon and Shepard, Secretan, Moberly, Schreiber, Crowfoot, Fleming, and Lacombe. Lord Dunmore, who tried and failed to
secure the original contract, has his name so enshrined along with Lord
Revelstoke, who came to the company's rescue by underwriting a bond
issue. Harry Abbott, the general superintendent, has a street named
after him in Vancouver, along with Henry Cambie, the surveyor, and
Lauchlan Hamilton, who laid out most of the CPR towns; Thomas
Shaughnessy has an entire subdivision. Macoun, Sifton, and even Baron
Pascoe du P. Grenfell, one of the more obscure and reluctant members
of the original Syndicate, are recognized in stations along the main
line. Rosser and Dewdney are immortalized in the names of the main
streets in the towns they founded. Most of the leading figures in the
railway's story had mountain peaks named after them; Van Horne,
indeed, had an entire range. But the connoisseur of place names will
search in vain in mountain village, park, avenue, subdivision, plaque,
or swamp for any reference to the man who built the railway between
Eagle Pass and Port Moody through some of the most difficult

country in the world. There is not so much as an alleyway named for Andrew Onderdonk.

Perhaps he would have wanted it that way, for he was a remarkably reticent man. He did not inspire the kind of anecdote that became part of the legends of Van Horne, Rogers, and Hill. No biographer appeared before or after his death to chronicle his accomplishments, which included the San Francisco sea wall, parts of the Trent Valley Canal in Ontario, and the first subway tunnels under New York's East River. In the personal memoirs of the day he remains an aloof and shadowy figure, respected but not really known. Rogers, Hill, and Van Horne were each referred to by their underlings, with a mixture of awe, respect, and terror, as "the old man." Onderdonk was known to everybody, from the most obscure navvy to the top engineers and section bosses, by the more austere title of "A.O."

If those initials had a Wall Street ring, it was perhaps because Onderdonk looked and acted more like a broker than a contractor. In muddy Yale, which he made his headquarters while his crews were blasting their way through the diamond-hard rock of the Fraser Canyon of British Columbia, he dressed exactly as he would have on the streets of his native New York. He took considerable care about his personal appearance. His full mustache was neatly trimmed and his beard, when he grew one, was carefully parted in the middle, as was his curly brown hair. He was tall, strapping, and handsome, with a straight nose, a high forehead, and clear eyes—an impeccable man with an impeccable reputation. "Onderdonk," recalled Bill Evans, a pioneer CPR engineer, "was a gentleman, always neat, well dressed and courteous." When he passed down the line, the white workers along the way—Onderdonk's lambs, they were called—were moved to touch their caps. A woman in Victoria who knew him socially described him as very steady and clearheaded, but added that he did not have much polish. In that English colonial environment, few Americans were thought to be polished. But to the men sweating along the black canyon of the Fraser, Andrew Onderdonk must have seemed polished indeed. Henry Cambie, the former government engineer who went to work for him, described him, as many did, as "a very unassuming man" and added that he was both clever and a good organizer and was "possessed of a great deal of tact." In short, Onderdonk had no observable eccentricities unless one counts the monumental reticence that made him a kingdom unto himself and gave him an air of mystery, even among those who were closest to him.

But no one was really close to him. If any knew his inner feelings, they left no record of it. If he suffered moments of despair—and it is clear that he did—he forbore to parade them before the world or even before his cronies. It was not that he shunned company; the big two-story, cedar home, with its gabled roof and broad verandas, which he built in Yale to house his wife and four children, was a kind of social center—almost an institution, which in fact it later became. Onderdonk was forever entertaining and clearly liked to play the host. "We lived as if we were in New York," Daniel McNeil Parker, Sir Charles Tupper's doctor and friend, wrote of his visit there with the Minister of Railways and Canals in 1881. The contractor and his wife were described by a friend as "a happy-go-lucky couple . . . fond of enjoying themselves." Cambie, in his diaries, notes time and again that he dined at the Onderdonks'. But Cambie, who had a good sense of anecdote, never seems to have penetrated that wall of reserve.

Onderdonk's modesty was matched by that of his wife, Delia, a short, plump, and pretty blonde, who was "the most modestly dressed woman in Yale," a frontier town where all the engineers' wives, having precious little else to occupy them, vied with each other in the ostentation of their frocks and gowns. "A nice, unaffected American lady," Dr. Parker wrote of her.

If Onderdonk presented a cool face to the world, it was partly because he did not need to prove himself over and over again. He had been raised in security; in his daughter's words, "his family on both sides were gentle people of education." Onderdonk differed from most of the contractors of his time and from all the other major figures in the story of the railway. Each one of them—Donald A. Smith, Duncan McIntyre, John S. Kennedy, Norman Kittson, James J. Hill, George Stephen, Sandford Fleming, and William Van Horne, right on down to Michael Haney and A. B. Rogers—had been a poor boy who made it to the top on his own. Most were either immigrants or the sons of immigrants; but Onderdonk came from an old New York family that had been in America for more than two centuries. He was a direct descendant of Adriaen van der Donck, the first lawyer in New Netherland, who in 1646 was granted what is now the southern part of Westchester County, New York. His mother was pure English—a Trask from Boston. Fourteen members of his immediate family had degrees from Columbia. His ancestral background was studded with bishops, doctors, and diplomats. Onderdonk himself was a man of education with an engineering degree. He did not need to swear loudly, smoke oversize cigars, act flamboyantly, or throw his weight around. It was not in his nature to show off; he was secure within himself.

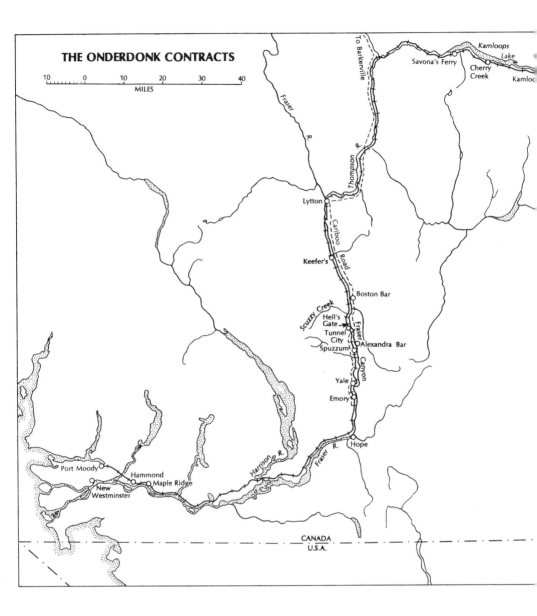

THE ONDERDONK CONTRACTS

That sense of security was also sustained by the knowledge that he had almost unlimited funds behind him. He was front man for a syndicate that included the New York banker H. B. Laidlaw; Levi P. Morton (later Vice-President of the United States) of Morton, Bliss and Company, a prominent eastern banking house; S. B. Reed, the immensely powerful vice-president of the Oregon Railway and Navigation Company; and, last but by no means least, Darius Ogden Mills, the legendary San Francisco and New York banker.

Mills handled the financial end of the Onderdonk syndicate. He was everything that Onderdonk was not, having clawed his way to his position as one of the boldest and most astute financiers in America by striking it rich in California in 1849—not by finding gold but by chartering a sailing vessel, loading it with all the commodities likely to be in short supply in the California camps, and sailing it successfully around the Horn. Mills sold out his stock to the eager miners at fabulous prices and went on swiftly to fame and fortune, becoming the first president of the Bank of California and marrying off his daughter to Whitelaw Reid, proprietor of the New York *Tribune*.

In 1880, when he and Onderdonk were securing their first contracts in British Columbia from the Canadian government, everybody was talking about Mills's palatial office building being planned on Broad Street, New York (the finest in the world, it was said: thirteen structures had to be demolished to accommodate it), and his even more palatial private home opposite St. Patrick's Cathedral, "a mansion of which a Shah of Persia might be proud," for which, it was reported, he had paid the highest frontage price in history. The carved woodwork, painted ceilings, and inlaid walls and floors cost him an additional four hundred and fifty thousand dollars. As for his office building, it was garish with Corinthian pillars, red Kentucky marble, and Italian terra cotta. No wonder the Canadian government was impressed when it learned who was bankrolling Andrew Onderdonk. Charles Tupper, the Minister of Railways, had had his fill of underfinanced contractors.

At thirty-seven, Onderdonk was known as a seasoned contractor with a reputation for promptness, efficiency, and organization. He had just completed the massive sea wall and ferry slips in San Francisco on time, in spite of serious troubles with the incendiary labor chieftain Denis Kearney, a former sailor who rose to power as a coolie hater and was prominent in the riots of 1877. Onderdonk made it clear to the government that he would have all four contracts covering the entire 127 miles between Emory's Bar, at the start of the Fraser Canyon, and Savona's Ferry, on Lake Kamloops, or else he would pull out. He got what he asked for.

Some time later, when the government let the rest of the British Columbia line from Emory's Bar to Port Moody on the coast, Onderdonk was again awarded the contract, though again he was not the lowest bidder. Certainly in this instance, if not before, the government made use of some fancy sleight of hand to ensure that he was successful. The lowest bidder was passed over on a flimsy excuse and the job given to Onderdonk, whose bid was $264,000 higher. This was barefaced favoritism but Tupper made it stick. There was another suspicious aspect to the case. For the first time the contract was let as a lump sum, without being broken down into component parts. This method, as the

Globe pointed out, "is essentially a corrupt method, and is so considered by contractors." For one thing, it made it difficult to check up on extras. Clearly, the government wanted Onderdonk to have the job, which was, admittedly, as difficult a one as had ever faced a contracting firm in the Dominion. As Henry Cambie wrote: "No such mountain work had ever been attempted in Canada before."

The first four Onderdonk contracts were signed in 1880, before the Canadian Pacific Railway Company came into being. The CPR, under the terms of its contract, would inherit the Onderdonk line. Unlike Van Horne, this contractor was building a railway that he would never have to manage himself once it was completed. It was a salient distinction and the basis of a long and bitter dispute between the CPR and the government in the years that followed the driving of the last spike.

By the time the CPR turned its first prairie sod in May, 1881, Onderdonk had been at work for a year, but he had not laid a mile of track. For all those twelve months, the people of Yale had grown accustomed to the ceaseless reverberations caused by rock being blown to bits twenty-four hours a day. There were, within a mile and a half of the town, four tunnels to be drilled; it took Onderdonk eighteen months to blast them out of the rock of the canyon—a compact granite, striped with extremely hard veins of quartz. Mountains of this granite, the toughest rock in the world, border both sides of the river, rising as high as eight thousand feet. In the first seventeen miles upriver from Yale there were no fewer than thirteen tunnels; between Kamloops and Port Moody there was a total of twenty-seven. The sixty-mile stretch of road between Emory and the Thompson River was considered to be the most difficult and expensive on the continent. The blasting was painfully slow; even when the big Ingersoll compressed-air drills were used, it was not possible to move more than six feet a day. The flanks of the mountains were grooved by deep canyons; as a result, some six hundred trestles and bridges were required above Yale. To build them, Onderdonk would need to order forty million board feet of lumber.

The approaches to many of the tunnels had to be galleried. Gallery work was only slightly less demanding than tunneling. The trains were destined to travel on the very lip of the precipice, into which a kind of notch had been blasted, the roof consisting of solid rock which was usually several hundred feet thick and sometimes several thousand. One such gallery ran for one hundred feet; at its rim was a perpendicular wall of rock, two hundred feet high.

At Hell's Gate on the Fraser, a traveler could watch the agony of construction taking place directly across the foaming waters. Splintered trees toppled into the muddy gorge, huge rocks catapulted into the sky, vast chunks of mountainside slid into the river. It seemed impossible that a road could be carved out of those dripping black cliffs. Here men could be seen suspended at dizzy heights against the rock walls, clinging to ladders roped to trees on the summit, so that they could drill blasting holes into the face of the escarpment. Each time a shot was fired, the men had to clamber swiftly up the ladders to escape the effect of the explosion. Engineers made their measurements and took their cross sections suspended for hours and sometimes days "like Mahomet's coffin between heaven and earth." They often worked in their bare feet, which they believed ensured them a better footing. A break or a slip in the rope, a rock toppling from above, or a premature blast meant certain death.

High above the grade and sometimes below it was the old corduroy road to the Cariboo mines, which Sir James Douglas, Governor of British Columbia, had caused to be built in the 1860's. It was jammed with traffic. Twelve-mule teams thudded by. Ungainly prairie schooners, pulled by sixteen oxen with six spares plodding behind, rattled past, loaded with everything from rice for the coolie labor to portable sawmills for the construction camps. The road itself had been an engineering miracle in its day—a crazy, unbelievable highway cut into the cliffs, the only link between the coast and the interior plateau of British Columbia. In some spots in the Fraser Canyon it had to be carried around the precipice on trestlework, like the balcony of a house, so that passengers on the Cariboo stage were traveling directly over the boiling waters three hundred feet below.

Onderdonk was pledged to keep the road open; without it the economy of the Cariboo would be throttled. Besides, he needed it himself to bring supplies to his construction camps. The difficulty of sparing the road while the blasting and the building were going on all around —above it, below it, and right beside it—was indescribable. Great chunks of the road sometimes slid into the Fraser. Sometimes the railway itself required the right of way; when that happened, construction had to be halted until a new section of road was built.

The traffic on the Cariboo Road presented a constant problem. Two covered wagons linked in tandem and hauled by nine yoke of oxen made a cavalcade well over a hundred feet long. It was bad enough getting around the tight curves, but added to this was the loose rock blown from tunnel openings or cuts, which often held up the stages or caused accidents.

By June of 1882, when Van Horne launched his record-breaking push across the prairies, Onderdonk had driven scarcely twenty miles of steel. An explosives factory was turning out four thousand pounds of nitroglycerine a day. Ten vessels containing six thousand Chinese coolies were on their way from the Orient to swell his labor force. Expenses were mounting alarmingly. The freight rates on the old Cariboo corduroy road were strangling him. As a result he had decided, in the spring of 1882, to attempt a task that almost everyone else considered impossible: he proposed to build a steamer that could actually negotiate the most treacherous section of the Fraser Canyon, known as Hell's Gate. Veteran rivermen all believed Hell's Gate to be impassable, for here the river reached a peak of fury, hurling itself at ten knots over a ledge of black basalt between twin ramparts only eighty feet apart. It was Onderdonk's plan to force a steamboat through this chute and put her into service between Lytton and Boston Bar.

The sturdy little craft that he ordered was to be built at Spuzzum near Tunnel City (named for the Big Tunnel, sixteen hundred feet long, being drilled twenty miles upriver from Yale). She was to be called *Skuzzy*, after a mountain stream "that comes dancing and falling through the opening in the rocks at times causing attractive falls and finally uniting its clear stream with the less pleasant waters of the Fraser." The little vessel was launched on May 4 by Mrs. Onderdonk, modestly dressed in a long skirt and a plain whaleboned blouse.

It was easier to construct such a craft than it was to persuade a crew to man it. Old river hands pleaded with Onderdonk to abandon the scheme. The river was in spring flow, rising rapidly day after day, spilling over its banks and endangering small settlements. At the last moment a skipper, Asbury Insley, was found to attempt the feat. He set off on May 17, using every trick he had learned to pit the *Skuzzy* against the furious waters. Time after time he was beaten back until he turned the boat about and returned defeated to Spuzzum.

To the astonishment of all, Onderdonk announced that another attempt would be made to force the boat through the canyon. He had gone all the way to the upper Columbia to find three expert boatmen foolhardy enough to make the attempt. These were Captain S. R. Smith of Lewiston, Idaho, his brother David, and J. W. Burse, who was to act as engineer. Smith had taken the steamer *Shoshone* one thousand miles down the Snake River to the Blue Mountains—the only boat in history to make such a perilous passage. If anyone could battle through Hell's Gate, Smith and his colleagues were the men to do it.

On September 7, Onderdonk brought five flatcars loaded with guests from Yale to witness the ordeal. They rattled over the newly laid track, the train swaying around the sharp curves and plunging into the recently driven tunnels where water dripped steadily from, the jagged roofs of black rock. They crowded the high banks of the Fraser, laying wagers of gold and timber and other merchandise on the outcome—the odds running as high as a hundred to one against the boat's getting through.

The crowds could not stay to witness the full struggle. After four days, only a few miles of headway had been made and after ten days, it became apparent that the *Skuzzy* was losing the battle. At this point Andrew Onderdonk took command. He ordered ringbolts driven into the rock walls of the canyon, then stationed one hundred and fifty Chinese laborers at intervals along the banks to pass heavy ropes through the bolts. These ropes were attached to the ship's capstan. Finally on September 28, with the aid of the engines, the steam winch, fifteen men on the capstan, and the mass of coolies tugging and straining along the bank (to cling to the ropes and pull was imperative, for to lose one's grip and fall meant certain death), the boat finally got through, and a public holiday was declared in Yale.

It took the *Skuzzy* another seven hours to fight her way upstream to Lytton before she went into freighting service. The current was so swift that it required only an hour to make the run back to Boston Bar, and on her first voyage she was badly damaged, with a gaping hole in her hull, and her sides, it was said, scraped almost to the point of transparency. She limped into berth, had her wounds repaired, and for the next year worked the river, emerging splintered and battered after every journey.

All this time men were being mangled or killed by falling rock, by slides, by runaway horses, and above all by the incessant blasting. Some whose hands were covered with blasting powder suffered severe burns when they recklessly tried to light their pipes. Others, returning prematurely to a half-finished tunnel following a blast, were met by a second, which blew them to pieces. One hid behind a tree two hundred feet from a tunnel about to be blasted and thought himself perfectly safe; a flying splinter sheared off his nose. Often, huge rocks came hurtling out of the mouths of tunnels like cannonballs. One sank a boat, causing a man to drown. Another knocked down a bridge. The larger blasts touched off avalanches and mud slides. Almost every time heavy shots were fired inside a tunnel, great boulders were ripped free from the mountainside by the reverberations. One of these tore through the roof of the engine house at Number One Tunnel, "somewhat injuring a couple of men," in the casual report of the Yale *Inland Sentinel.* One slid down from such a height that it carried part of an oak forest and an entire Indian burying ground into the river, allowing the oaks to continue to grow "and the dead men's bones to rest without being in the least disturbed—fences, roots, images and all."

Another rockslide actually blocked the Thompson River, forming a dam half a mile long and a hundred and fifty feet wide, raising the water two hundred feet and flooding several farms while leaving the channel below almost dry. The Chinese and Indians working in the vicinity dropped their tools and rushed to the river bed to collect the hundreds of fish wriggling and gasping in the mud and also to recover the gold, which was still plentiful and, with the water down, easy to pan. Some made two hundred dollars a day in this manner until the river, working its way round the barrier of rock, formed a new channel. Another slide in November, 1882, blocked the track east of the Big Tunnel to a depth of sixty feet; it was mid-April before the debris could all be cleared away. An unexpected slide near Keefers Station was struck by a train with such impact that the locomotive became detached. It hurtled over a 250-foot embankment, did a full somersault, and landed upright at the river's edge. The fireman and engineer climbed out unhurt.

There was a curious accident at Cherry Creek caused by the near-desert conditions of the Interior Plateau of British Columbia. To one teamster hauling blasting powder by wagon, the rocks on the roadbed beneath suddenly seemed to take fire. The sight caused the horses to plunge forward, breaking loose from the wagon and pulling the driver, who held fast to the reins, right off his seat and away from the vehicle, which blew up with a roar. Later the mystery was unraveled: the dry weather had shrunk the staves of the powder barrels so that every seam leaked explosive. Thus both the floor of the wagon and the road beneath it were covered with loose powder, which was finally ignited by sparks made by the horses' shoes striking the rocks.

There were other odd mishaps caused by the treacherous terrain. It was not even safe to get drunk. One veteran railroader who did staggered to the top of a bluff not far from the Big Tunnel one January day and toppled to his death. Even as careful and experienced an engineer as Henry Cambie was not immune. His horses bolted on the Cariboo Road —a fairly common occurrence—his carriage struck a new stump, and he, his wife, and his child were thrown out. The child escaped unhurt but both parents were injured, Mrs. Cambie suffering a severe concussion.

The danger was so great that it became difficult to get men who were willing to be suspended by ropes to drill holes in the chasm walls for explosives. The Indians were the most fearless; fortunately, they turned out to be first-class rock workers. Their task was to go down first and blast out the footholds in which other men could stand and work. But the Indians had a habit of working until payday and then quitting to spend their earnings.

Six months after Onderdonk began his contract, the hospital at Yale had to be enlarged to take care of the accident victims. Mrs. Onderdonk, capable and unpretentious, acted as superintendent. Most of the injured arrived in bad shape because of the difficulty of conveying them back to Yale over the impossible terrain. By August, 1881, the *Inland Sentinel*, which had been reporting deaths almost weekly, had become alarmed at the accident rate: "Life is held too cheap, generally, in this country, and it will evidently require severe punishment to teach parties that they cannot trifle with other people's lives even if they are careless of their own existence." Exactly one week after those words were written, two more men working in Number Seven Tunnel were killed by falling boulders.

2 · *"The beardless children of China"*

WHEN ANDREW ONDERDONK ARRIVED IN British Columbia there were perhaps thirty-five thousand white citizens in the province. Since he would need at least ten thousand able-bodied men to build his part of the railway—and actually many more, because of the turnover—it was clear that he would have to look elsewhere for much of his labor force. From the very outset there was a kind of terror that he would solve the problem by importing and employing Chinese.

As soon as he arrived in Victoria in April, 1880, Onderdonk was met by a deputation from the Anti-Chinese Association. It was his intention, he assured the delegation, to give white labor the preference in all cases. The difficulty was that there was very little surplus white labor because of the railroad boom in the western United States and in Canada. When the white labor of the province was exhausted, Onderdonk said he would, if necessity compelled him, fall back on the French Canadians of eastern Canada. Should that not be sufficient, he would with reluctance engage Indians and Chinese.

The first Chinese had come to British Columbia from California in 1858, attracted by the gold of the Fraser and Cariboo. Anti-Chinese feeling had been rising steadily since the early 1860's and had reached a peak in 1878, when the legislature passed a resolution banning their employment in the public works of the province. At that time there were some three thousand Chinese in British Columbia, all of them prepared to work for lower wages than any white laborer; that was the chief cause of the discontent. There was no politician in the province who could have been elected had he advocated, even in the most tentative terms, the continued admittance of any Chinese to Canada. Indeed, it was considered political suicide to take any stand but one that was anti-Oriental.

The feeling elsewhere in Canada, though less intense, was generally against the Chinese. Almost all newspapers were editorially opposed to Oriental immigration. In Winnipeg, where Chinese were all but unknown, the *Times* published a fairly typical series of opinions about "the beardless and immoral children of China," as it called them; they possessed "no sense whatever of any principle of morality"; their brains were "vacant of all thoughts which lift up and ennoble humanity"; and "it is an established fact that dealings with the Chinese are attended with evil results."

The Prime Minister himself agreed that the Chinese were "an alien race in every sense that would not and could not be expected to assimilate with our Arian population," but he was far too pragmatic to exclude Orientals from Canada until the railway was built. He put it bluntly to Parliament in 1882: "It is simply a question of alternatives: either you must have this labour or you can't have the railway."

The vanguard of Onderdonk's white labor force came from San Francisco, then the only real source of supply. Some of these men, sent up by employment agents, had never done a hard day's work before. To quote Henry Cambie, they were for the most part clerks out of employment, "broken-down bar-keepers, or men of that class," men who had never handled a shovel before and who often appeared on the scene attired in fashionable garments in a rather tattered state. Some of these new laborers actually went into the cuttings wearing patent-leather shoes with trousers sprung over the foot.

Onderdonk was operating on a tight budget. He had been forced to accept four contracts at bids which were more than a million and a half dollars lower than his own tendered price. He had paid out an additional two hundred and fifteen thousand dollars to purchase the contracts of the successful bidders. In short, he had almost two million dollars less to work with than he had contemplated when he undertook to tender on the Fraser River section of the CPR.

Moreover, he was asking men to come all the way to the wilds of British Columbia for wages that were lower than those the Northern Pacific was offering through more settled country. Onderdonk paid his laborers between $1.50 and $1.75 a day; the American railway was offering between $1.75 and $2 a day. For skilled labor, the gap was even greater.

Chinese coolies, on the other hand, could be employed for one dollar a day. The contracts, furthermore, stipulated that they must buy their provisions at the company stores, where the prices were inflated; if they took their custom elsewhere they were to be paid only eighty cents. White workers required all the paraphernalia of a first-class camp, including cooks, flunkeys, and a wide variety of supplies but the coolie was prepared to take care of himself. He could move about in the wilderness, set up his own camp, and pack all his belongings, provisions, and camp equipment on his back. Michael Haney, who went to work for Onderdonk in 1883, discovered that it was possible to move two thousand Chinese a distance of twenty-five miles and have them at work all within twenty-four hours. The same task could not be performed with a similar number of white workmen in less than a week. It is small wonder, then, that almost from the outset Andrew Onderdonk began hiring Chinese in spite of a volley of protests.

In the Report of the Royal Commission on Chinese Immigration in 1885, J. A. Chapleau wrote that "as a railway navvy, the Chinaman has no superior." Long before that, the United States transcontinental railway system had already established the efficiency of coolie labor. Onderdonk's first consignment came from the Northern Pacific Railroad in Oregon in 1880, the second from the Southern Pacific in California in 1881.

In the winter of 1881–82, Onderdonk chartered two sailing ships to bring an additional two thousand coolies from Hong Kong. They arrived after a long, rough winter passage—"the men below decks slept in closed hatches with bad ventilation," Cambie recalled—but in good physical condition. In New Westminster they were "penned in the wharf overnight like so many cattle" and then packed aboard the little stern-wheeler *William Irving*—as many as 642 to a boatload—transferred to flatcars at Emory, and sent directly out along the line. All together in 1882, Onderdonk brought in ten shiploads of Chinese, a total of about six thousand.

The coolies came from eight districts of Kwangtung Province, whose capital, Canton, until 1842 was the only port in the country through which foreign trade was permitted. The crowded conditions of the coolies who were hived together, 241,000 to the square mile, made the prospect of emigration attractive. All it took to ensure financial independence in Kwangtung, where the average wage was seven cents a day, was three hundred American dollars. It was the ambition of almost every immigrant to save that much money and then return to his homeland after perhaps five years of work on the railroad or in the mining camps, a situation which helps explain the British Columbians' continuing complaints about money leaving the province.

The Chinese were not hired individually but in large groups of as many as a thousand through agents representing the Six Companies of Kwangtung. These companies were rather like commercial guilds. They handled the shipment of Chinese to North America as well as their contracts with their employers and their eventual return to China. Each Chinese paid a fee of 2.5 per cent of his wages to the company, together with his passage money—about forty dollars. The company, in its turn, was pledged to look after each man's welfare in North America, protecting him, for instance, if he got into legal difficulties.

This was certainly not "slave" labor, as many British Columbia politicians and newspapers called it, or even indentured labor. Undoubtedly the companies were a good deal more than mere benevolent associations: they made a good profit and, through an arrangement with the steamship companies, rendered it impossible for any Chinese to return home before he had paid his debts. On the other hand, from the point of view of the individual coolie, who could speak not a word of English and who was totally uninformed about North American customs and society, the Six Companies represented the only real method of getting to the promised land.

Michael Haney declared that in his entire experience of dealing with the Chinese he could not recall one case of dishonesty. They lived up to their contracts, and if there was a dispute with a subcontractor, "it only needed the presence of a representative of the contractor to assure them that their grievances would be considered, to send them cheerfully to work again." Nor did Haney know of a single instance of disagreement between the individual worker and the Chinese company that paid the wages. The experience of the contractors with the Chinese on the job was in marked contrast to the general feeling against them in Victoria. Everybody who dealt with them as laborers, from Andrew Onderdonk down, praised them. George Munro, who had charge of a construction gang from Yale east to Sicamous, echoed the general attitude when he said they "were easy to handle if they were properly dealt with." But woe to any white boss who dealt with them improperly! If they thought their rights were being trampled on, they ceased to be docile. After all, in the days of Imperial China, Kwangtung had a persistent reputation for disaffection; most of the active leaders of the subsequent revolution, including Sun Yat-sen himself, were Cantonese. Munro ruefully recalled his first payday, when, through an error in the payroll department, the Chinese workers received one cent less per hour than had been agreed upon. ". . . there was a little war declared right there. They stormed the Company's stores like madmen, and it didn't take the men at fault long to discover their mistake. The Chinamen were paid their cent and peace reigned once more."

Such incidents were not uncommon. The coolies were divided by the company that provided them into gangs of thirty laborers plus a cook, an assistant cook, and a bookman, whose task it was to keep count of the payments to be made to each individual. In charge of each work gang was a white boss or "herder," who dealt directly with the bookman. Any foreman who did not get along well with his Oriental laborers could expect trouble. Once when a white boss refused to allow his coolies to build a fire along the grade to heat their big teapots, they quit en masse and headed for Yale. On several occasions, white foremen were physically assaulted. One foreman who tried to fire two Chinese over the head of the gang's bookkeeper precipitated a riot near Lytton. He and the white bridge superintendent, the timekeeper, and a teamster were attacked by the entire gang, which mangled one man with a shovel. The following night a party of armed whites attacked the Chinese camp, burned their bunkhouses, and beat several coolies so severely that one died.

In such instances feeling ran high against the coolies. The Chief Justice of the province, Matthew Baillie Begbie, was horrified by "the terrible outrages against Chinamen" in the neighborhood of Lytton. One case, he said, "in its wholesale unconcealed atrocity equalled anything which I have read of agrarian outrage in Ireland." Begbie was aghast that in all cases "the perpetrators have escaped scot free." In one instance the ringleaders were positively identified by four of the surviving victims but were acquitted by the jury "upon evidence of an *alibi* which the prosecutors might well deem perjured."

The Chinese could also escape detection; since all coolies looked alike to whites, it was difficult and sometimes impossible to swear out warrants for their arrest. The *Inland Sentinel* reported in August, 1882, that "the Chinese workers below Emory went this week for another boss and he had to make tracks for Yale. An effort has been made to get out 8 warrants in the names of the Chinamen, but they could not be had, consequently the effort failed."

Two Chinese who attacked a foreman near Maple Ridge in February, 1883, were summonsed but later released "by a howling mob of Chinamen holding in their hands . . . axes, picks, shovels . . . [who] declared that unless the prisoners were released they would tear the houses to pieces and rescue them." The prisoners were let go but were later recaptured, fined sixteen dollars each, and returned to camp without further trouble.

Many of these incidents occurred because of accidents along the line, for which the Chinese blamed the white foremen. At Hammond, after a big slide killed several coolies, the foreman had to hold their angry co-workers at bay with a leveled revolver. Another time, about ten miles below Hope, a foreman named Miller failed to give his gang proper warning of a coming explosion; a piece of rock thrown up by the subsequent blast blew one coolie's head right off. His comrades took off after Miller, who plunged into the river to save himself. Several Chinese dived in after him while others on the bank pelted him with stones. Miller was saved by a tunnel contractor who rowed a boat through the hail of missiles and hauled him in, but not before one of the Chinese had gotten off two shots from a pistol. Miller and his rescuer rowed desperately upstream, followed for two miles by an angry mob, before they made good their escape. Commented the *Inland Sentinel*: "Not even Chinamen should be unnecessarily exposed to injury or loss of life."

Fatalities appeared to be more frequent among the Chinese laborers than in the white group. A single month in the late summer of Onderdonk's first season, culled from Henry Cambie's diary, gives an idea of their frequency:

"*August 13* [*1880*]—A Chinese drilling on the ledge of a bluff near Alexandra Bar is killed when a stone falls from above and knocks him off."

"*August 19*—A log rolls over an embankment and crushes a Chinese to death at the foot of a slope."

"*September 4*—A Chinese killed by a rock slide."

"*September 7*—A boat upsets in the Fraser and a Chinese is drowned."

"*September 11*—A Chinese is smothered to death in an earth cave-in."

Yet, in that last week—on September 9—the *Sentinel* proudly announced that "there have been no deaths since the 15th of June." Clearly it did not count Chinese.

The coolies were generally fatalistic about death. Haney, calling one day at a tent where a sick Chinese lay, asked the bookman, "Will he die to-day?" The bookman shook his head. "No, to-morrow, three o'clock." Haney claimed that at three, to the minute, the man expired.

The Chinese would not work in the presence of death, which they considered bad luck. When a man died on the job, the gang that worked with him usually had to be moved to another section of the line. Haney once came upon two thousand Chinese all sitting idle; one of their number had fallen off the bank and his corpse lay far below, spread-eagled on the rocks. In vain the walking boss argued and swore. He pointed out that it was impossible to reach the body. The bank was a sheer precipice, and no boat could approach it through the boiling waters.

"Well," said Haney, "what do you propose to do? Can't have these Chinamen standing around until that Chinaboy disintegrates."

The walking boss scratched his head. "There's an Indian who promises to move that body for ten dollars. I've tried to make a deal with him but he won't budge on that price and it's too much."

"Never mind how much it is," Haney retorted. "Pay it and get those men back to work."

He moved off down the line. During the evening a sharp explosion was heard in the canyon. When Haney returned, the Chinese were back at work and the body had vanished. The Indian had stolen some dynamite and caps, lowered them with a smoldering fuse down the canyon wall, and blown the cadaver to bits.

The Chinese subsisted mainly on a diet of rice and stale ground salmon, scorning the white man's fresh meat and vegetables. As a result they died by the score from scurvy, and no real attempt was made to succor them. Two hundred who came over from China died during their first year in Canada, causing a panic among the citizens of Yale, who believed the newcomers were suffering from smallpox. As in other deaths of Chinese from accident or illness, there was no coroner's inquest and no medical attention was supplied by either the government or the contractor.

The cold winters caused the Chinese great hardship. Most found it impossible to work after mid-November. Cambie, on November 22, noted: "Chinamen who are still at work (only a few gangs) appear to suffer dreadfully from cold. They work in overcoats and wrap their heads up in mufflers." In the winter of 1883–84, when Onderdonk's work force was diminished, the suffering was very great. When the contractors had no more need of them, the Chinese were discharged and left to scrabble for pickings in the worked-out sandbars of the Fraser or to exist in near destitution in the dying towns along the completed track.

Not all of the Chinese who came to Canada with the hope of securing financial independence achieved their dream. The sudden completion of the Onderdonk contract made return to Asia impossible for thousands who had not been able to raise the price of passage home or the minor fortune of three hundred dollars that they had expected to amass. Although a Chinese laborer was paid about twenty-five dollars a month on the railway, it was difficult for him to save very much. He was not paid for the three months of winter when work was at a near standstill. His expenses were considerable: for clothes, $130; for room rent, $24; for tools and fares, $10; for revenue and road taxes, $5; for religious fees, $5; for doctors and drugs, $3; for oil, light, water, and tobacco, $5. These typical charges (given to a Royal Commission by an informed Chinese witness) left the average coolie with exactly forty-three dollars after a full year of toil on the railway. That scarcely covered his debt to the steamboat company. The census figures of 1891 indicate that some five thousand coolies were unable to go back to Asia in the years following the completion of the Onderdonk contract.

Because the Chinese left home expecting to return in a few years, they made no attempt to learn the language or alter their mode of life. They clung to the simple coolie jacket, loose trousers, cloth slippers, and pigtail. They kept to their own ways, for they had no intention of losing their character in what they believed would be a temporary abode. Thus they were forever strangers in a foreign land and their continued presence gave to British Columbia a legacy of racial tension that was to endure for more than half a century.

The Chinese railway workers who remained left few descendants (since they brought no women with them) and few, if any, memories. Some, however, returned to Kwangtung and then came back to Canada with their families to settle permanently in British Columbia. One of whom there is some slight record was a farmer from Toyshan named Pon Git Cheng. One of his sons became a houseboy for Benjamin Tingley Rogers, the Vancouver sugar magnate. And one of *his* sons, Dr. George Pon of Toronto, was in 1972 a vice-president of Atomic Energy of Canada. Dr. Pon was told something of his family background and was able to return to China to visit his grandfather's village in Toyshan. But he never discovered exactly what it was his grandfather did on the railway—how he was hired, where he worked, or what he felt about the strange, raw land which was to become his home. Such details were not set down and so are lost forever—lost and forgotten, like the crumbling bones that lie in unmarked graves beneath the rock and the rubble high above the Fraser's angry torrent.

3 · *Michael Haney to the rescue*

CHEAP ORIENTAL LABOR UNDOUBTEDLY saved Onderdonk from bankruptcy. Without the Chinese he would have had enormous difficulty in finding enough manpower to do the job, and the competitive market would certainly have forced up the cost of white labor. Between 1880 and 1884, at their lower rate of pay, the coolies saved him between three and five million dollars. Their presence also acted as a damper on wage demands. In 1884, for example, when workmen near Port Moody struck, they were instantly replaced by a gang of Chinese rushed down from Yale.

The Governor General believed that the presence of the Chinese was keeping costs down by at least 25 per cent, but even with this advantage Onderdonk's operation was a marginal one. By 1883 he was clearly in financial trouble. Marcus Smith, the government engineer who acted as Ottawa's watchdog on the line, reported that winter that "it was painfully apparent to myself and even to outsiders that the men were not working to advantage nor were they being well directed. . . ." Smith had his staff estimate the amount of work being done per man and found—on the basis of cubic yards of earth moved—that the averages were very low. Unless some drastic changes were made, he felt, Onderdonk could not pull through without heavy loss.

By March, 1883, when Onderdonk hired Michael Haney, he was showing a book loss of two and a half million dollars on the work completed. Haney was given the management of the entire operation from Port Moody to Kamloops.

The crusty Marcus Smith was of two minds about Haney. "He seems to fully realize the gravity of your position and is anxious to improve it," he told Onderdonk, but he also warned that if Haney thought he could save the situation by evading or curtailing essential portions of the work, "he is bordering on dreamland."

"I hope Mr. Haney has not caught the disease of the American mind to do something rapid or astounding," Smith wrote. Haney, after all, was given to bold escapades. He did, however, know a good deal about saving money. Many of Onderdonk's problems, he quickly discovered, had come about through slack organization, slow handling of materials, and delays in transportation. He immediately tightened up discipline and speeded deliveries. He introduced his invention, the wing plow, which unloaded gravel from a line of open cars at bewildering speed. He developed a large nitroglycerine factory at Yale, and when it blew up, breaking every window in town, he rebuilt it. He traveled the line on horseback, using relays of steeds so that he could inspect as much as a hundred miles of track a day. In this way all of the work in progress came under his personal inspection twice each month.

One of the chief reasons for the delays, Haney discovered, was the inordinate amount of trestle bridging required. Timbers had to be shaped and cut at each bridging point, always at enormous cost. Haney streamlined the operation by building a mill capable of producing one hundred and fifty thousand board feet of lumber a day with every stick marked and numbered for its exact position on the bridge for which it was destined. By this method, the great trestles, fabricated in advance, were sent forward ready for immediate erection. At the scene, an ingenious foreman named Dan McGillivray had worked out a method of sending each marked timber to its destination by means of a cable and pulley system stretched across the trestle.

Haney was a man who did everything with flair, a characteristic that helps explain why he was viewed as a kind of walking accident. On the Thunder Bay line he had survived at least four brushes with death. When the new Governor General, the Marquess of Lansdowne, came out to inspect the line shortly before its completion, Haney insisted on taking him on a wild ride to the coast. The viceregal train rattled along at seventy miles an hour, careering around the tight curves which the government had insisted upon in the interests of cutting costs. Lansdowne, a quiet man, scarcely uttered a word as Haney enthusiastically pointed out to him how well the track was laid.

Finally, when they stopped at a small station to take on water, His Excellency spoke up: "How far is it to Port Moody?"

Haney replied that it was another forty-eight miles.

"Will we be running as fast the balance of the way?"

Haney responded that he thought he could better the pace.

"I have a wife and family in Ottawa and I am rather anxious to see them again," the Governor General replied, "so if you are continuing that rate of travel, I think I will just stay here." A chastened Haney brought the train crawling into Port Moody.

In spite of Haney's cost cutting, Onderdonk's financial problems continued. In the fall of 1883 he set off for Ottawa to lobby for a further subsidy for the unfinished line. In Victoria he ran into one James Hartney, who had been cutting timber for him and who had not yet been paid. It says something for the state of Onderdonk's finances that the railway builder, who had a continent-wide reputation for prompt payment, kept putting Hartney off. He was preparing to leave for San Francisco with his family on a Sunday evening, but just before the ship sailed, Hartney served him with a writ. Thus was the island community treated to the strange spectacle of the province's biggest employer of labor being pulled from his bunk at two in the morning, hauled back to shore, and lodged in jail, where he languished for two hours before his friends bailed him out.

4 · *The* Sentinel *of Yale*

THE OPTIMISM OF FRONTIER COMMUNIties along the line of the railway in the 1880's knew no bounds. The transitory aspect of railway building did not seem to impress itself on those who settled in the small towns, which boomed briefly and just as quickly faded. When it became clear that the Pacific railway was finally to be built and the details of the Onderdonk contract were made public, the price of lots rose swiftly in Emory, the steamboat landing at the head of the navigable section of the Fraser—a town that had seen an earlier period of prosperity flare and fade during the gold rush of 1858.

Emory, the real-estate ads announced, "cannot fail to become one of the most important and prosperous Cities on the Pacific slope." But Emory was not destined to be a city. It soon became clear that the real center of the Onderdonk operations would be at Yale. "Next summer will be a boom for Emory sure," the paper wrote wistfully in January, 1881. But in May the *Sentinel* itself moved its offices to Yale —a roaring, wide-open community which for the next three years was to be the railway center of British Columbia. Then it too would fade as merchants, workers, and major institutions—once again including the *Sentinel*—packed up and moved to Kamloops.

The *Sentinel*'s editor, a black Irishman named Michael Hagan, belonged to that vanishing breed, the itinerant journeyman newspaper Jack-of-all-trades. When he arrived at Emory in the spring of 1880, there was not much about a newspaper office that he had not mastered. He was prepared to write every word himself, set it all in type, buck the hand press, and trudge up and down the line between Emory and Yale, a stout staff in his hand, drumming up business. Apparently he was attracted by railway construction towns. Six years before, he had launched another *Sentinel* at Thunder Bay.

Hagan's assistant, George Kennedy, always remembered his first sight of Yale. The paper was still being published at Emory when he and Hagan, with the latest edition strapped to their backs, poled and paddled a canoe through the ripples of the canyon the four miles to the neighboring community.

"The town of Yale was *en fête* that day in a 'wild and woolly' sense, and the one long main 'business' street fronting the river, presented a scene and sounds, at once animated and grotesque—bizarre and risqué. The shell like shacks of saloons, whereof every third building, nearly, was one, fairly buzzed and bulged like Brobdignagian wasps' nests, whose inmates, in a continual state of flux, ever and anon hurled in and out, in two's and three's or tangled wrangling masses. Painted and bedizened women lent a garish color to the scene. On the hot and dusty road-side, or around timbers, rails, and other construction debris, men in advanced stages of intoxication rolled and fought or snored in bestial oblivion. One drunken duel assumed a gory and tragic guise, when one of the sweating, swearing gladiators started sawing at his antagonist's neck with a jack knife. A tardy conservor of the peace, at this stage, separated the bloody belligerents, while a handy medicine man did a timely mending job on the lacerated connecting-piece of the chief victim."

It was a brilliant scene. Every shape of face and every kind of costume was observable along the main street. The saloons, with names like the Rat Trap, Stiff's Rest, and the Railroader's Retreat, were packed with gamblers playing faro, poker, chuck-a-luck, and dice. Three-card monte, the confidence man's game, was to be found everywhere. Against the incessant hammering of drills and the periodic crump of blasting powder, there was a cacophony of foreground noises —saw, mallet, and hammer, mouth organ, fiddle, and concertina, blending with the harsher music of rattling wheels. The air reeked with the mingled pungencies of fresh salmon, sawdust, black powder, and tobacco smoke. Yale, in short, was very like any raw frontier town in Wyoming, Montana, or Arizona save for one thing: all the saloons were shut tight on Sunday.

The Irish were everywhere. There were five local characters named Kelly, all unrelated. Big Mouth Kelly had the contract for burying dead Chinese. Kelly the Rake was a professional gambler who seemed to have been sent out by a casting office: he dressed totally in black from his wide sombrero and knotted silk tie to his leather leggings and narrow boots. Silent Kelly was so called because he played solitaire day after day. Molly Kelly ran a bawdyhouse. Long Kelly worked for her.

The Toronto *Mail* dispatched a man to examine the phenomenal community. He observed that "people don't walk in Yale, they rush. Yale is no place for a gentleman of leisure. From 'peep o' day' til long into the night the movement of men, horses and wagons along the one business street goes on scarcely with intermission. As we gaze at the hurrying throngs we wonder how on earth they all find beds or even space in which to lie down when they seek repose."

Although prices were double and triple those in San Francisco, nobody seemed to grudge spending a dollar. Hagan continually warned his readers—one suspects in vain—of the dire consequences of spending all their wages the day they received them: ". . . such abuse will undermine health and leave disease and want in train. Once the money is squandered very little care need be expected and . . . a premature death is the result. . . . Let those unfortunately addicted to strong drink take heed."

It was a strange and rather artificial world. Almost everybody must have known that it was a temporary existence, but no one voiced that feeling. Hagan wrote optimistically about the town's great future from vague mining properties, but in his editorial columns there was a growing peevishness towards the Onderdonk company as the railway out of Yale neared completion. The feeling of optimism gave way to a kind of carping against established forces. On May 3, 1883, following a rumor that the roundhouse and machine shops were to be moved, Hagan called a meeting to discuss "this desertion of the town." But a year later, he too was forced to desert.

The impermanence of the community was underlined by the shifting population and by the terrible fires that ravaged the business section. Seen from the steamer, the chief characteristic of the community was its newness. The buildings were always new; so were the fences, the sidewalks, and the people. Yale had no opportunity to grow old.

In its three-year joy ride, the town suffered two disastrous fires, both started by drunks. On July 27, 1880, a third of the town was burned to the ground, only a month after Hagan had warned the townspeople of the dangers of just such a conflagration. But ebullient communities rarely look to the future, being concerned with the pleasures and profits of the moment. Hagan was ignored. It took a second fire in August of 1881, which reduced half the town to ashes in three hours, before there was any serious talk about gathering funds to buy a steam pumper.

The news of such disasters took some time to leak to the outside world, for, in spite of the human traffic, Yale existed in a kind of vacuum. There was no telegraph or telephone service; as a result, almost every item carried in the weekly *Sentinel* was a local one. Mail from the East came by way of San Francisco and took weeks to arrive. Much of the news from Europe was two months old. A simple journey from Victoria could be an exhausting undertaking.

After the town burned down for the second time, it began to take on a more sober and less flamboyant appearance. Concerts, recitals, lectures, and minstrel shows began to vie with the saloons for patronage. An entertainment institute was formed, for whose first recital Mrs. Onderdonk kindly lent her piano. The Chinese opened their own Freemasons' Lodge with an ornamental flagstaff, as well as a joss house. Grand balls were held, in which people danced all night—and even longer—to the music of scraping violins. "A ball out here means business," wrote Dr. Daniel Parker, Charles Tupper's traveling companion. "The last one . . . commenced at 12 o'clock on Monday morning and lasted continuously day and night until 12 o'clock the next Saturday."

On the great fête days the community, bound by a growing feeling of cohesion, turned out en masse. The Queen's Birthday on May 24 was an occasion for a half holiday for whites and Indians. Chinese New Year, celebrated by the coolies early in February, ran for an entire week and "favourably impressed the white people of Yale." The biggest event of all was the Fourth of July, since Yale was very much an American town; indeed, Hagan declared in his newspaper that the large number of Americans working on the railway "have caused the B. Columbians to worry about the possibility of the Americans forcing the province into American hands."

Nonetheless, everyone turned out to honor the day that, again in Hagan's words, "gave birth to free America—the home of the oppressed of all nations." Half the population of New Westminster chugged up the river for the occasion on the *William Irving*, decked with greenery and flying pennants, a band playing on her upper deck. Cannons roared. Locomotives pulled flatcars crammed with excursionists from neighboring Emory. Indians climbed greased poles. "The Star-Spangled Banner" was enthusiastically rendered outside the Onderdonk home. Couples tripped "the light fantastic toe" on a special platform erected on the main street. There were horse races, canoe races, caber tossing, and hurdles. "It was conceded on all hands that the day was a gala one." By comparison, July 1, celebrating a Confederation that was less than a generation old, passed almost unnoticed. British Columbia was part British and part American; it would require the completion of the railway to make her part of the new Dominion.

Far off beyond the mountains—beyond the rounded bulks of the Gold Range, beyond the pointed peaks of the mysterious Selkirks—the rails were inching west; but as far as Onderdonk's navvies were concerned, that land was almost as distant as China. ". . . we really knew very little about what they were doing on that side," Henry Cambie recalled. Any letters, if such had been written, would have had to travel down the muddy Fraser by boat, on to Victoria, and thence to San Francisco, across the United States to St. Paul, north into Winnipeg, and then west again until they reached End of Track. The distance involved was more than five thousand miles, and yet in 1883 End of Track, in the foothills, was only about three hundred miles away.

15

1 · The Promised Land

BY THE SPRING OF 1883, CANADA WAS A country with half a transcontinental railroad. Between Port Moody and Ottawa, the track lay in pieces like a child's train set—long stretches of finished road separated by formidable gaps. The easiest part of the CPR was complete: a continuous line of steel ran west for 937 miles from Fort William at the head of Lake Superior to the tent community of Swift Current in the heart of Palliser's Triangle. To the west, between Swift Current and the half-completed Onderdonk section in British Columbia, was a gap of 750 miles on parts of which not even a surveyor had set foot. The section closest to civilization was graded, waiting for the rails to be laid. The remainder was a mélange of tote roads, forest slashings, skeletons of bridges, and engineers' stakes. An equally awesome gap, of more than six hundred miles, extended east from End of Track near Fort William to the terminus of the newly completed Canada Central Railway on Lake Nipissing. Again, this was little more than a network of mired roads chopped out of the stunted timber and, here and there, some partially blasted tunnels and rock cuts.

By the time the snows melted, almost the entire right of way for twenty-five hundred miles, from the rim of the Shield to tidewater, was abuzz with human activity. In the East, the timber cutters and rock men who had endured the desolation of Superior's shore the previous winter were ripping a right of way out of the Pre-Cambrian wilderness.

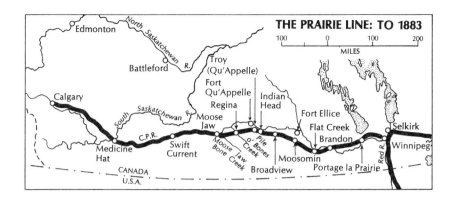

THE PRAIRIE LINE: TO 1883

In the Far West, more thousands were invading the land of the Black-foot tribes and clambering up the mountains. Little steel shoots were sprouting south, west, and east of the main trunk line in Manitoba. And wherever the steel went, the settlers followed with their tents and their tools, their cattle and their kittens, their furniture and their fences.

From the famine-ridden bog country of Ireland, the bleak crofts of the Scottish hills, and the smoky hives of industrial England, the immigrants were pouring in. They clogged the docks at Liverpool—three thousand in a single record day, half of them bound for Manitoba—kerchiefed women with squalling infants, nervous young husbands, chalky with the pallor of the cities, and the occasional grandmother, all clutching in a last embrace those friends and relatives whom they never expected to see again. They endured the nausea of the long sea journey, emerged from the dank holds of Sir Hugh Allan's steamships at Halifax and Montreal, and swarmed aboard the flimsy immigrant cars that chugged off to the North West—the "land of milk and honey," as the posters proclaimed it. Occasionally some sardonic newcomer would scribble the qualification "if you keep cows and bees" beneath that confident slogan; but most of the arrivals cheerfully believed it, enduring the kennels of the colonist cars in the sure knowledge that a mecca of sorts awaited them.

The land moved past them like a series of painted scenes on flash cards—a confused impression of station platforms and very little more, because the windows in the wooden cars were too high and too small to afford much of a view of the new world. They sat crowded together on hard seats that ran lengthwise and they cooked their own food on a wood stove placed in the center of the car. They were patient people, full of hope, blessed by good cheer. In the spring and summer of 1883, some 133,000 of them arrived in Canada. Of that number, two-thirds sped directly to the North West.

No one, apparently, had expected such an onslaught. The demand for Atlantic passage was unprecedented. The CPR found it had insufficient rolling stock to handle the invading army and was obliged to use its dwindling reserves of cash to buy additional colonist cars secondhand. In Toronto, the immigrant sheds were overflowing; in May alone ten thousand meals were served there—as many as had been prepared in the entire season of 1882. The young Canada postal service was overtaxed with twelve thousand letters destined for the North West. The number had quadrupled in just two years.

Off to the West the trains puffed, every car crammed—some people, indeed, clinging to the steps, and all singing the song that became the theme of the pioneers: "One More River to Cross." The CPR by April was able to take them as far as the tent community of Moose Jaw, four hundred miles to the west.

It was not always easy to tell blue blood from peasant. The man on the next homestead or the waiter serving in a tent restaurant might be of noble birth; the son of Alfred Lord Tennyson, the poet laureate, was breaking sod on a homestead that spring. The journalist Nicholas Flood Davin on his first day in Regina was struck by the gentlemanly bearing of the waiter in the tent where he breakfasted. He turned out to be a nephew of the Duke of Rutland, engaged in managing a hastily erected hotel for the nephew of Earl Granville, who had opened a similar establishment in Brandon.

The most singular settlement of all was Cannington Manor, founded forty miles south of Moosomin and named for a village in Somerset. Here a group of former English public-school boys, led by a British officer, Captain E. M. Pierce, attempted to re-create the folkways of the aristocracy on the bald prairie. In its heyday Cannington Manor boasted a twenty-two-room mansion, a private race track (complete with imported steeplechase jockeys), and a hunt club replete with authentic foxhounds and thoroughbred horses. The residents played cricket, rugger, and tennis, engaged in amateur theatricals, raised game fowl, and established a stock farm, a pork-packing plant, two cheese factories, and a variety of village trades. But when the CPR branch line, which all had hoped for, was built ten miles to the south, Cannington Manor became a ghost town.

The immigrants brought everything to the prairies, including pets. One enterprising arrival from Ontario, sensing the loneliness of the settler's life, brought in a crate of cats. They were snapped up at three dollars apiece. An early pioneer, Esther Goldsmith, always remembered the wild scene at the Brandon station when a bird cage was snatched from a woman's hand in the scramble for the train. Another recalled her first real view of the prairie driving eighty-five miles north from

Broadview with a canary in a cage on her lap. A typical menagerie was that brought to Moosomin in April, 1883, by the Hislop family. It included two horses, four cows, three sheep, a little white sow, a dog, a cat, eleven hens, and a rooster.

"Freedom?" wrote William Oliver sardonically. "There never was such a thing; every acre was won by hard toil and the sweat of man." The breaking up of the prairie sod was grueling work. Oliver noted that the land was dotted with small rosebushes, whose interwoven roots added to the toughness of the turf. A man with a good team of oxen was lucky if he could till three-quarters of an acre in a day. It was a harsher life than many would-be pioneers had bargained for. Oliver, who was a carpenter, was asked by one well-to-do young Englishman to build him a home not far from Regina on two sections of land. It was a substantial house for those parts, complete with carpeting, window drapery, and furniture from England. But when the job was finished, the settler's wife arrived with two maids and a manservant and stared at the results with something approaching horror. "I cannot describe her arrival," Oliver wrote. "It was pathetic in the extreme." She lasted exactly six months and then left her husband, who, having wasted a fortune, could not face returning to England and instead took a job with the Indian Department.

Government land was free up to a limit of a quarter section, or 160 acres; the homesteader who worked it for three years was given title to it and could, in addition, pre-empt an adjoining quarter section; that is, he could take an option to purchase it in the future and thus prevent himself from being hemmed in.

In the North West, as the rails pushed steadily toward the mountains, new communities began to take shape. "These towns along the line west of Brandon are all the same," the Fort McLeod *Gazette* reported. "See one, see all. There are some board houses, but most of them are board frames (rough) with a canvas roof." Both Moose Jaw, with its "bare, freckled and sunburnt buildings," and Medicine Hat, another canvas town on a coulee of that name, were in this category. The former, in spite of its youth, already had three newspapers by 1883. The latter, by July, boasted six hotels, though most of them were mere tents sheltering half a dozen bunks.

This was Sam Steele's territory. The remarkable Mounted Policeman had been named acting adjutant of the Fort Qu'Appelle district the previous year and placed in command of detachments along the line of CPR construction. As the rails made their way from the coulees of Saskatchewan to the final spike at Craigellachie, Steele would always be on hand to keep the peace. A huge man with deep chest and bristling mustache Steele had a solidly military background: one ancestor had fought with Wolfe at Quebec, another with Nelson at Trafalgar, a third with Wellington at Waterloo. At seventeen, Steele had joined the militia, serving against the Fenians in 1866 and taking part in General Garnet Wolseley's Red River Expedition against Riel in 1870 (when he managed to hoist three-hundred-pound barrels of flour onto his massive shoulders to negotiate the portages of the Pre-Cambrian Shield). Steele was a perennial volunteer. When the first permanent force unit was formed in 1871, he rushed to the colors. When the North West Mounted Police was organized in 1873, he joined immediately, becoming the force's first sergeant-major. He had a habit of being present when history was being made: he took part in the thousand-mile march to the Rockies in 1874; he bargained with Sitting Bull after the Custer affair; now he was presiding at the building of the first transcontinental railway; he would go on to become "the Lion of the Yukon" during the Klondike gold rush. Steele was the prototype Mountie, one of several who gave the force its traditions and turned it into an international symbol of the Canadian frontier. Even his name had a ring of romance to it: "Steele of the Mounted." James Oliver Curwood, the American novelist, borrowed the phrase for one of his books about the North.

In his capacity as police magistrate, Inspector Steele worked without rest under primitive conditions. In Regina his courtroom had been a tent, sixteen by fourteen feet. It was so cold that winter that the clerks had to keep their ink bottles on the tops of stoves. Between Moose Jaw and Medicine Hat, Steele had no courtroom at all. At Swift Current he tried cases while seated on a Red River cart, with planks stretched across it for a bench and the evidence taken down on the flap of his dispatch bag. As he worked he counted the trains roaring by to End of Track, loaded with ties, rails, and spikes. He could tell by the number how many miles were being laid that day.

By July, the organization had been perfected to the point where ninety-seven miles of track were laid instead of the monthly average of fifty-eight. As Langdon and Shepard approached the end of their contract, the track-laying guides were seized by a kind of frenzy; on July 28, about two weeks out of Calgary, they set a record that has never been surpassed for manual labor on a railroad: 6.38 miles of finished railway—earthworks, grading, track laying, and ballasting— were completed in a single day.

It was, of course, a stunt, theatrically produced by an organization that had reason to feel cocky. Special men were brought in for the job: the tireless Ryan brothers, world champion spikers, who could drive a spike home with two blows, and Big Jack, a Herculean Swede who was said to be able to hoist a thirty-foot rail weighing 560 pounds and heave it onto a flatcar without assistance. The statistics of that day have been preserved. Sixteen thousand ties and more than two thousand rails (totaling 604 tons) were used. A platoon of bolters, fifteen in all, each put in an average of 565 bolts, followed by thirty-two spikers, averaging four blows to a spike, which meant that in fourteen hours they each delivered an average of eighty-four hundred blows with a sledge hammer. The first two miles of material were hauled ten miles across the prairies and the remainder came up from a two-thousand-foot siding three miles away, which was itself installed that same day by the regular sidetrack gang. Such was the organization that the contractors had perfected in fewer than eighteen months.

The whole country marveled over the feat of building the railway across the prairies in just fifteen months—everybody, that is, except the people it was displacing. To the Indians, the road symbolized the end of a golden age—an age in which the native peoples, liberated by the white man's horses and the white man's weapons, had galloped at will across their untrammeled domain, where the game seemed unlimited and the zest of the hunt gave life a tang and a purpose. This truly idyllic existence came to an end with the suddenness of a thunderclap just as the railway, like a glittering spear, was thrust through the ancient hunting grounds of the Blackfoot and the Cree. Within six years, the image of the Plains Indian underwent a total transformation. From a proud and fearless nomad, rich in culture and tradition, he became a pathetic, half-starved creature, confined to the semiprisons of the new reserves and totally dependent on government relief for his existence.

The buffalo, on which the entire Indian economy and culture depended, were actually gone before the coming of the railway; but the order of their passing is immaterial. They could not have existed in a land bisected by steel and crisscrossed by barbed wire. The passing of the great herds was disastrous, for without the buffalo, which had supplied them with food, shelter, clothing, tools, and ornaments, the Indians were helpless. By 1880, after the three most terrible years they had ever known, the emaciated natives were forced to eat their dogs and their horses, to scrabble for gophers and mice, and even to consume the carcasses of animals found rotting on the prairie.

On top of this the Indians were faced with the sudden onslaught of a totally foreign agrarian culture. In eastern Canada, the influence of the white strangers had made itself felt gradually over a period of generations. In the North West the railway made it happen almost instantaneously. It did not matter that the various treaties guaranteed that the old, free life would continue and that the natives would not be forced to adopt white ways. With the buffalo gone and the grasslands tilled and fenced, such promises were hollow.

The government's policy, born of expediency, was a two-stage one. The starving Indians would be fed temporarily at public expense. Over a longer period, the Indian Department would attempt to bring about a sociological change that normally occupied centuries. It would settle the Indians on reserves and try to turn a race of hunters into a community of peasants. The reserves would be situated on land considered best suited for agriculture, all of it north of the line of the railway, far from the hunting grounds. Thus the CPR became the visible symbol of the Indians' tragedy.

It was a tall order. Only terrible privations could have caused thousands of once-independent people to abandon so meekly an entire way of life. The famine of 1879–80 forced thousands of reluctant Indians onto the new reserves. Others, led by such free spirits as the Cree chieftains Big Bear and Piapot, continued to defy the authorities and follow the will-o'-the-wisp of the buffalo through the Cypress Hills and into the United States. It was not the buffalo they were chasing but the shadows of the past; the great herds were always over the next hill. By the winter of 1882–83, five thousand disillusioned Indians were starving in the neighborhood of Fort Walsh. In the end, all the tribes moved north to the reserves. To the south lay the line of the railway: a steel fence barring them from their past.

Some of the chiefs accepted the coming of steel with a certain amount of fatalism; Poundmaker, for one, urged his Cree followers to prepare for it. Early in 1882, he told his people to work hard, sow grain, and take care of their cattle: "Next summer, or at latest next fall, the railway will be close to us, the whites will fill the country, and they will dictate to us as they please. It is useless to dream that we can frighten them; that time is past; our only resource is our work, our industry, and our farms. Send your children to school . . . if you want them to prosper and be happy."

It was sensible advice, given the inevitability of settlement, but not every chieftain took it, not even Poundmaker himself. His fellow Cree leader, Piapot, ran afoul of Secretan's survey crews in 1882, pulling up forty miles of the surveyors' stakes on the line west of Moose Jaw. Secretan, who had little patience with or understanding of the Indians, threatened to shoot on sight any "wretched ill-conditioned lying sons of aborigines" if they pulled up more stakes—a statement that caused consternation in Ottawa. That year Piapot was further disillusioned by what he considered government betrayal. In May, he ordered the

Major A. B. Rogers.   James Jerome Hill.

After crossing the first great barrier of the Rockies in 1884, the grade began to creep up the broad valley of the Columbia toward its rendez-vous with the vast mountain island of the Selkirks.

Blasting through the Pre-Cambrian Shield north of Lake Superior.

Men toiling at three levels on a tunnel in the Rockies.

Building the Nepigon Bridge, north shore of Lake Superior.

The 200-foot Stoney Creek Bridge, North America's tallest.

A bawdy house at Donald, where the railway crossed the Columbia.

A settler's sod home on the prairie in 1884. Note the buffalo bones.

Rogers Pass village at the summit of the Selkirks in 1885.

Inspector Sam Steele of the N.W.M.P.   *Gabriel Dumont, prairie general.*

A war artist depicts the ordeal of the troops heading west in 1885.

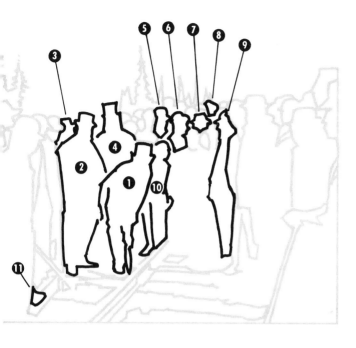

1. Donald A. Smith.
2. William Cornelius Van Horne.
3. Michael Haney.
4. Sandford Fleming.
5. Henry Cambie.
6. John McTavish, land commissioner.
7. John Egan, western superintendent.
8. Tom Wilson.
9. James Ross, mountain boss.
10. Edward Mallandaine.
11. Major Rogers's foot just visible.

Donald A. Smith drives home the Last Spike at Craigellachie.

The first excursion out of Yale, over the rickety trestles and under the shattered rock galleries of the Fraser canyon.

The first train from the east is greeted by the citizens of the new Pacific terminus of Vancouver, then less than a year old.

railway workmen to advance no farther into his hunting grounds. When they ignored him, he ordered his followers to camp directly upon the right of way. The railway, he said, was the cause of all his troubles.

There followed one of those gaudy little incidents that helped to build the growing legend of the North West Mounted Police—a scene that was to become the subject of one major painting and a good many romantic illustrations:

The two young men from the Maple Creek detachment ride up on their jet-black horses. There squats Piapot in front of his tepee, quietly smoking his pipe, directly in the line of the railroad. Around him the young braves wheel their horses, shouting war cries and firing their rifles into the air, egged on by a crowd of shrieking women. The prairie, speckled with spring wildflowers, stretches off to the low horizon. From somewhere in the distance comes the ominous sound of hammers striking on steel.

The sergeant tells the chief that he must make way for the railway. The brown old man refuses to budge. The sergeant takes out his watch. "I will give you just fifteen minutes," he says. "If by the end of that time you haven't begun to comply with the order, we shall make you."

The braves jostle the policemen, trying to provoke them into a fight. The two young men in the pillbox hats and scarlet tunics quietly sit their horses. The minutes tick by. Birds wheel in the sky. The chief remains impassive. The young Crees gallop about. Finally, the sergeant speaks again. "Time's up!" he says, and, throwing his reins to the constable, he springs from his steed, strides to the tepee, and kicks down the tent poles. The painted buffalo skin collapses. Other tepees topple under the kicks of his polished boot. "Now git!" says the sergeant, and, astonishingly, the Indians obey. Piapot has been stripped of his dignity.

This incident, told and retold in most of the books about the early days of the North West Mounted, helped to bolster the tradition of the redcoats as fearless upholders of the law. Yet, in the light of the Indians' tragedy, it is inexpressibly sad; and the day was swiftly approaching when no Mounted Policeman would again dare to act in such a fashion. The Indians, already beginning to feel that they had nothing to lose, were growing bolder.

Not far from Calgary, the railway builders encountered the most remarkable Indian leader of all, the sagacious Crowfoot, chief of the Blackfoot nation—a slender, intelligent man who carried himself with great dignity and was renowned for his many feats of bravery. He had fought in nineteen battles, had been wounded six times, and had once rescued a child from the jaws of a grizzly, dispatching the animal with a spear while the whole camp watched. Crowfoot had many good qualities—eloquence, political skill, charity, and, above all, foresight. Long before his fellows he saw what was coming: the end of the buffalo, the settlement of the West, the spread of the white man's style of living across the plains. Crowfoot pinned his hopes on the government and signed a treaty in 1877.

Thus, when the tents of the construction workers went up on the borders of the Blackfoot reserve, the tribe was in a ferment. The chief sent envoys to warn the foremen that no further construction work would be permitted and that seven hundred armed braves stood ready to attack.

At this point, Albert Lacombe stepped into the picture. For some time Lacombe had been concerned about the creeping advance of civilization, which would change his own way of life as surely as that of the natives. "Now that the railway gangs are coming nearer to our poor Indians," he confided to his diary in May, 1883, "we can expect all kinds of moral disorders." When Lacombe learned of the trouble at the Blackfoot reserve, he rode immediately to the construction camp —a homely priest in a tattered cassock, bumping over the prairie, his silver curls streaming out from beneath his black hat.

He was met with a brusque rebuff. The Indians, he was told, could go to the devil. Lacombe decided to make his appeals to higher authority. He had met Van Horne during his period as chaplain to the railway workers on the Thunder Bay Branch. The general manager had been impressed.

"Near the Lake of the Woods at sunrise one morning in 1882," Van Horne wrote some years later, "I saw a priest standing on a flat rock, his crucifix in his right hand and his broad hat in the other, silhouetted against the rising sun, which made a golden halo about him, talking to a group of Indians—men, women and papooses—who were listening with reverent attention. It was a scene never to be forgotten, and the noble and saintly countenance of the priest brought it to me that this must be Father Lacombe of whom I had heard so much."

Lacombe dispatched telegrams to Van Horne, Donald A. Smith, and Edgar Dewdney. The answers were not long in coming; nobody wanted another Custer-style massacre. The orders went straight to End of Track: cease all work until the Indians are placated. Lacombe was asked to appease them any way he could.

The priest had known Crowfoot for years. They had met first under dramatic circumstances near Rocky Mountain House on a snowy December night in 1865, after a band of Crees had attacked a Blackfoot camp where Lacombe was sleeping. After ten hours of bloody fighting, in which Lacombe himself had been temporarily felled by a spent bullet, the outnumbered Blackfoot warriors had been saved by a strong relief force under Crowfoot. The incident, besides launching a lifelong friendship between the two men, also helped foster the legend of Lacombe's invincibility—he appeared to have risen from the dead. This legend was strengthened in the years that followed. In 1867, Lacombe led a party of starving Crees for twenty-two days through a blizzard to apparently miraculous safety. On another occasion, when an entire Blackfoot camp was succumbing to scarlet fever, Lacombe worked tirelessly among the stricken for twenty days before he himself contracted the disease; he recovered. Again, in 1870, when smallpox ravaged the North West, Lacombe exhausted himself in succoring the victims, his only protection against the disease being a piece of camphor held in his mouth. Fellow priests died and so did three thousand Indians, but Lacombe kept working, scraping out mass graves with knives, axes, or his own hands, comforting the sick, solacing the dying. Hundreds of Indians were so moved that they became Christians in tribute to his selflessness.

At the CPR's behest the priest set out to placate his old friend. He arrived at Crowfoot's camp with half a ton of sugar, tobacco, tea, and flour. At Lacombe's suggestion, the chief called a grand council where the priest, standing before the squatting braves, spoke: "Now my mouth is open; you people listen to my words. If one of you can say that for the fifteen years I have lived among you, I have given you bad advice, let him rise and speak."

No one budged. It was a dangerous, electric situation.

Lacombe kept on: "Well, my friends, I have some advice to give you today. Let the white people pass through your lands and let them build their roads. They are not here to rob you of your lands. These white men obey their chiefs, and it is with the chiefs that the matter must be settled. I have already told these chiefs that you were not pleased with the way in which the work is being pushed through your lands. The Governor himself will come to meet you. He will listen to your griefs; he will propose a remedy. And if the compromise does not suit you, that will be the time to order the builders out of your reserve."

Lacombe sat down and Crowfoot stood up. "The advice of the Chief of Prayer is good. We shall do what he asks." He had already consulted with Lieutenant-Colonel A. G. Irvine, the Commissioner of the North West Mounted Police, and asked him if he thought he, Crowfoot, could stop the railway. Irvine replied by asking Crowfoot if all the men in the world could stop the Bow River from running. The chief resigned himself to the inevitable. He did not believe in foolhardy gestures. Not long afterward, Dewdney arrived and agreed to give the Indians extra land in return for the railway's right of way.

2 · *Prohibition*

IN A CURIOUSLY ROUNDABOUT WAY, THE presence of the Indians in the North West had aided the railway in its swift progress across the plains. Without the Indians it is doubtful whether prohibition would have existed; without prohibition it would have been impossible to drive steel so efficiently. The entire North West Territories (but not Manitoba or British Columbia) were dry by law— a law that had its roots in the scandalous era of the American whiskey forts, which had been established in the Canadian far west before the days of the Mounted Police. Long before the railway was commenced, the liquor traffic west of Manitoba had been driven underground.

A. C. Forster Boulton, a CPR land examiner, gave in his memoirs a remarkable picture of a bone-dry Medicine Hat as he first came upon it in 1883: "It was a rough place then. . . . Miners, cowboys, trappers, prospectors gathered in the saloons to drink soft drinks and play cards. I remember I thought at the time what a fine thing it was that no spirits could be bought for love or money. If whiskey had been allowed, then life, with the men gathered in these saloons, would have been cheap." It makes an incongruous spectacle—the rough frontier town full of men in outlandish dress crowding into the saloons to purchase mugs of sarsaparilla.

Lively they certainly were, and never entirely dry, but the prairie railway camps, in contrast to those south of the border, were relatively tame. The contractors, American and Canadian, were grateful. "When a man breaks the law here," one American boss told George Grant, "justice is dealt to him a heap quicker and in larger chunks than he has been accustomed to in the States." What he was praising, of course, was the Canadian passion for order imposed from above—a British colonial heritage—as against the American concept of localized grass-roots democracy. There were no gun-toting town marshals keeping the peace in the Canadian West; instead there was a federally appointed, quasi-military constabulary. The Mounties did not have to run for election, they were relatively incorruptible, and they were fair; that was one of the reasons why the Canadian West lacked some of the so-called color of its American counterpart. Many an American felt some of his basic freedoms curtailed when he crossed the border. He could not buy a drink in a saloon, he could not carry a gun on his hip, and he could not help select the men who enforced the law. On the other hand, he was safe on the streets and in the bars from hoodlums and bandits, and on the lonely plains from painted savages. If he did overstep the mark he could be sure that no hastily organized mob of vigilantes would string him up to the nearest tree.

Though the prohibition laws had been made originally to protect the natives, they were enforced as strictly as possible for the railroad workers. In Maple Creek a man was charged because a druggist without his knowledge put six bottles of vanilla in a case of chemicals he was carrying. He was clapped into jail overnight and fined one hundred dollars. Another was haled before a magistrate for having a small bottle of peppermint in his possession. It may be that both were not as innocent as was supposed, since explanations tended to be ingenious. One man in Medicine Hat, arraigned as a drunk, pleaded that he had got high from drinking Worcestershire sauce.

For all of the railway construction period, the Mounted Police were locked in a battle of wits with the whiskey peddlers. Every device that human guile could devise was used to smuggle liquor into the North West and to keep it hidden from official eyes. Eggshells were blown of their contents and alcohol substituted. Imitation Bibles, made of tin, were filled with intoxicants and peddled aboard CPR passenger cars; metal kegs of alcohol were concealed in the center of barrels of kerosene; mincemeat soaked in brandy and peaches marinated in Scotch were also common. At Silver City, not far from Calgary, the police seized nineteen cans of corn, peas, and tomatoes which on inspection were revealed to contain alcohol, not vegetables—all shipped by an Ontario distiller. Eleven barrels supposedly filled with pork, imported into Calgary, were found to contain 1,584 bottles of liquor, which, at five dollars a bottle—the regulation price there in those days—would have realized almost eight thousand dollars, a tidy profit at a time when whiskey sold for something like fifty cents a gallon in eastern Canada.

On the treeless prairie where concealment was difficult, the ingenuity of the bootleggers met its greatest test. One favorite hiding place was the boiler of a disabled or wrecked locomotive laid up on a siding. Another was one of the many carcasses of packhorses that lay strewn along the route of the line. It was said that hundreds of these dead animals were used to conceal bottles of liquor. The dives, as they were called, were always close at hand—innocent-appearing log huts unmarked by any sign and totally empty of whiskey. A thirsty man knocking on the door might be met by a rough-looking proprietor, who, on being asked for a drink, would crawl out to the apparently empty prairie, poke around for a loose sod, lift it, and producing a small bottle, actually pump the liquor from the bowels of the earth with a pocket instrument.

"The low cunning . . . used by these serpents . . . is marvellous," one eyewitness declared. "Nothing but the able assistance of his satanic majesty himself could enable these men to conceive of half their truly unique schemes." One good-looking man in a plug hat, white tie, and black coat shipped an organ to End of Track, ostensibly for the use of the navvies during divine service. It was actually a hollow shell lined with tin and loaded with spirits. Another walked the line carrying the familiar knapsack which apparently contained nitroglycerine canisters; he bore a red flag in his hand, which kept the Mounties away—as well as everybody else. As the *Globe* remarked, there was not much deceit in that: "The whiskey will kill almost as quick as dynamite." Known variously as Chain Lightning, Tangle Foot, Death on Wires, and Injin Killer, it was generally a fearsome concoction made by mixing a gallon of good liquor and nine gallons of water into which was sunk a quantity of copper sulphate crystals and oil of smoke and later, for coloring, a little black tea. The price, in the dives, was twenty-five cents a glass.

Perhaps the most ingenious of the whiskey peddlers on the prairies was a Mrs. Hobourg of Regina, "a woman of daring and originality" who used to arrive back in town from a trip to the wet cities of Winnipeg and Brandon looking more than pregnant from a circular rubber bag she wore around her waist. Another of her devices was to dress up a keg of liquor to resemble one of her offspring asleep on the seat beside her or to disguise it as a pillow on which she might rest her head while the police rummaged vainly through her old-fashioned bag. Mrs. Hobourg boasted that she "could down all the police in the Northwest," but she was finally caught one June day and fined two hundred dollars and costs for importing two barrels of "beef and beans."

Under the prohibition laws, the Mounted Police in the North West Territories could legally enter and search any premises at any hour of the day or night. This "detestable duty," as Sam Steele called it, did not add to the popularity of the force. Some of the constables themselves indulged in private bootlegging. When the former British Army trooper John Donkin first went out to Regina to join the Mounties, he noticed that his escort had purchased in Winnipeg "a cargo of whiskey," which he stored in his baggage to distribute to his fellow policemen. "Each member of the force," Donkin wrote, "is expected by his comrades when entering the territory to bring a libation of 'old rye' or 'bourbon' with him, from the more favoured regions. This is a pretty commentary upon the prohibition law."

Donkin's gloomy description of Regina's sporting life explains the fervor with which the occasional furtive bottle, no matter how villainous, was welcomed: "The solemnity which perennially reigns in a North-West hotel is beyond words. Long-faced men sit silent around the stove, only varying the grim monotony by an occasional expectoration of tobacco juice. Sometimes they may break out, and engage in the congenial pastime of 'swapping lies.' The bar dedicated to teetotalism (cider is sold and hop beer) makes a ghastly attempt at conviviality and jocoseness, by having an array of bottles of colored water and cold tea marshalled upon a series of shelves and labelled 'Old Tom,' 'Fine Old Rye,' Hennessy's 'Silver Star,' or 'Best Jamaica.' With what hideous humour do these tantalizing legends taunt the thirsty tenderfoot from 'down East.' "

In sharp contrast to this sober spectacle were the occasional orgies of drinking that broke out in the North West, especially when a party of surveyors or traders was leaving Manitoba for "the purity of the uncontaminated prairie," as the *Globe* called it:

"It is generally night. As the men feel the affects [*sic*] of the treacherous mixture the noise becomes dreadful. Indians, Half-breeds, camp followers, and navvies join in the hideous orgy.

"Men have been known to be torn from their beds, dragged to the spot, and forced to drink. Yells, curses, howlings, ribald songs fill the air and if a pile of ties can be fired it adds hugely to the effect. This lasts all night but morning finds them strewn everywhere in a drunken stupor or deadly sick. Men have died after one of these terrible orgies."

Brandon, on the edge of Manitoba, was the farthest western point at which liquor could be sold. That, no doubt, explained why a visitor from Fort McLeod remarked on the number of men "staggering about the streets considerably under the influence of the juice of Bacchus." The first station west of Brandon was Moosomin. Here the train was supposed to be searched for whiskey but, according to Donkin, "a constable or corporal merely promenades with clanking spurs down the aisles of the cars."

Sometimes, however, the search was more intensive, as Nicholas Flood Davin, the editor and publisher of the Regina *Leader*, discovered. Davin had been attacking the Mounted Police vigorously in his paper, especially Superintendent W. M. Herchmer. He had the ill luck to be on the same train as Herchmer on August 4, 1884, when a constable came through on a routine liquor check at Moosomin. Davin had a small flask of whiskey lying on the seat behind him. The constable pounced. Normally, the practice was to order the offender to pour the liquor out and leave it at that, but Davin got special treatment. He was charged and haled into court in Regina, where the magistrate was none other than Herchmer himself. He was fined $50 and $15.50 costs.

The following day in the *Leader*, Davin struck back at "the tyranny of Colonel Herchmer," attacking "the alarming powers temporarily placed in his hands." Herchmer had "caused the law to be strained in order to gratify what everybody knows, was a desire to avenge fancied wrongs suffered by himself . . . because of comments imposed on us from time to time as public journalists, by the conduct of this or that member of the N.W.M.P." In this, Davin was supported by most of the North West and Manitoba newspapers, many of which had been attacking him on the subject of Regina as a capital city.

Davin was probably more embarrassed at being publicly found with liquor than he was by being arrested, since, in his newspaper, he had been a strong temperance advocate. Most frontier editors were hard drinkers, but because temperance was as popular a cause in the eighties as pollution was ninety years later, the majority publicly embraced it. Everybody, indeed, seemed to pay lip service to the principle, including the worst topers. Davin himself thrived on whiskey. Before preparing one of his eloquent speeches it was his habit to lock himself in his room with a shelf of books and a full bottle.

Prohibition or no, a good deal of liquor was consumed along the CPR right of way during the construction period. Sam Steele, who resented the strict laws and the nuisance of enforcing them, went so far as to claim that "the prohibitory law made more drunkards than if there had been an open bar and free drinks at every street corner." That is scarcely credible. When Edwin Brooks, migrating from Quebec, reached Regina in August, 1883, he was able to write to his wife, Nellie: "I can tell you they [the police] look after these whiskey dealers awfully sharp. One never sees a drunken man in this N.W.T. or if ever very seldom." The truth was that because of prohibition the CPR was able to keep its men on the job and, in spite of occasional sprees, stabilize a work force whose training and precision made it possible to drive almost nine hundred miles of steel in fifteen months. When it was all over and the trains were running from Winnipeg to the base of the Rockies, the Moose Jaw *News* summed it up:

"The order and quiet which have prevailed during the construction of the Canadian Pacific, where thousands of men, proverbially not of the tractable kind, have been employed far in advance of civilization and settlement, have been unexampled in the history of any similar enterprise."

3 · *The magical influence*

LANGDON AND SHEPARD COMPLETED their contract in mid-August, 1883, when the rails reached Calgary. Until that moment, the old Hudson's Bay fort and its cluster of adjacent log buildings—Roman Catholic and Methodist missions, freighters' cabins, I. G. Baker store, and two hotels—had been more closely linked with the United States than with Canada. The chief mode of travel to Fort Benton, Montana, was by trains of bullocks, an American transportation device, rather than by Red River ox-cart, and all the mail carried United States stamps because it was posted south of the border. Fresh fruit was so rare that when half a box of apples arrived they were sold at fifty cents each (the equivalent of more than two dollars in modern terms); they were the first that had been seen in that part of the North West.

The railway was to change all that. It was even to change the location of the town, as it had in the cases of Brandon and Regina.

Until the railway arrived, Fort Calgary was situated on the east bank of the Elbow River near its confluence with the Bow. As usual, there were squatters living in rough shanties, hired by Winnipeg land speculators to occupy the most likely ground until the townsite was subdivided.

The settlement watched the railroad approach with mingled apprehension and anticipation. Where would the station be located? Under the terms of its contract, the CPR had title to the odd-numbered sections along the right of way. The fort and surrounding log structures, together with all the squatters' shacks, were situated on an even-numbered section—Number Fourteen. However, the adjacent section, Fifteen, on the opposite bank of the Elbow, had been reserved by Order in Council as pasturage for the police horses. Surely, everyone reasoned, the town would have to be put on the east bank, where the fort was located.

The scrapers, clearing the right of way, lumbered through on June 21, followed by an army of graders. The tension began to mount. The bridge across the Bow was completed on August 10; two days later a construction train puffed in. On August 15, a train carrying a temporary station arrived, and the community held its breath. Where would it stop? To everyone's dismay it shunted directly through the settlement, crossed the new bridge, and was established, together with a siding, on Section Fifteen on the far side of the Elbow.

A state of uncertainty existed at this point on the banks of the

Elbow. Nobody quite knew what to do. No survey had been taken. The ownership of Section Fifteen was in dispute. The town was growing rapidly on the east bank, but because everyone wanted to wait for the decision about the townsite, no one wanted to go to the expense of erecting anything permanent; and so for all of 1883 Calgary was a tent city.

On August 20, two young men arrived from the East, erected a tent, and prepared to publish a newspaper, the *Herald*. In its first edition, the paper announced the arrival, on August 27, of Stephen, Angus, Donald A. Smith, and Van Horne. The trip had been made from Winnipeg over the new track at an average rate of more than thirty-five miles an hour, and at some points the locomotives, fed from recently discovered coal deposits near Medicine Hat, had pulled the cars at a clip of sixty miles an hour.

The directors invited Father Lacombe, who had saved them so much grief, to be their guest at luncheon in Van Horne's private car. On a motion by Angus, Lacombe was made president of the CPR for one hour. Taking the chair, the priest immediately voted himself two passes on the railroad for life and, in addition, free transportation of all freight and baggage necessary to the oblate missions, together with free use for himself for life of the CPR's telegraph system.

The directors were happy to grant Lacombe what he asked. He was the one man who had the full confidence of the Indians. All the promises made that day were honored by the railway. Moreover, Lacombe's rather cavalier use of the passes, which he lent out indiscriminately (as he did most of his belongings), was regularly tolerated. On one occasion the two passes, which became familiar along the line, were presented by two nuns, newly arrived in the West. "May I ask," the conductor politely inquired, "which one of you is Father Lacombe?" He let the blushing sisters go on their way.

After honoring the priest, the distinguished visitors departed Calgary without leaving the questioning settlers one whit the wiser about the future over which they themselves clearly had no control. The state of indecision continued all that fall, with half the community swearing that it would not budge an inch to accommodate the railway. "There are some people here who have a mind of their own and do not propose to follow the meanderings of the CPR," the Fort McLeod *Gazette* declared. The *Herald* continued to demand, in vain, that the matter be settled one way or the other. In December it reported that "we have much pleasure in announcing that our friends east of the Elbow have definitely decided upon the permanent location of the city in that quarter. Already the surveyors are hard at work upon the sub-division of the Denny Estates, and our next issue will contain the date of the sale of this beautiful spot so well adapted for the future capital of Alberta."

But the CPR itself, not anyone else—editor, banker, merchant, or real-estate man—would make the decision where Calgary was to be. In January, when the Order in Council regarding the NWMP pasturage was finally rescinded, the CPR spoke. The city would be on the west side of the Elbow River and not on its original location on the east side. To underline that point, the government, which stood to profit equally with the railway, moved the post office across the river to the west.

In vain the Denny subdivision on the east side advertised that it was "the centre of Calgary City." As soon as the post office crossed the river, James Bannerman followed with his flour and feed store. All the solemn pledges about staying put and refusing to follow the meanderings of the railway were forgotten and a kind of wild scramble ensued as butcher shop, jeweler, churches, billiard parlor, and hotels packed up like gypsies and located on the favored site. The *Herald* reported that buildings were suddenly springing up "as though some magical influence were being exerted" and that what had been barren prairie just three weeks before "is now rapidly growing into the shape of a respectable town."

Once again the railway, in truth a "magical influence," had dictated the lineaments of the new North West.

4 · *George Stephen's disastrous gamble*

WHEN GEORGE STEPHEN RETURNED TO Montreal from the North West on October 1, 1883, the company's financial situation was even darker than before. Van Horne had spent the thirty million dollars raised the previous year. Hill had left the company and was selling out most of his stock. One of his reasons, and probably the major one, for this abrupt and unexpected withdrawal was the CPR's announced intention of taking the route north of Lake Superior, and it was reinforced by Van Horne's decision to order three lake streamers to compete with American railways south of the border and to carry railway materials across the lakes to the men building the line. Hill, who expected to get all the freight to the North West for his St. Paul road, had never contemplated such a turn of events. Both Donald A. Smith and George Stephen resigned simultaneously from the board of Hill's St. Paul, Minneapolis and Manitoba Railway, though they retained their stock and their friendship with the ex-Canadian. Smith replaced Hill as a director of the CPR. J. S. Kennedy's subsequent resignation from the CPR board—it was inevitable that the New York banker would follow Hill—made a bad impression on Wall Street, since Kennedy's firm had made its reputation in railroad securities. Moreover, the country was entering a depression. CPR stock began to drop. On June 25, 1883, when the international syndicate formed the previous year by Stephen to raise funds had picked up its last option for another ten millions, the stock had reached a peak of 65½ on the New York exchange. There were few takers. By October 31, it had slipped back to 49⅜.

That same fall, the North West, still reeling from the collapse of the real-estate bubble, was struck a second blow. An early frost wiped out the wheat crop. In the United States, the Northern Pacific was teetering on the edge of insolvency. By December, its president, Henry Villard, who had risen in a few years from obscurity to commanding financial leadership, would be deposed—his health wrecked, his worldly goods abandoned to his creditors. On October 26, the *Globe* used the word "depression" to describe the economic crisis. If the CPR was to throw any more of its outstanding common stock on the market it would be sacrificed. Stephen was as concerned about the shareholders as he was about the company. He was afraid that many of them, egged on by speculators, would rush to dump their stock on the market at great personal loss—and to their later regret. He decided upon a bold gamble.

He saw the Prime Minister on October 24. Macdonald was seriously concerned over his friend's appearance. It was the first time he had seen him so depressed. But the plan the CPR president unfolded was a tribute to "his enormous pluck."

Stephen had forty-five million dollars' worth of unissued stock. At the moment no one would buy it, except at a price so low the company could not benefit. Stephen wanted to force the stock up; only in that way could he secure adequate funds to finish the railway. He had decided upon a plan he thought would work: with the government's help, the CPR was prepared to guarantee a 5 per cent dividend for the next ten years on all issued and unissued stock.

Stephen wanted the government to guarantee 3 per cent; the remainder, he felt, could be paid out of the company's resources. Because the government had had a disastrous experience with previous railway guarantees, Stephen was prepared to pay in advance for the privilege; he was in effect buying a government annuity. He had reckoned the cost as an insurance company reckons a policy: the price tag came to twenty-five millions. He was prepared to pay fifteen million dollars down, an additional five million the following February, and the rest in securities and assets, including postal subsidies. All this would be deposited with the government, which would be acting merely as trustee for the fund.

This was exactly the kind of daring gambit that had won for Stephen a reputation for financial wizardry in international banking circles. But it *was* a gamble. If the gamble succeeded, then Stephen could sell the rest of the company's stock at something close to par and get enough money—he calculated that he needed about thirty millions—to finish the railway. But if he lost, he would be tying up a huge block of cash at a time when the railway was desperately short of money. The situation out along the line was already serious. At Brandon, eighty men on the staff of the freight office had not been paid for three months; at the end of that period the company was able to give them only one month's back wages. Brandon's storekeepers had no other choice but to carry them. As one put it: "We've got to carry them. If the CPR goes bust, we will all have to pack up and go back to Bruce County, Ontario."

In theory, Stephen's plan was workable. He was proclaiming to the financial world that CPR shares were gilt-edged and that the Canadian government had confidence in them. All during the construction period the company had never passed a dividend. With 3 per cent guaranteed and only 2 per cent for the company to raise from current revenue, the investing public would look favorably on the proposition.

Macdonald liked the idea and the Cabinet approved it. The Prime Minister felt that the guarantee would boom the CPR's stock to seventy or more, but these rosy predictions did not come true. Canadian Pacific stock shot up briefly to a little over sixty-three dollars. It hovered at that price for a few days and then began to drop back again until, by the end of 1883, it was down to fifty-two.

Long before that point was reached, Stephen was forced to revise his plan. He would guarantee a dividend, not on one hundred million dollars' worth of stock but only on sixty-five millions. That meant that, since fifty-five millions were already issued, he had only ten million dollars' worth of unissued stock available to him. He dared not put that up for sale at the reduced price but was able to use it as security to get a loan of five million dollars in New York through J. S. Kennedy's firm.

The gamble had been disastrous. To raise five million dollars, George Stephen had put up nine millions in cash and pledged another seven millions in securities. The railway was worse off than it had been before he took the plunge. And in December it was hit by another blow: the Canada North-West Land Company was in difficulties. The CPR, to keep it alive, was obliged to take back about half of the land-grant bonds that it had sold to the company on time, and an equivalent amount of land.

The CPR's situation was critical. Stephen realized that the railway had scarcely a friend left in the international financial capitals: "Things in New York are simply disgusting, every fellow there and in London too is ready to cut our throats if he could be sure of robbing us." He tried to keep his spirits up: "I am not discouraged and confident that in some way we shall triumph over all obstacles and disappoint all our *enemies* and pretended *friends*." But Macdonald, to whom he poured out his feelings, knew that he was close to despondency. The incurable Stephen optimism was beginning to wear thin in banking circles, as Sir John Rose confided to the Prime Minister in his oblique way: "Mostly strictly between us, our friend Stephen's assurances are rather regarded now with less trust than I like to see." Stephen's reputation for financial wizardry had suffered a bad blow as a result of the gambit that failed. Rose wanted to know about CPR securities. Many of his friends were "foolishly sacrificing" their shares as a result of adverse reports. Would he be warranted in advising them to hang on? Even a hint from Macdonald would help.

Macdonald had already, though with great reluctance, made his decision: the government would have to come to the company's aid and find some way of forcing a new loan down the throat of Parliament. But it had taken considerable persuasion to budge the Prime Minister. One evening late in November a powerful CPR delegation visited him at his private residence, Earnscliffe. Stephen, Angus, McIntyre, Van Horne, and J. J. C. Abbott, the lawyer, were all present to make the case, but Macdonald could not be moved. Van Horne later described the scene and its aftermath to the historian O. D. Skelton.

"Gentleman, I need not detain you long," the Prime Minister told the group. "You might as well ask for the planet Jupiter. I would not give you the millions you ask, and if I did the Cabinet would not agree. Now, gentlemen, I did not have much sleep last night, and should like to go to bed. I am sorry but there is no use discussing the question further."

Stephen and the others tried to argue; Macdonald refused to listen. The five men went dolefully back to the city to wait for the four o'clock morning train to Montreal. It must have seemed to them that their careers were at an end.

They stopped in at the old Bank of Montreal cottage to spend the intervening hours. There they encountered John Henry Pope, the acting Minister of the Railways, stretched out on a couch reading, a strong habitant cigar between his teeth and a glass of whiskey at his side.

"Well, what's up?" Van Horne remembered Pope saying.

While McIntyre pranced nervously about, Stephen gave him the bad news.

Pope rose slowly, lit a new cigar, heaved his gaunt frame into his shaggy coat, clapped his old otter cap on his head, and called for a carriage.

"Wait till I get back," was all Pope would say. It was now past one o'clock.

He returned an hour and a half later, poker-faced, kicked off his rubbers without a word, doffed his cap and coat, poured out another pony of whiskey, with maddening deliberation lit a fresh cigar, and finally broke the tension: "Well, boys, he'll do it. Stay over until to-morrow."

Pope, who had gotten the Prime Minister out of bed, had used the one argument that could convince his chieftain that the CPR must get its loan: "The day the Canadian Pacific busts the Conservative party busts the day after," he told him.

The following day Stephen and his colleagues appeared before the Council to find the Prime Minister out of sorts, Alexander Campbell, the Senate Leader, totally opposed to further help, and Leonard Tilley, the finance minister, openly advocating that the government take over the railway. Macdonald desperately needed Tupper at his side. Sir Charles, though still a Member of Parliament, had been dispatched to London to replace Sir Alexander Galt as High Commissioner. On December 1, Macdonald sent him a curt cable: "Pacific in trouble. You should be here." The new High Commissioner was handed the message just as he was rising to speak at a dinner in his honor, but he was not long in dispatching a reply: "Sailing on Thursday." When he arrived in Ottawa, he "found everybody in despair."

Stephen was frantic: "Something must be done at *once*," he told the Prime Minister; otherwise he must give up and let the government take over the railway. He needed $3,850,000 cash by January 1, 1884, to pay immediate debts. By January 8, he needed an additional $3,812,-240 to pay off a short-term loan in New York. Another payment was due the government—$2,853,750—by February 1. The company's total short-term debt was fifteen millions.

A bank crisis was not inconceivable. Stephen himself feared that if the heavy advances to the railroad, made without adequate security, became known to the public, there would be a run on the Bank of Montreal. The bank's chief executive officers were in a state of terror.

Tupper privately told them that they must advance the railway the money it needed; the government would guarantee payment. That was not good enough for the bankers. Confidence in the CPR had reached such a low point that they demanded a secret memorandum, which they insisted be signed not only by Tupper but also by Leonard Tilley, the finance minister, and by the Prime Minister himself. They had to be satisfied with a paper signed by Tupper alone; in a close vote they agreed to extend the loan. It was, as Stephen realized, "a narrow squeak." Several of the directors were determined to refuse the application and "smash the whole thing up." Stephen was convinced that they were under the control of the Grand Trunk's Joseph Hickson and also were motivated by "envy, hatred and malice."

This short-term aid did not solve the railway's long-term problems. There could, in fact, be only one solution. In mid-January, Stephen formally requested a government loan of $22,500,000, repayable May 1, 1891, and further relief in the form of a five-year postponement on the second installment of more than seven millions that he had so recklessly promised in order to guarantee the dividend. This was a tremendous sum for any Canadian company to raise in 1884; it represented almost a whole year's revenue of the Dominion government. In addition, Stephen asked that both the remainder of the subsidy and the extra money provided by the loan be paid out to the CPR, not on a mileage basis but on the basis of actual work done. In return, he promised to finish the job in exactly half the time stipulated in the original contract. To get the necessary working capital, Stephen was forced to mortgage the main trunk line, all the rolling stock, and everything else connected with the railway, including outstanding stock and land-grant bonds. With this loan, the CPR had exhausted all further means of raising capital.

This was the medicine that Macdonald and Tupper had to force their reluctant followers to swallow. It would not be easy. A platoon of powerful forces was arrayed against the railway: the Opposition under Edward Blake; half the newspapers in the country; the great international press associations—Reuters and AP—which seemed to be spokesmen for the Grand Trunk; the large financial houses; and a good many of Macdonald's own followers, including several Maritimers (who had no interest in a western railroad), most of the Quebec *bleus*—Conservatives, who wanted an equal share in any largesse the government intended to dispense—and the Manitobans, who represented a growing popular antagonism to the CPR.

The building of the railway had laid a bundle of annoying problems at the Prime Minister's door that Christmas season of 1883–84. Andrew Onderdonk was haunting the lobbies trying to get a further subsidy. He had arrived at a singularly unpropitious moment. A few days before Christmas, disgruntled Manitoba farmers had organized themselves into a pressure group, the Manitoba and North-West Farmers' Union. Its formation marked the beginning of a vexing and perennial Canadian problem: the disaffection of the agrarian West with the industrial East. The symbol of that disaffection was the CPR.

There were a good many reasons for western discontent in 1883, not all of them the fault of the railway: the collapse of the Manitoba real-estate boom, the killing frost of September, 1883, speculators' disappointment over the change of route, and the desire of the farmers to run their own show.

The railway was seen mainly as an arm of the eastern industrialists. The CPR would haul away the prairie's great natural resource, grain, to eastern Canada and, in turn, deliver the protected manufactured goods of Ontario and Quebec to the prairie consumers. As the farmers saw it, they were paying through the nose in two ways. First, they felt the prices on manufactured goods—especially agricultural implements—to be exorbitant because of the protective tariffs. Secondly, they felt the freight rates to be equally excessive because of the CPR's monopoly.

They had cause to be suspicious of the CPR's motives in the matter of freight rates, for the CPR Syndicate was the lineal descendant of the hated Kittson Line, whose steamboats had charged such outrageous rates in the seventies. Its successor was the Pembina Branch of the CPR and its corporate cousin south of the border—Hill's "Manitoba Line." Since no competing line was allowed, the two connecting railways linking Winnipeg with St. Paul charged what the traffic would bear. Van Horne's letters indicate that a rate-fixing agreement between the two companies existed.

The farmers believed, with reason, that the Monopoly Clause in the contract kept rates high, in addition to frustrating the building of other lines. But in 1883, Macdonald, at Stephen's prompting, had disallowed the provincial charters of three Manitoba railways because they came too close to the international border. The farm agitation did not die down. By March, 1884, when the Farmers' Union held a second, larger convention, the Brandon *Sun* forecast either emancipation or open rebellion. "There can be no middle course now," the paper said.

In addition to the disaffected Manitobans, Macdonald had the

Quebeckers to contend with. If the CPR was to get a loan, then how about French Canada? The province intended to use the situation as a lever to get further federal assistance.

Stephen, meanwhile, was struggling to keep the company afloat. On January 22, 1884, he scribbled a note to Macdonald that he was going back to Montreal to try to "keep things moving . . . until relief arrives." There was a note of resignation, even despair, in this letter: ". . . you must not blame me if I fail. I do not, at the moment, see how we are going to get the money to keep the work going. . . . If I find we cannot go on I suppose the only thing to do will be to put in a Receiver. If that *has* to be done the quicker it is done the better."

It was the first time that the responsibility of bankruptcy had been mentioned, and Stephen sounded almost comforted at the prospect: "I am getting so wearied and worn out with this business that almost any change will be a relief to me."

When the CPR president reached Montreal, he picked up a copy of the *Star* in which, to his fury, he read an editorial which insinuated that he, Smith, McIntyre, Angus, and the others had been robbing the company for their own benefit. Since all of them had pledged their own stock in the St. Paul Railway against the CPR's bank loan, the words cut deep. The fact that he had recently completed, at a cost of some three million dollars, a mansion on Drummond Street "fitted up and furnished with regal magnificence" did not help the company's image.

There was also the matter of the guaranteed dividend. The CPR's critics were not slow to point out that, in guaranteeing an annual 5 per cent on the par value of the issued stock, the members of the Syndicate were ensuring a cozy income for themselves since all of them owned large blocks of shares. As Blake put it later in the House: "They invest money with one hand for the purpose of taking it out with the other."

The real rate of return, of course, was far higher than 5 per cent, since all but the fifty thousand shares had been sold at a heavy discount. One block of 200,000 shares had sold for twenty-five cents on the dollar, much of it to insiders. Stephen got most of his stock at that price—about 23,000 shares out of his total of 31,000-odd. A study of his holdings during this period indicates that he was enjoying an average return on all of his CPR shares of almost 12 per cent—an enormous rate of interest for that or any time. His annual income from CPR stock alone came to about one hundred and fifty thousand dollars, all of it guaranteed and none of it taxable. In 1972 that would represent a *net* income of close to three-quarters of a million. No wonder, then, that the "scribblers," as Stephen contemptuously called them, were carping.

But he had to put up with them as he had to put up with the politicians. Macdonald warned him in mid-January that it would take another six weeks to get the loan through Parliament. Stephen was aghast. Six weeks, when every day counted! "Had I supposed it would take to 1st of March before help could reach us I would not have made the attempt to carry on."

In Montreal, he learned the magnitude of the railroad's financial dilemma. Every cent coming in from the government subsidy had to go directly to the Bank of Montreal to cover the loan of three and a half millions. Nothing could be diverted to pay wages or meet the bills for supplies that were piling up in the office of Thomas Shaughnessy, Chief of Commissariat. He must have an advance of at least three and a half millions by February 8 in order to pay off the bank. "If this cannot be obtained," he told Tupper, "it is not a bit of use of my trying to carry on any longer."

But he had to carry on as he had been carrying on all that year, putting off creditors, trimming costs, postponing expenses. In spite of further threats to Macdonald, cries of despair, and attacks of fatigue and nerves, he would continue to carry on. It was not in his nature to give up.

5 · *The CPR goes political*

THERE WAS TROUBLE NORTH OF LAKE Superior. On December 15, 1883, John Egan had been forced to cut off the cost-of-living bonuses that Van Horne had instituted in that unprepossessing environment. The men were bluntly asked to sign a new contract agreeing to the reduction or to leave their jobs. Some thirty-five hundred refused, and the work on the line was suspended. In the end, however, most of the men were forced to return to work because it was hard to find employment in winter.

In his brusque interviews with the press, the general manager exuded confidence. In Chicago the previous August, he had announced that the CPR was employing twenty-five thousand men and spending one hundred thousand dollars a day.

"How much will it cost per mile through the Rockies?" a reporter asked him.

"We don't know," Van Horne replied.

"Have you not estimated the amount beforehand?"

"The Canadian Pacific Railway," declared Van Horne, "has never estimated the cost of any work; it hasn't time for that; it's got a big job on hand, and it's going to put it through."

"Well, but if you haven't estimated the cost of the construction through the mountains how do you know that you have sufficient funds to push the road as you are currently reported to have?"

"Well," replied Van Horne airily, "if we haven't got enough we will get more, that's all about it."

The reporter retired, "forcibly impressed with the resolute frankness of character displayed by the man who is the administrative head of this great Canadian enterprise."

Van Horne was not being frank. He too was scrambling for cash and pinching every penny possible. There scarcely seemed to be an expenditure in 1883 that did not come under his personal scrutiny, from the cost of the paymaster's revolvers to the hiring of a cab at Portage la Prairie. He could berate a man for sending a telegram "containing 35 words and costing this Coy about $2.00 and which could have just as well have been sent by mail," and he could also give orders for mammoth savings north of Superior, where construction had just got under way. His general superintendent there was another Ross—John, no relation to the James Ross in charge of mountain work. When John Ross asked for sixteen steam shovels in addition to the two he had working, Van Horne turned him down. They cost ten thousand dollars each and the company could not afford to tie up that amount of money. The general manager suggested the number could be reduced by putting in trestles of round timber. The trestles would last for seven or eight years. This would mean that large earthworks—filling in and replacing the temporary bridging—would not be required immediately. Steel trestles, at that point, were out of the question.

Van Horne's idea was to get a workable line through—one that would stand up for at least six years—make it pay, and then begin improving it. Masonry could certainly wait. Van Horne gave orders that all rock quarrying, dressing of stone, and installation of masonry should cease except in those places where an iron bridge was absolutely essential. The CPR could not afford that kind of luxury. And when John Egan wanted an extra telephone wire installed between Winnipeg and the lakehead, Van Horne turned him down: "I think you will be able to get along without difficulty as two wires properly worked under a strict censorship as to unnecessary telegrams and telegrams of unnecessary length can do an enormous amount of work. . . . We must not spend one dollar where it can possibly be helped."

Van Horne was in the House of Commons visitors' gallery on

February 1, with Stephen and Donald A. Smith, when Tupper rose to propose the new Canadian Pacific Railway resolutions. The *Globe* was quick to note sardonically that Smith could lean down "and hear the man who in 1878 denounced him in the most infamous manner in the same chamber labouring hard to show the company of which Mr. Smith is a leading member is composed of men of great wealth, enterprise, unblemished honour and undoubted integrity. Time certainly brings its revenge."

It was time, Stephen realized, for a reconciliation. Stephen felt he owed it to his cousin; Smith was not greatly interested in railways and took little part in the CPR's affairs, but in desperate times he was like a rock. When extra money was needed, Smith raised it. When he was asked to put up his personal fortune to back a loan, he signed it away without so much as raising one of his tangled eyebrows. And yet, beneath that hard shell, tempered in the service of the great fur company and in the hurly-burly of politics, there was a childlike sensitivity. The disaffection of the Prime Minister clearly irked him; he wanted to make up. Now his grateful cousin handed him that prize. Macdonald's reception was kind and cordial and Stephen thanked him for it; the two, it was said, settled their differences over a bottle of good Scotch. Smith did not mention the particulars to Stephen; that was not his way, but "I know he *felt* a good deal and I know—without his saying it—that he is today a much happier man."

That was the only gleam of light in an otherwise gloomy month. The debate on the railway resolutions turned into a bitter and lengthy parliamentary wrangle, sparked by a daily diet of rumor, speculation, and minor sensation fed to the country through the Opposition press.

One thing was clear to the public: the CPR was in deep trouble. As the *Globe* had not failed to point out, the people of Canada at the time of the signing of the contract had been told that "this Company possessed vast resouces; that its credit was unlimited; that they would never, never ask for any further aid from the country; that the people should rejoice because the amount of their burdens and obligations on account of this road were absolutely and immutably fixed." The news from Ottawa made the declarations of 1881 sound hollow indeed. "The thirty millions once gone will be gone for ever," mourned the *Globe*.

The tension grew. On February 17, a mass meeting was held in Quebec City to protest the Government's railway policy. On February 20, there were rumors that several Quebec ministers would resign. Forty-two Quebec Members, it was whispered, had bolted the Conservative Party. The Prime Minister himself looked drawn and pale but determined. When a vote was finally taken at two-thirty the following

morning on an Opposition amendment, the Quebec Members surprised
the Opposition by falling faithfully, if sullenly, into line. Macdonald
had given and promised a retroactive subsidy to Quebec on the somewhat dubious premise that the line between Montreal and Ottawa,
now owned by the CPR, was a work of national importance.

To a casual newspaper reader, it must have seemed as if the debate
was tearing the country apart. The following Tuesday the *Globe*,
which never let up, summed up the state of the nation in an editorial
that was only too accurate: "To what a sad condition Sir John Macdonald and his colleagues have reduced the country! Quebec, separating herself from the other Provinces, compels the Government to yield to her
demands. Manitoba talks secession, and is certainly discontented. The
other Provinces, including Ontario, are dissatisfied, and the Indians—
ill-treated, cheated and half-starved by the partisans whom Sir John
tries to satisfy at their expense—threaten hostilities. Perhaps it is sufficient offset to all this that the Grand Old Schemer maintains his
serenity, that Lieut. Governor Dewdney has received an increase of
salary, that Sir C. Tupper is content, and that the C.P.R. Syndicate
are satisfied." Only British Columbia, once "the spoilt child of Confederation," appeared to be at peace.

It was the first time, really, that Canadians had become aware of
the new kind of nation they were tying together through the construction of the railway—an unwieldly pastiche of disparate communities,
created under varying circumstances, tugged this way and that by
a variety of conflicting environmental and historical strains, and all now
stirred into a ferment by the changes wrought through the coming of
steel. Macdonald had been used to governing a tight, familiar community from the federal capital. Until the coming of the railway he
had known most of it intimately—the people, the places, the problems.
Suddenly he was faced with an entirely different political situation.
Far out along the half-completed line of track, new political leaders
whom he had never heard of in communities he had never visited were
demanding a say in matters which he only partially understood. It is
significant and tragic that though the Prime Minister was also Superintendent General of Indian Affairs, he himself had never been to the
North West or entered a Cree or Blackfoot tepee.

He had not taken much part in the loan debate; the public argument he left to Tupper. His own labors took place behind the scenes
and in the party caucus. To the French Canadians he had offered
conciliation. To the remainder of his irresolute followers he offered a
familiar threat: if they did not support him, Parliament would be
dissolved and they would face the prospect of going to the country

on the heels of a Government defeat in the House. Meanwhile, he told Stephen, "the CPR *must* become political and secure as much Parliamentary support as possible." The Grand Trunk was now in opposition to the Government and would use its considerable political influence to fight Macdonald. All railway appointments in Ontario and Quebec henceforth must be made on a political basis: "There are plenty of good men to be found in the ranks."

This was something that both Stephen and Van Horne had fought against—the almost universally accepted Canadian business practice of hiring a man on the basis of his party affiliation. Stephen considered himself above politics. As for Van Horne, he placed ability before any other consideration. Now, however, they were both forced to bow to the inevitable. "It has always been a matter of principle with me never to enquire into a man's politics in transacting business," the general manager wrote ruefully to the Honourable Peter Mitchell that spring, "but I must say that our past winter's experience at Ottawa has somewhat staggered me." Before the debate was over, Macdonald was able to write to a political friend that Stephen had informed him that Van Horne "is fully aware now of the necessity of not appointing anybody along the line who has not been 'fully circumcized'—to use his own phrase."

Van Horne's conversion to politics is fascinating. At first he pretended to have nothing to do with it. But by 1887 he was secretly aiding the political cause of Arthur Wellington Ross, who had so strongly supported the CPR in the loan debate of 1884. From that point on, he appeared to plunge into politics, apparently throwing caution to the winds. The CPR not only persuaded its men to vote for Conservative candidates (and made sure that the Liberal-minded employees did not get to the polls) but also pumped large sums of money into Conservative election funds. In 1890, Stephen somewhat ruefully reminded the Prime Minister of the fact that since 1882 he had "personally and otherwise, through Pope *alone* spent over one million dollars" aiding the Tories. Macdonald's advice, given in the heat of a critical loan debate of 1884,. that the CPR "*must* become political," certainly bore fruit.

For George Stephen, watching that debate from the galleries one day and hurrying back to Montreal to stave off creditors the next, the political arguments dragged on interminably. The president wanted another extension on his Bank of Montreal loan, but, notwithstanding Tupper's intercession, the bank refused. On February 27, 1884, the CPR president wrote another desperate note to the Prime Minister: "McIntyre goes down to N.Y. tonight to raise by way of a loan for a few days $300,000 which we think will keep us out of the sheriff's hands till Tuesday or Wednesday. I hope he will manage this, though he may not be able. In that case I do not know what we shall do."

The following day, the CPR relief bill passed the House. How soon could Macdonald get it through the Senate? Again Stephen implored the Prime Minister to move swiftly. It would have to be made law by Wednesday, when McIntyre's short-term loan (negotiated successfully in New York) fell due; and on Wednesday it was done. At the very last moment the company had been saved from ruin. That denouement was reminiscent of one of the cheap yellow-backed thrillers that Macdonald liked to read to clear his mind from the cares of the day.

Those cares were very real ones. The Prime Minister was in his seventieth year and was complaining more and more of being tired every night. When he had driven the original CPR contract through Parliament in 1881 he had believed his main worries to be at an end, at least as far as the railroad was concerned. Stephen, he thought, would take the responsibility off his back. But the railroad, which was wearing Stephen down too, was pressing upon Macdonald's stooped shoulders like a great weight, as it had a dozen years before in the days of Sir Hugh Allan and the first, abortive Canada Pacific Company. "He is the slave to the C.P.R. Syndicate, and dare not do anything they dislike," the *Globe* was declaring. This was not true, but Macdonald *was* a slave to the railway idea; until the last spike was driven, there would be no relief. Once again the papers were hinting that he would retire and accept the job of High Commissioner in London. He was suffering once again from an old nervous disease, inflammation of the stomach; but he could not retire while the railway remained unfinished. "It is only because I want to be *in* at the completion of the CPR that I remain where I am," he had told Stephen the previous November. "I may say I groan for rest."

By the summer of 1884, Macdonald was worried that Stephen himself might give in. "I would leave the Govt. tomorrow," he admitted to Tupper in July, "if it were not that I really think George Stephen would throw in the sponge if I did. He was so worried & sleepless that his wife became alarmed." The Prime Minister insisted that Stephen go off to the seaside for a vacation. A few days later, he himself came down to visit him, and for three days the two men on whom so much depended basked in the sun and talked about the railroad and the future of the country. Macdonald thought Stephen has "chirped up a good deal" as a result of his rest. He would need to, to survive the trials that lay ahead.

16

1 · The armored shores of Lake Superior

THE PRICE OF BUILDING THE LINE NORTH of Lake Superior was appalling. One ninety-mile section ate up ten million dollars, and one single memorable mile of track was laid through solid rock at a cost of seven hundred thousand. By the summer of 1884, John Ross had close to fifteen thousand men and four thousand horses working between Lake Nipissing and Thunder Bay; every month the company sent a pay car out along the line with $1,100,-000 in wages. To save money and time, Van Horne had three dynamite factories built in the Caldwell-Jackfish area, each capable of turning out a ton a day. The bill for dynamite, nitroglycerine, and black powder came to seven and a half million dollars. The awesome quantities of food consumed by the workmen flabbergasted old-time traders. In winter it required three hundred dog teams, working incessantly, to keep the railroad supplied. Gilbert Spence, who was working for the Hudson's Bay Company near Peninsula Harbour, "seemed somewhat upset" when Harry Armstrong, the engineer, told him that the navvies in the vicinity were consuming twelve tons of food a day and using four tons of tobacco a month. At that point the country was so primitive that Spence's Indian wife had never seen a horse or cow or even heard of a telegraph line. But all this was about to change.

The line hugged the armored shores of Lake Superior, where the type of construction was very heavy but supply relatively easy. Van Horne had ordered three big lake boats built in Scotland, each with a burden of two thousand tons and a speed of fifteen knots. Two were delivered in 1883 but the third capsized in the middle of the Clyde during the launching ceremonies, drowning a hundred workmen. The others, on arrival at Montreal, were cut in two and reassembled on the upper lakes in time to do duty between Algoma Mills and Thunder Bay in the early summer of 1884. In this way freight could be shipped by water from Montreal to Port Arthur (formerly Prince Arthur's Landing) and by rail from Port Arthur to Winnipeg—a distance of 1,320 miles—in sixty-six hours. This was the start of the Canadian Pacific Steamship service, under Henry Beatty, whose son was to become president of the CPR at a time when it was able to advertise itself as "The World's Greatest Travel System."

To Stephen, watching every penny in Montreal, the whole operation must have been disturbing. This was the section that almost everybody, Stephen included, had once said should not be built. This was the section that had caused Hill's disaffection—and Kennedy's. Now it was devouring the millions that the company had managed to pry loose from Ottawa. In May, John Ross was brought to a meeting in Montreal to see if the vast army of men, crawling over the somber rock of the Shield, could be reduced. It was not really possible. To get his loan, Stephen had promised that the job would be completed in five years instead of ten; they had to press on with it.

There was no thought of stopping for winter. Track had to be laid in all seasons, in snow five feet deep and in temperatures that dropped to forty and fifty degrees below zero. Sometimes the drifts were so high that in the absence of an embankment it was impossible to locate the center line of the roadbed, the markers themselves being hidden. At first the contractors sent gangs of men ahead with shovels to try to locate the route, but this wasted too much time and held up construction. In the end, the ties and rails were laid directly on top of the snow, the center being determined by the perimeter of the clearing. Sometimes, when spring came, it was found that the rails had not been laid on the grade at all.

All sorts of short cuts were attempted. There was one rock cutting seven hundred feet long and thirty feet deep, about ten miles east of White River, on which the contractors were well behind. A delay of a month or more seemed inevitable until it was decided to lay the track directly on top of the rocky escarpment, to one side of the half-finished cut. It was not easy to get a locomotive over this barrier. The first that attempted to reach the top slipped back. The rails were sanded and the track smoothed out a little until finally a single car was pulled over safely. When the engine crews grew used to the hazard they were able to cross it easily with two cars. By the time the cut was finished, the track had moved on thirty miles.

In the interests of greater speed, Van Horne imported a track-laying machine. This was really a train loaded with rails, ties, and track fastenings. Shallow, open-top chutes, with rollers spaced along the bottom, were hung on either side, and the ties and rails were rolled along by manpower to the front of the device, where they were man-handled onto the grade. Joint bars and bolts accompanied the rails, which moved along on one side of the machine, while the track spikes, in long narrow boxes, together with the ties, were rolled along on the other side. (In later years the rollers were powered by machinery.)

The usual method of cut and fill was abandoned in the interest of saving money. It would have cost more than two dollars a cubic yard to cut through the hills and fill up the hollows with horses hauling the rock and gravel thus removed. Van Horne had decided at the outset to carry the line high, building timber trestles over the intervening valleys, gullies, and clefts, and filling them in later with materials brought in by rail rather than by the more expensive teams. The cost of these trestles was about one-tenth the cost of the filling operation.

To Alan Brown, a pioneer in Ontario railway development, "the rock cuttings were wonderful." Brown, who traveled the line shortly after it was completed, said he felt weak in his powers of description: "It is impossible to imagine any grander construction. . . . Everything is synonymous with strength. . . . The bridges, the tunnels, the rock cuttings almost make you aghast, and after seeing the tunnel work I was not surprised to think that the Hon. Alexander McKenzie at one time spoke of them as 'impassable barriers.' . . . What has been done in that part of the line proves that nothing is impassable or impossible in engineering and construction."

The blasting of the Shield was done, as always, at a considerable cost in men's lives. Dynamite had largely replaced the more dangerous nitroglycerine, but even dynamite, carelessly handled, can bring trag-edy. One man tried to pack a dynamite cartridge tighter by tamping it down with an iron crowbar; he was blown to pieces. A hotel proprietor from Port Arthur on a fishing expedition reached into the water and encountered a live discarded dynamite cap among the rocks; it blew his hand off. In another instance a man asleep in a cabin near McKay's Harbour was killed when a rock from a blast tore through the roof and crushed him.

Harry Armstrong, making camp in the summer of 1884, pulled a heap of green boughs over his fire to keep it going and discovered, to his horror, that they had concealed a half box of explosives, the side of which was already ablaze. His first impulse was to flee, but fearing that he would not get far enough before the box exploded, he picked it up, raced to the lake, flung it in, and escaped. John Macoun had a similar close call that same year while walking the line near Rossport with his son. He arrived at one cutting to discover that the men were heading for a shelter because of the impending blast. Macoun's fleet-footed boy gained cover, but the botanist was caught on a plank crossing a stream and deluged by a shower of stones.

Macoun wrote that his journey down the unfinished line of the railway that year was "indescribable, as we were tormented by flies, and our path was not strewn with roses." Yet there was a kind of perverse grandeur about the country through which the steel was being driven. The dark, contorted rocks—riven at times as if by a giant cleaver—and the sullen little lakes wearing their yellow garlands of water lilies had a beauty that existed nowhere else in the world. Superintendent John Egan found himself waxing poetical about it to the press: "The scenery is sublime in its very wildness; it is magnificently grand; God's own handiwork stands out boldly every furlong you proceed. The ravines and streams are numerous and all is picturesqueness itself. As to the character of the work, it will remain an everlasting monument to the builders."

To the men on the job—throats choked with the dust of shattered rocks, ears ringing with dynamite blasts, arms aching from swinging sledges or toting rails, skin smarting and itching from a hundred insect bites, nostrils assailed by a dozen stenches from horse manure to human sweat—the scenery was only a nuisance to be moved when it got in the way. The summers were bad enough but the winters were especially hard; in the flat light of December, the whole world took on a dun color, and the chill wind blowing off the great frozen inland sea sliced through the thickest garments.

Because of the isolation, conditions in the camps north of Lake Superior were undoubtedly the worst of any along the line of the railway. The track-laying gangs on the prairies enjoyed the relative comfort of the boarding cars. Together with the mountain crews, they were supplied directly by rail from Winnipeg. But the men who drove steel across the Shield lived like creatures on another planet in gloomy and airless bunkhouses which were little better than log dungeons.

The traditional Canadian bunkhouse was a low-walled building, sixty feet long and thirty feet wide, built of spruce logs chinked with moss and plastered with clay or lime. Into these hastily constructed temporary structures, often badly situated and inadequately drained, between sixty and eighty men were crammed. They slept in verminous blankets on beds of hay in double-decker bunks that extended around three sides of the building. The atmosphere was oppressive and the ventilation meager. The faint light that entered from two small windows at either gable was rarely sufficient for reading or writing. The nights were fetid with steam from the wet clothes that chronically hung over the central stove. In the summer, the air was rancid with smoke from burning straw and rags set afire to drive off the maddening hordes of mosquitoes and black flies. The board floor was generally filthy and the roof often leaked. Baths and plumbing were unknown; men washed and laundered or not as they wished. Medical attention was minimal.

Although Van Horne believed in feeding his men well, the conditions north of Superior, especially in the winter, made for a monotonous and unhealthy menu. The only real delicacy was freshly baked bread; otherwise the staples were salt pork, corned beef, molasses, beans, potatoes, oatmeal, and tea, varied by an occasional carcass of frozen beef. There was little if any fresh or green food to lighten this excessively coarse and heavy diet, which, when it did not lead to actual scurvy, produced in most men a feeling of sluggishness and lassitude.

In spite of these circumstances it was not usually difficult to get cheap labor. Economic conditions were such that in the summer of 1883, ordinary shovelmen were being paid $1.50 for a ten-hour day along Lake Superior and in some instances as little as $1 a day, which was the going rate in the eastern cities. Any attempt at labor organization brought instant dismissal; Van Horne had a reputation as a union buster. In the rare instances when strikes did occur, they were quickly broken.

As the winter of 1883–84 approached, however, the company discovered that, in spite of considerable unemployment, prospective navvies were not eager to be locked up for an entire season on the Lake Superior line. Wages rose again to $1.75 a day for shovelmen and $2 for rockmen. Board, however, was increased to four dollars a week; as Van Horne put it, "the difference in wages . . . will not amount to much on account of the difference in board but it looks much better to the men."

The cost of board was only one of several factors that made the pay seem better than it was. Men were paid only for the days on which they worked; if the weather, sickness, or construction delays kept them in the bunkhouses, they received no wages. Eight wet days a month— a not uncommon situation—could reduce a navvy's net pay, after board was deducted, to four dollars a week. In addition he had the cost of his clothing and gear, much of it purchased at company stores at inflated prices, and sometimes his meals and transportation en route to the site.

The company held him in thrall because the company controlled both the shelter and the transport. If he complained, he could be fired out of hand. If he wanted to quit, he had to continue to pay board until the company was ready to transport him to civilization; then he had to pay his departure fare as well. Under such a system it was difficult for a man to accumulate much money.

Yet the conditions of the wage earners were far superior to those of the men who worked for themselves on small subcontracts, grading short strips of right of way with shovel and wheelbarrow, or clearing the line of brush and stumps for fixed prices, arrived at by hard bargaining. Such work might involve two partners, or a group of a dozen or more. These subcontracts had one apparent advantage: the men were their own bosses. They could work or not as they wanted. The advantage was generally illusory; most of the self-employed men worked much longer hours under worse conditions than the wage earners, yet made no more money. The real beneficiaries were the larger contractors, who got the job done at minimal cost.

Living arrangements for those employed on small subcontracts were especially squalid. Harry Armstrong came upon one such camp of French Canadians that he thought was the worst he had ever seen. It was a log cabin without windows or floor. The only light was supplied by a sort of candle made from a tin cup filled with grease with a rag as a wick. The men ate at a long hewn-plank table. In one corner stood a cookstove. In another was a straw mattress occupied by an injured man waiting for a doctor. There was nothing in the way of a floor except black mud, kept thawed by the heat of the stove. To bridge the mud there were several scattered poles across which the men were supposed to pick their way; if they slipped off the poles they sank into the mud to their ankles. Armstrong had dropped in looking for something to eat. Dinner was over, "but I was welcome to the best they had, all the refuse from table had been scraped off after each meal which didn't improve the mud."

The camps of the Italian immigrants—who suffered badly from scurvy—were even worse. One group, which took a contract clearing the line, lived during the winter in a kind of root cellar, dome-shaped and without windows. To enter, they crawled through an opening in the bottom, and there they lay most of the time playing cards, going out into the snow when the sun shone to do a little work. Once a week they bought a sack of flour and a little tea on credit. By spring they had managed to clear half an acre; the proceeds may or may not have paid for the winter's provisions.

Under such conditions the navvies turned inevitably to alcohol.

By special act (separate from the one governing the North West Territories) the government had banned the sale of liquor along the line of the railway as far east as the Manitoba border. Here, as on the prairies, government agents fought a running battle with whiskey peddlers. In May, 1881, the Thunder Bay *Sentinel* estimated that no fewer than eight hundred gallons of spirits were sold every month to the twenty-five hundred people living between Whitemouth River and Lake Wabigoon. The price was fifteen dollars a gallon, compared with as little as fifty cents in Toronto. The methods used to deceive the police were as ingenious as those employed on the prairies and led to much greater lawlessness because the North West Mounted Police did not patrol the Ontario section of the line, and many of the local constabulary were plainly corrupt. A regular count made by the company revealed that there were five thousand revolvers and three hundred shotguns and rifles, together with the same number of dirks and bowie knives, in the possession of railroad workers on the Lake Superior line.

The peddlers tried every possible scheme to stay in business, even going to the length of getting railway foremen drunk and bribing them with cheap liquor to act as salesmen. Another method derived from the American frontier tradition of seizing control of the local police force and thus controlling the town through a vigilante committee. Both Peninsula Harbour (described by one visitor as "the worst place in the world") and Michipicoten were for several months under the control of gangs of desperadoes who terrorized the citizens and held a tight rein on the whiskey trade, keeping out all competition and running the communities for their own personal profit.

In Michipicoten, the vigilante gang that ran the town was headed by the former police chief, Charles E. Wallace. In October, 1884, the gang attempted to shoot the local magistrate, whose life had been frequently threatened. He took refuge in the construction office, ducking bullets that were fired directly through the walls. A force of Toronto police was called to the scene by telegraph. They arrived by boat on October 23 and were met at the docks by a rowdy crowd that would give them no information as to the identity of the culprits.

By nightfall the police had seven prisoners in custody. As a result, the boardinghouse being used as their headquarters became the target of hidden riflemen who pumped a fusillade of bullets into it, grazing the arm of the cook and narrowly missing one of the boarders. When the police emerged from the building, revolvers drawn, the unseen attackers departed. It was said that forty men armed with repeating rifles were on their way to rescue the prisoners. The police maintained an all-night vigil but there was no further trouble.

Meanwhile, about thirty prostitutes, driven out of Peninsula Harbour by Magistrate Frank Moberly, the redoubtable brother of Walter Moberly, had descended on Michipicoten, seeking refuge. They had no sooner debarked from the steamer than they learned that the police were in control. The gaudy assembly wheeled about and re-embarked for another destination.

The police destroyed one hundred and twenty gallons of rye whiskey, captured and dismantled a sailboat used in the illicit trade, and laid plans to capture the four ringleaders of the terrorist gang, including the ex-police chief, Charles Wallace. After some careful undercover work they descended upon a nearby Indian village where the culprits were supposed to be hiding. The police flushed out the wanted men, but Wallace and his friends were too fast for them. A chase ensued in which the hoodlums, apparently aided by both the Indians and the townspeople, easily evaded their pursuers.

No sooner had the big-city constabulary departed the following day with their prisoners than Wallace and his three henchmen emerged from the woods and instituted a new reign of terror. Wallace, "in true bandit style," was carrying four heavy revolvers and a bowie knife in his belt and a Winchester repeating rifle on his shoulder. The four finally boarded the steamer *Steinhoff* and proceeded to pump bullets into the crowd on the dock before departing for Sault Ste Marie. Their target was actually the CPR ticket office and, more specifically, the railway's agent, Alec Macdonald, who had taken refuge within it. Before the steamer departed, Wallace and his friends had managed to riddle the building with a hundred bullets without, fortunately, scratching their quarry.

Frank Moberly arrived shortly afterward with a posse and cleaned up the town, but Wallace himself and his partners were not captured until the following February, after a gunfight in the snow in which one of the arresting constables was severely wounded. Wallace was sentenced to eighteen months in prison. By the time he was released, the railway was completed and the days of the whiskey peddlers were over forever.

2 · *Treasure in the rocks*

BETWEEN THUNDER BAY AND LAKE Nipissing there was no single continuous line of track. The contractors, supplied by boat, were strung out in sections of varying length, depending on the terrain; indeed, some contracts covered country so difficult that only a mile was let at a time. For administrative purposes, the Lake Superior line was divided into two sections: the difficult section led east from Fort William to meet the easier section, which ran west from Lake Nipissing, the point at which the Canada Central, out of Ottawa, joined the CPR proper.

In the summer of 1882, a young Scot of eighteen named John McIntyre Ferguson arrived on Nipissing's shore. Ferguson was the nephew of Duncan McIntyre, president of the Canada Central and vice-president of the Canadian Pacific—an uncle who knew exactly where the future railway was going to be located. The prescient nephew purchased 288 acres of land at a dollar an acre and laid out a townsite in the unbroken forest. He also built the first house in the region and, in ordering nails, asked the supplier to ship them to "the north bay of Lake Nipissing." Thus did the settlement unwittingly acquire a name. By 1884, when the CPR established its "company row," North Bay had become a thriving community. Ferguson went on to become the wealthiest man in town and, after North Bay was incorporated, its mayor for four successive terms.

The land between North Bay and Lake Superior was generally considered to be worthless wilderness. For years, the politicians who opposed an all-Canadian railway had pointed to the bleak rocks and stunted trees of the Shield country and asked why any sane man would want to run a line of steel through such a sullen land. The rails moving westward from North Bay cut through a barren realm, denuded by forest fires and devoid of all color except the occasional somber russet and ocher that stained the rocks and glinted up through the roots of the dried grasses on the hillsides. There were the oxides of nickel and copper and the sulphides of copper and iron, but it needed a trained eye to detect the signs of mineral treasure that lay concealed beneath the charred forest floor.

By the end of 1882, the rails of the Canada Central, following the old voyageurs' route up the Ottawa and Mattawa rivers from Pembroke, had crossed the height of land and reached Lake Nipissing. By the end of 1883 the first hundred miles of the connecting CPR were completed. Early that year the crudest of tote roads, all stumps and mud, had reached the spot where Sudbury stands today. Here, as much by accident as by design, a temporary construction camp was established. It was entirely a company town: every boardinghouse, home, and store was built, owned, and operated by the CPR in order to keep the whiskey peddlers at bay.

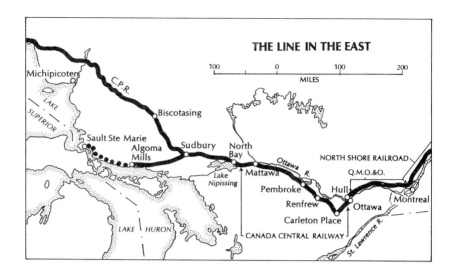

THE LINE IN THE EAST

The first men to examine the yellow-bronze rocks in the hills around the community made little or nothing from their discoveries. The earliest to take heed of the mineral deposits was probably Tom Flanagan, a CPR blacksmith, who picked up a piece of ore along the right of way about three miles out of town and thought that he had found gold. He failed to realize, of course, that he was standing not only on a copper mine but also on the largest nickel deposit in the world. Flanagan did not pursue his interest, but John Loughrin, who had a contract for cutting railroad ties, was intrigued by the formations and brought in three friends. In February, 1884, they staked the land on what became the future Murray Mine of the International Nickel Company. It subsequently produced ore worth millions, but not for the original discoverers.

Other company employees became millionaires. One was a gaunt Hertfordshire man named Charles Francis Crean. Crean, who had been working on boats along the upper Ottawa carrying provisions to the construction camps, arrived on the first work train into Sudbury in November, 1883, walked into the company store and noticed a huge yellow nugget being used as a paperweight by the clerk behind the counter. The clerk said the ore was probably iron pyrites—fool's gold —but he let Crean have a piece of it. Crean sent it to a chemist friend in Toronto, who told him it was an excellent sample of copper. In May, 1884, Crean applied for a mining claim and staked what was to become famous as the Elsie Mine.

A month later, the observant Crean spotted some copper ore in the ballast along the tracks of the Sault Ste Marie branch of the railroad. He checked back carefully to find where the material had come from and was able to stake the property on which another rich mine, the

Worthington, was established. Later he discovered three other valuable properties.

A week after Crean staked his first claim, a timber prospector named Rinaldo McConnell staked some further property which was to become the nucleus of the Canadian Copper Company's Sudbury operation—the forerunner of the International Nickel Company. (It was copper, of course, that attracted the mining interests; nickel had few uses at the time.) Another prospective millionaire that year was a railway-construction timekeeper named Thomas Frood, who acted on a trapper's hunch and discovered the property that became the Frood Mine, perhaps the most famous of all.

For every fortune made at Sudbury a dozen were lost. In the fall of 1883, well before the staking rush, Andrew McNaughton, the first magistrate of the new settlement, arrived with the CPR construction crew. McNaughton went for a stroll in the hills and became lost in a heavy fog. The search party that found him also picked up some copper-stained rocks. The newly arrived physician had the rocks analyzed and was told they were worthless. He learned later that he had been standing on the site of the Murray Mine when his searchers found him.

But then the story of northern Ontario mining is the story of happenstance, accident, and sheer blind luck. Sudbury itself was an accident, located by error on the wrong side of a lake and named by the contractor, James Worthington, after his wife's birthplace in England. Worthington had not intended to use such an unimportant spot on the map to honor his spouse, for Sudbury at the time was seen as a transitory community. However, the station up the line that was expected to be the real center of the area had been named for Magistrate McNaughton, and Worthington had to settle for the lesser community. He was not the only man to underestimate the resources of the Canadian Shield. Long before, when John A. Macdonald had talked of running a line of steel through those ebony scarps, Alexander Mackenzie had cried out that that was "one of the most foolish things that could be imagined." Right up until the moment of Sudbury's founding, some members of Macdonald's Cabinet, not to mention a couple of the CPR's own directors, were opposed to such madness. It was only when the land began to yield up its treasure that the fuss about the all-Canadian line was stilled.

3 · *The Big Hill*

IN THE ROCKIES, THAT SUMMER OF 1884, the weather was wet and miserable. The naked peaks were masked by clouds, and the numbing, incessant rain turned the milky Kicking Horse into a torrent that spread itself across the Columbia flats, cutting the tote road so badly that it was almost—but not quite—impossible for the teams to struggle through. Severe frosts persisted until late June. Snow swept the upper slopes of the mountains. In the shacks that did duty as offices near the summit, roaring fires had to be maintained well into the early summer.

The rails had sped out of Calgary the previous fall along the easy incline of the Bow Valley at the same rapid rate that had taken them across the plains. Indeed, another record had been set. The CPR gangs set out to better the achievement of the Northern Pacific, one of whose track-laying teams had captured the short-distance record by laying six hundred feet of track in six and a half minutes. Not far from Bow Gap, where the roadbed entered the Kicking Horse Pass, the Canadians managed to lay six hundred feet in four minutes and forty-five seconds. It was a considerable feat; whereas the Northern Pacific had achieved its result by sponsoring a race between two gangs, on the Canadian line, as one onlooker noted, "it was accomplished in cold blood and without the least preparation except putting more than the ordinary quantity of rails on the car."

When the steel reached the pass, the track laying slowed down as the incline steepened. The rails crept to within a few miles of the summit and came to a halt for the winter. For all of the summer of 1884, the construction headquarters of the Mountain Division of the CPR remained near the summit where End of Track had stood the previous fall. The community that sprang up was at first known as Holt City, after Tim Holt, who ran the company store, and whose brother, Herbert, was one of the major contractors on the division. Later on it acquired the name of Laggan; today it is known as Lake Louise Station.

Holt City, surrounded by acres of lodgepole pine, sat on the banks of the Bow—the beautiful Bow, "swift and blue, and heavenly and crystal, born of the mountains and fresh from snowfield and glacier." It was to this little camp, raucous with the pandemonium of squeaking fiddles, that the pay car came on its monthly rounds; and it was here that men crowded in on payday to squander their earnings at the three hotels, or at the poker, faro, and three-card monte tables, or at the

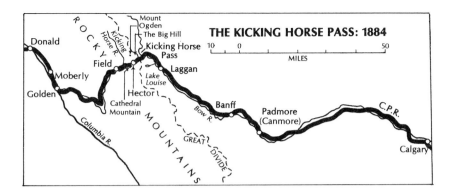

THE KICKING HORSE PASS: 1884

surreptitious little cabins along the route that did duty as blind pigs.

James Ross had announced that he would need twelve thousand men in the mountains in the summer of 1884. By June they were pouring in. Every train brought several carloads of navvies who had come across the plains from Winnipeg. Turner Bone, who worked for Herbert Holt that summer, recalled that the scene "might well have been compared to a gathering of the clans in response to the call of the fiery cross; all keyed up and ready to go." They tumbled off the cars and trudged up the right of way to the construction camps, in a land hitherto seen by only a handful of men, singing the song of the construction men in the mountains:

> *For some of us are bums, for whom work has no charms,*
> *And some of us are farmers, a-working for our farms,*
> *But all are jolly fellows, who come from near and far,*
> *To work up in the Rockies on the C.P.R.*

Morley Roberts, the British novelist, who arrived that summer, watched the tenderfeet from the cities heading off up the line to the various camps—a miscellaneous throng of about a hundred, loaded down with blankets and valises—and noted that many had never worked in the open air at all. Some indeed had not done a hard day's work in their lives:

"It was quite pitiful to see some little fellow, hardly more than a boy, who had hitherto had his lines cast in pleasant places, bearing the burden of two valises or portmanteaus, doubtless filled with good store of clothes made by his mother and sisters, while the sweat rolled off him as he tramped along bent nearly double. Perhaps next to him there would be some huge, raw-boned labourer whose belongings were tied up in a red handkerchief and suspended from a stick."

Behind the laborers came the first tourists, some of them traveling all the way from Winnipeg to gaze upon the wonders of the mountain scenery, which the construction of the railway had suddenly disclosed. "Every week now sees excursions, walks, horseback rides, picnics, mountains scaled, scenery explored, and a dance or two." The government's Engineer-in-Chief, Collingwood Schreiber, was ecstatic, as all were, about the scenery: it "far surpasses the scenery upon the other transcontinental lines, if I mistake not it will be a great resort for tourists and madmen who like climbing mountains at the risk of breaking their necks."

Some of that scenery was fast disappearing under the human onslaught. "Round me," wrote Morley Roberts, "I saw the primaeval forest torn down, cut and hewed and hacked, pine and cedar and hemlock. Here and there lay piles of ties, and near them, closely stacked, thousands of rails. The brute power of man's organised civilisation had fought with Nature and had for the time vanquished her. Here lay the trophies of the battle."

The mountainsides that year were ablaze with forest fires started by the construction workers. At times the entire pass, from the summit to the Columbia and westward, seemed to be aflame. The Grand Trunk's Sir Henry Tyler, making a careful inspection of the rival line, was horrified to learn that some of the fires had been purposely ignited in his honor.

The most distinguished tourists that summer were the members of the British Association for the Advancement of Science, who held their annual meeting in Canada in 1884. The association, including the future Lord Kelvin, then plain William Thompson, went to End of Track and beyond, where they almost lost Alfred Selwyn, a distinguished geologist. Selwyn was crossing a temporary wooden scaffold over a ravine when an avalanche thundered down, tearing the bridge apart. The geologist was carried a considerable distance, caught in a mass of broken and dislocated timber, but emerged unhurt.

Avalanches were frequent in the Rockies that season, many of them set in motion by the continual blasting that went on along the line. Everyone who witnessed a Rocky Mountain avalanche was awestruck. "They resembled exactly a large mow taken down with a scythe in the fields," Alexander Mackenzie wrote to his daughter. (The former Liberal Prime Minister was on a tour of the North West as a guest of the railway and, as a result, was to change his mind about the barrenness of prairie land.) Sam Steele described glaciers that broke away and tore pathways half a mile wide through the forest. He saw one avalanche descend five thousand feet from a summit with such velocity that it tore directly across a valley and up the opposite side for another eight hundred feet.

Under such conditions, the work went on at a killing pace from dawn to dusk. On one contract the workmen averaged more than ten hours of labor a day every day for a month. Some of them had thirteen or fourteen hours a day to their credit. If rain made work impossible, they caught up in sunny weather. Some even worked by moonlight.

As always, a good portion of many men's wages was spent on illegal liquor. Gamblers, whiskey peddlers, and criminals of all sorts were filtering into the mountains from the Northern Pacific's territory south of the border and establishing their dens on every creek and gully along the right of way.

The railway workers lived in every kind of accommodation along the line—in tents of all shapes and sizes, in boxcars rolled onto sidings, in log huts and in mud huts, in shanties fashioned out of rough planks, and in vast tents with hand-hewn log floors, log walls, and a box stove in the center. Over the whole hung the familiar pungency of the bunkhouse, an incense almost indescribable but compounded of unwashed bodies, strong tobacco, steaming wool, cedar logs, and mattress straw. Such communities had an aura of semipermanence, unlike the portable towns of the prairies; the track did not move mile by mile or even yard by yard. On some days it seemed to creep along inch by inch as the contractors attacked the granite bulwarks with tons of dynamite and hordes of workmen.

The work was often as dangerous as it was backbreaking. Near one of several tunnels along the Kicking Horse the cut in the hill was so deep that the men worked in three tiers. At the very top, the route was being cut through gravel; in the center the gravel gave way to blue clay; below the clay was hard rock. The men on the lowest tier, working just above the layer of rock (which would have to be dynamited), attacked the clay from beneath. Twenty to thirty feet above them a second gang worked, chopping out the gravel and wheeling it away in barrows. The high gang removed the top layer of sand and stumps. Those at the very top worked in comparative safety; the middle gang was in some peril because they had to watch out for rocks that might topple down on them; but the lowest gang was in constant danger —from both benches above them came a constant shower of rocks. Morley Roberts, who worked on the lowest tier, reported that he never felt safe for a single moment. Every sixty seconds or so, all day long, a warning cry would be heard and a heavy stone or boulder would come thundering down the slope, scattering the men on both sides. On his third day on the job an eighty-pound rock put him out of action for five days. The literate vagabond whiled away his convalescence with a copy of Thomas Carlyle's *Sartor Resartus*.

The *Globe*, always waspish where the CPR was concerned, wrote that summer that it would be a miracle if the road reached Kamloops before 1886, but Van Horne had a schedule and he meant to keep to it. He had told Stephen that the job could be completed by the end of 1885; Stephen had translated that advice into a pledge to the Government. They could not afford to let the work lag. Fortunately, they had some remarkable generals at the head of that mountain army. The CPR was a spawning ground for an amazing generation of entre-preneurial talent whose influence became world-wide.

They sprang from varied backgrounds, these future captains of industry. The thirty-six-year-old James Ross, a short, compact man, thickly bearded and good-humored, was the son of a Tyneside ship-owner and had had engineering experience on both sides of the ocean. Van Horne regarded him as one of the ablest builders on the con-tinent, probably unequaled by any other man. Ross became one of the most successful financiers in Canada, a kind of capitalist's capitalist—a coal and steel baron, a traction magnate, a yachtsman, commodore, and philanthropist.

Herbert Samuel Holt, a huge Irishman who walked with a rolling gait and spoke as little as possible to anyone, went on to become the richest man in Canadian history. Holt hated publicity and had no intimates: in the twenties and thirties he became a mystery man who controlled an unprecedented empire of three hundred companies on four continents—a kind of Canadian Basil Zaharoff. Knighted in World War I for planning the railway system for the army in France, he was, in the words of the *Daily Express* of London, "the business brain of Canada . . . certainly a more important figure in the Canadian world than the prime minister is in that of Britain."

Two other mountain contractors, whose names were to become familiar after the turn of the century, were William Mackenzie and Donald Mann. Mackenzie, who held several bridging contracts along the Kicking Horse, had begun his career as a schoolteacher in Kirk-field, Ontario. His future partner, Mann, was a powerful figure with dark, brooding eyes and with arms like hams, capable of picking up a man and holding him at arm's length, feet off the ground. Mackenzie and Mann became railway promoters, capping a long career by con-structing the Canadian Northern, a transcontinental line which was designed to rival the Canadian Pacific but which went gloriously bank-rupt at considerable expense to the Canadian taxpayer.

There was another future tycoon working along the line that year but in a more humble capacity, "a young raw Highland Scotch boy" from New Westminster named Jack Stewart. Stewart, an engineer's assistant, came out of World War I a major-general and went on to become the largest contractor in the West, helping to build another ill-fated transcontinental railroad, the Grand Trunk Pacific, and founding, for the Liberal Party of British Columbia, a lively newspaper, the Vancouver *Sun*.

The contractors were forced to improvise to push the line through on time. Since it was impossible to take heavy drills down the dizzy inclines of the Kicking Horse, all blasting holes had to be punched out by hand. The men hammered the broken rocks into smaller pieces and shoveled them into carts and barrows. In spite of such primitive techniques, Ross's work force managed to move a million and a half cubic yards of earth and rock and, in addition, drill half a mile of tunnels during the 1884 season.

Van Horne had decreed that all bridges be made of timber in order to save money. Even without the cost factor, the necessity of pushing the line through on time would have dictated this swifter method of construction. There was no way in which iron girders or quarried stone could be transported down the gorge of the Kicking Horse until the rails were laid.

It was a considerable feat to cross an unfinished bridge, as hundreds of men were forced to do. Along the crosspieces lay stringers, placed on edge and at varying distances, some close together and some so far apart that a man could scarcely leap from one to the next. These were lying loose, unbolted and trembling with every movement. Some fifty feet below, the water could be seen swirling around the sharp rocks. If a man fell, nothing could save him, especially if he was carrying a load, for there was nothing below to seize hold of except the great timbers of the understructure.

In order to get around the face of some of the bluffs without drilling tunnels or making expensive cuts, the railway resorted to "grasshopper trestles," so called because the outer posts extended far down into the gorges, standing in steps cut in the rock, while the inner posts, like a grasshopper's forelegs, were very short and sometimes nonexistent. Later on, these trestles were replaced by walls of masonry built by Scottish stonemasons.

On its queasy descent from the Great Divide, the road switched back and forth across the Kicking Horse by truss and trestle eight times. Before the right of way could be cleared, a tote road had to be constructed to replace the dangerous surveyors' trail cut into the cliffside. This in itself was a major construction job. The tote road ran a few feet above the bed of the railway, winding in and out along the face of a slope that topped the almost sheer cliffs above the river. In one place it was notched right into the cliff above the stream bed. It was almost as perilous as the Golden Stairs, which had scared the wits out of Grant and Fleming the summer before; often it was that same pack trail, slightly widened. On their first journey down the hazardous thoroughfare, men involuntarily hugged the upper side and uttered a sigh of relief when the journey was over. Herbert Holt was almost killed on the tote road in 1884 when his horse slipped on a stone and fell over the edge of a perpendicular cliff seventy feet above the river. The future mystery man had a miraculous escape; he plunged twenty-eight feet, turned a complete somersault, and landed on his stomach on the trunk of a dead tree caught in the canyon's wall. Had the tree not been present to break his fall, the financial history of the nation in the early twentieth century would have been considerably altered.

The choice of the Kicking Horse Pass had presented the CPR with a formidable dilemma. The river drops eleven hundred feet in the first three and a half miles of its headlong race down the western slopes of the Rockies. Under the terms of its contract with the government, the CPR was pledged to a maximum gradient of 2.2 per cent, or about 116 feet to a mile. But to build the line as Rogers had located it, the railway would have been forced to cross several unstable boulder slides, and to pass under an immense, unpredictable glacier. In addition, it would have been necessary to drill a tunnel fourteen hundred feet long through solid rock. That, the engineers predicted, would delay the railway for almost another year. Sandford Fleming suggested to Van Horne that the company build a temporary line dropping quickly down from the summit into the comparative level of the valley of the Kicking Horse by means of a grade of 232 feet per mile—twice as steep as that allowed by the contract and four times as steep as the ideal maximum. Fleming's suggestion was accepted, and thus was born the "Big Hill" between the stations of Hector and Field. It was an eight-mile horror.

In submitting the plan to the Minister of Railways, Van Horne dealt airily with the problem. The ruling gradient on the CPR had been set at 1 per cent. But on the Big Hill the gradient for almost four miles would be 4.4 per cent. This would be followed by a comparatively level stretch, and then, for an additional three and a half miles, the gradient would run between 3.5 and 4 per cent. In his memorandum Van Horne claimed that the Northern Pacific had used a steeper gradient without difficulty pending the completion of a long tunnel and that similar gradients had been used across western American mountain ranges on one or more other railways. The heavy gradient, he said, occurred in a section where traffic—mainly local—would be light for a number of years; only three or four trains a day would pass by. It would be cheaper to wait for a time when wages were not inflated by the railway's labor requirements and the pressure of time would no longer be a factor.

Van Horne was scrupulously correct, but he was leaving a great deal unsaid. The Northern Pacific and Santa Fe lines had built temporary switchbacks of the same grade, but these had been used for comparatively short periods. There *was* one short scenic railway that operated on grades as high as 7 per cent, but this was a freak. No major line, even those crossing the Great Divide in Colorado, exceeded a 4 per cent grade; nor did the lines that crossed the Andes out of Peru. The grades on the Big Hill would be the steepest ever regularly operated for any considerable period by a standard-gauge railroad. Van Horne's "temporary line"— an eight-mile diversion from the original location—would last for a quarter of a century.

It was the beginning of a twenty-five-year nightmare for the railway's operating department. Even a 2.2 gradient can cause runaways. The first train that tried to descend the Big Hill—a construction outfit consisting of two locomotives and three boxcars—ran away, climbed the rails on a curve, and plunged to the river below, killing three men. Safety switches were installed every two miles and manned twenty-four hours a day so that if a train got out of control, the man in charge of the switch could turn the track onto a spur, which would lead the runaway up the side of a hill until it came to a halt. Still, a second construction train lost control after passing over a safety switch and headed straight into a tunnel where sixty men were working. The engineer slammed the engine into reverse, set the whistle, and jumped. When the tender derailed, the train came to a stop.

The various rituals established by the railway to ensure safety held up operations in the mountains. At the top of the Big Hill, every passenger train was required to stop to have its air brakes and sanding apparatus tested and inspected. Brakemen jumped off at intervals and trotted beside the train to make sure the wheels were not sliding or heating unduly. Boxcars and flatcars, always difficult to manage, were restricted to a speed of six miles an hour. All trains were required to stop at the safety switches. The bigger engines were limited to seventeen loaded cars in daylight and twelve at night; smaller engines could not even pull these loads. Every car was set by hand, the brakeman using a pick handle for extra leverage to apply the brake as tightly as possible without causing the wheels to slide. Powerful water brakes were brought into service when the steeper inclines were reached and the trains began to slide downhill like toboggans. The air brakes were retained as a last resource. In spite of these precautions, and in spite of the safety switches and a complicated system of whistle warnings, runaways continued to occur. One train lost a forty-ton wing plow, which plunged three hundred feet into the river. And there were several cases of locomotives roaring down the slope so fast that the men tending the safety switches could not operate them in time to save train or crew.

The upward journey was a slow and difficult operation. At least four 154-ton engines were required to pull a train of 710 tons to the summit. Under such conditions it took an hour to move eight miles. Such a train could not be long—fourteen to twenty freight cars or eleven passenger coaches. When the Prince of Wales visited Canada, it took five engines to pull his entourage back over the summit of the Rockies.

All of this was expensive and time-consuming; the use of four locomotives meant that there were four times as many chances for delay through engine failure. And in the winter, when the winds shrieked off the Yoho ice fields in forty-below weather, smothering the mountain slopes in immense drifts of cement-hard snow, the difficulties were compounded. But it was not until 1909 that the CPR decided to return to the original location and drill the remarkable spiral tunnels, which make a figure 8 deep within the bowels of Cathedral Mountain and Mount Ogden. It took ten thousand men two years to do the job, but there was not an employee in the operating division of the CPR who did not believe that it was worth it.

Nonetheless, the steeper line allowed Van Horne to push the railroad down the Kicking Horse to its junction with the Columbia (the site of Golden) by September, 1884. By the following January it had moved on down the Columbia for seventeen miles to the point where the line would cross over to the mouth of the Beaver at the foot of the Selkirks.

Here, at a spot known simply as First Crossing (it would later be named Donald, after Donald A. Smith), the work came to an end for the season and another garish little community sprang into being on the frozen riverbank, a "gambling, drinking, fighting little mountain town," mainly shacks and saloons with ambitious names like the Cosmopolitan, the Queen of the West, the Sweet Hotel, the Italian Restaurant, and the French Quarter. Here on November 15, Jack Little, the telegraph operator, set down on paper the events of one single moonlit night:

". . . the Italian saloon . . . [is] a little hut, 12 × 16, and it dispenses beer, cigars, and something more fiery, in unlimited quantities. The barkeeper is a woman . . . there is an accordion squeaking in the corner, and it and the loud coarse laugh of the barmaid make an angelic harmony. . . . On all sides we hear the music of the dice box and the chips . . . the merry music of the frequent and iniquitous drunks; the music of the dance and the *staccato* accompaniment of pistol shots; and the eternal music, from the myriad saloons and bars along the street, of the scraping fiddle. In the French Quarter a dance is going on. The women present are Kootenai Squaw, 'the first white lady that ever struck Cypress' and two or three of the usual type of fallen angels. A gang of men and boys line the walls and a couple of lads dance with the damsels in the centre. There is a lamentable want of a sense of shame at Columbia Crossing. . . .

"During our walk we met plenty of 'drunks.' The contractor is as drunk as his employees, and the deadbeats are as drunk as usual. There is a good deal of card-playing . . . all through the night. . . .

"Below the high bank, on the dry land left by the receding river, several teamsters have camped for the night preparatory to crossing in the morning. The ferry boat with its one light is making its last trip for the night across the narrow space of water, becoming narrower day by day as the ice encroaches from the banks. On the opposite side of the river lights shine out from rafts and shacks, while above them the dark pine forest stretches its gloomy line. The scene behind is growing livelier as the hours grow shorter. There is a row at one of the card tables. A pistol shot follows. A man is seen standing back a rough crowd with drawn revolver while another man is lying in a pool of his own blood. Well, it is all very interesting, no doubt, and has the great charm of being 'western' which makes up for a multitude of sins."

4 · *"The ablest railway general in the world"*

ALL DURING THE SPRING OF 1884, VAN Horne, who had moved his headquarters to Montreal, was trying his best to get out to British Columbia to settle on the Pacific terminus of the railroad. A variety of problems kept forcing him to postpone the journey, not the least of which was the continual need to stave off creditors, cut costs, reduce staff, and cheapen the immediate construction of the line. None of this particularly perturbed the general manager. As Charles Tupper once said, "No problem that ever rose had any terrors for him."

He was faced daily in Montreal with a mixed bag of executive decisions, many of them niggling but all, apparently, requiring his personal intervention. No detail was too small for Van Horne to handle. To a Brockville man who wrote to him asking for a job as a clerk, he sent a swift rejection accompanied by a piece of personal advice: "Perhaps you will permit me to say, that in seeking employment in the shape of office work, I think you will find that your hand writing will militate against you." The bill of fare on the newly acquired lake boats offended his palate: ". . . altogether too many dishes offered," he told Henry Beatty. "Fewer varieties, but plenty of each, I have always found to be better appreciated than a host of small, made-up dishes. Poultry of any sort when it can be had is very desirable. Two entrees will be plenty. Deep apple, peach and etc., pie should be the standard in the pastry line; and several of the minor sweets should be left out. Plenty of fresh fish . . . is what people expect to find on the lakes and it is, as a rule, the scarcest article in the steamers' larders." From that moment, Lake Superior trout and whitefish became standard Canadian Pacific fare.

Many of his actions in 1884 were designed to further the interests of the railway in the years to come. He worried about grain buyers swindling prairie farmers and told Egan that if the buyers would not pay a fair price the market must be stimulated by dropping in outside buyers with private assistance to shake it up. He was distressed by the erection of flat warehouses. His experiences in Minnesota had convinced him that far more modern elevators would be needed to clean and grade the grain; otherwise the reputation of Manitoba as a wheat producer would be ruined. The first elevator built by the company at Fort William had a capacity of one million bushels. Van Horne also did his best to persuade the farmers to forget soft wheat and concentrate on harder varieties. The best of these was Red Fife, and as an inducement Van Horne offered to carry the seed free of charge to any farmer who ordered it.

The general manager was equally solicitous of the immigrants pouring into Winnipeg. Like the farmers, they were the railway's future customers. He wrote to an assistant in April urging that they be lodged and treated as comfortably as possible. "It is exceedingly important," he said, "that no bad reports go back from these first parties." In order that incoming settlers could get immediate access to supplies on the prairies, he had sidings built at intervals along the line on which he placed railroad cars fitted up as stores. As soon as anyone came along who seemed to be a good storekeeper, the business was transferred to him and the store car moved elsewhere.

In spite of the need to cut costs—and Van Horne had already been forced to cheapen the line—he had no intention of pinching pennies where the railway's public image was concerned. To the president of the Michigan Central, who asked that he use a certain type of economical sleeping car exclusively, he replied that he would not: "It should be understood that we cannot consent to the use of inferior cars in this line. If the business is to be successfully worked up, the very best cars will be needed." He was determined that the interior woodwork of the passenger cars be hand carved, going so far as to import craftsmen from Europe to do the job. "We can't have a veneer, it's too expensive," he told the board of directors. "Every foot of imitation carving will affect the opinion and attitude towards us of the Company's employees. We want them to have confidence in us —we want every clerk, conductor and brakeman to regard this Company as above all mean pretense. So everything must be of the best material, and be exactly what it pretends to be. Otherwise, their attitude and their service to us will not be what it ought to be."

Van Horne took special delight in personally designing sleeping cars and parlor cars, which he believed should furnish a maximum of comfort as well as aesthetic appeal. To this end he engaged noted artists to handle the interior decoration. As for comfort, he once, as an object lesson to his own people, made a comic illustration showing a tall, fat man attempting to squeeze into one of the short berths provided by United States railroads. He made sure that CPR cars were constructed of larger dimensions with longer and wider berths. Van Horne himself thought in terms of bigness. He liked big houses, "fat and bulgy like myself," with big doors, big roofs, big windows, big desks, and vast spaces.

In matters of the CPR's future, his whole philosophy was based on permanence. He wanted everyone in the company's employ to work for the continuance of the enterprise. The railway, as he saw it, was to become a kind of religion among the men who worked on it and also among the people who traveled on it. Conductors, telegraph clerks, freight- and expressmen, senior executives—all these were to be missionaries spreading the gospel of the omnipotent, generous company. "You are not to consider your own personal feelings when you are dealing with these people," he told a trainman who had engaged in a dispute with an irritable passenger. "You are the road's while you are on duty; your reply is the road's; and the road's first law is courtesy."

Van Horne was one of the first railroad executives to realize the value of retaining such auxiliary utilities as the telegraph, express, and sleeping-car departments. These, he used to say, were not the big tent but the sideshows, and "I expect the sideshows to pay the dividend." It was the custom of other railways to franchise these departments to independent firms which took the cream, as Van Horne put it, off the business and left the skim milk to the railway.

This forthright attitude led him into a head-on collision with Western Union, in the person of Erastus Wiman, the president of one of its subsidiaries, the Great North Western Telegraph Company. Wiman met with Van Horne and some of the executive committee to try to buy the CPR's telegraph system "for next to nothing," in Van Horne's words. When Van Horne demurred, Wiman approached Stephen, charging that the general manager was prompted by personal motives and was acting out of spite. Wiman went on to charge that Van Horne intended to "run out all other telegraph companies" and that his whole career indicated his desire in the direction of "disregarding all vested right or interests of those unable to defend themselves."

Van Horne replied to Wiman's complaints in a spirited letter to J. J. C. Abbott, the company's counsel: "I do not like to write in anger, but the whole day has passed and I have hardly yet worked down to a suitable state of mind to answer your note of yesterday. I am appalled at Mr. Wiman's impudence. . . . [He] wanted our telegraph system for next to nothing while I wanted full value for it, and I think I know what that is as well as he does. . . .

"Our Directors have not as yet seriously discussed our telegraph policy, but when they do, I shall strongly represent the great value of their telegraph privileges and implore them to protect, develop and utilize them to the fullest extent and advantage and not in any event to part with them for less than their full value, considering all their possibilities, and not to be seduced by Mr. Wiman's soft words, deceived by his false words, or frightened by his bluster into discounting one cent in price or yielding one inch in advantage: and in my opinion the Western Union Company will not accomplish much in this matter until they set some honourable man at work upon it, which I am free to say Mr. Wiman is far from being. You have my full permission to forward this letter to him."

In mid-June, Van Horne decided that he must inspect the line between Lake Superior and Nipissing before making his journey to the Pacific Coast. The inspection covered everything, right down to the quality of the lake steamer's coffee, which he complained "contained a considerable percentage of burnt peas."

Accompanied by the government's Engineer-in-Chief, Collingwood Schreiber, Van Horne took off on an eighty-two-mile walking trip to look over the stretch between Nepigon and Jack Fish Bay. He was a corpulent man by this time, spending most of his days at a desk in Montreal, but he amazed Schreiber by his energy and endurance. After walking for miles through fire-blackened rock country, the two men finally reached an engineer's camp at dusk, limp and sore. Van Horne promptly challenged the chief engineer to a foot race. On their return journey by steam launch from Jack Fish Bay to Red Rock, the boiler began to leak, but Van Horne would not be thwarted. He and Schreiber and the boat's engineer paddled the launch through the wave-flecked waters of the lake, and when the engineer met with an accident the two companions paddled the rest of the way themselves.

In the camps along Superior's shore and later in the mountains, Van Horne fitted in easily. He probably preferred the workmen to some of the stuffier members of Canadian society with whom he was forced to put up from time to time. He often used to test acquaintances for their sincerity. He liked to sign one of his own paintings with the name of Théo Rousseau, a fashionable French artist, and listen sardonically to the oohs and ahs of pretentious guests who praised his judgment.

His power, by 1884, was enormous. Lord Dunmore said of him: "I don't know a man living who exercises the patronage that man does at this moment. No other man commands the same army of servants or guides the destiny of a railway over such an extent of country." Dunmore spoke truly. Van Horne, "the ablest railway general in the world," was in charge of the equivalent of several army divisions. At the same time he continued to indulge his various exotic tastes. His collection of Japanese porcelain was rapidly becoming the finest in the world; it was chosen carefully to illustrate historically the development of the art. He liked to demonstrate his connoisseur's skill, especially when in a dealer's shop for the first time. He would have himself blindfolded and, as each piece was put into his hands, he would name the artist, place of origin, and approximate date, using only his sense of touch; he managed to be right about 70 per cent of the time. His taste extended to French paintings (he collected Impressionists long before they were popular or valuable) and to the design of CPR stations. When he discovered, to his chagrin, that his architects had designed the Banff Springs Hotel so that it faced away from the mountains, he sketched in a rotunda that could redress the oversight. The famous station at Sicamous in British Columbia, which rose like a trim ship from the lake's edge, and the log station

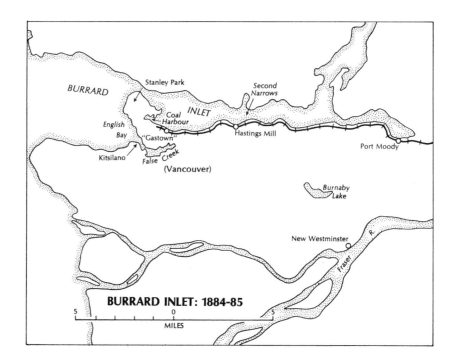

BURRARD INLET: 1884-85

houses and chalets in the Rockies and Selkirks were also his idea. He scribbled a sketch on a piece of brown paper and turned it over to a designer with a brief order: "Lots of good logs there. Cut them, peel them, and build your station." Thus in various subtle ways did Macdonald's "sharp Yankee" help to transform the face of his adopted land.

5 · *The Pacific terminus*

VAN HORNE'S EXPEDITION TO BRITISH Columbia was finally arranged in late July of 1884, and on August 4 a distinguished party arrived at Victoria and moved swiftly across the Strait of Georgia to Port Moody, then designated as the terminus of the transcontinental line. The little village, perched on the rim of a narrow bank at the head of Burrard Inlet, was basking in the glow of optimism brought on by the unquenchable belief that it was to become the greatest metropolis on the Pacific Coast. Until the summer of 1882, the site had been unbroken forest. When Van Horne arrived—with ships emptying their holds of steel rails, with the new railway terminal wharf heaped with supplies, with streets being hacked out of the bush and gangs of men at work grading the track toward Yale—the community was enjoying a mild boom.

"Port Moody . . . has no rival," exulted the *Gazette*, the settlement's pioneer newspaper. "There is no place upon the whole coast of British Columbia that can enter into competition with it . . . these declarations are sweeping but incontrovertible."

The paper could hardly wait for Van Horne to arrive so that the new metropolis could be laid out. Its editor became carried away by the magnitude of it all and began to envisage gigantic markets, theaters, churches, paved streets, hotels, shops, and warehouses rising "like magic."

It was all tragically premature. In Victoria, Van Horne was disturbingly noncommittal about Port Moody as a terminus. Before making a decision, he said, he wanted to visit the mouth of Burrard Inlet and examine its geography. There were two settlements straggling along the inlet, the tiny community of Hastings, surrounding the mill of that name, and another properly called Granville but dubbed "Gastown" after a former saloonkeeper, John "Gassy Jack" Deighton.

Van Horne did make one thing clear: wherever the terminal was situated, a large city would spring up, second only, in his opinion, to San Francisco. Together with the Premier of British Columbia, William Smithe, and the ever-present realty man, Arthur Wellington Ross, late of Winnipeg, he arrived at Port Moody on the evening of August 6. That evening the general manager was met and interviewed by most of the prominent citizens. He kept his own counsel; he could, he said, express no opinion on the matter of the terminus. Nevertheless everyone believed that he had made up his mind in favor of Port Moody.

But Van Horne's immediate reaction was that Port Moody would not do. There was no room on that crowded ledge for a substantial city. The railway alone would require four hundred acres of level ground, and even that much space did not exist. The following day he traveled to the mouth of the inlet by boat and found there was plenty of level ground in the vicinity of Coal Harbour and English Bay. If Van Horne could persuade the provincial Government to subsidize the continuation of the line from Port Moody, then it was his intention to build the terminus at that point.

Van Horne's decision ensured the swift decline of the little settlement at the head of the inlet. As the truth began to dawn upon them, Port Moody's merchants sent off petitions of protest. These were in vain; the general manager could not be moved. He was already planning to name the new terminus Vancouver, because the proximity of Vancouver Island would help to identify its geographic position in the minds of world travelers. More than that, Van Horne, the romantic, wanted to give his new metropolis a name he considered worthy of its future—that of the daring explorer, George Vancouver, who had sailed those shores back in the 1790's, long before any railway was contemplated.

One of the influences working upon Van Horne in the selection of a terminus was that of Marcus Smith, who was the government's watchdog on the Port Moody–Emory's Bar section of the Onderdonk contract. At the end of April, 1884, Smith urged the general manager to select English Bay as the terminus rather than Port Moody and suggested that the company purchase land for a station and siding as soon as possible. What Smith was at pains to keep secret was that he himself had secretly held property along the future right of way since the previous July.

The spectacle of Marcus Smith secretly dabbling in real estate and repeatedly urging Van Horne to place the terminus where it was best designed to enrich him is particularly unedifying in that Smith was a man who proclaimed his own honesty repeatedly and loudly in the face of what he believed to be almost universal corruption. His own surreptitious dalliance in railway land speculation did not weaken the venom of his personal suspicions. He told his banker that sale of the land would give him a chance "of making a few thousand dollars which will be very acceptable as the Govt. service is becoming very irksome through corruption connected with the Onderdonk contracts so that I fear I cannot stand it much longer." Smith was forever predicting his imminent resignation or dismissal; actually, he survived in the government service longer than most of his colleagues.

Marcus Smith clearly believed that corners were being cut on the Onderdonk section of the line and that many of his colleagues and superiors were purposely ignoring inferior work in accepting without question or further investigation the estimates of the contractor's men. Although his witness cannot be taken as gospel, it is obvious that, for one reason or another, the government engineers did not hold Andrew Onderdonk to the letter or even the spirit of his contract and that they allowed a good deal of shoddy work to go unremarked. Certainly Van Horne was appalled at what he saw that August. The timber trusses were "the worst I ever saw in a railway. In the attempt to strengthen them they have been patched and spliced in a most wonderful manner—boulders and debris are continually coming down on the track."

The situation led to a series of disagreeable battles between Van Horne and John Henry Pope, who was Charles Tupper's successor as Minister of Railways. Pope was in a difficult position. He felt duty bound to stand behind his own people, who had told him that the work was properly done. "It seems to be a very sore question with him," Van Horne told Stephen, "and he usually gets into a rage within ten minutes after we touch upon it." When the Onderdonk contracts were completed, Pope refused Van Horne's suggestion of a board of arbitration to examine the contentious points and swore "he would find some way to compel the Company to take over the road in its present condition." The dispute led to an open breach between Pope, who had been the railway's greatest friend and supporter within the Cabinet, and Van Horne. Their feud was so bitter that they did not speak for many years and shook hands only on Pope's deathbed.

Marcus Smith was so scathing in his comments about this section —between Port Moody and Emory—that he was transferred to the section east of Kamloops (which Onderdonk had contracted to build not for the government but for the CPR). That, at least, was Smith's explanation for the move. Certainly he was impolitic in his official correspondence in charging Onderdonk, and by inference Collingwood Schreiber himself, with corruption. "It is . . . generally believed," he wrote, "that Onderdonk by corrupt means had the power to get any engineer removed from his contract and that I was removed at his instance." Smith warned that if a public scandal arose he would "if driven to extremity" make public everything he knew, "even if I have to leave the Government service." But in the complicated dispute that followed over the Onderdonk contracts, he was not called. Nor did he speak up or leave the service.

There is no doubt that along the Fraser Canyon, the government shaved costs to the bone to the detriment of the line, as Henry Cambie's diaries make clear. The curves were not to exceed four degrees and the grades were not to exceed 1 per cent, but Cambie had scarcely located two miles when he received a telegram from Ottawa to "locate the cheapest possible line with workable curves and grades." Cambie and his assistant, T. H. White, stopped the survey and began adopting eight-degree curves, thereby avoiding tunnels and expensive cuts. According to White, when the curves reached ten degrees, Andrew Onderdonk, "throwing up his arms to high heaven declared that he refused to accept the order to run construction trains on so impossible a curvature." A short time later, the Government went so far as to permit reverse double curves, the bane of railroad engineers and operating crews. A reverse double curve occurs when one curve follows another in an "S" figure without any intervening straightaway. The resultant unequal wear and tear on both tracks and wheels is considerable. Between Kamloops and Lytton there were 430 curves and virtually no straight track. Not only would the maintenance be costly on such a section but the operating speed would also be slower.

The result of all this parsimony was a long and acrimonious debate between the CPR and the government which finally resulted, in 1888, in a board of arbitration. The company claimed twelve million dollars from the government; the final settlement, in 1891, was $579,-255. The dispute embittered Stephen, who felt that he had been betrayed by Pope and Tupper, both of whom swore before the arbitrators that the line was built as intended, yet admitted under cross-examination that if the company had taken the full ten years to complete the transcontinental the government would have been forced to rebuild the Onderdonk section. As a reward for building the line swiftly, Stephen felt he was "forced and cheated into accepting a temporary road, utterly unfit to be operated as a through trunk line." This was certainly one of the reasons why Stephen finally left Canada and returned to his native Scotland, disgusted with politics and with politicians and estranged even from Macdonald.

As for Van Horne, he told a United States Senate inquiry in 1889 that if the CPR had had control of the British Columbia section, "we would not have built it where it is." He would have found a way to circumvent the Fraser Canyon, which he described, not inaccurately, as "one of the worst places in the world."

6 · Not a dollar to spare

THE GENERAL MANAGER HAD HIS FIRST view of the Fraser Canyon on August 9, 1884, after a record run from Port Moody in which the train traveled at speeds approaching sixty miles an hour. He was accompanied by Collingwood Schreiber, supervising engineer Joseph W. Trutch, Major A. B. Rogers, Marcus Smith, Henry Cambie, Michael Haney, and S. B. Reed—as quarrelsome, temperamental, and jealous a company of engineers as it was possible to assemble. Smith had quarreled with Rogers, bullied Cambie, questioned Schreiber's integrity, and called Trutch an incompetent. The Canadians were all jealous of Rogers, whose crusty personality did not endear him to either casual acquaintances or colleagues. Haney and Smith had fought eyeball to eyeball on several occasions. Reed was known as the man who did the hatchet job in Winnipeg in 1882. In addition, several of the group had apparently been engaged to spy on one another. When the CPR decided to give Onderdonk the sub-contract to build east from Savona's Ferry towards the Eagle Pass, it sent Rogers out as supervising engineer. Van Horne, in April, decided to send Cambie out to check up on Rogers. Later he sent Reed to check on Cambie and then, to cap it all, dispatched Marcus Smith to look over Reed's work.

In spite of all this it was a reasonably harmonious octet that arrived at Kamloops on August 10, having inspected the steel cantilever bridge across the Fraser near Lytton, "one of the great wonders of the C.P. railway," as the *Inland Sentinel* rightly described it. Designed by C. C. Schneider of New York, it was the first bridge of its kind in North America; the second (which was actually installed first) crossed the Niagara Gorge just below the famous falls. Until the bridge was finished, a cable was stretched across the boiling Fraser, and freight and passengers were carried over in a basket suspended from pulleys. The basket ran for six hundred feet from the high bank to the lower opposite bank under the force of gravity, was stopped by a bale of hay at the far end, where it discharged its cargo, and was then hauled back by a horse. Cambie actually made the crossing before the basket was used, sitting in the body of a wheelbarrow slung by ropes from its four corners. As he came hurtling down the cable Cambie to his dismay saw a man roll two bales of hay into his path and, fighting back the inclination to scream, threw his legs into the air to protect them. The barrow struck one bale and sent it flying; the second brought it to a stop.

Yale was all but finished as a community. Kamloops was the new mecca. The community was delighted to see the general manager. An attempt was even made to change the name of neighboring Savona's Ferry to Port Van Horne in his honor. He would have none of it. When he noticed the new signboard on the station, he growled: "Somebody pull that thing down." But Kamloops, which had suffered a decline after the gold rush of the 1860's, perked up with his announcement that it would be a divisional point and the site of extensive yards and railroad facilities. Here were repeated all the spectacles attendant on the construction period—the hotels jammed with men, some sleeping in the barroom and some on billiard tables, some gambling their savings away and some drinking them up. Cambie had noted the previous month that there were so many drunken men in town he was loath to leave his hotel room. The courts were crowded with liquor cases, presided over by the former Premier, little George Walkem, himself no mean toper. "Judge Walkem carried away dead drunk at 7 a.m. when everybody was looking on," Cambie scribbled in his diary one day, noting, however, that Walkem recovered sufficiently to open court at 10:30 A.M. and, presumably, to levy the usual fines for intoxication.

It was Onderdonk's job to continue the railroad for the CPR from the end of the government section at Savona's Ferry to meet the railway builders coming from the east, probably in the vicinity of the Eagle Pass in the Gold Range. On August 11, Van Horne, together with Major Rogers and S. B. Reed, set off along the route of the line that would take them directly through Eagle Pass and then on across the mountains to the Columbia. A wagon was expected to meet them at Sicamous Landing to convey them as far as the road was completed; when it failed to arrive on time, Van Horne insisted that the expedition set off on foot in the drenching rain. Rogers went ahead, leading a cayuse loaded with the party's baggage. Reed followed, with his coat and vest rolled into a small package. The general manager brought up the rear, enveloped in a waterproof and smoking the inevitable long cigar.

It was a truly fearful trip. The members of the party were forced to leave most of their spare clothing at End of Track and push on by freight team, scow, and, finally, pony train. An early fall of snow had deposited three feet of slush on the mountain trails, already littered with the castoffs of other travelers—blankets, saddles, personal belongings, and the corpses of pack ponies. Sometimes Van Horne found himself sinking waist deep in icy mud. While crossing Summit Lake, Van Horne tumbled into water that was only a degree or so above freezing. The engineer, John Stevens, who was present, wrote: "I have never forgotten, after 48 years, the vigorous and breezy comments about the country and everybody connected with it which he made when we had pulled him back onto the raft."

The entire trip from Kamloops to the Rockies was one that few people had ever made. In another fifteen months the railway was complete and it was no longer necessary to make the journey on foot.

The party was without food for two days, probably as a result of Rogers's eccentric provisioning. When they finally arrived at the most forward of the camps on Rogers Pass, the general manager's sensitive nostrils detected the aroma of ham cooking. "It was then," he later recalled, "that I learned that a man can smell ham ten miles away."

On this journey several new Van Horne legends were born. When the general manager reached the Mountain Creek trestle he was told that a few days before, several men had crashed to their deaths in the ravine below. The floor of the trestle, suspended one hundred and sixty feet above the torrent, consisted at that time of two loose planks and nothing more. One of the general manager's companions was barely able to negotiate the bridge by crawling inch by inch on his hands and knees, but Van Horne stepped confidently out on the shaky planks, strode across the trestle, and returned just as imperturbably.

He liked to take curves on the newly constructed road at the highest possible speed. Once, with a dangerous trestle looming up ahead, the engineer balked at taking the locomotive across.

"Here," Van Horne said, "get down and I'll take her over myself."

"Well," said the engineer, "if you ain't afraid, guess I ain't neither."

When the general manager left the mountains and rolled across the prairies in the comfort of his private car, he was able to witness the by-products of his handiwork: Calgary, Medicine Hat, Moose Jaw, and Regina slowly changing from tent and shack towns to permanent communities; crops being harvested; sod houses going up; and a veneer of civilization spreading out over the raw prairie. As he sped toward Winnipeg (a city of twenty-five thousand, of whom six thousand were dependent on the railway) Van Horne could note at every siding along the line the bleak symbols of a vanished past —great stacks of buffalo bones being loaded into boxcars. The general manager had made his knowledge of gardening pay off in a minor way for the hard-pressed railway. Cleaned and bleached in the sun, the bones were shipped in Minneapolis, where they were sold as fertilizer for seven dollars a ton.

Back in his Montreal office, he plunged once again into the routine of executive decisions. Had Alexander Mackenzie been impressed by his trip to the North West? Then a letter giving his impressions would be "of very great use in killing the villanous slanders that are being published about 'alkali deserts,' 'sandy stretches,' etc." Jim Hill, Van Horne learned, had spies within the company and was boasting that he was in possession of full reports on all the business the railway did at Port Arthur. The general manager moved swiftly to stop the leakage. In British Columbia, Arthur Wellington Ross, the railway's real-estate representative, had overstepped the bounds of propriety and had taken a piece of property on the Hastings Mill Tract in trust for Van Horne, with some secret agreement involved. The general manager declined to accept the property. "I do not like transactions of this kind and do not intend to take any chances whatever of having my name smirched by my connection with them," he told Ross.

As always, no matter was too small to occupy the general manager's attention. "I am afraid I shall never get exactly what I want until I take up wood engraving myself," he informed Thomas H. Lee of the American Bank Note Company after poring over some drawings and engravings of the mountain section. He wanted to see steam and not black smoke issuing from the locomotives pictured in the foreground of Mount Stephen; that would give more emphasis to the presence of the railway.

He could be sarcastic. To Harry Abbott he shot off a withering note: "You have on your Engineering Staff an inspired idiot by the name of Gribble, who is writing letters here complaining of the desecration of the Sabbath Day by barbarians in your employ. These letters are very long and must have taken a considerable time to write; if they were written during the work the time must have been stolen from the company's time, if they were written on the Sabbath he too must have desecrated the Sabbath."

And then there was his forthright reply to one George Wainwright, who wanted to launch a winter carnival at Winnipeg, complete with ice palaces, dog trains, and Indian mushers: "You will pardon me if I express my opinion very strongly on this subject.

"I think the combination of attractions referred to would have the most damaging possible effect upon the North West. Ice Palaces, Indians and Dog Trains are not popular features in our foreign advertising, and I think the less said about them in Manitoba, the better.

"For some inscrutable reason nearly everybody in Canada has his photograph taken in furs with salt scattered over to represent snow. Many of these go abroad and few people in England have ever seen a Canadian picture except in Winter dress. For this reason the name of Canada is almost universally associated with an Arctic climate and this idea is one of the most difficult to remove from the minds of people abroad.

"Individually I will be disposed to contribute liberally to a 'shirt-tail' carnival and will furnish a large proportion of the necessary linen dusters and palm leaf fans; but when it comes to the other thing, the like of which has already worked more harm than good in Montreal, I must decline any aid or encouragement.

"All the advantages, for the time being, to the hotel keepers and the Railways would not outweigh the loss to the North West of one settler."

More and more, however, Van Horne was concerned with the need to keep costs down. Over and over, in his wide-ranging correspondence, he used the expression "we have not a dollar to spare." Staffs were reduced to the bone: ". . . we are at all points discharging every man who can be possibly spared." Repairs to locomotives were cut back to the minimum: "The financial situation pinches us severely and every corner must be clipped now, even if it costs in the end." Costs on the Kamloops Lake section of the railway had to be shaved drastically. "Please go over the matter carefully and see how long it can be figured—every dollar counts," Van Horne instructed Cambie. Similar orders went to John Ross: "By cutting every corner and cheapening the work in every practicable way, we may be able to build the line for the money available. . . . If we cannot do that, we must stop the work."

As the months went by, Van Horne's communications with his deputies in the field became more and more insistent. ". . . we are again very near our *danger line*," he informed John Ross in October. Failure to complete the work within the limits of the government loan would be "disastrous." All pretense of building a first-class line had been abandoned. Even the ballasting of the rails had to be discontinued. The roadway would be made safe for trains running at a moderate rate of speed and nothing more. Van Horne issued instructions to all general superintendents limiting their power to spend money. No structure could be moved without Van Horne's permission; not even a fence could be built, or a nail driven. That was how tight money had become.

Outwardly, the general manager maintained his air of bluff confidence. When a Scottish friend of W. B. Scarth of the North West Land Company asked if the CPR was a good investment, Van Horne replied: "I have no hesitation in expressing my opinion in the strongest possible terms that it will pay handsomely"—and he went on to say why: its entire debt was only a third that of the Northern Pacific on a mileage basis, and even less in comparison with other United States transcontinental railways. The CPR's advantage as a through line was greater, and the road itself was far better built.

But Van Horne's real expression of confidence in the railroad went much further than words. He himself had sunk almost every dollar he had in Canadian Pacific stock. If the road failed, he was prepared to go down with it.

7 · *The edge of the precipice*

ONCE AGAIN, THE RAILWAY WAS IN A critical financial position. "I *feel* like a man walking on the edge of a precipice with less 'nerve' than is comfortable or even *safe* in such a case," George Stephen wrote to the Prime Minister at the end of 1884. "The uncertainty is too much for me with all our other difficulties. On

Saturday we got a telegram from Port Arthur that the men had struck and would go off the work if we did not send them their pay. We sent a man up on Saturday and hope to gain time till our next estimate comes. But the ordeal I am going through is not easy to stand."

The ordeal had begun that summer—only a few months after Parliament had reluctantly passed the loan of $22,500,000. By September the credit of the company at home and abroad was gone. Stephen and Donald A. Smith had been dipping deeply into their private fortunes in an attempt to sustain it. They were close to the bottom of the barrel.

Almost all of the spring loan had been gobbled up by the railway builders on the Shield and in the mountains; what was left was being paid out only as the work was done; often these payments were very late. In addition there was a whole variety of unseen expenses. The grain elevator at the lakehead, for instance, had to be built if the CPR was to capture the grain traffic from its United States rivals. The cost came to three hundred thousand dollars. Then there were the terminals, shops, and equipment, spread over more than two thousand miles. In the first ten months of 1884 the company found it had spent eight million dollars on essential work that had not been contracted for.

The railway was working on a margin that was terrifyingly narrow. A few days' delay in the payment of the subsidy could mean that thousands of men would not be paid. Yet for a variety of reasons, all based on the government's strict arrangement with the company, the payments were often slow or slender.

The Pacific Scandal still haunted Macdonald and his colleagues. They were fearful of seeming to show any sign of favoritism to the Canadian Pacific; it was safer to err on the side of caution.

Such delays, the exasperated Stephen pointed out, were damaging the credit and reputation of the company and they "cruelly add to my already questioning anxieties and labours."

There were other problems connected with the subsidy payments brought on by the remoteness of the country into which the railroad was probing. Expensive tote roads had to be constructed out of Lake Nipissing and Michipicoten and across the Selkirk Mountains. Vast quantities of construction equipment and supplies had to be brought in, especially before the onset of winter. For all of this the company was forced to lay out funds months in advance; but in Schreiber's strict interpretation of the contract terms, the subsidy did not apply to these preliminary steps of construction.

The government's method of estimating the subsidy was also a bone of contention. The supervising engineer checked the work completed and reckoned in dollars and cents how much remained to be done.

Enough money was held back by the government, in each instance, to complete the road, and the difference was paid out to the company: the subsidy could not cover all the work done. Stephen wrote to Macdonald at one point that he was flabbergasted to learn that Schreiber's estimates for one month were half a million dollars less than the railroad had actually spent on construction. Van Horne finally prevailed on Schreiber to relax certain standards, especially on steel and masonry bridges, but he was then faced with the problem of making temporary trestles appear permanent, because the government paid no subsidy on temporary construction.

The real fear was that the government would stop payment altogether. This it was empowered to do if its engineers estimated that there were not enough funds left to complete the line. By October, 1884, it was becoming increasingly clear that if the company had to find funds to repay its loan of the previous November, together with interest and dividends, the coffers would be empty and construction must cease.

Wages were suspiciously slow. Van Horne gave Schreiber an ingenious explanation of why thousands of men on the Lake Superior section were facing long delays in pay. For three hundred miles, he pointed out, the area was accessible only by boat or by temporary roads. Since monthly disbursements amounted to a million dollars or more, "it has been no easy matter to distribute and pay the large sums required."

The truth was that the company was using every possible excuse to stave off creditors and employees. At the end of October, in Thunder Bay, the CPR announced that the men in the eastern division would henceforth be paid by checks drawn on the Bank of Montreal; the reason given was that it was too dangerous to carry around more than a million dollars in cash. The real reason was that Van Horne had decided on a daring though ruthless plan. He intended to keep nine thousand men at work all winter in the remotest areas with plenty of good food. They would be paid by checks, which they would be unable to cash. If any man wanted to get away he would find it almost impossible to do so; the isolated conditions would make it difficult to leave before spring, at which time the general manager believed funds must be forthcoming.

In those desperate months, Van Horne and Stephen leaned heavily on Thomas Shaughnessy, a man apparently able to make one dollar do the work of a hundred. Shaughnessy was rising rapidly in the ranks; one day he would be president. He sprang from humble beginnings. Both his parents were immigrants; his father, a Limerick Irishman, was a policeman on a beat in Minneapolis. This modest start undoubtedly contributed to Shaughnessy's later love of ostentation. He was a dapper man, always bandbox fresh, immaculately turned out, a pearl in his tie, a gray hat on his head, a gold-handled cane in his gloved hand. An autocrat who remained aloof from all but his closest intimates, he was, in a contemporary journalist's assessment, "a man almost bloodless in the intensity of his devotion to material ends." He was a company man through and through. In his view, what was good for the CPR was good for Canada; he held no personal or political views except those of the institution he served. That he served it well in the financial crisis of 1884–85 is beyond doubt. He never appeared to show the slightest tremor of panic as he kited checks, kept creditors at bay, denied funds, made partial payments, and generally held the company together. In Toronto, the heads of the big wholesale houses, through Van Horne's and Shaughnessy's persuasion, extended millions of dollars in credit so that supplies could go forward.

Shaughnessy would go to almost any lengths to keep the CPR solvent. There is an illuminating story, still told in the Shaughnessy family, that illustrates his devotion. At a board meeting one day, so the tale has it, George Stephen solemnly read a letter from an American railway-supply company complaining that they had tried to do business with the CPR without success, even though they had on several occasions in 1884–85 made out large checks to Thomas Shaughnessy. The implication was clear: Shaughnessy had been taking money under the counter for favors rendered, supposed or real.

The board of directors called Shaughnessy in and demanded an explanation. He excused himself quietly, went to his office, and returned with a sheaf of deposit slips from the Bank of Montreal, all endorsed by him to the account of the Canadian Pacific. The slips tallied to the penny with the total amount the American firm said that it had paid him.

"Would these by any chance have been bribes?" asked Stephen incredulously.

"Of course," came the cool reply, "but, by God, we needed the money, didn't we?"

While Shaughnessy was using extraordinary measures to keep the company solvent, Stephen was slowly committing his entire personal fortune and those of his closest colleagues to its further support. The previous winter, he, Donald Smith, Angus, and McIntyre had put up a total of $2.3 million in their own bonds and securities as collateral against CPR bank loans. But in May, McIntyre dropped right out of the Canadian Pacific, refusing to stay even as a director or to have anything to do with the management of a company he clearly believed would go to the wall. Baron Reinach, one of the original European members of the Syndicate and a charter investor, went with him. Stephen, who had already bought out Hill and Kennedy, was forced to use more of his fortune to buy out both the Reinach and the McIntyre stock. In the president's opinion, these men had "deserted"; they were little better than traitors. Contemptuously, he told Macdonald that he could get along without McIntyre. Later he went into more detail about his feelings. The vice-president had been "coarsely selfish & cowardly all through these 5 years. Ruthless in disregarding the interests of others when he could advance his own. . . . When McIntyre deserted the Coy he made up his mind that it would '*burst*' and that Smith & I would lose every dollar we had, in the collapse." Stephen in future years was forced occasionally to do business with his erstwhile vice-president but otherwise did his best to avoid him; as he said, he could not stand to be in the same room with him. The unkindest cut came a few months after the defection when, in the CPR's darkest days, McIntyre was the first to refuse it credit and threatened to sue immediately unless his firm's accounts for dry goods was paid at once.

In the face of these defections, the loyalty and steadfastness of Donald A. Smith was refreshing and touching. Smith never failed his cousin when personal guarantees were needed at the bank. A story told of that time describes how at every directors' meeting Stephen would begin by asking, "Has anyone found anybody to buy any of the stocks and bonds since we last met?" One day Smith, coming in late and observing the gloom on the faces of his fellow directors, suggested a twenty-four-hour adjournment. When the morrow came, a jaunty Smith entered and asked, "Has anyone raised any money?" His colleagues gloomily shook their heads. Whereupon Smith announced, "I've stolen another million and that will last us till somebody gets some more."

Though this tale, which made the rounds of Montreal clubs, may be apocryphal, Smith was prepared, like Stephen, to invest all of his own money in the Canadian Pacific. Stephen, who went to London in July, was able that month to "*melt*," as he put it, a number of land-grant bonds into cash by giving the personal guarantee of Smith, Angus, and himself to a British bank for a four-month loan. "Smith," he told Macdonald, "has behaved splendidly, promptly doing what I asked him to do."

The continued attacks on the Canadian Pacific affected Canada's own credit position on the other side of the Atlantic. Leonard Tilley, the Finance Minister, arriving in London in June and hoping to float a loan of five million pounds, was alarmed at the propaganda campaign that had been organized. "A desperate effort is being made here, and successful too," he reported, "to force down both Govt. bonds and CPR stocks, and the knowing ones say they will be forced still lower. All kinds of unfriendly statements are sent here from the U States & Winnipeg . . . and I fully expect that when the prospectus of our loan appears to-morrow we will have a heavy GT blast against it." The expected blast came: a "fierce article" in the *Standard* and a "vile article" in the *Mining & Financial Register*, which referred to the loan as "another crutch for the CPR." A man actually paraded in front of the great financial house of Baring, where the bonds were being offered, advertising the article by means of huge handbills. Tilley, who blamed the Grand Trunk for planting the story, got his money only with difficulty and not at the rate he had expected. A week later CPR stock dropped to a record low of 39 on the New York board. The railway's enemies, determined to drive it into bankruptcy, were also apparently prepared to bruise the country as well.

Stephen, whose skin was never very thick when attacks were being made on his railway, responded with fury to the "malicious venom" in the Toronto *Globe* that summer. It was "simply damnable that they should be allowed to live and pursue such hellish work." There was no doubt in his mind as to who was behind the *Globe*'s continuing attacks: "Hickson is at the bottom of it all." Finally, Stephen was stung to the point of reply. The *Globe* published his letters in full and then turned them against him:

"If Mr. George Stephen's statements that the last loan of $30,-000,000 will build and equip the road, why is he so sensitive about the attacks of the Globe? To be frank with Mr. Stephen he has humbugged the public as much as he can. He has a corrupt government and the corrupt Parliament at his mercy; but a few years hence he will have to appeal to the electors of Canada who make and unmake governments and parliaments. He had better make good use of the power he has at present over the creatures who have so shamefully betrayed the taxpayers of this country. Mr. Stephen has lost caste; Mr. Stephen is looked upon now as a pocket edition of Jay Gould. It is his own fault. He has betrayed the public for a fortune for himself and his friends. He has sullied the reputation he once had as a high-toned businessman. He has no one to blame but himself. He sees his downfall near at hand, and hopes that by blaming the Globe newspaper he may fall upon a bed of doom; but we sincerely hope it won't be, as it deserves to be upon something harder."

To the sensitive Stephen, who valued his personal integrity and reputation above all else—far more than he valued his own fortune or possessions—these aspersions were almost too much. During that year he seemed to swing from depression to elation and back to depression again. In August he confidently told the press that the government loan of the previous spring was quite sufficient to finish the railway. In October, the Prime Minister found that "he is in high spirits over the CPR." At that point he had just seen the company's balance sheet, which showed that the railway was making money in all its divisions—a net of $563,374 on earnings of $4,017,209 in the first nine months of 1884.

Stephen's euphoria was short-lived. Soon he was a mass of nerves again. The company could certainly make money, but the shortage of ready cash was killing it. In mortgaging the railroad, Stephen had made it impossible to raise any further funds except through the sale of outstanding stock. But the government lien and the Grand Trunk campaign had frightened off potential buyers. Unless he could make an arrangement to get rid of that lien, he faced an impossible situation. It was a maddening dilemma: as soon as the CPR became a through line the profits would roll in, for it held a mileage advantage over other transcontinental railroads. Goods arriving from the Orient could speed across Canada to the Atlantic far faster than on any rival road. But could the CPR be completed? By October, Stephen realized that there simply was not enough money to do the job.

He set off for England for the third time that year. The loan he had negotiated in July would shortly be due. Worse, the five-million-dollar loan he had raised in New York the previous year by pledging ten million dollars' worth of CPR stock was also due in November. And in February, the company would be forced to pay its guaranteed dividend of 5 per cent. The government was responsible for 3 per cent, but the CPR would somehow have to find the cash for the remainder—an amount in excess of one million dollars.

The situation looked almost hopeless. Only a few months before, the air had crackled with brave promises about the future of the CPR and of the country. Now, to have to admit that the railway was again in financial trouble! It was too much, Stephen suspected, for Macdonald to swallow politically.

Nevertheless, he began to see some pinpoints of light at the end of the dark tunnel down which he had set his course. He disposed of the New York loan by the now familiar device of using his own funds and those of some of his friends. He simply bought up the stock held as collateral and paid off the debt. Then in London, the doughty Charles Tupper came to his aid. As Tupper put it, "the prosperity of Canada is involved in this gigantic enterprise." It could not be allowed to fail. He drafted a plan for relief of the railway and shot it off to Ottawa. Finally, by pledging $385,000 worth of the bonds of the Toronto, Grey and Bruce Railway, which he, Donald Smith, and R. B. Angus held among them, Stephen was able to raise a loan of a quarter of a million from a Scottish financial institution. It was this small bit of Highland good cheer that prompted the president to send off to Donald Smith one of the most memorable cablegrams in Canadian history—and certainly the shortest.

Both Stephen and Smith had come from small Scottish towns in the countryside drained by the River Spey, in a land once dominated by the Clan Grant. Stephen remembered, and knew that Smith would remember also, a great rock which dominated the valley no more than three miles from Dufftown, in Banffshire, where he had been born. Everyone knew the meaning of that rock: it was a symbol of defiance. In the brave old days, when clan battled clan, a sentinel had kept watch on its stark promontory, and when the enemy was sighted and a fiery cross was borne through Speyside, this rock had become a rallying place for the Clan Grant. The rock was known as Craigellachie, and it was this defiant slogan that Stephen dispatched to his cousin. Into one brief, cryptic sentence, the CPR president managed to convey all the fierce passions, bold defiance, dark hatreds, and bright loyalties inherited from his Scottish forebears. "Stand fast, Craigellachie!" the cable advised, and Donald Smith, when he read it in Montreal, must himself have heard, as in the distance, the clash of warring claymores and the wild skirl of battle.

17

1 · Eighteen eighty-five

EIGHTEEN EIGHTY-FIVE WAS PERHAPS
the most significant year of the first Canadian century. After that year
nothing could ever be the same again, because for the first time Canadians would be able to travel the length of their nation without setting
foot in a foreign land. Van Horne's two hundred miles of engineering
impossibilities and Edward Blake's sea of mountains would both become authentic Canadian tourist attractions. Names like Lake Louise,
Banff, and Yoho would stand for the ultimate in scenery; Kenora and
North Bay would symbolize hunting and fishing paradises; Sudbury
would be emblematic of mineral wealth; Regina and Moose Jaw would
conjure up visions of golden wheat; Calgary would automatically mean
cowboys and rodeos. Three years before, most of those names had not
existed on the map.

A series of devices came into being that year that would help to
bind the country together. The single-pole electric trolley had just been
invented and was demonstrated for the first time at the Toronto Agricultural Fair of 1885. That same year Gottlieb Daimler took out his his-
toric patent for an internal combustion engine and Karl Benz built his
pioneering four-stroke automobile—a three-wheeler. The presence of
radio waves was confirmed and the long-distance telephone put into
use. Like the railway, these new aids to communication would help
stitch the awkward Canadian archipelago of population islands into
a workable transcontinental reality.

The concept of a transcontinental railway was also responsible for changing the casual attitude toward time. Theretofore every city and village had operated on its own time system. When it was noon in Toronto, it was 11:58 in Hamilton, 12:08 in Belleville, 12:12½ in Kingston, 12:16½ in Brockville, and 12:25 in Montreal. In Michigan alone there were twenty-seven different times, most of them established by local jewelers. In some cities (Pittsburgh was one) there were as many as six versions of the correct time, varying by as much as twenty minutes.

As the railways lengthened across the continent, the constant changing of watches became more and more inconvenient. Worse, railway passenger and freight schedules were in total confusion. Every railroad had its own version of the correct time, based on the time standard of its home city. In the United States, a hundred different time standards were used by the various railroads. In order that passengers could compare the various times, large stations were forced to install several clocks.

On New Year's Day, 1885, the Universal Time System was adopted at Greenwich, England. About a year earlier the major American railways and the Canadian Pacific had brought order out of chaos as far as their own schedules were concerned by adopting "railway time." The change was a fundamental one, for it affected in a subtle fashion people's attitudes and behavior. Promptness and tardiness took on a new meaning. Schedules became more important when they became more precise. Canada began to live by the clock in a way it had not previously been able to do.

Much of the credit for this went to Sandford Fleming, the man who had originally planned the transcontinental railway in Canada. When Fleming was first contemplating the idea of the Canadian Pacific, he had realized that the plan would immediately raise difficulties in the computation of time. His views were confirmed as the railway project took shape. In 1876 he prepared a widely circulated memorandum on the subject. Two years later he made energetic efforts to read a paper on the concept before the British Association for the Advancement of Science but was rebuffed as an unknown and a colonial. Nonetheless, he persevered in his study of time and the Canadian Institute recognized him in 1885 as "unquestionably the initiator and principal agent in the movement for the reform in Time-Reckoning and in the establishment of the Universal Day."

Because of the railway, the settled and stable community of Canada was entering a new period of instability. The closed frontier society of 1850–85 was being replaced by the open frontier society of 1885–1914. After 1885, the Canadian Shield ceased to be a barrier to westward development. The railway would be a catalyst in new movements of population (such as the Klondike gold rush) and in a variety of social phenomena that would destroy the established social order.

Eighteen eighty-five was as dramatic a year as it was significant. As the nation became vertebrate, events seemed to accelerate on a collision course. In Montreal, George Stephen, teetering on the cliff edge of nervous collapse, was trying to stave off personal and corporate ruin. In Ottawa, John A. Macdonald faced a Cabinet revolt over the railway's newest financial proposals. In Toronto, Thomas Shaughnessy was juggling bills, checks, notes of credit, promises, and threats like an accomplished sideshow artist in order to give Van Horne the cash he needed to complete the line. On Lake Superior, Van Horne was desperately trying to link up the gaps between the isolated stretches of steel—they totaled 254 miles—so that the CPR might begin its operation as a through road. In Manitoba, the political agitation against both the government and the railway was increasing, in spite of Macdonald's promise that the hated Monopoly Clause would be dropped from the contract once the job was finished. In St. Laurent on the Saskatchewan, Louis Riel, the leader of the Red River uprising of 1869, was back from his long exile and rousing the métis again. On the far plains and in the foothills, the Cree chieftains Big Bear and Poundmaker were petitioning for new concessions from an unheeding government. And in the mountains, the railway builders faced their last great barrier, the snow-shrouded Selkirks.

The Selkirks remained a mystery almost to the moment when the steel was driven through. There was something uncanny about those massive pyramidal peaks, scoured by erosion and rent by avalanche. As late as 1884, when the rails reached the mouth of the Beaver, powerful voices had been raised urging that the road circumvent the mountains by following the hairpin valley of the Columbia. The uneasiness was felt in the highest echelons of the company, and with good reason: for the very first time the locomotives, rather than the Indians, were blazing a pioneer trail.

Van Horne had thought long and hard about using the Rogers Pass in preference to the longer but easier Columbia Valley. Publicly he called it "one of the finest mountain passes ever seen," but privately he had reservations. On the one hand there would be heavy gradients—probably greater than 2 per cent—for some forty miles. That would mean heavy assisting engines and costly wear and tear on the track. Against that there was the saving of the cost of operating nearly seventy-seven miles of additional line, which meant a reduction of two hours in passenger time and four hours for freight trains. This latter considera-

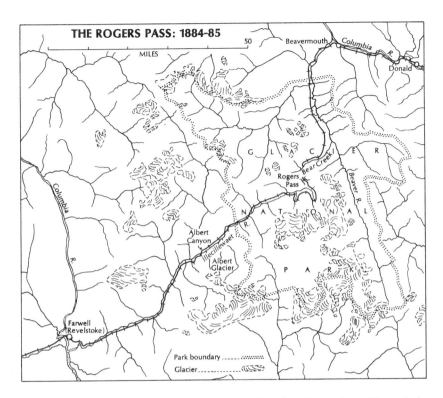

THE ROGERS PASS: 1884-85

tion was of great importance when competing for through traffic and, in the general manager's opinion, "would alone be sufficient to justify the use of heavier gradients." Van Horne, who disdained circumlocution, opted for the Rogers Pass.

There were problems in the Selkirks, however, on which no one had reckoned, and these began to manifest themselves in the first months of 1885. By that time the right of way had been cleared directly across the mountains, from the mouth of the Beaver River at its junction with the Columbia on the east to the mouth of the Illecillewaet at its confluence with the Columbia on the west. More than a thousand men, strung out in scattered construction camps and individual shacks along the tote road, were toiling away in the teeth of shrieking winds that drove snow particles like needles into their faces. Seen from the top of the pass, the location line resembled a wriggling serpent, coiling around the hanging valleys, squeezing through the narrow ravines, and sometimes vanishing into the dark maw of a half-completed tunnel. High above, millions of tons of ice hung poised on the lip of the mountains, the birthplace of the avalanches and snowslides that constantly plagued the area.

The snowslides occurred largely on the western slopes. Like the lush vegetation—the gigantic cedars and huge ferns, which astonished every traveler who crossed the Rogers Pass—they were the result of an extraordinary precipitation. The moist winds, blowing across British Columbia from the Pacific, were blocked by the mountain rampart, which relieved them of their burden of water vapor. The rainfall each summer was heavy and the subsequent snowfall phenomenal. An average of thirty feet of snow fell each winter at the Illecillewaet Glacier; at the summit the average fall was fifty feet.

This natural phenomenon posed a threat to the entire operation of the railway. In midwinter, the Rogers Pass—a mass of avalanches, slides, and fallen glaciers—was almost impossible to breach. The snowslides were solid packs of ice and were sometimes fifty feet in thickness. Through this frozen jungle the railroad builders intended to force the line. On February 8, a slide six miles west of the summit buried the camp of William Mackenzie, killing the cook. On the same day a second slide, four miles west of the summit, buried three men alive. A third slide, closer to the summit, destroyed a company store. As the situation grew worse, the panic-stricken men refused to work. Herbert Holt lost sixty-five thousand dollars' worth of supplies, all swept away by a vast slide at the end of February. By that time all communication between the summit and Second Crossing was cut off; supplies could no longer come in from Kamloops but had to be hauled up from Beavermouth.

A Selkirk snowslide was a terrifying spectacle. A quarter of a million cubic yards of snow could be detached from a mountain peak and come tearing down the slopes for thousands of feet, ripping out great cedars, seizing huge boulders in its grip, and causing an accompanying cyclone more fearful than the avalanche itself. This cyclone extended for a hundred yards or more outside the course of the slide and was known as the flurry, a term that scarcely did credit to its intensity. A few seconds before the body of the avalanche struck, the pressure of this gale-force wind snapped off huge trees several feet in diameter fifty feet above the base without uprooting them. The accompanying cloud of fine snow particles was impacted like moss against the windward side of the trunks. One such flurry was known to have picked up a man and whirled and twisted him spirally and so rapidly that when he dropped he was a limp mass without a bruise or a break in skin or clothing yet with every bone in his body either broken or dislocated. One snowslide, which stopped just short of the track near Glacier, was preceded by a flurry so powerful that it knocked eight loaded freight cars off the rails. The railway builders sometimes cut right through small mountains of debris left by such slides. One cut, about forty feet deep, was full of tangled trees and presented such a strange appearance when gulleted—the sawn stumps sticking out like raisins in a cake—that it was known as Plum Pudding Cut.

Apart from the slides, the prodigious falls of snow presented a considerable hazard. In one six-day period, eight and a half feet of snow fell. Sometimes three weeks could pass without the blizzard ceasing. Even in mid-May there might be two feet of snow remaining in the summit area. In the winter, the scene from the Rogers Pass was eerie. A traveler gazing westward looked down into a two-thousand-foot gorge, muffled in a white blanket twenty feet deep. Above and around him the glaciers dangled, shimmering in the sunlight. At one spot, forty-two glaciers were visible, the largest being the vast Illecillewaet, which would for more than half a century be one of the great Canadian tourist attractions until the changing climate caused it to recede. (One lady from Seattle gazing upon it in awe wanted to know whether the CPR had installed it for advertising purposes.)

This scenery, an uncalculated asset for the railway in the summer season, was an uncalculated liability in the winter. It became obvious that no trains could operate in safety during January and February; but even if the company had fully comprehended the problem in 1885, it is doubtful that it could have raised the money to solve it. The problems of the Selkirks delayed the opening of through passenger service to the Pacific by at least six months. In the winter of 1885–86 entire sections of completed track were swept away by snowslides and the line had to be closed. The scene of desolation was described by Michael Phillips, a rancher who traveled the line on foot: "A deserted house or cabin looks dreary in these mountains, a deserted town more dismal yet; but imagine, if you can, a railway deserted! Hundreds of miles of line abandoned! Signal boxes, stations, small towns lifeless, and fast being buried beneath the snow, all battered to pieces by fierce mountain storms!"

It took Herculean efforts to open the track in the early years of its operation. Specially designed ice chisels were used to burrow into the snow; the resulting tunnels were filled with sacks of black powder and the snow packed in behind so that the entire right of way could be blasted clear. In the end, the company was forced to construct almost six miles of snowsheds—fifty-four of them, built of heavy timbers. Even then there were unforeseen accidents—a tree driven right through the roof of one shed, a ten-ton boulder crashing through another. The sheds cost forty dollars a foot to construct, an expenditure Van Horne had not foreseen when he adopted the Rogers Pass route.

For the next quarter century, this westward descent, like that of the Big Hill in the Rockies, was an operating nightmare. In March, 1910, a snowslide which caused the loss of fifty-eight lives finally convinced the CPR that it must abandon the Rogers Pass. This resulted in a second engineering feat, equal to the drilling of the spiral tunnels— the boring of the longest double-track tunnel on the continent, the five-mile-long Connaught. Passing under Mount Macdonald, the tunnel lowered the grade by 540 feet, shortened the line by four and a half miles, and reduced the track curvature by an amount corresponding to seven complete circles. The man who did the job was the same Jack Stewart who worked as a youth in helping build the mountain line.

Snow or no snow, the line had to be driven to completion somehow by the end of 1885. As winter gave way to spring, every mile of the right of way was throbbing with activity—teamsters jogging in with wagonloads of supplies, other teams plowing up the rough, root-ridden earth, small armies of men swinging picks and shovels, others blasting out cuts and tunnels—trees toppling, stumps flying sky-high, boulders splintering, and always the reek of smoke and horse manure blotting out the subtler scent of the cedar forest.

Along the gorge of the Kicking Horse, the railway had kept close to the river, crossing it at the most economical spots, with the tote road suspended above. But in the valley of the Beaver, which led up toward the Selkirks, the line rose high above both road and river, as much as two and three hundred feet in places. The mountain streams tumbling down from the glaciers above had cut deep gouges in the naked rock, and it was over these gulches that the longest and the highest bridges were required. Built entirely of timber cut on the spot, they had few counterparts in the world. The Mountain Creek Bridge, which rose more than 175 feet above the torrent, was one of the largest wooden structures ever built, being twelve hundred feet long. The bridge over Stoney Creek was the highest in North America, supported on wooden towers two hundred feet high, set in concrete.

There is a tale of Van Horne arriving at the half-completed Stoney Creek bridge when it was imperiled by rising floods. Men were felling trees, dragging logs to the site, and building new trestle braces and bulwarks when the general manager appeared. He plunged in to help, assisting with his own hands the positioning of heavy blocks of stone, instructing the carpenters as to the best method of securing the huge wooden braces, showing the blacksmiths how to fashion their iron clamps, and never once losing his demeanor of cool authority. He drove the men all day until the light faded and the bridge was saved. By that time his private car was drawn up on the rails and Van Horne retired to it. Not long afterward, the sounds of violin music came drifting through the night air. The general manager was playing an aria by Gounod, a sure sign that he was satisfied with the day's labor.

On the far side of the pass, where the Prussian blue waters of the Illecillewaet raced downhill between thick jungle walls, the line made a double loop, curving first to the left, then swinging back across the valley to the very tip of the great glacier and then, a mile farther on, twisting back again in the shape of an inverted "S." This was three more miles of railway than Van Horne had counted on; it took nine and a half miles to reach the level of the stream four miles from the summit. But it was necessary to avoid the snowslides. For the future tourists, swaying down this dramatic slope from the vantage point of an observation car in what was shortly to become Glacier National Park, the experience would be electrifying—the awesome cedars rising like great pillars from the thick beds of ferns, the mountainsides sprinkled with wild columbine and pigeonberry, the glittering ice fields, the sword points of the mountain peaks, the cataracts pouring off the cliffs as airily as wood smoke, and the shining track coiling through the dark cuts and over the slender bridges on its journey to the Columbia. This was the same trail, bestrewn with devil's-club and skunk cabbage, up which Major Rogers and his nephew Albert had toiled on their voyage of discovery in 1881; that Fleming and Grant, badly lacerated by thorns, had managed to negotiate in 1883; and that a hungry Van Horne had struggled over in 1884. Nobody except an enthusiastic mountaineer would ever have to make that journey again; and only a few, gazing up at the shattered rock of the clefts and tunnels and the pilings of the matchstick bridges, would let their thoughts rest upon the thousands of sweating workmen who made it possible.

2 · *The return of the Messiah*

To those who had known the North West before the time of the steel, the railway was a symbol of the passing of the Good Old Days. To the Indians it was a new kind of boundary, as solid in its own way as a wall. To the white settlers of northern Saskatchewan, its change of route had meant disappointment. To the farmers of Manitoba it spelled monopoly and grinding freight rates. To the half-breeds, it stood for revolutionary social change.

From Winnipeg to Edmonton, the North West was in a ferment. Whites, Indians, and half-breeds were all organizing. At the end of July, 1884, the Crees of the North Saskatchewan, who had come to the point of rebellion earlier in the year, were welded into an Indian council by Big Bear, the most independent of the chiefs. The Indians felt that the Government had deceived and betrayed them, and the Indians were right. Ottawa had promised to save them from starvation, yet already their meager rations had been cut back as part of an official policy of retrenchment brought on by economic conditions. It was plain that the eastern politicians had little understanding of conditions in the North West. The new Minister of the Interior, Senator David Macpherson, had not even ventured as far as Winnipeg.

The white settlers and farmers were equally disaffected. In addition to the burgeoning Manitoba and North-West Farmers' Union, which was threatening secession, or even rebellion, other organized groups were petitioning Ottawa for redress. Their demands were similar: local autonomy, reform of the land laws, control of their own railways, reduction of protective tariffs, and an end to the CPR monopoly.

The English and Scots half-breeds and the French-speaking Roman Catholic métis had another grievance. Since 1873, they had been demanding in the North West Territories what the government had recognized and granted in Manitoba after the first collision with Louis Riel—a share in the aboriginal title of the land. They had been put off, time after time, with the maddening reply that consideration would be given to their demands. Nothing concrete was done.

The coming of the railway marked for the métis the end of a social order that had been based on hunting and freighting. With the Red River cart obsolete, they could no longer occupy themselves in the freighting business, long an auxiliary source of income. By 1884 they were in a state of frustration and alarm because of the government's stumbling land policy. One of the problems was the difficulty of acquiring title to land on which many had squatted for years.

By the spring of 1884, protest meetings were becoming common at St. Laurent, the strongest and best established of the métis communities. ". . . the N. W. Ter. is like a volcanoe ready to erupt," one métis wrote to the exiled Louis Riel in May, 1884. By that time, the united half-breed community in the forks of the Saskatchewan had decided that Riel was the only man who could lead them—peacefully, it was hoped—in an agitation to force the Government's hand. He had done it fifteen years before. He must be persuaded to do it again. No one else had his magnetism, his sense of tactics, his eloquence, and, above all, his reputation.

Riel was far away and many years out of touch, living in poverty and teaching school at Sun River, Montana. But distance held no terrors for the métis. Four of them saddled up their horses that May and set out on a seven-hundred-mile ride to meet their Messiah.

The most interesting member of the delegation was Gabriel Dumont, the most popular and respected man along the Saskatchewan—a
natural leader, though totally unlettered and almost apolitical. For
years Dumont, "the Prince of the Prairies," had been chief of the
buffalo hunt. He was a legendary rider, sharpshooter, drinker, gambler,
and even swimmer—a rarity among métis—and he had acquired the
knack of "calling" buffalo into a trap, a skill lost by most Indian tribes.

There were many tales circulating about the plains regarding
Dumont's exploits as a youth. At eighteen, he had led a posse of Cree
to an armed camp of twenty-five Blackfoot to recapture the kidnapped
wife of a friend. Dumont and one man entered the camp, jumped the
guards, and carried off the woman safely. On another occasion he had
flabbergasted a Blackfoot encampment by creeping in out of the shadows
at the height of a pot dance and joining the male dancers who were
spearing meat in the central pot and boasting of their exploits in killing
Crees. "I am Gabriel Dumont," he shouted, spearing a piece of meat
on his own, "and I have killed eight Blackfoot! What do you think of
that?" The chief was so astounded he invited Dumont to stay and even
suggested a peace treaty.

In 1884, when he set off to see Riel, Dumont was forty-seven years
old, a swarthy man with bull's shoulders and a handsome, kindly face.
He had been a chief of his people since the age of twenty-five, much
beloved by all who knew him, including Sam Steele, the Mounted
Policeman, who thought him one of the kindest and best of men, flawed
only by an obsession for gambling: he was quite capable of playing
cards for three days and nights without stopping to eat. Dumont knew
the prairies, Steele said, "as well as a housewife knows her kitchen,"
and was universally respected: "One might travel the plains from one
end to the other and talk to the métis hunters and never hear an unkind
word said of Dumont. He would kill bison by the score and give them
to those who were either unable to kill or had no buffalo. Not until
every poor member of the hunting-parties had his cart filled with meat
would he begin to fill his own. When in trouble the cry of all was for
Gabriel."

In 1884 there was trouble, and the cry was for Gabriel again. He
knew that he could not lead his people in a battle with the government
of Canada. He spoke several Indian dialects as well as he spoke his
native French, but he had no English and no gift for oratory. He was
a man of action, a prairie general who would shortly become the tactician of the last stand of the métis empire against the onrush of civilization.

The four métis delegates arrived at Riel's small home on June 4,

1884. Riel was plumper than he had been in the days of the Manitoba uprising. His features had filled out and he now wore a curly, red-brown beard. He was still handsome, with a high, intelligent forehead, a straight nose, and eyes that, when he recalled the stirring days of 1869 and 1870, "danced and glistened in a manner that riveted attention."

He was under doctor's orders to behave quietly and avoid excitement, a counsel he only occasionally remembered to follow. Exiled in 1875 for five years as a result of his role in the Red River troubles, he had been subjected to such stresses that he had gone insane at times, bellowing that he was a prophet, suffering hallucinations, and sometimes running naked down the corridors of the institutions in which he was confined. Twenty months in Quebec asylums (hidden from his pursuers) had calmed him down, but his sense of personal mission was never quenched. Moving west, he had plunged briefly into Montana politics before settling down with his dark little métis wife, Marguerite, to the penniless life of a parish schoolmaster.

Riel was clearly aroused by the message the delegation brought to him. The sense of power, which he had enjoyed in his brief time as master of Fort Garry, was still within him; so was the mystic conviction that he had a divine mission to perform. Undoubtedly he felt keenly the plight of his people, as he had fifteen years before. Added to that was his own sense of injury at the hands of the Canadian government. Canada, he believed, owed him both land and money while he himself had been living in penury. After some consideration he told the delegation that he would return to Canada temporarily (he was at this point a naturalized American) to fight not only for his personal rights and those of his people but also for the white settlers and the Indians. Significantly, his first public meeting in the North West, in July, was held at an English-speaking settlement, Red Deer Hill. W. H. Jackson, secretary of the Settlers' Union, shared the platform with him. Later that month Riel and Jackson met with Big Bear and incorporated in their subsequent petition to Ottawa the Indians' grievances and demands.

On the surface Riel did not appear to sanction trouble and probably did not contemplate it at that time. His meetings were outwardly peaceful. The métis demands were sent to Ottawa; they included requests for land scrip, better treatment for the Indians, parliamentary representation, reduction of the tariff, and the building of another railway to Hudson Bay. In spite of the clamor, the government remained curiously inattentive.

The resident priest at St. Laurent, Father André, wrote three letters to the Indian Commissioner, Edgar Dewdney, in January and February, 1885, stating clearly that unless the government took some action to redress grievances there would be an uprising under Riel in which the Indians would join. By this time Riel was acting very strangely. From the first of January, it was said, he had fed exclusively on blood instead of flesh, the blood being cooked in milk. It was done, Charles Nolin later swore in court, to excite a feeling of awe in the minds of his followers, "no doubt with a view to making them believe that he was acting under Divine instructions." There is not much doubt that Riel himself believed that he was God's envoy. He prayed daily, told of revelations he had experienced in the night, recounted the visitations of saints, and periodical conversations he said he had had with the Holy Ghost.

Father André's repeated warnings were supplemented by others from Joseph Howe, the Mounted Police inspector at Prince Albert; from Major L. N. F. Crozier, his superior at Battleford; and from D. H. McDowell, the representative of the district on the Territorial Council. The government's response was a vague set of promises and the establishment of a commission, to examine the question of land scrip for the métis. This served only to infuriate Riel and his followers.

Crozier's advice was that "if this man Riel was out of the country the normal quiet would be restored." The truth of the matter seems to be that Riel could have been bought off easily for a few thousand dollars. The evidence suggests that he was prepared to desert the métis cause and return to Montana for hard cash and that he did his best to negotiate that return with the Government's representatives. Councillor McDowell reported that "his claims amount to the modest sum of $100,000 but . . . I believe myself that $3,000 or $5,000 would cart the whole Riel family across the boundary."

To John A. Macdonald, this was simple blackmail, and he refused to countenance it although fourteen years before he had had no such qualms. The Prime Minister's mood that spring seemed to be delay, as George Stephen was finding to his own frustration. Macdonald appeared to exhibit a strange blindness toward the North West. He had shown it in 1869 at the time of the first Riel trouble. He had shown it repeatedly in the settlement of prairie communities, when the rights of the settlers were ignored. He had shown it with the Indians and now he was showing it with the métis. There was a curious ambivalence about the Prime Minister's attitude toward the new Canada west of Ottawa. At the time of Confederation he had ignored it totally, believing it unfit for anything but a few Indians and fur traders. Then, when the Americans

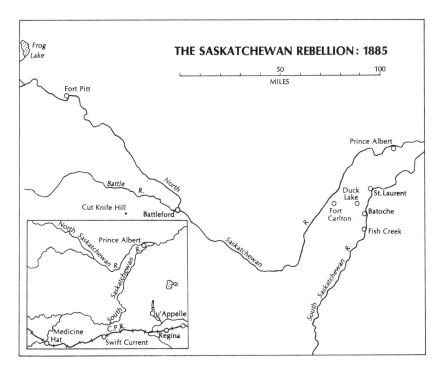

THE SASKATCHEWAN REBELLION: 1885

seemed on the point of appropriating it by default, he had pushed the bold plan for a transcontinental railway. Suddenly once again he seemed to have lost interest. The railway was floundering in a financial swamp; the West was about to burst into flame. Macdonald vacillated.

Riel's memory went back to those intoxicating moments in December, 1869, when he had been able to secure concessions for his people as the result of a bold *fait accompli*. Something along the same lines was in his mind in the early months of 1885. He would not need to resort to bloodshed; the threat of it would bring the Canadian government to its senses.

But times had changed; Riel ignored the presence of the railway. In 1869, the Red River had been an isolated community, separated from Canada by the rampart of the Shield. He and his métis had existed almost in a vacuum and worked their will because the Canadian minority in the settlement could not be reinforced by soldiers from the East. Those conditions no longer held.

By March 13, Major Crozier was expecting a rebellion to break out at any moment. The Mounted Police Commissioner, A. G. Irvine, dispatched a hundred reinforcements to Prince Albert. Rumor, winging across the prairies, raised that number to five hundred, so that Riel came to believe that the government had replied to his demands by raising an army against him. Events now began to accelerate. On

March 18, the day before the festival of St. Joseph, the patron saint of the métis, Riel took prisoners, seized arms in the St. Laurent–Batoche area, and cut the telegraph line between Batoche and Prince Albert. The following day, with his people assembled for the festival, he set up a provisional métis government, as he had done in 1869. He did not want bloodshed; and when Gabriel Dumont urged him to send messengers to enlist Indian support, Riel overruled him, believing Ottawa would now yield to the threat of insurrection.

He was, however, becoming more inflammatory. He told his people that five hundred policemen were on the way to slaughter them all. In the week that followed he and his followers, in Crozier's words, "robbed, plundered, pillaged and terrorized the settlers and the country." They sacked stores, seized and held prisoners, and stopped the mails. Riel and Crozier exchanged emissaries on March 21; the rebel leader's clear intent was to convince the policeman that he was committed to a violent course of action. Dewdney wired Macdonald the following day that the situation looked very serious and that it was imperative that an able military man be in the North West in case the militia had to be called out. On March 23, Macdonald dispatched Major-General Frederick Dobson Middleton to the Red River with orders that the militia should move. Macdonald, who incredibly was "not aware of any causes for discontent," belatedly dispatched his dilatory commission to the spot to investigate the métis land claims.

It was Riel's intention to seize Fort Carlton and establish it as the capital of his new government. He demanded unconditional surrender from Crozier: "We want blood! blood! If Carlton is not surrendered it will be a war of extermination; I must have an answer by 12 o'clock or we will attack and take the fort."

Crozier decided to hold Fort Carlton with his policemen and a detachment of volunteers from Prince Albert. But on March 25 he sent a sergeant and seventeen constables with eight sleighs to get provisions and ammunition from the trader's store at nearby Duck Lake. It was a strange move, since it was inevitable that the métis under Dumont, who had already occupied and looted the store, would repulse them. Three miles from Duck Lake, four of the Mounted Police scouts were turned back by a large number of pursuing métis and Indians. The sleighs halted. Dumont and his followers drew up, behaving "in a very overbearing and excited manner." The Prince of the Plains actually went so far as to prod the ribs of the Mounted Police interpreter with a cocked and loaded rifle while the Indians jeered at the police: "If you are men, now come in." The party retreated.

This was too much for the impatient Crozier. The Force had been slighted. No one who wore the scarlet coat could countenance such a breach of the law. Without waiting for Irvine and his reinforcements, the superintendent set out with his fifty-five Mounted Policemen, forty-three Prince Albert volunteers, and a seven-pound cannon in tow.

Dumont, on horseback, watched them come. His métis dismounted and began to creep forward through a curtain of falling snow, partially encircling the police. Crozier drew his twenty sleighs up in line across the road and ordered his men to take cover behind them. A parley took place under a rebel white flag with Dumont's brother Isidore and an Indian on one side and Crozier and a half-breed interpreter, John McKay, on the other. When Crozier extended his hand to the Indian, the unarmed native made a grab for McKay's rifle. Crozier, seeing the struggle, gave the order to fire. Isidore Dumont toppled from his horse, dead. The rebels were already on the move, circling around the police left flank. Crozier put spurs to his horse and galloped back to the police lines through a hail of bullets. The Indian had also been killed.

At this moment, with the métis pouring a fierce fire on the police from two houses concealed on the right of the trail and outflanking them on the left, Louis Riel appeared on horseback through the swirling snow, at the head of a hundred and fifty armed métis. He was grasping an outsize crucifix in his free hand, and when the police fired at him he roared in a voice that all could hear: "In the name of God the Father who created us, reply to that!"

Within thirty minutes Crozier had lost a quarter of his force killed and wounded. The métis had suffered only five casualties. The North West Mounted Police were in retreat. The Saskatchewan Rebellion had begun.

3 · *"I wish I were well out of it"*

SUNDAY, JANUARY 12, 1885, WAS THE Prime Minister's seventieth birthday, and on Monday all of Montreal celebrated his anniversary, which also marked his fortieth year in politics. It was almost fifteen years since he had promised British Columbia a railway to the Pacific, and in that period he had moved from the prime of life to old age. The rangy figure was flabbier; the homely face had lost some of its tautness; the hair was almost white; deep pouches had formed beneath those knowing eyes; the lines around the edges of the sapient lips had deepened; and on the great nose and full cheeks were the tiny purple veins of overindulgence.

He was a Canadian institution. There were many grandparents at that birthday celebration in Montreal who could not remember a time when Macdonald had not been in politics. The reports of his imminent retirement through illness, fatigue, incompetence, scandal, or political maneuver had appeared regularly in the press for all of the railway days. His suicide had been rumored, his death predicted, his obituary set in type ready for the presses to roll; but Macdonald had outlasted one generation of critics and spawned a second. He had left the country the previous fall, weary to the point of exhaustion, suffering once again from the stomach irritation that seemed to be the bane of Canadian political leaders. Now he was back, miraculously revived, jaunty as ever, making jokes about his health and telling his friends and supporters that as long as his stomach held out the Opposition would stay out.

He would need a healthy stomach for the days that lay immediately ahead; but as he drove through two miles of flaming torches on that "dark soft night," under a sky spangled by exploding rockets, to a banquet in his honor, he was in the mellowest of moods. In his speech he could not help amplifying the eulogies that he heard on all sides about the great national project, which was nearing completion. "In the whole annals of railway construction there has been nothing to equal it," he said. Only a few of those in attendance—George Stephen was one—could appreciate the irony of that statement. The Prime Minister might just as easily have been referring to the immensity of the financial crisis that the railway faced.

Just the previous Friday, Stephen had dispatched one of his frantic wires to the Prime Minister: "Imminent danger of sudden crisis unless we can find means to meet pressing demands." That week, rumors of the company's financial straits began to leak out. On January 16, one of the Montreal papers reported that the CPR could not meet its April dividend, that attacks on the London market had caused another drop in the price of its stock, and that the company was paying for its normal cash purchases with notes at four months. The rumors were true. Within a fortnight the stock was down below 38; not long after it hit a new low of 33⅛.

Stephen had worked out a scheme whereby the unissued stock of the CPR would be canceled by government legislation, the lien on the railway removed, and a more or less equivalent amount of cash raised by mortgage bonds applied to the entire main line of the railway, with principal and interest on them guaranteed by the government. About half the cash from these bonds would be used to help pay off the loan of 1884. The rest would go to the company as a loan to pay for expenditures not included in the original contract. The remainder of the 1884 loan would be paid off in land-grant bonds.

Financially, it was an ingenious scheme. Politically it was disastrous. The previous year, Blake had taunted the Government about the CPR loan: "Don't call it a loan. You know we shall never see a penny of this money again." This was strong meat; Macdonald could foresee the hazards of allowing the Opposition to cry, "We told you so!"

The Prime Minister at seventy was a different man from the fifty-five-year-old who in 1870 had firmly believed that no time should be lost in building a railway to the Pacific. Then, if anything, he had been overly rash in his promises to British Columbia; now the aging chieftain seemed weary and confused, hesitant of taking any political risk, insensitive to the problems of the North West, and apparently sick unto death of the railway he had helped to create. The picture of Macdonald in 1885 is that of a leader who has lost his way, stumbling from one crisis to another, propped up by bolder spirits within his Cabinet and by the entreaties of men like Stephen and Van Horne. His policy of delay which from time to time had worked in his favor was disastrous in 1885; it brought bloodshed to the North West and came within an hour of wrecking the CPR.

The Prime Minister had been doing his best to avoid Stephen, whose letters, telegrams, and personal visits were becoming more importunate as the crisis grew. Stephen, however, would not be put off. He shuttled back and forth between Montreal and Ottawa, plaguing Cabinet Ministers and government servants, such as Collingwood Schreiber, when he could not see their chief. His letters had taken on a waspish, old-womanish quality. "It is as clear as noonday, Sir John," he wrote in January, "that unless you yourself say what should be done, nothing but disaster will result." But Old Tomorrow would not say. In vain, Stephen pleaded, cajoled, promised, and threatened. Tilley, the Finance Minister, who did not believe the company's plan was politically feasible, exasperated him. Could Macdonald do nothing with Tilley? "What alarms me is the apprehension that the patient will die while the doctors are deliberating on the remedy." Stephen was almost at the end of his tether—or thought he was: "I feel *my* ability to save it has gone. I am sorry to confess this even to myself."

The specter of the dividend hovered over the CPR's executive committee. Default, the president knew, would be fatal. The company's books were about to close. If it did not advertise the dividend, the world would assume that the Canadian Pacific was bankrupt. Again, the only hope was the government. Surely it would come to the assistance of the company on a temporary basis, making an advance on supplies before the end of January; those funds could be paid back out of the monthly estimates. If Stephen could have that assurance he would take the risk of advertising the dividend. He wired Macdonald on January 20: "The dividend must be cabled tonight. . . . Can I trust to this? Please answer. I cannot delay advertizing dividend any longer."

Now the Prime Minister was forced into a corner. He had to break the news to Stephen that there was no chance of any further government assistance. He faced a revolt in his Cabinet and he was not prepared to do battle for the railway. Three Ministers were obdurately opposed to further relief for the CPR; and one of these, Archibald McLelan, a Nova Scotian, the Minister of Fisheries, had given notice that he would resign if any further public monies were advanced to the CPR. The Prime Minister wired Stephen that there was little chance of legislation that session. He would, however, be able to carry an advance of enough money to pay the dividend if it would enable Stephen to postpone matters until 1886. With an election behind him, Macdonald felt he could change many minds.

This was worse than no answer at all. There was no way the railway could stay afloat until 1886 without further funds over and above the subsidy. Stephen knew what he had to do.

In one of his directors' meetings, when bankruptcy was imminent and real, Stephen, in a speech that Van Horne later characterized as the finest he had ever heard, turned to Smith and said simply: "If we fail, you and I, Donald, must not be left with a dollar of personal fortune." Smith had silently agreed. Now the two Scotsmen prepared to go down with the railway. They pledged the remainder of their joint fortunes and all their personal assets—everything they possessed down to their gold cuff links—to raise the six hundred and fifty thousand dollars necessary to pay the dividend and an additional million dollars on a five-month note to provide the short-term funds the company would need to carry it over the coming weeks.

When the treasury officers arrived at Stephen's new home on Drummond Street in Montreal to take an inventory of his personal possessions, he stood quietly by. They had already counted his cash and securities. Now they brought along experts who valued his growing art collection, his marble statuary, his furniture, and his famous imported piano. Then they catalogued his household linen, his china, and his silverware. Stephen carefully examined the long list of his material possessions acquired over a period of thirty-five years in Canada, and then, in the words of an eyewitness, "without a flicker of an eyelid signed it all away."

It was a remarkable act, given the business morality of that day, or indeed of any day, as Stephen himself well knew. What he and Smith had done was "simply absurd on any kind of business grounds."

"I venture to say," he told Macdonald, "that there is not a business man in all Canada, knowing the facts, but would say we were a couple of fools for our pains. But as long as we are able to save & protect the Company against its enemies who seem bent on its destruction we shall not grudge any risk, or loss that may occur. Personal interests have become quite a secondary affair with either of us."

This attitude was unique in North American railway annals. Among the various United States transcontinental lines, bankruptcies had been the rule. The directors and promoters, however, had rarely lost a penny. Railways were not generally viewed by their promoters as a method of developing the nation but merely as an easy way of siphoning money out of the public purse. But to Stephen, money was truly secondary.

". . . it is killing to have any of our friends think we are simply doing our bare duty by the Coy & are making money out of it," he told the Prime Minister. Making money was for Yankees like Jay Gould and the notorious Russell Sage—railway bandits who wore no masks. Stephen shared Macdonald's contempt for the stereotype. To be likened to Gould, as he had been, was particularly mortifying. The thing that Stephen prized most was his reputation; the idea that he might be the means whereby his friends and business associates would lose money bothered him far more than the possible financial ruin he now courted. It was not enough that he be a man of honor in the business world; he must be *seen* to be a man of honor. If the CPR crashed, Stephen must crash with it. At least, if he ended up selling pencils in the streets (an unlikely outcome), the world would know that he had done his duty at great personal sacrifice.

Stephen was becoming more emotional as the days wore on and the government dallied. At one point, when he was at his most despondent, he began to cry while sitting in Schreiber's office. His tears of despair were the outward sign of an inner sense of impending personal doom. "I am not *sure* of *myself* being able to stand the strain for an indefinite time," he confessed to Macdonald. "I have had warnings of which no body knows but myself which I will fight against to conceal to the last."

No such melodramatic disclosures issued from Donald Smith's compressed lips. As always, he remained imperturbable. If he had physical warnings, he never betrayed them; if he had emotions, he never revealed them. He was a lonely man, subject to considerable gossip about his "strange and complicated" family relationships. "His wife," Sir Henry Tyler of the Grand Trunk wrote to Lady Tyler in

1888, "is said to have another husband, & his daughter, lately married against her mother's wishes, not to be his own." But he was always present in the background when needed, as solid and unmoving as the great rock of Craigellachie; and Stephen undoubtedly drew strength from that presence.

The two Scotsmen could provide relief only on a short-term basis; they could not, unaided, save the railway with a million dollars. The demands of the contractors in the mountains and along Lake Superior would consume that sum in a few weeks. Already the three-month notes given to satisfy clamorous creditors were coming due, and Macdonald was still vacillating on the "rearrangement scheme," as Stephen called it.

Stephen continued to hammer away at Macdonald, modifying his original proposal for relief here and there but in essence asking for the removal of the lien and a further loan of five millions.

"I don't know how Council . . . will take it," a weary Macdonald wrote to Tupper in London. ". . . our difficulties are immense . . . we have blackmailing all round." As the price of acceptance the hungry Quebeckers were again demanding that the provincial government lines be subsidized, while the Maritimers were clamoring for another railway. "How it will end God knows," Macdonald said, "but I wish I were well out of it."

Macdonald was dispirited, Tilley indifferent, Stephen close to collapse, and even the normally ebullient Van Horne in a private state of gloom. Outwardly, the general manager remained supremely confident. One morning when a creditor approached, asking for payment and expressing fear as to the outcome of the railway's financial crisis, Van Horne turned to him bluntly and said, "Go sell your boots, and buy C.P.R. stock." Inwardly he must have had his doubts. The absence of the pay car in the Selkirks and on the shores of Lake Superior was threatening to close down the railway. At Beavermouth, the rowdy construction camp on the Columbia, there was already talk of a mass strike. On the Lake Superior section, men were threatening to lynch a contractor whom they blamed for holding back their wages.

When he was not on the road, the general manager haunted Ottawa, visiting the Russell House and the Rideau Club, working to secure the faith of the politicians and the contractors by painting word pictures about the future of the North West and the railway. To an inner circle of intimates he pointed out the disastrous effect the railway's collapse would have on the country. The major banks would totter; wholesale houses would crash; an army of men would be thrown out of work; Canada's credit would be damaged for years.

Van Horne had more difficulty in getting to Macdonald himself.

There is a story of how he managed, at last, to intercept the Prime Minister in the lobby of the House.

"Sir John," he said, "we are and you are dangling over the brink of Hell."

"Well, Van Horne," Macdonald replied, "I hope it will be delayed a while. I don't want to go just yet."

As they strode along the corridor the elusive Tory leader slipped away to speak to "an old friend." That was the last Van Horne saw of him. When he turned back to speak again, Macdonald had vanished, leaving behind a somewhat baffled stranger, flattered at having been so suddenly buttonholed by the Prime Minister.

Van Horne's own future was secure enough. As a friend told him at the time, he could always return to the United States, where several good posts were available for him. To this suggestion he made a characteristic answer: "I'm not going to the States. I'm not going to leave the work I've begun, and I am going to see it through. I'm here to stay and I can't afford to leave until this work is done no matter what position is open to me."

On March 18, Stephen made an official application to the Privy Council for a loan of five million dollars. The application was considered and at length rejected. Stephen vowed that he would leave Ottawa, never to return. The railway was done for. Its directors were ruined men.

Van Horne this time made no attempt to hide his feelings. Percy Woodcock, an artist friend who painted with him, remembered that his hobby no longer was powerful enough to take his mind off the railway's troubles: "Sometimes in the midst of a joyous bit of painting the thought of the road would come to him like a shot and hang over him, holding him totally absorbed and still."

Collingwood Schreiber recalled with some emotion a scene in his office with Van Horne—"the only time I believe his iron nerve was ever shaken." A close friendship had grown up between the two as a result of their several journeys together, especially the hard excursion along the shores of Lake Superior in the summer of 1884. Now the general manager looked up at Schreiber and, very slowly and very softly, revealed the depth of his despair: "Say, if the Government doesn't give it [the loan] we are finished." Van Horne, who had never cast a vote in his life, felt that he had been beaten at the one game he did not understand—the game of politics. He had come within an ace of commanding the greatest single transportation system in the world, and now his ambition had been thwarted, not by any act of his but by a combination of subtle forces which he could not control. No one had seen him reveal his feelings to such an extent since that dark day, so many years before, when his small son William had died, and his friend John Egan, driving him in absolute silence to the funeral, noticed a tear fall onto his hand.

And then, as if the railroad itself had given the cue, succor came from the North West in the most perverse and unexpected form. The métis under Louis Riel had raised the flag of insurrection.

Earlier that year, Van Horne had held a significant conversation with John Henry Pope.

"Why not put us out of our misery?" Van Horne asked the Minister. "Let us go off into some corner and bust."

Pope replied that the government was so concerned about Riel and his followers that it could not undertake further entanglements. An outbreak was possible.

"I wish your CPR was through," Pope said.

Van Horne wanted to know when the government might expect to have troops ready to move to the North West. Pope told him it might be in the first or second week in March. Van Horne immediately declared he could get troops from Kingston or Quebec, where the two permanent force units were stationed, to Qu'Appelle in ten days.

In late March, Van Horne was reminded of this promise when Schreiber remarked to him that Macdonald seemed more concerned about the troubles in the North West than he did about the railway. A thought occurred to the general manager: *How could the government refuse to aid a railway that sped troops out to the prairies, took the métis unawares, and crushed a rebellion?*

Van Horne immediately offered to the Privy Council the services of the railway to move troops, if needed, from Ottawa to Qu'Appelle. He made only one stipulation: he and not the army was to be in complete control of food and transport. His experience in moving troops during the American Civil War had taught him to avoid divided authority and red-tape interference.

It sounded like a foolhardy promise. There were four gaps, totaling eighty-six miles, in the unfinished line north of Lake Superior. Between the unconnected strips of track—much of it unballasted and laid hastily on top of the snow—was a frozen waste of forest, rock, and hummocky drifts, whipped up by the icy winds that shrieked in from the lake. Could men, horses, artillery pieces, and military supplies be shuttled over the primitive tote roads which crossed that meeting place of blizzards? The members of the Council refused to believe it.

"Has anyone got a better plan?" Macdonald asked. There was no answer. Van Horne was told to prepare for a massive movement of men, animals, arms, and equipment.

The first intimations of the impending Saskatchewan Rebellion appeared in fragmentary reports in Ontario newspapers on March 23, jammed in between the inevitable advertisements for such patented cure-alls as Dr. Radway's Sarsaparillan Resolvent, which promised cheap and instant relief for every known disease from cancer to salt rheum. By the following day, Van Horne's plan was in operation, although Joseph-Philippe-René-Adolphe Caron, the Minister of Militia and Defence, was still unsure it would work. The engagement at Duck Lake took place on March 26; when the news burst upon the capital, the country was immediately mobilized.

In Ottawa on the very morning of the Duck Lake tragedy, George Stephen had just finished scribbling a note to Macdonald confessing failure and asking that the Privy Council decision rejecting his proposal be put into writing, so as "to relieve me personally from the possible charge of having acted with undue haste." There was nothing more that the CPR president could do. The fate of the CPR now lay with the railway itself. If Van Horne's gamble worked, then the politicians and the public would have the best possible proof that the presence of a transcontinental line could hold the nation together in time of trouble.

4 · *Marching as to war*

ON MARCH 27, ALL OF SETTLED CANADA learned from its newspapers that a bloody rebellion had broken out in the North West. Ten members of Crozier's mixed force of police and volunteers lay dead at Duck Lake. Thirteen more were wounded, two mortally. Gabriel Dumont's victory was beyond dispute. The Indians were about to rise. Prince Albert, Fort Carlton, Batoche, Fort Pitt, and perhaps Fort Qu'Appelle, Calgary, Edmonton, Moose Jaw, and Regina were all threatened. A wave of apprehension, anger, patriotism, and excitement washed over eastern Canada.

The Government had already called out A and B Batteries stationed in Quebec and Kingston—the only permanent military force in all of Canada; on March 27, several militia regiments were ordered to be ready to move immediately to the North West. This aroused a flurry of speculation. How on earth were they to get there? By Canadian Pacific Railway? How could troops, baggage, guns, horses, and equipment be shuttled over those trackless gaps?

Van Horne was nevertheless determined to move 3,324 men from London, Toronto, Kingston, Ottawa, Montreal, Quebec, Halifax, and a dozen smaller centers. Harry Abbott and John Ross, his deputies on the Superior section, were not in the least perturbed by the problem Van Horne faced them with; they had regularly moved seven hundred workmen over gaps in the line during the winter. Caron warned Abbott to be ready to receive eight hundred troops on March 28. The remainder would move on a staggered schedule over a two-week period.

When the news was confirmed that the entire force was to be shipped west on the new railroad, a kind of frenzy seized the country. To a considerable extent the social life of the cities and towns of settled Canada revolved around the militia. Young officers were in demand at the highly stratified winter sports that marked the era. *The* great social event of the year was the militia ball. One saw uniforms everywhere. Tailors' advertisements featured military fashions over civilian, and the most popular weekend entertainment for the general public was watching the local militia parade through the streets or listening to a military-band concert in the park.

Now, suddenly, the militia was parading through the streets for the first time in earnest, for the country had not yet fought a war of any kind. Never before had Canadians witnessed the kind of spectacular scenes that took place in every major town in the East during late March and early April—the cheers for Queen and Country, the blare of martial music, the oceans of flapping banners, the young men in scarlet and green marching behind the colors, the main streets jammed with waving thousands, the roll of drums, the troop trains puffing through the small towns and off into the Unknown—the singing, the cheering, the weeping and the kissing and the bittersweet good-bys. All this sound and spectacle, pumped up by a fanfaronade of military oratory—together with the terrible news on April 2 of a massacre of priests and civilians by Big Bear's Indians at Frog Lake—kept the country on an emotional binge for the better part of a fortnight.

The first militia units called out were the Queen's Own Rifles, the Royal Grenadiers, and the Infantry School, all of Toronto. The scenes that Monday morning, March 30, when the troops prepared to leave, were chaotic and extravagant. It seemed as if every single citizen who could walk or crawl had come from miles around to line the route of march from the drill shed to the Union Station. The crowd had stood for hours waiting to see the troops. Hundreds offered to pay for positions in the flag-decked windows, but these could no longer be purchased. Women and children fainted continually and had to be removed by the police. Many were weeping.

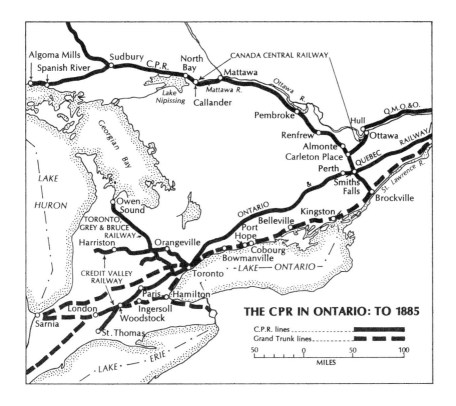

THE CPR IN ONTARIO: TO 1885

C.P.R. lines
Grand Trunk lines

50   0   50   100
MILES

About 11:30, the cheering of the troops was heard from the drill shed, and the entire mob of more than ten thousand broke into an answering cry. The cheering moved like a wave along King Street, so loud that the band of the Tenth Royal Grenadiers could not be heard from half a block away. The crush made it impossible to move. Somebody spotted the first uniform—that of a member of the Governor-General's Body Guard on horseback, followed by Colonel William Dillon Otter, marching on foot at the head of his men. Now the sound of martial music came through at last, and this had a quieting effect on the crowd. A group of about five hundred civilians rushed ahead of the marching men, clearing the way through the dense mass of spectators. Then came the ultimate spectacle: the glittering brass of the band's instruments, the straight rows of fur caps, and the sharp outlines of rifles, drifting above the craning heads "like a float in the water."

Down the streets the young men came, as the crowd around them and above them, before them and behind them, shouted themselves hoarse. Bouquets drifted down from windows. Handkerchiefs fluttered. A thousand flags flapped in the breeze. Those who could not move along beside the troops began to cry "Good-by, good-by!" as the musicians struck up the song that became a kind of theme all over Canada that month, "The Girl I Left Behind Me."

To the foot of York Street, by the station, the crowd had been pouring in an unending stream—all kinds and conditions of people, in carriages, hacks, and express vans, on foot and pushing perambulators, all hoping to catch one last glimpse of brother, son, or sweetheart. The immense crowd filled the Esplanade from one end of the station to the other, swarming over the roofs of freight cars and perching in every window. The morning had started warm and pleasant; then, as if to mirror the crowd's changing mood, it began to rain. The rain increased and changed to a heavy sleet, but the people did not move. The *Mail* reported that of some ten thousand gathered at the station, most of them without umbrellas, fewer than a dozen sought shelter.

Jammed into the cars, the men leaned out of windows and waved at the throng pressed up against the train. The cars began to crawl forward. Arms appeared above the crowd, waving final greetings, and these were answered from the windows by an assortment of fluttering handkerchiefs, toques, forage caps, side arms, socks, and even underwear. Above the continual roaring, individual good-bys could be heard. Then the band of the Queen's Own struck up "Auld Lang Syne" and the men joined in. Slowly the train drew away through the yards, where the top of every freight and passenger car was black with waving and cheering well-wishers, and then through the driving sleet and the whirling snow toward the dark forests and the unballasted track of the new Canada.

These scenes were repeated over and over again during the days that followed. In Kingston, on March 30, hundreds, "flushed and fervent," crammed the town square to greet the incoming troops. In Montreal the crush of onlookers was so great that a vast double window burst out from a three-story building, injuring twelve persons. In Ottawa, the station platform was "a dense mass of enthusiastic, patriotic, jostling, laughing, shouting and war-fever-stricken individuals of all ages, sizes, sexes and complexions." In Quebec, "the scene presented beggars description." The Ninth Voltigeurs, having attended Mass at the basilica on April 2, marched through a wild crowd, escorted by the city's snowshoe clubs in uniform, carrying torches and singing "*La Marseillaise*" and "The British Grenadier."

Only the Governor-General's Body Guard, the oldest cavalry regiment in Canada, departed in comparative quiet and secrecy, the authorities fearing for the safety of the seventy horses among the press of the crowds. The Guard was kept on the *qui vive* for several days while final arrangements were made to get the horses over the gaps in the line. When the regiment left, their colonel, George T. Denison, and his officers had not slept for three nights, having remained booted and spurred and ready to move on the instant for all of that time.

The men from the farms and cities were hard-muscled, keen, and young enough to laugh at the kind of ordeal they would shortly face along the uncompleted route of the CPR. They were also woefully undertrained and underequipped. The York Rangers, huddled in the Toronto drill shed, looked more like sheep than soldiers. In Kingston, the most military of cities, it was noticed that the members of the composite Midland Regiment were badly drilled. Among the 65th, in Montreal, there were men who had never fired so much as a blank cartridge.

Few battalions left for the North West properly equipped. The belts and knapsacks of the Queen's Own had done duty in the Crimean War, thirty years before. Their rifles were old Snider Enfields, most of them totally unreliable because of years of wear and tear. Any man who wanted to be a sharpshooter brought along his own weapon. The clothing of the York Rangers was old and rotten, the knapsacks ill-fitting and so badly packed that a day's marching would break men down. Several of the Midland companies had no knapsacks at all and were forced to wrap their belongings in heavy paper. Others had no helmets. One battalion had suffered a fire, so that the entire force set out without uniforms. Many of the 65th lacked trousers, tunics, and rifles; indeed, there was not a company in that battalion properly equipped for service—ammunition was so scarce that each man could be allotted only three rounds. Even the crack Governor-General's Body Guard had not been issued satchels for their mounts and so the men were forced to submit to the ignominy of wrapping their personal belongings in blankets. Until this moment, membership in a militia unit had been a social asset. Nobody, it appeared, had ever considered the possibility that one day his unit would march off to war. To a great extent, the soldiers had to depend on the bounty of a grateful civilian populace. All the government was obliged to issue was a greatcoat, a tunic, trousers, and a rifle.

The trains sped off toward Dog Lake, where the real ordeal would begin. The officers, at Van Horne's insistence, were given first-class accommodation even though the government's requisition did not cover sleeping cars and Van Horne doubted if he could collect for it. But he was looking further ahead than the bills for the mass movement of some three thousand troops. For the sake of the railway's long-term image it was "important that the report of the officers as to the treatment of the troops on our line should be most favourable." For that reason the CPR was prepared to carry free any clothes or goods sent out to the

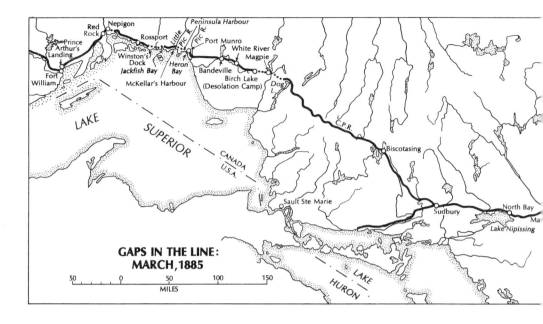

GAPS IN THE LINE:
MARCH, 1885

soldiers by friends or relatives. As for the men themselves, Van Horne
ensured that there would, whenever possible, be mountains of food and
gallons of hot, strong coffee. Better than anybody else, he knew what
the troops were about to face. He could not protect them from the chill
rides in open flatcars and sleighs, or from the numbing treks across the
glare ice, but he could make sure that his army marched on a full
stomach.

5 · The cruel journey

AS THE TRAINS ROLLED WESTWARD AND
the cheering faded, the men from the cities, farms, and fishing villages
of the East began to glimpse the rough face of the new Canada and
comprehend for the first time the real dimensions of the nation. Out of
North Bay the land stretched off to the gray horizon, barren and desolate. The first gap in the line began near Dog Lake and here the railway
had prepared a Lucullan feast of beef, salmon, lobster, mackerel, potatoes, tomatoes, peas, beans, corn, peaches, currants, raisins, cranberries,
fresh bread, cakes, pies, and all the tea and coffee needed to wash it
down. It was the last night of comfort the soldiers would know for
several days and the start of an adventure that all would remember
for the rest of their lives.

The men, packed tightly in groups of eight in sleighs, set off behind
teams of horses down the uncompleted right of way. At every unbridged

ravine and unfilled cut the sleighs were forced off the graded surface, sometimes for several miles, and onto the tote road, a roller-coaster path that cut through forests, ran over stumps, windfalls, and rocks, dipped up and down through gorges, and wound through stretches of tightly packed trees. In some places the sleighs encountered boulders seven or eight feet high; in others they pitched into holes as deep as graves, with the riders flung over the dashboards and into the steaming haunches of the terrified horses. "No description," wrote one man, "could give an idea of the terrible roads through the woods." Spills and accidents were so frequent they were taken as normal. One sleigh carrying members of the 65th overturned no fewer than thirteen times in the forty miles between Dog Lake and the end of track at Birch Lake. Men already half frozen in the twenty-degree-below weather were hurled out and submerged in six feet of powdery snow, often with all their equipment. Caps, mitts, mufflers, side arms, and other articles of luggage were lost in the white blanket through which the sleighs reared and tumbled. One member of the London Fusiliers was completely buried under an avalanche of baggage; a comrade was almost smothered when a horse toppled onto him. When sleighs carrying troops westward encountered empty sleighs returning eastward for a second load, chaos resulted: the detours were only wide enough to permit a single team to pass through without grazing the trees on either side. If a horse got a foot or two out of the track, the runners would lock onto a tree trunk or, worse still, rise up on a stump, tilting occupants and baggage into the snow.

Generally, this trip was made by night when the sun was down and the weather cold enough to prevent the snow from turning to slush. The men crouched in the bottoms of the sleighs, wrapped in their greatcoats and covered with robes and blankets; but nothing could keep out the cold. To prevent themselves from freezing, officers and men would leap from the careening sleighs and trot alongside in an attempt to restore circulation. For some units, the cold was so intense that any man who left any part exposed even for a few minutes suffered frostbite. "What they passed through that night all hope will never require to be repeated," a reporter traveling with the Grenadiers wrote back.

The teams were changed at Magpie camp, a halfway point along the unironed right of way. Here was more food—pork, molasses, bread, and tea, the staples of the construction workers. Many arriving at Magpie thought they had reached the end of their ordeal and were chagrined when the bugle blew and they realized that it was only half over. Scenes of confusion took place in the darkness—the men scrambling about seeking the sleighs to which they had been assigned, the snow dropping so thickly that friends could not recognize each other in the dark, the horses whinnying and rearing, the half-breed teamsters swearing, the officers and noncoms barking orders, the troops groaning with the realization that everything they owned was soaking wet and that they would have to endure four more hours of that bone-chilling journey.

Out of the yard the horses galloped, starting along a route utterly unknown to them, depending solely on their guides and their own instincts, tumbling sometimes—sleighs and all—over the high embankment, righting themselves, and plunging on. The entire gap between Dog Lake and Birch Lake took some nine hours to negotiate, and at the end stood a lonely huddle of shacks, which was promptly named Desolation Camp.

It deserved its title. A fire had swept through the scrub timber, leaving the trees naked of bark and bleached a spectral white. A cutting wind, rattling through the branches, added to the general feeling of despair. The only real shelter was a tattered tent, not large enough to accommodate the scores who sought refuge in it. Yet some men had to remain there for hours, their drenched clothing freezing to their skins in temperatures that dropped as low as thirty-five below.

The 10th Royal Grenadiers arrived at Desolation Camp at five one morning after a sleigh journey that had begun at eight the previous evening. There were no trains available to take them farther, and so they endured a wait of seventeen hours. They did not even have the warmth of a fire to greet them. Tumbling out of the sleighs like ghosts —for the falling snow had covered them completely—they tried to huddle in the tent through whose numerous apertures bitter drafts blew in every direction. The tent was so crowded that it was not possible to lie down. Some men lit fires outside in three feet of snow, only to see the embers disappear into deep holes melted through the crust. Others rolled themselves in their blankets like mummies and tried to sleep, the snow forming over them as it fell.

Every regiment that passed through Desolation Camp had its own story of hardship and endurance. Some members of the Queen's Own were rendered hysterical by the cold; when the trains finally arrived they had to be led on board, uncomprehending and uncaring. Although most of the troops had had very little sleep since leaving civilization, they were denied it at Desolation Camp because sleep could mean certain death when the thermometer dropped. The Halifax Battalion, the last to arrive, had to endure a freezing rain, which soaked their garments and turned their greatcoats into boards. When men in this condition dropped in their tracks, the guards were ordered to rouse them by any means, pull them to their feet, and bring them over to the fires to dry. There they stood, shivering and half conscious, until the flatcars arrived.

In these cars, sleep again was all but impossible, especially for those who traveled at night in below-zero weather with a sharp wind blowing. The cars were the same gravel cars used by construction crews to fill in the cuts. Rough boards had been placed along the sides to a height of about six feet, held in place by upright stakes in sockets. There was no roof, and the wind and snow blew in through the crevices between the planks. Rough benches ran lengthwise and here the men sat, each with his two issue blankets, packed tightly together or huddled lengthwise on the floor. The officers were provided with a caboose heated by a stove, but many preferred to stay with the men.

For the Governor-General's Body Guard, such a journey was complicated by the need to minister to the animals. There were no platforms or gangways in the wild; the men were obliged to gather railway ties and construct flimsy inclined planes up which the horses could be led to the cars. Because the snow was generally three or four feet deep and the ties were sheathed in ice, the makeshift ramps had to be covered with blankets so that the animals would not lose their footing. All had to be watered and fed before the men could rest. Nor could they be moved by sleigh across the Dog Lake gap to Desolation Camp at Birch Lake; the cavalrymen rode or led their animals the entire distance. When the cavalry moved by train, the horses were placed in exactly the same kind of flatcars as the men. Unloading them at each point occupied hours. It was necessary to remove all the hind shoes to prevent injuries to men and steeds; even with that precaution, one fine black stallion was so badly injured by a kick from another horse that he had to be destroyed.

The track that led from Desolation Camp to the next gap at Port Munro was of the most perfunctory construction. The ties had been laid directly onto the snow, and in some sections where a thaw had set in, four or five ties in succession, spiked to the rails, would be held several inches off the ground. One man likened the train's movement to that of a birchbark canoe. Trains were thrown off this section of track daily and the rails were slowly being bent by the heavy passage, which rarely exceeded five miles an hour. "It was," a member of the Queen's Own Rifles wrote home, "about the longest night any of us ever put in."

At Bandeville, the halfway point, the men were fed sandwiches and hot tea. Some were so stiff with cold they had to be lifted out of the cars. Others were so bone-weary that when they reached the warmth of the eating house, the change in temperature was too much for them, and they dropped off into a sleep so deep it was almost impossible to awaken them to eat. One man fell into the snow on the way into the shanty. When his comrades picked him up, he seemed to be insensible. They carried him inside and found there was really nothing wrong with him; he had simply gone to sleep on his feet.

Warmed by this brief respite, the men made ready for the next leg of the journey—a chilling seven hours to Port Munro, a construction station on Lake Superior.

Here was a deep natural harbor, dominated by a thousand-foot crag. In the harbor lay a leaky schooner, *Breck*, capable of sleeping some two hundred troops. Here the troops slumbered in comparative comfort, huddled together in the hold on mattresses composed of equal parts of hay and dirt, and later of water. The leakage was probably caused by the weight of the human cargo grinding the vessel down through the ice. By the time the Halifax battalion arrived, the floor was afloat and the pumps could not be worked because of the frost.

The second gap in the line—about twenty miles—began at Port Munro and continued to McKellar's Harbour, a small inlet near the mouth of the Little Pic River. There were not enough sleighs in the area to carry more than the baggage, and so the troops were forced to march across the glare ice of Lake Superior to the next piece of track, a journey of some eight hours. They began it, generally, in high spirits:

> *The volunteers are all fine boys and full*
> *of lots of fun*
> *But it's mighty little pay they get for*
> *carrying a gun;*
> *The Government has grown so lean and the*
> *CPR so fat*
> *Our extra pay we did not get—*
> *You can bet your boots on that!*

The Grenadiers, well fed and rested, moved out onto the ice in light marching order at dawn on Easter Sunday—a long, wavering line of men with the teams drawn up all around the bay. Above them, a cloud of purest white encircling its midriff, towered the black mountain from whose high head the sun's first rays, red as blood, streamed down on the ice and lit up the crags on the far side of the harbor. A bugle split the sharp morning air and the men began to sing "Hold the Fort, for We Are Coming" as they moved out onto the cold bosom of the lake.

But the very sun that had greeted them that morning was to prove the worst of enemies. For those who had been issued snow glasses the glare on the ice was searing enough; they arrived at their destination, their faces scorched and blistered sometimes almost beyond recognition. Others managed to make eye coverings, Indian fashion, out of strips of birchbark with thin slits cut into them. But there were others who were rendered painfully blind, a red haze blotting out all vision, the corneas smarting as if sandpapered. Colonel Otter himself, at the head of his troops, was almost totally blind when End of Track was reached again.

The troops, buffeted by piercing winds on one side and blistered by the sun's glare on the other, were eventually strung out for seven miles across the lake. Marching was almost impossible on the glassy surface; then, after ten miles, the texture changed: deep cuts, broken blocks of ice, and rocks frozen into the surface began to lacerate the feet of the men and officers, especially those who had the misfortune to leave home in light shoes. Some threw their kits away, bit by bit; some collapsed in their tracks; others became temporarily deranged; one man was ruptured. The baggage sleighs, following behind, gathered up the casualties.

"I can tell you I'll never forget that march," a member of the Queen's Own Rifles wrote home. "We dared not stop an instant as we were in great danger of being frozen, although the sun was taking the skin off our faces. One man of our company went mad and one of the regulars went blind from snow glare. We arrived at our destination about 9 p.m. My boots and leggings were frozen to my feet."

Those units that traveled the same gap by night endured equally fearful conditions. "That night was indeed a terrible one," a member of A Battery recalled. "You have heard of soldiers in the Sudan wandering away from the column on the march while in a somnambulistic condition. Well that is just how our men were. . . . The night was dark, the temperature freezing and a heavy snow storm with a wild, piercing wind made the march a fearful undertaking." Any man who drifted away from the column knew that he faced almost certain death. To prevent this, guards were assigned to ride around the column to head off drifters and stragglers. At that, the night was so dark and the way so difficult that the guide appointed to lead the troops across lost his way and the ordeal was lengthened by several hours.

The travail of the cavalry was again far more strenuous. The infantry was marched across the ice as far as McKellar's Harbour, where a short piece of line had been laid to Jackfish Bay. But because of the nuisance of loading and unloading horses for such a short span, the Governor-General's Body Guard decided to ride or walk their steeds the full distance to Jackfish on the ice of the lake.

For twenty miles the horsemen faced "a vast prairie or desert of ice," with snow and drifts everywhere and no track of any kind. The permanent surface was obscured by a crust under which two or three inches of water lay concealed. Above the crust there was as much as a foot of light snow. This uneven and treacherous surface was broken by equally treacherous patches of smooth ice. Through this chill morass the horses, all of them lacking hind shoes, slipped, floundered, and struggled for mile after mile.

An entirely different but equally uncomfortable set of circumstances presented itself to the York Rangers. They crossed the same gap in a driving storm of rain and sleet, trudging up to their knees in a gruel of snow and water, in gutters eight inches deep left by the runners of the sleighs. At McKellar's Harbour the men were forced to wait six hours for the flatcars to return. Fortunately the rain ceased, but the temperature dropped and the soaking-wet clothes began to freeze on the men's backs. They built roaring fires and clustered around them, scorching in front and freezing behind, until the train finally arrived.

These long waits without shelter were among the cruelest privations suffered by the soldiers en route to the North West. The Queen's Own endured three: a two-hour wait in blinding sleet when a train broke down at Carleton Place, a nine-hour wait in the freezing cold at McKellar's Harbour, and a four-hour wait in driving sleet at Winston's Dock. Most of these waiting periods were spent standing up; it was too cold and too wet to sit down.

At Jackfish Bay, where the next gap began, the soldiers, badly sunburned and frostbitten—their faces masses of blisters, their feet bruised and swollen—were billeted in shanties, freight houses, and empty transport cars. Here was more hot food, and then, for the lucky ones, a twenty-seven-mile sleigh ride through the wet sleet to Winston's Dock, and for the rest another forced march through the heaped snow.

Now the bone-weary troops, gazing from the rims of the cutters and through the slats of the flat cars, began to gain some understanding of Van Horne's feat of railway construction. At Jackfish they could see the gaping mouth of one of the longest tunnels on the road, piercing a solid wall of rock, one hundred and fifty feet high, for five hundred feet. For miles on end the roadbed had been blasted from the billion-year-old schists and granites—chipped into the sheer surface of the dark cliffs or hacked right through the spiny ridges by means of deep cuts. In some places it seemed as if the whole side of a mountain had been ripped asunder by dynamite and flung into the deep, still waters of the lake.

The voyage between Winston's Dock and Nepigon was again made on rails laid directly over the snow. The scenery grew grander as the cars crawled along and the soldiers began to stand up in their seats to see "sights which we will never forget"—the road torn out of the solid rock for mile after mile, skirting the very lip of the lake, from whose shores the mountains rose up directly for hundreds of feet above the track. Though the condition of the road was such that the engines were sometimes derailed, the troops did not seem to mind: "The delay was vexatious, and yet accommodated us, for we had ample opportunity as we steamed slowly along to observe and admire the grandeur and grim majesty of the scenery along the line." On some of the cars, the soldiers produced Moody and Sanker and YMCA songbooks and began to sing.

There was one final gap yet to come, and for many it would be the most terrible of all. This was the short march over the ice of the lake between Nepigon and Red Rock. It was no more than ten miles but it took some troops as long as six hours to cover it.

The 10th Grenadiers started out in the evening "into the solemn darkness of the pines and hemlocks," along a trail so narrow that any attempt to move in column of fours had to be abandoned. It was almost impossible to stay on the track, and yet a single misstep caused a man to be buried to his neck in snow. When the troops emerged from the woods and onto the ice of the lake they were met by a pitiless, pelting rain that seemed to drive through the thickest clothing. The rain had softened the track made by the sleighs, covering it with a slush so deep that every step a man took brought him into six inches of icy porridge. All attempts to preserve distance under such conditions had to be abandoned; the officers and men linked arms to prevent tumbling. To move through the slush the men were forced to raise their knees almost to their waists; in effect, they waded the entire distance.

As the rain increased, the lights of Red Rock, beckoning in the distance, winked out behind a wall of water. Now and then a man would tumble exhausted into the slush and lie immovable and unnoticed until somebody stumbled over him. Captain A. Hamlyn Todd, of the Governor-General's Foot Guards, counted some forty men lying in the snow, many of them face down, completely played out.

Some actually fell asleep as they marched. "One brave fellow had plodded on without a murmur for three days. He had been suffering, but through fear of being left behind, in the hospital, refrained from making his case known. He tramped half way across . . . reeling like a drunken man, but nature gave out at last, and with a groan he fell on the snow. There he lay, the pitiless rain beating on his upturned face, until a passing sleigh stopped behind him. The driver flashed his lantern . . . [and] said he was dead. 'Not yet old man,' was the reply of the youth as he opened his eyes. 'I am not even a candidate for the hospital yet.'" The soldier—he was a member of the 10th Royal Grenadiers—was placed on a sleigh and carried the rest of the way.

Some men who fell by the wayside could not speak. A member of the York Rangers described one such case: "On the way across one of the boys of the 35th was so fagged out that he laid down on the sleigh and could not move an inch. Captain Thomson asked him to move to one side but not one inch would he stir, so he caught hold of him like a bag and baggage, and tossed him to one side to let him pass."

When Red Rock was finally reached, the men were like zombies. They stood, uncomprehending, in ankle-deep ice water, waiting for the trains; and when these arrived they tumbled into cars—not flatcars this time, but real passenger cars—and dropped in their tracks, lying on the floor, twisted on the seats all of a heap, sleeping where they fell. One man, the son of a British general, crumpled up onto the floor in such a position that his head was under the seat, "and no amount of shaking would wake him to improve his situation." There was tea ready for them all but, cold and wet as they were, many did not have the strength to drink it. The ordeal was at an end; the track, as they well knew, lay unbroken all the way to their destination at Qu'Appelle. There would be no more marching until the coulees of Saskatchewan were reached—time enough then to reckon with Dumont's sharpshooters. For the moment, at least, they had no worries; and so, like men already dead, they slept.

18

1 · *The Westerner is born*

WILLIAM VAN HORNE WAS NOT A MAN given to rash or boastful promises. When he said that he could move troops from eastern Canada to Qu'Appelle in ten days, he was. actually giving himself a cushion of twenty-four hours. The first troops to leave Ottawa on March 28 arrived in Winnipeg exactly one week later. Within two days they were on the drill ground at Qu'Appelle. Two hundred and thirty miles to the north at Batoche, Riel was in control, resisting Dumont's repeated requests to cut the line of the railway and institute guerrilla warfare. Battleford was under siege by Poundmaker's Indians—five hundred and twelve persons, some three hundred of them women and children, confined to the stockade. Big Bear's Crees, following the massacre at Frog Lake, were roaming the country around Fort Pitt, killing, looting, and taking prisoners. But by mid-April, not much more than a fortnight after Duck Lake, the entire Field Force except the Halifax Battalion was in Saskatchewan and ready to march north.

The rebellion wrenched the gaze of settled Canada out to the prairie country. Every major newspaper sent a war correspondent with the troops, and for weeks the pages of the dailies were full of little else. The hardships, the condition of the soldiers, the state of their morale, together with those illuminating tales of human interest that are the journalist's grist—all these were reported. But interlaced with such dispatches there was something else—a new awareness of the land and of the railway's relation to it, comments on the thoughtfulness and courtesy of the CPR attendants, which Van Horne had been at such pains to foster, amazement at the engineering marvels along the lake shore and at the speed and efficiency with which the troops reached Winnipeg. For week after week in the columns of the daily press, as the journalists dilated on the grandeur of the scenery, the impressive size of the newly created cities, and the wonders of the plains, Canadians were treated to a continuing geography lesson about a land that some had scarcely considered part of the nation. Until 1885, it had been like a foreign country; now their boys were fighting in it and for it, and soon anyone who wanted to see it could do so for the price of a railway ticket.

The Halifax Battalion was especially delighted and surprised to discover so many fellow Nova Scotians working along the line and living in the western towns. "I was surprised at the size of the city of Winnipeg," one Nova Scotian wrote home, "and the magnificent character of the buildings and the splendid wide streets, three times as wide as in Halifax. The stone and brick stores on every hand indicate a surprising degree of enterprise in this city. . . . The police have the finest body of men I ever saw, and the fire department is in an excellent state of efficiency. . . . There are a great many Nova Scotians in both the police and fire departments." No longer would these Maritimers think of the North West as the exclusive property of Ontario.

Until the coming of the railway, all of the North West and the land beyond the mountains had been like a great desert with scattered oases of population, separated by many days' travel and each sufficient unto itself. Now the cross-fertilization process had begun. At last Canada had an accessible frontier from which to draw new strength, new blood, and new ideas. A new kind of Canadian, the "Westerner," was making his first impact on the men from the sober East. He belonged to a more openhanded and less rigid society; over the century that followed he would help to change the country.

One war correspondent's description of a prairie town, written that April, mirrored the astonishment of an Ontario city man on first coming up against western life: "Here is where the man who has a turn that way can study the human face divine, and the human dress astonishing. Men well dressed, fully dressed, commonly dressed; awfully dressed, shabbily dressed, partly dressed; men sober, nearly sober, half drunk, nearly drunk, quite drunk, frightfully drunk, howling drunk, dead drunk; men from Canada, the States, the United Kingdom and from almost every state in Europe, men enormously rich and frightfully poor, but all having a free and easy manner which is highly refreshing to a man fresh from the east who is accustomed to the anxious expressions of men in our silent streets at home."

The western Canadian was still in embryo, living often in a hovel of sod or earth or in one of those lusty, tented dormitories that had no counterpart in the East. "The 'Hotel,' itself," wrote the *Globe*, "is a revelation. It is of canvas and is like nothing under the earth. The beds are in tiers one above the other and a man generally bursts into tears when he gets into one of them. In such a camp there is always a poker saloon, a billiard saloon, and a number of the most villainous whiskey dives under canvas that can possibly be imagined."

In such crucibles was the western character tempered. Its influence had yet to be felt, but here and there in the growing settlements were men who would help to shape the country: Pat Burns out in Calgary, laying the basis of a vast fortune by selling meat to CPR contractors; James Lougheed, the lawyer and future Cabinet Minister, whose grandson would be Premier of Alberta, hanging out his shingle in the same city; Charles Whitehead, the railway contractor's son, in Brandon; the Sifton brothers, sons of another railway contractor, also in Brandon, setting out to practice law together—both would go on to distinguished political careers; Rodman Roblin, late of Prince Edward County, Ontario, a future Premier of Manitoba and the grandfather of another Premier, tilling his farm near Carman. The railway, or the promise of the railway, had brought them all to the North West.

If Riel's rebellion helped change eastern attitudes toward the prairies, it also helped change them toward the CPR. Van Horne was later to remark in his dry way that the railway should have erected a statue of the métis leader. As early as April 6, he was able to tell a friend in Scotland that "there is no more talk about the construction of the Lake Superior line having been a useless expenditure of money, nor about the road having been built too quickly. Most people are inclined to think it would have been better had it been built three or four weeks quicker."

Yet—and Van Horne must have felt the irony of the situation— the CPR was in worse financial shape than ever. It had cost almost a million dollars to ship the troops west, and that bill was not immediately collectable. (The CPR charged the government $882,331.32 for the entire job; in July, 1886, after the inevitable war-claims commission had duly deliberated, the government paid $760,648.13.) The railway, in Van Horne's words, was making sacrifices "to the great detriment of our regular business," keeping engines under steam and cars waiting empty for as long as twenty-four hours at a time when it had scarcely a dollar in the bank.

It was a strange situation: at the moment of its greatest triumph, while the troops were speeding west on the new steel to the applause of the nation, the CPR's financial scaffolding was collapsing, and scarcely anybody in Ottawa appeared to be concerned. Indeed, on April 11 Van Horne discovered to his dismay that, in spite of his contribution to the nation, somebody in the government service was continuing to send surveyors, public officials, and freight to Manitoba by way of Chicago on the Grand Trunk rather than by the CPR's Toronto and St. Thomas line, which connected with the Canada Southern and Michigan Central at London. While the Canadian Pacific was straining every effort to move the troops, its rival was pocketing a profit.

2 · *Stephen throws in the towel*

GEORGE STEPHEN WANTED OUT; OTTAWA had become painful to him. He could no longer bear the varnished atmosphere of the East Block, whose outer offices he had been haunting since December. Those two political nerve centers, the Russell House and the Rideau Club, had become agonizing symbols of setback and defeat. He was determined to shake the slush of the capital from his boots, never to return.

On March 26, the day of the bloody engagement at Duck Lake, dispirited and sick at heart, he went to his room in the Russell House and packed his bags. He had already dispatched a letter to the Prime Minister explaining that, as a result of a conversation that morning, he was satisfied the government could not give the railway the aid it required. There was in that letter none of the desperation that characterized so much of his correspondence with Macdonald. Stephen was drained of emotion; all that remained was a kind of chilly aloofness, a sense of resignation: "I need not repeat how sorry I am that this should be the result of all our efforts to give Canada a railway to the Pacific ocean. But I am supported by the conviction that I have done all that could be done to obtain it." That was it. The great adventure was over. Stephen prepared to return to Montreal to personal ruin and public disgrace.

Among the crowd in the lobby that evening were a CPR official, George H. Campbell, and two Cabinet Ministers—Mackenzie Bowell, Minister of Customs (who had originally opposed the railway loan), and Senator Frank Smith, Minister Without Portfolio. Campbell was one of several CPR men working on members of the Government to try to change their minds regarding further aid to the railway. Bowell had already been converted; Smith did not need to be. He was the head of a firm of wholesale grocers in Toronto which was a supplier to the CPR; also, he was personally involved in railways as well as in allied forms of transportation. Of all of Macdonald's inner circle, with the exception of Charles Tupper and John Henry Pope, he was the most enthusiastic supporter of the railway.

As the three men chatted, they spotted Stephen walking toward the office to pay his bill. He was clearly downcast and exhausted with mental strain and anxiety. Smith was alarmed at his appearance and his obvious intentions.

He hurried toward Stephen and urged him not to leave. "No," said Stephen, "I am leaving at once; there is no use—I have just come from Earnscliffe and Sir John has given a final refusal—nothing more can be done. What will happen tomorrow I do not know—the proposition is hopeless."

But Smith, whose powers of persuasion were considerable, managed to dissuade Stephen from leaving by promising that he and Bowell would make a final effort that evening to change the Prime Minister's mind. They drove to Earnscliffe for a midnight interview, leaving Campbell with orders to remain with Stephen and not allow any other person access to him.

Smith was one of the most powerful politicians at Ottawa, a handsome, large-hearted Irishman with a vast following among the Roman Catholics of Ontario. He had worked himself up from immigrant farm hand to the ownership of one of the largest wholesale houses in Canada. He owned the Toronto horsecar system and was president of a bank and of a railway. He had also become a close friend and confidant of the Prime Minister, who believed that Smith could personally deliver the Catholic vote in Ontario, or withhold it. If any man could swing the Prime Minister and the Cabinet, it was Smith.

He and Bowell arrived at Earnscliffe and attempted for more than an hour to persuade the Prime Minister to reconsider the matter of the loan. It was the second time within a year that a midnight attempt had been made to reprieve the CPR. Apparently, Smith was less successful than Pope had been in 1884. Macdonald may have been shaken, but he would not move. Nevertheless, when Smith returned at 2 A.M. he was able to convince Stephen that he should not give up the ghost. Guarded by the vigilant Campbell, whose instructions were to keep him incommunicado, the CPR president agreed to revise his proposal for relief while Smith worked on Macdonald and the Cabinet. It was said that for Campbell the three days that followed were the most

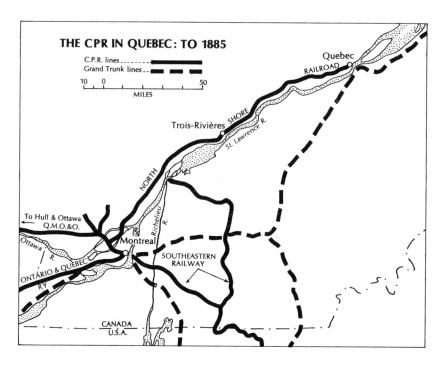

THE CPR IN QUEBEC: TO 1885

C.P.R. lines
Grand Trunk lines

10 0   50
MILES

Quebec
RAILROAD

Trois-Rivières

SHORE

St. Lawrence R.

NORTH

To Hull & Ottawa
Q.M.O.&O.

Ottawa R.

Richelieu R.

Montreal

ONTARIO & QUEBEC RY.

SOUTHEASTERN
RAILWAY

CANADA
U.S.A.

anxious of his life. He was the constant companion of "a man torn with anguish and remorse whose heart seemed to be breaking with compassion for friends whose downfall he felt himself responsible for."

Stephen had his revised proposition ready for the Privy Council the following day. That it was not rejected out of hand must be seen as a victory for Frank Smith. It was no wonder that years later Van Horne wrote to Smith that everybody connected with the railway felt a debt of gratitude to him "which they can never hope to repay." McLelan of Fisheries might resign if the loan went through, but Smith made it clear that he would resign if it did not; and Smith controlled more votes.

Over the next fortnight, as the troops from eastern Canada were shuttled off to the plains, a series of protracted and inconclusive negotiations took place regarding the exact terms of the proposed loan. With every passing day, Stephen grew more distraught. The government had him in a corner and was driving a hard bargain. Among other demands, it would insist that the CPR take over the North Shore line between Montreal and Quebec City. Under pressure from Ottawa, the Grand Trunk could be persuaded to give up the line to the Quebec government, which in turn would lease it back to the CPR at an annual cost of $778,000. It was doubtful, Stephen thought, if it could earn one hundred thousand dollars annually, it was so run down. (Later that year the CPR bought the line outright.)

But there was no help for it. Reports were coming in of a serious strike at Beavermouth in the shadow of the Selkirks; an angry mob of laborers, demanding their pay, was marching on the CPR's construction headquarters. Stephen saw Tilley immediately, gave him the news of the trouble, and warned the Finance Minister of the "utter impossibility of averting an immediate & disastrous collapse" unless some way could be found to give the company temporary aid to tide it over while the matter was being discussed at painful length in the Cabinet and in Parliament. Tilley was not helpful; he was one who believed that the government would have to take over the railway.

Once again the CPR president was at the end of his tether. Once again he told Macdonald: ". . . it is impossible for me to carry on this struggle for life, in which I have now been for over 4 months constantly engaged, any longer." The delay had finished him, he said—rendered him "utterly unfit for further work." He was sick at heart, fed up with politicians, betrayed by the very man in whom he had placed his confidence. Yet he could not quite bring himself to leave. He waited four more days. Silence. Finally, on April 15, Stephen gave up. That evening he took the train back to Montreal, to the great mansion on Drummond Street, in which he must have felt a trespasser since it was, in effect, no longer his. And there the following morning the dimensions of the disaster the railway faced were summed up for him in a curt wire from Van Horne:

"Have no means paying wages, pay car can't be sent out, and unless we get immediate relief we must stop. Please inform Premier and Finance Minister. Do not be surprised, or blame me if an immediate and most serious catastrophe happens."

3 · *Riot at Beavermouth*

OF ALL THE MERCURIAL CONSTRUCTION camps along the CPR's mountain line, the one at the mouth of the Beaver River was the most volatile. It was dominated by saloons—forty of them—all selling whiskey at fifty cents a glass, and each taking in as much as three hundred dollars a night.

The gamblers and whiskey peddlers had originally concentrated at Donald, on the east side of the Columbia. In order to remove his men from temptation, James Ross caused the track to be taken across the river. There, along the Beaver flats, where the pale green waters meandered out of the mountains through a carpet of ferns and berries, he established a company store and a postal car. The plan did not work. The coarser elements soon moved across the Columbia bridge and began to build saloons, dance halls, and brothels out of cedar logs. Under British Columbia law the saloons were legal as long as they were licensed by provincial authorities. Under Dominion law it was illegal to sell liquor within the forty-mile railway belt. This caused a series of comic-opera disputes between representatives of the two jurisdictions all along the line in British Columbia.

Ross refused to allow CPR trains to provide the gamblers, saloon-keepers, and prostitutes with food or supplies. An upsurge of petty thievery and discontent followed. Sleighs left unguarded were robbed; subcontractors were tempted to sell provisions illegally at black-market prices. The town was awake most of the night to the sound of dancing, singing, and revelry. Sam Steele, the Mounted Police inspector in charge, remembered that "we were rarely to bed before two or three a.m., and were up in the morning between six and seven." Steele spent the forenoon disposing of prisoners—mainly drunks who had been lodged in jail overnight for their own safety—and the afternoon with summary trials for petty theft and assault.

By late March, the complaints over lack of pay began to gather into a rumble of discontent that moved up and down the line in angry gusts. The men had resigned themselves to going without pay in the winter, but by early spring funds were needed for homesteads in Manitoba, Minnesota, and the Dakota Territory. Steele counseled patience. He feared that a strike could swiftly develop into a riot, sparked by a large number of "ruffians, gamblers and murderers from the Northern Pacific who had left it on the completion of that road." He warned Ross of the danger and wired the Prime Minister that a strike was imminent but got no action; Macdonald had more serious troubles in Saskatchewan on his mind. At this critical point Steele was felled by a massive attack of Rocky Mountain fever and was forced to take to his bed. He was so ill he could scarcely lift his head from the pillow.

At this very moment, with the strongest force for law and order incapacitated, thousands of men struck and began marching up the line toward Beavermouth.

The news of the work stoppage had barely reached Steele when a frantic wire arrived from the mayor of Calgary: the entire North West seemed to be up in arms; Riel and Dumont had struck; the Crees under Big Bear and Poundmaker were on the verge of joining the rebellion; Crowfoot and his braves were camped on the very edge of Calgary. "For God's sake, come; there is danger of an attack by the Blackfeet!" Everything seemed to be crowding in on Steele at once. He could only reply that the situation at Beavermouth was so dangerous that he could not spare a man. He had only eight as it was.

The workmen had not been paid because the contractors had not been paid. Those who quit first were in the farthest outpost of the section of the line then under construction. They set out to march to End of Track, gathering others to their cause as they passed through the various camps. By the time they reached Mountain Creek, they numbered several hundred.

Track laying, which had come to a halt with winter's onset, was about to recommence. Carpenters were strung out on top of the great Mountain Creek trestle, trying to complete it before the track reached that point. The strikers massed on the edge of the ravine below and called to the men to stop work and come down off the bridge. The carpenters, intent on finishing the job, refused. One of the strikers seized an ax and slashed the rope that held the block and tackle used to hoist bridge materials to the top of the trestle. That meant the carpenters could do no further work.

The strikers moved resolutely on to Beavermouth, gathering strength as they went. The ailing Steele received a deputation and warned them that "if they committed any act of violence, and were not orderly, in the strictest sense of the word, I would inflict upon the offenders the severest punishment the law would allow me."

Three hundred of the strikers, armed with revolvers, began to police the line, ordering the tracklayers to cease work, the teamsters to leave their teams, and the bridge workers to lay down their hammers. A trainload of men sent to End of Track was driven back. James Ross himself mounted the engine, told the engineer to put on all steam, and ran it through the armed mob as bullets whistled past his cab. The train entered the narrow canyon of the Beaver, an easy place to defend with a few men. Here the tracklayers began again.

On came the strikers, firing as they advanced, while the tracklayers worked in the canyon. Steele's second in command, a thickset sergeant with the appropriate name of Fury, drew his party across the mouth of the canyon to meet the advance. When they arrived, Fury announced that he would shoot the first man to cross the line. An uproar followed, but the strikers were cowed and returned to Beavermouth, allowing the tracklayers to finish their day's work.

Sergeant Fury returned at the end of the day and reported to his bedridden superior. Steele, still racked by fever, rose unsteadily and sat down in a camp chair. Both men were awaiting a Constable Kerr, who had gone to End of Track for a supply of medicine for the ailing inspector. Kerr attempted to arrest a contractor named Behan, "a well known desperado," for being drunk and disorderly but was immediately attacked by a crowd of strikers who threw him to the ground and forced him to retreat without his prisoner.

No Mounted Police officer could allow such humiliation to go unnoticed. Said Steele: ". . . we must take the man at any cost. It will never do to let the remainder of the gang know they can play with us." He told Fury to take what men he needed to arrest Behan. Fury set off with two constables to arrest the offending contractor, whom they found in a saloon "in the midst of a gang of drunken companions." The constables seized their quarry and dragged him out, surrounded by an angry mob of two hundred armed men. Fury was hesitant about using his pistol; as a result, the strikers were able to retrieve Behan and the police retreated.

Fury, badly mauled and with his jacket torn, returned to the police barracks and asked Steele for orders. "Take your revolvers," Steele said, "and shoot anyone who interferes with the arrest!"

Events were now building to a climax. Steele, still bedridden, was too weak to watch what happened from the window, but the local stipendiary magistrate, George Hope Johnston, gave him a running account. He watched Fury and three policemen start off for the bridge across the Beaver that separated the CPR store and police barracks from the saloon town on the other side. The men entered the log community and disappeared between cabins. A few moments later the sharp crack of gunfire echoed through the valley.

"There is one gone to hell, Steele," Johnston said.

Sick or not, Steele had to see for himself. He forced himself out of bed and crawled to the window in time to see two of his men dragging a prisoner across the bridge. The prisoner was "fighting like a fiend, while a woman in scarlet followed . . . with wild shrieks and curses." Sergeant Fury and the third constable brought up the rear, trying to fend off the crowd, which had swollen to seven hundred.

It was time for Steele to act. He called on Johnston to get the Riot Act and, seizing a Winchester from the constable on guard at the jail, ran to the bridge, leveled his rifle at the crowd, and told the strikers to halt.

"Look at the ———," someone cried, "his own death bed makes no difference to him!" Nonetheless, everybody stopped. One of the constables knocked out the struggling prisoner with a heavy blow and pulled him by the collar the rest of the way, "insensible as a rag." The woman in red started to scream: "You red-coated ———!" Steele turned to his men: "Take her in, too!" Then he started forward onto the bridge to face the sullen mob.

Johnston had been forced to kick the orderly-room door in, the constable with the key having been too busy with the riot. He arrived at last, took up a position beside Steele, and opened the book at the Riot Act. Steele said: "Listen to this and keep your hands off your guns, or I will shoot the first man of you who makes a hostile movement." There was silence. Sergeant Fury had already put a bullet into the shoulder of a man who tried to keep him from taking his prisoner.

After the Riot Act was read, Steele spoke again: "You have taken advantage of the fact that a rebellion has broken out in the North West and that I have only a handful of men, but, as desperate diseases require desperate remedies, and both disease and remedy are here, I warn you that if I find more than twelve of you standing together or any large crowd assembled, I will open fire upon you and mow you down! Now disperse at once and behave yourselves!"

Steele's full force of eight Mounted Police now stood in line behind them, rifles cocked. Steele stood his ground with Johnston and watched the grumbling mob slowly break up. The following morning the town and all the line "was as quiet as a country village on Sunday." Steele arrested all the ringleaders in the riot, brought them to court, and fined them each one hundred dollars or six months in jail.

The men remained off work until arrangements were made to pay them, but there was no further violence. Steele, still convalescent, donned his uniform and headed for Calgary. James Ross implored him to come back, but this was not possible. The North West was at war. Three columns of troops were preparing to move north to the fertile valley of the Saskatchewan, now held in thrall by roaming bands of Crees and a more disciplined force of métis under Riel and his adjutant general, Dumont. Out from Calgary went Major-General T. Bland Strange, brought out of retirement from his ranch to keep the restive Blackfoot in check with the six hundred volunteers of the Alberta Field Force. North from Qu'Appelle marched the first division of the North West Field Force—nine hundred men under General Middleton, determined to strike at Riel's headquarters in Batoche. The second division—five hundred men and two hundred teamsters—entrained for Swift Current and then moved north under Colonel Otter (happily recovered from his snow blindness) to relieve the besieged stockade at Battleford. Steele himself was given a unique command. His task was to organize, as swiftly as possible, a calvary detachment known as Steele's Scouts and strike off in pursuit of the rebel Cree chieftain, Big Bear. It was perhaps the most remarkable case on record of instant recovery from Rocky Mountain fever.

4 · *The eleventh hour*

WHEN STEPHEN LEARNED FROM VAN Horne on April 16 that the CPR pay car could not be sent out, he immediately wired the news in cipher to John Henry Pope in Ottawa. Van Horne had hinted at the imminence of a "serious catastrophe." Another riot was likely if wages were again held up. The Minister of Railways was Stephen's last hope. Not long before, the CPR president had sat in Pope's drawing room, his head in his hands, and said to Rufus, Pope's son: "We are ruined—there is only one man who understands the seriousness of our position and that is your father—It is through him that we must be saved."

On first acquaintance, John Henry Pope was a curiously unimpressive man—angular of feature, ungainly in manner, slow in speech, awkward of gesture, and hesitant in his parliamentary oratory. He had only elementary schooling, a deficiency that made his correspondence seem almost childlike. Yet he was one of the most powerful men in the Government. There was a patriarchal simplicity and dignity about him which inspired liking and respect. His features were Lincolnian and so was his manner. He might be an awkward speaker but he did not fall into the trap of making dangerous admissions; nor could he be provoked into hasty or angry statements. Macdonald listened to him and trusted him.

Pope went straight to the Prime Minister with Stephen's decoded telegram and again pointed out the obvious: if the CPR went bankrupt, the Government could not survive. At last the vacillating party leader was forced into a decision. Until this moment he had believed, not without good reason, that any further relief to the company would be politically disastrous. The exhausting debate of 1884 had been bad enough, but it would be nothing compared to the national uproar occasioned by further public handouts to a faltering railroad. Whichever course Macdonald took, he knew he was going to face a storm. If the CPR collapsed, it would undoubtedly touch off a wave of bankruptcies and personal tragedies—men without pay, suppliers overextended, entire communities facing depression, the country demoralized by the failure of its great national endeavor. And then there was Blake, the man who always had the facts and figures at his fingertips and who used them to devastating effect. Blake would appear as a Cassandra, reminding the nation of his famous prediction that the CPR would never pay for its axle grease; Macdonald did not care to face that taunt. He had two choices, both of them politically unpalatable, but one was slightly less distasteful than the other. With very little heart he decided that once again he must help to bail out the CPR.

Fortunately, the mood of the country was beginning to change. Because of the swift action of the railway, the government had a good chance of localizing the Saskatchewan Rebellion and preventing it from spreading throughout the North West. First, however, there was a nasty wrangle in the Conservative caucus. The majority of Macdonald's followers were in favor of the government's taking over the road. McLelan resigned, as he had said he would. Macdonald had to use all his charm and all his political muscle to bring the party into line. He personally spoke or wrote to every recalcitrant Conservative, threatening his own resignation if they failed to back his proposal for another loan.

In one crowded week, events took on momentum of their own. The railway still had no money to pay its men and not much hope of getting any: the relief bill, which was not yet before the House, would not be passed before a long debate in Parliament. Macdonald privately asked the Bank of Montreal to advance five million dollars to the CPR, explaining that he intended to bring some resolutions before Parliament regarding financial aid "at an early date." The bank bluntly refused to advance a penny.

The same day—April 24—at Fish Creek, a coulee not far from Batoche, a handful of métis under Gabriel Dumont fought General Middleton's superior force to a standstill. The métis lost six men, the Canadians fifty; Middleton was immobilized for a fortnight. There was better news from Battleford, where the five hundred people cooped up in a stockade less than two hundred yards square were finally released by Colonel Otter's division. In London the Grand Trunk, eying events in Canada, was waiting to pounce on its hapless rival. On April 27, Sir Henry Tyler told a Grand Trunk meeting that the CPR was finished—that it would be taken over by the government and when that happened his company would gladly come forward and "*assist.*"

The CPR's secretary, Charles Drinkwater, diplomatically suggested that the bank might take a different view if the railway relief bill were actually placed before Parliament. Finally, the reluctant Prime Minister acted. He gave notice to the House on May 1 of the resolutions he proposed to submit. It came at a singularly dramatic moment. The press that day was proclaiming that Britain and Russia were on the eve of war. Stephen had just opened a telegram from the Imperial War Department: Was the CPR in a position to transport war matériel to the Pacific Coast? The CPR president instantly wired an affirmative response. Then, on May 2, there was more bad news from Saskatchewan: Colonel Otter had suffered a defeat at the hands of Poundmaker and his Crees.

Still there was to be a delay. Macdonald was determined to postpone the debate on the railway resolutions until he had forced his pet franchise bill through the House. This measure was designed to substitute a single, uniform, federal franchise for the varying provincial franchises that were still being used in federal elections. To Stephen, desperately trying to "tide over matters," it seemed as if the Prime Minister was putting a petty squabble with the provinces ahead of what he was prone to call "this great national undertaking."

Stephen was beside himself at this politicking. Abbott had "fairly scared" him with the news that it might be five or six weeks before the CPR resolutions became law. The railway could not hold out for anything like that time. Stephen felt that Macdonald had lost faith in him, that the imminent collapse of the company was no longer of much moment. Certainly the Prime Minister, harried by events in the North West and obsessed with his battle over the franchise bill, was weary of Stephen's chronic injured carping.

It was essential that the government guarantee a loan at the bank. Even a million dollars would help. That sum in Shaughnessy's hands could give the company perhaps three weeks' breathing space. On May 5, at the government's request, the Bank of Montreal advanced three-quarters of a million dollars. It was not much; but it was something.

The real problem was wages. The pay car with the March wages, due to leave from Montreal on April 15, had not been sent out. A month passed; by that time the April wages were also due. Still there was no sign of any payment. All along the line the grumblings began to be heard, mingled with reports of real privation. Single men had not been able to pay their board for two months. Grocers, bakers, butchers, and dry-goods and hardware merchants began to deny further credit to married employees. In the CPR shops at Toronto a number of men were forced to cut themselves down to one meal a day. They had been unable to get extensions from local shops because these, in turn, had been denied further supplies from wholesale houses that had advanced credit. Everybody from office clerk to dispatcher felt the pinch. For the ordinary laborer, who received only a dollar a day and was therefore unable to save any money, the lack of pay was especially severe.

A listlessness seemed to have seized the employees of the railway in Ontario. They continued to work because they had no recourse. Unlike the track gangs farther west, they were not essential to the survival of the CPR. When a group of mechanics at Perth told Van Horne that they would quit work unless the pay car came along, the general manager simply informed them that if that happened, he would close down the works. That message, traveling up and down the line, killed all talk of a general strike.

In Parliament, the debate on the franchise bill dragged on and on. Speeches lasted for seven hours; one sitting went on for three days without a break; there were ninety-three divisions of the House. It was clear that the CPR would have to have a government advance or another guarantee at the bank if it was to stay alive until the relief measure could pass the House and Senate. "It is very hard having to fight both enemies & friends," Stephen wrote in a bitter and urgent letter to Macdonald. Somehow the railway had to find money, not just for wages but also for the interest payments on the bonds of the Ontario and Quebec Railway. It was the twelfth of May: the interest was due on the first of June. "If we default," Stephen reminded the Prime Minister, ". . . then goodbye to the C.P.R."

The resolution of the CPR's various financial crises was always theatrical, fraught with the same kind of tension that audiences had come to expect from the stage melodramas of the era, in which the heroine was saved at the last instant from the onrushing locomotive, the big saw, or the Fate Worse Than Death. Such a moment came, again at the eleventh hour, less than a week before the interest on the O. & Q. bonds was due. Most of the directors of the company waited breathlessly outside the Privy Council door while the Cabinet argued over whether or not the government could guarantee another bank loan. In later years, Van Horne liked to describe that scene to his friends:

"I guessed that sound would come best to me if I stood in the room opposite the glass door which would help to act as a resonator. But though I could hear each voice as it spoke, I was unable to make out clearly what anyone said. It was an awful time. Each one of us felt as if the railway was our own child and we were prepared to make any sacrifice for it, but things were at a dead-lock and it seemed impossible to raise any more money. We men ourselves had given up twenty per cent of our salaries and had willingly worked, not overtime but double-time, and as we waited in that room, we thought about these things and wondered whether all our toil was going to be wasted or not, and what would happen if Canada were ruined. . . . At last Joe Pope came with a yellow paper in his hand. He said that the Government was prepared to back the Bank of Montreal to the extent then required. I think we waited until he left the room. I believe we had that much sanity left us! And then we began. We tossed up chairs to the ceiling; we trampled on desks; I believe we danced on tables. I do not fancy that any of us knows now what occurred, and no one who was there can ever remember anything except loud yells of joy and the sound of things breaking!"

Van Horne raced to the company's office to telegraph the news to Shaughnessy. The operator seemed too slow and so the general manager pushed him aside and began ticking off the message himself. It had been a near thing. "The advance we are now making is quite illegal and we are incurring the gravest responsibility in doing so," Macdonald wrote to Stephen.

The resolutions for the relief of the railway were still not before the House, and John Henry Pope was not able to present them until June 16. By that time the rebellion in Saskatchewan had been crushed. Riel and Poundmaker were both prisoners. Dumont, whose small band of sharpshooters had held off the militia for a surprisingly long period, had vanished over the border. Sam Steele was in hot pursuit of Big Bear. Schreiber had already informed Tupper (in England) that "the House and country are both in favour of the CPR and that should now be doubly the case when the fact is patent to the world [that] but for the rapid construction . . . Canada would have been involved in a frightful waste of blood and treasure quelling the rising in the North West."

Edward Blake had no intention of giving in without a fight. He was prepared to oppose the relief bill as he had opposed the whole concept of a privately owned transcontinental railway from the very beginning. His speeches were now lasting for six hours and wearying the House, but they made Stephen almost apoplectic: "The *meanest* thing of the kind that has ever come under my notice . . . an ill-conditioned, vindictive effort. . . . I am so furious with Blake that I cannot at the moment write coherently about him or his speech. What a miserable creature he must be!"

The Prime Minister had his own problems. Tupper, the greatest of all parliamentary fighters, was out of the picture in London. Pope was ill. Campbell, the Minister of Justice, was incapacitated by splitting headaches. Tilley, also ill, was off to Europe. Macdonald had remarked earlier that year that he could not be away for an hour without "some blunder taking place." He had just come through a savage debate on the franchise bill; now he must gird himself up for another struggle. This time, however, he was in a stronger position. The railway had proved itself. No matter what Blake and his colleagues said, it had saved the country.

He made that point when he rose to speak: "Late events have shown us that we are made one people by that road, that that iron link has bound us together in such a way that we stand superior to most of the shafts of ill-fortune, that we can now assemble together, at every point which may be assailed, or may be in danger, the whole physical force of Canada by means of that great artery, against any foreign foe or any internal insurrection or outbreak."

The debate that followed, as Joseph Pope recalled it, was "acrimonious and unpleasant." It was a foregone conclusion that the measure would pass; what was less certain was the company's ability to survive during the time it would take to turn the bill into law. If the Opposition kept on talking, the CPR could collapse.

The loan from the bank ran out, and the chances of another were slim. Stephen was so hard pressed that he was forced to delay his continuing visits to Ottawa; they were not productive anyway. There is a story told of him and Abbott sitting in the anteroom of the Council chamber one hot afternoon, patiently awaiting the outcome of a final desperate appeal for help, only to discover that the Ministers, rather than face them, had vanished by another door.

"I feel like a ruined man," said the dejected Stephen. Yet, in spite of all his dark predictions about imminent collapse, in spite of his sinister warnings about his own physical condition, in spite of his pledge never again to visit the capital, even in spite of his declarations that he would turn negotiations over to Van Horne, he somehow hung on and the company somehow hung on.

The melodrama continued literally until the very last hour. By July, the CPR's credit had reached the snapping point. One creditor would wait no longer. The company owed him four hundred thousand dollars and could not meet its obligations. On July 10, it is said, the debt was due. If it was not paid, the CPR was faced with all the confusion of a complicated receivership: a scramble of creditors all demanding payment, the total collapse of the company, a halt on all railroad construction, and a legal and financial tangle that could drag on for months before a new corporation with new government arrangements could be formed and the work resumed.

The debate had occupied the best part of a month. The morning of July 10 came and the bill still had not passed the House, which did not sit until 1:30 that afternoon. According to O. D. Skelton, Van Horne's sometime confidant, the four-hundred-thousand-dollar debt was due at three o'clock. There were the usual maddening parliamentary formalities before a division could be taken, but at two that afternoon a majority of the Commons voted in favor of railway relief. That affirmation of confidence was good enough for any creditor; the measure would become law in a matter of days. With the Lake Superior line complete and only a few dozen miles remaining in the gap between the Selkirks and the Gold Range, the railway was saved. It is doubtful if history records another instance of a national enterprise coming so close to ruin and surviving.

In England, Tupper was working on the great financial house of Baring to market the new CPR bonds when they were issued. Here, too, the climate had changed. Stephen was on board ship when at last the CPR relief bill received royal assent on July 20. By the time he reached London, he found that Tupper had done his work for him. Baring Brothers took the entire issue of the bonds, half at 90 and the remainder at 91. In Canada the CPR got the money it needed to finish the line, and it never had to ask for a Government loan again.

For once, luck was with the company. The bond issue was floated at exactly the right moment. The brief British boom was short-lived, and Baring had trouble disposing of the issue, only half of which was actually subscribed by the British public. The remainder of the bonds were taken up by members of the firm and by George Stephen and Donald A. Smith, who bought half a million dollars' worth between them. It was small wonder that the CPR changed the name of the new town at the second crossing of the Columbia from Farwell to Revelstoke, after the baron who was born Edward Charles Baring and who headed the firm that came to the rescue of the impossible railway.

5 · A land no longer lonely

THE FRONTIER WAS MELTING AWAY before the onslaught of steel. The old free days when whiskey peddlers hid in every thicket, when gambling ran unchecked, when towns were constructed of tents and logs and the prairies were unfenced, were vanishing. On the heels of the railway came Timothy Eaton's new catalogue, devised in 1884 by that most revolutionary of merchants. For as little as two dollars the ladies of Moose Jaw or Swift Current could order one of several models of the new Grand Rapids Carpet Sweeper or for twenty-five cents a patented Hartshorn window shade with spring rollers.

A rough kind of sophistication was making itself felt. Methodist halls where temperance speakers held court invaded the old frontier. Amateur theatricals came into vogue, along with skating carnivals, musical recitals, and educational lectures. The sudden transformation of Winnipeg from a muddy little village into a glittering metropolis astonished the soldiers who poured through on their way to do battle with Dumont and Poundmaker. They were "surprised at the splendid buildings and enormous plate glass fronts of Main street, which is said to remind one of Boston or New York."

This was still the West, high, wide, and handsome, but it was no longer the frontier. It would have been unthinkable in 1885 for Van Horne to pull a pistol on General Rosser in the Manitoba Club, as he had done only three years before. The violent days were over—gone with the buffalo and the antelope, gone with Red River carts and the bullock trains and the nomads who once roamed so freely across that tawny sea of grass.

The native peoples of the plains had made their final futile gesture against the onrushing tidal wave of civilization in the deep coulees of the North Saskatchewan country in May. The impetuous Gabriel Dumont, restrained only by a leader who was becoming increasingly mystic and irrational, finally broke out and met the militia at Fish Creek on April 23, luring them into a kind of buffalo pound and vowing to treat them exactly as he had treated the thundering herds in the brave days before the railway. Here his force of one hundred and thirty métis, armed for the most part with shotguns and muzzle-loaders, held back some eight hundred trained men under General Middleton, the bumbling and overcautious British Army regular. On May 2, at Cut Knife Hill, Chief Poundmaker and 325 Cree followers emerged victorious against cannon, Gatling gun, and some 540 troops under Colonel Otter.

These were the last contortions of a dying culture. The Canadian government had eight thousand men in the field, transported and supplied by rail. The natives had fewer than one thousand under arms, and these were neither organized nor in all cases enthusiastic. Riel, the prairie prophet—some called him a prairie pontiff—planned his campaign according to the spiritual visitations he believed he was receiving almost daily. The more practical and pugnacious Dumont used his knowledge of the ground, his skill at swift maneuver and deception, and his experience in the organization of the great hunts to fend off superior forces. It is possible, had Riel given him his head, that he could have cut the main CPR line, derailed the trains, and harried the troops for months in a running guerrilla warfare that would have blocked western settlement for a period of years; but the outcome in the end would have been the same.

In mid-May Dumont fought his last battle at Batoche. It lasted for four days, until the métis' ammunition ran out. It was remarkable, among other things, for the use of the first and only prairie warship.

It also brought about Riel's surrender and the flight of his adjutant general, who subsequently re-enacted the incidents of 1885 in Buffalo Bill's Wild West Show.

In the weeks that followed, the Indian leaders surrendered too, or fled over the border—Poundmaker, Little Poplar, Lucky Man, Red Eagle, Poor Crow, Left Hand, Wandering Spirit, and finally Big Bear. There was no place any longer for a wandering spirit, as Crowfoot, the wisest of them all, had thoroughly understood. Two days before the Duck Lake engagement, a worried Macdonald had asked Father Lacombe to try to ensure the neutrality of the Blackfoot chief and his followers. Crowfoot, who believed he could get more from the government by remaining loyal, forbore to take up arms. His steadfastness was rewarded in various ways, not the least of which was the present of a railway pass from Van Horne. Thus was seen the ironic spectacle of the withered Indian riding back and forth across the prairies on the same iron monster that had changed his people's ways and caused them to be driven into the corrals of the northern reserves.

Deep in the broad evergreen valley between the Selkirk Mountains and the Gold Range, through which the olive Columbia flowed on its southerly course to the sea, the old frontier life still existed along the line of the unfinished railway. The last rail was laid on the Lake Superior section on May 12, so that the troops would be able to return to the East in considerable comfort; but in British Columbia construction continued for most of 1885. As the months wore on, the gap between the two groups of tracklayers shrank. On the Onderdonk side, the rails were ascending the western slope of the Gold Range from Eagle Pass Landing on Shuswap Lake. On James Ross's side, the rails were moving up the eastern slopes of the same mountains from Farwell on the Columbia, soon to be renamed Revelstoke.

It was said that the population of Eagle Pass Landing was sober only during the monthly visits of the stipendiary magistrate from Kamloops. Everybody, it was claimed, purposely avoided drink on those occasions so as to enjoy it with greater license the rest of the time. The community's existence was short but merry. In order to prevent cardsharps from corrupting the settlement, it was an unwritten rule that packs of cards be thrown out of the window after every game and a fresh pack opened. A visitor reported that they lay in heaps in the dirt "until the road was actually covered with hearts, spades, diamonds and clubs."

At Farwell, on the second crossing of the Columbia (named after the government surveyor who originally laid out the townsite), board shacks and cabins, euphemistically named "hostess houses," sprang up, presided over by such interesting ladies as Madame Foster, an enormous black woman, and Irish Nell, described as being "tough as nails but with a heart of gold."

Here, as in every other new community along the line of the railroad, the CPR brooked no opposition from local merchants or speculators in the matter of real-estate profits. A. S. Farwell, the surveyor, had secured one hundred and seventy-five acres for himself on the banks of the Columbia; as he had anticipated, the railway location went right through his property. However, he refused the terms offered by the CPR, and a long and expensive lawsuit followed, which he eventually won. For practical purposes he lost. The company followed its practice of moving the location of the station and laid out another townsite which became the heart of the business section of Revelstoke.

What the CPR wanted in British Columbia was a gift of land in return for establishing a town or divisional point. The general manager had no intention of locating the smallest station where "it will benefit anybody who had imposed upon us in the matter of the right of way." It was Van Horne's principle that the entire cost of setting up a divisional point should be recouped through the sale of adjacent real estate donated by grateful citizens who were really beholden to the railway for the future prosperity of their community.

In his dealings with William Smithe, the Premier of British Columbia, the general manager was characteristically hardheaded. He knew that the provincial government was anxious to see the CPR extend its line to a new terminus at Granville on Burrard Inlet because it would help the sale of public land in the area. In return, Van Horne asked for almost half the peninsula on which the present metropolitan area of Vancouver is situated. He settled for an outright gift of six thousand acres from the government, including almost all of the waterfront between the Second Narrows and the military reserve, which shortly became Stanley Park. In addition, the Hastings Mill had to give up immediately four thousand acres of land and an additional one thousand acres annually in return for an extension of its lease to 1890.

To get what he wanted, Van Horne resorted to tough measures. He told Henry Beatty to intimate to private speculators east of Granville that if they did not deal liberally with the company, the CPR shops and all terminal works of any consequence would be moved away from their property to the area of English Bay. In the end the landholders had to yield a third of the lots in each block they held. The railway, in short, would dominate the new city. No street could be continued to tidewater without its permission.

"Keep your eyes open," Van Horne is said to have told a colleague after an all-night poker session in which he himself had been badly taken. "These damned Vancouver fellows will steal the pants off you." But Van Horne was engaged in a larger game for higher stakes. He held all the unalienated lots in Granville township, the right of way from New Westminster to English Bay, the vast grant from Hastings Mill, and, far back in the forest, a valuable tract of residential property, which he named Shaughnessy Heights. He also had the entire foreshore of the future city, which he had insisted upon because, he said, the depth of the water made piers impossible; the railway would need all that land for dock facilities. Future events were to prove that this was not necessary, and, as later generations slowly realized, the railway would have had to come to the mouth of the inlet anyway, whether or not it was given as much as an acre of free real estate. Van Horne may have been skinned at poker in the last of the frontier railway towns, but he was the real winner in a much more important game of skill and bluff.

6 · The last spike

EDWARD MALLANDAINE WANTED TO FIGHT the Indians. When the news of the rebellion reached Victoria, where he lived and went to school, there was no holding him; and his father, a pioneer architect and engineer, did not try to hold him. He booked passage to New Westminster, got aboard the new CPR line out of Port Moody, and took it as far as Eagle Pass Landing. He was just seventeen years old, small for his age, with a thin, alert face half hidden by a black cap. He trudged over the line of the partly finished road until he reached Golden, at the foot of the Kicking Horse, and there he learned, to his intense disappointment, that the rebellion was over.

He headed west again, through the Rogers Pass and into Farwell, with its single street lined with log and frame shacks. There was a feeling of excitement in Farwell that summer of 1885. The town was the halfway point between the two Ends of Track: freight outfits bustled in from the Rogers and the Eagle passes; boats puffed into the new docks from the mines at the Big Bend of the Columbia; a new post office was opening. Young Mallandaine decided to stay for a while in Farwell and go into business for himself. He opened a freighting service between the town and Eagle Pass Landing, taking a pony through the Gold Range twice each week along the tote road carved out by the railway contractors and soliciting orders for newspapers and supplies from the navvies along the way. It was hard going but it made a profit.

It was an exciting time in which to live and an exciting place in which to be—especially for a teen-age boy. Mallandaine was bright enough to realize that history was being made all around him and he noted it all in his mind for later reference: the spectacle of fifty men hanging over the face of the cliffs at Summit Lake, drilling holes in the rock; the sound of thunder in the pass as hundreds of tons of rock hurtled through the air; the sight of a hundred-foot Howe truss put together in a single day; the long, low huts where the navvies, mostly Swedes and Italians, slept "huddled in like bees in a hive with little light and ventilation"; the accidents, brawls, drinking, and gambling in the camps, "with men of all nationalities throwing away their hard-earned pay at faro, stud poker and other games of chance"; a gun battle with two men shot in a gambling den not far from the Farwell post office; and, toward the end of the season, the rough pageantry of the Governor General, Lord Lansdowne himself, riding on horseback through the gap between the two lines of steel on his way to the coast.

Each time Mallandaine made his way through Eagle Pass, that gap was shorter. He noted "day by day the thousands of feet of earth removed and . . . the swarms of men slaving away like ants for the good of the gigantic enterprise." By October it became clear that the road would be finished by the first snow. The mushroom towns began to lose their inhabitants and a general exodus took place as the contractors discharged more and more men. Now, as the boy moved through the mountains, he noticed the wayside houses shut up and deserted, contractors' equipment being shifted and carted away, and hundreds of men traveling on foot with all their belongings to the east or to the west. Some of the rougher characters, who had operated saloons and gambling dens, became outlaws, "and many a poor man who had been toiling all summer, was obliged to deliver up his earnings."

All the activity that had excited Edward Mallandaine on his arrival began to die away, and an oppressive silence settled on the pass —a silence broken only by the hideous shrieking of the construction locomotives echoing through the hills as they rattled by with flatcars loaded with steel rails. Mallandaine felt a kind of chill creeping into his bones—not just the chill of the late October winds, sweeping down through the empty bunkhouses, but the chill of loneliness that comes to a man walking through a graveyard in the gloom.

The pass became so lonely that Mallandaine almost began to dread the ride between Farwell and the Landing. There was something eerie about the sight of boarded-up buildings, dump cars left by the wayside, and portions of contractors' outfits cast aside along the line of the tote road. And the silence! Not since the days of the survey parties had the mountains seemed so still. Mallandaine decided to pack it in; there was no business left to speak of anyway. He made plans to return to his parents' home in Victoria. There was, however, one final piece of business, which he did not want to miss. He was determined to be on hand when the last spike on the Canadian Pacific Railway was driven.

On the afternoon of November 6, the last construction train to load rails—an engine, a tender, and three flatcars—left Farwell for Eagle Pass. Mallandaine was one of several who climbed aboard and endured the "cold, cheerless, rough ride" that followed. A few miles out of Farwell, it began to snow. The rails became so slippery that when one gumbo grade was reached the locomotive could not creep over it and, after three attempts in which the train slid backwards down the incline, one car had to be abandoned.

Far into the darkness of the night the little train puffed, its passengers shivering with cold. Mallandaine, lying directly upon the piled-up rails and unable to sleep, was almost shaken to pieces as the train rattled over the unballasted roadbed. Finally it came to a stop. The youth tumbled off the flatcar in the pitch dark, found an abandoned boxcar, and managed a short sleep. At six that morning the track crews were on the job. By the time Mallandaine awoke, the rails had almost come together.

At nine o'clock, the last two rails were brought forward and measured for cutting, with wagers being laid on the exact length that would be needed: it came to twenty-five feet, five inches. A peppery little man with long white whiskers, wearing a vest with a heavy watch chain, cut the final rail with a series of hard blows. This was the legendary Major Rogers. One of the short rails was then laid in place and spiked; the second was left loose for the ceremony. The crowd, which included Al Rogers, Tom Wilson, Sam Steele, and Henry Cambie, waited for the official party to appear.

It is perhaps natural that the tale of the driving of the last spike on the CPR should have become a legend in which fancy often outweighed fact; it was, after all, the great symbolic act of Canada's first century, a moment of solemn ritual enacted in a fairyland setting at the end of a harrowing year. Two days before the spike was driven, George Stephen had cabled in cipher from England: "Railway now out of danger." The bonds had risen to 99, the stock to 52½. Nine days after the spike was driven, Louis Riel kept his rendezvous with the hangman at Regina. In more ways than one the completion of the railway signaled the end of the confined, comfortable nation that had been pieced together in 1867.

It is not surprising, then, that some who were present that day in the mountains should have recalled half a century later that the spike was made of gold. But there was no golden spike. The Governor General had had a silver spike prepared for the occasion; it was not used, and His Excellency, who had expected to be present, had been forced to return to Ottawa from British Columbia when weather conditions caused a delay in the completion of the line.

"The last spike," said Van Horne, in his blunt way, "will be just as good an iron one as there is between Montreal and Vancouver, and anyone who wants to see it driven will have to pay full fare."

The truth was that the CPR could not afford a fancy ceremony. It had cost the Northern Pacific somewhere between $175,000 and $250,-000 to drive its golden spike. The CPR might be out of danger, but it had enormous expenditures facing it. Stephen proposed paying off the five-million-dollar temporary loan almost immediately. Van Horne's whole purpose was to get a through line operating to the Pacific so that he could tap the Asian trade. There would be time for ceremonies later on.

The very simplicity and near spontaneity of the scene at Eagle Pass—the lack of pomp, the absence of oratory, the plainness of the crowd, the presence of the workmen in the foreground of the picture—made the spectacle an oddly memorable one. Van Horne and a distinguished party had come out from Ottawa, Montreal, and Winnipeg for the occasion. The big names, lounging at their ease in the two parlor cars "Saskatchewan" and "Matapedia," included Donald A. Smith, Sandford Fleming, John Egan, John McTavish, the land commissioner, and George Harris, a Boston financier who was a company director. Because of the incessant rains the party was held up for several days at Farwell until the work was completed.

Meanwhile, on the far side of the mountains, Andrew Onderdonk's private car "Eva" came up from Port Moody with Michael Haney aboard, pulling the final load of rails to the damp crevice in the mountains which the general manager, with a fine sense of drama, had decided years before to name Craigellachie. The decision predated Stephen's memorable telegram to Donald A. Smith. When Van Horne first joined the company the word was in common use because of an incident in 1880, when the Syndicate was being formed out of the original group that had put the St. Paul railway together. One of the members had demurred at the idea of another railway adventure and suggested to Stephen that they might only be courting trouble. Stephen had replied with that one word, a reference to a Scottish poem which began with the phrase: "Not until Craigellachie shall move from his firm base." Van Horne, hearing of the incident, decided that if he was still with the CPR when the last spike was driven, the spot would be marked by a station called Craigellachie.

It was a dull, murky morning, the tall mountains sheathed in clouds, the dark firs and cedars dripping in a coverlet of wet snow. Up puffed the quaint engine with its polished brass boiler, its cordwood tender, its diamond-shaped smokestack, and the great square box in front containing the acetylene headlight on whose glass was painted the number 148. The ceremonial party descended and walked through the clearing of stumps and debris to the spot where Major Rogers was standing, holding the tie bar under the final rail. By common consent the honor of driving the connecting spike was assigned to the eldest of the four directors present—to Donald A. Smith, whose hair in five years of railway construction had turned a frosty white. As Fleming noted, the old fur trader represented much more than the CPR. His presence recalled that long line of Highlanders—the Mackenzies and McTavishes, Stuarts and McGillivrays, Frasers, Finlaysons, McLeods, and McLaughlins—who had first penetrated these mountains and set the transcontinental pattern of communication that the railway would continue.

Now that moment had arrived which so many Canadians had believed would never come—a moment that Fleming had been waiting for since 1862, when he placed before the government the first practical outline for a highway to the Pacific. The workmen and the officials crowded around Smith as he was handed the spike hammer. Young Edward Mallandaine was determined to be as close to the old man as possible. He squeezed in directly behind him, right next to Harris, the Boston financier, and directly in front of Cambie, McTavish, and Egan. As the little hunchbacked photographer, Ross of Winnipeg, raised his camera, Mallandaine craned forward so as to see and be seen. Fifty-nine years later, when all the rest of that great company were in their graves, Colonel Edward Mallandaine, stipendiary magistrate and reeve of the Kootenay town of Creston, would be on hand when the citizens of Revelstoke, in false beards and borrowed frock coats, re-enacted the famous photograph on that very spot.

The spike had been hammered halfway home. Smith's first blow bent it badly. Frank Brothers, the roadmaster, expecting just such an emergency, pulled it out and replaced it with another. Smith posed with the uplifted hammer. The assembly froze. The shutter clicked. Smith lowered the hammer onto the spike. The shutter clicked again. Smith raised the hammer and began to drive the spike home. Save for the blows of the hammer and the sound of a small mountain stream gushing down a few feet away, there was absolute silence. Even after the spike was driven home, the stillness persisted. "It seemed," Sandford Fleming recalled, "as if the act now performed had worked a spell on all present. Each one appeared absorbed in his own reflections." The spell was broken by a cheer, "and it was no ordinary cheer. The subdued enthusiasm, the pent-up feelings of men familiar with hard work, now found vent." More cheers followed, enhanced by the shrill whistle of the locomotives.

All this time, Van Horne had stood impassively beside Fleming, his hands thrust into the side pockets of his overcoat. Though this was his crowning moment, his face remained a mask. In less than four years, through a miracle of organization and drive, he had managed to complete a new North West Passage, as the English press would call it. Did any memories surface in that retentive mind as the echoes of Smith's hammer blows rang down the corridor of Eagle Pass? Did he think back on the previous year when, half starved and soaking wet, he had come this way with Reed and Rogers? Did he reflect, with passing triumph, on those early days in Winnipeg when the unfriendly press had attacked him as an idle boaster and discussed his rumored dismissal? Did he recall those desperate moments in Ottawa and Montreal when the CPR seemed about to collapse like a house of cards? Probably not, for Van Horne was not a man to brood or to gloat over the past. It is likelier that his mind was fixed on more immediate problems: the Vancouver terminus, the Pacific postal subsidy, and the Atlantic steamship service. He could not predict the future but he would help to control it, and some of the new symbols of his adopted country would be of his making: the fleet of white Empresses flying the familiar checkered flag, the turreted hotels with their green château roofs, boldly perched on promontory and lakefront; and the international slogan that would proclaim in Arabic, Hindi, Chinese, and a dozen other languages that the CPR spanned the world.

As the cheering died, the crowd turned to Van Horne. "Speech! Speech!" they cried. Van Horne was not much of a speechmaker; he was, in fact, a little shy in crowds. What he said was characteristically terse, but it went into the history books: "All I can say is that the work has been done well in every way."

Major Rogers was more emotional. This was his moment of triumph too, and he was savoring it. In spite of all the taunts of his Canadian colleagues, in spite of the skepticism of the newspapers, in spite of his own gloomy forebodings and the second thoughts of his superiors, his pass had been chosen and the rails ran directly through it to Craigellachie. For once, the stoic major did not trouble to conceal his feelings. He was "so gleeful," Edward Mallandaine observed, "that he upended a huge tie and tried to mark the spot by the side of the track by sticking it in the ground."

There were more cheers, some mutual congratulations, and a rush for souvenirs—chips from the tie, pieces of the sawn rail. Young Arthur Piers, Van Horne's secretary, spotted the twisted first spike lying on the track and tried to pocket it. Smith, however, told him to hand it over; he wanted it as a souvenir. Smith had also tossed the sledge aside after the spike was driven but before he left, one of the track crew, Mike Sullivan, remembered to hand it to him as a keepsake. Then the locomotive's whistle sounded again and a voice was heard to cry, "All aboard for the Pacific." It was the first time that phrase had been used by a conductor from the East, but Fleming noted that it was uttered "in the most prosaic tones, as of constant daily occurrence." The official party obediently boarded the cars and a few moments later the little train was in motion again, clattering over the newly laid rail and over the last spike and down the long incline of the mountains, off toward the dark canyon of the Fraser, off to the soft meadows beyond, off to the blue Pacific and into history.

Aftermath

SIR JOHN A. MACDONALD finally visited the North West in 1886, when the railway was finished, riding through a portion of the Rockies on the cowcatcher of a CPR locomotive, a hazard he did not greatly enjoy. He survived two more elections, in 1887 and in 1891. Three months after the latter victory, at the age of seventy-six, he died of a stroke. He was succeeded by J. J. C. Abbott, the CPR's lawyer, who had once been Sir Hugh Allan's legal adviser in the days of the Pacific Scandal.

EDWARD BLAKE remained as leader of the Liberal Opposition until 1887. Gloomy about the future of his country, he retired from active politics in 1890, moved to Ireland in 1892, and was elected to the British House of Commons as an Irish nationalist. He sat until 1907 and died, five years later, in Toronto.

ALEXANDER MACKENZIE remained a member of the House of Commons until his death at seventy, but failing health and partial paralysis, some of it undoubtedly attributable to the strains of office, kept him in the shadows. He thrice refused a knighthood (as did Blake) and died in 1892, ten months after the passing of his great Conservative rival.

SIR CHARLES TUPPER served as High Commissioner in London until 1896 (except for a brief period as Minister of Finance). In 1896 he became Secretary of State in the Cabinet of Mackenzie Bowell, who had been Prime Minister. When Bowell resigned in April, Tupper became Prime Minister briefly. His party was defeated at the polls in June by the Liberals under Sir Wilfrid Laurier, and Tupper was leader of the Opposition until his retirement in 1900. He died in England in 1915.

LORD DUFFERIN, on leaving Canada, held a series of ambassadorial posts in Russia, Turkey, Italy, and France. But the pinnacle of his not inconsiderable ambition was reached in 1884 when he was created Viceroy of India, a post he had always coveted above the viceregal seat in Ottawa. When he died, at the family seat at Clandeboye, Ireland, in 1902 at the age of seventy-six, he was remembered as one of Victorian England's most eloquent and distinguished diplomats.

GEORGE STEPHEN was knighted in 1886 for his contribution to the building of the CPR. He continued as president until 1888, when he became chairman of the board and moved to England. It was said that one of his reasons for leaving Canada was his disaffection with politicians, who had forced the Onderdonk section on him and caused him to build the uneconomic "Short Line" through Maine to connect Quebec with the Maritime Provinces. In 1891 Stephen was elevated to the peerage and became Baron Mount Stephen. He stepped down from the CPR board in 1899 and died in 1921.

JAMES J. HILL's real career did not begin until he quit the CPR. His grand adventure was the extension of the St. Paul, Minneapolis and Manitoba Railway westward to Great Falls, Montana (a community he helped found), in 1887 and to Seattle in 1893. By then the line had been consolidated into the Great Northern Railroad Company. Hill's feat of railroad building—free of bankruptcy, financial scandal, and Government assistance—was perhaps the greatest in the history of the United States. He helped reorganize the Northern Pacific after that company again went bankrupt in 1893 and in 1901 won a memorable financial battle against his great rival, E. H. Harriman. Hill, who maintained his friendship with Stephen and Donald A. Smith for all of his life (they both retained their holdings of St. Paul and later Great Northern stock), died in 1916.

RICHARD B. ANGUS remained as a director of the CPR for more than forty years. In 1910, when he was seventy-nine, he became president of the Bank of Montreal, which had hired him as a junior clerk in 1857. That same year he refused a knighthood. He died in 1922.

DONALD A. SMITH had reached his sixty-fifth birthday at the time the last spike was driven—an age at which most men retire. He had already enjoyed several careers as fur trader, politician, financier, and railway executive. With the railway behind him, he entered on a variety of new ventures. Already vice-president of the Bank of Montreal, he became president in 1887. He was elected chancellor of McGill University in 1889 and founded Royal Victoria College at McGill in 1896. Knighted in 1886 for his services to the CPR, he was created Baron Strathcona and Mount Royal in 1897. The unit of mounted rifles which he equipped for the Boer War, Lord Strathcona's Horse, still survives in Calgary. Smith, who became Canadian High Commissioner to London in 1896, was made Lord Rector of Aberdeen University in 1899 and chancellor in 1903. He died in London in 1914 in his ninety-fourth year.

WILLIAM CORNELIUS VAN HORNE succeeded Stephen as president of the CPR in 1888 and as chairman of the board in 1899. By this time he had become a leading figure in the Canadian financial world—involved in concerns as varied as the Windsor Salt Company and Laurentide Paper. He piloted the company through a turbulent period of financial crisis and expansion which saw him personally write the copy for the CPR's ebullient advertising (" 'How High We Live,' said the Duke to the Prince on the Canadian Pacific Railway"). Retirement did not suit the restless nature of this remarkable man. He tried to fill in the time with travel, but this was not enough for him. One day in Florida he spotted a vessel at the dock and asked its destination. He was told it was bound for Cuba. "All right," said Van Horne, "give me a ticket." It was as a result of this incident that Van Horne built another railway —this time across Cuba. Van Horne was knighted in 1894 after his wife overcame what he called her republican tendencies, but he himself, it is said, refused a peerage because of his American birth. When he died in Montreal on September 11, 1915, every wheel in the CPR's vast transportation network stopped turning.

MAJOR A. B. ROGERS went to work for James J. Hill's railroad after the last spike was driven. In the summer of 1887 in the Coeur d'Alene Mountains of Idaho his horse stumbled and fell on a steep trail. Rogers was thrown onto a stump. He died from the effects of his injury in May, 1889.

TOM WILSON never left the mountains. He spent his whole life as a packer and guide, making his home at Banff, where he became a fixture. He had expected to meet his friend Al Rogers in the summer of 1931 to visit the spot near Lake Wapta where, fifty years before, the "vow of twenty" had been made on the Great Divide, but Al Rogers died on May 16, 1929. Tom Wilson, who dictated his memoirs to W. E. Round in 1931, died September 22, 1933.

THOMAS SHAUGHNESSY, in his turn, succeeded Van Horne as president and later chairman of the CPR. Under his tenure—he was known as the King of the Railway Presidents—the CPR became the leading transportation system on the globe, building a chain of great hotels, establishing an Atlantic shipping service to match its Pacific fleet, and acquiring other companies, notably in the mining and smelting field. A staunch Imperialist, who gladly accepted a peerage in 1916, Baron Shaughnessy organized Imperial transport and purchasing for Canada during World War I and put the CPR's credit behind $100 million worth of Allied war loans. He died in 1923, shortly after naming his successor, Edward Beatty, and telling him to "take good care of the Canadian Pacific Railway."

ANDREW ONDERDONK went from British Columbia to Argentina, where in 1886 he built the Entre Rios railway north of Buenos Aires. His later construction work included nine miles of drainage tunneling in Chicago, the Chicago Northwestern Elevated Railway, a double-track tunnel in Hamilton, part of the Trent Valley Canal system (which included one of the largest rock cuts on the continent), and part of the rebuilding of the Victoria Bridge over the St. Lawrence. He was a partner, at one time, of G. W. Ferris and, it is believed, helped build the famous wheel which was a feature of the World's Columbian Exposition at Chicago in 1893. In 1905 he was general manager of the New York Tunnel Company, building a subway tunnel under the East River between Manhattan and Brooklyn, said at the time to be one of the most difficult pieces of work ever undertaken by a contractor. He died on June 21 of that year at Oscawana-on-Hudson, near Croton. He was fifty-six years old. The cause of death was given as "overwork."

SAMUEL BENFIELD STEELE continued to preside at the most color-ful incidents in the history of the Canadian North West. He was sent to the Kootenays in 1887 to settle the Indian troubles. In 1897 he manned the passes on the international boundary between Alaska and the Yukon during the stampede to the Klondike. He ran the stampede like a military maneuver, saving untold lives and keeping the city of Dawson, in the boom year of 1898, under tight control. (This aspect of his career is chronicled in detail in the author's *The Klondike Fever*.) During the Boer War he commanded Lord Strathcona's Horse and remained in the Transvaal as head of the South African Constabulary there. On returning to Canada in 1906 he commanded the Calgary and later the Winnipeg military districts. When war broke out he was promoted to major-general, raising and training the Second Canadian Division, which he took to England in 1915. He retired and was knighted in 1918. He died at Putney, England, the following year.

JOHN MACOUN traveled about Canada and continued collecting botanical specimens for most of his life. In 1887 he became assistant director and naturalist of the Geological Survey. In 1912 he retired and moved to British Columbia. After his death at Sidney in 1920, his autobiography was published posthumously by the Ottawa Field Naturalists' Club. There are forty-eight species of flora and fauna named after Macoun as well as a mountain in the Selkirks.

SANDFORD FLEMING remained as a director of the CPR and chancellor of Queen's University until his death. His most notable achievement after the CPR construction period was the part he played in planning the Pacific Cable, which was completed in 1902. He represented Canada at colonial conferences in London in 1888 and Ottawa in 1894 and at the Imperial Cable Conference in 1896. Knighted in 1897, he died in Halifax in 1915 at the age of eighty-eight.

GEORGE MONRO GRANT carried on as principal of Queen's until his death. His reputation in both political and educational circles was outstanding. He was elected moderator of the Presbyterian Church in 1882 and president of the Royal Society of Canada in 1901. He died in 1902.

MARCUS SMITH, in spite of his many protestations, did not leave the government service nor was he dismissed. He remained as a consulting engineer until his retirement in 1892 and died in Ottawa in 1904 in his ninetieth year.

WALTER MOBERLY continued in Manitoba as a railway engineer but returned to Vancouver in the late 1890's and spent his declining years there in a small furnished room on Hornby Street. He completed several books in retirement, and his bitterness over the naming of the Rogers Pass, as expressed in several newspaper interviews, increased in old age. He died in 1915, of cancer of the larynx, aged eighty-three.

LOUIS RIEL was hanged on November 16, 1885. He remains the most controversial figure in Canadian history, the subject of dozens of books, novels, histories, at least one play, and one opera. His adjutant, GABRIEL DUMONT, escaped to the United States, became a leading performer in Buffalo Bill's Wild West Show (where he reenacted the stirring days of 1885), returned to Canada under a general amnesty, and died in Batoche at the age of sixty-eight. BIG BEAR and POUNDMAKER, the rebel Cree chiefs, were given prison sentences for felony but were released in 1887. Neither survived his freedom by more than a few months.

CROWFOOT lived on his reserve until his death in 1890. Although he was thought of as an ancient chieftain, he was only fifty-six years old. His great friend, FATHER LACOMBE, lived to be eighty-nine. After the coming of the railway, Lacombe's career was anticlimactic. He became a settled parish priest, first at Fort McLeod and later at St. Joachim, near Edmonton. He retired in 1897 to a hermitage at Pincer Lake, emerged in 1899 to help negotiate Treaty No. 8 with the northern Indians, traveled to Europe and the Holy Land, and, in 1909, founded the Lacombe Home at Midnapore, Alberta, for derelicts of all races who had never been able to make an adjustment to the new North West. When he died in 1916, the eulogy he read over Crowfoot's grave a quarter of a century before might have been his own: "Men, women and children, mourn over your great parent; you will no more hear his voice and its eloquent harangues. In your distress and misery you will no more rush to his tent for comfort and charities. He is gone. There is no one like him to fill his place."

The "last spike" was removed, after the dignitaries departed, by roadmaster Frank Brothers. Brothers was afraid that souvenir hunters would tear up his track to secure the prize. (As it was, chunks of the tie were chopped away and the remaining piece of the sawn rail was split up by memorabilia seekers.) Brothers later presented the spike to Edward Beatty, but it was stolen from Beatty's desk. What happened to the spike cannot be ascertained with any accuracy, but it may be the one in the hands of Mrs. W. H. Remnant of Yellowknife. According to Mrs. Remnant, Henry Cambie came into possession of the spike and gave it to W. J. Lynch, chief of the patent office in Ottawa, to keep for his son Arthur, who was serving with the British Army Medical Corps. When Arthur returned home, his father presented him with the spike, which by this time had been worked into the shape of a carving knife with the handle silvered. His daughter Mamie, now Mrs. Remnant, inherited it. The other spike, which Donald Smith bent and discarded and then appropriated as a souvenir, was cut into thin strips which were mounted with diamonds and presented to the wives of some of the members of the party. Several ladies who did not receive the souvenirs were so put out that the diplomatic Smith had another spike cut up into similar souvenirs. These, however, were made larger so that the recipients of the original gifts would be able to tell the difference. Lord Lansdowne's original unused silver spike was presented to Van Horne and is still in the Van Horne family.

The CPR was immortalized by Hollywood in 1949 when Twentieth Century-Fox made *Canadian Pacific*, a film purportedly about the building of the railway. The star was Randolph Scott, who played the role of Tom Andrews, a surveyor who, unassisted, discovers a pass in the Rockies, thus allowing railway construction—held up in the prairies—to proceed once more. There are only two historical figures in the film: Van Horne, depicted as a weedy construction boss with his headquarters in Calgary, and Père Lacombe, shown as a stout and rather comical Irish priest. The conflict revolves around the attempt by the métis (pronounced "mett-isse" in the film) living around Lake Louise(!) to prevent the railway from coming through the mountains. Dirk Rourke, the métis leader (played by Victor Jory), rouses the saloonkeepers along the line of the road to cause a strike, which Scott breaks up singlehandedly by the use of his six-shooters. Then Rourke persuades the Indians to attack the railroad as if it were a wagon train; they appear in full feathered headdress, waving tomahawks and shooting flaming arrows from their primitive bows. Scott rallies the railroad workers, who in a pitched battle destroy or disperse the redskins. Love interest is supplied by a woman doctor, whom Scott eventually rejects because she believes in nonviolent methods, and a pretty métis girl who saves the day by disclosing her people's plans and thereby winning Scott's affections. This is perhaps the only Hollywood film ever made about the Canadian West in which the North West Mounted Police are conspicuously absent. That may explain why almost every railroader in the picture carries two six-shooters on his hip. The film lists a Canadian technical adviser in the person of John Rhodes Sturdy, at one time a public-relations officer for the Canadian Pacific Railway.

CHRONOLOGY,
NOTES,
BIBLIOGRAPHY,
ACKNOWLEDG-
MENTS
AND INDEX

Chronology

1871

1872

February 24	Allan reports to American principals that he has made an offer to Senator David L. Macpherson.
February 29	Senator Macpherson turns Allan down.
March 28	Allan authorized by Americans to spend $50,000 on "influence."
April	Fleming settles on Yellow Head Pass as the best route through the Rockies.
June 12	Allan reports to McMullen that he has George Étienne Cartier on his side.
July 1	Allan reports to General George Washington Cass on his use of the Americans' funds to bring Cartier to heel.
July 17	Fleming meets John Macoun, the botanist, aboard lake steamer.
July 26	Macdonald authorizes Cartier to tell Allan that government influence will be used to get him the presidency of the CPR.
July 30	Allan and Cartier reach an understanding. Cartier asks Allan for campaign contributions.
August 2	Fleming's party leaves Fort Garry.
August 9	Allan helps Cartier open his election campaign.
August 26	Macdonald wires, "I must have another ten thousand."
September 1	Macdonald Government returned in federal election.
September 14	Fleming meets with Moberly in Yellow Head Pass.
September 16	McMullen learns that Allan has spent $343,000.
October 11	Grant and Fleming end their journey in Victoria.
October 24	Allan breaks news to McMullen that Americans can have no part in Canadian Pacific Railway.
December 31	McMullen meets Macdonald in Ottawa and tells him of Allan's double dealings.

1873

January 23	McMullen and associates return to Ottawa for second meeting with Macdonald.
February 25	Hincks reports to Macdonald from Montreal that Allan has paid off McMullen and purchased his indiscreet correspondence.
March 6	Parliament opens.

April 2	Lucius Seth Huntington's motion touches off the Pacific Scandal.
April 8	Macdonald announces select committee to investigate Huntington charges.
May 23	Parliament adjourned until August 13.
July 3	Select committee meets again; refuses to take evidence.
July 4	*Globe* (Toronto) and *Herald* (Montreal) publish Allan correspondence.
July 17	Opposition papers publish McMullen revelations.
July 19	Esquimalt named as terminus for CPR.
August	Jesse Farley appointed receiver of St. Paul and Pacific Railroad.
August 13	Parliament meets and is prorogued.
August 14	Royal commission appointed to take evidence based on Huntington charges.
September 17	Jay Cooke's banking firm fails, touching off financial panic.
October 1	Royal commission ends hearings.
October 23	Parliament opens "short session."
November 3	Macdonald's speech.
November 5	Macdonald Government resigns.
December	Donald Smith passes through St. Paul and asks Norman Kittson to investigate bankrupt St. Paul and Pacific Railroad.

1874

January	Party under E. W. Jarvis prepares to explore Smoky River Pass in Rockies.
January 22	Liberal Party under Alexander Mackenzie re-elected.
February 3	Edward Blake resigns from Mackenzie Cabinet.
February 15	Jarvis party reaches Smoky River Pass.
April 3	Jarvis party manages to reach Edmonton.
June 12	Lord Carnarvon offers to arbitrate dispute between British Columbia and Ottawa.
June 29	Some two hundred angry passengers on Dawson Route are stranded at North West Angle without transportation.
August 30	First contract on transcontinental railway—for the Pembina Branch—signed.
November 17	Lord Carnarvon lays down terms of settlement between Ottawa and British Columbia.

1875

February 19	Adam Oliver and friends awarded telegraph contract between Fort William and Red River.
May 14	Blake re-enters Mackenzie Cabinet.
June 1	First sod of main line of Canadian Pacific Railway turned at Fort William.

1876

January 10	British Columbia rejects Ottawa overtures, threatens secession.
March 17	James J. Hill leaves St. Paul for meeting with Donald A. Smith in Ottawa regarding purchase of bankrupt St. Paul railway.
May	Fleming given leave of absence; goes to England.
August 16	Lord Dufferin arrives at Esquimalt for viceregal visit.
September 20	Bids opened for Section Fifteen contract, CPR.
November 18	Dufferin, Mackenzie, and Blake almost come to blows over British Columbia issue.
December	Fleming called back from leave.

1877

January 9	Joseph Whitehead awarded contract for Section Fifteen.
January 29	First proposal by Jim Hill to Dutch bondholders.
May	Hill and Smith meet George Stephen in Montreal.
May 22	Marcus Smith orders Henry Cambie to launch a secret expedition to examine the Pine River Pass.
May 26	Hill and Kittson make a second offer to the Dutch which is construed as an offer to purchase.
September 1	George Stephen visits the St. Paul and Pacific Railroad for the first time.
October 9	*The Countess of Dufferin*, first locomotive on the prairies, arrives in Winnipeg.

December 25   Stephen, back from Europe, reports his failure to raise funds to buy bankrupt St. Paul line.

1878

March 13   Final agreement of sale between Dutch bondholders and Stephen-Hill group.

March 18   Mackenzie introduces bill into Parliament to lease Pembina Branch of CPR to unspecified. parties.

March 27   "Montreal Agreement" among partners in St. Paul syndicate: Stephen, Hill, Smith, and Kittson.

March 29   Marcus Smith's official report urges acceptance of Pine Pass–Bute Inlet route but asks year's delay for more surveys.

April   Fleming is once again called back from sick leave in England to deal with Marcus Smith.

May 10   Tupper and Macdonald call Donald A. Smith a liar and a coward in a stormy scene as Parliament is prorogued.

July 22   Mackenzie government selects Fraser River–Burrard Inlet route for CPR.

July 31   Hill completes first section of St. Paul line and secures land grant.

September 17   Conservative Party returned to power in federal landslide.

    Last spike of Pembina Branch driven.

November 11   First train of St. Paul and Pacific crosses border at St. Vincent and arrives at Emerson, Manitoba.

December   Macdonald government restores Esquimalt as CPR terminus.

1879

May 10   Tupper in House outlines Government's railway policy, rejects Burrard route, and announces 125 miles will be built at once in British Columbia.

June 21   Donald A. Smith's election controverted for corruption.

October 4   Burrard route readopted.

November 20   Andrew Onderdonk arrives in Ottawa to negotiate for four British Columbia contracts.

1880

March 1	Government relieves Joseph Whitehead of contract.
April 22	Onderdonk arrives at Yale, B.C., to commence construction.
April 28	Alexander Mackenzie resigns as Liberal leader. Edward Blake named new leader.
May 22	Fleming resigns and is replaced by Collingwood Schreiber.
June 15	Charles Tupper's memo to Privy Council urges that capitalists be found to build CPR.
June 29	Macdonald, at political picnic, Bath, Ontario, announces capitalists in Britain stand ready to build railway.
August 12	CPR royal commission begins hearings.
September 4	Macdonald signs a provisional agreement in London with Stephen-McIntyre-Hill syndicate.
September 11	Donald A. Smith defeated in Selkirk by-election.
September 27	Macdonald arrives back in Montreal.
October 21	Final contract signed with Stephen syndicate.
November 2	Father Albert Lacombe arrives at his new mission at Rat Portage.
December 9	Parliament opens; details of contract made public.
December 11	Tupper rallies Conservative caucus.
December 13	Debate on contract opens.
December 23	Christmas recess.

1881

January 5	Parliament reconvenes.
January 12	Pacific Railway Bill read for first time.
January 14	New tender from Howland syndicate reaches government.
January 17	Macdonald's speech in Parliament.
January 18	Blake's speech.
January 27	Bill passes first reading.
January 31	Bill passes second reading.
February 1	Bill passes final reading.
February 15	Bill passes Senate.
February 16	Canadian Pacific Railway Company incorporated.

April 29	Major A. B. Rogers leaves Kamloops for Selkirks.
May 2	First sod turned at Portage la Prairie by General T. L. Rosser.
May 18	George Stephen, R. B. Angus, and James J. Hill meet with John Macoun in St. Paul and discuss change of route.
May 21	Rogers party begins ascent of Selkirks.
July 15	Rogers meets Tom Wilson.
October 7	Hill takes W. C. Van Horne on brief tour of CPR line out of Winnipeg.
November 1	Van Horne's appointment as general manager confirmed.
December 13	Van Horne arrives in Winnipeg to take up duties.

1882

January 12	Van Horne and Rogers meet with CPR board in Montreal. Change of route made public.
February 1	Van Horne fires General Rosser by telegram.
March 13	Fire destroys CPR offices and Bank of Montreal building, Winnipeg.
April 12	Edmonton lots go on sale in Winnipeg.
April 14	Jim Coolican and Winnipeg "boomers" leave for St. Paul.
April 19	Crest of Red River flood hits Winnipeg, sweeps away Broadway Bridge.
May 4	Andrew Onderdonk launches *Skuzzy*; it fails to breach Hell's Gate on the Fraser.
May 22	Rogers makes vain attempt to locate pass in Selkirks by ascending eastern slopes.
June 17	Last spike driven on government line between Fort William and Selkirk, Manitoba.
June 18	CPR acquires Montreal–Ottawa section of Quebec, Montreal, Ottawa and Occidental Railway.
June 20	Conservative Party under Sir John A. Macdonald wins sweeping victory.
June 30	Lieutenant-Governor Edgar Dewdney posts notice at Pile o' Bones Creek reserving the land as site of new capital of North West Territories.
	Great Western stockholders approve merger with Grand Trunk.

July 17	Rogers sets off from Columbia River on second attempt to locate pass in the Selkirks from the east.
July 24	Rogers reaches summit of Selkirks and finds pass.
August 23	First train arrives at Regina with official party for dedication ceremonies.
September 7	Second launching of *Skuzzy* at Hell's Gate.
September 28	*Skuzzy* breaches Hell's Gate.
December 29	CPR issues $30 million of stock to New York syndicate.

1883

March 15	Onderdonk hires Michael Haney to manage work between Yale and Port Moody.
May 3	James J. Hill quits CPR board; sells most of his stock.
July 28	CPR tracklayers set a record: lay 6.38 miles in a day.
August 17	CPR issues 200,000 shares of stock at twenty-five cents on the dollar.
August 18	Langdon and Shepard complete prairie contract.
August 27	Official party arrives at Calgary.
October 24	Stephen outlines guaranteed dividend plan to Macdonald and lodges formal petition for financial aid.
December 1	Macdonald wires Tupper in London: "Pacific in trouble."

1884

January 15	George Stephen asks for government loan of $22,500,-000.
February 1	Tupper proposes new CPR loan resolutions to Parliament.
February 28	CPR relief bill passes House.
May	Duncan McIntyre quits CPR.
June 4	Gabriel Dumont and métis delegation arrive at home of Louis Riel in Montana to invite him to return to North West.
July 11	Riel holds his first public meeting at Red Deer Hill.
July 31	Big Bear convenes first Indian council at Duck Lake.
August 6	Van Horne visits site of Vancouver on Burrard Inlet.

August 10	Van Horne inspects Onderdonk line and arrives at Kamloops.
September 16	Van Horne in Montreal asks CPR directors to approve choice of Vancouver as CPR western terminus.

1885

January 1	Universal Time adopted at Greenwich, England.
January 12	John A. Macdonald celebrates his seventieth birthday in Montreal.
March 18	Stephen asks Privy Council for another loan and is rejected.
March 19	Riel sets up provisional métis government in Saskatchewan.
March 23	Macdonald orders Major-General Frederick Middleton to move militia north from Winnipeg to scene of métis unrest.
March 26	Major L. N. F. Crozier's force of Mounted Police defeated by métis under Gabriel Dumont at Duck Lake. Saskatchewan Rebellion begins.
March 28	Permanent forces in eastern Canada ordered to move. Militia units called out.
April 1	CPR workmen strike at Beavermouth, British Columbia.
April 2	Group of Big Bear's Crees massacres priests and other whites at Frog Lake.
April 5	First troops reach Winnipeg.
April 7	Strike at Beavermouth ends.
April 16	Van Horne wires Stephen that CPR pay car cannot be sent out.
April 23	Dumont defeats General Middleton at Fish Creek.
May 1	John A. Macdonald gives notice in Parliament of new measures for financial relief of CPR.
May 2	Chief Poundmaker defeats Colonel Otter's troops at Cut Knife Hill.
May 15	Riel surrenders to Middleton.
May 16	Last rail laid on Lake Superior line.
May 26	Poundmaker surrenders.
June 16	John Henry Pope moves resolutions for CPR aid in Parliament.
July 2	Big Bear surrenders.

July 10   CPR aid bill passes House of Commons.

July 15 *(approx.)*   CPR floats $15-million bond issue with Baring Brothers in London.

July 20   Louis Riel goes on trial for his life in Regina.
CPR aid bill gets royal assent.

July 29   Andrew Onderdonk completes government contracts; line is finished from Port Moody to Savona's Ferry.

August 13   CPR acquires North Shore line between Montreal and Quebec.

September 18   Louis Riel sentenced to hang.

September 30   Onderdonk completes contract with CPR between Savona's Ferry and Eagle Pass.

November 7   Last spike driven at Craigellachie.

Notes

I have tried to arrange the notes in such a way that narrative flow will not be interrupted for the lay reader while, at the same time, the scholarly researcher can, without too much difficulty, establish the sources of my material. For this reason I have not followed the usual method of sprinkling the text with small numbers—a practice that I find irritating. I have also discarded another annoying tradition, that of using *op. cit.* for all but the first reference to any work. It is maddening for a researcher to struggle back through all the *op. cits.* in his search for the original citation. In the abbreviated notes that follow, the scholar can always go directly to the bibliography.

I have tried to give a source for every quotation in the book and, in addition, for facts that are not self-evident and for anecdotes that may be disputed.

page *line*

FROM SEA TO SEA

3	*19*	*Islander*, Dec. 31, 1870.
4	*7*	*British Colonist*, Jan. 2, 1871.
4	*17*	*Globe*, Jan. 2, 1871.
4	*31*	*Ibid.*, Jan. 4, 1871.
5	*25*	Southesk, p. 70.

CHAPTER 1

7	*6*	*Parliamentary Debates*, Fourth Session, 1871, Vol. 2, p. 681.
8	*13*	*Ibid.*, p. 745.
8	*30*	*Ibid.*, p. 681.
8	*37*	*Macdonald Papers*, Vol. 252, Morris to Macdonald, April 1, 1871.
9	*28*	*Parliamentary Debates*, 1871, p. 745.
9	*35*	*British Columbia and the Canadian Pacific Railway*, Complimentary Dinner to the Hon. Mr. Trutch, Ottawa, Monday, April 10, 1871.
10	*32*	Pope, *Correspondence*, p. 124, Macdonald to Charles Brydges, Jan. 28, 1870.
10	*37*	Quoted in Stanley, *Louis Riel*, p. 40.
11	*8*	Willson, p. 182.
11	*11*	*Watkin*, p. 17.
11	*23*	*Irwin*, pp. 120 and 128.
11	*30*	*St. Paul Press*, Feb. 8, 1870, quoted in Gluek, p. 262.
12	*16*	Johnson, p. 27.
12	*20*	Macdonell, p. 3.
13	*9*	Hind, *et al., Eighty Years Progress*: Keefer, *Travel and Transportation*, p. 227.
13	*21*	Fleming, *Practical Observations*.
14	*4*	*Ibid.*, p. 46.
14	*32*	Quoted in Smith, *Political Destiny*, p. 62.
15	*2*	Quoted in *Lower*, p. 296.
15	*9*	Quoted in Smith, *Political Destiny*, p. 62.
15	*14*	*Leader*, Toronto, April 28, 1870.
16	*25*	Berry, p. 191.
18	*9*	Quoted in Young, Vol. 2, p. 83 *n.*
18	*21*	*Ibid.*, p. 81.
18	*23*	Pope, *Memoirs*, p. 43, Macdonald to Watkin, March 27, 1865.

page *line*

23	*11*	Palliser, *Journals*, p. 16.
23	*13*	Palliser, *Further Papers*, p. 5.
23	*21*	Gladman, p. 164.
23	*23*	Hind, *Narrative*, p. 220.
23	*26*	*Ibid.*, p. 234.
23	*30*	*Ibid.*
23	*42*	Hind, *et al., Eighty Years Progress*, p. 80.
25	*20*	Trotter and Hawkes, p. 291.
25	*24*	D'Artigue, p. 45.
26	*9*	Southesk, p. 92.
26	*20*	*Luxton Papers*, Memoirs of Mrs. David McDougall, p. 3.
26	*37*	Wolesley, *Blackwood's*, p. 178.
27	*21*	Butler, p. 7.
28	*11*	*Ibid.*, p. 197.
28	*17*	*Ibid.*
28	*24*	*Ibid.*, pp. 200–1.
28	*29*	*Ibid.*, pp. 199–200.
29	*5*	*Ibid.*
29	*16*	*Ibid.*, p. 351.
30	*13*	Grant and Hamilton, pp. 47–8 *n.*
30	*23*	*Ibid.*, p. 143.
32	*2*	Grant, *Ocean to Ocean*, p. 74.
32	*14*	*Fleming Papers*, Folder 131, Grant to Fleming, Sept. 30, 1880.
34	*19*	*Macoun*, p. 73.
34	*37*	*Ibid.*, p. 81.
35	*12*	Grant, p. 272.
35	*15*	*Ibid.*, pp. 272–3.
36	*24*	Butler, pp. 103–4.
36	*40*	*Malhoit Manuscript*, pp. 108–9.
37	*35*	Willson, p. 197.
37	*39*	*Nor'wester*, July 6, 1874.
38	*6*	*Ibid.*
38	*13*	Trow, pp. 12–13.
40	*1*	Begg, *History*, Vol. 2, p. 261.
40	*8*	Marchioness of Dufferin, *Journal*, p. 343.
40	*13*	*Fitzgibbon*, pp. 110–11.

CHAPTER 2

43	*29*	Irwin, p. 120.
43	*34*	*Ibid.*, p. 165, Ogden to Cooke, June 17, 1871.
44	*7*	*Macdonald Papers*, Vol. 519, Macdonald to George Jackson, July 17, 1871.
44	*16*	*Report of Royal Commis-*

page *line*

sioners, p. 11, Hincks's testimony.

44 *31* *Globe*, March 14, 1873.

44 *37* Quoted *Montreal Daily Star*, Nov. 27, 1926.

46 *13* *Globe*, July 4, 1873.

46 *15* Quoted in Stewart, p. 235.

46 *22* *Report of Royal Commissioners*, p. 4, Hincks's testimony.

46 *30* *Dufferin Papers*, Dufferin to Kimberley, Sept. 26, 1873.

46 *39* *Globe*, July 17, 1873, McMullen's statement.

46 *42* *Ibid.*

47 *3* Quoted in Willson, p. 183.

47 *13* Quoted in Irwin, pp. 171–2, Jay Cooke to H. C. Fahnestock, Jan. 16, 1872.

47 *17* *Ibid.*

47 *26* Josephson, p. 57.

47 *38* Quoted in Oberholtzer, Vol. 2, p. 296, Cooke to Gen. B. Sargent, Feb. 25, 1870.

47 *42* *Ibid.*

48 *13* *Globe*, July 4, 1873, Allan to Gen. Cass, July 1, 1872.

48 *22* *Ibid.*

49 *33* *Ibid.*

50 *3* *Ibid.*

50 *13* *Ibid.*, Allan to McMullen, June 12, 1872.

50 *18* Pope, *Public Servant*, p. 40.

51 *13* *Globe*, July 4, 1873, Allan to Gen. Cass, Aug. 7, 1872.

51 *15* *Ibid.*, Allan to McMullen, Aug. 6, 1872.

51 *31* Boyd, p. 320.

52 *22* Clarke, p. 103.

52 *28* *Ibid.*

52 *35* *Report of Royal Commissioners*, p. 119, Macdonald's testimony.

53 *9* *Ibid.*, p. 134, Allan's testimony.

53 *21* *Ibid.*, p. 134.

53 *27* *Ibid.*, p. 160, Abbott's testimony.

53 *31* *Ibid.*

54 *11* *Ibid.*, pp. 136–7, Allan's testimony.

54 *22* *Ibid.*

55 *4* *Ibid.*, p. 181, Thomas White's testimony.

55 *20* *Macdonald Papers*, Vol. 123, Macpherson to Macdonald, July 27, 1872.

55 *27* *Ibid.*, Allan to Macdonald, Oct. 7, 1872.

55 *31* *Report of Royal Commissioners*, pp. 132–3, Allan's testimony.

56 *10* *Dufferin Papers*, Macdonald to Dufferin, quoted in Dufferin to Kimberley, Sept. 29, 1873.

56 *17* *Globe*, July 4, 1873, Allan to McMullen, Sept. 16, 1872.

56 *36* *Dufferin Papers*, Dufferin to Kimberley, Oct. 9, 1873.

57 *25* *Report of Royal Commissioners*, p. 108, Macdonald's testimony.

58 *2* *Ibid.*, p. 109.

58 *5* *Globe*, July 17, 1873, McMullen's statement.

58 *21* *Report of Royal Commissioners*, p. 109, Macdonald's testimony.

58 *42* Irwin, p. 196.

59 *6* *Ibid.*

59 *17* Pope, *Memoirs*, p. 557, Macdonald to Cartier, April 9, 1873.

59 *27* Pope, *Correspondence*, pp. 204–5, Macdonald to Rose, Feb. 13, 1873.

60 *5* *Macdonald Papers*, Vol. 224, Hincks to Macdonald, Feb. 25, 1873.

CHAPTER 3

61 *7* *Dufferin Papers*, Dufferin to Kimberley, March 7, 1873.

61 *12* Ross, George, p. 61.

62 *2* *Dufferin Papers*, Dufferin to Kimberley, March 7, 1873.

62 *7* *Ibid.*

62 *17* *Globe*, March 6, 1873.

62 *19* *Ibid.*

62 *25* *Ibid.*, April 1, 1873.

62 *27* *Ibid.*

63 *19* *Ibid.*, April 3, 1873.

63 *25* *Message*, p. 4, Dufferin to Kimberley, Aug. 15, 1873.

63 *30* *Dufferin Papers*, Dufferin to Kimberley, April 4, 1873.

63 *35* Stewart, p. 131.

63 *40* Rose, *Cyclopaedia*, p. 164.

64 *16* Pope, *Memoirs*, p. 556, Macdonald to Cartier, April 9, 1873.

65 *21* *Dufferin Papers*, Dufferin to Kimberley, Sept, 29, 1873.

66 *2* *Ibid.*, Sept. 12, 1873.

66 *7* Biggar, p. 84.

66 *17* Willison, p. 188.

page *line*

66 *31* Creighton, *Old Chieftain*, pp. 56–70.

69 *17* Pope, *Correspondence*, Macdonald to Dufferin, July 4, 1873.

69 *26* *Mail*, July 6, 1873.

69 *34* *Gazette*, Picton, Aug 1, 1873.

71 *14* *Dufferin Papers*, Dufferin to Kimberley, July 23, 1873.

71 *18* De Kiewiet and Underhill, p. 12, Dufferin to Carnarvon, March 18, 1874.

71 *28* Willison, p. 24.

71 *33* *Macdonald Papers*, Vol. 79, Macdonald to Dufferin, Aug. 7, 1873.

72 *7* *Ibid.*, Vol. 125, Abbott to Macdonald, July 22, 1873.

72 *16* *Ibid.*, Day to Macdonald, July 24, 1873.

72 *22* *Globe*, Aug. 2, 1873, Aug. 8, 1873.

72 *25* *Dufferin Papers*, Dufferin to Kimberley, Nov. 6, 1873.

72 *35* *Ibid.*

73 *12* *Globe*, Aug. 19, 1873.

73 *16* *Ibid.*

73 *30* *Dufferin Papers*, Dufferin to Kimberley, Oct. 9, 1873.

73 *42* *Report of Royal Commissioners*, p. 2, Starnes's testimony.

74 *10* *Globe*, Sept. 4, 1873.

74 *30* *Report of Royal Commissioners*, p. 39, Daker's testimony.

74 *39* *Ibid.*, p. 125, Langevin's testimony.

74 *41* *Ibid.*

75 *12* Careless, Vol. 2, p. 307.

75 *14* *Report of Royal Commissioners*; Macdonald's testimony runs from p. 99 to p. 121.

75 *29* *Ibid.*, p. 119, Macdonald's testimony.

75 *36* Quoted in *Globe*, Sept. 29, 1873.

75 *38* *Report of Royal Commissioners*; Allan's testimony runs from p. 129 to p. 155.

77 *5* *Ibid.*, pp. 156–72, Abbott's testimony.

77 *28* Hutchison.

77 *32* Pope, *Public Servant*, p. 81.

77 *38* *Ibid.*, p. 43.

78 *20* *Dufferin Papers*, Dufferin to Kimberley, Sept. 26, 1873.

78 *26* Young, Vol. 2, p. 150.

78 *30* *Citizen*, Oct. 23, 1873.

79 *37* Ross, George, p. 55.

81 *8* *Dufferin Papers*, Dufferin to Kimberley, Oct. 26, 1873.

81 *25* *Globe*, Oct. 28, 1873.

81 *34* *Dufferin Papers*, Dufferin to Macdonald, Sept. 20, 1873, Sept. 30, 1873.

82 *13* *Globe*, Oct. 28, 1873.

82 *30* *Ibid.*, Oct. 29, 1873.

82 *35* *Ibid.*

82 *41* *Dufferin Papers*, Dufferin to Kimberley, Nov. 6, 1873.

83 *5* *Ibid.*

83 *11* *Ibid.*

83 *40* *Globe*, Nov. 4, 1873.

84 *17* *Dufferin Papers*, Dufferin to Kimberley, Nov. 6, 1873.

84 *22* *Globe*, Nov. 4, 1873.

84 *27* Thomson, p. 166 *n*.

86 *38* *Mail*, Nov. 6, 1873.

87 *6* Pope, *Correspondence*, Dufferin to Macdonald, Nov. 4, 1873.

88 *5* Ross, George, p. 144.

88 *20* Young, Vol. 2, p. 153.

88 *30* *Dufferin Papers*, Dufferin to Kimberley, Nov. 6, 1873.

89 *8* Ross, George, p. 71.

89 *11* *Globe*, Nov. 7, 1873.

89 *23* Thomson, p. 167.

89 *33* *Globe*, Nov. 7, 1873.

89 *37* Preston, *My Generation*, p. 92.

90 *4* *Globe*, Nov. 7, 1873.

90 *23* *Dufferin Papers*, Dufferin to Kimberley, Nov. 13, 1873.

90 *37* Pope, *Memoirs*, pp. 195–6.

91 *13* Ross, George, p. 80.

91 *27* Pope, *Public Servant*, p. 29.

CHAPTER 4

92 *8* *Hargreaves Diary*, July 5, 1872.

92 *18* *Rylatt Manuscript*, pp. 176–177.

93 *13* Fleming, *CPR Report*, 1877, p. 87.

93 *25* *Ibid.*, 1878, pp. 88 and 104.

93 *33* *Ibid.*, 1872, App. 6, p. 58.

93 *38* *Moberly Diary*, Oct. 8, 1872.

94 *3* *CPR Royal Commission*, 1882, Vol. 2, p. 1685, Fleming's testimony.

94 *8* *Ibid.*, p. 1315, Fleming's testimony.

page *line*

94 *12* Fleming, *Letter to Secretary of State*, App. 3, p. 23.

94 *14* *CPR Royal Commission*, Vol. 2, p. 1242, Horetzky's testimony.

94 *20* *Ibid.*

94 *22* *Ibid.*, Vol. 2, p. 1700, Fleming's testimony.

94 *33* *Marcus Smith Papers*, PABC, *Diary*, July 20, 1875.

94 *37* Fleming, *CPR Report*, 1872, App. 6, p. 58.

94 *40* *Ibid.*, p. 68.

95 *4* *Marcus Smith Papers*, PABC, Smith to Hunter, May 27, 1874.

95 *17* *Ibid.*, PAC, Letterbook, Vol. 5, Smith to Fleming, Feb. 25, 1878.

95 *24* Gosnell, p. 102.

95 *29* Allard.

96 *5* Quoted in Begg, *History*, Vol. 2, pp. 181–2.

96 *10* *CPR Bulletin*, Feb. 1, 1936.

96 *36* Fleming, *CPR Report*, 1872, App. 6, p. 63, Rowan's testimony.

97 *3* *CPR Royal Commission*, Vol. 1, p. 126, Carre's evidence.

97 *11* *Ibid.*, Vol. 1, pp. 538–9, Kirkpatrick's evidence.

97 *14* Fleming, *CPR Report*, 1872, App. 4, p. 42, by R. McLennan.

97 *15* *Ibid.*, p. 48.

97 *23* Fleming, *CPR Report*, 1877, App. H, pp. 148–61, Jarvis narrative.

98 *11* *Ibid.*, p. 153.

98 *16* *Ibid.*, p. 155.

98 *18* *Hanington Papers*.

98 *27* *Ibid.*

98 *29* Fleming, *CPR Report*, 1877, App. H, p. 157, Jarvis narrative.

98 *37* *Ibid.*, p. 147.

99 *31* Moberly, *Rocks and Rivers*, p. 44.

100 *4* Robinson, *Blazing the Trail*, pp. 66–7.

100 *22* Robinson, *Walter Moberly*.

100 *32* *Moberly Diary*, Jan. 4, 1872.

100 *36* Moberly, *Rocks and Rivers*, p. 42.

101 *26* Fleming, *CPR Report*, 1872, App. 3, p. 31, by Walter Moberly.

101 *34* *Moberly Diary*, Jan. 1, 1872.

101 *36* Fleming, *CPR Report*, 1872, App. 3, p. 34.

102 *2* Robinson, *Blazing the Trail*, p. 74.

102 *7* *Ibid.*, p. 75.

102 *36* *CPR Royal Commission*, Vol. 3, p. 57.

104 *9* Robinson, *Blazing the Trail*, p. 77.

104 *23* *Ibid.*, p. 84.

104 *29* Grant, *Ocean to Ocean*, p. 249.

104 *39* *CPR Royal Commission*, Vol. 2, p. 1678, Fleming's testimony.

105 *5* Moberly, *Address*, p. 10.

105 *10* *Ibid.*, p. 13.

105 *16* *CPR Royal Commission*, Vol. 2, p. 1826, Moberly's deposition.

105 *30* *Moberly Diary*, Sept. 8, 1872.

105 *39* Moberly, *Address*, p. 13.

106 *6* *CPR Royal Commission*, Vol. 2, p. 1828, Moberly's deposition.

106 *12* Moberly, *Address*, p. 14.

106 *15* *Ibid.*, p. 15.

106 *16* *Ibid.*

106 *21* *Ibid.*

107 *1* *Hanington Papers*.

107 *2* Markwell.

107 *5* *Armstrong Manuscript*, p. 33.

107 *7* *Ibid.*, p. 97.

107 *10* *Rylatt Manuscript*, p. 20.

107 *13* *Fawcett Diary*, June 29, 1872

107 *16* *Hargreaves Diary*, July 3, 1872.

107 *19* *McLennan Papers*, Smith to McLennan, Aug. 23, 1872.

107 *20* *Marcus Smith Papers*, PAC, Letterbook, Vol. 6, Smith to Helmcken, Jan. 12, 1880; Letterbook, Vol. 4, Smith to J. H. Pope, July 20, 1883.

107 *21* *Ibid.*, Letterbook, Vol. 6, Smith to Brydges, Oct. 28, 1879.

107 *22* *Ibid.*, Letterbook, Vol. 4, Smith to Schultz, March 21, 1885.

107 *23* *Marcus Smith Papers*, PABC, Smith to Joseph Hunter, Feb. 23, 1885.

107 *23* Quoted in Fleming, *Letter to Secretary of State*, pp.

page *line*

24–5, Smith to Fleming, March 24, 1875.

107 *25* *Marcus Smith Papers*, PAC, Letterbook, Vol. 5, Smith to Fleming, Dec. 28, 1877.

107 *26* *Ibid.*, Smith to Helmcken, May 25, 1877.

107 *27* *Ibid.*, Letterbook, Vol. 6, Smith to Helmcken, Jan. 12, 1880.

108 *19* Fleming, *CPR Report, 1874*, App. E, p. 109, by Marcus Smith.

108 *28* *Marcus Smith Papers*, PABC, *Diary*, July 20, 1873.

108 *32* *Ibid.*, June 25, 1872.

109 *4* Fleming, *CPR Report, 1874*, App. E, p. 120.

109 *29* *Marcus Smith Papers*, PAC, Autobiographical note, Manuscript Group 29, A19, Vol. 12.

109 *34* *Hargreaves Diary*, July 3, 1872.

109 *42* *Ibid.*, June 23, 1872.

110 *13* *Ibid.*, Oct. 30, 1872.

110 *17* *Ibid.*, June 23, 1872.

110 *22* *Ibid.*, June 26, 1872.

110 *25* *Ibid.*, July 3, 1872.

110 *32* *Ibid.*, July 5, 1872.

110 *36* *Fawcett Diary*, June 29, 1872.

111 *5* *Hargreaves Diary*, June 23, 1872.

111 *12* *Marcus Smith Papers*, PAC, Letterbook, Vol. 5, Smith to Helmcken, Dec. 8, 1876.

111 *21* *Fawcett Diary*, June 16, 1872.

111 *24* *Ibid.*, June 22, 1872.

111 *26* *Ibid.*, June 29, 1872.

111 *30* *Hargreaves Diary*, Sept. 12, 1872.

112 *3* *Marcus Smith Papers*, PABC, *Diary*, July 13, 1872.

112 *13* *Ibid.*, Aug. 11, 1872.

112 *18* *Ibid.*, Smith to Hunter, July 8, 1875.

112 *32* Fleming, *CPR Report, 1877*, App. 1, pp. 164–5, by Marcus Smith.

112 *39* *Ibid.*, p. 166.

CHAPTER 5

114 *2* Preston, *My Generation*, p. 112.

114 *6* *Bryce Papers*, James M.

Coyne to Bryce, Sept. 9, 1915.

115 *16* Goldwin Smith, *Reminiscences*, p. 436.

115 *18* De Kiewiet and Underhill, p. 13, Dufferin to Carnarvon, March 18, 1874.

115 *40* Willison, p. 19.

116 *29* Josephson, p. 169.

117 *12* *Hansard*, p. 1715, April 23, 1877.

117 *13* De Kiewiet and Underhill, p. 259, Dufferin to Carnarvon, Sept. 24, 1876.

117 *18* Quoted in Grant and Hamilton, p. 137.

117 *33* Fleming, *CPR Report, 1874*, p. 23.

117 *35* *Ibid.*, p. 153.

117 *38* *Ibid.*

117 *39* De Kiewiet and Underhill, p. 267, Dufferin to Carnarvon, Oct. 8, 1876.

118 *39* Fleming, *CPR Report, 1877*, p. 19.

119 *32* *Edgar Papers*, Mackenzie to Edgar, Feb. 21, 1874.

119 *34* *Mackenzie Papers*, Letterbook, Vol. 11, Mackenzie to Holton, Sept. 26, 1876.

122 *5* Blake.

122 *23* *Order in Council*, App. A.

123 *6* De Kiewiet and Underhill, p. 232, Dufferin to Carnarvon, May 26, 1876.

123 *18* Pope, *Correspondence*, p. 177, Macdonald to Lord Lisgar, Sept. 2, 1872.

123 *22* De Kiewiet and Underhill, p. 232, Dufferin to Carnarvon, May 26, 1876.

123 *28* Marchioness of Dufferin, *Journal*.

124 *2* Smith, *Reminiscences*, p. 458.

124 *20* De Kiewiet and Underhill, p. 264, Dufferin to Carnarvon, Oct. 8, 1876.

124 *26* *Ibid.*, p. 238, Dufferin to Carnarvon, June 1, 1876.

124 *33* *Ibid.*, p. 274, Dufferin to Carnarvon, Oct. 8, 1876.

124 *37* *Mackenzie Papers*, Littleton to Mackenzie, Aug. 27, 1876.

124 *41* De Kiewiet and Underhill, p. 274, Dufferin to Carnarvon, Oct. 8, 1876.

125 *9* *Ibid.*, p. 261.

page *line*

125 *15* *Ibid.*
125 *21* *Ibid.*, p. 331, Dufferin to Carnarvon, Jan. 19, 1877.
125 *36* *Ibid.*, p. 310, Dufferin to Carnarvon, Nov. 23, 1876.
125 *42* *Dufferin Papers*, Mackenzie to Dufferin, Nov. 19, 1876.
126 *23* Fleming, *CPR Report*, 1877, p. 74.
126 *37* Burpee, p. 8.
127 *11* *Fleming Papers*, Vol. 50, Fleming to Tupper, Feb. 9, 1880.
127 *35* Fleming, *CPR Report*, 1877, App. "I", p. 169, by Marcus Smith.
127 *42* *Marcus Smith Papers*, PAC, Letterbook, Vol. 5, Smith to Mackenzie, April 17, 1877.
128 *8* *Ibid.*, Smith to Cambie, May 22, 1877.
128 *13* *Mackenzie Papers*, Film M.199, Robson to Mackenzie, Sept. 26, 1879.
128 *19* *Marcus Smith Papers*, PAC, Letterbook, Vol. 5, Smith to Hunter, Dec. 7, 1877.
128 *30* *Ibid.*, Smith to Fleming, Dec. 7, 1877.
128 *32* *Ibid.*
128 *41* *Ibid.*
129 *17* *Ibid.*, Smith to Helmcken, Dec. 7, 1877.
129 *32* *Ibid.*, April 22, 1878.
130 *5* *Public Accounts Committee*, p. 121, Rowan's testimony.
130 *7* *Ibid.*, p. 117, Fleming's testimony.
130 *16* *CPR Royal Commission*, Vol. 2, p. 1628, Fleming's testimony.
130 *25* *Marcus Smith Papers*, PAC, Letterbook, Vol. 5, Smith to Helmcken, May 25, 1877.
130 *33* Fleming, *CPR Report*, 1878, pp. 13–14.
130 *42* *Marcus Smith Papers*, PAC, Letterbook, Vol. 6, Smith to Helmcken, Jan. 12, 1880.

CHAPTER 6

131 *23* Ham, p. 44.
133 *6* Healy.
134 *27* Willson, p. 153.
134 *39* *Nor'wester*, May 17, 1875.
135 *21* Ham, p. 29.
135 *34* McWilliams, pp. 161–2.

page *line*

137 *17* Rutledge, April 1, 1920, p. 73.
138 *14* Mitchell, p. 21.
138 *33* *Globe*, June 10, 1875.
138 *37* *Ibid.*
139 *11* *Ibid.*
139 *32* *Ibid.*
140 *17* *Mail*, Sept. 3, 1877.
140 *23* Biggar, p. 170.
140 *34* *CPR Royal Commission*, Vol. 3, pp. 139–48.
142 *19* *Senate Committee*, 1878, p. vii.
142 *30* *CPR Royal Commission*, Vol. 1, pp. 657–9, J. S. Caddy's testimony.
142 *30* *Hansard*, 1877, p. 1725.
143 *13* *CPR Royal Commission*, compiled from evidence.
143 *18* Willison, p. 36.
145 *29* *Nor'wester*, Sept. 6, 1875.
145 *35* *CPR Royal Commission*, Vol. 3, p. 245.
146 *8* *Ibid.*, p. 236, Whitehead to Mackenzie, Nov. 28, 1876.
146 *13* *CPR Royal Commission*, Vol. 1, p. 220, Whitehead's testimony.
146 *26* *Ibid.*, Vol. 3, p. 242.
146 *33* *Ibid.*, p. 241, also Vol. 1, pp. 221–2, Whitehead's testimony.
146 *41* *Ibid.*
146 *42* *Ibid.*, Vol. 1, p. 227, Whitehead's testimony.
147 *21* *Ibid.*, Vol. 2, p. 1351, Fleming's testimony.
148 *28* Willson, pp. 34–5.
148 *34* Bernard.
149 *15* MacKay, p. 302.
150 *14* *Hansard*, 1878, Vol. 2, p. 1675.
150 *21* *Ibid.*, p. 1682.
150 *29* *Ibid.*, p. 1689.
150 *36* *Ibid.*, pp. 1690–1.
150 *39* *Ibid.*, p. 1691.
151 *7* *Ibid.*, p. 2556.
151 *11* *Ibid.*, pp. 2558 to 2564.
151 *38* Preston, *Strathcona*, p. 108.
152 *38* *Ibid.*, p. 112.
153 *1* Ross, George, p. 100.

CHAPTER 7

154 *19* Pope, *Public Servant*, p. 36.
155 *4* *Ibid.*, *Memoirs*, Vol. 2, p. 202.
155 *24* *Dufferin Papers*, Dufferin to

page *line*

Sir Michael Hicks-Beach, Sept. 20, 1878.

155 *26* *Ibid.*, Sept. 28, 1878.

155 *27* *Edgar Papers*, Mackenzie to Edgar, Sept. 24, 1878.

155 *38* Biggar, p. 202.

156 *2* *Ibid.*, p. 203.

156 *27* Quoted in Porritt, p. 247.

156 *41* Pope, *Correspondence*, p. 240.

157 *10* *Hansard*, 1879, p. 1909.

157 *22* *Ibid.*, p. 1893.

157 *30* *Ibid.*, p. 1892.

157 *38* *Tupper Papers*, Vol. 5, Memorandum, Department Railways and Canals, March 4, 1880.

158 *6* *CPR Royal Commission*, Vol. 2, p. 1020, Vol. 3, pp. 443, 448.

158 *20* *Marcus Smith Papers*, PAC, Letterbook, Vol. 5, p. 26, Confidential Memo: Location of the Canadian Pacific Railway, Jan. 20, 1879.

158 *21* *Ibid.*, Smith to Tupper, Jan. 23, 1879.

158 *26* *Ibid.*, Smith to Macdonald, May 12, 1879.

158 *37* *Ibid.*, Vol. 6, Smith to Brydges, Nov. 4, 1879.

159 *1* *Ibid.*, Smith to Macpherson, Oct. 27, 1879.

159 *5* *Ibid.*, Smith to Hewson, Oct. 30, 1879.

159 *9* *Hansard*, 1880, p. 52.

160 *23* *CPR Royal Commission*, Vol. 3, p. 70.

160 *27* *Ibid.*, p. 711.

160 *36* *Ibid.*, p. 78.

161 *8* *Select Committee*, *1879*, pp. xii and xiii.

161 *16* *CPR Royal Commission*, Vol. 2, p. 1711, Horetzky's testimony.

161 *21* *Fleming Papers*, Folder 162, Horetzky to Fleming, Sept. 24, 1880.

161 *25* Fleming, *Letter to Secretary of State*, App. 3, p. 25.

162 *23* *Armstrong Manuscript*, p. 73, Aug. 14, 1931.

163 *27* *Ibid.*, pp. 77, 79.

164 *42* *CPR Royal Commission*, Vol. 1, p. 161.

165 *10* *Sentinel*, Nov. 5, 1880.

165 *18* *CPR Royal Commission*, Vol. 1, p. 543, Kirkpatrick's testimony.

page *line*

165 *42* Keefer, *Address.*

166 *16* *Armstrong Manuscript*, p. 109.

166 *37* *Ibid.*

166 *41* *Sentinel*, Nov. 12, 1880.

167 *2* *Times*, July 20, 1880.

167 *10* *Ibid.*, Sept. 4, 1880.

167 *25* Rutledge, April 15, 1920, p. 21.

167 *33* *Ibid.*

168 *34* *Ibid.*

168 *42* *Ibid.*

170 *14* Fleming, *England and Canada*, p. 173.

170 *28* Fitzgibbon, pp. 163–4.

170 *41* *Times*, Aug. 2, 1881.

171 *4* Rutledge, April 15, 1920, p. 66.

171 *14* *Sentinel*, Aug. 8, 1877.

171 *35* *Globe*, Sept. 24, 1883.

172 *29* *Armstrong Manuscript*, p. 101.

173 *23* Rutledge, April 15, 1920, pp. 22 and 66.

173 *40* *Armstrong Manuscript*, p. 85.

174 *8* *Times*, Dec. 29, 1880.

174 *27* *Ibid.*, Aug. 14, 1880.

174 *29* *Globe*, Sept. 24, 1883.

174 *38* *Ibid.*

175 *2* *Times*, Nov. 8, 1880.

175 *17* *Ibid.*, Aug. 14, 1880.

177 *4* *Ibid.*

177 *10* *Ibid.*

177 *29* Hughes, p. 250.

177 *31* *Ibid.*, p. 251.

177 *38* *Ibid.*, p. 252.

178 *13* *Ibid.*, p. 256.

178 *18* Breton, p. 78.

CHAPTER 8

181 *16* Myers, *American Fortunes*, p. 672.

181 *29* Pyle, Vol. 1, p. 164.

183 *7* *Ibid.*, p. 114.

186 *22* *Farley vs. Kittson et al.*, p. 572, Hill's testimony.

187 *14* *Ibid.*, p. 1488, Saunders's evidence.

188 *30* *Ibid.*, p. 1318, Newel's evidence.

189 *8* *Ibid.*, p. 826, Hill's testimony.

189 *24* *Ibid.*, p. 1139, Smith's testimony.

189 *27* *Ibid.*, pp. 1227–8, Stephen's testimony.

189 *32* *Ibid.*, p. 1229.

page *line*

191 *11* Gilbert, p. 7.
191 *24* Collard, p. 186.
191 *34* Pyle, Vol. 1, p. 203.
192 *40* Creighton, *Old Chieftain*, p. 305.
193 *19* Gilbert, p. 17.
194 *36* *Macdonald Papers*, Vol. 271, Stephen to Macdonald, June 4, 1889.
195 *11* *Farley vs. Kittson et al.*, p. 944, Defendant's Exhibit No. 39, Stephen to Hill, Jan. 17, 1879.
196 *15* Pyle, Vol. 1, p. 206.
196 *20* Gibbon, p. 193.
196 *22* Pyle, Vol. 1, p. 206.
198 *9* *Farley vs. Kittson et al.*, p. 1192, Smith's testimony.
198 *26* *Circuit Court, Judgement of July 15, 1882.*
198 *31* *Farley vs. Kittson et al.*, p. 1785, Opinion of Judge Brewer, Sept. 13, 1889.
199 *6* *Ibid.*, 317, Complainant's Exhibit No. 162, Kennedy to Farley, Feb. 25, 1878.
200 *3* Gilbert, p. 49.
200 *23* *Farley vs. Kittson et al.*, p. 919, Defendant's Exhibit No. 20, Stephen to Hill, Feb. 10, 1878.
200 *29* *Ibid.*, p. 631, Hill's testimony.
201 *41* Pyle, Vol. 1, p. 256.
203 *32* Myers, *Canadian Wealth*, p. 257.
204 *3* *Bryce Papers*, James M. Coyne to Bryce, Sept. 9, 1915, reporting Smith's remarks to Winnipeg Canadian Club.
204 *15* Moody, p. 170.
204 *21* Pyle, Vol. 1, p. 303.
205 *6* Skelton, *Railway Builders*, p. 139.

CHAPTER 9

207 *18* Willson, *Lord Strathcona*, pp. 204–5.
207 *23* Fleming, *CPR Report, 1880*, App. 23, p. 353, Tupper to Fleming, April 15, 1880.
207 *24* *Ibid.*, p. 354.
207 *41* *Tupper Papers*, Vol. 5, Memorandum dated June 15, 1880.
208 *4* *Campbell Papers*, Campbell to D. O. Mills, Aug. 2, 1880.

208 *35* *Macdonald Papers*, Vol. 127, McIntyre to Macdonald, July 5, 1880.
208 *39* Collins, p. 177.
209 *15* *Macdonald Papers*, Vol. 267, Stephen to Macdonald, July 9, 1880.
210 *22* *Campbell Papers*, Onderdonk to Campbell, Aug. 3, 1880.
210 *33* Saunders, p. 286.
211 *21* *Macdonald Papers*, Vol. 267, Stephen to Macdonald, Sept. 27, 1880.
211 *28* *Ibid.*
211 *34* *Free Press*, Manitoba, Sept. 7, 1880.
211 *36* *Daily Witness*, Sept. 23, 1880.
212 *7* Quoted in *Free Press*, Ottawa, Oct. 2, 1880.
212 *40* *Mail*, Sept. 27, 1880.
213 *2* *Times*, Sept. 27, 1880.
213 *16* Biggar, p. 218.
214 *9* Preston, *Strathcona*, p. 132.
214 *21* *Macdonald Papers*, Vol. 267, Stephen to Macdonald, Dec. 16, 1880.
214 *27* *Ibid.*, Vol. 259, Morton, Rose & Co. to Sir John Rose, July 6, 1883.
214 *33* *Ibid.*, Vol. 267, Stephen to Macdonald, Dec. 16, 1880.
214 *42* *Ibid.*, Oct. 9, 1880.
215 *7* *Ibid.*, Oct. 18, 1880.
215 *22* *Ibid.*, Nov. 13, 1880.
215 *24* *Ibid.*
216 *2* *Free Press*, Ottawa, Dec. 20, 1880.
216 *5* *Daily Witness*, Dec. 13, 1880.
216 *6* Quoted in *Times*, Dec. 14, 1880.
216 *6* Quoted in *Times*, Dec. 24, 1880.
217 *18* Quoted in Hutchison, p. 941.
217 *22* *Free Press*, Ottawa, Dec. 20, 1880.
217 *28* *Macdonald Papers*, Vol. 267, Stephen to Rt. Hon. W. E. Forster, Feb. 22, 1881.
217 *40* *Globe*, Jan. 5, 1881.
218 *27* *Free Press*, Ottawa, Dec. 13, 1880.
219 *19* Lyall, Vol. 1, p. 215.
219 *30* *Free Press*, Ottawa, Dec. 6, 1880.
220 *11* *Citizen*, Dec. 9, 1880.

page *line*

220 *36* *Hansard*, 1880–81, p. 2, Dec. 9.
221 *36* *Macdonald Papers*, Vol. 267, Stephen to Macdonald, Dec. 16, 1880.
222 *6* *Hansard*, 1880–81, p. 50.
222 *18* Ross, George, p. 116.
222 *37* *Hansard*, 1880–81, p. 74.
223 *4* *Ibid.*, p. 75.
223 *12* *Ibid.*, p. 142.
223 *19* *Daily Witness*, Dec. 18, 1880.
224 *41* *Hansard*, 1880–81, p. 302.
225 *32* *Ibid.*, p. 281.
225 *38* Ross, George, p. 119.
226 *5* Pope, *Correspondence*, p. 277.
226 *9* Saunders, p. 294.
226 *16* *Free Press*, Ottawa, Jan. 8, 1881.
226 *29* *Mail*, Jan. 15, 1881.
226 *35* *Hansard*, 1880–81, p. 398.
228 *10* *Ibid.*, p. 488.
229 *20* Macdonald's speech runs from p. 485 to p. 495 in *Hansard*, 1880–81.
229 *25* *Canadian Illustrated News*, Jan. 29, 1881.
230 *5* *Hansard*, 1880–81, pp. 495 to 518, Blake's speech.
234 *16* *Ibid.*, p. 708.
234 *11* Quoted *Free Press*, Ottawa, Jan. 29, 1881.
234 *12* *Ibid.*, Jan. 21, 1881.
235 *4* *Free Press*, Ottawa, Feb. 1, 1881.

CHAPTER 10

238 *19* *Free Press*, Ottawa, Feb. 18, 1881.
238 *21* *Tupper Papers*, Vol. 5, Tupper to Macdonald, July [n.d.], 1881.
238 *23* *Ibid.*, Tupper to Macdonald, March 31, 1881.
238 *27* *Free Press*, Ottawa, June 24, 1882.
242 *6* J. A. Chapleau, *Hansard*, 1885, p. 2566.
242 *24* Macoun does not name them but it is clear from newspaper accounts that Stephen and Angus were both in St. Paul in May just before Macoun went north.
243 *2* Macoun, *Autobiography*, p. 182.
243 *30* *Taylor Papers*, Microfilm

Roll M-118, Taylor to R. B. Angus, Nov. 20, 1880.
243 *39* *Ibid.*
244 *28* Macoun, *Autobiography*, p. 185.
245 *23* *Hansard*, 1882, p. 953.
246 *3* *Ibid.*, p. 974.
246 *14* *Globe*, Jan. 3, 1882.
246 *31* See Pyle, Vol. 1, pp. 299–300.
246 *42* Macoun, *Autobiography*, p. 185.
249 *10* Edward Blake, *Hansard*, 1885, p. 2600.
249 *33* Hedges, p. 90.
250 *12* See Roe, "Early Opinions."
250 *29* *Times*, March 24, 1881.
252 *12* Secretan, p. 127.
252 *16* Shaw and Hull, p. 89.
252 *21* Trotter and Hawkes, p. 89.
253 *30* *Ibid.*, p. 160.
253 *40* *Ibid.*, p. 169.
254 *17* *Ibid.*, p. 159.
254 *37* *Ibid.*, p. 157.
255 *30* Secretan, pp. 133–5.
255 *37* Kavanagh, p. 115.
255 *39* *Ibid.*, p. 116.
256 *2* Shaw and Hull, p. 89.
258 *30* Quoted in *Free Press*, Ottawa, March 3, 1881.
259 *32* *Macdonald Papers*, Vol. 267, Stephen to Macdonald, Dec. 13, 1881.
259 *34* *Ibid.*, Dec. 10, 1881.
260 *34* *Ibid.*, Dec. 20, 1881.
261 *11* *Ibid.*
261 *41* *Ibid.*, Vol. 524, Macdonald to Stephen, Oct. 19, 1881.
262 *8* *Ibid.*, Vol. 267, Stephen to Macdonald, Sept. 12, 1882.
262 *39* *Ibid.*, Aug. 27, 1881.
263 *9* *Ibid.*, Nov. 5, 1881.
263 *23* *Ibid.*, Nov. 4, 1881.
263 *37* Pyle, Vol. 1, p. 318, Hill to Angus, July, 1880.
263 *40* Pearce Memo.
264 *15* Vaughan, p. 74.
264 *22* Tupper in *Hansard*, 1882, p. 1007.
265 *7* Vaughan, p. 148.
265 *30* *A Year in Manitoba*, p. 72.
265 *32* *Free Press*, Manitoba, Aug. 6, 1881.
265 *37* Miller, *Diary*, p. 65.
265 *42* *Free Press*, Manitoba, Oct. 8, 1881.
266 *4* *Ibid.*, Sept. 15, 1881.
266 *14* *Ibid.*, Aug. 10, 1881.
266 *30* Vaughan, p. 62.

page *line*

267 9   *Ibid.*, pp. 108-9.
267 14 Pearce Memo.
267 35 Vaughan, p. 75.

CHAPTER 11

269 7   *Free Press*, Manitoba, Jan. 2, 1882.
269 20 *Times*, Jan. 26, 1882.
269 21 *Globe*, Jan. 19, 1882.
269 23 *Ibid.*, March 3, 1882.
270 10 *Times*, March 23, 1882.
270 13 *Globe*, April 29, 1882.
270 26 Quoted in *Times*, Feb. 3, 1882.
270 30 *Sentinel*, Nov. 11, 1881.
270 36 *Globe*, Jan. 18, 1882.
270 41 Quoted in *Times*, Feb. 7, 1882.
271 15 *Sentinel*, Nov. 11, 1881.
271 28 *Times*, Sept. 16, 1881.
271 34 Armstrong Manuscript, p. 121.
271 40 *Sun*, Winnipeg, Feb. 24, 1882.
272 3   *Ibid.*
272 6   *Ibid.*, March 16, 1882.
272 20 Ham, pp. 51-2.
272 23 *Times*, Feb. 7, 1882.
272 25 *Ibid.*
272 34 Trotter and Hawkes, p. 229.
272 39 Quoted in *Times*, Sept. 26, 1881.
273 2   *Globe*, Feb. 10, 1882.
273 9   Tway thesis.
273 21 *Globe*, Feb. 2, 1882.
273 33 *Ibid.*, March 3, 1882.
273 35 *Ibid.*, Feb. 24, 1882.
273 37 *Sun*, Winnipeg, Feb. 20, 1882.
274 3   *Times*, Feb. 27, 1882.
274 9   Ham, p. 51.
274 23 McLagan, p. 519.
274 31 *Globe*, March 3, 1882.
275 4   Steele, *Forty Years in Canada*, p. 164.
275 27 *Sun*, Winnipeg, Feb. 24, 1882.
275 34 *Globe*, Feb. 10, 1882.
276 10 *Sun*, Winnipeg, May 12, 1882.
276 18 *Times*, March 3, 1882.
276 22 *Sun*, Winnipeg, March 7, 1882.
276 26 *Times*, Feb. 21, 1882.
276 30 *Ibid.*, Feb. 16, 1882.
276 41 *Globe*, March 13, 1883.
277 15 White.

277 22 *Times*, Sept. 16, 1881.
277 26 Quoted in *Times*, Sept. 26, 1881.
277 29 McWilliams, p. 128.
278 5   *Sun*, Winnipeg, Feb. 24, 1882.
278 15 *Globe*, March 13, 1882.
278 27 *Ibid.*, Feb. 10, 1882.
278 30 *Times*, Feb. 7, 1882.
278 39 *Ibid.*, June 14, 1882.
278 41 *Ibid.*, Jan. 28, 1882.
278 42 Quoted in *Sun*, Winnipeg, March 7, 1882.
279 5   *Ibid.*, March 23, 1882.
279 13 *Globe*, March 17, 1882.
279 24 Trotter and Hawkes, p. 91.
279 29 *Ibid.*, p. 221.
279 34 *Globe*, March 21, 1882.
279 38 *Ibid.*, March 3, 1882.
279 40 *Ibid.*, April 11, 1882.
280 12 *Times*, May 19, 1882.
280 40 *Ibid.*, Nov. 13, 1882.
281 8   *Globe*, March 28, 1882.
281 14 *Ibid.*
281 17 *St. Paul Pioneer Press*, quoted in *Times*, March 23, 1882.
282 32 Trotter and Hawkes, p. 94.
282 37 *Ibid.*, p. 95.
282 40 *Globe*, Feb. 1, 1882.
282 42 *Times*, Feb. 28, 1882.
283 8   Hill, *Manitoba*, pp. 432-3.
283 15 *Ibid.*
283 33 *Times*, May 30, 1882.
283 38 *Bulletin*, April 29, 1882.
283 42 *Times*, Feb. 27, 1882.
285 1   *Globe*, Jan. 4, 1882.
285 9   *Ibid.*, Feb. 1, 1882.
285 20 *Times*, Feb. 11, 1882.
286 3   White.
286 37 Quoted in *Times*, March 25, 1882.
286 39 *Ibid.*
287 21 *Globe*, April 4, 1882.
287 35 *Times*, April 12, 1882.
287 37 *Ibid.*, April 13, 1882.
288 6   *Bulletin*, April 29, 1882.
288 7   *Times*, April 13, 1882.
289 4   *Globe*, April 20, 1882.
289 38 McWilliams, p. 128.
290 6   Hill, *Manitoba*, p. 449.
290 10 Armstrong Manuscript, p. 121.
290 13 *Globe*, April 11, 1882.
290 28 Hill, *Manitoba*, p. 445.
290 17 *Ibid.*, p. 448.
290 29 *Ibid.*, p. 449.
290 41 Ham, p. 31.

page *line*

CHAPTER 12

page *line*

Stephen to Macdonald,
Feb. 26, 1882.
323 27 *Ibid.*, Vol. 267, Stephen to
Macdonald, Jan. 23, 1881.
323 32 CPR *Reports*, 1881–89, p.
21, Shareholders' Proceedings, May 10, 1882.
324 28 *Macdonald Papers*, Vol. 268,
Stephen to Macdonald,
Aug. 27, 1882.
324 31 *Ibid.*, Sept. 29, 1882.
324 34 *Ibid.*, Oct. 5, 1882.
324 38 *Ibid.*, Macdonald to Stephen,
Oct. 20, 1882.
325 1 *Ibid.*, Stephen to Macdonald,
Nov. 21, 1882.
325 3 Hedges, p. 37.
325 13 *Sessional Paper*, No. 31A,
1884, pp. 99–105.
325 15 *Macdonald Papers*, Vol. 159,
Rose to Macdonald,
Feb. 1, 1883.
325 18 *Ibid.*, Vol. 259, Rose to
Macdonald, Jan. 18, 1883.
325 25 *Sessional Paper*, No. 31A,
1884, pp. 225–33.
325 32 *Ibid.*
326 13 *Macdonald Papers*, Vol. 268,
Stephen to Macdonald,
Jan. 4, 1883.
326 18 Taché, p. 453.
326 26 Stevens, *Canadian National
Railways*, Vol. 1, p. 332.
326 33 Taché, p. 452.
327 3 Lovett, p. 114.
327 28 *Hickson Papers*, Macdonald
to Hickson, June 17, 1882.
327 31 *Ibid.*, June 20, 1882.
327 33 *Ibid.*, Aug. 14, 1882.
327 37 *Ibid.*, Hickson to
Macdonald, Oct. 9, 1882.
328 21 *Macdonald Papers*, Vol. 268,
Stephen to Macdonald,
Jan. 4, 1883.
328 23 *Ibid.*, Feb. 1, 1883.
328 29 *Ibid.*, Vol. 277, clipping:
Money Market Review,
Feb. 2, 1883.
329 3 *Van Horne Letterbooks*,
No. 9, Van Horne to
Hickson, Dec. 22, 1884.
329 9 *Ibid.*, No. 12, Van Horne to
Begg, June 22, 1885.

CHAPTER 13

331 32 *Secretan*, p. 187.
331 34 Wilson Manuscript, p. 17.

page *line*

332 1 McKelvie, "Thousands of
Last Spikes."
332 5 McKelvie, "They Routed
the Rockies."
332 7 Stevens, *An Engineer's
Recollections*, p. 7.
332 12 *Ibid.*, pp. 12–13.
332 22 Secretan, p. 192.
332 39 Wilson Manuscript, p. 22.
333 15 *Ibid.*
334 3 Moberly, *Journals*, 1866,
p. 15.
334 10 Rogers, p. 418.
334 24 Minneapolis *Tribune*,
quoted in *Times*, March 15,
1882.
335 8 Rogers, p. 419.
335 13 Grant, *Week*, March 6, 1884.
336 10 Rogers, p. 420.
336 31 *Ibid.*, p. 421.
336 35 Flaherty.
336 40 Wilson Manuscript, p. 11.
340 4 *Ibid.*
340 25 *Ibid.*, p. 17.
341 4 *Ibid.*
341 21 *Ibid.*, p. 21.
342 8 *Ibid.*, p. 23.
342 24 *Ibid.*, p. 24.
342 33 *Ibid.*
343 32 *Ibid.*, p. 27.
344 40 *Ibid.*, p. 4.
345 40 *Ibid.*, p. 5.
346 12 Secretan, p. 189.
346 27 Wilson Manuscript, p. 30.
346 32 *Ibid.*
347 13 Grant, "The Canada Pacific
Railway," p. 886.
347 36 Grant, *Week*, May 1, 1884,
p. 341.
348 25 CPR Archives, Rogers to
Van Horne, Jan. 10, 1883.
349 1 Quoted on Canadian Pacific
Railway Company, Souvenir
Menu.
349 22 Wilson Manuscript, p. 41.
349 41 *Ibid.*, p. 42.
350 9 *Ibid.*
351 22 *Ibid.*, pp. 48–9.
351 31 *Ibid.*, p. 57.
352 8 *Ibid.*, pp. 57–8.
352 20 Gilbert, pp. 101–2.
352 29 Vaughan, p. 82.
353 20 *Van Horne Letterbooks*,
No. 7, Van Horne to
Onderdonk, Sept. 10, 1884.
353 29 *Ibid.*, No. 1, Van Horne to
A. B. Rogers, Feb. 6, 1883.
354 8 Shaw and Hull, p. 70.
354 31 Vaughan, p. 81.

page *line*

355 3 Shaw and Hull, p. 139.
355 32 Secretan, p. 105.
355 42 Shaw and Hull, p. 149.
357 5 *Ibid.*, p. 150.
357 10 *Ibid.*, p. 154.
357 18 See, for example, Shaw, "A Prairie Gopher Makes Reply."
357 31 Shaw and Hull, p. 155.
357 40 Moberly, *Rocks and Rivers*, p. 102.
358 2 Robinson and Moberly, p. 73.
358 22 Fleming, *England and Canada*, p. 244.
358 26 *Ibid.*, p. 229.
358 28 *Ibid.*, p. 244.
358 38 Roberts, *The Western Avernus*, p. 83.
359 20 Fleming, *England and Canada*, pp. 248–9.
359 26 *Ibid.*, p. 258.
359 30 *Ibid.*, p. 249.
360 13 Grant and Hamilton, p. 254.
360 37 Grant, "The Canada Pacific Railway," p. 887.
361 7 Fleming, *England and Canada*, p. 270.
361 13 Grant, "The Canada Pacific Railway," p. 887.
361 23 Grant, *Week*, May 22, 1884, p. 391.
362 16 Wilson Manuscript, p. 64.
362 31 *Ibid.*, p. 67.

CHAPTER 14

364 27 Evans Memorandum.
364 31 Vincent Memorandum.
364 36 Cambie to Fairbairn.
364 37 Robinson and Moberly, p. 105.
365 8 Parker, p. 353.
365 12 Vincent Memorandum.
365 17 Cambie to Fairbairn.
365 20 Parker, p. 353.
365 24 Weekes to Miller.
367 15 Clews, p. 457.
367 42 *Globe*, Feb. 16, 1882.
368 2 *Ibid.*, Feb. 4, 1882.
368 6 Robinson and Moberly, p. 105.
369 10 Parker, p. 353.
370 20 *Inland Sentinel*, Dec. 7, 1882.
371 40 *Ibid.*, Sept. 2, 1880.
372 3 Parker, p. 354.
373 19 Rutledge, May 1, 1920.

page *line*

373 14 *Inland Sentinel*, Aug. 4, 1881.
373 32 Quoted in *British Colonist*, April 13, 1880.
374 15 *Times*, April 30, 1879.
374 18 *Hansard*, 1882, p. 1477.
374 21 *Ibid.*
374 26 Cambie, "Reminiscences," p. 473.
374 41 *Inland Sentinel*, advertisement, March 31, 1881.
375 1 *Ibid.*, April 7, 1881.
375 7 *Ibid.*, Aug. 30, 1883.
375 14 Rutledge, May 1, 1920.
375 20 *Report of Royal Commission on Chinese Immigration*, 1885, p. cxxx.
375 28 Cambie to Fairbairn.
375 30 *Globe*, May 11, 1882.
376 29 Rutledge, May 1, 1920.
376 37 Pugsley, June 15, 1930.
377 5 *Ibid.*
377 14 *Inland Sentinel*, Nov. 30, 1882.
377 21 *Ibid.*, May 17, 1883.
377 30 *Report of Royal Commission on Chinese Immigration*, 1885, p. lxxxiv.
377 37 *Inland Sentinel*, Aug. 17, 1882.
377 42 *Ibid.*, Feb. 22, 1883.
378 18 *Ibid.*, Dec. 14, 1882.
379 1 Rutledge, May 1, 1920.
379 23 *Ibid.*
379 29 *Inland Sentinel*, May 5, 1881.
379 37 *Cambie Diary*, Nov. 22, 1880.
380 13 *Report of Royal Commission on Chinese Immigration*, 1885, Huang Sic Chan's testimony, p. 366.
381 16 *Marcus Smith Papers*, PAC, Letterbook No. 4, Smith to Onderdonk, June 5, 1883.
381 31 *Ibid.*
382 32 Rutledge, May 1, 1920.
383 17 *Colonist*, March 4, 1880.
383 20 *Inland Sentinel*, Jan. 13, 1881.
384 18 Kennedy, "When History Was A-Making," p. 45.
385 12 *Inland Sentinel*, Feb. 3, 1881
385 21 *Ibid.*, May 3, 1883.
386 11 Parker, p. 356.
386 16 *Inland Sentinel*, Feb. 8, 1883.
386 21 *Ibid.*, Feb. 15, 1883.

page *line*

386 24 *Ibid.*, July 7, 1881.
386 33 *Ibid.*
386 41 Robinson and Moberly, p. 107.

CHAPTER 15

389 18 "The Good Old Days of Broadview."
391 6 Oliver.
391 18 *Ibid.*
391 31 *Gazette*, Fort McLeod, Jan. 13, 1883.
391 32 *News*, July 4, 1884.
393 12 *Quarterly Review*, Jan. 1887, pp. 129–30.
394 2 Stanley, *Birth of Western Canada*, p. 218.
394 33 Stobie, p. 6.
395 3 *Globe*, May 4, 1883.
395 29 Haydon, pp. 105–6.
396 17 Breton, p. 87.
396 33 Van Horne, Preface to Hughes, p. vi.
397 38 Breton, p. 88.
398 1 *Gazette*, Fort McLeod, May 24, 1883.
398 21 Boulton, *Adventures*, p. 30.
398 30 *Quarterly Review*, Jan. 1887, p. 136.
399 13 *Leader*, Regina, Aug. 30, 1883.
399 29 *Herald*, Calgary, Oct. 1, 1884.
399 33 *News*, Jan. 18, 1884.
400 8 *Globe*, April 25, 1885.
400 32 Powers, p. 27.
400 35 Steele, *Forty Years in Canada*, p. 177.
401 2 Donkin, pp. 14–15.
401 15 *Ibid.*, p. 20.
401 27 *Globe*, April 25, 1885.
401 31 *Gazette*, Fort McLeod, Jan. 13, 1883.
401 35 Donkin, p. 16.
402 11 *Leader*, Regina, Aug. 16, 1883.
402 27 Steele, *Forty Years in Canada*, p. 177.
402 32 Brooks, Part I, Brooks to wife, Aug. 23, 1882, p. 111.
402 42 *News*, Jan. 25, 1884.
404 36 *Gazette*, Fort McLeod, 1883.
405 2 *Herald*, Calgary, Dec. 26, 1883.
405 12 *Ibid.*, Jan. 2, 1884.
405 19 *Ibid.*, Feb. 13, 1884.
405 21 *Ibid.*, Feb. 20, 1884.

page *line*

406 10 Advertisement of T. E. Hanrahan & Co., *Globe*, July 4, 1883.
406 27 *Tupper Papers*, Vol. 5, Macdonald to Tupper, Nov. 22, 1883.
407 17 Vancouver *Province* clipping, 1932, quoting F. W. Peters, ex-General Superintendent, CPR, Vertical Files, PABC.
408 7 *Macdonald Papers*, Vol. 168, Stephen to Macdonald, Dec. 18, 1883.
408 15 *Ibid.*, Vol. 259, Rose to Macdonald, Dec. 29, 1883.
409 19 Skelton, *Life and Letters of Laurier*, Vol. 1, p. 273.
409 28 Pope, *Correspondence*, Macdonald to Tupper, Dec. 1, 1883, p. 308.
409 30 *Ibid.*, Tupper to Macdonald, Dec. 2, 1883, p. 308.
409 31 Harkin, p. 115.
409 32 *Macdonald Papers*, Vol. 268, Stephen to Macdonald, Dec. 15, 1883.
409 42 *Ibid.*, Dec. 23, 1883.
410 8 *Tupper Papers*, Vol. 5, Stephen to Tupper, Dec. 28, 1883.
410 9 *Ibid.*, Vol. 6, Jan. 5, 1884.
410 25 Tupper, *Hansard*, 1884, pp. 98–113.
411 39 *Sun*, Brandon, March 8, 1884.
412 15 *Macdonald Papers*, Vol. 268, Stephen to Macdonald, Jan. 22, 1884.
412 19 *Tupper Papers*, Vol. 6, Stephen to Tupper, Jan. 24, 1884.
412 23 *Leader*, Regina, June 7, 1883.
412 31 *Hansard*, 1885, p. 2618.
412 39 See *Sessional Paper* No. 31A for 1884, which gives Stephen's holdings in 1883 and 1884.
413 8 *Tupper Papers*, Vol. 6, Stephen to Tupper, Jan. 24, 1884.
413 17 *Ibid.*
413 30 *Sentinel*, Dec. 15, 1883.
414 11 Quoted in *Globe*, Aug. 10, 1883.
414 18 *Van Horne Letterbooks*, No. 1, Van Horne to W. Horder, April 9, 1883.

page *line*

414 *26* *Ibid.*, No. 4, Van Horne to John Ross, Feb. 23, 1884.
414 *32* *Ibid.*, No. 5, April 15, 1884.
415 *8* *Globe*, Feb. 1, 1884.
415 *23* *Macdonald Papers*, Vol. 268, Stephen to Macdonald, Feb. 10, 1884.
415 *36* *Globe*, Feb. 2, 1884.
416 *20* *Ibid.*, Feb. 26, 1884.
417 *3* Gibbon, p. 261.
417 *17* *Van Horne Letterbooks*, No. 5, Van Horne to Mitchell, April 21, 1884.
417 *21* Quoted in Waite, *Arduous Destiny*, from H. H. Smith Papers, Macdonald to Smith, March 3, 1884.
418 *3* *Macdonald Papers*, Vol. 269, Stephen to Macdonald, Feb. 27, 1884.
418 *22* *Globe*, March 8, 1884.
418 *30* *Stephen Papers*, Macdonald to Stephen, Nov. 26, 1883.
418 *35* *Tupper Papers*, Vol. 6, Macdonald to Tupper, June 28, 1884.

CHAPTER 16

419 *8* *Sentinel*, Oct. 31, 1884.
419 *16* Armstrong Manuscript, p. 133.
421 *29* *Adam Brown Papers*, "Trip to Pacific Coast by Canadian Pacific Railway, 1888," pp. 4–5.
422 *4* *Armstrong Manuscript*, p. 151.
422 *12* Macoun, *Autobiography*, p. 216.
422 *22* *Sentinel*, Jan. 14, 1885.
423 *32* *Van Horne Letterbooks*, No. 3, Van Horne to Harry Abbott, Sept. 21, 1883.
423 *34* *Ibid.*, No. 2, Van Horne to John Ross, Sept. 2, 1883.
424 *32* *Armstrong Manuscript*, pp. 145–7.
424 *41* *Ibid.*, p. 147.
425 *23* *Sentinel*, Nov. 8, 1884.
426 *19* *Ibid.*, Nov. 3, 1884.
429 *33* *Parliamentary Debates*, Fourth Session, Vol. 2, p. 745.
430 *22* *Free Press*, Manitoba, Oct. 3, 1884.
430 *34* Roberts, p. 57.
431 *8* Bone, p. 70.
431 *15* Roberts, p. 79.

page *line*

431 *28* *Ibid.*, p. 57.
432 *3* *Globe*, Aug. 22, 1884.
432 *8* *Tupper Papers*, Vol. 6, Schreiber to Tupper, Sept. 29, 1884.
432 *15* Roberts, p. 55.
432 *35* Buckingham and Ross, pp. 609–10.
433 *42* Roberts, p. 69.
434 *3* *Globe*, June 24, 1884.
434 *41* Stevens, *An Engineer's Recollections*, p. 12.
436 *25* *Van Horne Letterbooks*, No. 6, Van Horne to Minister of Railways and Canals, May 19, 1884.
438 *7* Carter, pp. 13031–2.
439 *28* *Herald*, Calgary, Nov. 15, 1884.
439 *37* MacBeth, p. 102.
440 *7* *Van Horne Letterbooks*, No. 4, Van Horne to G. T. Breackenridge, Feb. 8, 1884.
440 *16* *Ibid.*, No. 6, Van Horne to Beatty, June 7, 1884.
440 *31* Vaughan, p. 139.
440 *37* *Van Horne Letterbooks*, No. 5, Van Horne to W. Whyte, April 28, 1884.
441 *7* *Ibid.*, Van Horne to H. B. Ledyard, March 26, 1884.
441 *16* Thompson and Edgar, p. 143.
441 *23* Vaughan, p. 142.
441 *27* Collard, p. 253.
441 *39* MacBeth, p. 144.
442 *4* Vaughan, p. 138.
442 *34* *Van Horne Letterbooks*, No. 5, Van Horne to J. J. C. Abbott, March 15, 1884.
442 *39* *Ibid.*, No. 6, Van Horne to Beatty, July 5, 1884.
443 *12* Vaughan, p. 109.
443 *26* *Ibid.*, p. 148.
443 *35* Collard, p. 252.
444 *6* Vaughan, p. 152.
445 *4* *Gazette*, Port Moody, Dec. 22, 1883.
445 *13* *Ibid.*, Aug. 16, 1884.
446 *12* *Marcus Smith Papers*, PAC, Letterbook No. 4, Smith to Van Horne, April 28, 1884.
446 *25* *Ibid.*, Smith to Brock, Oct. 13, 1884.
446 *40* *Van Horne Letterbooks*, No. 14, Van Horne to Stephen, Nov. 24, 1885.
447 *5* *Ibid.*
447 *9* *Ibid.*

page *line*

447 *12* Pope, *Memoirs*, p. 75.
447 *16* *Marcus Smith Papers*, PAC, Letterbook No. 7, Smith to Brock, Aug. 11, 1893.
447 *24* *Ibid.*, No. 4, Smith to Schreiber, March 14, 1885.
447 *32* Cambie, "Reminiscences," p. 473.
447 *38* Markwell.
448 *15* *Macdonald Papers*, Vol. 272, Stephen to Macdonald, Sept. 3, 1889.
448 *23* *Senate Committee in Inter-state Commerce*, Van Horne's testimony, p. 229.
449 *9* *Inland Sentinel*, April 10, 1884.
449 *30* Matthews.
449 *38* Cambie Diary, July 16, 1884.
450 *2* *Ibid.*, May 30, 1884.
450 *28* Stevens, *An Engineer's Recollections*, p. 14.
450 *36* Gibbon, p. 274.
451 *9* Vaughan, p. 111.
451 *28* *Van Horne Letterbooks*, No. 7, Van Horne to Beatty, Sept. 17, 1884.
451 *38* *Ibid.*, No. 8, Van Horne to Ross, Nov. 21, 1884.
451 *42* *Ibid.*, No. 9, Van Horne to Lee, Dec. 26, 1884.
452 *36* *Ibid.*, No. 8, Van Horne to George Wainwright, Dec. 2, 1884.
452 *41* *Ibid.*, No. 6, Van Horne to Hon. John Carling, July 15, 1884.
453 *1* *Ibid.*, Van Horne to Egan, July 15, 1884.
453 *4* *Ibid.*, No. 7, Van Horne to Cambie, Aug. 30, 1884.
453 *8* *Ibid.*, Van Horne to John Ross, Aug. 28, 1884.
453 *11* *Ibid.*, No. 8, Van Horne to John Ross, Oct. 19, 1884.
453 *20* *Ibid.*, Oct. 31, 1884.
453 *29* *Ibid.*, No. 7, Van Horne to W. B. Scarth, Oct. 6, 1884.
454 *4* *Macdonald Papers*, Vol. 269, Stephen to Macdonald, Dec. 29, 1884.
454 *30* *Ibid.*, March 16, 1884.
455 *23* *Van Horne Letterbooks*, No. 8, Van Horne to Schreiber, Oct. 17, 1884.
455 *29* *Sentinel*, Oct. 31, 1884.
455 *36* Vaughan, p. 114.
456 *6* *Standard*, Montreal, Jan. 4, 1908.

456 *34* Told to the author by the present Lord Shaughnessy.
457 *5* CPR Archives, Lord Mount Stephen to "Arthur," Aug. 18, 1909.
457 *7* *Macdonald Papers*, Vol. 269, Stephen to Macdonald, March 31, 1884.
457 *12* *Ibid.*, Nov. 7, 1885.
457 *21* CPR Archives, Lord Mount Stephen to "Arthur," Aug. 18, 1909.
457 *30* Bernard.
457 *38* *Macdonald Papers*, Vol. 269, Stephen to Macdonald, July 23, 1884.
458 *6* *Ibid.*, Vol. 277, Tilley to Macdonald, June 12, 1884.
458 *9* *Ibid.*, June 19, 1884.
458 *18* *Tupper Papers*, Vol. 6, Stephen to Tupper, Aug. 13, 1884.
458 *40* *Globe*, Sept. 5, 1884.
459 *5* *Ibid.*, Aug. 16, 1884.
459 *6* *Lorne Papers*, Macdonald to Lorne, Oct. 18, 1884.
459 *9* *Van Horne Letterbooks*, No. 8, "Statement of Earnings and Expenses, from 1st January to 30th Sept. 1884," Oct. 29, 1884.
459 *42* *Macdonald Papers*, Vol. 129, Tupper to Tilley, Nov. 28, 1884.
460 *22* Gibbon, p. 278.

CHAPTER 17

462 *38* CPR Archives, Biographical Note on Fleming.
463 *36* Reprinted from Chicago *Tribune* in *Sentinel*, Sept. 1, 1883.
464 *3* *Van Horne Letterbooks*, No. 1, 1882–83, Memorandum on gradients, undated, p. 2.
465 *12* *Herald*, Calgary, Feb. 19, 1885.
465 *38* Keefer, p. 73.
466 *16* Wheeler, *Canadian Alpine Journal*, p. 41.
466 *31* *Phillips Papers*, "A Winter Trip on the Canadian Pacific Railway," by Michael Phillips.
466 *41* Keefer, *Address*, pp. 72–3.
468 *2* Lewis.

page *line*

468 *31* *Dewdney Papers*, PAC, Vol. 6, "T.Z." to Riel, May 20, 1884.

470 *34* Steele, *Forty Years in Canada*, p. 93.

471 *6* *Sun*, Winnipeg, June 29, 1883.

471 *37* *Dewdney Papers*, PAC, Vol. 1, copy of letter to Major Crozier from Sgt. H. Keenan, Sept. 25, 1884.

472 *9* *Return to an Address*, Deposition of Charles Nolin, p. 392.

472 *22* *Dewdney Papers*, PAC, Vol. 1, Crozier to Dewdney, Jan. 7, 1885 (copy).

474 *10* *Return to an Address*, Deposition of Charles Nolin, p. 393.

474 *12* *Sessional Paper*, No. 8A, Crozier to Irvine, May 29, 1885, p. 43.

474 *19* *Dewdney Papers*, PAC, Vol. 3, Dewdney to Macdonald, March 22, 1885.

474 *21* *Ibid.*, Macdonald to Dewdney, March 23, 1885 (copy).

474 *23* *Ibid.* (telegram).

474 *28* *Sessional Paper*, No. 8A, Crozier to Irvine, May 29, 1885.

474 *41* *Ibid.*, Irvine to Macdonald, April 1, 1885.

475 *23* Howard, p. 391.

476 *17* Pope, *Correspondence*, Macdonald to Tupper, Jan. 24, 1885, p. 332.

476 *22* Hughes Manuscript, p. 139.

476 *28* *Macdonald Papers*, Vol. 269, Stephen to Macdonald, Jan. 9, 1885.

476 *33* Hughes Manuscript, p. 139.

477 *6* Pope, *Correspondence*, p. 330.

477 *29* *Macdonald Papers*, Vol. 269, Stephen to Macdonald, Jan. 17, 1885.

477 *36* *Ibid.*, Jan. 14, 1885.

478 *5* *Ibid.*, Jan. 20, 1885.

478 *17* *Macdonald Papers*, Vol. 269, Macdonald to Stephen, Jan. 20, 1885.

478 *25* Bonar, quoting Randolph Bruce, Lieutenant-Governor of B.C., who was told the story by Van Horne.

478 *41* Coleman, p. 14.

479 *8* *Macdonald Papers*, Vol. 269, Stephen to Macdonald, Feb. 9, 1885.

479 *17* *Ibid.*

479 *36* *Ibid.*

480 *2* *Tyler Papers*, Tyler to wife, Aug. 29, 1888.

480 *21* *Tupper Papers*, Vol. 6, Macdonald to Tupper, March 17, 1885.

480 *28* Vaughan, p. 120.

481 *6* Hughes Manuscript, p. 142.

481 *18* *Ibid.*, p. 145B.

481 *29* Vaughan, p. 179.

481 *32* Hughes Manuscript, p. 146.

482 *20* Skelton, *Laurier*, pp. 276–7.

482 *23* Vaughan, p. 121.

482 *41* Skelton, *Laurier*, p. 277.

483 *17* *Macdonald Papers*, Vol. 269, Stephen to Macdonald, March 26, 1885.

484 *8* *Caron Papers*, Caron to Abbott, March 27, 1885.

485 *14* *Globe*, March 31, 1885.

486 *26* *British Whig*, April 1, 1885.

486 *31* *Citizen*, April 1, 1885.

486 *32* *Globe*, April 3, 1885.

487 *40* *Van Horne Letterbooks*, No. 11, Van Horne to William Whyte, April 23, 1885.

489 *10* *Globe*, April 6, 1885.

489 *35* *Ibid.*, April 13, 1885.

491 *35* *Ibid.*

491 *38* *Ibid.*, April 11, 1885.

492 *31* Howard, p. 101.

493 *24* *Globe*, April 18, 1885.

493 *31* *Sentinel*, April 10, 1885.

494 *2* Denison, *Soldiering in Canada*, p. 274.

495 *3* *Morning Chronicle*, May 5, 1885.

495 *10* *Ibid.*, May 1, 1885.

495 *18* *Mail*, April 9, 1885.

495 *35* Archer, April 6, 1885.

496 *3* *Mail*, April 9, 1885.

496 *10* *Globe*, April 23, 1885.

496 *18* Archer, April 6, 1885.

CHAPTER 18

498 *22* *Morning Chronicle*, May 18, 1885.

499 *2* *Globe*, April 25, 1885.

499 *38* *War Claims Commission Report*, Nov. 3, 1886.

499 *42* *Van Horne Letterbooks*, No. 11, Van Horne to Caron, April 11, 1885.

page *line*

500   *11*   *Ibid.*
500   *30*   *Macdonald Papers*, Vol. 269,
             Stephen to Macdonald,
             March 26, 1885.
501   *16*   Hughes Manuscript,
             p. 146A.
502   *3*   Preston, *Strathcona*, p. 140.
502   *8*   *Sunday World*, Toronto,
             May 18, 1918.
502   *21*   *Macdonald Papers*, Vol. 269,
             Stephen to Macdonald,
             April 15, 1885.
503   *5*   *Ibid.*, April 9, 1885.
503   *13*   *Ibid.*, April 11, 1885.
503   *14*   *Ibid.*, April 15, 1885.
503   *26*   *Ibid.*, Stephen to Pope,
             April 16, 1885.
504   *16*   Steele, *Forty Years in
             Canada*, p. 195.
504   *27*   *Ibid.*, p. 196.
504   *41*   Steele, *Forty Years in
             Canada*, p. 197.
507   *22*   *Macdonald Papers*, Vol. 269,
             Stephen to Pope, April 16,
             1885.
507   *28*   Gibbon, p. 287.
508   *17*   Willison, p. 196.
509   *13*   *Stephen Papers*, Macdonald
             to Stephen, May 26, 1885.
509   *21*   *Macdonald Papers*, Vol. 129,
             Macdonald to C. F.
             Smithers, April 24, 1885.
509   *32*   *Ibid.*, Vol. 269, Stephen to
             Macdonald, April 30, 1885.
509   *35*   *Ibid.*, Vol. 268, Drinkwater
             to Macdonald, April 27,
             1885.
509   *42*   *Ibid.*, Vol. 269, Stephen to
             Macdonald, May 1, 1885.

page *line*

510   *8*   *Ibid.*, May 4, 1885.
510   *13*   *Macdonald Papers*, Vol. 269,
             May 9, 1885.
510   *23*   Denison, *Canada's First
             Bank*, Vol. 1, p. 224.
511   *15*   *Macdonald Papers*, Vol. 269,
             Stephen to Macdonald,
             May 12, 1885.
512   *2*   Morris, pp. 57–8.
512   *8*   *Stephen Papers*, Macdonald
             to Stephen, May 26, 1885.
512   *20*   *Tupper Papers*, Vol. 6,
             Schreiber to Tupper.
512   *35*   Saunders, Macdonald to
             Tupper, Feb. 27, 1885,
             Vol. 2, p. 46
513   *4*   *Hansard*, 1885, p. 2504.
513   *6*   Pope, *Correspondence*,
             p. 331.
513   *16*   Vaughan, p. 129.
513   *17*   *Ibid.*
513   *39*   Skelton, *Laurier*, Vol. 1,
             p. 281.
515   *3*   *Morning Chronicle*, May 5,
             1885.
516   *39*   Daem and Dickey, p. 8.
517   *3*   *Ibid.*, p. 9.
517   *38*   *Van Horne Letterbooks*,
             No. 9, Van Horne to Beatty,
             Dec. 19, 1884.
518   *2*   Morley, p. 72.
519   *9*   Mallandaine.
521   *10*   Vaughan, p. 131.
523   *7*   Fleming in Wheeler's *The
             Selkirk Range*, Vol. 1,
             p. 173.
524   *3*   Mallandaine.
524   *15*   Fleming in Wheeler's *The
             Selkirk Range*, Vol. 1,
             p. 173.

Bibliography

A LIST OF ABBREVIATIONS:

CPRA Canadian Pacific Railway Archives
PAC   Public Archives of Canada
PABC Public Archives of British Columbia
PAM   Public Archives of Manitoba
PAO   Public Archives of Ontario
PAS   Public Archives of Saskatchewan
TPL   Toronto Public Library
VA   Vancouver Archives

UNPUBLISHED SOURCES

ANON.: Manuscript, "The Good Old Days of Broadway," PAC
ARMSTRONG, Harry William Dudley: Papers, PAC
BROWN, Adam: Papers, PAC
BRYCE, Dr. George: Papers, PAM
CAMBIE, Henry J.: Letter to J. M. R. Fairbairn, September 24, 1923, VA
     Papers and diary (privately held)
CAMPBELL, Sir Alexander: Papers, PAO and PAC
CARON, Joseph P.: Papers, PAC
DALLIN, Helen Marion: Manuscript, "What I Remember," 1884, PABC
DEWDNEY, Edgar: Papers, PAC and Glenbow-Alberta Institute Museum
DUFFERIN, First Marquis of, and Ava: Papers (microfilm), PAC
DUNCAN, W. H.: Letter to Mrs. Austin Bothwell, Legislative Librarian, Regina
EDGAR, Sir James David: Papers, PAO
EVANS, W. H.: Memorandum, VA
FAWCETT, Edgar: Diary, "Three Months on Survey, CPR–Bute Inlet," 1872, PABC

FLEMING, Sir Sandford: Papers, PAC

HANINGTON, Major C. F.: Papers, PABC

HARGREAVES, George: Diary, "Bute Inlet, 1872," PABC

HICKSON, Sir Joseph: Papers, PAC

HUGHES, Katherine: Manuscript, "Biography of Sir William Van Horne," PAC

LORNE, Marquis of: Papers, PAC

LUXTON, Norman H.: Papers, PAC

MACDONALD, Sir John A.: Papers, PAC

MACKENZIE, Alexander: Papers, PAC

McLENNAN, Roderick: Papers, TPL

MALHOIT, Zéphirin: Manuscript, "Seventy Years of Growth with Canada," PAC

MOBERLY, Walter: Diary, December, 1871 to February, 1873, PBAC

MOUNT STEPHEN, Lord (see also STEPHEN, George): Letter to "Arthur," August 18, 1909, CPRA, Montreal

PEARCE, William: Manuscript (privately held)
      Memo, November, 1924, CPRA
      Papers, PAS

PEYTON, Charles Alfred: Papers, PAM

RYLATT, Robert M.: Manuscript, "Leaves From My Diary," PABC

SMITH, Marcus: Papers, PAC and PABC

STEPHEN, George: Papers, PAC

TAYLOR, James Wickes: Papers, PAC

TUPPER, Sir Charles: Papers, PAC

TWAY, Duane Converse: "The Influence of the Hudson's Bay Company upon Canada, 1870–1889," unpublished Ph.D. thesis, University of California, 1963

TYLER, Sir Henry W.: Papers, PAC

VAN HORNE, Sir William Cornelius: Letterbooks, PAC

VINCENT, Mrs. F. W.: Memorandum, PABC

WEEKES, Gladys Onderdonk: Letter to Mrs. W. O. Miller, August 23, 1934, PABC

WILSON, T. E.: Manuscript, "The Last of the Pathfinders, as related to W. E. Round" (privately held)

PUBLIC DOCUMENTS

CANADA

Parliamentary Debates, 1870–72, and Debates of the House of Commons of the Dominion of Canada, 1875–1885 (Hansard)

Message to Parliament from the Governor-General (Lord Dufferin)

Report of the Royal Commissioners Appointed by Commission, addressed to them under the Great Seal of Canada, bearing date the Fourteenth day of August, A.D., 1873, Ottawa, 1873

Public Accounts Committee, House of Commons, 1877

Reports and Minutes of Evidence Taken Before the Select Committee of the Senate Appointed to Inquire into and Report upon the Purchase of Lands at Fort William for a Terminus to the Canadian Pacific Railway, Ottawa, 1878

First Report of the Select Standing Committee on Public Accounts in Reference to Expenditure on the Canadian Pacific Railway Between Fort William and Red River, Ottawa, 1879

Report of the Canadian Pacific Railway Royal Commission Evidence, 3 volumes, Ottawa, 1882

Sessional Paper No. 31A, 1884: Second Session of the Fifth Parliament of the Dominion of Canada, Ottawa, 1884

Report of the Royal Commission on Chinese Immigration, Ottawa, 1885

Sessional Paper No. 8A: Report of the Commission of the North-West Mounted Police Force, 1885, Ottawa, 1886

War Claims Commission Report, July 19, 1886

Return of an Address for Documents re the North-West Rebellion, Ottawa, 1886

Instrument No. DB 21001, Land Titles Office, Regina

SIR SANDFORD FLEMING

Progress Report on the Canadian Pacific Railway Exploratory Survey, Ottawa, 1872

———, Canadian Pacific Railway, A Report of Progress on the Explorations and Surveys up to January, 1874, Ottawa, 1874

———, Report on Surveys and Preliminary Operations of the Canadian Pacific Railway up to January, 1877, Ottawa, 1877

———, Reports and Documents in Reference to the Location of the Line and a Western Terminal Harbour, Ottawa, 1878

———, Report and Documents in Reference to the Canadian Pacific Railway, Ottawa, 1880

———, Memorandum Addressed to the Honourable, The Minister of Railways and Canals by the Engineer-in-Chief of the Canadian Pacific Railway, Ottawa, 1880

———, Letter to the Secretary of State, Canada, in Reference to the Report of the Canadian Pacific Royal Commission, Ottawa, 1882

BRITISH COLUMBIA

Columbia River Exploration, 1865, New Westminster, 1866

UNITED STATES

Circuit Court of the United States for the District of Minnesota, Jesse P. Farley, complainant, and Norman W. Kittson, James J. Hill and the

St. Paul, Minneapolis and Manitoba Railway Company, defendants, 15th day of July, A.D. 1882

No. 6, Supreme Court of the United States, October Term, 1886, Jesse P. Farley, appellant, vs. Norman W. Kittson, James J. Hill and The St. Paul, Minneapolis and Manitoba Railway Company (Appeal from the Circuit Court of the United States for the District of Minnesota)

U.S. Congress, Senate, Committee on Interstate Commerce, *Transportation Interests of the United States and Canada, Statements taken before the Committee*, Washington, D.C., 1890

NEWSPAPERS AND PERIODICALS

British Colonist	Victoria, 1871
British Whig	Kingston, 1885
Bulletin	Edmonton, 1882–83
Canadian Illustrated News	Montreal, 1873–81
Citizen	Ottawa, 1873–85
Daily British Colonist and Victoria Chronicle	Victoria, 1878–80
Daily Witness	Montreal, 1880–81
Free Press	Manitoba, 1873–85
Free Press	Ottawa, 1880–82
Gazette	Fort McLeod, 1883
Gazette	Picton, 1873
Gazette	Port Moody, 1883–84
Globe	Toronto, 1871–85
Herald	Calgary, 1883–85
Inland Sentinel	Emory, Yale, and Kamloops, 1880–85
Islander	Charlottetown, 1870
Leader	Regina, 1883–84
Leader	Toronto, 1870
Mail	Toronto, 1873–85
Morning Chronicle	Halifax, 1885
News	Moose Jaw, 1884
Nor'wester	Winnipeg, 1874–75
Sentinel	Thunder Bay, 1875–85
Standard	Montreal, 1908
Sun	Brandon, 1882–84
Sun	Winnipeg, 1881–84
Times	Winnipeg, 1879–83

PUBLISHED SOURCES

ANON.: *A Year in Manitoba*, London, 1881 (pamphlet)
The Canadian Biographical Dictionary and Portrait Gallery of Eminent and Self-Made Men, 2 volumes, Toronto, 1880–81

"The Indians Liked Lemonade," Regina *Leader-Post*, September 29, 1936

"The Canadian Pacific Railway," *Quarterly Review*, January, 1887

ALLARD, Jason O., and McKELVIE, B. A.: "Breaking Trail for Iron Horse," *Maclean's*, August 1, 1929

ARCHER, John H., ed.: "Recollections, Reflections and Items from the Diary of Captain A. Hamlyn Todd," *Saskatchewan History*, Vol. XV, No. 1 (Winter, 1962)

BARNEBY, W. Henry: *Life and Labour in the Far, Far West; Being Notes of a Tour in the Western States, British Columbia, Manitoba, and the North-West Territory*, London, 1884

BEGG, Alexander: *History of the North-west*, 2 volumes, Toronto, 1894

BERNARD, Kenneth: "Lord Strathcona," *Wide World Magazine*, March, 1907

BERRY, C. B.: *The Other Side, How It Struck Us*, London, 1880

BIGGAR. E. B.: *Anecdotal Life of Sir John A. Macdonald*, Montreal, 1891

BLAKE, Edward: *A National Sentiment*, Ottawa, 1874 (pamphlet), reprinted in *Canadian Historical Review*, September, 1921

BONAR, James C.: *The Inauguration of Trans Canada Transportation*, Montreal, 1936 (pamphlet)

BONE, P. Turner: *When the Steel Went Through: Reminiscences of a Railroad Pioneer*, Toronto, 1947

BOULTON, A. C. Forster: *Adventures, Travels and Politics*, London, 1939

BOYD, John: *Sir George Étienne Cartier, Bart., His Life and Times*, Toronto, 1914

BRETON, Paul-Émile, O. M. I.: *The Big Chief of the Prairies: The Life of Father Lacombe*, trans. by H. A. Dempsey, ed. by G. A. Morgan, Edmonton, 1955

BRIDLE, Augustus: *Sons of Canada, Short Studies of Characteristic Canadians*, Toronto, 1916

BROOKS, Edwin J.: "Edwin J. Brooks' Letters," Pt. I. *Saskatchewan History*, Vol. X. No. 3 (Autumn, 1957); Pt. II, Vol. XI, No. 1 (Winter, 1958)

BUCKINGHAM, William, and ROSS, George M.: *The Hon. Alexander Mackenzie: His Life and Times*, Toronto, 1892

BURPEE, Lawrence J.: *Sandford Fleming, Empire Builder*, Toronto, 1915

BUTLER, Lieutenant William Francis: *Report of His Journey from Fort Garry to Rocky Mountain House*, Ottawa, 1871
The Great Lone Land, London, 1872

Canadian Pacific Railway Company: CPR *Reports*, 1881–89
Souvenir Menu, Chateau Lake Louise, Seventy-Fifth Anniversary Luncheon, August 21, 1957
Staff Bulletin, February 1, 1936

CAMBIE, Henry J.: "Reminiscences of Pioneer Life in the West," *The Engineering Journal* (of the Engineering Institute of Canada), Vol. II (October, 1920)

CARELESS, J. Maurice: *Brown of the Globe*, 2 volumes, Toronto, 1959, reprinted 1963

CARTER, C. F.: "The Passing of the Big Hill," *World's Work*, Vol. XX (June, 1910)

CLARKE, Charles: *Sixty Years in Upper Canada*, Toronto, 1908

CLEWS, Henry: *Fifty Years in Wall Street*, New York, 1908

COLEMAN, D'Alton C.: *Lord Mount Stephen (1829–1921) and the Canadian Pacific Railway*, New York, 1945 (pamphlet of the Newcomen Society)

COLLARD, Edgar A.: *Canadian Yesterdays*, Toronto, 1955
Montreal Yesterdays, Toronto, 1962

COLLINS, J. E.: *Canada under the Administration of Lord Lorne*, Toronto, 1884

CREIGHTON, Donald: *John A. Macdonald, the Young Politician*, Toronto, 1952
John A. Macdonald, the Old Chieftain, Toronto, 1955

D'ARTIGUE, Jean: *Six Years in the Canadian North-West*, Toronto, 1882

DAEM, M., and DICKEY, E. E.: *A History of Early Revelstoke*, Revelstoke, B.C., 1962

DE KIEWIET, C. W., and UNDERHILL, F. H., eds.: *Dufferin–Carnarvon Correspondence 1874–1878*, Toronto, 1955

DENISON, George T.: *Soldiering in Canada*, Toronto, 1901

DENISON, Merrill: *Canada's First Bank; a History of the Bank of Montreal*, 2 volumes, Toronto, 1966–67

DONKIN, J. G.: *Trooper and Redskin in the Far Northwest*, London, 1889

DRAKE, Earl G.: *Regina: the Queen City*, Toronto, 1955

DUFFERIN, Marchioness of (Ava): *My Canadian Journal 1872–1878*, London, 1891

FITZGIBBON, Mary: *A Trip to Manitoba, or Roughing It on the Line*, Toronto, 1880

FLAHERTY, Norman: "Rogers Pass—Scenic Wonder," Vancouver *Colonist*, October 29, 1961

FLEMING, Sandford: *England and Canada*, London, 1884
Appendix E in A. O. Wheeler, *The Selkirk Range*, Vol. I, Ottawa, 1905
"Practical Observations on the Construction of a Continuous Line of Railway from Canada to the Pacific Ocean on British Territory" (Appendix to Henry Youle Hind's book *A Sketch of an Overland Route to British Columbia*, Toronto, 1864)

GIBBON, John Murray: *Steel of Empire*, Toronto, 1935

GILBERT, Heather: *Awakening Continent: The Life of Lord Mount Stephen*, Vol. I, Aberdeen, Scotland, 1965

GLADMAN, George: *Report on the Exploration of the Country Between Lake Superior and the Red River Settlement*, Toronto, 1958

GLUEK, Alvin C., Jr.: *Minnesota and the Manifest Destiny of the Canadian North West*, Toronto, 1965

GOSNELL, R. E.: *Sixty Years of Progress, British Columbia*, Vancouver and Victoria, 1913

GRANT, George Monro: *Ocean to Ocean*, Toronto, 1873
"The C.P.R., by the Kicking Horse Pass and the Selkirks," *Week*, 1883 and 1884

"The Canada Pacific Railway," *Century Illustrated Monthly Magazine*, Vol. XXX (October, 1885)

GRANT, William Lawson, and HAMILTON, Frederick: *George Monro Grant*, Toronto, 1905

HAM, George H.: *Reminiscences of a Raconteur*, Toronto, 1921

HAMILTON, Z. M. and M. A.: *These Are the Prairies*, Regina, n.d.

HARKIN, W. A., ed.: *Political Reminiscences of the Right Honourable Sir Charles Tupper, Bart.*, London, 1914

HAYDON, A. L.: *The Riders of the Plains*, Toronto, 1910

HEALY, W. J.: "Early Days in Winnipeg," *Beaver*, June, 1949

HEDGES, James B.: *Building the Canadian West: The Land and Colonization Policies of the Canadian Pacific Railway*, New York, 1939

HILL, Alexander Staveley: *From Home to Home: Autumn Wanderings in the North-West in the Years 1881, 1882, 1883, 1884*, London, 1885

HILL, Robert B.: *Manitoba: History of Its Early Settlement, Development, and Resources*, Toronto, 1890

HIND, Henry Youle: *Narrative of the Canadian Red River Exploring Expedition of 1857 and of the Assiniboine and Saskatchewan Exploring of 1858*, 2 volumes, London, 1860

HIND, Henry Youle, with Thomas Keefer, C. Robb, J. G. Hodgins, M. H. Perley, and W. Murray: *Eighty Years Progress of British North America*, London [Toronto Printing], 1863

HOWARD, Joseph Kinsey: *Strange Empire: A Narrative of the Northwest*, New York, 1952

HUGHES, Katherine: *Father Lacombe: The Black-Robe Voyageur*, Toronto, 1920

HUTCHISON, Paul P.: "Sir John J. C. Abbott," *Canadian Bar Review*, Volume 26, 1948

INNIS, Harold: *A History of the Canadian Pacific Railway*, Toronto, 1923

IRWIN, Leonard B.: *Pacific Railway and Nationalism in the Canadian-American Northwest, 1845–1873*, Philadelphia, 1939

JOHNSON, George: *Alphabet of First Things in Canada*, Ottawa, 1897

JOSEPHSON, Matthew: *The Robber Barons*, New York, 1962 reprint

KAVANAGH, Martin: *The Assiniboine Basin*, Winnipeg, 1946

KEEFER, Thomas: "Address on the CPR," American Society of Civil Engineers *Transactions*, Vol. XIX (August, 1888)

KENNEDY, George: "When History Was A-Making," Kamloops *Sentinel*, Souvenir Edition, May 29, 1905

LEWIS, H. H.: "Sir William C. Van Horne," *Ainslie's Magazine*, reprinted in *Daily World*, December 29,1900

LOVETT, H. A.: *Canada and the Grand Trunk, 1849–1924*, Montreal, 1924

LOWER, A. R. M.: *Canadians in the Making*, Toronto, 1958

LYALL, Sir Alfred: *The Life of the Marquis of Dufferin and Ava*, 2 volumes, London, 1905

MacBETH, R. G.: *The Romance of the Canadian Pacific Railway*, Toronto, 1924

MacDONELL, Allan: *The North-West Transportation, Navigation and Railway Company: Its Objects*, Prospectus, Toronto, 1858

MacKAY, Douglas: *The Honourable Company*, New York, 1936

McKELVIE, B. A.: "Thousands of Last Spikes at Craigellachie," Vancouver *Province*, November 18, 1944
"They Routed the Rockies at Summation Point," Vancouver *Province*, February 3, 1945

McLAGAN, J. C.: "Sketch of the Rise and Progress of Winnipeg," in John Macoun, *Manitoba and the Great North-West*, Guelph, 1882

MACOUN, John: *Autobiography of John Macoun, M.A., Canadian Explorer and Naturalist, 1831–1920*, Ottawa, 1922
Manitoba and the Great North-West, Guelph, 1882

McWILLIAMS, Margaret: *Manitoba Milestones*, Toronto, 1928

MALLANDAINE, Colonel Edward: "Youngest Boy to See 'Last Spike' Driven Still Alive," Revelstoke *Review*, June 29, 1940

MARKWELL, Mary: "An Adventure in Railway Building," *Saturday Night*, March 1, 1930

MATTHEWS, Major J. C.: "One Man Stands Up for CPR," Vancouver *Province* September 26, 1966

MAVOR, James: "Van Horne and His Sense of Humour," *Maclean's*, November 15, 1923

MILLER, Arthur Rowe: "The Diary of Arthur Rowe Miller," *Saskatchewan History*, Vol. X, No. 2 (Spring, 1957)

MITCHELL, Peter: *The West and North-west: Notes of a Holiday Trip*, Montreal, 1880

MOBERLY, Walter: Journals, 1865–66, in *Columbia River Exploration, 1865–66*, 2 volumes, New Westminster, 1866, and Victoria, n.d.
Picture of the Canadian Pacific Railway, address December 8, 1908, to the Art, Historical and Scientific Association of Vancouver; Vancouver, 1909
The Rocks and Rivers of British Columbia, London, 1885

MOODY, John: *The Railroad Builders*, Vol. 38, "Chronicles of America," New Haven, 1919

MORLEY, Alan: *Vancouver: from Milltown to Metropolis*, Vancouver, 1961

MORRIS, Keith: *The Story of the Canadian Pacific Railway*, London, 1920

MYERS, Gustavus: *History of the Great American Fortunes*, New York, 1936 (reprint)

MYERS, Gustavus: *History of Canadian Wealth*, Chicago, 1914

NOTMAN, W., and TAYLOR, Fennings: *Portraits of British Americans*, 3 volumes in 2, Montreal, 1865

OBERHOLTZER, Ellis P.: *Jay Cooke, Financier of the Civil War*, 2 volumes, New York, 1968, reprint from 1907, Philadelphia

OLIVER, William: "Westward Ho," Lethbridge *Herald*, July 11, 1935 (Golden Jubilee Edition)

PALLISER, John: *Journals, Detailed Reports and Observations Relative to the Exploration of British North America*, London, 1859
Further Papers Relative to the Exploration of British North America, London, n.d.

PARKER, William F.: *Daniel McNeil Parker, M.D.: His Ancestry and a Memoir of His Life*, Toronto, 1910

POPE, Sir Joseph: *Memoirs of the Right Honourable Sir John Alexander*

Macdonald, G.C.B., First Prime Minister of the Dominion of Canada, 2 volumes, Ottawa, 1894 (reprint Toronto, 1930)

The Correspondence of Sir John Macdonald: Selections from the Correspondence of the Right Honourable Sir J. A. Macdonald, G.C.B., First Prime Minister of the Dominion of Canada, Toronto, 1921

POPE, Maurice, ed.: *Public Servant: The Memoirs of Sir Joseph Pope*, Toronto, 1960

PORRITT, Edward: "Sixty Years of Protection in Canada," *The Grain Growers Guide*, Winnipeg, 1913

POWERS, J. W.: *The History of Regina*, Regina, 1887

PRESTON, W. T. R.: *My Generation of Politics and Politicians*, Toronto, 1927

Strathcona and the Making of Canada, New York, 1915

PUGSLEY, Edmund E .: "Pioneers of the Steel Trail," Pt. 2, "Two Streaks of Rust," *Maclean's*, June 15, 1930; Pt. 4, "Fighting the Snow Menace," *Maclean's*, August 15, 1930

PYLE, Joseph Gilpin: *The Life of James J. Hill*, 2 volumes, New York, 1916

ROBERTS, Morley: *The Western Avernus*, London, 1887

ROBINSON, Noel: "Walter Moberly Knew B.C. as 'Sea of Mountains,' " *Daily Province*, January 5, 1946

ROBINSON, Noel, and MOBERLY, Walter: *Blazing the Trail Through the Rockies*, Vancouver, 1915

ROE, F. G.: "Early Opinions on the 'Fertile Belt' of Western Canada," *Canadian Historical Review*, Vol. XXVII (June, 1946)

ROGERS, Alberta: Appendix E in A. O. Wheeler, *The Selkirk Range*, Vol. I, Ottawa, 1905

ROSE, George Maclean: *A Cyclopaedia of Canadian Biography*, 2 volumes, Toronto, 1886–91

ROSS, George W.: *Getting into Parliament and After*, Toronto, 1913

RUTLEDGE, J. L.: "Binding the West with Bands of Steel: The Eventful Story of Michael John Haney," *Maclean's*, April 1 and 15, and May 1, 1920

SAUNDERS, E. M., ed.: *The Life and Letters of the Rt. Hon. Sir Charles Tupper, Bart., K.C.M.G.*, 2 volumes, London, 1916

SECRETAN, J. H. E.: *Canada's Great Highway: From the First Stake to the Last Spike*, London, 1924

SHAW, Charles Aeneas: "A Prairie Gopher Makes Reply," Vancouver *Province*, October 7, 1934

SHAW, Charles Aeneas, and HULL, Raymond, eds.: *Tales of a Pioneer Surveyor*, Toronto, 1970

SKELTON, Oscar D.: *The Railway Builders: A Chronicle of Overland Highways*, Vol. 32, *Chronicles of Canada*, Toronto, 1916

The Life and Letters of Sir Wilfrid Laurier, 2 volumes, Toronto, 1921

SMITH, Goldwin: *Reminiscences*, New York, 1910, edited by Arnold Haultain

The Political Destiny of Canada, Toronto, 1878

SOUTHESK, Earl of: *Saskatchewan and the Rocky Mountains*, Toronto, 1875

STANLEY, George F. G.: *The Birth of Western Canada: A History of the Riel Rebellion*, Toronto, 1936
Louis Riel, Toronto, 1963

STEELE, Samuel B.: *Forty Years in Canada*, Toronto, 1915

STEVENS, G. R.: *Canadian National Railways*, Vol. I, *Sixty Years of Trial and Error, 1836–1896*, Toronto, 1960

STEVENS, John F.: *An Engineer's Recollections (reprinted from Engineering News-Record)*, New York, 1936

STEWART, George, Jr.: *Canada Under the Administration of the Earl of Dufferin*, London, 1878

STOBIE, Margaret: "The Formative Years: 1. Struggle for Rights," *Beaver*, No. 286 (Summer, 1955)

TACHÉ, Louis J. C. H., ed.: *Men of the Day: A Canadian Portrait Gallery*, Montreal, *c.* 1890

THOMPSON, Norman, and EDGAR, J. H.: *Canadian Railway Development from the Earliest Times*, Toronto, 1933

THOMSON, Dale C.: *Alexander Mackenzie, Clear Grit*, Toronto, 1960

TROTTER, Beecham, and HAWKES, Arthur: *A Horseman and the West*, Toronto, 1925

TROW, James: *A Trip to Manitoba*, Quebec, 1875

VAN HORNE, William Cornelius: Preface to Katherine Hughes, *Father Lacombe: The Black-Robe Voyageur*, Toronto, 1920

VAUGHAN, Walter: *The Life and Work of Sir William Van Horne*, New York, 1920

WAITE, Peter B.: *Arduous Destiny: Canada, 1874–1896*, Toronto, 1971
"Sir John A. Macdonald: The Man," *Dalhousie Review*, Vol. XLVII (Summer, 1967)

WALLACE, W. S.: *The Dictionary of Canadian Biography*, Toronto, 1926
The Growth of Canadian National Feeling, Toronto, 1927

WATKIN, Sir E. W.: *Canada and the States, Recollections, 1851 to 1866*, London, 1887

WHITE, William: "I Might Have Owned Regina," *Maclean's*, June, 1935

WILLISON, Sir J. S.: *Reminiscences, Political and Personal*, Toronto, 1919

WILLSON, Beckles: *Lord Strathcona: The Story of His Life*, London, 1902

WOLSELEY, Garnet: "Narrative of the Red River Expedition by an Officer of the Expeditionary Force," *Blackwood's Edinburgh Magazine*, January–June, 1871

YOUNG, Hon. James: *Public Men and Public Life in Canada*, 2 volumes, Toronto, 1912

Acknowledgments

This book is an abridgment of the two-volume work that was published in Canada in 1970 and 1971 under the titles *The National Dream* and *The Last Spike*. The research was done in the various archives and libraries of Canada, chiefly at the Public Archives of Canada at Ottawa, the British Columbia Archives at Victoria, the Glenbow-Alberta Institute Museum at Calgary, the Public Archives of Ontario, and the Metropolitan Toronto Central Public Library. My research assistant was Norman Kelly, M.A., and the manuscript was read critically by Professor Michael Bliss of the History Department, University of Toronto. The Canadian Pacific Railway, while not opening all of its archival material to me, facilitated the trips that both Mr. Kelly and I made across Canada by rail and gave us expert advice in the technical areas of railroading. In addition, several other people deserve my gratitude, notably Ennis Halliday and Ann Michie, who typed notes and manuscripts; T. E. Price of Vancouver and his son, Alex, both CPR history buffs; Mrs. John D. Ross, for letting me read the Cambie diaries; and Tom Wilson's son, Ed, of Calgary, who gave me permission to quote from his father's manuscript. A more complete bibliography and acknowledgment appears in the Canadian editions.

Index

A Note About the Author

Pierre Berton is at home in all media. A former magazine editor, newspaper columnist, and book editor, he has been seen regularly on Canadian television for the past fifteen years. His daily interview program travels the globe and his radio commentary is heard each morning in Toronto. He is also the country's best-selling author, with an unprecedented trio of Governor General's Awards (equivalent to the U.S. Pulitzer Prize) to his credit.

Berton's two books on the building of the Canadian Pacific Railway (here condensed into a single volume for American readers) broke all publishing records in Canada. His history of the Gold Rush, *The Klondike Fever*, is considered the definitive work on that subject and the National Film Board documentary *City of Gold*, which he wrote and narrated, has won some forty international awards including the Grand Prix at Cannes. Mr. Berton also holds two National Newspaper Awards and the Stephen Leacock medal for humor. He is the father of seven children and lives with his family at Kleinburg, Ontario, a small village not far from Toronto.

A Note on the Type

This book was set in Monticello, a linotype revival of the original Roman No. 1 cut by Archibald Binny and cast in 1796 by the Philadelphia type foundry, Binny & Ronaldson. The face was named Monticello in honor of its use in the monumental fifty-volume *Papers of Thomas Jefferson*, published by Princeton University Press. Monticello is a transitional type design, embodying certain features of Bulmer and Baskerville, but it is a distinguished face in its own right.

Composed, printed, and bound by
The Haddon Craftsmen, Inc., Scranton, Pa.

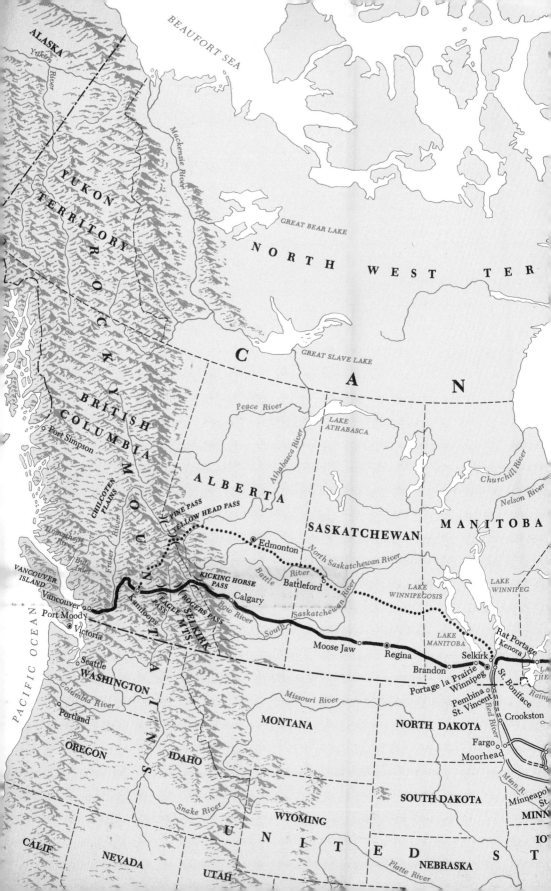

ALASKA

Yukon River

BEAUFORT SEA

YUKON TERRITORY

R O C K Y

BRITISH COLUMBIA

Mackenzie River

GREAT BEAR LAKE

N O R T H   W E S T   T E R

C A N A

GREAT SLAVE LAKE

Peace River

Port Simpson

Homathco River

CHILCOTEN PLAINS

Butte Inlet

Fraser River

Athabasca River

LAKE ATHABASCA

A L B E R T A

M O U N

PINE PASS

YELLOW HEAD PASS

Edmonton

KICKING HORSE PASS

Calgary

Battle River

North Saskatchewan River

Battleford

SASKATCHEWAN

M A N I T O B A

Churchill River

Nelson River

LAKE WINNIPEGOSIS

LAKE WINNIPEG

VANCOUVER ISLAND

Vancouver

Port Moody

Victoria

Kamloops

EAGLE PASS

ROGERS PASS

SELKIRK MTS.

Bow River

South   *Saskatchewan River*

Moose Jaw

Regina

LAKE MANITOBA

Brandon

Portage la Prairie   Winnipeg

Selkirk

Rat Portage (Kenora)

St. Boniface

LA

THE

Rainy

PACIFIC OCEAN

Seattle

WASHINGTON

Columbia River

Portland

OREGON

T A I N S

IDAHO

Snake River

Missouri River

MONTANA

Pembina

St. Vincent

Red River

NORTH DAKOTA

Crookston

Fargo

Moorhead

Minn. R.

Minneapol

St.

MINN

SOUTH DAKOTA

WYOMING

U N I T E D

Platte River

NEBRASKA

S T

IO

CALIF

NEVADA

UTAH

COLOR